THE INTERNET
INTERNATIONAL DIRECTORY

THE <u>INTERNET</u>
INTERNATIONAL DIRECTORY

Mitzi Waltz

Ziff-Davis Press
Emeryville, California

Copy Editors	Kelly Green and Nicole Clausing
Technical Reviewers	Eric D. Berg and Paul R. Freedman
CD-ROM Technical Reviewers	Michael DeLacy and Carol Burbo
Project Coordinator	Barbara Dahl
Proofreader	Vanessa Miller
Cover Illustration and Design	Regan Honda
Book Design	Meredith Downs
Word Processing	Howard Blechman
Page Layout	Tony Jonick and M.D. Barrera
Cover Copy	Kate Langer
CD-ROM and HTML Page Production	Michael Botts, Michael Ealey, and Bill Smith
Indexer	Ted Laux

Ziff-Davis Press books are produced on a Macintosh computer system with the following applications: FrameMaker®, Microsoft® Word, QuarkXPress®, Adobe Illustrator®, Adobe Photoshop®, Adobe Streamline™, MacLink®Plus, Aldus® FreeHand™, Collage Plus™.

For information about U.S. rights and permissions, contact Chantal Tucker at Ziff-Davis Publishing, fax 212-503-5420.

If you have comments or questions or would like to receive a free catalog, call or write:
Ziff-Davis Press
5903 Christie Avenue
Emeryville, CA 94608
800-688-0448

ISBN 1-56276-329-6

Manufactured in the United States of America
10 9 8 7 6 5 4 3 2 1

To Ian

and to my research assistants:

Laure Akai

Lee Doyle

Chris Hughes

John LeClerk

Joseph Morris

Casey Muller

Steve Schultz

Raj Shah

Andrew Sleigh

Douglas Squirrel

Brian Thomas

Carmen Waltz

Table of Contents

Part 2: International Internet Sites 69

Appendixes

Acknowledgments

Writing a book like this is not a one-person endeavor. My first thanks go to Wayne Ause, my able, affable Internet wizard and editorial assistant. He interpreted arcane software settings for me, made sure the chaotic mass of incoming listings was organized, and kept his nose to the grindstone despite a tough schedule.

I relied on a wonderful staff of research assistants to collect the listings for this volume: Laure Akai, Lee Doyle, Chris Hughes, John LeClerk, Joseph Morris, Casey Muller, Steve Schultz, Raj Shah, Andrew Sleigh, Douglas Squirrel, Brian Thomas, and Carmen Waltz all came through with the goods. Even better, they all grasped the notion that a good sense of humor was the essential factor in surviving the rapid-fire Netsurfing challenge that I handed them, forwarding hilarious Net-finds and lots of funny e-mail—although the practical joke that subscribed me to the origami mailing list went just a little too far…. You're a great crew; you deserve an eternal-flame Web page in your honor.

My wonderful agent, Karen Nazor, accomplished miracles on my behalf in a very short period of time—thank you.

Suzanne Anthony, Kelly Green, Nicole Clausing, and Barbara Dahl, my editors at Ziff-Davis Press, and the rest of my publisher's excellent editing, production, design, and marketing team also deserve thanks. This group knows how to work together in pursuit of a common goal. They went above and beyond the call of duty to make this project happen.

And no Internet book should be without a big thank-you to the thousands of people who work, often without pay, to create innovative new software and hardware that make the Net work better; the many Usenet moderators, systems operators, and site managers who contribute their skills and receive little recognition in return; the free-speech and free-thought advocates who are working hard to make sure this worldwide resource remains available to us all; and those who take the time and effort to provide files, sites, and Web pages for our education and enjoyment.

On a personal note, my partner Steve Schultz has also been instrumental in making this book a success. He was both supportive and critical when needed—without a doubt the best editor I've got.

—**Mitzi Waltz**
Portland, Oregon

Introduction

This directory is different from other Internet guides and directories that you may have seen. Because the Internet began in the United States, for its first decade almost all Internet sites and the information they offered were domestic. The Net has now expanded to include sites around the world. The result: More people suddenly have more access to the world's information resources that ever before.

All of the sites listed in this directory were chosen because they offer at least some content with an international orientation. From ways to check the weather in Ghana to the latest underground music archives in Finland, there's probably a listing that will help you find what you're looking for. I've tried to make the lists as all-inclusive as possible by including sites from many geographical locations, by making sure that various viewpoints are represented, and by trying to balance "official" government and military archives with those maintained by individuals or by scientific and academic institutions, and with archives stored outside the nation's borders.

Although the opinions stated in the reviews of the sites are entirely my own, inclusion in this volume does not mean that I (or Ziff-Davis Press) endorse a site or its offerings. You should take care to investigate thoroughly any information you find on the Internet before using it, just as you would not act on the advice of an investment book without checking out the author's claims and recommendations with a financial counselor or other sources. The type of information you find will depend heavily on each archivist's point of view: what he or she deems important; his or her political, social, and economic views; and, in the case of government and other institutional sites, formal policies and even outright censorship of opposing views. One of the Internet's strengths is that providing information is inexpensive, and the technology to do so is becoming more widespread. That's great when it comes to creating a freewheeling, uncensored marketplace of ideas—but it also opens the door to charlatans, crackpots, and disinformation artists. Let the browser beware!

The listings are in subject order, and are arranged alphabetically. This made more sense than any other organizational method, but doesn't always tell the entire story about each entry. One of the great things about Internet sites is that they can hold incredible volumes of data. It's rare for a site to be so strongly focused as to cover just one aspect of the human experience. I strongly encourage you to make time for goal-free exploration: Navigating the Net this way is like wandering through the stacks of the world's hugest library, opening an intriguing volume here, checking out a book there, playing a tape here as you go. For information junkies, it's like being a kid in a candy store.

To help you find your way, there are three indexes to the listings: subject, alphabetical by site name, and geographical.

Ziff-Davis Press hopes to make this book an annually updated affair. If you discover fabulous Internet resources that fit its international theme, please send them along! We'd also love to hear suggestions and comments from readers, particularly about how they've used this book. You can direct your mail to Mitzi Waltz c/o Ziff-Davis Press, 5903 Christie Avenue, Emeryville, California 94608; or send e-mail to infobahn@teleport.com.

Subject Index of Internet Sites

Note: Page numbers indicate the beginning of subject sections.

BON VOYAGE

Alphabetical Index

Geographical Index

Fiji

Jamaica

Japan

Middle East

Cosimini

Part 1

The Internet:
An International
How-to Guide

INTERNATIONAL CONNECTIVITY MAP

This map illustrates the levels of connectivity available around the world. The four types of connectivity are BITNET, Internet Protocol, UUCP, and FidoNet. The shadings represent the number of types of connections (from zero to four) that can be found in a given region. For a more detailed description of how each region is connected, please see Chapter 3.

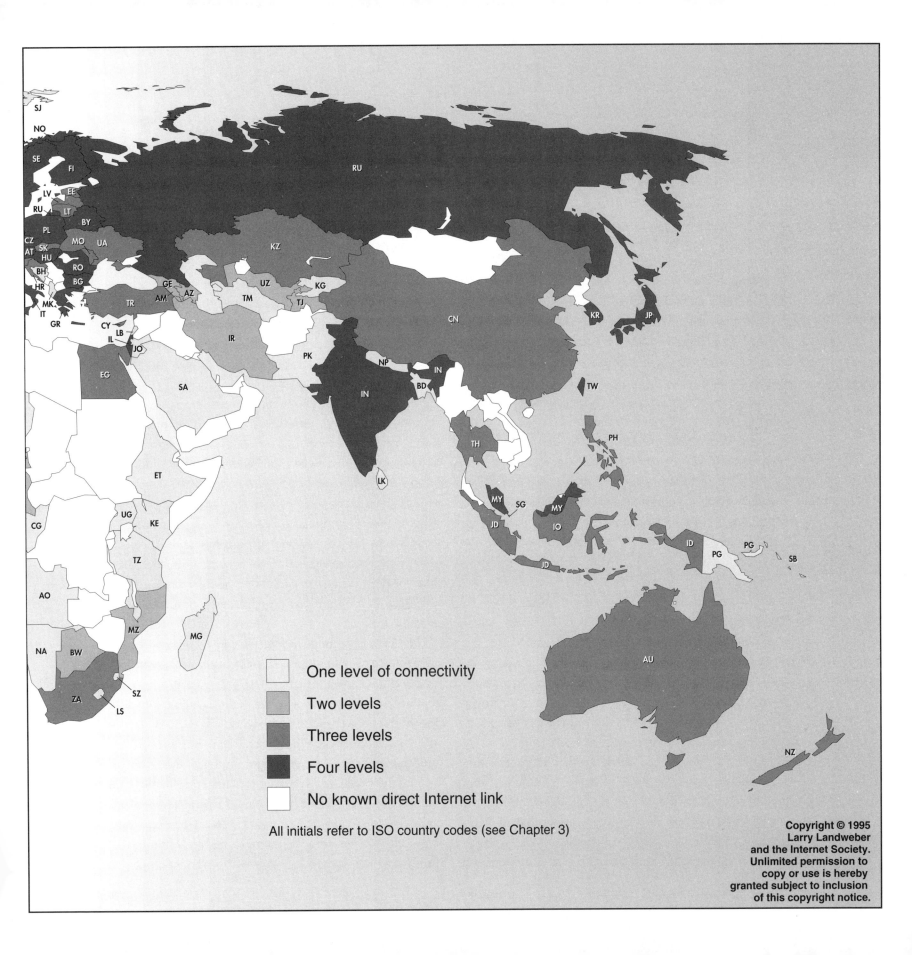

One level of connectivity

Two levels

Three levels

Four levels

No known direct Internet link

All initials refer to ISO country codes (see Chapter 3)

Chapter 1:
Introduction to the Internet

A few years ago the word *Internet* barely registered on the public radar screen—and now you can't escape it. The local news flashes e-mail addresses at you, the prefix *cyber* and the "information superhighway" metaphor are beginning to wear out their welcome, and even your grandmother has gotten the word that a computer, a telephone, and this Internet thing can be combined to provide unprecedented access to information. What kind of information? Just about anything: recipes, wiring diagrams, bibliographies, full-length articles, photos, entire online magazines, databases of all sorts, satellite photos of the weather patterns on Earth—you name it.

If you have electronic mail at work, you're already aware of how easy it is to communicate with people through your computer. An Internet account can extend this ability to send digital letters beyond the bounds of your office or corporate network, making it as quick and cheap to exchange love letters with the Sultan of Brunei as it is to notify Joe down the hall that a meeting is scheduled for 2:00 p.m.

But e-mail is just the beginning.

An account with full Internet access, combined with a few nifty software tools, can literally put the world's knowledge—and the world's population—at your fingertips. From library catalogs to the archives of the planet's great museums and universities, any data, text, chart, or image that can be stored electronically is probably online somewhere, or soon will be. Nearly every nation has some type of connection to the Net, which in many places actually provides more reliable communications than the voice telephone system. You can even turn the Net into an entertainment center with online games played simultaneously by people all over the world, or treat it like an international CB radio with Internet Relay Chat and similar features.

It's precisely this ability of the Internet to reach out beyond the arbitrary borders of the United States that led to the creation of this guide. Dozens of books have been published that concentrate on the Internet resources available in the United States, but for most people who are not online as academics or professional researchers, those books simply do not offer enough international spice. And spice is nice. Few of us will ever have the opportunity to travel the globe in person—at least not for more than a week here and there—but the Internet can open doors to places we'd love to go.

Once you learn how to open these doors, your way is clear to "meet" and talk to fascinating people around the world, to undertake personal or professional research projects using resources on other continents, to practice a second (or third) language, and to contribute to cross-cultural understanding in an environment that is immediate and uncensored.

The listings included in this book are by no means complete. Every single day new collections of information come online, while others disappear. A relatively recent method of delivering words and pictures online called the World Wide Web—also known as WWW, W3, or the Web—has accelerated the process, because simple software now makes it easy for even programming novices to create and make available Web pages. When they're on your screen, these electronic pages look a lot like magazine pages, with text, graphics, and photos. They use a nifty idea called *hypermedia*: Click on a highlighted word or image that you want to know more about and it's linked to an explanation, a document, an archive of hundreds of documents, or another Web page halfway across the world that can tell you more. And because they're multimedia, Web pages can offer sound and even video in addition to words and pictures.

Using this new Internet tool is like taking a virtual-reality world tour with a ticket that offers unlimited stops: around the world in 80 minutes, if you'd like. Unlike a trip that relies on the airlines, however, trekking the World Wide Web can provide serendipitous and strange discoveries. A single click of your mouse can send you from Michigan to Manitoba, then to Mauritius via Mexico and back again. And WWW also works as an easy interface for searching information archives that otherwise require learning special commands or installing extra software.

In the computer biz, marketing types refer to software so great and unique that it creates a whole new business category or activity as a "killer application," or "killer app." When the first desktop publishing programs came out years ago, they were referred to as killer apps. Mosaic, the WWW browser included in the CD-ROM that accompanies this book, is getting the nod as the Internet's first killer app. Mosaic was originally developed by programmers working for the University of Illinois's National Center for Supercomputing Applications (NCSA) and is still available at no charge; you now have the enhanced commercial version. It lets people who have Macintoshes, PCs with Windows, or UNIX machines running X-Windows use their graphical interfaces to see and understand the Internet in a more visual way. Like your favorite spreadsheet or word processing program, it uses color, icons, pull-down menus, and push-buttons to make navigating around easy, and it keeps track of where you've been and where you're going now.

Mosaic actually wasn't the first Web browser, and it has since been joined by several others that might work better for you. For more about current browser options and more detail on how to use WWW, see Chapter 12.

Right now, just for fun, I'd like to show you an evening's Internet home travel movies. After all, you picked up this book because you want to see other places, learn about new cultures, and take a ride on that (stop me before I say it again!) information superhighway, right? Well, here we go. I'll include the Web addresses (properly known as Universal Resource Locaters, or URLs) for our destinations in parenthesis: They're the strings of letters, numbers, and symbols that start with *http://* (the parenthesis are not part of the address).

Around the World in 80 Minutes

Our trip begins at my home computer. With a cup of coffee and a late-night snack close at hand, I click on an icon that opens up an Internet connection through Teleport, the company from which I buy Internet access. Once I'm online, I launch NCSA Mosaic, which instantly takes me to the place I have designated as my jumping-off point for Web exploration, my friend Dwayne Jones-Evans's page in North Fitzroy, Australia (http://www.latrobe.edu.au/nexus/HTML/dwayne.html).

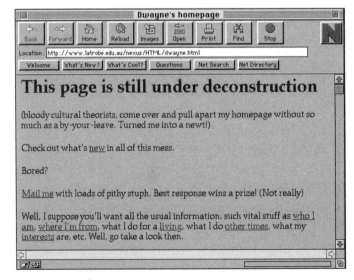

Dwayne's home page

Dwayne is one of thousands of individuals who have created their own Web pages. Like most of these "personal" pages, Dwayne's takes a humorous approach, and has links to other Web pages that feature his favorite subjects, which range from full-dress Viking reenactments to sustainable agriculture. A click on the highlighted words *the WorldWideWeb* takes me to the center of it all: the European Laboratory for Particle Physics, or CERN (http://www.w3.org/).

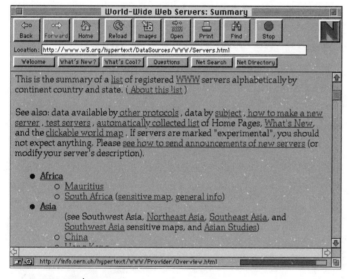

CERN Web page

Located near Geneva in Switzerland, CERN maintains a group of pages that are among the most popular stops on the Web for both casual travelers and serious students of Internet programming. From here you can access information about hypertext programming and WWW tools, get helpful hints on navigation, find exhaustive lists of other Web pages, and basically be overwhelmed by the sheer volume of stuff and nonsense that's out there.

Clicking on the words *W3 Servers* here brings up a list of known Web servers arranged by continent and country. Being in a mood for some art, I head for France and choose the WebMuseum (http://www.emf.net/louvre/rh/1.html) from the long list of French servers.

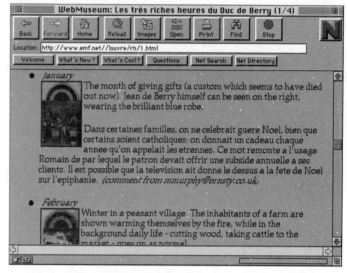

Les Très Riches Heures du Duc de Berry on the Web

I decide to view *Les Très Riches Heures du Duc de Berry*, tonight's feature exhibit at the WebMuseum. This illustrated medieval book of days limns life in the fields and home of the Duke through the course of a year. The delicate manuscript is housed at a museum in Chantilly, France, but can't be seen by the public anymore—except by Internet, or in printed reproductions.

The pictures take their time to reach my screen, first as small "thumbnails" and then, with a double-click of my mouse, in their full glory. The text, printed in English and French, is quite interesting, and even with my high school *français* I can tell that there are substantial differences between the two. The French commentary is long, more biting, and quite opinionated… intriguing.

I could stay here for hours, but there's a world of art, beauty, and strangeness waiting for me out there. My next planned stop is Isfahan, Iran. There's no direct link between Paris and this historic Islamic city, so I type in the address for an exhibition of Islamic architecture that a friend told me about (http://www.anglia.ac.uk/~trochford/isfahan.html).

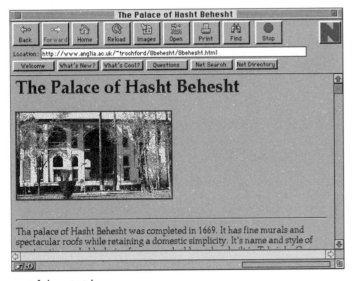

Isfahan Web page

This page is located at Anglia Polytechnic University at Cambridge, England, but as the lovely photos begin to reveal themselves I feel like I'm taking a virtual tour of someplace that I will almost surely never see in person, considering the political and social climate in Iran.

I could download some color photos here, but although I'm tempted, I decide to tour a decidedly different metropolis, albeit one with a similarly rich history. Pointing Mosaic in the direction of the Ministry of Tourism of Slovenia (http://www.ijs.si/slo.html), I opt for a stroll around the old-fashioned avenues of the almost-unspoiled European city of Ljubijana.

Tito may have blemished the rest of the former Yugoslavia with concrete tenements (and who knows what the suburbs of Ljubijana look like—for all I know it could be Cabrini-Green, Eastern Europe style), but thankfully he left this jewel alone. A clickable city map takes you around to the sights, of which there are many, while text menus offer business, travel, and cultural information.

Ljubijana on the Web

Unfortunately, there's nothing on my favorite Slovenian music group, Laibach. I jump back to the W3 Servers page to browse the list of music resources, and after several twists and turns on the information superhighway that reveal nothing about Laibach's brand of theatrical, industrial pop, I pull up at the Afro-Caribbean Music Guide, based in Bry-sur-Marne, France (http://www.ina.fr/Music).

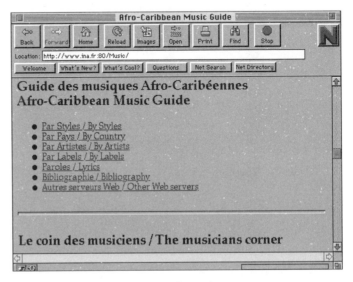

Afro-Caribbean Music Guide Web page

I've only heard a little of this type of music, but I know it's immensely popular in Europe and, of course, Africa. The names of the variants are rhythmic enough to start a song with: Soukouss, Makossa, Bukutsi, Zouk....

The page offers concert listings, sound files, bibliographies and discographies, scores, lyrics, and links to info on the nations of origin of each style and performer. It's a simply designed page, but an excellent introduction to these unique sounds.

I find here that I'm missing an add-on utility for Mosaic that I need to check out the audio clips that are available, so I scoot over to another site recently recommended by a friend. Travels in Hypermedia (http://www.york.ac.uk/~jjrk1/), subtitled "A Snapshot of the Techno Subculture," is a cyberpunk-flavored offering that also has quite a bit of information on Internet navigation, finding WWW tools, and generally turning yourself into an online expert.

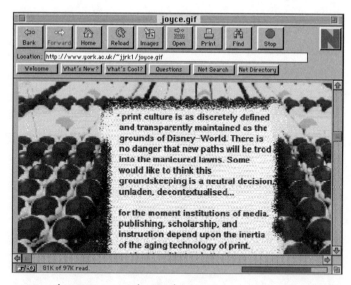

Travels in Hypermedia Web page

On the down side, the folks who built this page used some huge graphics, which are extremely slow to appear. When they do show, they were worth the wait, but my eyelids are drooping.

I decide that a trip to the wild side of the Net is in order if I'm to stay up any longer. One of the adjectives often used in press accounts to describe the Internet is "anarchy," and in many respects that's an apt way to characterize a system that exists largely without laws, governments, or national borders. A trip to the Spunk Press Web page (http://www.cwi.nl/cwi/people/Jack.Jansen/spunk/Spunk_Home.html), which holds an archive of anarchist texts and graphics, provides access to more literally revolutionary applications of the term. It's an interesting view of the kind of ideas that, once placed on the Internet, are instantly as accessible as more mainstream views.

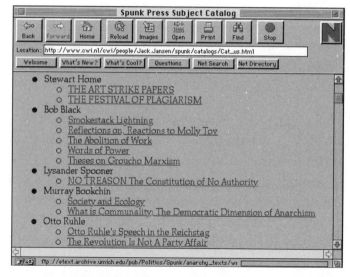

Spunk Press Web page

Because this page is created and maintained by an international collective, text comes in a number of languages—mainly English and Spanish, but with a smattering of Catalan, Russian, Esperanto, Dutch, Finnish, and German. I spend a while browsing through this library-style listing of text and graphics, but it's obviously not incendiary enough to make up for coffee deficiency at this late hour. I decide it's time to call it a night before I turn from cyberpunk to cyberpumpkin.

It's been an interesting journey, and different choices anywhere along the path might have taken me to even more exciting or unusual spots. I wrote down six more addresses to investigate later on as I navigated: There seems to be no end to new and worthwhile stuff to see on the World Wide Web.

By now I hope you feel like jumping up to book your own Grand Tour—if so, that's the spirit! Think of this book as your Internet travel resource. The next few chapters will give you enough of the particulars needed to understand how the transportation system works and how to get moving; the listings will give you some intriguing ideas about what your destination could be.

Bon voyage—and don't forget to take the side roads and back alleys. As in real-life travel, these spontaneous detours are often the best part.

Chapter 2: Internet History

When you read a magazine article about the Internet, it is often described as a "global computer network." In reality, it's a multitude of different computer networks that can talk to each other, and therefore seem like a seamless whole, by way of a specially developed interface protocol. (An *interface protocol* is a set of standards that lets different kinds of computers talk to each other.)

In the United States, it all started with ARPANET, a government-sponsored network for the U.S. Department of Defense's semi-independent Advanced Research Projects Agency (semi-independent in that it did most of its research without much Department of Defense scrutiny). ARPANET was set up in 1969 to foster communication between big military research facilities, government bureaus, and the research departments of major American universities. ARPANET grew steadily throughout the 1970s. In 1975, ARPANET was taken over by the Department of Defense proper, which used it as the basis for an expanded network called the Defense Data Network, or DDN.

Both systems switched over to using a new communications protocol called Transmission Control Protocol/Interface Protocol (TCP/IP) in 1983. TCP/IP lets computers of many types talk to each other despite having different internal communications systems. This breakthrough made it much easier to forge links with similar networks worldwide.

In 1980, the National Science Foundation (NSF) came on the scene with another network it dubbed *The Internet*. This network combined with the ARPANET/DDN family of networks in 1987 to form a more widely distributed successor, NSFNET. This initially included mostly academic sites all around the country, NASA, the Department of Energy, and the research departments of large companies that often undertook joint projects with their academic and military counterparts.

Usenet, a discussion network, was established as an unofficial project in 1977, while BITNET sprung up for nonscience academic chat in 1981. And big companies were growing networks of their own that were, in turn, linked in various ways to these semipublic nets as the 1990s grew near. The NSF then went to work on establishing a national infrastructure that would allow this network to continue increasing in size.

Of course, students at Internet-linked universities soon discovered that this was a cool tool. Games appeared, and Usenet discussion groups branched out to include the wacky and the forbidden.

At the same time, computer bulletin boards were beginning to spread. These systems were based on a single PC or Macintosh attached to one or more modems, allowing people to call in, leave e-mail for other BBS users, and contribute to discussions. At first, there was no way for e-mail and online discussions to go beyond the BBS machine itself, but a young hacker named Tom Jennings changed that in 1983 with his FidoNet system.

The FidoNet concept was simple: Each Fido BBS is a node in the network, and is set up to call one or more other Fido nodes nightly to transfer mail and news. Eventually messages and posts wend their way around the world. It can be slow, but it's cheap; it requires nothing fancier than a modem to link up, and it works.

FidoNet took off like a shot, with new nodes springing up everywhere from Mongolia to Montana by 1991. In many ways, FidoNet was—and often still is—the perfect connectivity system for regions where phone service is abysmal and conventional Internet service providers are but a pipe dream. Best of all, the basic software itself is super cheap, although support will cost you, as will prepackaged software components that make things work smoothly and quickly. But a dedicated hacker with adequate knowledge of communications and programming can create a system able to send and receive international newsfeeds and mail, using whatever computer equipment happens to be at hand and with little to no cash outlay.

Makers of other BBS software have borrowed from the FidoNet model to build their own round-robin networking systems. Like Fido boards, these phone-linked BBS networks can be connected with the Internet, at least via an occasional call-up connection, and are therefore part of the global construct that we think of as the Internet. Even the smallest BBS can now add UNIX-to-UNIX Copy Program (UUCP) software to give all its users Internet mail and Usenet feeds for as low as $20 per month for the entire group.

In fact, some BBSs are getting so large that their incomes and number of users can support a full-time Net connection. This category of "Internet nodes" includes well-known services like the Whole Earth 'Lectronic Link, or WELL, in Sausalito, California; New York City's ECHO and MindVox; and many other big regional bulletin boards.

Internetworking Goes Worldwide

The Internet proper may have begun in America, but during its period of gestation sister networks were coming online all over the world. Their development generally followed a pattern quite similar to that of the American Internet: First military and scientific institutes linked their computers with a large technical university or two; then the network spread to include other colleges and perhaps a few private companies, then individual users began to come on board through commercial Internet providers or sneaky arrangements with bonafide members.

Academic networks sprung up like daisies in the 1970s and early 1980s, including the European Academic Research Network (EARN), which got its initial funding from IBM; the Irish Universities Network; the Joint Academic Network (JANET) in England, which is currently managed by British Telecom and has since grown to include major research hospitals and the like; NORDUnet, which links the universities of five Scandinavian countries; and the Finnish University Network (FUNET).

The first nations outside North America to officially connect up with ARPANET were England and Norway, both of which cemented their initial links way back in 1973. But other such connections were gradually forged as the networks evolved, bringing them all under one umbrella as they are today. There have been arguments about standards, but pragmatic network designers seem to be working those out as time goes by.

Asia and the Near East Get on Board

Asia wasn't part of the plan when the Net began, perhaps because some of the biggest contributors to the growth of the Internet in the States were large manufacturers and defense contractors that were in competition with their semi–state-sponsored counterparts in Japan, Taiwan, and Korea. It took a shoestring-budget initiative by a renegade computer scientist at the University of Hawaii to bring the Far East into the mix. The University of Hawaii provided the first Internet links for Korea, Japan, and several of Asia's smaller nations as well, and is still the most important transfer point for United States/Asia traffic.

Japan already had an excellent internetwork called WIDE (Widely Integrated Distributed Environment) in place. Like the Internet, WIDE is a combination of several smaller networks, including BITNET Japan; the education-oriented National Center for Science Information network; JAIN, which links university networks; the Todai International Science Network for physicists and chemists; and JUNET, the first academic-technical internetwork, which is linked to both the University of Hawaii and to CSNET, a U.S. scientific network.

WIDE was created through corporate donations, and keeps going thanks to the tireless labor of graduate students at Keio University in Fujisawa, located in southern Japan. It's highly unusual in that it was not an initiative of the Japanese government and was not based in Tokyo, which is usually the center of everything in this island nation. In fact, that internetworks exist at all in Japan is something of a fluke: The country's land-line phone system was a monopoly run by Nippon Telephone & Telegraph (NTT) until the mid-1980s, and NTT did not even allow privately owned modems on its lines.

Now NTT itself has gotten on the Internet bandwagon—in fact, it offers some excellent Internet resources, including well-designed Web pages. And Japanese consumers have already gotten high-speed ISDN service nationwide, creating a boom in Internet hookups.

Singapore has taken a different approach than Japan's rather free-form one. Its authoritarian government has ordered up a national telecommunications infrastructure that rivals any other nation's, but you won't find private Singaporeans online, unless it's to access government-approved services such as sanitized entertainment offerings or information provided by the government itself. Straight Internet access is available only with a government license, and they are reserved for corporate and government customers. As a result, there's a growing underground Net-hacking movement in Singapore, which must be made up of some the world's braver telecommunicators. Often the instigators are Australian, English, and American programmers working there on contract, infecting their equally curious and information-starved Singaporean peers with their enthusiasm and illicit know-how.

Taiwan is implementing a program similar to Singapore's.

Unless you work in the computer industry, you may not know just how important the programming and design talent of near Eastern countries like India, Bangladesh, and Malaysia is becoming. With national commitments to technical education and a corps of eager students attending the best universities of both their home nations and those abroad, these countries are poised to become major players on the Internet. Malaysia, for example, spent the

early 1990s laying fiberoptic cable whenever a hole was being dug for a new road or other public-works project. And Indian and Bangladeshi programmers are highly visible at every single company involved in producing hardware and software for the Internet's infrastructure.

You can bet that many of the best and brightest will want to take their knowledge home, where they can be stars of a burgeoning industry instead of second assistant to the vice-president of networking services.

Israel is also a major player in computing, especially in the graphics, imaging, and military electronics fields. Naturally, as a U.S. ally Israel was early on the list for networking. Israeli citizens are expressing a high degree of interest in the technology, and can often be found on Internet Relay Chat (IRC) chatlines. 1995 has also seen rapid deployment of a huge number of Israel-themed World Wide Web pages.

As of yet, few Arab nations have become full partners in the Internet club. This has a great deal to do with military regulations on commerce with nations not allied with the United States or Europe, although the Asian nations are doing a brisk trade in our absence.

Recently, Iran has begun to make its presence felt on the Net. It had excellent technical universities before the Ayatollas took over, and perhaps these tentative first steps indicate that they are once again turning out up-to-date graduates. Turkey is also pinning its hopes for a more prosperous future on building up its technological expertise, often with assistance from its European allies.

Iraq and Libya, of course, occupy an Internet no-man's land.

Many observers agree that Vietnam, Cambodia, and Thailand are poised to be the Internet's rising stars as the decade closes. These countries have embraced the latest telephone and computer technology, and in many ways are ahead of their Western peers when it comes to thinking up ingenious, high-tech solutions to deal with a patched-together infrastructure. Not content to wait for Western and Japanese investors to jump in, small start-ups and entrepreneurial efforts beginning here will, by the end of the century, be felt on the Net in a major way.

As of now, China is a big question mark. The government imported its first supercomputer from the United States in early 1995 and is certainly industrializing at an astonishing rate. One of those industries is computer manufacturing, and a good many of those computers are being used within China rather than being exported. On the other hand, you won't be seeing too many private PCs with modems attached in China. Computer links with the outside world, along with the more well-known use of fax machines, were an important conduit for news about the Tienanmen Square massacre and the operation of an "underground railroad" to support and spirit away hunted student radicals afterward. The government is now keeping a tight lid on any technology that might serve to embarrass it in some future situation of similar import.

When you start to explore the World Wide Web, you'll begin to see the nation suffix *au* attached to an awful lot of the most intriguing educational resources. That's because the Australian government is going full speed ahead with a program to put as many of its government, research, and educational archives online as possible.

If you know much about Australian geography, it makes sense. It's a huge continent, but almost all of the population is concentrated in a few coastal cities. Extreme weather conditions in the jungle north and desert center make travel by land difficult. Even driving between major cites like Melbourne and Brisbane can be a grueling ordeal (and since cars and gasoline are quite expensive, a large part of the population relies instead on an excellent public transportation system). The Internet offers a way to make the nation's resources available to schoolchildren in remote Alice Springs, to mining-town doctors, and to average citizens, no matter whether they live in the outback or in cosmopolitan Sydney.

New Zealand shares this zeal for telecommunications, and is also pursuing its place on the Net with a vengeance.

Where the Internet Lags Behind

Networking in the nations of the Southern Hemisphere, with the exceptions of Australia and New Zealand, is just now reaching the point where Europe was in the 1970s. Part of the reason is lack of cash, and lack of a home-grown computer industry to supply the equipment. Another part of it has to do with the legacy of racism and colonialism. Brazil, whose government's policy of favoring home-grown computers over imports worked to build a strong national computer industry, is the loudest voice on the Internet in South America.

Too many of the smartest kids from the nations that make up Latin America, Central America, and Africa still look to the United States or Europe when they dream of a career in computers—and who can blame them? Unstable governments were propped up and used as pawns during the Cold War of the 1960s and 1970s, and are now playing another losing role in the War of the Multinationals. In fact, the harsh economic reality facing the South as the year 2000 approaches is that most of their countries are tied to a diet of no infrastructure-building and no growth in higher education for the forseeable future, thanks to huge debts owed to the World Bank, the EMF, and private banks, and to the austerity programs these entities have imposed.

This paints a bleak picture, but there is activity on the horizon, much of it coming from actions taking place at technical universities, actions much like those that made the cash-starved University of Hawaii into a high-tech hotbed once upon a time. Outsiders are also playing a part, including the Institute for Global Communications (IGC), the San Francisco–based company that runs the PeaceNet, LaborNet, ConflictNet, and EcoNet networks. IGC is a company committed to social change, so it's providing networking assistance and in some cases equipment where it can't otherwise be gotten. This project has so far included support for network building in many Third World countries, including Brazil, Cuba, Nicaragua, Panama, and Ecuador.

Individual entrepreneurs and, of course, multinationals like IBM that see the South as ripe for computer and networking equipment sales, are also doing some network building of their own.

France has had a hand in starting up networks in Africa, where the former colonial power still maintains a business, educational, and military presence. Through the auspices of ORSTOM, a national research institute originally formulated to come up with solutions to problems in "the colonies," it has seeded major African technical universities with bright young engineers. Of course, these universities have plenty of homegrown whiz kids of their own, itching for news on the latest technology and a chance to get even the meager start-up budgets provided with the French personnel. The result is Réseau Informatique de l'OESTOM, or RIO, a network that relies mainly on dial-up connections. Among the countries linked via RIO are Nigeria, Benin, and the Ivory Coast.

The United Staes has gotten involved in Mexico, Central America, and South America, often as part of military-industrial ventures. Mexico has a particularly good university network, linked into the United States and the Internet via the University of Texas at Austin and other schools. In fact, recent events in the southern state of Chiapas may give a clue as to new and perhaps disquieting ways the Net can be used. The Zapatista revolutionaries have used a satellite phone, a portable PC running Windows, and a dial-up Internet account supplied by an academic sympathizer to communicate with the world during and since the rebellion of 1994, effectively circumventing a government-imposed news ban.

In both the Third World and Eastern Europe, FidoNet has frequently played a prominent role in jump-starting the process, often at the hands of scientists, researchers, and educators who have been up against nonexistent budgets and antinetworking bureaucracies. Fido boards provided, and in many cases are still providing, links with networks emerging in Europe or the United States to bring in Internet information and make sharing in global debate and education possible.

Fido is the de facto standard for BBSs in Russia, the former republics of the U.S.S.R., and Eastern Europe. The entire Eastern Bloc was barred from joining the Net during the Cold War, and exporting computer equipment to the region was also illegal. Glasnost opened the doors just enough to set up a rudimentary web of connections, although those who have to contend with it on a daily basis are forthright in saying that the network resembles an information footpath, not a superhighway.

The phone system itself is a Byzantine mess, and the computers aren't much better. Russian computer engineers had few chances to come up with innovative solutions in the 1970s, because their government set them to work copying Western PCs instead of conducting independent research. Despite it all, the excellent system of technical institutes produced an entire generation of bright young computer scientists. The addictive computer game Tetris was the first inkling most westerners had of this programming prowess, but you can be sure it won't be the last.

An important part of the developing Internet connection for ex–Eastern Bloc residents is GlasNet, a Russian network that runs on equipment donated by Sun Microsystems, one the United States's largest computer companies. GlasNet became famous when, during the 1991 coup and ensuing blackout on traditional news media, it was an important avenue for exporting uncensored news.

GlasNet maintains a Gopher server, which includes information in English about getting an account from the United States and how to set up an Internet connection in Russia.

Where the Internet Is Going

In the United States, the most publicized Internet changes occurring now are government involvement beyond the military-academic level and commercialization of the Net. Politicians like Vice President Al Gore have proposed, preached about, and passed a scheme to bring government data and services to the people via a high-speed, public-access network. Gore's "information superhighway" plan has a hidden catch, however, in that it includes a proposal for metered Internet use that could drive costs sky-high for average users not accessing government information.

Big business has also discovered the Internet's potential as an advertising medium, and once-stringent rules against blatant commercial activity have been loosened to allow this type of use. The World Wide Web is proving to be especially fertile ground for advertisers, including record companies, film studios, brokerage houses, and fast-food chains.

Some countries, including the United States and England, have seen calls to add policing functions to the Net, some of which would put restrictions on free speech and political expression that would be far more stringent than those applied to print media or public speakers. Such efforts have met with overwhelming opposition from Net users and civil libertarians, who believe that the Internet's discussion groups and information services are the closest thing to a truly free market of ideas to happen since the Greek *agora*. Their anticensorship ideas are catching on in nations where such restrictions are already in place, either in regards to the entire phone system or to computer communications specifically. India and Italy are two countries that have cracked down on unauthorized telecommunications, only to find that Internet users can bite back. France dealt with its computer sex-chat "problem" by slapping a tax on the companies involved, since censorship seemed impractical at best.

The countries that have been on the Net the longest are now seeing a movement for low-cost, grassroots telecommunications. In the United States and Canada this includes the Freenet system of municipally supported, Internet-linked computer networks. The linkage of private

BBSs and the Internet will also be interesting to watch, as will new uses for the World Wide Web. Already at least one site in the United Kingdom is setting up a WWW interface to a Telnet connection that will allow multiple callers to talk to each other, read or hear online lectures and then discuss them, and enjoy music and visuals as it all happens.

This is only one of the new activities happening on the Net. Internet Radio is another intriguing concept that's only just seeing the light of day. It allows for audio broadcasts, including real-time call-in shows and music, to be "broadcast" via Internet. Radio with a multinational audience, uncensored content and none of the restrictions attached to shortwave and Ham broadcasts is undeniably hot stuff. Another important application will be long-distance telephone conversations over the Net (yes, some people are already doing it), bypassing phone system tariffs and no doubt causing a bit of a hullabaloo with Ma Bell and her global relatives if it catches on.

This next decade on the Internet is going to be very interesting, to say the least.

Chapter 3:
State of the International Net

As the history covered in previous chapters shows, the Internet is still a growing enterprise, with some countries well connected and others still in the early stages of getting online. The following country-by-country list owes a heavy debt to the International Connectivity List maintained by Net pioneer Larry Landweber, which can be obtained from ftp://ftp.cs.wisc.edu/connectivity_table. You can contact Mr. Landweber directly with any comments or additions. (Larry Landweber, Computer Sciences Dept., University of Wisconsin—Madison, 1210 W. Dayton St., Madison, WI 53706; lhl@cs.wisc.edu).

Of course, this listing gives you a picture in time: Changes are occurring rapidly. I've included comments about restrictions on only those countries where such restrictions are well known; I'm sure there are many less-known restrictions as well.

I have used Mr. Landweber's convenient convention of letting the generic term *BITNET* stand in for all BITNET-style networks, which include EARN, NETNORTH, GULFNET, and many others worldwide, and I have retained his coding system. I have added comments about restrictions on use of these networks and special difficulties where such information is known.

Four categories of connectivity are represented by the four letters that precede each entry. A *b* in the first position indicates that the nation has between one and five BITNET sites; a *B* indicates over five BITNET sites. An *I* in the second position indicates a direct international IP (Internet Protocol) link. A *u* in the third position indicates five or fewer domestic UUCP sites (UUCP sites transfer e-mail and newsgroups from BBSs or local networks to the global Internet), while *U* means there are more than five domestic UUCP sites. An *f* in the fourth position means there are five or fewer FidoNet nodes with connections to the global Net, while an *F* indicates more than five such FidoNet nodes. If a country does not have any sites that fit one of these categories, you'll see a - in that position instead.

After the connectivity codes described above, you'll see a two-letter abbreviation. These are the country codes adopted by the International Standards Organization (ISO); confusingly, they are not necessarily the same as the domain name codes used in e-mail addresses for that country.

CONNECTIVITY	ISO COUNTRY CODE	COUNTRY
-I—	DZ	Algeria (People's Democratic Republic of)
—-f	AO	Angola (People's Republic of)
-I—	AQ	Antarctica

CONNECTIVITY	ISO COUNTRY CODE	COUNTRY
—u-	AG	Antigua and Barbuda
BIUF	AR	Argentina (Argentine Republic)
-IU-	AM	Armenia
—-f	AW	Aruba
-IUF	AU	Australia; interactive games banned from Australia's overburdened link with the Internet.
BIUF	AT	Austria (Republic of)
b-U-	AZ	Azerbaijan
—u-	BS	Bahamas (Commonwealth of the)
b—-	BH	Bahrain (State of)
—U-	BD	Bangladesh (People's Republic of)
-Iu-	BB	Barbados
bIUF	BY	Belarus
BIUF	BE	Belgium (Kingdom of)
—U-	BZ	Belize
-IUF	BM	Bermuda
—UF	BO	Bolivia (Republic of)
—u-	BA	Bosnia-Herzegovina
—uf	BW	Botswana (Republic of)
BIUF	BR	Brazil (Federative Republic of)
bIUF	BG	Bulgaria (Republic of)
—U-	BF	Burkina Faso (formerly Upper Volta); Burkina Faso also has dial-up IP access.
—Uf	CM	Cameroon (Republic of)
BIUF	CA	Canada; laws against "hate speech" restrict some types of political discourse, the government has barred online discussion of some court cases, and strict anti-pornography statutes also apply to the Internet.
BIUF	CL	Chile (Republic of)

CONNECTIVITY	ISO COUNTRY CODE	COUNTRY
-IuF	CN	China (People's Republic of); government restricts private-citizen access.
bIu-	CO	Colombia (Republic of)
—U-	CG	Congo (Republic of the)
—u-	CK	Cook Islands
-Iuf	CR	Costa Rica (Republic of)
—Uf	CI	Cote d'Ivoire (Republic of)
-IuF	HR	Croatia
—U-	CU	Cuba (Republic of)
bI-f	CY	Cyprus (Republic of)
bIUF	CZ	Czech Republic
bIUF	DK	Denmark (Kingdom of)
—Uf	DO	Dominican Republic
-Iu-	EC	Ecuador (Republic of)
bIU-	EG	Egypt (Arab Republic of)
—u-	SV	El Salvador (Republic of)
—-f	ER	Eritrea
-IUF	EE	Estonia (Republic of)
—-f	ET	Ethiopia (People's Democratic Republic of)
-Iu-	FO	Faroe Islands
-Iu-	FJ	Fiji (Republic of)
BIUF	FI	Finland (Republic of)
bIUF	FR	France (French Republic); government taxes online sex services but does not prohibit them.
—u-	GF	French Guiana

CONNECTIVITY	ISO COUNTRY CODE	COUNTRY
—u-	PF	French Polynesia
—-f	GM	Gambia (Republic of the)
—UF	GE	Georgia (Republic of)
BIUF	DE	Germany (Federal Republic of)
—uF	GH	Ghana (Republic of)
BIUF	GR	Greece (Hellenic Republic)
-I-f	GL	Greenland
—u-	GD	Grenada
b-uf	GP	Guadeloupe (French Department of)
-I-F	GU	Guam
—u-	GT	Guatemala (Republic of)
—u-	GN	Guinea (Republic of); Guinea also has dial-up IP access.
—u-	GY	Guyana (Republic of)
—u-	HT	Haiti (Republic of); Haiti's UUCP connection is actually just a ccMail e-mail system.
BI-F	HK	Hong Kong
BIUF	HU	Hungary (Republic of)
-IUF	IS	Iceland (Republic of); government restricts sexually explicit material online.
bIUF	IN	India (Republic of); a prohibitive government licensing scheme makes starting a BBS or private service provider extremely expensive, and the government can censor and survey online communications.
-IUF	ID	Indonesia (Republic of); government restricts private-citizen access, content.
bI—	IR	Iran (Islamic Republic of); government probably restricts private-citizen access, content—can't be confirmed.
BIUF	IE	Ireland
BIUF	IL	Israel (State of)
BIUF	IT	Italy (Italian Republic); government is said to use software-piracy laws to seize equipment from BBSs critical of government and its alleged Mafia connections.

CONNECTIVITY	ISO COUNTRY CODE	COUNTRY
-Iu-	JM	Jamaica
BIUF	JP	Japan
—-f	JO	Jordan (Hashemite Kingdom of)
-IUF	KZ	Kazakhstan
—-F	KE	Kenya (Republic of)
—u-	KI	Kiribati (Republic of)
BIUF	KR	Korea (Republic of)
-I—	KW	Kuwait (State of)
—U-	KG	Kyrgyz Republic
-IUF	LV	Latvia (Republic of)
—U-	LB	Lebanon (Lebanese Republic); Lebanon also has dial-up IP services.
—u-	LS	Lesotho (Kingdom of)
-I-F	LI	Liechtenstein (Principality of)
-IUF	LT	Lithuania
bIUF	LU	Luxembourg (Grand Duchy of)
-I-F	MO	Macau (Ao-me'n)
—u-	MK	Macedonia (Former Yugoslav Republic of)
—U-	MG	Madagascar (Democratic Republic of)
—-f	MW	Malawi (Republic of)
bIUF	MY	Malaysia
—U-	ML	Mali (Republic of); Mali also has dial-up IP access.
—u-	MT	Malta (Republic of)
—u-	MH	Marshall Islands (Republic of the)
—uf	MU	Mauritius

CONNECTIVITY	ISO COUNTRY CODE	COUNTRY
BIuF	MX	Mexico (United Mexican States)
-IuF	MD	Moldova (Republic of)
-I—	MC	Monaco (Principality of)
—Uf	MA	Morocco (Kingdom of)
—Uf	MZ	Mozambique (People's Republic of)
—U-	NA	Namibia (Republic of)
—u-	NR	Nauru (Republic of)
—u-	NP	Nepal (Kingdom of)
BIUF	NL	Netherlands
—u-	AN	Netherlands Antilles
—U-	NC	New Caledonia
-IUF	NZ	New Zealand; legislation proposed in late 1994 could impose severe content and access restrictions.
-Iu-	NI	Nicaragua (Republic of)
—U-	NE	Niger (Republic of the); Niger also has dial-up IP access.
—Uf	NG	Nigeria (Federal Republic of)
—u-	NU	Niue
bIUF	NO	Norway (Kingdom of)
—U-	PK	Pakistan (Islamic Republic of)
-IuF	PA	Panama (Republic of)
—u-	PG	Papua New Guinea
—u-	PY	Paraguay (Republic of)
-IUf	PE	Peru (Republic of)
-IuF	PH	Philippines (Republic of the)
BIUF	PL	Poland (Republic of)

CONNECTIVITY	ISO COUNTRY CODE	COUNTRY
bIUF	PT	Portugal (Portuguese Republic)
bIUF	PR	Puerto Rico
-Iu-	RE	Réunion (French Department of)
BIuF	RO	Romania
bIUF	RU	Russian Federation
—u-	LC	Saint Lucia
—u-	VC	Saint Vincent and the Grenadines
—u-	WS	Samoa (Independent State of)
B—-	SA	Saudi Arabia (Kingdom of)
—Uf	SN	Senegal (Republic of); Senegal also has dial-up IP services.
—u-	SC	Seychelles (Republic of)
bIuF	SG	Singapore (Republic of); government restricts private-citizen access, content.
-IUF	SK	Slovakia
-IUF	SI	Slovenia
—u-	SB	Solomon Islands
-IUF	ZA	South Africa (Republic of)
BIUF	ES	Spain (Kingdom of)
—U-	LK	Sri Lanka (Democratic Socialist Republic of)
—u-	SR	Suriname (Republic of)
-I—	SJ	Svalbard and Jan Mayen Islands
—u-	SZ	Swaziland (Kingdom of)
BIUF	SE	Sweden (Kingdom of)
BIUF	CH	Switzerland (Swiss Confederation)
BIuF	TW	Taiwan, Province of China

CONNECTIVITY	ISO COUNTRY CODE	COUNTRY
—uf	TJ	Tajikistan
—-f	TZ	Tanzania (United Republic of)
-IUF	TH	Thailand (Kingdom of)
—u-	TG	Togo (Togolese Republic)
—u-	TO	Tonga (Kingdom of)
—u-	TT	Trinidad and Tobago (Republic of)
-IUf	TN	Tunisia
BI-F	TR	Turkey (Republic of)
—u-	TM	Turkmenistan
—u-	TV	Tuvalu
—-f	UG	Uganda (Republic of)
-IUF	UA	Ukraine
bIUF	GB	United Kingdom (United Kingdom of Great Britain and Northern Ireland); BBS licensing has been proposed for the UK, as have content restrictions for sexual and political matter and a ban on private-citizen encryption.
BIUF	US	United States (United States of America); content restrictions regarding sexual matter have been proposed, as have digital surveillance laws.
-IUF	UY	Uruguay (Eastern Republic of)
—UF	UZ	Uzbekistan
—u-	VU	Vanuatu (Republic of, formerly New Hebrides)

Nations without Direct Internet Links

The following countries, many of them remote island nations, have no form of direct Internet access at all—or at least their status was unknown at press time. That is not to say that private citizens or governments do not use dial-up services based elsewhere to access the Internet. The cost of long-distance phone calls might limit such access but does not prevent it, except in countries without long-distance phone service, such as Pitcairn. It is also possible to use Internet-Ham packet-radio connections to reach these nations. I have been told that

some individuals in the Cayman Islands have set up UUCP access via links with U.S. BBSs.

In addition, official and unofficial representatives of several countries on this list, including East Timor, Myanmar (Burma), and Mongolia, maintain an Internet presence in the United States, Europe, or elsewhere to provide information to the international community. Others may have temporary connections through international aid organizations, private individuals, or businesses.

ABBREVIATION	COUNTRY
AF	Afghanistan (Islamic Republic of)
AL	Albania (Republic of)
AL	Albania (Republic of)
AS	American Samoa
AD	Andorra (Principality of)
AI	Anguilla
BJ	Benin (People's Republic of)
BT	Bhutan (Kingdom of)
BV	Bouvet Island
IO	British Indian Ocean Territory
BN	Brunei Darussalam
BI	Burundi (Republic of)
KH	Cambodia
CV	Cape Verde (Republic of)
KY	Cayman Islands
CF	Central African Republic
TD	Chad (Republic of)

ABBREVIATION	COUNTRY
CX	Christmas Island (Indian Ocean)
CC	Cocos (Keeling) Islands
KM	Comoros (Islamic Federal Republic of the)
DJ	Djibouti (Republic of)
DM	Dominica (Commonwealth of)
TP	East Timor
GQ	Equatorial Guinea (Republic of)
FK	Falkland Islands (Malvinas)
TF	French Southern Territories
GA	Gabon (Gabonese Republic)
GI	Gibraltar
GW	Guinea-Bissau (Republic of)
HM	Heard and McDonald Islands
HN	Honduras (Republic of)
IQ	Iraq (Republic of)
KP	Korea (Democratic People's Republic of)
LA	Lao People's Democratic Republic

ABBREVIATION	COUNTRY
LR	Liberia (Republic of)
LY	Libyan Arab Jamahiriya
MV	Maldives (Republic of)
MQ	Martinique (French Department of)
MR	Mauritania (Islamic Republic of)
YT	Mayotte
FM	Micronesia (Federated States of)
MN	Mongolia
MS	Montserrat
MM	Myanmar (Union of, formerly Burma)
NT	Neutral Zone (between Saudi Arabia and Iraq)
NF	Norfolk Island
MP	Northern Mariana Islands (Commonwealth of the)
OM	Oman (Sultanate of)
PW	Palau (Republic of)

ABBREVIATION	COUNTRY
PN	Pitcairn
QA	Qatar (State of)
RW	Rwanda (Rwandese Republic)
SH	Saint Helena
KN	Saint Kitts and Nevis
PM	Saint Pierre and Miquelon (French Department of)
SM	San Marino (Republic of)
ST	Sao Tome and Principe (Democratic Republic of)
SL	Sierra Leone (Republic of)
SO	Somalia (Somali Democratic Republic)
SD	Sudan (Democratic Republic of the)
SY	Syria (Syrian Arab Republic)
TK	Tokelau
TC	Turks and Caicos Islands
AE	United Arab Emirates

Chapter 4:
Hardware and Software Needs

If your computer can be hitched up to a modem—and you'd be hard-pressed to find a current or recent model that can't be—you can get access to the Internet. That doesn't mean it'll be a solid, reliable, fast, and easy-to-use link. The minimum configuration for a high-speed link using software that supports graphics is 4 megabytes of RAM and enough space on your hard drive to hold your communications software and the occasional downloaded item. In other words, all Macs and any 286, 386, or 486 PC can be made to work, with perhaps a memory or storage upgrade. Of course, recent top-of-the-line computers using the Pentium or PowerPC chip will have no difficulties either.

I hate to suggest it, but if your system doesn't meet these base requirements it might be time to upgrade. But if that simply isn't feasible, you can still get basic Internet capabilities, which is really nothing to sneeze at. You'll have access to most of the same information; it just won't look as pretty or be as easy to find.

Choosing a Modem

The modem is your most essential piece of equipment. Your computer thinks digitally; specifically, in terms of 1s and 0s. You don't see a screen full of numbers because software translates these codes into text and graphics (thank goodness!). Similarly, a modem translates codes coming out of your computer into a format that your phone line can understand and moves them along to their destination.

If all this seems a bit too technical for you at the moment, take a look at a fax machine for a more visual example of how the process works, one that almost everyone has had a chance to deal with at work over the past decade. A fax machine combines three devices—a telephone, a modem, and a scanner—into one little box. When you feed in a letter that you want to send, the scanner part copies it and stores a "picture" of it in digital form. The modem part converts that digital file into analog information that can be sent out over the phone line. With a computer modem, your commands or files can be translated without the need for a scanner.

What kind of modem should you buy? Well, if you want to move along at a pace that's faster than glacial, I recommend getting nothing that runs slower than 14,400 kilobytes per second, or 14.4 Kbps. A 9,600-bps modem will be considerably slower, but it's adequate if you can't get a faster one.

Modem speeds are usually measured in terms of how many thousands of tiny chunks of data, or *bits*, they can convert from analog to digital and send out in one second. Each bit represents a 1 or a 0; 1,000 bits is called a *byte*. *Kilobytes*, or K, refers to thousands of bytes, while *megabytes*, or MB, refers to millions. The first models were 300 bps, and speeds went up rapidly from through 1,200 bps, 2,400 bps, and 4,800 bps to 9,600 bps. At the time this book was going to press, 14.4-Kbps modems were readily available for prices as low as $99. Using a slightly less expensive but slower model will cost you more in connect charges from your Internet service provider every time you get online, and you will quickly tire of waiting for 20, 30, 40 minutes and longer to download software or large text files.

In addition, faster modems have some extras that can boost their usefulness, such as compression capabilities built in to squeeze more data through than the actual transmission speed indicates. With 14.4-Kbps modems, this means that you can push through files at rates up to 19.2 Kbps. The chips in the newer modems are also less prone to transmission errors, because they have various error-checking procedures built in that adjust for line noise and other typical problems.

There are also modems rated at 28.8 Kbps (also called V.Fast or V.FC) out there, at prices about twice that of 14.4-Kbps models. I use one of these myself. There's just one problem with 28.8-Kbps modems: Most of today's off-the-shelf computers can't send or receive uncompressed data any faster than 19.2 Kbps. The serial port that funnels information in and out of your computer just can't hack it. A few V.FC modems come equipped with an extra chip called a 16550 buffered UART (Universal Asynchronous Receiver Transmitter), which adds a data buffer to your system to make sure your computer isn't pushed faster than it can go, losing data in the process. The same chip is found in high-speed serial interface cards, likes Hayes's ESP Communications Accelerator for the PC.

There are also some nifty add-ons that can sneak by this potential bottleneck. Cards like the Hustler from Creative Solutions for the Macintosh's NuBus slot, for example, and Microcom's V.FC Deskporte Fast modems for the PC's parallel port bypass the serial port to bring data in faster.

Since 28.8-Kbps modems can, with compression, move things along at speeds up to 57.6 Kbps, you can see why some Netsurfers would choose to go through the hassle and extra expense of adding a high-speed interface to make them work. If you can afford it, you won't regret it. But if you're unsure, start out with a 14.4. You can always sell it or give it to your kids later on.

ISDN: THE COMING WAVE

Of course, the only constant about computer hardware is that it never stops getting better and faster. The same thing is about to happen to modems.

You may have seen the initials *ISDN*, which stand for Integrated Services Digital Network, in connection with telephone service before. ISDN lines are super-fast fiber-optic cables, the kind that the telephone companies are installing in large cities just as fast as they can dig holes for them. ISDN lines can carry multiple conversations at speeds far surpassing today's phones wires; they're ready to handle multimedia information, too, like videoconferencing for businesses and faster and more reliable Internet access for anyone.

To take advantage of ISDN lines, your phone company or a private phone-line provider has to offer them. If you're in a major metropolitan area, they could be in place already, but the ISDN connection may not go all the way to your phone. You can change that, and you might want to, since with ISDN and a data service unit you can get speeds of up to 128 Kilobytes per second.

ISDN phone service costs between $50 and $500 per month, so it pays to shop around. The first few compatible modems are in the $400 price range, and are usually in the form of an adapter card that also helps your PC handle higher-speed data. You may also have to pay more for your Internet connection.

For now, the cost of ISDN-based Internet access is a little high for most home users, although home-business users might want to give it a look. But with prices for both equipment and service falling rapidly, it's definitely on its way.

Communications Software

Most modems purchased at a computer store or via mail-order come with communications software. Many also have a fax program that lets you receive faxes via your modem and computer and send out computer documents to fax machines. This is a nice extra, and in my opinion it's well worth paying a little more for. Some of the top-of-the-line fax/communications packages and modems can also be set up to put corporate-style voice-mail services on your phone, as in, "To leave a message for Mary, press 1."

Communications software relates to the Internet only if you plan to get a dial-up account. (Read on to the next section for an in-depth explanation on the difference between dial-up and IP Internet accounts.) It'll handle the dialing up part for you, and can also be used for transferring files directly between two computers over the phone and for calling computer bulletin board services (BBSs).

If you purchase your modem used, it may not have software with it. In that case, there are many programs you can buy that will make it work for you. Old PC standbys like Zterm are fine for use with a dial-up account, and dial-up Mac users can choose from Software Ventures's MicroPhone Pro, White Knight from The Freesoft Company, and several others. For IP access, the software you need will often be available for free or at a nominal cost through your service provider. You'll need software that lets your computer communicate using the TCP/IP protocol, plus an application that supports connecting with a SLIP or PPP account (more on these later in the section).

Several "Internet package deals" are available that include a set of IP account tools. Among the most popular PC options are Superhighway Access from Frontier Technologies and Spry's Internet In A Box; full-access accounts for Macs can be enhanced with the applications included in Ventana Press's Internet Membership Kit and other collections.

This book comes equipped with a complete package of IP software, including the World Wide Web browser Enhanced NCSA Mosaic, on the accompanying CD-ROM.

Choosing an Internet Service Provider

Settling on a service provider is the second part of the Internet hook-up equation. Internet service providers are companies that have several dedicated lines installed at their central offices, and rent the use of these lines to customers by the hour or by the month. Customers use modems to call up the service provider's computer system, which controls access to the lines. There are hundreds of service providers available throughout the world, and competition is driving down their prices to such a point that purchasing an unlimited-use IP account may very well be less expensive than paying the basic monthly rates (with their time limits and high per-hour charges) of one of the commercial online services.

How to choose? It depends on what kind of service you want, where you are located, and how much hand-holding you think you'll need.

It's possible to hook up your computer to the Net by installing an actual dedicated high-speed phone line in your home—creating a permanent, 24-hour-a-day link. It costs quite a bit, and unless you plan on spending every waking hour on the box there's really no point. Among home users, there are exceptions to this rule: running a home business that relies on the Internet for orders, or telecommuting for eight hours each day via the Internet, for example. Of course, if you're planning some sort of commercial, charitable, or artistic enterprise that will require full-time connectivity in the future, you can always start small and move up when that time comes. And ISDN service, as outlined in the box on the previous page, could be an alternative to expensive leased lines for those who need more speed.

Dial-up Internet Accounts

The simplest type of connection is called a *dial-up account*, also known as a UNIX account. As the first moniker indicates, with this kind of account you dial up a central computer at your service provider using your favorite communications software. What you'll probably get on your screen is a UNIX shell that helps you navigate around to send e-mail, look for files, and get out on the Net.

UNIX is a computer operating system developed by Bell Labs. It's the language used to program computer equipment that runs the phone system, and the Internet's pioneers settled on it as the best choice for creating their communications vision as well. It's not lovely to look at, but it does have certain advantages. One is that a great deal of UNIX code is in the public domain, meaning that programmers don't necessarily have to pay a royalty to some software company every time they come up with a new program written in UNIX. Another is that it is almost infinitely extensible through just such new programs. If something isn't working right, a smart UNIX programmer can probably come up with a patch of some sort—and since it's royalty free, he or she can give it away to the rest of the world, enabling everyone to solve their similar problems.

Did I mention that UNIX isn't pretty? Yes, I did—but it's a good thing to say it twice, because sometimes UNIX can be downright plug-ugly. The good part is, you don't have to learn to be a programmer to use UNIX-based Internet services. That's where that UNIX shell I mentioned comes in. Shell programs put a slightly better face on UNIX, hiding some of its complexity. With a shell, all you have to learn is a few basic commands, which vary a little depending on the shell and the service provider. Typically, these are two-key combinations, like *Control-X* (which might save an e-mail message in your provider's system) or *ls* (which might list the files you have stored on your provider's computer).

A good provider will have a manual that includes a short list of the basic stuff you need, with more detailed explanations in case you want to know "why" as well as "how." Often this same information is available online by entering *?* or *help* at a command prompt—a *command prompt* is a character like the greater-than sign (>), at which you tell the computer what you want it to do.

If these last few paragraphs started to give you the willies, don't worry. You won't need to call in your 12-year-old whiz-kid nephew to explain this stuff, although in all honesty, the best way to avoid frustration and get online with a minimum of psychic pain is to invite your smartest, most Internet-savvy friend over for a drink and some hands-on help and advice. In addition, all major service providers have technical support people you can call during certain hours for a little help over the phone. Sometimes these folks are way overworked, though, so be sure to read the manual, check if help files are available online, and maybe call that smart friend first. Most of the problems you will encounter will be the result of not following directions to the letter. Computers insist on that sort of thing, unfortunately.

IP Internet Accounts

Dial-up accounts are an inexpensive way to get started, but they don't support the latest Internet software, programs that make navigation easier by putting a graphical interface on the whole shebang. This set of software includes NCSA Mosaic, Netscape, and other graphics-based

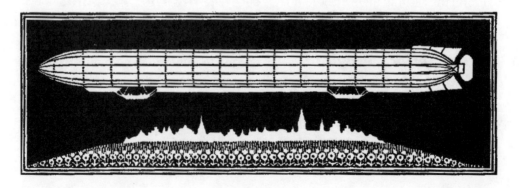

browsers for the World Wide Web, Fetch and Ws_ftp for FTPing, TurboGopher or WsGopher for revving up your Gopher searches, and Eudora and other programs for managing your e-mail. To make these snazzy programs run, you'll need an IP connection.

IP stands for *Internet Protocol*, the communications protocol that the Internet uses to talk to connected devices. Having an IP account means that you'll get a much more direct connection, giving you increased room to maneuver.

There are two types of IP accounts out there: SLIP and PPP. SLIP stands for Serial Line Internet Protocol, while PPP is the acronym for Point-to-Point Protocol. Each of these connects via IP, but in a slightly different way. Along with most service providers, I strongly recommend choosing the PPP option if you can. PPP is more standardized, more reliable, and supported by more Internet software than SLIP. That said, many users still prefer SLIP.

Your service provider can explain how to hook up your computer with SLIP or PPP and will generally provide you with the software to do so, but here are a few helpful hints to get you started.

Macintosh users will need a Control Panel in their System called MacTCP, which is sold by Apple Computer and is also available (often at a considerable discount) in some commercial "instant Internet kits." You'll also need either MacSLIP or MacPPP, depending on which type of account you have, both of which are freeware. (*Freeware* is software distributed at no charge; its cousin, *shareware*, is software distributed free of charge for testing, but you are expected to pay for it if you find it useful.) Other versions of SLIP and PPP software are available from commercial developers, such as InterSLIP from Intercon Systems.

For Windows users, the freeware program Trumpet Winsock is the most common connection program.

Regardless of which computer you use, these programs behave like bridges. They establish the connection between your computer and your service provider, and then they

WHY SHAREWARE RULES

Let me put in a plug for the programmers who write shareware. This Internet thing would not be happening without them, because few people until recently had reason to spend lots of money on Internet software. Shareware bypasses computer stores and advertising hype. If it stinks, the word is out on the Net before the developer responsible has time to turn around. If it needs work, early users tend to give freely of their time and suggestions (and complaints), and these great programmers fix it and put out better stuff. It's always reasonably priced, and if you find yourself relying on it you really should pay up. It's the right thing to do, and I like the thought of kitchen-table entrepreneurs making a good living from people honest enough to pay on the honor system. Don't you?

more or less disappear into the background. You're online: What to do now?

What you do is graphically achieve all those things poor dial-up users have to slog through using an obnoxious, hard-to-remember command-line interface. The way you do it is by running programs that give you a point-and-click face for common Internet procedures, from obtaining free software from an FTP archive to browsing through the World Wide Web. Almost all such programs are available as freeware or shareware.

Your service provider will no doubt have a hefty archive of such programs, and can suggest which are best for your needs and their specific set-up. One category that will be essential is software that can decompress files. To save valuable space, not mention uploading and downloading time, many files found on the Internet have been squished to fit with a variety of software programs. Until you bring them back to their normal size, you can't use them. By the way, be sure to remember that compressed files are *binary*, not text files, and set your software to download them as such or they'll be unusable anyway.

You can tell which software was used, and in turn what you'll need to expand the file, by the suffix at the end of the file's name. For example, if it says .zip, you'll need WinZip or a compatible program; while the suffix *.sit* refers to StuffIt, either StuffIt, StuffIt Deluxe, or the freeware UnStuffIt will do the trick. UnStuffIt also decodes BinHexed files—binary files that have been compressed and encoded as ASCII text for easy transfer via e-mail—and files with the .hqx suffix.

Accessing the World Wide Web with graphics requires a Web browser; see Chapter 11 for more on these and other WWW tools.

Well, there you have it: If you can pull together a computer, a modem, software, a phone line, and a service provider, you have everything you need to get started. Your service provider should be able to answer any specific questions that are beyond the scope of this necessarily brief and basic discussion; if they can't, you may have the wrong service provider!

Chapter 5:
Getting an Internet Account

You'll find a list of better-known U.S. and international service providers in Appendix A, but with the exponential growth of this mode of communications, it seems that new ones are springing up faster than anyone can keep track of them.

If you live in a major metropolitan area, choosing will mainly be a matter of comparing several companies on the basis of price, technical support, and services. Some providers offer a beginner-level handbook and training; others expect you to figure it out on your own. Some provide Internet software; others expect you to buy your own. Regardless, be sure that the service provider you pick does offer both dial-up and IP accounts, even if you're quite sure that the former is all you want for now. If you change your mind, switching providers can be a real hassle.

If you don't see a company on the list that's located in or very near your town, that doesn't mean you're out of luck. Several of the companies listed offer service nationwide, often with local access numbers. Also, be sure to check out any free local or regional computer publications you may find at your nearest computer shop. These will almost always have an ad or two for a company with local connections.

Your yellow pages phone directory may have listings as well: check under *Internet*, *communications*, *online*, and even *BBSs* and *bulletin board systems*. It is now relatively easy for even small BBSs to add an Internet link and resell their service to you. Sometimes all they offer is a UUCP connection for e-mail and Usenet newsgroups, but many are now providing full dial-up access to the Net. In any case, the local BBSs are an excellent place to ask about a service provider.

Computer users groups, if you happen to belong to one, are also a good information resource. They may maintain a list of providers, or at least give you a name of the local Internet guru. Such groups meet monthly to talk about new hardware, troublesome software, and job opportunities. They generally are listed in free computer magazines; the manufacturer of your computer should also have a national list of users groups. In some areas, users groups are forming specifically to deal with Internet software and activities.

If you live in a small town or rural area, your choices may be few and not as appealing as those available to your big-city counterparts. You may have to pay not just connect-time charges and monthly fees, but long-distance bills as well. Yuck! If there's no alternative but to deal with a provider outside your area, look into using TymeNet or SprintNet, two services that can provide cut-rate long-distance hours to online-service users. All national service providers are familiar with these money-saving calling plans, and most have contracted with one or the other for customers just like you. The extra charges will appear on your online-service bill.

You might also purchase Internet service through CompuServe, Delphi, America Online, or another national online service, if it offers a local access number.

Payment

Many providers insist that you pay by credit card, which can be a problem for some of us. In my experience, most service providers can be persuaded to take payment by check *if* you will be paying in advance. Too many companies have been burned by customers who run up huge bills on their accounts, then disappear into thin air. I can hardly blame them for not giving others a chance!

One thing to look out for is the aforementioned high connect-time charges, fees for "special" services such as receiving large files or downloading files, and higher prices for accessing the service with a high-speed modem. You will be shocked by how quickly these little extras can mount up, especially during your first couple of months online, when you are sure to bungle about and spend lots of time in what should be carefree exploration. Flat-fee accounts with either a limited or an unlimited number of hours usually end up being a better bargain, even if the base monthly fee is higher than the competition's.

Freenets and Other Ways to Get Online Really Cheap

In a few parts of the United States, you can get Internet access for free, or almost free. The access is generally by way of a dial-up account, not an IP connection, but free and cheap are both very good prices.

One such service is called a *freenet*. These are municipal information networks supported by governments or private foundations. Often they have been set up to provide access to government services and documents, such as information on how to pay your property taxes, but end up providing a wide array of resources. Some have quite the online-community feel to them. Call your public library to see if there's such a network in your town—contrary to the stuffy image many folks have about librarians, they are probably the most "wired" people in the United States today. If your town has a freenet, you can bet that the library was the first institution to sign on.

In fact, many public libraries offer Internet access themselves. The Seattle, Washington and Portland, Oregon libraries, for example, have Internet terminals in the library and also offer dial-up service to patrons from home. Their Internet systems are connected to the libraries' own electronic card-catalog systems, which are linked up with local universities and are geared toward public use for research and educational purposes. Enterprising dial-up users in these and other cities have discovered ways to "work the system," however, discovering "secret" pathways that lead to Telnet access to university systems that allow e-mail accounts and personal file archives to be set up. Except in cases of extreme abuse, most libraries have chosen to turn a blind eye to such examples of typical American ingenuity.

University and college Internet systems are generally restricted to students, faculty, employees, and alumni. If none of these categories fits, you may be able to get around this by signing up for a campus library card. Most people are unaware of it, but almost all public universities and many private ones will make their library collections available to "guest researchers" for a modest fee, perhaps $50 to $100 per year. If library access includes a dial-up or on-campus Internet connection, there you have it. Auditing or taking a single class can work the same way: Perhaps you can talk a sympathetic professor into letting you take an independent study course in Research via the Internet?

Don't neglect the local community college or high school, either, as many are getting online and offering inexpensive access to students and, in a few cases, even parents.

Then there's the workplace. Now, far be it from me to advocate playing Netsurfer on the company system while you're supposed to be working. But if your employer has Internet access, you may be able to legitimately use the system after hours from your home. Talk to the guys and gals in the computer room. If it's out of the question for security or expense reasons, they'll be quick to tell you. If not, they can explain the procedures and get you going. It will no doubt help your cause if you can come up with some work-related reason for needing access, such as "I'm trying to build up my online research skills so I can be more of an asset to my department in that area." You know the drill.

Of course, the problem with free and cheap access is that everybody wants it. Sooner or later, busy signals will increase, and you'll be faced with slow operation times as thousands of cheapskates compete for the same limited bits of bandwidth. Using these systems to check out the Net is a great idea, but if you find that it's something you'd like to keep exploring, why not contact a commercial provider about a personal account? It's not terribly expensive, and it'll be well worth it in terms of improving the quality and quantity of your Internet experience.

Getting Online from an International Location

If you need to access your account from overseas, or if you are going abroad for an extended period and want to set up an account there, check in with the service providers listed for the continent you'll be on for specific options. As indicated in Chapter 3, the greatest obstacle you may face is the state of the local phone system. In many areas, practically the only way to get phone service within a reasonable period of time is to invest in a cellular phone. A friend of mine who moved to the Czech Republic found that having a line installed at her rural dwelling would take about two years (and that's two years in Czech bureaucrat time, which could translate into three or four).

In the developing world, there often isn't even the option of waiting for the phone company. In response, the number of cellular phones in Vietnam long ago outstripped the number of land lines in that country, while in India satellite phones have become all the rage in remote villages.

You may also face some interesting problems with equipment compatibility. Adapters are available to make U.S. telecommunications equipment work with standard European phone jacks, of which there are several models. They don't always work. You'll find Euro-style jacks in most of Africa, while the American model or something similar predominates in Central and South America. Sometimes this means the *old* American phone jack, the kind with two wires that run into a box. You'll have to wire in your modem manually if that's the case.

Dealing with phone systems that use the old-fashioned switchboard with a human operator can also be a royal pain. You'll have to arrange in advance to have the connection made, then make your modem call. Party lines and modems don't mix, of course.

You'll also need to call in an electronics whiz to make the connection in Russia, in the republics that once made up the U.S.S.R., and much of Eastern Europe. I'm told that marrying a modem and a vintage Soviet phone jack requires two wires, one alligator clip, considerable patience, lots of luck, and some good vodka for both the electrician and you. And even then, you'll find that your phone goes dead on a regular basis for no reason, that (in the words of Laure Akai, Moscow resident and one of the researchers who contributed to this book) your screen will "freak out" repeatedly due to line noise, and that calls to your service provider often simply don't go through. It's enough to make an expensive cellular phone and modem look less like a yuppie luxury and more like a lifeline!

In truly remote locations—such as in the middle of the ocean on a yacht—you may be able to link in via packet radio. This is a computer-enhanced variant on Ham radio. My husband's parents have used this with some success while living on their boat in Mexico. They've learned how to call up weather data and send out emergency calls, and I suspect they're avoiding adding e-mail only to keep their retirement as quiet and idyllic as possible.

Finding a Service Provider on the Internet

The Internet itself is your best resource for finding a service provider. For PDIAL, a frequently updated list providers maintained by Peter Kaminski, send an e-mail message to the address info-deli-server@netcom.com— the body of the message must read *PDIAL*.

Separate lists of European, Eastern European, African, and Asian service providers are maintained by Carl Benoit, a Belgian Nethead. These can be obtained in several ways:

- Try the World Wide Web at http://www.earth.org/ ~lips/
- FTP to sumex-aim.stanford.edu and track down the correct path:
    - /info-mac/comm/information/internet-dialin-Europe-2.1
    - /info-mac/comm/information/internet-dialin-Exussr-2.1
    - /info-mac/comm/information/internet-dialin-Africa-1.3
    - /info-mac/comm/information/internet-dialin-Asia-1.0
- Gopher to rip.psg.com/1m/networks/connect/
- See the Usenet newsgroups alt.internet.access. wanted or alt.internet.services, and look for the appropriate associated file:
    - Directory of Internet access in Europe.2.1
    - Directory of Internet access in ex-USSR.2.1
    - Directory of Internet access in Africa.1.3
    - Directory of Internet access in Asia.1.0

The service providers listed in Appendix A were culled from these exhaustive lists, which run into the dozens of pages. The lists are updated monthly.

Chapter 6:
Internet Addresses and How to Find Them

An Internet e-mail address usually contains a number of clues about where it's from. It may indicate a person's name (*btraven@mexico.com* might belong to B. Traven), the company they work for (as evidenced by suffixes like *ibm.com, apple.com,* and *hp.com*), how they connect to the Net (the suffixes *panix.com, netcom.com, compuserve.com,* and *aol.com* are all based on the names of popular Internet service providers or online services), or even what country they live in.

Here's how the address system works. Let's take this fictitious address as an example:

```
pneruda@poetsinc.santiago.cl
```

The first part of the address, *pneruda*, is called the *username*. Sometimes it's a full name, sometimes a contraction or initials, sometimes a nickname or even a number. No matter what the username is, it denotes an actual e-mail box on a system somewhere. The @ in the middle stands for *at*, because the second part of the address tells you precisely where pneruda's mailbox is located. The words after @ name either the host computer or a *domain*, which could be a network, a subnetwork on a computer, or simply a name chosen by the user or an entity they work for. In computerese, that's called a *Domain Name Service*, or DNS, address.

Domain names can be reserved through many service providers; generally, a modest fee will be levied. The provider registers the name for you, which might be the name of your business, something amusing, or even the name of someone else's business! One prankster registered "mcdonalds.com" before the Big Mac people got around to it, just to see what would happen—let's just say the results were predictable and involved expensive lawyers.

In the case of pneruda's address, the domain is something called *poetsinc*. Perhaps that's a corporation or literary society called *Poets Inc.*? There are no further clues in this address, although many addresses include a suffix that denotes what kind of entity the user is affiliated with. Here's a short list of commonly used domain suffixes:

.com	Businesses
.edu	Schools and research facilities
.gov	Government agencies
.mil	Military facilities
.net	Major service providers
.org	Organizations, such as clubs and service groups

Pneruda's address uses a different kind of identifying suffix. It tells you what city and country it emanates from: Santiago, Chile. Countries are identified on the Net by two-letter country codes, such as *CL* for Chile, *CA* for Canada, and *FI* for Finland. Most, but not all, of these codes are identical to the ISO country codes listed in Chapter 3.

Mailing List and Listserv Addresses

Addresses with that telltale @ in the middle can be e-mail conduits to an individual, a group, a company, or even a robotlike software program called an *automailer*, which performs a special function when it receives mail, such as putting you on the subscription list for an electronic newsletter or kicking out a price list that you have requested for a company's products. If you see an address with the username *Listserv* or with a destination that's preceded by *mailer*, you're definitely dealing with an automailer. A Listserver address may be accompanied in print by a second, similar address, which is the one you would use to post (add your own comments) to the list rather than to subscribe to it (arrange to receive it). Also, you may need to include specific text in your e-mail message to subscribe (such as *subscribe COOL LIST*).

Internet Resource Addresses

Other resources on the Internet have addresses that look much like the last half of an e-mail address. This makes sense, because when you call up an FTP site, Gopher server, or Web page, you are trying to contact a computer rather than a human being. Here's an entry from this catalog that we can use as an example:

Name:	Archive of French comics, including *Valerian* and *Tintin*.
Type:	FTP
Address:	ftp.funet.fi/pub/culture/comics/

The address tells you that a) it's an FTP server, a computer set up to let you grab files using software that supports the File Transfer Protocol; b) the computer is called ftp.funet.fi; and c) the computer is located in Finland (FI). The part divided by slash describes the route you will take to find the archive dedicated to the brave boy detective Tintin. You'll open the *pub* directory, where you will find and open the *culture* directory. From there you'll open the *comics* directory and choose from a list of items found therein.

Addresses for computers that you can Telnet to will have a similar format to the one listed above, as will Gopher sites; Telnet sites will also have a port number. Such names do not always include hints like "ftp" or "gopher" to let you know how to access the site; if faced with a mystery address, you may just have to experiment with different methods.

Computers linked to the Internet also have a numerical address called an IP (Internet Protocol) address. You're unlikely to bump into one of these, but if you do they are pretty recognizable. They take the form of numbers divided by periods, such as 131.112.172.15. These are simply a numerical code for the written address, and you can use them the same way.

World Wide Web addresses are slightly different from all others, but are easy to recognize because they always start with the prefix *http://*, as in:

```
http://www.msen.com/~pauleric/mist.html
```

This is the address of a neat site called Mysteries of the Web. The prefix *http* denotes the method you'll use to access the archive. The *://* divides it from www.msen.com, which is a the address of the computer where the page resides (and since you now know .com means it's a commercial entity, *msen* must be a contraction of the corporate name). The last part of the address, */~pauleric/mist.html*, is the path to the Web page.

Web addresses can be terribly long, and are known both technically and colloquially as URLs, which stands for *Universal Resource Locaters*.

Wide Area Information Server (WAIS) addresses are the simplest. Since you will already be using a WAIS search engine to find them, all the information the software needs to reach the requested site is the name of the online database to be searched. This will be a single word or a hyphenated phrase, such as *anthropology* or *supreme-court*.

Usenet newsgroups have simple addresses that attempt to display the interest discussed therein. These can be as simple as *rec.heraldry*, or as long and silly as the infamous *alt.barney.dinosaur.die.die.die*. There are several classes of newsgroups, including rec (recreational), comp (computer related), news (for news, of course), sci (scientific), social (social issues), talk (pure debate), and misc (everything else). The alt category (for "alternative" subjects) is not Usenet proper, but it looks just like it and can be requested in the same way.

The dedicated searcher will find that there are other types of "alternative" newsgroups. *Clari* is the prefix for newsgroups originating on the ClariNet system (ClariNet is United Press International's foray into electronic journalism), *bit* denotes BITNET newsgroups, *de* precedes the names of Usenet-style groups in German, *fj* is the designation for Japanese newsgroups, and so on.

How to Find (Almost) Anyone's E-Mail Address

Getting someone's e-mail address can be as easy as opening the phone book. It all depends on how carefully the person you're trying to contact guards his or her privacy.

At the furthest extreme, people have the choice of sending their mail and Usenet posts through devices called automatic remailers (see Chapter 8 for more information on these). But most people, for better or worse, allow their e-mail addresses and some associated personal information to become public by default.

WHOIS is a service that can be reached via Telnet, a local client, or e-mail. You must know what company, school, or government office the person is at. Most of the people in the WHOIS directory are involved in some way with creating or maintaining the Internet. Obviously, this limits the usefulness of WHOIS searches. A list of WHOIS servers is available by e-mail; just send a message to mhpower@athena.mit.edu.

Generally called *white pages* directories, X.500 directories keep track of e-mail addresses via their X.500 attributes. X.500 is a standard for mail transfer. These directories are available via a local client or Gopher server: look for an item like */Phonebook* on any Gopher menu.

KIS stands for *Knowbot Information Service*, an automated e-mail address information system that's fairly new. It searches archives of addresses at several predetermined sites using Telnet or e-mail. Developed by the Corporation for National Research Initiatives, it checks out WHOIS, X.500, and finger lists (lists that use a special protocol to tell you who's behind an e-mail address) to track down your person, based on their last name. You will see a name, location, e-mail address, and sometimes even a street address and phone number if the person is found.

Netfind is a program that searches many databases to find a name that you enter. Telnet to bruno.cs.colorado.edu and log in as *netfind*. It's a hard program to use, so start your journey by entering *h* for help!

CWIS (*Campus Wide Information System*) is used by universities to keep track of ever-changing e-mail addresses on campus. If the person you're searching for is a student, employee or faculty member, they should be here. It's available via Gopher or CWIS servers.

CSO name servers, named after their developers at the Computing Services Office of the University of Illinois at Champagne-Urbana, are available through Gopher menus or through special software at some sites (mostly U.S. universities).

If you have an e-mail address for a mystery person, you can identify the owner by "fingering" them. A *finger search*, available through the menu of your UNIX shell account or many Gopher menus, brings up public information on Internet users.

If you want to identify a person who posted something on Usenet, you can feed the name you see in the *From:* line at the top of the post into a system at MIT that may or may not have an e-mail address or other information to send back to you. To do so, send an e-mail message to mail-server@pit-manager.mit.edu. The body should read

```
send usenet-addresses/name
```

with *name* being the last name or one-word alias of the mystery poster. Here's an example:

```
send usenet-addresses/waltz
```

might turn up information on me. You will receive a reply from MIT with the info if it does, or a note that says there were no matches.

Chapter 7: Netiquette, FAQs, and Emoticons

When in Rome, do as the Romans do" is age-old travel advice. If you're traveling in cyberspace, I hope you'll amend it a bit. Not all of the "Romans" there behave as the rest of us wish they would.

There's no Emily Post robot online to make you shape up, but there are a few simple rules (some call them "netiquette") that will help you avoid causing a scene.

- Don't type in ALL CAPITAL LETTERS; it's considered the equivalent of shouting.
- If you are asked for someone else's e-mail address, please ask the owner of that address before you pass it along.
- If you are going to quote e-mail you received from someone else in a public forum, such as a newsgroup, you would be wise to ask permission beforehand. At the very least, make sure you attribute the quote properly and show it in context.
- Do not flood the Net with your resume or business solicitations. This goes beyond rude, and the response you'll get will no doubt be beyond rude as well!
- When participating in newsgroups and mailing lists, try to resist the urge to post "I agree" and "me too!" responses to other people's posts. You can imagine how annoying it is to find a mailbox full of these.
- It is illegal to post copyrighted images, text, or software online. Major corporations (Playboy, Disney, Microsoft, and so on) now employ many Netsurfers

whose job it is to find such items and find out who uploaded them. You don't want your name to end up on their lists.
- Don't type in the heat of the moment; you will regret it later. There's a time and a place for *flaming* (spouting off angrily at someone), but public forums are probably not it.
- Be careful about overusing resources: This includes those of your service provider, your school or employer, and the sites that provide Internet resources.

Frequently Asked Questions (FAQs)

If you have a question about how to do something on the Net, chances are you're not the first to ask it. One of the more pleasant customs on the Internet, and one of special significance to new users, is the provision of FAQs (pronounced *faks*). These files contain the answers to your questions, from the basics of playing Multi-User Dungeons (MUDs) to everything you ever wanted to know about the inner workings of Telnet systems.

The Usenet newsgroup news.answers is one place to find FAQs. You can subscribe to news.answers; it is also archived at the Johns Hopkins University Gopher server, at merlot.welch.jhu.edu. Choose *Usenet News and FAQS*. If you prefer to FTP, use anonymous FTP to visit rtfm.mit.edu, and follow the path /pub/usenet/news.answers for a list. There's also a complete list of

FAQs, updated regularly, available by anonymously using FTP to go to rtfm.mit.edu and following the path /pub/usenet/news.answers/index.

Look for the FAQ before you ask the question. You will get better advice and avoid looking silly.

Emoticons

Lots of old Internet users think emoticons are too cutesy-pie, but emoticons still get plenty of use. The main reason is that it's hard to express complex emotions like irony online. We forget that much of what we convey in face-to-face conversation is communicated by facial expression, body language, or tone of voice, and we feel at a loss when we don't have those tools at our disposal. These little combinations of keyboard symbols are intended to bridge the gap.

Here are a few of the most frequently used emoticons. Creating new ones is an art form, and jokesters have come up with enough to fill a small book. Emoticons are also called *smileys*.

:) or :-)	Your basic smiley face; means you're happy or speaking in jest; some people also use <grin>
:-(	Sad face
:-X	Sending kisses
:-0	Wow!
;) or '-)	Winking face, for sly remarks
%-)	Crazy or blotto, as in "I have an excuse for typing so badly"
:-@	Screaming face

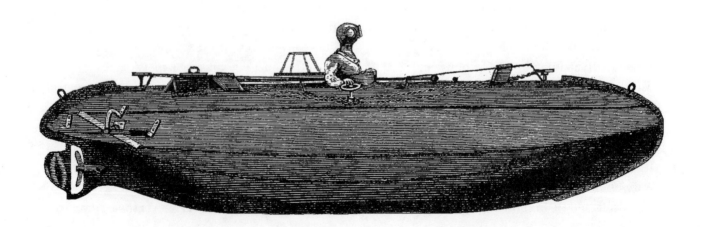

Chapter 8: Security and User Safety

Especially for parents with children, user safety is a very real concern. Obviously, someone you bump into on the Internet can't reach out and knock you over the head, steal your wallet, and take off in your car. It does occasionally happen that people are defrauded over the Internet, however. And as in any place that offers some measure of anonymity, a few antisocial types are out there.

Much has been made in the popular press of "cyber-rape," something that has occurred in the course of interactive role playing in at least one Multi-User Dungeon game. Unpleasant though such events must be for those involved, there is a simple solution to any kind of "cyber-attack" attempted on your person or gaming character when you are online: Pull the plug on the session.

Another kind of annoyance is the online masher, a guy who notices that a woman is present in an interactive forum or chat room and sends her unwanted romantic or sexual overtures. I have yet to have this happen to me in a decade of online activity, but I do know others who have been sexually harassed electronically. It seems to be more prevalent on commercial online systems than on the Internet per se, since commercial systems often display data about persons online, including their age, gender, and perhaps a description. Just because a company asks you for such information doesn't mean you need to provide it, of course, and not doing so may offer you a measure of invisibility. Some women choose names that do not telegraph their femaleness, and I don't think that's a bad idea, although I wish we lived in a world where it wasn't necessary.

I don't like to be hassled on the street, and when it happens there I'm pretty forthright about telling Mr. Offensive where to go. I recommend that any woman (or man—it could happen to anyone!) who is the recipient of rude or raunchy overtures online take the same tack. Most other users do not find this behavior acceptable, so embarrass the jerk if you can. Hopefully, he or she will go away. There are technological solutions too, which can be especially useful for filtering out the boors who occasionally infest a favorite Usenet newsgroup. Known by the colorful name of "Bozo Filters," these programs can tell your computer to automatically delete any message posted by Mr. or Ms. Pottymouth. Ah, sweet relief!

If the behavior is carrying over into your e-mail box, try simply deleting every message until the sender gets the message. Responding may only exacerbate the problem. In extreme situations, you might ask your service provider— or theirs—for help in pounding it in.

In a very few cases people have had the misfortune to encounter outright psychopaths online. This type of person may use his or her manipulative personality to worm personal details out of you, such as your name, address, or phone number. I recommend never giving out such information except under controlled circumstances. You don't want some weirdo to show up at your door next Wednesday night, right? It has happened a couple of times, and I'm sure we can all imagine how frightening it must have been for the person who had to face down the cyber-weirdo in the flesh.

Even worse, there are some real creeps who prey on children online. Pedophiles have found that the Net's anonymity and easy access to kids computing alone can be a powerful combination. They may represent themselves as someone the child's own age, perhaps a virtual "pen pal," or as an adult mentor with access to cool software or other treats. Teenagers are generally aware enough to steer clear of these hazards, but I think a lecture on the possibility for danger is in order. In particular, you should make it clear that any first meetings with new online friends are to take place under your supervision. Younger kids really need more adult involvement than a one-time lecture can provide. Why not spend most of your online time together if you're worried about their vulnerability?

I don't want to make too much of these "dangers." Because fear sells, many magazines, newspapers, and TV news programs have run scare stories about the Internet and about computer BBSs. You are probably *less* likely to run into a dangerous character on the Internet than you would at a real-life gathering of a similar size, such as Mardi Gras in New Orleans or the World Cup soccer finals. And in most cases the remedy is simple, instantaneous, and requires no lethal force: Just break the connection.

Online Cons

Con artists and the Internet are a truly dangerous combo. Flim-flammers are already realizing the Net's potential, much as they have with the telephone and the fax machine. It's a real annoyance to have to wade through messages inviting you join some pyramid sales scheme—I mean scam—or to buy condo timeshares, stocks, commodities, or what have you, sight unseen. Obnoxious sales pitches are not as uncommon as they should be on newsgroups, and they occasionally come by way of e-mail, too. Con artists are even putting up glitzy Web pages, inviting you to spend your dough on their dubious invention or venture.

Many businesspeople are legitimately trying to leverage on the Internet's popularity by using it as a sales tool. As long as no sales pitch comes to you unbidden, as long as you are not harassed by repeated e-mail inquiries after you check out and discard such pitches, and as long as the transaction is on the up-and-up, hardly anyone has a problem with this. Even though the Internet was conceived of as a noncommercial entity, it's a given that some measure of business activity will intrude over the next several years. All of the regular laws apply, there's just no online fraud investigators or cops to enforce them. This fact puts you in charge of your own financial well being.

As with the shady salesman at your door, don't invite anyone into your online life who seems to be selling a too-good-to-be-true dream. If you are considering an investment of some sort, insist on receiving the proper documentation in writing, by "paper" mail, and go over it with a professional financial advisor. Don't give out your home or business phone number without thinking twice. Check out the credentials of a company before sending them a nickel. Even job offers or what appear to be "for sale" listings by private parties online can be a rip-off.

Businesspeople who do cross the line have found that Internet users have a tendency to retaliate, flooding their e-mail boxes with nasty complaints, and even resorting to old juvenile stand-bys like ordering unwanted pizzas delivered to their offices. It may be immature, but I'll bet it's effective.

Security

There are impediments to running a legitimate business online, and these problems also affect consumers. The most crucial of these is that the Net is not a secure channel for distributing personal financial information or credit card numbers without first hiding your data from prying eyes. These eyes are out there. And they are looking for credit card numbers or other information they can use to get their hands on your money. Large corporations have been burned by hackers who set up programs in their networks, including their Internet connections, that searched out and snagged credit card transaction information. Don't let it happen to you!

To avoid getting ripped off in this way, you can learn from the big corporations. When they want to transact important business online or send sensitive documents, they use encryption.

Encryption software translates your

message into a code that only a recipient with the proper code key can break. An often-used metaphor for an unencrypted Internet message is that of a postcard—and as one of my former roommates learned to his chagrin when his girlfriend sent him a spicy postcard and I thought it was for me, you'd better not send anything sensitive in a way that any postal employee or passer-by can read! An encrypted message, like a letter in an envelope, is safe from most snoops. Even the government's supercomputers have a hard time cracking the codes of the latest public-key encryption software, which requires two "code keys" to open.

Which leads us to a delicate problem. The Internet needs secure data transfer, but encryption is considered to be a "weapon" by the National Security Administration of the United States. That means that heavy-duty encryption software is not to be exported, although the paradoxical reality is that, due to illegal export, such programs are even more widely available abroad than they are here. The result? Companies and individuals are forced to use weaker, less safe encryption programs for any message that goes outside the borders of the United States. Software developers are reluctant to invest in building better encryption software, because sales will be limited to the domestic market. And Internet crooks and Nosy Nellies continue to have a field day.

Whether and how you use encryption is up to you. I personally would not purchase anything with a credit card over the Net unless I was sure that the number would be encrypted for its entire journey. Online sales systems under development will do just that. In the meantime, perhaps it's best to shop by Net, then pay by mail or phone. (Phones aren't secure either, particularly the cellular variety, but there are fewer listeners to worry about.)

If you are interested in adding encryption to your software arsenal, one of the most popular and widespread programs in use on the Internet is Pretty Good Privacy, better known as PGP. Written by a fiercely independent programmer named Phil Zimmerman, who is having some problems with the government as we speak, PGP is a highly secure public-key encryption system. For information on how to get and use PGP, which is available for many computer types, see the listings under "Encryption and Privacy Issues" in Part 2.

I understand that Zimmerman is currently working on a version of PGP that can encrypt phone calls made via computer as well—maybe someday he will get around to solving the cellular security problem, too!

It is illegal to distribute PGP outside the United States, although it was available for sale on floppy disks at street kiosks in Moscow when a friend visited there many years ago, and it is routinely found on overseas Internet servers.

I wish I could say that PGP is easy to use, but it's not: Explaining the intricacies of setting up a PGP key ring and encrypting messages is beyond the scope of this book. I highly recommend downloading the readily available PGP documentation file.

Protecting Your Privacy

Credit card numbers and love letters aren't the only thing you might want to protect online. Many people do not want their names, addresses, work affiliations, and other personal data displayed to the world, and perhaps added to electronic databases for advertising or more sinister purposes.

If you don't want your e-mail address to be visible on your mail, you could try using an *automatic remailer*. These are computers that strip out all the identifying address information from a message, then send it on to its destination with the remailer's address where the sender's used to be.

Lest you think that anyone who tries such a ploy is up to no good, there are many reasons that someone might wish to use a remailer. If you are Bill Gates, billionaire owner of Microsoft, you certainly don't want your private Internet address appearing on the Net. It's a sure bet that you'd be greeted the next day by umpteen notes begging for a share of your cash. The same goes for people who have good reasons to avoid being listed in any kind of directory, such as former spouses of abusive partners, lottery winners, and political refugees.

Many automatic remailer users simply want to avoid having their e-mail address gathered for commercial purposes without their permission. And some truly do have nefarious purposes, such as evading Interpol (the international police force) or the FBI. It should be noted, for anyone who fits into the latter category, that the operators of remailers can be (and have been) subpoened to get the name and true e-mail address of a criminal suspect who uses their service.

For more detailed information about remailers and how to use them, FTP to ftp.csua.berkeley.edu:/pub/cypherpunks/remailer, where you can download the text "hal's.remailer.gz" and other information.

Privacy laws governing the use of information gathered online differ from nation to nation, and the few that exist are new and untested. Some service providers have tried to sell information about their customers, and have been met by a great deal of flak. If your privacy is truly important to you, you'll think twice about volunteering information via online questionnaires and the like. Developing a database is usually what these are there for.

A Word about Viruses, Hackers, and Crackers

The word *virus* makes everyone nervous, whether you're talking about computers or the common cold. Viruses are out there, although most are fairly benign. But why take chances? You can't get a virus from a text file, but a binary file (a computer program) could carry one. It's prudent to have the latest virus-protection software installed on your computer, and to run any downloaded programs through it before they go on your hard drive. My computer once "caught" a virus called WDEF right in the middle of a crucial project, and it ended in a tragedy of lost files, missed deadlines, and sobbing editors. No fun.

Until recently, when a newbie asked if hackers could invade your home computer when you were hooked up to the Internet, the standard answer from oldtimers was derisive laughter. However, events in the spring of 1995 proved that it can, in some special cases, be done. Infamous computer cracker Kevin Mitnick (a *hacker* is an enterprising programmer; a *cracker* is a malicious enterprising programmer) used a sneaky technique called spoofing to gain access to the home workstation of a well-known computer security expert, then ransacked files and left boastful messages in his wake. He didn't boast for long, though, because the wronged party immediately joined the manhunt for Mitnick, already on the run from the FBI, and helped them make the arrest. Mitnick'll be cooling his heels for a long time, but there are more where he came from.

The typical home user has little to worry about regarding "home invasion"–style cracking. Crackers are more interested in stealing corporate data for competing companies, or in making a very public spectacle of themselves, than in rummaging through your hard drive.

Security and privacy are in many ways the hottest issues on the Internet right now, with the spectre of censorship and, as Internet personality John Perry Barlow so eloquently put it, "Jackboots on the Infobahn" giving these issues an essential push. A number of newsgroups cover these topics in depth, and concerns have even spawned a movement of sorts, whose members are known as "cypherpunks." These advocates of privacy and encryption are leading the charge for your ability to choose who sees your files and who gathers files on you, and what they have to say bears listening to.

Chapter 9: Internet Resources, Tools, and Navigation Tips

There are many ways to find information on the Internet, and it also offers the possibility of setting up interactive exchanges between individuals for fun, business, or educational purposes. This chapter presents a run-down of the various navigation methods, with some extra tips about software and procedures that can make the task of finding and meeting easier.

If you find that my simplified explanations leave out more than you'd like, see Internet listings under "Internet Resources Online" (in Part 2), which includes Internet FAQs. A FAQ denotes a file that includes the answers to those questions. When you're stumped, downloading one of these can be a lifesaver! In addition, Appendix B has a bibliography of books that go into various online operations in considerably more detail than this directory.

Instant Mail

Let's start with the most common Internet service, electronic mail. It's also the easiest to use: You simply compose a message and add the address, then ask your software to send it. Precisely how that message is composed will depend on your software. If it uses UNIX commands, you'll need to learn a couple of basic ones, while office e-mail programs like Microsoft Word, QuickMail, and Lotus Notes can be set up to give workers e-mail access to the Internet using the same familiar interface they compose interoffice missives with. If you have an IP account, graphical mail applications with offline mail readers are available for the Mac, Windows, and UNIX platforms.

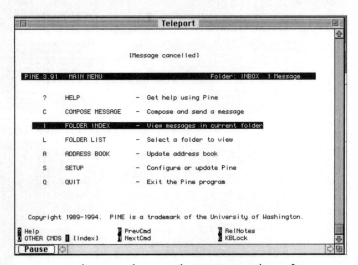

An e-mail screen showing the PINE e-mail interface

Mailing documents and software, either as a simple item or as an attachment to an e-mail note, is often difficult. Not every e-mail system used by people with Internet addresses can handle messages with a file attached. With text files, the easiest solution is copying the text and pasting it into an e-mail message. For binary files, you can compress and convert the binary code with BinHex, resulting in a type of text that the recipient can turn back into a binary file with a software utility. Common examples of BinHex utilities are uuencode and btoa for PCs and UNIX machines, and BinHex or UnStuffIt for the Mac. These are all available as freeware.

If BinHexing the file sounds like too much trouble or the person you want to send it to doesn't have the right utility, it may be time to bite the bullet and send it on a disk via "snail mail" (the postal system).

Some e-mail systems have the added disadvantage of restricting the length of messages. You may have to break up your text into several parts if you're dealing with one of these systems.

E-mail can do more for you on the Internet than you think. If you have only e-mail access to Internet (through your job or a local computer BBS, for example), you can still take advantage of some of the other resources you read about in magazine articles or books like this one. You can subscribe to electronic magazines and mailing lists—more info on that below—and you can request specific files from FTP archives.

FTP is an acronym for *File Transfer Protocol*. If you have dial-up or IP Internet access, you can use your computer to go to an FTP archive and retrieve text files or programs, as outlined in the section below. These archives are also reachable by using an an e-mail FTP application gateway, ftpmail. Setting up your request is a tad complex, but it *does* work. To get a free tutorial on ftpmail, send an e-mail message containing only the word *help* in the body of the message to ftpmail@decwrl.dec.com.

Telnet Access

When you *Telnet* into a computer system, you literally log on as if you were working at a machine on the network you're calling. You can therefore do all the things that other people there can do. The most frequent use for Telnetting on the Internet is logging onto Internet-connected information services, such as PeaceNet, ECHO, The WELL, and so on. If you enjoy contributing to an "online community" but find that those long-distance calls are decimating your pocketbook, see if you can get Telnet access.

Some computers also allow Telnet access to their archives. Quite a few public and university libraries allow people to Telnet into their card catalogs, which is a great way to hunt down books, dissertations, and magazine articles about your favorite subjects. You can use the Interlibrary Loan system to order these from your local library, if they are available in the United States.

Telnetting is quite simple, and can be done via a UNIX shell account. Your service provider will probably have a list of Internet options that includes "Telnet"; choosing this will give you a prompt. Depending on what type of shell you have, you might enter the string

```
open nameof.computer.todial
```

in which nameof.computer.todial is, of course, the address you're trying to dial into, such as well.com or echo.nyc.com. Some systems allow you to enter the name alone.

A Telnet screen

If your attempt is successful, you'll see text on your screen that tells you so, and asks you to log in. If you are calling a system where you have an account—The WELL, perhaps—this is where you would enter your username and password. If you don't have an account, try using *guest* or *new* and press Return after the password prompt. You may be granted admittance.

Telnet can be used to dial up not just the kinds of archives and services that we usually think of as Internet resources, but all sorts of computers that are attached in some way to the Net. I know systems analysts who Telnet into their favorite mainframe at work while on the road, for example. If you'd like to know more about how to access particular species of computers, the Telnet instructions in *The Whole Internet User's Guide and Catalog* (listed in Appendix B) make the most sense of any that I've read.

FTP: File Transfer Protocol

FTP is the workhorse of the Internet. It's a *protocol*, or set of communications standards, that lets you browse through data archives stored on remote computers and download items of interest to your home computer. These can be computers where you have an account, such as computers at your place of business or school, or computers that allow the general public to drop in at will. The latter are called *anonymous* FTP servers, because they allow you to give the name *anonymous* at the login prompt and simply press Return when you see the password prompt.

Once you're online, "regular" FTP and anonymous FTP work the same way, although there may be files that anonymous users cannot see or download. If you are FTPing using a UNIX shell account, you'll need to learn a few simple commands. There's actually quite a list of FTP commands out there, but most of them won't be important to you. You can see the whole list anytime you're on an FTP server by entering *help* at a prompt, and you can get info on specific commands by entering help and the command name (for example, >help mget will get you a blurb about using the mget command).

An anonymous FTP screen

The first thing you'll want to do when you are admitted to an FTP server is use the command ls or dir. *ls* will show you a basic list of files, while *dir* will show you a more detailed directory. You can continue using these commands to browse through the contents of successive directories until you find what you're looking for, or you can move around by using the *cd* command to change your directory location. In books like this one, the path you want to take to a file area is usually spelled out. Here's an example:

Name:	Japanese aviation archives
Type:	anonymous FTP
Address:	ftp.spies.com/Library/Article/Aero/

This listing indicates that you can log into the FTP server ftp.spies.com as "anonymous," open the Library directory, find and open the Article directory within, then open the Aero directory to find a list of salient files.

Once you have found the file you want—in this hypothetical case we'll call it aero.japan—you can download it using the *get* command. First, you need to specify what kind of file you're grabbing at the prompt. If it's a text file, enter *ascii* at the prompt. If it's a binary (application) file, enter the command *binary*. At the next prompt, enter *get aero.japan*, and the FTP server will download it to your system. You can download multiple files with the mget command. The files you receive may be compressed.

Because FTPing can be a royal pain, especially when there are many layers of directories to dig through to get the "gold" you seek, several helpful applications have been created to make your task easier. Applications like Fetch can be used with an IP account to take the hassle out of FTPing. Fetch puts a friendly interface on the process that can save you hours of mental anguish.

Alternatively, you can use the archie FTP-search resource to find and get a file, or try using a Gopher server or Web browser, which also puts a more pleasant face on the process. There's more on these and other search tools, such as HYTELNET and WAIS, later in this book.

Mailing Lists

Being on an Internet mailing list is a surefire way to fill your mailbox daily. These lists are made up of several people who correspond with each other about a certain topic, such as a scientific process, technology, or favorite pop star. Anything you send to the mailing list address goes out to all the other recipients, and everyone broadcasts their comments and suggestions back to the group.

I have occasionally had to take myself off of a list when the volume became too intense. But at their best, they are an interesting way to have an ongoing conversation interspersed with useful news bulletins.

To see if there's a mailing list that covers some of your favorite hobbies or interests, search through the mailing list archive at the Nova Scotia Technology Network Gopher. The Gopher server's address is nstn.ns.ca; choose Internet Resources from the first menu, then open Mail

Lists. Another Gopher site with mailing list info is the UK Mailbase Gopher at mailbase.ac.uk. Last but not least, you can use anonymous FTP to search at ftp.nisc.sri.com. Follow the path /netinfo/interest-groups. And, of course, I've included many mailing lists in this book.

Electronic Media

This may be the wave of the future. Someday you might receive a personalized newspaper on your computer every morning, perhaps with all "happy news" if you're having one of those I-can't-stand-any-more-depressing-world-events days.

For now, you can subscribe to many electronic publications. Some are scientific or technical journals; others fall into the broad category of "e-zines," noncommercial publications usually created by a single person or a couple of friends, often with a counterculture viewpoint.

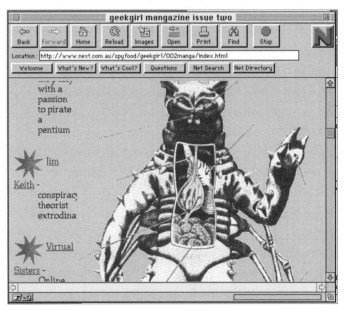

A screen from the Australian e-zine "GeekGirl"

The University of Michigan maintains a famous archive of such publications. Use anonymous FTP to access etext.archive.umich.edu and follow the /pub/* path to find a long, long list of choices. You can also check out Factsheet 5 Electric for names and reviews of both electronic and traditionally published zines. It's on The WELL's Gopher server at gopher.well.sf.ca.us. Choose Publications, then Factsheet Five Electric.

For electronically delivered news, including a daily paper, check out the news section on IGC's web page (http://www.igc.apc.org/).

See the "Digital Media" sections in Part 2 for many more electronic publications you can subscribe to or download.

Newsgroups

Newsgroups are ongoing discussions, interspersed with news and data, that you can read and contribute to. They come in educational, no-nonsense forms, and they come in irreverent and even profane forms. Some service providers refuse to carry certain newsgroups, such as those containing frank discussions about sex or those that carry graphics files that may be copyrighted pictures.

Usenet is the main system in the United States; there's also BITNET, ClariNet, and several overseas options.

To receive and contribute to newsgroups, you'll need a newsreader program. Ask your service provider which they recommend; there are dozens to choose from for Macs, PCs, and UNIX.

Your newsreader software will determine how to subscribe to these groups. If you'd like to check out the incredibly long (and growing) list of newsgroups currently available, Telnet to kufacts.cc.ukans.edu and log in as kufacts. You'll find descriptions of each and every one. There's also a quarterly (!) book available at most bookstores called *What's On Internet*, which is devoted to the Usenet scene. It's listed in Appendix B.

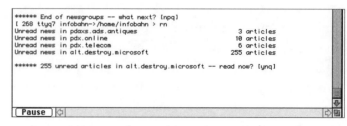

A newsgroup reader screen

You can post to Usenet groups anonymously. For information on how to do so, send an e-mail message to help@anon.penet.fi. This is just one of several anonymous remailer sites. (For more information about this option, see Chapter 8.)

The collected postings of many Usenet groups are available on Gopher servers. For American groups, try the Michigan State University Gopher at gopher.msu.edu. Choose News & Weather from the menu, then USENET News. Many European and English newsgroups are archived at the University of Birmingham's Gopher. Its address is gopher.bham.ac.uk. Choose Usenet News Reader, then European/UK Groups. There's also a selection of newsgroup archives from around the world at the Johns Hopkins University Gopher (merlot.welch.jhu.edu). Choose Usenet News and FAQs, then Read USENET News Groups. There are some really interesting items here, especially for students of foreign cultures. You can use these Gopher resources to check the intelligence level of the group before involving yourself, and considering the experiences many people have had on Usenet, that's not such a bad idea.

MUDs

Multi-User Dungeons (MUDs) are actually quite nice places to be, ominous name aside. They are online interactive games in which you take part by assuming the identity of a character you create. This character will meet other people's characters and have adventures in an environment that can itself be created in part by long-time users. All of this takes place by way of Telnetting to the computer where the MUD is in place. If you're a dial-up user, you can likely do this from a menu in your shell program. IP users will need to know the address of the MUD they'd like to check out. You might start by subscribing to the Usenet groups rec.games.mud.misc and rec.games.mud.admin for leads. Several Web pages have also sprung up to serve the MUDding craze: See the listings under "Games" for a few to try.

The first MUDs were swords-and-sorcery style games similar to the popular game Dungeons & Dragons. Participants masqueraded as elves, adventurers, and wizards, and gamboled in text-based environments reminiscent of Tolkien's *Lord of the Rings*. Later, shoot-'em-up variants came along, followed by most any sort of environment for fun and adventure that innovative gamers/designers could come up with. Some of the newer ones are "adult-oriented," while some others are bizarrely surreal. The concept is also being extended to use for educational or non-gaming entertainment purposes.

MUD is often used as a catch-all term for any role-playing game on the Internet, but there are several other varieties. Object-oriented MUDs are called MOOs, and then there are MUCKs, MUSHes, and even more.

MUDders use simple commands like "left" and "emote" to move around in their fictitious environments and interact. In some cases they can also use their programming skills, if they've got 'em, to enhance their characters, create useful or amusing objects, and extend their environments.

The wider use of multimedia computers with plenty of power will bring to life a new kind of MUD, one where the environment is fully visual and auditory instead of text based.

I have a feeling that MUDding is going to be bigger than video games. The endless complexity and personal interaction can be dangerously addictive—so much so that Australia has actually banned the practice from its public Internet links. Some campuses have also had to crack down on MUDs and other games that hook players into tying up important computer resources for hours on end.

Check 'em out—but don't say I didn't warn you.

The World Wide Web

The World Wide Web (or WWW) is a method of accessing and searching diverse sources of information via multimedia "Web pages" created using hypertext software. These pages act as interfaces to a variety of Internet resources, including WAIS databases and traditional FTP archives. As the "Around the World in 80 Minutes" excursion in Chapter 1 showed, it's highly visual, easier to use than other search and retrieval tools, and lots of fun. As a result, it has been embraced by the Internet community, with new and inexperienced users particularly appreciating its simplicity.

WWW deserves some special attention, because for the kind of cross-cultural exploration this book is intended to foster it's the best Internet resource of all. See Chapter 11 for all you need to know to get started.

Navigation Tips

When you're just getting going on the Internet, think of yourself as an explorer. Maps and guides like this one can help you reach your destination. It's also important to keep records as you feel your way along. If your communications software allows you to save your session to a capture file that can be opened as text later on, you can keep a record of your learning process.

I often find myself taking notes in the margins of books or on sticky notes. Why not? Unless you are a computer communications professional, you don't have to memorize all the FTP commands or master every nuance of your Internet software. The important thing is knowing where to find the information that will help you get around when you need it. You might find it useful to keep a small notebook nearby to write down the addresses of places you'd like to revisit, or tips you don't want to forget.

Some Internet software, such as the Web browsers Mosaic and Netscape, are set up to keep track of your online travels. Both will let you record the addresses of favorite Web sites in a helpful "hotlist." Gopher tools let you save archives as "bookmarks," as does the text-based Lynx browser for the World Wide Web.

Keeping these records will be especially important during your first few forays on the Net. You'll find that tutorials, guidebooks, and friendly advice aside, much of your learning will involve trial and error. Keeping track of where you've been, what you've tried to do, and what worked will keep the error part to a happy minimum.

Chapter 10: Searching the Net

The Internet is such a vast resource that searching for a specific bit of data can be a daunting task. There are far too many computers and databases online at this point for even the world's greatest brains to keep it all "upstairs." So a few of those brains have turned their attention toward coming up with various ways to index the information stored online, and providing methods for accessing the indexed resources. Here are a few of the solutions they've developed:

- **Gopher** Developed by researchers at the University of Minnesota, Gopher servers can, as the name indicates, "go fer" items that you request. Gopher searches take you on a trip through a series of hierarchical menus. You can assign bookmarks to places on the sever that you want to return to. These bookmarks are also handy as a way to keep your place when trundling through layer upon layer of files. When you find what you're looking for, you can download it. You can use Gopher servers to access other computers via telnet, do FTP searches with archie, consult WAIS databases, and read (but not post to) Usenet newsgroups. There are many such servers, some of which are subject- or nation-specific. HGopher for Windows and TurboGopher for Mac add a graphical interface to "Gopherspace," making it easier to navigate. You can also do Gopher searches from many WWW pages.

NOTE: For regular updates on the latest and greatest Gopher servers in Cyberspace, subscribe to the Gopher Jewels mailing list. Send an e-mail message to listproc@einet.net. The body of the message should say SUBSCRIBE GOPHERJEWELS FIRSTNAME LASTNAME, with "FIRSTNAME LASTNAME" replaced by your full name.

- **Veronica** Just what Gopherspace needed most: an indexing system that lets you search on single or compound terms instead of dragging through endless menus only to find out you're looking in the wrong place.
- **Archie** This index to FTP sites is a command-driven search program developed at McGill University. It's available via WAIS, Gopher, and WWW.
- **HYTELNET** Developed at University of Saskatchewan, HYTELNET is a hypertext search resource that can point to a variety of data resources and set up a Telnet connection to them. Access it via Telnet, Gopher, or WAIS, as well as through HYTELNET servers.
- **WAIS** This is another search engine that can check out specific databases for text documents. Developed by Thinking Machines, Apple Computer, KMPG Peat Marwick, and Dow Jones & Company, WAIS demands a keyword query. WAIS does the looking for you—unlike Gopher, it doesn't let you dawdle around and see what else you can find, but goes straight to the requested info. For a master index of WAIS servers, use your Web browser to visit http://info.cern.ch/hypertext/Products/WAIS/Sources/Overview.html.

- **The WebCrawler**   If you give this tool a few key-words it will generate a page of links that might be what you're looking for. In the process, it builds up its own list of indices. The number of entries can be overwhelming unless you narrow down the search, though. Use your Web browser software to go to the Crawler's lair at http://www.biotech.washington-.edu/WebCrawler/WebQuery.html.

- **World Wide Web Worm**   This searcher cross-references all known WWW resources worldwide. It's located at http://www.cs.colorado.edu/home/mcbryan/WWWW.html.

One problem with all of these search methods is that indexes can only be updated every so often. And even with regular updates, it's close to impossible to index the resources of all the computers linked directly to the Net, much less the thousands of resources available via the Internet that are not linked in directly. The WebCrawler is a clever experiment to test a self-updating search engine.

Even if it doesn't turn up all possible Internet resources at once, doing a general subject search (or several) can usually get you started on a voyage of discovery. Out of four listings for "bioregionalism" found via veronica, for example, visiting the Gopher sites suggested may turn up lists of even more resources, and so on.

See "Internet Resources Online" in Part 2 for leads to other Net indexes (including commercial services).

Chapter 11:
Special Focus on the
World Wide Web

The World Wide Web is almost certainly the easiest way yet discovered to access the contents of the Internet. It's based on a concept called *hypermedia*, which means linking data, graphics, audio, and video files together in an endlessly searchable pattern. The hypermedia overlay now taking shape atop the Internet's almost unfathomable resources is allowing users to find more information with less effort. This overlay is called the World Wide Web.

Hypermedia is the natural outgrowth of the *hypertext* concept, which has been around considerably longer. Hypertext was designed to work the way the human mind works. When we read about something new, we may encounter unfamiliar terms or find our thoughts taking off on a slightly related tangent prompted by one word or sentence. Wouldn't it be neat if you could simply click on that word or item of interest and get a definition or more information? With hypertext, you can.

Of course, someone has to write up and connect all those layers of information. You can imagine how difficult it might be to create, say, a hypertext version of an encyclopedia. It would be an organizational nightmare to manage such a project, and as a result there are few such works commercially available as of yet.

The World Wide Web lets information providers set up connections between data as they go, and as more sites are linked to each other the "web" of interconnected information can become endlessly complex and layered, without any one person or organization having to do it all. And the items connected can be more than just text.

Hypertext is not a new idea: Ted Nelson, a well-known and highly creative California programmer, has been evangelizing about it since the mid-60s. The first real commercial application of the concept was in Apple Computer's HyperCard, a computer program that used the metaphor of linked index cards to create layered information. HyperCard was originally thought of as a note-taking system, but savvy users made it their own to build everything from digital magazines to complex games. For a look at how far HyperCard can be pushed, I highly recommend *If Monks Had Macs*, a Voyager CD-ROM created by Brian Thomas, a contributor to this book—it weaves together items ranging from a translation of "The Imitation of Christ" to an existential pinball game, using the metaphor of a modern monastery library. Brilliant!

Hypertext eventually came to be used at CERN, a Swiss physics lab that relies on an international workforce and necessarily huge amounts of data to do its experimental research. CERN originally thought of hypertext as a research tool useful only to its own far-flung staff, and perhaps to researchers at similar institutions. But because the lab made information about its hypertext project easily available, because it was quickly realized that the same techniques could be used to link more than just text files, and because visually appealing software has since been created to make hypermedia more accessible to nonscientific Internet users, the concept has literally swept the world since its debut in 1991. Of course, it didn't hurt that CERN plays the unofficial role of Internet service provider to several countries, giving anything it does a rather high profile on the Internet.

What's a Web Page?

The basic links in the World Wide Web are called Web pages. These documents display the information items that are linked directly to that page. Some are literally just lists with perhaps a headline or a graphic, but these pages can be as beautifully designed as a magazine story, a pamphlet, or a slick advertising brochure. These days, most pages present their hot links (links to other Web pages) in the form of text set off from the rest of the document with color. They can also be represented by clickable graphics, icons, or buttons.

For an educational and lovely example, take a look at the Islamic Architecture of Isfahan Web page I visited in Chapter 1. The first page you receive on your screen after calling up this Web site is an introduction to its contents, much like the table of contents in a book, but with small illustrations. Some words are in color to indicate that they are gateways to more information. Clicking on the word

Minarets takes you to a page with specific information about Isfahan's historic minarets. You can click on the name of a certain minaret for information about the structure. Clicking on another highlighted word might take you to an archive of historical information about the golden age of the Persian Shahs.

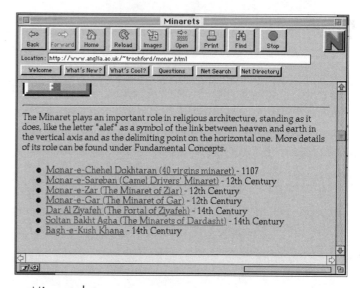

Minarets home page

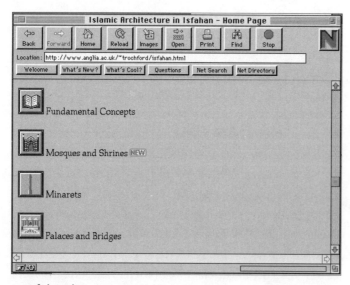

Isfahan home page

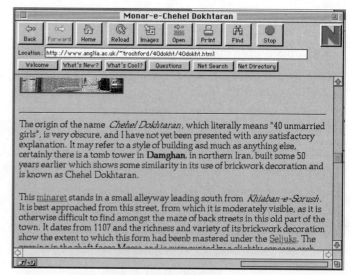

Monar-e-chechel Dokhtaran page

At any click you could be leaving the computer that holds the page you first saw and entering another one, perhaps at a university in Iran or a museum in France. The creator of the Islamic Architecture of Isfahan page linked his words and pictures to existing Internet resources that he felt might be of interest. This is usually an ongoing process, as scholars and visitors e-mail the Web page's creator about new links that might be appropriate.

By following these ever-unwinding threads as your interest takes you, you can explore the archives of human history, science and research in a fashion that's much like the way a child explores his or her environment. Remember when looking at a color illustration of a sailing ship in *Treasure Island* could set you to thinking of sailing the seven seas, which made you think about tropical islands and dining on tropical fruit, which then reminded you that there was a pineapple upside-down cake in the kitchen? Schools have taught us to gather our thoughts and plod along in a linear fashion, which is often useful. But one of the lessons you learn when studying the backgrounds of great intellectual discoveries is that the most creative thinkers almost always have their flashes of brilliance when they let their minds wander, allowing serendipity and even dreams to work their magic. The Web may help many people to harness once again that childlike power of following what are seemingly disparate interests, only to find that elements learned along the way suggest a solution for some otherwise unrelated problem.

World Wide Web Software

To let your mind wander the Web, you'll need a Web browser. This is software that puts Web pages on your screen and supports the concept of hypermedia links.

If you have a dial-up account you will be stuck with a text-only browser, generally the one known as Lynx. That means that the colors, sounds, videos, and pictures will not be visible on your screen as you explore, just the words. On the positive side, you can download some of these nontext elements. If you can delay gratification, that's not so bad—at least you can get to the raw data, and Lynx is much easier software for open-ended searches than, say, a straight FTP command-line search.

Web pages can, in fact, be FTP servers, Gopher servers, and other "old-fashioned" Internet information repositories in disguise. They just give these resources a new look, providing a "one-stop shopping" approach to the data hunt.

Without a doubt, seeing Web pages in their full visual glory is a heck of a lot more interesting than checking out screen after screen of text. That's why there's so much buzz about Web browsers like NCSA Mosaic, Netscape, WinTapestry, Cello, and others. Mosaic is the best known, because it was one of the first. It also has the benefits of a strong support system for new users and an interface that's easy enough to help beginners to grasp the basic concepts right away.

Since its introduction as a free software package for the X Windows graphical front-end for UNIX workstations, Mosaic has been rewritten for PCs with Windows and for the Macintosh. More recently, commercial versions (like Enhanced NCSA Mosaic on the CD-ROM that accompanies this book) have added a few extra features.

If you choose to use the original NCSA Mosaic, you can download it directly from NCSA or many other sites on the Internet, including the freeware archives provided by most service providers. NCSA maintains several Web pages with information about how to use its popular program, and FAQs are also available. In addition, there is now a long shelf of books for sale that cover the World Wide Web in general or certain Web browsers in particular.

Below are screens from NCSA Mosaic and Netscape, its most prominent commercial competitor. Both feature an

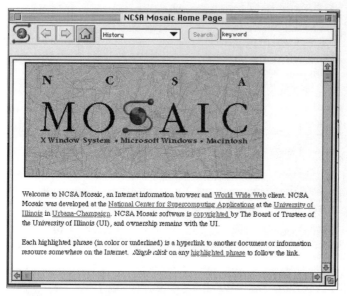

NCSA Mosaic's home page screen

An example of a Netscape screen

attractive interface and a number of tools for accessing various types of data via World Wide Web.

These browsers are extensible with smaller, specialty applications (*utilities* or *helper applications*) that can read data stored in various formats. You'll probably want to include readers that let you decompress and look at graphics in the GIF, JPEG, and TIFF formats; an application for playing QuickTime digital video clips; and an application that supports sound files. If you run into a problem with reading or translating a particular file, chances are that someone has written a utility that can handle it. One of the best things about the Internet is that no matter where the programmer has uploaded his or her creation, you can almost surely find it, get it, and have the benefit of using it.

Since each Web browser has its own interface, I won't go into the specifics of what buttons or menus perform which operation: You'll have to consult the vendor or, in the case of freeware like Mosaic, public information like FAQs and self-instruction books. Suffice it to say that I've seen about eight different Web browsers now, and all of them are simple enough that even a rank amateur at computing could figure them out within 15 minutes. That's not to say that there won't be extra features to learn as you go along: There will be. But you can definitely learn the rudiments of "Netsurfing" and be on your way in practically no time at all. What a nice change from other computer software!

Web Training Wheels

Here are some resources for the beginning Netsurfer. You might want to make one of these Web pages your first port of call, and keep all of them in your bookmarks list or hotlist as touchstones while you're learning:

- **Mosaic Starting Points Home Page** This page sends you on your way with Mosaic, leading you through helpful hints on navigation, and providing lists of sites to visit. It includes links with search engines like the World-Wide Web Worm.

```
http://www.ncsa.uiuc.edu/SDG/Software/
Mosaic/StartingPoints/NetworkStarting-
Points.html
```

- **CERN WWW Virtual Library**   This is one of the best places to start if you're searching for specific information. It has exhaustive (and sometimes exhausting) lists of Web sites arranged by subject.

  ```
  http://info.cern.ch/hypertext/DataSources/
  bySubject/Overview.html
  ```

- **WWW FAQ List**   The FAQ List provides a single interface for obtaining all the Web FAQs you're looking for.

  ```
  http://www.cis.ohio-state.edu/hypertext/
  faq/usenet/FAQ-List.html
  ```

- **The Mother-of-all BBS**   This is a gigantic index of home pages. WAIS search tools are available, and you can add your own page to the list. It is heavy on commercial sites.

  ```
  http://www.cs.colorado.edu/homes/mcbryan/
  public_html/bb/summary.html
  ```

- **Mysteries of the Web**   An alphabetical list by subject of cool Net resources with hot links.

  ```
  http://www.msen.com/~pauleric/mist.html
  ```

Several World Wide Web veterans I know recommend an English magazine called *3W: Global Networking Newsletter*, which concentrates on the latest WWW developments and sites. The magazine is available on many magazine stands, particularly at technical bookstores, and it also maintains a Web page at http://www.3W.com/3W/.

Chapter 12: Making Personal Connections Online

The spread of the Internet has brought the wonders of the online world to lots of folks who would never proudly wear the label of geek or nerd, and (I hope that saying this doesn't offend any of my fellow nerdlings) I believe it's broadened the horizons of many hard-core computer nuts as well.

There's an unfortunate stereotype concerning computing enthusiasts that has them fixated on a glowing screen night and day, breaking only for caffeine and vending-machine sandwiches as they pursue the ultimate programming breakthrough. Even more unfortunate is the fact that for a few benighted souls, this stereotype rings all too true. But most computer fans also have wide-ranging interests in art, literature, games, sports, and hobbies of all kinds. In fact, it's these interests among the scientific and technical elite at American research institutes and universities that built the foundation for Usenet newsgroups, which quickly branched out from research and techie topics to include other subjects.

The first online discussions and non–work-related files to make the rounds concerned subjects like science fiction, Star Trek, and related futuristic topics. Of course, then somebody started talking about sex, and you can guess what that lead to: an exponential increase in interest in this nifty new uncensored medium. As I write this, discussions and files relating to sex are probably outstripping the actual science-and-technology-and-education business that takes place on the Internet.

But interesting as that topic may be, it's certainly not the only one that brings people together. Owners of exotic pets, lute players, women working in the computer sciences, users of obscure and ancient computers—these are just a few of the groups that chat daily via Usenet and mailing lists.

In fact, the Internet's capacity for bringing like-minded individuals together despite geographical distances may be its most compelling capability.

For example, Web pages can offer an international community resources of value in their work, and a central meeting place that fosters a sense of camaraderie. The Animation 2000 project is a case in point. Sponsored by the Institut National de l'Audiovisual in France, the project uses a Web page (http://www.ina.fr/Ina/Recherche/Anim2D/A2000/) to reach artists in the field of two-dimensional animation throughout the world. The Animation 2000 working group now includes French, Spanish, and German animators, visual artists, and researchers, working together to create a global solution for producing 2-D animation with computer software.

Reaching out to friends scattered around the world is the theme of the Fudan University Alumni page (http://odin.pat.dcu.ie:8080/fudan.html). Former students of this Chinese college can log in through Web pages in Europe and the United States to catch up on what old classmates are doing, pass on news from back home and from their new lives, and debate issues of special interest to

Chinese expatriates. The first screen they see is a color photo of the tranquil grounds at their beloved alma mater.

Here's a sample message:

```
<<Hi, Wang Hai -
Congratulations to your marriage, I heard
of that from Zhengzhong Dong. Do you
happen to know Zhu Wei Wen's email
address?
- Limin Wang (at U Penn).>>
```

The page includes a regularly updated list of alumni, with their current street and e-mail addresses (except for Mr. Zhu, apparently). The homesickness is palpable, but having a chance to talk with each other really seems to help.

Political activists of all stripes have also discovered that the Net is an excellent organizing tool. Causes mainstream and obscure have taken up residence, with almost every international disaster relief, political, social, religious, and investigative group listing an e-mail address at the very least, and often maintaining file archives, discussion groups, and Web pages as well.

For causes that may not get much attention from the press, and particularly in cases where access to timely information is stymied by political repression, censorship, or poor communications systems, the Internet has made some things possible that might not otherwise be.

For example, when the Indonesian army committed a massacre in East Timor back in 1991, several individuals who heard about it on the news posted to newsgroups or on the PeaceNet network, looking for information and ways to assist the Timorese. Local groups were also forming independently in several major cities. When they noticed each other online, the East Timor Action Network was formed. "Many of us still haven't met each other," chuckles John Miller, coordinator of the New York chapter. "Now there's a conference on East Timor on PeaceNet that has become the place to get your daily 'information overload.' Even though not much appears in the U.S. media, there is a lot of information out there through the wire services, or called, mailed, or faxed out of East Timor," he said.

East Timor itself is not on the Net, but sympathizers in Indonesia are able to use the Internet as a conduit for underground reports about arrests, battles, and political campaigns, he explained. As a result, ETAN has become a worldwide player, getting the latest news out to interested parties within minutes. The Internet has also allowed it to coordinate media and letter-writing campaigns in an effort to protect the Timorese.

In sum, there's something online for almost everyone, and the Net's international character seems to exert a broadening influence on those of us who travel there. You're no longer limited to seeking out kindred spirits in your hometown or region: You can search the entire world to find others who think and feel as you do, who share a particular passion, or who challenge your assumptions in ways that may make you think or even reconsider long-held beliefs.

All of the technical data, free software, and cool graphics available online pale in comparison to the value of these very real—and in our socially atomized world all too rare—personal connections.

Chapter 13:
Using the Net as a
Research Tool

Never before has the amateur researcher had the ability to grab so much information. Whether you're tracking down your family's geneology or compiling statistics on endangered fish stocks in the world's rivers, there are literally thousands of archives waiting for you to initiate a search.

Just don't lose sight of the fact that quantity and quality are not the same thing. There is plenty of disinformation, poorly documented information, and just plain wrong information out there online. Consider the source of your data, and don't assume that it has an official blessing just because it exists in an archive on a college campus or some prestigious research institute. I suspect that if some of the universities and other entities online had any idea what lurks in their FTP and Gopher servers, they would shut it all down without thinking twice.

That aside, it is nice to be able to gather information from all points of view, and the Internet is perfectly suited for that. You may want to start your search at a central indexing site: see Chapter 10 for a variety of handy search tools and Chapter 11 for some extremely useful sites on the World Wide Web. A broadly focused search is often more productive at first than an extremely specific one. It will let you identify a large number of potential resources, then query them for the specific item that you want.

Usenet newsgroups are also an essential resource. If you can find one or more newsgroups that relate to your topic, subscribing will give you a whole collection of self-appointed experts to answer your questions, help you find more information, and offer support during the search. You can post a query in the morning and have dozens of answers or comments waiting in your e-mail box by afternoon. The sci, bionet, and comp groups and many BITNET groups are dedicated primarily to research activities, as are a great many groups in the other categories. Mailing lists offer another method of making personal contacts helpful for your project and receiving regular news updates.

The World Wide Web's capacity for linking disparate resources and types of data is also a boon for researchers. Web pages related to your topic may point you in new directions; some also have an area where you can leave e-mail or messages for others who check into the page or for the page's author.

A wide variety of publications is available online, ranging from reputable scientific journals to direct news feeds from AP, UPI, and other news services. Many of these you can subscribe to electronically, while others reside as downloadable electronic text in archives. For some publications there may be a charge.

It's possible to connect with huge commercial databases like Lexis (legal case filings for the United States), Nexis (business data and news), and Dow Jones News/Retrieval through the Net as well. These services require an account and have steep hourly charges, but they contain a vast array of data that may not otherwise be available.

University libraries will allow you to run searches for dissertations, papers, and books online, as will the Library of

Congress and many local and foreign public libraries. Some texts may even be available electronically through the libraries—in the future, whole collections may be online.

In the U.S., several states and the Federal government are placing information, forms, and archives online; the same process is taking place overseas. These resources will be important to future researchers and to citizens who want to find out what their representatives have done or are planning.

Chapter 14:
Legal Issues in Cyberspace

The general attitude toward The Law in cyberspace could be summed up with the famous film quote, "Badges? We don't need no steenkin' badges!" from *Treasure of the Sierra Madre*. That said, it's not exactly true that there are no laws on the Internet. But there are no special laws made just for this new frontier—at least not yet in the United States. All of the old rules still apply, although the transnational nature of the medium and the potential for anonymity is giving them a serious tweak.

Who Governs the Net?

Despite being the descendant of dozens of government-funded projects, the Internet is not owned by any government or group of governments. Some of them own a piece of the pie here and there, and on their part of the highway they can quite easily set a speed limit.

The closest thing to an actual governing body on the Net is the Internet Society, a voluntary group that works to improve and expand the Internet. The only rules it's ever greatly concerned itself with are those regarding communications protocols and other programming decisions. That's not to say that no one ever calls on the Internet Society to step in when there's a problem, but it doesn't really have the authority to, say, stamp out offensive newsgroups or kick someone off the Net.

These kinds of actions can take place at the service-provider level, however. Most providers have a list of their own rules, better known as "acceptable use policies," which may

include such things as limiting you to a certain amount of time online, banning the use of certain programs on their system or, in the case of a few commercial online services with Internet connections, actually censoring your e-mail and posts.

There is, however, no law that says service providers *must* do these things, and many feel that not doing so gives them more protection in case of abuse, since they will honestly be able to say "I didn't know" if they really weren't looking.

Online Threats, Slander, and Libel

So what do you do if someone is using the Internet to harass or threaten you? If the person is outside of your country, you are probably out of luck. The best advice: Get a new Internet address, and keep your identity a secret. If you are in the same country, whatever laws your nation has regarding threatening communications by telephone or harassment calls applies equally to text delivered by phone. In the United States, posting a "fantasy" about murdering an actual person has been interpreted by the courts in one case as a death threat; it remains to be seen how an appeals court will rule.

It's the same with slander and libel law, and that's something to think about when you're posting to newsgroups. Newsgroups seem like a conversation, where defamatory remarks like "Hillary Clinton's a practicing witch" or "Rush Limbaugh's just a fat old drunk" may annoy your

friends, but won't get you busted. If you say those things online, however, it's the same as publishing them on a poster and tacking it up worldwide. And you could be sued for slander or libel should the injured party get wind of it.

What's Not a Crime Online

Misrepresenting yourself online is not a crime, although it's often a cause for complaint. It's not unusual for people to pretend to have a different sex, age, race, or occupation online than they actually do. It's probably fun to see how the other guy's shoes fit, but carrying a game like this on for long periods of time can end up hurting people—particularly when it comes to online romance, where these little masquerades can end in tragedy.

Sexual conversations and pictures online are also legal, as long as they do not involve people under the age of 18. It's not, however, legal to send smut to a minor in the United States, a fact that some courts are interpreting so liberally as to want to censor what adults can see just because an enterprising teenager might also figure out how to gain access. In addition, each American state has different laws on what's obscene, and in Georgia a judge recently put a California couple in jail for providing dirty pictures on their adults-only BBS that Georgia citizens could download over the phone. Obviously, this kind of ruling could have a serious effect on the Internet's seamier corners if his reasoning spreads.

Political speech has also been threatened as activists, including armed opposition groups such as Mexico's Zapatistas and terrorist groups like the Red Army Fraction, become more visible online. "Hate speech" on the Net, such as racist newsgroups or archives maintained by Holocaust deniers, are creating sticky situations for governments that ban such material. This category includes Germany, Canada, and several American states. It's not yet known how (and if) these governments will be able to deal with the availability of these ideas through an anonymous international medium.

There has been a corresponding rise in groups clamoring for freedom of electronic speech. The Electronic Freedom Foundation was the pioneer in the United States, but similar organizations now exist in Italy, Spain, India, the U.K., Canada, Brazil, and several other countries. These groups research current laws that affect Internet activities and try to head off proposals that could curtail online speech and access.

Dealing with Real Crime

Some serious crimes online can take on an international dimension. Security forces will almost always join together to bust pedophiles, murderers, Mafia dons, terrorists, and others who may try to use electronic communications to hide their activities. The United States government has the capability to eavesdrop on extranational electronic traffic, and is likely to use this ability to snare the occasional malfeasant.

Software piracy is another area where international cooperation is growing, since both software companies and police forces are well aware that the Net is a convenient vehicle for transporting illicit programs.

Fraud and theft are probably the most prevalent "real" crimes on the Net. Trafficking in stolen credit-card numbers, stealing information, perhaps even intercepting electronic cash as it travels across the cable are the high-tech heists these criminals are interested in. There are few agents in the FBI, RCMP, and similar agencies who understand the Internet well enough to effectively detect and capture data pirates as of yet, so you should take all the necessary steps to protect yourself rather than relying on the idea that someone else will look out for you.

Part 2
International Internet Sites

Please refer to the following indexes in the front of the book to quickly locate a particular site or subject of interest:

We have tried to provide as current and accurate a list of sites as possible. The Internet, however, is a dynamic network, and sites sometimes change addresses or disappear altogether.

If a site refuses your call, it may simply be busy or down for repairs. If it tells you that the Web page or archive you seek does not exist, try shortening the site's address and then search again. For example, turn "http://cwis.usc.edu/dept/elab/buidoi/vietgangs.html" into "http://cwis.usc.edu/"—perhaps the computer's files have been reorganized.

The "Editor's Choice" icon will draw your eye to certain sites that I especially enjoyed, or that offer exceptional resources. These are "don't miss" places to visit online.

AGRICULTURE

These sites provide information on plants, soils, pests, and methods of interest to both weekend and professional farmers. The discussion groups are actually quite active, which won't surprise modern farmers. Computers and databases have long been important tools for both agribiz types, and for small farmers trying to get the edge they need to compete.

Aberdeen University Department of Agriculture

This is an incredibly comprehensive assemblage of text, pictures, and links relating to agriculture and farming in the U.K. You can find information on everything from birds to water quality here. The section of animal images is worth a look.

Type: WWW
**Address: http://www.abdn.ac.uk/
           ~agr342/infoagric.html**
Region: Scotland, England

Agricultural Genome World Wide Web Server

Sponsored by the USDA's National Agricultural Library, this includes genome information on agriculturally important plant species for farmers and researchers. Full access to the library's genome databases is gradually being made available.

Type: WWW
**Address: http://probe.ralusda.gov:8000/
           index.html**
Region: U.S., World

AgriGator

AgriGator is a picturesque site whose alligator mascot oversees a nice list of agricultural and related material. More of a jump point than a destination, it provides links to information both international and domestic. The name is derived from its parent site "AlliGator," a page devoted to the Florida alligator population. These pages are both humorous and informative.

Type: WWW
**Address: http://gnv.ifas.ufl.edu/WWW/
           AGATOR/HTM/AG.HTM**
Region: U.S., World

Alternative Agriculture Grab-bag

If you're just getting into the subject of alternative agriculture, this is a good place to start learning. Fairly light load of daily messages—not just about organic farming, some "traditional" chat, too.

Type: Usenet newsgroup
Address: alt.agriculture.misc
Region: World

Aquaculture Discussion Group

This type of "farming" can include fish, crustaceans, and crops, all raised in water. This mailing list is a good place to learn what works and what doesn't.

Type: Mailing List
Address: listproc@upei.ca
**Send e-mail message with blank Subject
           line and body: SUBSCRIBE
           AQUA-L <Firstname Lastname>**
Region: World

Base de Dados Tropical

Celebrating Brazil's biodiversity with information on a wide range of topics from biological control to zoology; these pages are peppered with great graphics and tons of links to information both popular and technical. Lots of information on tropical edibles and farming.

Type: WWW
Address: http://www.ftpt.br/
Region: Brazil

Beijing Agricultural University

All about China's premier agricultural research college, including international exchange programs and its "experiment farm."

Type: WWW
Address: http://www.ihep.ac.cn/uni/BAU/agri.html
Region: China

City Farmer

This Canadian nonprofit promotes urban food production. Their fun site includes home composting, worm bins, and other backyard farming issues. There's also information on urban gardens in South Africa, Thailand, the U.K., and Australia.

Type: WWW
Address: http://unixg.ubc.ca:780/~cityfarm/urbagnotes1.html
Region: Canada, World

Consultative Group on International Agricultural Research

CGIAR pushes a high-tech approach to agriculture, and supports 16 international research centers, most in the developing world. This page offers access to the organization's latest meeting notes, directories, and news. CGIAR is based in Washington, D.C., and allied with the UN and the World Bank.

Type: WWW
Address: http://www.worldbank.org/html/cgiar/HomePage.html
Region: World

DINA: Danish Informatics Network in the Agricultural Sciences

DINA is an interdisciplinary research project involving several Danish colleges and research centers. It develops software and other high-tech methods for increasing and improving agricultural production, such as software that graphs and interprets the readings of agricultural sensors in a planted field.

Type: WWW
Address: http://www.dina.kvl.dk/
Region: Denmark

DLO-NL

Both conventional and sustainable agriculture research are undertaken by this Dutch institute. Site includes information on the Institute, its facilities and programs, and ag news.

Type: WWW
Address: http://www.bib.wau.nl/dlo/
Region: Holland

Food and Floods

Here, you'll find both general and specific regional data on floods, and their effect on food and agriculture.

Type: Telnet
Address: idea.ag.uiuc.edu
Login: flood
Region: World

Guide to Agriculture Resources on the Internet

This list is regularly updated to reflect the growing body of aggie information online.

Type: FTP
Address: ftp.sura.net/pub/nic/agricultural. list
Region: World

Hungarian Agricultural Biotechnology Center

Godollo Agricultural University's online with information about their research (and other institutions') into biosafety, biodiversity, genetically altered plants, and the like.

Type: Gopher
Address: hubi.abc.hu/
Region: Hungary

Institute of Arable Crops Research

This research organization runs three experimental farms to learn new ways to optimize crop production and maintain environmental quality. Links include photos and plans of the farms, related software, and research results.

Type: WWW
Address: http://www.res.bbsrc.ac.uk/
Region: England

Integrated Pest Management

IPM is the buzzword for balancing pesticides with organic methods to rid crops of harmful pests. This site offers the IPM Bulletin, a publication of the European IPM Working Group, an organization that does most of its field work in the developing world.

Type: WWW
Address: http://www.bib.wau.nl:80/ ipmnet/
Region: Europe, World

International Organization for Plant Information

IOPI is a group of botanists working on creating a hypermedia taxonomic database. IOPI's site also has an electronic news system for academics and professional farmers. Apply online according to your country.

Type: WWW
Address: http://www.csu.edu.au/ biodiversity/iopi/iopi.html
Region: Australia, World

Japanese Agriculture

Documents relating to agriculture, scientific farming, horticulture, and gardening. Notable is a folder on sustainable agriculture containing information on vermiculture, symbiosis, permaculture, and other topics. The site is highly technical but well-organized and easy to navigate. Hobby farmers and scientists alike will find much of interest here.

Type: FTP
Address: ftp.iij.ad.jp/pub/academic/ agriculture/
Region: Japan

Malaysian Ministry of Agriculture

A nicely written page about agriculture in Malaysia with information on the Ministry's history and organizational structure. Make sure to follow the link called "Agrotourism."

Type: WWW
Address: http://www.moa.my/
Region: Malaysia

Not Just Cows

The mother of all agriculture resources online. It's not pretty, and I'm not sure how frequently updated it is, but Not Just Cows is an unsurpassed list of ag resources. The items available include searchable library collections, links to agriculture-related BBSs, datasets, Usenet and BITNET newsgroups, newsletters, access to WAIS databases, and much, much more.

Type: WWW
Address: http://snymorvb.cs.snymor.edu/ hhgopher_root1:[librarydocs. htm]NOT_JU.S.T_COWS.html
Type: Gopher
Address: SNYMORVB.cs.snymor.edu:70
Region: U.S., Holland, Germany, England, Ireland, Australia, New Zealand, Canada, Hungary, World

PENpages

This database has lots of international agricultural information, including a special section for small and part-time farmers; weather statistics, and a schedule of the AG*SAT satellite; newsletters; and a link to an excellent international agricultural development database.

Type: Gopher
Address: PENPAGES.PSU.EDU/
Region: U.S., World

Russian Agricultural List

RUSAG-L discusses all aspects of agriculture in the former Soviet Union, not just Russia.

Type: Mailing List
Address: listserv@umdd.umd.edu
Contact: gage@umail.umd.edu (James Gage)
Region: Russia, CIS

Sustainable Agriculture Discussion

"Sustainable agriculture" means trying to minimize any negative impact on farmland and water resources. This newsgroup discusses alternatives to agricultural chemicals, building up the soil and preserving a diverse variety of seeds to protect against disease, and rampant gene-patenting, among other things. If you're looking for anything from organic cut flowers to hands-on advice, here's the place.

Type: Usenet
Address: alt.sustainable.agriculture
Region: World

Third World Academy of Sciences

This institute provides support for agricultural scientists and technologists in the developing world, and awards prizes and fellowships for outstanding achievements.

Type: WWW
Address: http://www.ictp.trieste.it/TWAS/ TWAS.html
Type: Gopher
Address: gopher.ictp.trieste.it/11/twas
Region: Italy, India, Africa, Asia, World

University of Western Sydney—Hawkesbury School of Agriculture and Rural Development

Home page for Australia's largest aggie school. Includes course information, who's on its prestigious staff, and news about agricultural developments on the island continent.

Type: WWW
Address: http://hotel.hawkesbury.uws. edu.au/HEART
Region: Australia

Zobler World Soils Data Set

All sorts of data and calculations to help you check out soil conditions worldwide, including yours, is here.

Type: WWW

Address: http://sun1.cr.usgs.gov/glis/ hyper/guide/world_soil

Region: World

ANIMALS

Animals can be man's best friend or—when sick or misbehaving—the bane of his existence. Many of the animal-related resources online are Usenet discussion groups, and they're a great place to go for help and a chance to chat with kindred spirits. I've included a long list of general ones, you may also find groups related to specific breeds of companion animals, such as schnauzers or Russian Blue cats.

Wildlife and conservation organizations are also making their presence known online. These sites are a good source for the latest statistics on preservation efforts and what you can do to help. One thing's certain: Affection for pets and a fascination with wild animals is a global phenomenon.

Animal Resources List

Animal-related businesses, such as Alpaca breeders, pet supply shops and aquarium-builders, are online here. Mostly U.S., but it's an interesting concept.

Type: WWW

Address: http://www.yahoo.com/ business/corporations/animals

Region: U.S., World

Animal Rights Resource Site

Animal rights and violations thereof, related actions, and political and philosophical information are the order of the day here. Vegetarian and vegan pages are linked in, as are reference materials, journals, and so forth.

Type: WWW

Address: http://envirolink.org/arrs/ index.html

Region: World

Animals and Politics

Here lies spirited, sometimes vitriolic debate on animal rights, hunting, speciesism, meat-eating, and the ethics of medical experimentation. Here PETA is vigorously denounced and just as vigorously defended. Here too may the like-minded and lonely meet over biscuits to trade recipes.

Type: Usenet newsgroup

Address: talk.politics.animals

Region: World

Antarctica and Its Critters

Marine mammals, birds, land animals, and their habitat on the Southernmost continent. There are no pictures, but the text is fascinating. It's a much richer environment than you might think.

Type: WWW

Address: http://icair.iac.org.nz/reports/ nz/visitor.html

Region: Antarctica, New Zealand

Badgers Can Be Fun

A badger fan may think he or she is the only one on earth to love this often maligned creature. Not so. Badgers are smart, brave, lovable, and worthy of respect: especially if you get too close to their pointy little teeth. Here's the place to meet people who know.

Type: Usenet newsgroup
Address: alt.animals.badgers
Region: World

Bears and Friends

This is a place for anecdotes and character sketches of the big, furry, personable king of the woods. Who can resist telling the world about their own unforgettable encounter?

Type: Usenet newsgroup
Address: alt.animals.bears
Region: World

Birding in the UK

This Welsh server has links to bird-related and natural history sites in Wales, England, Scotland, and beyond. Includes club information, where to go and what you'll see.

Type: WWW
**Address: http://www.aber.uk/~jgc3/
            birding.html**
Region: England, Scotland, Wales, Northern
            Ireland, World

Birding on the Web

Links to worldwide resources for bird-watching and ornithology, including EuroBirdNet (available in English, French, or German), can be found here. Daily news, book lists, information on tools, and more.

Type: WWW
**Address: http://compstat.wharton.upenn.
            edu:8001/~siler/birding.html**
Region: U.S., World

Birds and Their People

Here's a place for bird people (and wannabe bird people) to cross paths. This news group contains more technical advice on health and behavior, and fewer "cute" anecdotes than do most pet-oriented news groups.

Type: Usenet newsgroup
Address: rec.pets.birds
Region: World

BIYOT (Biyoloji Topulugu)

Translated from the Turkish, that's the Biology Society of Middle East Technical University Students. These avid birders offer great bird pictures and information.

Type: WWW
**Address: http://knidos.cc.metu.edu.tr/
            ~www38/biyothp.html**
Region: Turkey

Brazillian Zoos Directory

In Portuguese and some English. Learn here about all the zoos in Brazil, and their conservation efforts.

Type: WWW
**Address: http://www.ftpt.br/cgi-bin/
            bdtnet/zoocadastro**
Region: Brazil

Cat Lovers Online

The ever-popular felines generate a great deal of discussion. Cat people are never at a loss for anecdotes, or stingy with advice. Bereavement over the loss of a furry loved one is sure to draw sympathy. The irrepressible joy of a new little furball is gladly shared. Veterinary advice is never lacking. Some even comes from actual vets. And how much should you pay a cat sitter? Opinions vary.

Type: Usenet newsgroup
Address: rec.pets.cats
Region: World

Chia Pets

Some absurdist humor appears at this site dedicated to the 1990s answer to the Pet Rock, often apparently in some sort of code. alt.pets.chia may well be a virtual "drop box" in which various secret agents leave messages for each other. On the other hand, it may just be bored office workers running up the boss's phone bill whilst trolling for true love.

Type: Usenet newsgroup
Address: alt.pets.chia
Region: World

The Chihuahua Home Page

Here you can find a toally facetious history of the breed, which you will greatly enjoy if you feel the way I do about these yapping creatures. In fact, I think even chihuahua lovers will get a kick out of this.

Type: WWW
Address: http://www.icon-stl.net/~jbpeck /chp/chp.html
Region: Mexico, World

CITES-L

This list is for discussion of and posting about issues relating to the trade in wildlife and the Convention on International Trade in Endangered Species (CITES).

Type: Mailing list
Address: LISTPROC@WCMC.ORG.UK
Send e-mail message with body:
           SUBSCRIBE CITES-L <Firstname Lastname>
Contact: helen.corrigan@wcmc.org.uk (Helen Corrigan)
Region: World

Dog Activities

This group is for the discussion of activities involving dogs, such as conformation, obedience, field trials, herding trials, frisbee/disc competition, flyball, hunting, sledding, backpacking/camping, and hiking. Other appropriate topics include discussion of training for particular activities, physical conditioning, and how to hook up with activities available in your area.

Type: Usenet newsgroup
Address: rec.pets.dogs.activities
Region: World

Dogs and Their Health

This group is for health and medical questions related to dogs. This includes, but certainly is not limited to, questions on hip dysplasia, epilepsy, eye problems, diabetes, bloat, allergies and skin problems, and so on. Hereditary and acquired diseases may be discussed, as well as traumatic disorders. Questions about nutrition and feeding are also appropriate here. This newsgroup is not intended to replace veterinary care in any way, but is to help inform the dog owner about canine health.

Type:　　Usenet newsgroup
Address:　rec.pets.dogs.health
Region:　　World

Dog Behavior

This is a place to discuss training problems and techniques, as well as psychological phenomena and problems. Does your dog "hate" you? Do you want to stop your puppy from whining while you're at work? Is Fido jealous of your new squeeze? You're not alone.

Type:　　Usenet newsgroup
Address:　rec.pets.dogs.behavior
Region:　　World

Dog Breeds

Breeds and breeding are discussed here. Current prices can often be found, as can what to look for in order to insure you get your money's worth. Here's where to contact breeders and breeding associations worldwide.

Type:　　Usenet newsgroup
Address:　rec.pets.dogs.breeds
Region:　　World

Dog Information

Not a discussion group: This moderated group only posts FAQs and informational files relevant to rec.pets.dogs. FAQs that are already cleared for posting to news.answers are automatically eligible to be posted here, as are some others. Announcements of new e-mail lists are appropriate. This group is intended to make the FAQs and articles with useful information for dog owners more visible and easier to find, especially for newcomers.

Type:　　Usenet newsgroup
Address:　rec.pets.dogs.info
Region:　　World

Dogs—Miscellaneous

This group is for miscellaneous questions that are not appropriate for one of the other doggie groups. This includes chat, humor, and anything pertaining to canines not explicitly covered elsewhere.

Type:　　Usenet newsgroup
Address:　rec.pets.dogs.misc
Region:　　World

Dogs Who Help Humans

This newsgroup is for discussion of all aspects of dog rescue. General questions and answers on rescue dogs and procedures, general announcements from various rescue groups, methods to help a rescue dog adjust to its new home, idiosyncrasies of rescue dogs, training or retraining the rescue dog, and breed-specific information are all available here.

Type:　　Usenet newsgroup
Address:　rec.pets.dogs.rescue
Region:　　World

Dolphins: The Other Intelligent Mammal

Some say dolphins are smarter than humans: they don't pollute where they live, they never work unless unless they have to, and you'll never see one wearing platform shoes. This site is where to find out about dolphins, read accounts of encounters with wild dolphins, see reviews of dolphin books, and entertain speculations on the extent of dolphin intelligence and the nature of dolphin behavior. Dolphins in space? Find out why here.

Type: Usenet newsgroup
Address: alt.animals.dolphins
Region: World

EXOTIC-L

EXOTIC-L is a discussion list for and about all types and varieties of exotic pet birds. This list was created for the express purpose of discussing anything from the care and feeding of your beloved pet bird to the scientific research concerning any aspect of wild or domestic exotic bird populations. If you wish to discuss training, human-avian experiences, seek a bit of comfort over the loss of a cherished bird, or find the best way to handle any aspect of bird ownership, you'll be welcome on the EXOTIC-L list.

Type: Mailing List
Address: LISTSERV@PLEARN.EDU.PL
Send e-mail message with body:
            SUBSCRIBE EXOTIC-L <Firstname Lastname>
Region: World

Felines Wild and Domesticated

Behavior—both natural and unusual—is discussed, as are such topics as the chemistry of cat urine and the epidemiology of feline disorders. Though pets are discussed, the focus tends to be on their felinity

rather than their status as pets. If you've ever wondered about things like those travelers' tales of Tibetan temple cats, this group's for you.

Type: Usenet newsgroup
Address: alt.animals.felines
Region: World

Fishing Reports

Sagi's Outdoor News is an Arizona-based online newsletter for fishing, hunting, and outdoor recreation. Animal-right advocates come in for a bashing in stories here ("Freaks Target Rodeo," and so on) but it's an otherwise conservation-minded effort. Includes hotlinks to worldwide fishing information.

Type: WWW
Address: http://www.infop.com/outdoor/index.html
Region: U.S., Mexico, Canada, Germany, Iceland, Scotland

Foxes

For fox pictures, reviews of foxy books, and a place to discuss the sly little critters with others who find them endearing, this is it. The politics of fox hunting is discussed here, though not impartially.

Type: Usenet newsgroup
Address: alt.animals.foxes
Region: World

Hamsters Are Neat

The FAQ here contains nearly everything you need to know about keeping a hamster healthy and happy.

Posters wax eloquent about their pets' names and habits. There is even some ASCII art. A list of hamster owners' names is available for the bored and lonely.

Type: Usenet newsgroup
Address: rec.pets.hampster
Region: World

Hamsters Are Neat, Part 2

The FAQ from this group is also an electronic source guide for information on hamsters, a compendium of the information that passes through the group. And there is lots of discussion going on here about these cute and furry rodents.

Type: Usenet newsgroup
Address: alt.pets.hamsters
Region: World

House Rabbit Society

This group finds homes for abandoned bunnies. Includes pix and biographies of rabbits available for adoption, plus information on caring for rabbits as pets.

Type: WWW
**Address: http://www.psg.lcs.mit.edu/
             ~carl/paige/HRS-home.html**
Region: U.S.

Lampreys: Not Good Pets

Not even those who frequent this newsgroup are sure what it is about. Is it a biology group, a joke, a way to waste time between studies, or a place for clever opening lines for the amorously inclined? All agree, though, that lampreys suck. These sharp-toothed eels are an acquired taste (as you might be for them).

Type: Usenet newsgroup
Address: alt.animals.lampreys
Region: World

Lemurs

A place for those who love those "little guys with the big eyes" to trade stories, lemur jokes, reports of lemurs in the media, and scientific data. An "adopt a lemur" program is available.

Type: Usenet newsgroup
Address: alt.fan.lemurs
Region: World

National Anti-Hunt Campaign

This group seeks to end "blood sports" in the U.K. Since such activities have been closed to all but the blue-blooded for generations, the arguments occasionally take on a certain nasty class-based tone. Information on political and legal actions is available here, including about how England's new Criminal Justice Act is attempting to wipe out "hunt saboteurs" with hefty fines and jail time.

Type: WWW
**Address: http://envirolink.org/arrs/
             homepages.htm**
Region: England, Scotland

NetVet

Run by a veterinarian in St. Louis, this site has lots of information on animal health and related links. It's got a superb interface, too. Searchable, with links to the Electronic Zoo (information on wild animals), veterinary schools, and animal-welfare and breeding organizations. Other icons bring up tons of data about domestic species. For example, the horse list has over 60 information sources, with subjects ranging from breeding to racing to the genetics of coat color.

Type: WWW
Address: http://netvet.wustl.edu/
Type: Gopher
Address: vetinfo.wustl.edu:70/11n:/vet
Region: U.S., World

Pets of All Sorts

This is a popular place to discuss pets, from pot-bellied pigs to hedgehogs, and all the more common types as well. Charming anecdotes about posters' personal pets' adorable (and not so adorable) antics abound, as do serious inquiries about health and behavior problems.

Type: Usenet newsgroup
Address: rec.pets
Region: World

Rabbits for Fun and Profit

People with pet rabbits come here to brag, complain, and get to know each other. Does your bunny need a new home? Is your rug being chewed? Do you need to meet a vet who knows about bunnies' special problems? Are you still bored and lonely, even though you bought a bunny to share your life with?

Type: Usenet newsgroup
Address: alt.pets.rabbits
Region: World

Reptile and Amphibian Pets

This group is for those who fancy turtles, tortoises, snakes, and lizards. How do you determine the sex of a garter snake? Where do you obtain a gila monster permit? How long until those anole eggs hatch? How big a threat to the Galapagos tortoises is the burgeoning sea cucumber market? Find out here.

Type: Usenet newsgroup
Address: rec.pets.herp
Region: World

Tasmanian Tigers

This site gives the official line that this unique, dog-like marsupial carnivore is probably extinct. But sightings of the critter are occasionally reported. If one is finally found, I'm sure you'll hear it here. Includes links to information on endangered species in Australia and Tasmania.

Type: WWW
Address: http://kaos.erin.gov.au/life/ end_vuln/animals/thylacine.html
Region: Australia

Turtles, Tortoises, and Terrapins

Literally pages of resources regarding these hard-shelled creatures—even the Teenage Mutant Ninja kind—are in this Japan-based archive.

Type: WWW
Address: http://www.sfc.keio.ac.jp/ ~s93073no/site.html
Region: Costa Rica, Galapagos Islands, U.S., Japan

Wildlife Discussion Group

This newsgroup is a place where those interested in wildlife topics of any kind can get their questions answered, talk about various issues related to wildlife (note exceptions), converse with those involved in wildlife fields professionally, discuss scientific issues, and so on. This may include discussions by wildlife biologists, zoologists, and wildlife rehabilitators. The exceptions to this are hunting (except wildlife management topics), fishing, "wildlife as pets," and animal-rights topics. The use and abuse of animals sparks lively debate. It's a conduit for scientific data about animals and their lives, as well as a place for some fascinating (and some not-so-fascinating) personal anecdotes. It's also a

good place to let the world know if you are looking for work in the field, and home of the Raccoon Lovers mailing list.

Type: Usenet newsgroup
Address: rec.animals.wildlife
Region: World

World Conservation Monitoring Centre

Information on endangered species worldwide is available here, plus data on the status of parks, preserves, and other protected areas for wildlife.

Type: WWW
**Address: http://www.wcmc.org.uk/
index.html**
Region: England, World

World Equine Web Resources

Huge list, updated daily, of Internet resources about horses—feeding, care, shoeing, sales, and more.

Type: WWW
**Address: http://www.abdn.ac.uk/~src011
equine.html**
Region: Scotland, World

ANTHROPOLOGY

See also Art page 100; Folklore and Mythology page 274;
History page 324; Music page 390; Sciences page 438

Anthropology is the study of human cultures, and of how they interact and evolve. It includes the study of both ancient and modern societies. Some of the listings here, particularly the WWW pages, are incredibly rich repositories of information for the serious or casual student of humanity.

The Abayudaya Jews of Uganda

Songs, including some in English, photos and text about this unique Jewish African community. The Web page organizers are also hosting efforts to get a trained rabbi and Torah scrolls (scriptures) for the village, and have helped the villagers build a small synagogue already. Site was extraordinarily slow when I checked it, so be prepared.

Type: WWW
**Address: http://www.intac.com/
PubService/uganda/index.html**
Region: Uganda

African Studies at the University of Pennsylvania

This very extensive and well-linked African resource Web site from the African Studies faculty at UP provides graphics, information, and multimedia resources. It has K–12 education resources, basic web pages for almost 50 African nations (all with at least an entry from the CIA World Fact Book, a flag GIF, information on languages spoken and, in most cases, links to resources about or within the specified country), a Multimedia Archive with some 70 map GIFs, over 40 flag GIFs, a listing of African-oriented or -produced videos and films, a guide to on- and offline audiovisual and multimedia materials, plus satellite and weather images. Also featured are eight image collections, including Smithsonian and Vatican collections, African traditional masks, and wildlife images.

Links to the Library of Congress African collection, South African university libraries, and an online resource guide to African/African Studies net resources, including Middle East/North Africa online resources, are also here; as are links to several searchable databases located in Africa; the McGee "Black/African Sites" online resource list, and a large list of Web page links on a wide variety of African subjects.

Type: WWW
Address: **http://www.sas.upenn.edu/ African_Studies/AS.html**
Region: U.S., Africa

Al Mashriq—The Levant Multimedia Cultural Server

This is probably the largest online collection of Levantine Middle East (Lebanon, Jordan, Palestine, Iraq, Syria, and Egypt) multimedia resources. Available at this site are 27 subject-oriented menu items, which display flags, maps, or photos of the Levant; sound files of Arab music; documents on Levantine history and culture; and links to FTP and WWW servers in the Middle East.

Type: WWW
Address: **http://www.hiof.no/almashirq/**
Region: Lebanon, Jordan, Palestine, Iraq, Syria, Egypt

Amateur Anthropological Association List

Dubbed the "small-triple-a list," this focuses on issues of critical or radical anthropology from the perspective of those who are not anthropologists by trade. This is a nascent, very small list with little activity, but the pamphlets they have produced (archived with the list at the Gopher site listed below) are quite interesting.

Type: Gopher
Address: **nisp.ncl.ac.uk:70/11/lists-p-t/ small-triple-a**
Type: Mailing list
Address: **mailbase@mailbase.ac.uk**
Send e-mail bessage with blank Subject line and body: JOIN small-triple-a <Firstname Lastname>
Region: World

ANTHRO-L

This is the primary e-mail discussion list for general anthropological subjects. It is archived at the WWW site listed below.

Type: Mailing list
Address: **listserv@ubvm.cc.buffalo.edu**
Send e-mail message with blank Subject line and one-line body: subscribe ANTHRO-L <Firstname Lastname>
Type: WWW
Address: **http://www.anatomy.su.oz.au/ danny/anthropology/anthro-l/ index.html**
Region: Australia, World

Applied Anthropology Computer Network

The Applied Anthropology Computer Network archives are a source of excellent articles on applied anthropology, usually addressing primarily contemporary social issues from a very radical or critical perspective. These archives serve as the public clearinghouse for work produced by the Anthap Computer Network. Based in Rochester, Mich., the Anthap Network is jointly used by the Society for Applied Anthropology and the National Association for the Practice of Anthropology.

Type: Gopher
Address: **Gopher.acs.oakland.edu/
          1ftp%3avela.acs.oakland.edu%
          40/pub/anthap/**
Type: FTP
Address: **vela.acs.oakland.edu/pub/
          anthap**
Region: World

BASQUE-L

BASQUE-L is an e-mail discussion list for those interested in the unique culture, language, and history of the Basque region of Spain and its people.

Type: Mailing list
Address: **listserv@cunyvm.cuny.edu**
**Send e-mail message with blank Subject
          line and one-line body: subscribe
          BASQUE-L <your e-mail address>**
Region: Spain

Boriken: A Puerto Rican Mailing List

Boriken is an e-mail discussion list focusing on Puerto Rican culture and society. This list is not archived, and most of the discussion is in Spanish.

Type: Mailing list
Address: **listserv@enlace.bitnet**
**Send e-mail message with blank Subject
          line and one-line body: subscribe
          BORIKEN <your address>**
Region: Puerto Rico

Bui Doi: Life Like Dust

The film *Bui Doi* by filmmakers Nick Rothenberg and Ahrin Mishan traces the life of a Vietnamese immigrant who is a gang member, and his relationship to his community in the U.S. This display provides background on the film, a study guide for classroom use, background on the filmmakers, and digitized audio and video segments of the film. A good example of using multimedia to make anthropology more accessible.

Type: WWW
Address: **http://cwis.usc.edu/dept/elab/
          buidoi/vietgangs.html**
Region: U.S., Vietnam

Center for Social Anthropology and Computing Ethnographics Gallery

Based at the University of Kent in the U.K., the Center for Social Anthropology and Computing was founded to open up scholarly multimedia information on Social Anthropology to a much wider audience. The center is attempting to obtain out-of-print or open-copyright documents for electronic distribution via their site. Provided currently are several subject surveys, such as "45 Years in the Turkish Village," a well-written documentation of life in a rural Turkish village with illustrations; and "Traditions in the Cook Islands," which includes an extensive paper dealing with symbols in the Cook Islands' indigenous cultures plus a short QuickTime movie. Also here: a software archive, a bibliography of social anthropology publications, a forum for new papers and articles, book and film reviews, a very impressive linked hypertext list of "Anthropology Exhibits on the WWW," and links to a number of other major anthropology sites.

Type: WWW
Address: **http://lucy.ukc.ac.uk/index.html**
Type: Gopher
Address: **lucy.ukc.ac.uk:70**
Region: England

CENTRAL-ASIA-STUDIES-L

This Australia-based mailing list was organized to foster discussion about the language, history, politics, economics, and cultures of Central Asian nations.

Type: Mailing list
Address: majordomo@coombs.anu.edu.au
Send e-mail message with one-line body:
         subscribe CENTRAL-ASIA-STUDIES-L <Firstname Lastname>
Region: Central Asia

Classical Anthropology Discussions

The sci.classics newsgroup primarily focuses on classical literature and history, but also covers cultural, anthropological, and archaeological topics regarding Mediterranean civilizations of classical antiquity.

Type: Usenet newsgroup
Address: sci.classics
Region: Italy, Greece, Northern Africa

Cultural Studies and Critical Theory WWW at the Carnegie-Mellon: English Server

This is one of the best spots for radical academic literature on cultural theory, modern culture, and communications issues in general. This site also includes some more underground anarchist or post-leftist lit, like the e-journal *Bad Subjects*, which often touches on subjects of anthropological interest.

Type: WWW
Address: http://english-server.hss.cmu.edu/Theory.html
Type: Gopher
Address: english-server.hss.cmu.edu
Region: World

Cultural Discussions and Current Anthropology

Under the heading of "soc.culture." there are almost 200 newsgroups discussing the culture and contemporary social and political issues of countries, geographical regions, and ethnic groupings from around the world. A few examples are soc.culture.afghanistan, soc.culture.albania, soc.culture.arabic, soc.culture.estonia, soc.culture.latin-america, soc.culture.maghreb, and soc.culture.punjab. Each varies radically in content and style (for example, the soc.culture.afghanistan newsgroup is hot with discussion about the conflict there, with individuals from antagonistic parties going at each other, while in the soc.culture.native group discussion leans toward the traditions and history of native peoples and is much more subdued). Also covered by these groups are topics more political and technical, as well as attempts by people of certain ethnic or national backgrounds to maintain ties with friends or fellow citizens while abroad. See any complete listing of Usenet newsgroups to find a specific topic.

Type: Usenet newsgroup
Address: soc.culture
Region: World

EASIANTH for East and Southeast Asia

EASIANTH is an e-mail discussion group focusing on anthropological studies and activities in East and Southeast Asia.

Type: Mailing list
Address: listserv@u.washington.edu
Send e-mail message with blank Subject line and one-line body: subscribe EASIANTH <your address>
Region: East and Southeast Asia

East Timor Net

The East Timor Net Web page contains political and historical documents, but also has files charting the ethnic diversity of the island's native population, ethno-linguistic information, and biological and geological information about the island. The site is well-organized but still under construction, so don't be surprised if you run into an occasional blank page.

Type: WWW
Address: http://www.uc.pt/Timor/Timor Net.html
Region: East Timor, Indonesia

Electronic Antiquity

This e-journal, available at the Gopher site below, is a well-produced electronic scholarly publication dedicated to the study of the literature, art, history, and culture of the Mediterranean civilizations of classical antiquity.

Type: Gopher
Address: info.utas.edu.au:70/Publications/
Region: Italy, Greece, North Africa

Ethnographic Laboratory for Anthropology (E-Lab)

This site provides a view into the U.S.C. Ethnographic Lab, including examples from ongoing film and multimedia projects as well as abstracts of recent papers and books dealing with subject matter pertinent to their pursuits.

Type: WWW
Address: http://www.usc.edu/dept/elab/ welcome
Region: World

Fourth World Bulletin

This e-journal is the quarterly publication of the Fourth World Documentation Project, and contains up-to-date news on legal and political struggles of indigenous peoples around the world. Each issue comes in several parts of about 30K each. There's much here of interest to students of modern anthropology, particularly on the results of "culture clashes" between indigenous populations and their neighbors.

Type: Gopher
Address: gopher.native-ed.bc.ca:70/11/NEC
Region: World

Fourth World Documentation Project

FWDP is based out of the Center for World Indigenous Studies. The Center makes available to researchers documents concerning social, political, and human-rights issues faced by indigenous people throughout the world. Documents can be accessed by subject and geographic region, and all the archive documents are searchable via WAIS at this Web page. Over three dozen links to other archives of aboriginal and native studies archives are included here.

Type: WWW
Address: http://www.halcyon.com:80/ FWDP/fwdp.html
Region: World

Internet Resources of Interest to Anthropologists

There's a large collection of mailing lists, Usenet newsgroups, FTP servers, Gopher servers, Web pages, and e-zines here, making this page essential reading for anthropologists online.

Type: WWW
**Address: http://mayaquest.mecc.com/
            InternetResources.html**
Region: World

Iranian Culture and Information Center

Serving as a very basic Iranian cultural resource, this site provides maps and photos, modern and classical poetry, sound files of modern and classical Iranian music, art images, and general text files on Persian culture.
Type: WWW
Address: http://tehran.stanford.edu
Region: Iran

Journal of World Anthropology

Produced and published by the University of New York at Buffalo, the quarterly electronic *Journal of World Anthropology* provides a forum for discussion and propagation of academic anthropological studies and data. It's archived at the Gopher site below.
Type: E-journal
**Address: <listserv@ubvm.cc.buffalo.edu
Send e-mail message with body: sub jwa
            <Firstname Lastname>**
Type: Gopher
**Address: wings.buffalo.edu:70/11/
            academic/department/
            anthropology.jwa**
Region: World

Middle East Network Information Center

This University of Texas at Austin site has links via WWW and Gopher to Middle East Studies departments at academic institutions in the U.S., Israel, and the Arab world. Most of these Middle Eastern net links are set up by technical or scientific institutions,

hence there is little cultural information available, other than perhaps a few poetry examples, a recipe or two, and some digitized photos. However, as more humanities-oriented institutions of higher learning in this region develop connections to the net, MENIC will provide one of the best gateways to their computer systems. The Web page carries the same info as the Gopher, but is more conveniently organized.
Type: WWW
**Address: gopher://menic.utexas.edu:80/
            hGET%20/menic.html**
Type: Gopher
Address: inic.utexas.edu/11/menic
Region: Israel, Middle East

Middle East Studies Association Bulletin Gopher

Middle East Studies within any academic discipline is covered by MESA, and this Gopher site provides access to the Research Resources section of the MESA Quarterly Bulletin back to 1992. This provides tips on recently published information sources on the Middle East, including online resources. It also has links to a number of Middle East Studies departments, though these links are not very well stocked with online documents, instead providing guides to academic programs and library catalogs.
Type: Gopher
**Address: vmsgopher.cua.edu/11
            gopher_root_mesabul**
Region: Middle East

Native Americans

This fairly active newsgroup serves as a sounding board for topics and issues dealing with the indigenous peoples of the world, though primarily discussion focuses on Native North American (U.S. and

Canadian) issues. About half is political in nature, but a great deal of what is posted deals with historical and cultural issues relevant to anthropological inquiry. Open questions posted by outsiders seem to get a good deal of attention and serious response.

Type: Usenet newsgroup
Address: alt.native
Region: U.S., Canada

Native Net Server

The Native Net Server features general documentation on tribal government and Indian education in the U.S., as well as the charter and latest issue of the soc.culture.native Usenet news group FAQ, and the archives for the NATIVELIT-L mailing list.

Type: Gopher
Address: alpha1.csd.uwm.edu:70/11/ uwm%20Information/Native%20 American%20Net%20Server
Region: U.S., Canada

Netherlands Institute of the Near East

The home page for the Netherlands Institute of the Near East provides links to a number of Middle East Studies academic institutions, with an emphasis on Egyptology. The institute publishes a yearly Egyptology online bibliography, provides access to the Centre for Computer-aided Egyptology, plus archives and subscription information for MOinfo-l, a Dutch-language mailing list for Arabic and Middle East Studies, and the Institute's Department of Near Eastern Languages.

Type: WWW
Address: http://www.leidenuniv.nl/nino/ nino.html
Region: Netherlands, Near East

Oceana

This newsletter publishes scholarly works in the field of anthropology among the peoples of the Pacific Islands, New Zealand, and Australia. If you want to learn how Aborigines incorporate Catholicism into their native religion or better understand the role of female traditional health practitioners in New Guinea, read *Oceana*.

Type: WWW
Address: http://www.kun.nl/cps/
Region: Australia, New Zealand, New Guinea, Pacific Islands

Omnicultural Academic Resources

Based at St. Olaf Liberal Arts College in Northfield, Minn., this Gopher site features a collection of documents dealing with international and intercultural education topics, aimed at secondary level educators and students

Type: Gopher
Address: Gopher.stolaf.edu:70/Internet Resources/St. Olaf Sponsored Mailing Lists/
Region: World

Oxford Anthropology and Archaeology Corner

Organized by the Institute of Social and Cultural Anthropology at Oxford University, the Anthropology and Archaeology Corner Web page provides links to a number of major U.K. university anthropology archives, as well as a few very good local documents discussing the theory and merits of producing hypertext anthropological documentation, and examples of such documents.

Type: WWW
**Address: http://www.rsl.ox.ac.uk/isca/
            index.html**
Region: England, World

Palestine Gopher Server

This Gopher site holds primarily historical and political information regarding the situation of the Palestinian people and their struggle for political self-determination, but there is a small amount of cultural information, as well as some poetry by some of the great writers of the region.

Type: Gopher
Address: alquds.org/1
Region: Israel, Palestine, Jordan, Syria, Lebanon

Palestinian and Arab Anthropology Resources

Abed Khooli, a Palestinian physicist at the University of Oregon, has created an extremely well-organized personal Web page that has links to many Islamic and Arab cultural sites on the Net, as well as some excellent Palestinian historical documentation, an introduction to Islam, online Arabic language resources, and links to Gopher archives at AnNajah University in Nablus (a city in the West Bank), and soon other Palestinian institutes of higher learning.

Type: WWW
**Address: http://darkwing.uoregon.edu/
            ~alquds/whoami.html**
Region: Middle East

Polynesian Voyaging Society

The Hawaii-based Polynesian Voyaging Society is dedicated to the preservation of the cultural traditions of the societies that settled the islands of the South Pacific by traveling in huge outrigger voyaging canoes. Available through this Gopher site is information about the history of the Polynesian Voyaging Society, information regarding ongoing voyage projects, documentation on what life was like during the voyages, some history of the region, and information about the construction of the canoes themselves and ancient, noninstrument oriented, navigation techniques.

Type: Gopher
Address: nic2.hawaii.net/11/PVS
Region: U.S., Tahiti, South Pacific

The Science of Anthropology

The sci.anthropology newsgroup covers both topics of professional anthropological research as well as subjects of interest to amateur anthropologists. The sci.anthropology.paleo group covers the same territory for the discipline of paleo-anthropology. These Usenet newsgroups also have a WWW home page, which provides archival information, plus an online newsreader in a menu format that lets you browse the past few days' posts.

Type: Usenet newsgroup
**Addresses: sci.anthropology,
             sci.anthropology.paleo**
Type: WWW
**Address: http://www.anatomy.su.oz.au/
            danny/usenet/sci.anthropology/
            index.html**
Region: World

SDOMINGO

SDOMINGO is an e-mail discussion list focusing on the culture and society of the Caribbean island nation of Santo Domingo, most of which is in Spanish.

Type: Mailing list
Address: listserv@enlace.bitnet
Send e-mail message with blank Subject
**   line and one-line body: subscribe**
**   SDOMINGO <Your E-mail**
**   Address>**
Region: Santo Domingo

Seven Scenes of Plenty

This is an entirely digitized version of the film *Seven Scenes of Plenty* by world-famous ethnographic film-maker Michael Mascha. The film, the first in a planned trilogy of films dealing with life in the varied cultures of the South Pacific Islands, centers on the Fijian island of Matuka and the customs and lifestyle of its inhabitants, including the introduction of modern consumer goods and culture. Also included in the site is a background document about the filmmaker and the island of Matuka.

Type: WWW
Address: http://cwis.usc.edu/dept/elab/
**   mascha/index.html**
Region: Fiji

SHAMASH Project

Formerly known as the New York Israel Project, the SHAMASH server is subtitled "serving the Jewish Internet." This Gopher provides a number of very solid Jewish and Israeli cultural resources, including recent activities and dissertation abstracts carried through by the National Foundation for Jewish Culture, Holocaust historical archives, and geographic and travel resources regarding Israel.

Type: Gopher
Address: Israel.nysernet.org:71/1
Region: Israel

UC-Irvine Southeast Asian WWW Page

Dealing primarily with immigrant communities of Southeast Asians in the U.S., the U.C.I. Southeast Asian Archives are accessible via a contact given on this Web page. Also provided is the newsletter of the archive and a visual cultural online exhibit, which I believe changes subject periodically.

Type: WWW
Address: http://www.lib.uci.edu/sea/
**   seahome.html**
Region: Vietnam, Laos, Cambodia, Thailand

U.S.C's WWW Virtual Library Anthropology Pages

Choix
d'Éditeur

This site is the anthropology resources Web page for the University of Southern California's WWW Virtual Library, a WWW-accessible matrix of resources on a variety of academic subjects consisting of U.S.C.-based hypertext resources and links to other Gopher and web sites on both specified academic disciplines and general subjects. The WWW V-L Anthropology page has links to dozens of different WWW resources, including graphics, audio, and video resources.

Type: WWW
Address: http://www.usc.edu/dept/
**   v-lib/anthropology.html**
Region: World

XCULT-L

This list concentrates on issues brought up in the International Intercultural Newsletter, which is produced by graduate students at Penn State. The primary participants are educators in many different disciplines, though primarily from the Humanities.

Type: Mailing list

Address: listserv@psuvm.psu.edu
Send e-mail message with blank Subject
line and one-line body: subscribe
XCULT-L <Firstname Lastname>
Region: World

ARCHEOLOGY

See also Architecture page 93; History page 324

Into digging up artifacts, studying the relics of pre-historic cultures, or investigating dinosaurs and other long-extinct life forms? If so, there should be some sites of interest to you in this section. Hypermedia seems like a natural match for a field where interrelated text, graphics, and video can provide a much richer world of information than the typical textbook or popular-science magazine. I think there'll be many more resources before long.

Ancient Palestine

Want to take a walk through the buildings of ancient Palestine? Take a look at this Web site, which will let you take animated tours of various sites reconstructed by archaeologists. Includes Biblical references.
Type: WWW
Address: http://philae.sas.upenn.edu/
ANEP/ANEP.html
Region: Israel, Palestine, Syria

Archeology Discussion Online

Alternative views on archaeology, occasionally including various crackpot theories of the "ancient astronauts did it" or Velikovskian variety.
Type: Usenet newsgroup
Address: alt.archaeology
Region: World

ArchNet

Search for archaeological resources online by region from this site—very useful, frequently updated, and has a nice interface, too.
Type: WWW
Address: http://spirit.lib.uconn.edu/
ArchNet/Regions/Regions.html
Region: World

Arctic Circle

Great *National Geographic*-style graphics! The archaeological side of this site explores the colonial period in the transarctic region, and brings its impact up to the present day.
Type: WWW
Address: http://spirit.lib.uconn.edu/
ArcticCircle/index.html
Region: Siberia, U.S., Canada, Greenland, Iceland, Scandinavia, Russia

Ardeche Cave Art Discovery

Choix
d'Éditeur

Ardeche, France is the site of a celebrated December 1994 discovery of prehistoric cave paintings as powerful (and better preserved) than those of Lascaux. This Internet site is almost the only way you can see the paintings, as the site is totally closed to nonscientists. Ancient animals of Europe, in rippling ochres and blacks, with supporting text.
Type: WWW
Address: http://www.culture.fr/culture/
gvpda-en.html
Region: France

Avebury Department of Archaeology

This English school, itself located near one of the U.K.'s most spectacular megalith sites, maintains an excellent archive of archaeological material. Lots of links to sites around the world.

Type: WWW
Address: http://avebury.arch.soton.ac.uk/ NetStuff/archplaces.html
Type: FTP
Address: avebury.arch.soton.ac.uk
Type: Gopher
Address: avebury.arch.soton.ac.uk
Region: England, World

Cagliari (Sardinia) Archaeological Museum

In Italian, although I understand that an English version is being built. Includes lots of links to archaeological exhibits.

Type: WWW
Address: http://www.crs4.it/HTML/ RUGGIERO/MUSEO/mus_ind.html
Region: Italy

Classics and Mediterranean Archaeology

This is the definitive starting point for research online into world archaeology, with a focus on diggings in search of Classical-period Europe and related Eastern cultures. Includes archives of archeology journals, abstracts and data, plus information on materials viewable or obtainable from museums and libraries.

Type: WWW
Address: http://classics.lsa.umich.edu/ welcome.html
Type: Gopher
Address: rome.classics.lsa.umich.edu
Region: Italy, Greece, Tunisia, North Africa

Dinosaur

This is a list for those interested in dinosaur facts and discoveries; volume ranges up to maybe a dozen messages a week. Participants also discuss flying and swimming archosaurs and other animals that predated, coexisted with, or followed the mighty dinosaurs. Most participants are not paleontologists, but some are extremely well-versed.

Type: Mailing list
Address: LISTPROC@LEPOMIS.PSYCH. UPENN.EDU
Send e-mail message with one-line body:
SUBSCRIBE DINOSAUR
<Firstname Lastname>
Contact: rowe@lepomis.psych.upenn.edu (Mickey Rowe)
Region: World

Egyptian Artifacts Exhibit

Want to see a mummy tonight? You're in luck, a mummy is one of five Egyptian artifacts featured here at the University of Memphis.

Type: WWW
Address: http://www.memphis.edu/ egypt/artifact.html
Region: Egypt

El Pital

This site offers a look at a newly discovered "lost city" in the Mexican state of Veracruz. Includes an early look at artifacts, speculations about El Pital's importance in the advanced pre-Columbian civilization of Mexico, aerial views of the site, and information about the archaeologist in charge.

Type: WWW
**Address: http://infosphere.com/clients/
             smallworks/hiser/ElPital/ElPital
             .html**
Region: Mexico

Ethnohistory and Ethnoarchaeology at the University of Connecticut

This section of the University of Connecticut's ArchNet archaeology network provides a variety of historical and cultural documents pertaining to pre- and post-Columbian Northeastern U.S. indigenous nations. Ethnoarchaeology is the branch of the archaeological discipline that attempts to reconstruct cultures of the past from the artifacts they left behind, historical records, and any modern remnants of the group studied.

Type: WWW
**Address: http://spirit.lib.uconn.edu/Arch
             Net/Topical/Ethno/ Ethno.html**
Region: U.S., Canada

Institute of Egyptian Art and Archaeology

Here you can take a short color tour of Egypt, complete with pictures of many ancient buildings. You can also examine the Institute's collection of Egyptian art and artifacts.

Type: WWW
**Address: http://www.memst.edu/egypt/
             main.html**
Region: Egypt

Mesoamerican Archaeology Discussion

The sci.archaeology.mesoamerican newsgroup deals with Central American and Mexican archaeology and ancient civilizations from that region of the world. This is the place to discuss the Maya, Olmec, Toltec and related cultures, and the impressive ruins and artifacts they left behind.

Type: Usenet newsgroup
Address: sci.archaeology.mesoamerican
Region: Mexico, Guatemala, Central America

Newton: The Egyptology Resource

The best resource on Egyptology on the Web, from a branch of Cambridge University in England. Includes the latest news on new finds and changing interpretations of past data, and links to resources around the world. Regularly updated.

Type: WWW
**Address: http://www.newton.cam.ac.uk/
             egypt/**
Region: Egypt

Oriental Institute

The University of Chicago's archaeology department is one of the best-known and most respected in the world, so naturally it can provide an incredible amount of information through its Oriental Institute. This page has information on projects going on around the world, as well as on how international scholars can get money and scholarships for their own projects.

Type: WWW
**Address: http://www-oi.uchicago.edu/oi/
             default.html**
Region: World

Robotic Tele-Excavation Site

Talk about interactive—this is neat! Using a Web browser with a graphical interface plus a color or gray-scale monitor, the user can access a robotic arm at a remote site. It's stationed over a patch of earth that covers a variety of artifacts. By using the graphical controls on the screen and the images brought in via a closed-circuit camera on the robotic arm, you can manipulate the arm and its compressed-air jet to uncover the artifacts. Use is limited to about five minutes at a pop, but you can observe the efforts of others while queued up for your go at the robot.

Type: WWW
Address: http://www.usc.edu/dept/ raiders/story/index.html
Region: World

Turkish Village

The ancient village of Sos Hoyuk in northeast Turkey is the site of an ongoing investigation by an Australian archaeological team. Site surveys, photos, research results, and bibliographies are just part of the offerings here.

Type: WWW
Address: http://adhocalypse.arts.unimelb. edu.au/Dept/Arch/NETurkey/ home.html
Region: Turkey

World of the Vikings

Runes, history, artifacts, and even a runic font for Macs are here. Some text in Norwegian, Danish and Swedish as well as English. Links to museum exhibits, too: The Tromsø Museum is especially impressive and has an elegant Web interface for its online collections.

Type: WWW
Address: http://www.demon.co.uk/ history/index.html
Region: Denmark, Norway, Sweden, Russia, England

ARCHITECTURE

See also Archeology page 90; Art page 100; History page 324

I was once an architecture student, and I still love to study the myriad forms of local architecture. The Web may be just the tool to bring this activity to people who would never pick up an expensive retrospective volume on an obscure architect. Checking out some of these sites is a bit like combining the best of *National Geographic* and *Architectural Digest* in one eye-opening learning experience.

Several others are dedicated to information on specific schools of architecture, and will be of interest mainly to current, former, or prospective architecture students for now. Most of these college sites are quite new, and I expect that soon more information for laypeople will be added, such as photos, historical and biographical texts, and even multimedia stuff—especially as Computer Assisted Drafting (CAD) becomes commonplace at the college level.

Alternative Architecture

Dome houses, cob (rammed earth) construction, and solar energy are all cutting-edge ideas you'll find discussed in this newsgroup.

Type: Usenet newsgroup
Address: alt.architecture.alternative
Region: World

Alvar Aalto Museum

The Alvar Aalto Museum was founded in 1966 in Jyvaskyla, Finland. This site has beautiful pictures of the museum, which was designed by Aalto. Aalto was an architect who blended modern ideas about building as an art form with materials and designs rooted in traditional Finnish culture, creating clean, simple structures enhanced by light, folk-art colors, and local woods.

Type: WWW
Address: http://www.cs.jyu.fi/~jatahu/ aalto/homepage.html
Region: Finland

Architecture of Islam

Lots of photos take you on a guided tour of doors, arches, and other beautiful entryways to buildings in traditional Middle Eastern styles.

Type: WWW
Address: http://rubens.anu.edu.au/ islam2/Part1.html
Region: Iran

Architecture Pictures

Text and pictures (in GIF and JPEG formats) of a number of buildings around the world.

Type: FTP
Address: ftp.sunet.se/pub/pictures/ architecture
Region: World

Art and Architecture: Books in Print from Princeton University Press

Everything that Princeton University Press can sell you about architecture—which includes some neat titles with an international flavor.

Type: Gopher
Address: gopher.pupress.princeton.edu/ 11n%3a/discp/art
Region: World

Centre for Design (CfD) Home Page

This page is dedicated to the work of Environmental Design folks at Australia's Royal Melbourne Institute of Technology. You can find information on research, staff, and other environmental-design Internet sites.

Type: WWW
Address: http://daedalus.edc.rmit.edu.au/
Region: Australia

Chalmers School of Architecture

This Swedish school will tell you about their programs and research, as well as how to apply. Also includes a link to their library. Text available in English or Swedish.

Type: WWW
Address: http://www.arch.chalmers.se/ home-e.html
Region: Sweden

Classical Architecture of the Mediterranean Basin

This searchable index to architectural work allows you to specify the country, type of structure, and site you're interested in.

Type: WWW
Address: http://rubens.anu.edu.au/ architecture_form.html
Region: Greece, Italy, Europe, Africa, Middle East

Department of Interior Architecture and Furniture Design

A brief description of this department of the University of Art and Design Helsinki (UIAH).

Type: WWW

Address: http://www.uiah.fi/departments /intefurn/

Region: Finland

DESIGN-UQAM SOURCE

In French, it's the usual information on the Environmental Design programs at L'Université du Québec à Montreal.

Type: WWW

Address: http://meenakshi.design.uqam.ca/

Region: Canada

DIVA (Digital Images for the Visual Arts)

Go to the Images section, then to Australian Architecture. You can look at over 100 images of twentieth-century architecture in Melbourne, which are offered by the Visual Arts Library at Monash University in Melbourne.

Type: WWW

Address: http://www.monash.edu.au/ diva/images.html#ozarch

Region: Australia

Dome Project Page

This page is the work of some Japanese folks at the Synagetics Institute. They will send you pictures, text, and plans for a pine dome building based on R. Buckminster Fuller's classic geodesic dome.

Type: WWW

Address: http://cs1.sfc.keio.ac.jp/ ~t93827ya/dome/dome.html

Region: Japan

Energy Research Group

This group is part of the School of Architecture in the Faculty of Engineering and Architecture, of University College Dublin. They are working on research in energy utilization in buildings and climate-sensitive architectural design, and can tell you all about their projects.

Type: WWW

Address: http://erg.ucd.ie/

Region: Ireland

English Server Art Papers Archive

This Gopher site has a substantial archive of texts related to architecture and architects.

Type: Gopher

Address: english.hss.cmu.edu:70/1D-2% 3A241%3AArt%26Arch

Region: World

Fachbereich Architektur: Universitat Köln

In German, but it seems to be the usual directory of faculty, projects, and programs.

Type: WWW

Address: http://www.fh-koeln.de/fb-ar/ ar.html

Region: Germany

Fakultt 1: Architektur und Stadtplanung

In German, information about faculty and programs at the University of Stuttgart's excellent School of Architecture and Urban Planning.

Type: WWW

Address: http://www.uni-stuttgart.de/Cis/ Fakultaeten/fakultaeten.html

Region: Germany

FB10—Architektur: Universitat Wuppertal

In German, Wuppertal University's directory of faculty, projects, and programs.

Type: WWW
**Address: http://www.uni-wuppertal.de/
fachbereiche/FB10/welcome.html**
Region: Germany

Greek and Roman Cities of Western Turkey

This is a hypertext book placed online for your enjoyment. Unfortunately, it has no pictures, but it is useful to be able to jump around in the book as you like. Turkey has some beautifully preserved Classical ruins—less well-known than their counterparts in modern-day Italy and Greece, but equally beguiling.

Type: WWW
**Address: http://rubens.anu.edu.au/turkey
book/intro1.html#geography**
Region: Turkey

Interior Design

This low-traffic newsgroup covers the topic of interior architecture, including non-U.S. designers and trends.

Type: Usenet newsgroup
Address: alt.architecture.int-design
Region: World

Hong Kong Polytechnic's Building and Real Estate Pages

Maintained by the Department of Building and Real Estate at The Hong Kong Polytechnic University (it says something about the difference between the U.S. and Hong Kong that you would never find the sales and financing side of real estate and the "art" of architecture taught in the same department stateside, sometimes much to the detriment of fledgling architects.) You can find local new-construction news, a Gopher site with copious files, faculty research, and student projects online here. There's even an extensive collection of QuickTime movies that show off the school.

Type: WWW
Address: http://www.bs.hkp.hk/
Region: Hong Kong, China

Home Page for Wageningen University

The home page of the Department for Physical Planning and Rural Development of Wageningen University, the Netherlands, this offers details on programs, students, and research, with pictures. the Nethelands are well-known for innovative public planning and building projects, so this should be of interest to many.

Type: WWW
**Address: http://www.wau.nl/rpv/
dept-rpv.html**
Region: Netherlands

Ictinus Network Home Page

This site is maintained by the Faculty of Architecture, Building and Planning at the University of Melbourne in Australia. You can look at course lists, find library resources, and read faculty publications.

Type: WWW
**Address: http://www.arbld.unimelb
.edu.au/**
Region: Australia

Images from Japan

A gallery of photos of shrines, temples, and other buildings in Japan.

Type: WWW

Address: http://www.cs.uidaho.edu/ ~marc9442/japan.html

Region: Japan

IRC Home Page

This is the home page of the Institute for Research in Construction, which attempts to set Canadian standards for building construction. They can tell you how to light your building for safety or what foundation material is best to avoid earthquake damage.

Type: WWW

Address: http://www.irc.nrc.ca/

Region: Canada

Islamic Architecture in Isfahan

This site gives you a virtual tour of the town of Isfahan, which is a historic Islamic city in Iran. You can find photographs and descriptions of most of the buildings, which were built between the eleventh and nineteenth century. If you'd like a picture, you can download it as a GIF file.

Type: WWW

Address: http://www.anglia.ac.uk/ ~trochford/isfahan.html

Region: Iran

IUAV-CIDOC Venezia

The home page of the University Institute of Architecture in Venice, Italy. It's in Italian, but the images of this historic, romantic, and (of course) increasingly modern city speak an international language. Has student CAD projects and images and links to other WWW servers in Italy.

Type: WWW

Address: http://venice.iuav.unive.it/

Region: Italy

The Jerusalem Mosaic

A virtual tour of the city of Jerusalem, with lots of pictures and historical information.

Type: WWW

Address: http://www1.huji.ac.il/jeru/ jerusalem.html

Region: Israel

Moscow Kremlin Online Excursion

Text about and pictures of Moscow's Kremlin building, only recently opened by glasnost to the world's view, with a map of the Kremlin as well. Maintainers plan to add more images, with the goal of putting the entire Kremlin on CD-ROM, including movies and speech. You can also order floppies with the images (they are copyrighted, so you can't download them for free).

Type: WWW

Address: http://www.kiae.su/www/wtr/ kremlin/begin.html

Region: Russia

Musée du Louvre

In addition to its world-famous art collection, the Louvre building is, itself, an architectural treasure. And you can find images and historical data about it here (as well as a guide to the art that hangs on its walls).

Type: WWW

Address: http://www.Paris.org.:80/ musees/Louvre

Region: France

Musée National d'Art Moderne—Centre Georges Pompidou

Pictures and exhibition information from this art museum in Paris, France. Includes some images of the museum building, which "features" its water pipes and other utilitarian stuff on the outside. It raised quite an uproar when built, but has now become a much-loved landmark for Parisians.

Type: WWW
**Address: http://meteora.ucsd.edu:80/
~norman/paris/Musees/
Beaubourg/**
Region: France

Online Tour of Canada's Parliament—Introduction

Available in both French and English. You can play Canada's rousing national anthem and take a visual tour of the historic Parliament Buildings in Ottawa.

Type: WWW
**Address: http://www.cisti.nrc.ca/
programs/pio/intro.html**
Region: Canada

Persepolis HomePage

The home page of a photographer and linguist, this site contains several nice photographs of ancient ruins.

Type: WWW
**Address: http://copper.ucs.indiana.edu:80
/~dtorchin/**
Region: Iran

Pompeii Forum Project

Lots of big images of reconstructions of buildings in Pompeii, Italy, the swinging city that was buried under volcanic ash in the Roman era and only redis-covered in this century. Takes full advantage of the hypertext environment to bring out plenty of infor-mation on this fascinating subject.

Type: WWW
**Address: http://jefferson.village.virginia.
edu/pompeii/page-1.html**
Region: Italy

Public Works and Government Services Canada

Want to build in Canada or bid on a government construction project? These are the bureaucrats to talk to. You can also find accessibility regulations here for Canadian buildings. In both French and English.

Type: WWW
Address: http://www.pwc-tpc.ca/
Region: Canada

Resource Guide for Straw Bale Construction

Apparently there are lots of people who build straw bale houses. Here you can find all kinds of pointers to resources on this unusual and inexpensive con-struction method, which has some similarities to adobe and rammed earth.

Type: WWW
**Address: http://www.xmission.com/
~shea/straw/**
Region: World

Royal Melbourne Institute of Technology

Lots of pointers to information on building design, from a server in Melbourne, Australia. Particular emphasis on Environmental Design.

Type: Gopher
Address: daedalus.edc.rmit.edu.au/
Region: Australia

Straw House Herbals Home Page

This California company not only sells wildcrafted herbs, it makes organic straw bales and builds houses too. The one featured here is in Nova Scotia, Canada. You can see pictures of it, check out statistics on its moisture content, and find out how to build one of your own. Looks cozy!

Type: WWW
Address: **http://www.cfn.cs.dal.ca/ ~aa983/strawhouse.html**
Region: Canada

The University of Adelaide Department of Architecture

The home page of this Australian school of architecture offers information on local activities and research, as well as a link to the "trans-tasman-flux" mailing list (unfortunately down when reviewed, this is supposed to be an ongoing discussion between Victoria's University of Wellington and the University of Adelaide about architecture).

Type: WWW
Address: **http://www.arch.adelaide.edu. au/home.html**
Region: Australia

University of Canberra, Environmental Design Gopher

A locally oriented Gopher site, with menus on staff, notices, and programs in Environmental Design at this Australian university.

Type: Gopher
Address: **services.canberra.edu.au/11/ Faculty/Environmental%20Design**
Region: Australia

University of Calgary WWW Home Page

There's more to Calgary than cowboys and the annual Stampede. Here's information on the local university's programs in architecture, including Environmental Design.

Type: WWW
Address: **http://www.ucalgary.ca/~evds/**
Region: Canada

University of Manitoba's Faculty of Architecture

Descriptions of architectural programs offered by this Canadian school. Also has links to University collections of books, slides, and architectural models.

Type: WWW
Address: **http://cad9.cadlab.umanitoba. ca/UofM.html**
Region: Canada

U.S. Holocaust Memorial Museum

Not easy to visit, the museum reminds us of one of the great tragedies of the twentieth Century. This site includes a number of photographs of the unique and sobering museum building, as well as details about its construction.

Type: WWW
Address: **http://www.ushmm.org/**
Region: U.S., Germany, Poland

Vatican Exhibit: Rome Reborn

The virtual companion to the Library of Congress's exhibit on the Vatican and Rome. Lots of pictures.

Type: WWW
Address: **http://sunsite.unc.edu/expo/ vatican.exhibit/Vatican.exhibit .html**
Region: Italy

ART

See also Archeology page 90; Architecture page 93; Comics and Cartoons page 116; Craft page 147

What's art to one may be "le garbage" to another, but I think most of what's listed here is pretty classy stuff. The World Wide Web and art go so naturally together that I'm afraid other types of archives have been neglected. Now you have a good reason to get Webbed, if you haven't already. There's much more out there to be found, with many museums and universities leading the way by putting their collections online as digital images.

Academy of Media Arts in Cologne, Germany

This is the only arts academy in the Federal Republic of Germany that embraces all areas of visual media, including film and video. There is no art gallery, so this site is only of interest to those who might be interested in the school.

Type: WWW
Address: http://www.khm.uni-koeln.de/ homepage/ecommon.html
Region: Germany

The Amazon Project

Young artists from the Usko-Ayar Amazonian School of Painting use a traditional vision with "modern" techniques to document their world at this unique art school. The result is striking magical-realist imagery, most of which is for sale (at very reasonable prices, I might add).

Type: WWW
Address: http://www.egallery.com/ egallery/amazon.html
Region: Peru

ART+COM

ART+COM is a nonprofit, independent, interdisciplinary, and expensively equipped company that makes high-tech toys and other products for "ruling the information age." This page is where they promote and display their (very) creative wares. It's a good example of artists using the Internet as a promotional tool.

Type: WWW
Address: http://www.artcom.de/info.html
Region: Germany, World

Art at the University of Haifa, Israel

This server is still under construction. Currently it displays 120 images of Greek and Roman Art, 17 of Renaissance Art, 33 of Baroque Art, and 11 images of Modern Art.

Type: WWW
Address: http://lib.haifa.ac.il/
Region: Israel

Art and ASCII

It's nice to know that in this day of rendered 3-D imagery, people from all over the globe still ask for and type out art with no tools but a keyboard. One contributor to this newsgroup created in ASCII art a complete set of schematics and views of the Starship Enterprise from "Star Trek the Next Generation." I am impressed—really.

Type: Usenet newsgroup
Address: alt.ascii.art
Region: World

Art College of Korea's Kyungsung University

I only hope the school is not as boring as this Web page—but if you plan to study art in Korea (or Korean art), this is the place to look online.

Type: WWW
**Address: http://sarang.kyungsung.ac.kr/
aboutcollege/e-art.html**
Region: South Korea

Artcom

A very active discussion area for the international community about artists, art education, careers, happenings, and theory. This is the place to make pronouncements to the world—match this example, if you can: "Let's get off the future shock angst bandwagon and reclaim technology as our human creation, made by artists of technology, accessible to all people, appreciated by all people!"
Type: Usenet newsgroup
Address: alt.artcom
Region: World

Art Crimes

This graffiti art gallery features wall art from the U.S., Brazil, and the Czech Republic. They advertise this as "guerrilla art worth being arrested for" and then announce that "All photographs are © by the photographers. Please don't republish them without permission." In other words, we stole this art from its creators and we will sue you if use it. Bah. Enjoy the art anyway.
Type: WWW
**Address: http://www.gatech.edu/desoto/
graf/Index.Art_Crimes.html**
Region: World

Art Scenester Chat

This discussion of the international art scene is rarely attended. All the action is over in alt.artcom. It is a good place for making art announcements that won't get lost in a crowd of messages.
Type: Usenet newsgroup
Address: alt.art.scene
Region: World

Arts Database

To grab a file listing arts resources on the net, check here. I'm not sure how often this file is updated; some of the Web resources might be more current.
Type: FTP
**Address: nic.funet.fi/pub/doc/library/
artbase.txt.Z**
Region: World

Art Theft

I don't know if it's art thieves or art screamers that are lacking here, but I do know that the last time I checked, there were absolutely no messages in this newsgroup. Perhaps it was set up to discuss the theft of Munch's "The Scream," now recovered. A good place to post about the collected works of Karen Elliot, Stewart Home, and other accomplished plagiarists, I should think. Jeff Koons, anyone?
Type: Usenet newsgroup
**Address: alt.art.theft.scream.scream.
scream**
Region: World

Australian National University

The Australian National University offers a searchable database of 10,200 art images. Included are 2,800 from between the fifteenth century and the end of the nineteenth century; and 6,000 images of classical, medieval, and Renaissance architecture and sculpture.

Type: WWW
Address: http://rubens.anu.edu.au/
Region: Australia, England, France, Greece, Italy, World

Caribbean Arts Center

There's an online exhibition here, as well as interviews with and photos of some of the artists whose works are on display. The page is in English, while some of the interviews are in Spanish or both languages.

Type: WWW
Address: http://www.nando.net/prof/ caribe/Caribbean_Art_Center.html
Region: U.S. (Puerto Rico), Dominican Republic, Caribbean

Digital Art from Brazil

Here you can find artist Sandra Rey's online portfolio of computer-based designs. Lots of color and depth, they remind me of densely patterned fabric blowing in the wind.

Type: WWW
Address: http://tucano.inf.ufrgs.br/ilea/ Sandra/Sandra.html
Region: Brazil

Electronic Photo Gallery

Photographic works by contemporary Russian artists are on display here, including some computer-processed images.

Type: WWW
Address: http://www.kiae.su/www/wtr/ hotpictures/gallery.html
Region: Russia

European Media/Art Research Exchange

This site is a place worth keeping an eye on. Based in Canada, this site is well-organized and engaging. For example, one of this Web sites' seven sections is dedicated to answering the question "What are communities online?" It includes a well-thought-out online survey for you to fill out about your online community.

Type: WWW
Address: http://wimsey.com/anima/ EUROPROBE.html
Region: Canada

French Art

Choix
d'Éditeur

A very stylish design and a sophisticated interface makes this brief overview of the age of enlightenment as seen in the paintings of France's national museums very worthwhile.

Type: WWW
Address: http://dmf.culture.fr/files/ imaginary_exhibition.html.
Region: France

French Art, Part Deux

A handful of images by Degas, Monet, Renoir, and van Gogh. The text is all in French.

Type: WWW
Address: http://www-leland.stanford.edu /~golnas/impressionism/ impressionists.html
Region: France

French Stereograms

The text describing these stereograms is French, but the dozen or more 3-D images need no translation.

Type: WWW
Address: http://acacia.ens.fr:8080/home/ massimin/sis/sis.html
Region: France

Frida Kahlo

This site is dedicated to Frida Kahlo, the modern Mexican artist, who painted some of the most searching self-portraits this side of Vincent van Gogh. You can study those here, and also peruse an illustrated commentary on her struggle with polio, a tragic accident, and a marriage to the famed Mexican artist and muralist, Diego Rivera.

Type: WWW
Address: http://www.cascade.net/ kahlo.html
Region: Mexico

Galapagos' HyperCard Square

This site shares a beautifully set-up gallery of Japanese Interactive (HyperCard) art. Many of the stacks require Japanese System software or the Japanese Language Kit to display texts or messages correctly.

Type: WWW
Address: http://mtlab.ecn.fpu.ac.jp/ guru.html
Region: Japan

Indian Art

Extraordinarily ecstatic and vibrant contemporary Indian art, with titles like "The Divine Couple," "Cupid Disturbs Krishna," and "Krishna Embraces Gopa-kumar."

Type: WWW
Address: http://www.best.com/~rayk/ html/picidx.html
Region: India

Jan Vermeer

Only a few paintings by the great Dutch painter Jan Vermeer have survived, and this WWW site features small, medium, and large images of all of them, as well as a guide to the museums that own them and to Vermeer's hometown of Delft.

Type: WWW
Address: http://www.ccsf.caltech.edu/ ~roy/vermeer/
Region: Netherlands

Japanese Art

This directory of GIFs of prints in the Ukiyo-e style (seventeenth to nineteenth centuries) contains far more than 13 ways of looking at Mt. Fuji. It also features a "Kanji lesson of the day."

Type: FTP
Address: ftp.uwtc.washington.edu/pub/ Japanese/Pictures/Ukiyo-e/
Region: Japan

Le WebLouvre

Le WebLouvre is the unofficial, award-winning virtual Louvre Web network. It has mirror sites in Florida, North Carolina, California, Australia, Japan, Singapore, Korea, France, Italy, and Ireland. It has more engaging displays of art and music, and more of Paris (including the piles of skulls in the catacombs), than the official Louvre Museum Web site.

Type: WWW
Address: http://sunsite.unc.edu/louvre/
Region: France

Leonardo Net

This site set up by a commercial Internet provider in Santa Monica provides a guide to the work of the original Renaissance Man. Besides his most famous oil paintings, it introduces his drawings of fantastic flying machines and war machines.

Type: WWW
Address: http://leonardo.net/
Region: Italy

Louvre Web

The official Louvre Web site. You can access pictures of the Louvre's two most famous ladies—the Venus de Milo and the Mona Lisa—a few other images, a history of the museum, a detailed floor plan, current special exhibitions, hours, ticket prices, and the Louvre Metro stop.

Type: WWW
**Address: http://meteora.ucsd.edu:80/
            ~norman/paris/Musees/Louvre/**
Region: France

Luxembourg National Museum of Art and History

Preview the entry hall and the plan, and glance at a few highlights of the museum's collections.

Type: WWW
**Address: http://www.men.lu/~fumanti/
            LuxMusee.html**
Region: Luxembourg

Mexican Painters

This archive includes biographical and other information about 15 Mexican painters, including Olga Costa and Diego Rivera. In Spanish.

Type: Gopher
**Address: unicornio.cencar.udg.mx/11/
            cultfolk/pinturas**
Region: Mexico

Middle East and North African Index

A great index to Middle East and North African Internet culture sources, especially on art. Also includes virtual classrooms with titles like "Introduction to Judaism" and "Let's Learn Arabic."

Type: WWW
**Address: http://menic.utexas.edu/
            mes.html**
Region: Middle East, North Africa

Miscellaneous Arty Chat

A less-crowded forum than alt.art.com, where announcements for and concerns of the art community are discussed.

Type: Usenet newsgroup
Address: rec.arts.misc
Region: World

Netherlands Institute of the Near East (NINO)

This guide to NINO's collections currently provides a hypertext tour of the wall paintings of Christian Nubia, including paintings in situ as well as museum-held examples. Provided are digitized images of the paintings plus documentation about their site of origin and any known history.

Type: WWW
**Address: http://www.leidenuniv.nl/nino/
            nino.html**
Region: Netherlands, Sudan, Egypt

Oslo Net

This is avant-garde art. One piece on display is called Damaged 1–12. "The starting point for this series of images was the accidental transformation caused by a hard disk crash," says the text. What I like best here is the virtual English language "café" here in Oslo, Norway, where you can discuss what it all means.

Type: WWW
Address: http://www.oslonett.no/home/ atelier/
Region: Norway

OTIS

An online gallery and collaboration experiment are only part of what's at this humongous art site. Most of the artists involved are U.S.-based, many of them rather avant garde. Includes performance, comics, video, digital fine arts, sculpture, painting, all sorts of visuals. Cool T-shirts are available, too. Best of all, it's got extensive links to art sites worldwide.

Type: WWW
Address: http://sunsite.unc.edu/otis/ otis.html
Region: U.S., World

Papua New Guinea Meets Stanford University

During the summer of 1994, 10 master carvers from Papua New Guinea worked in Stanford, California, to create a permanent outdoor sculpture garden of New Guinean art at Stanford University. The stated goal is: to "rehumanize arts and artists that have been consistently dehumanized by western images and stereotypes of the 'primitive.'" This inspired me. A must-see Web site—masterpieces of woodcarving revealed in superb sepia-toned photographs, and with a fascinating commentary.

Type: WWW
Address: http://fuji.stanford.edu/icenter/ png/ngp.html
Region: New Guinea

Performance Piece with Caffeine

Is it the Web's most famous piece of performance art, or is it the dumbest thing since Pet Rocks? Come here to stare at a view, updated every second, of an electric drip coffee maker at the University of Cambridge, England. Contemplate the meaning of Caffeine and Art in modern life.

Type: WWW
Address: http://www.cl.cam.ac.uk/ coffee/coffee.html
Region: England

Peruvian Art before Columbus

Displays from private collections are now showing at this online gallery, sponsored by the Krannert Art Museum. The museum also has exhibits of African, European, and Asian art, which you can reach through this page as well.

Type: WWW
Address: http://www.ncsa.uiuc.edu/ General/UIUC/KrannertArt Museum/Guide/GuideContents .html
Region: Peru

REIFF II

This is a German museum of electronic art, located in Aachen. Some introductory information is available in English, but the museum tour itself is in German. Includes some links to other European art-scene sites.

Type: WWW
Address: **http://www.informatik.rwth-aachen.de/Reiff2/**
Region: Germany

Singapore Art

This, the official Web site of the government of Singapore, includes Cyberville, a deluxe 3-D interface to the Net. Themes of current online exhibitions include nineteenth-century prints of Singapore, and the influence of schooling in Paris on Malaysian and Singaporean artists.
Type: WWW
Address: **http://www.ncb.gov.sg/nhb/museum.html**
Region: Malaysia, Singapore

Surrealism, Dada, and Futurism

These twentieth-century art movements can be accessed through this very complete Web page. Resources include surrealist games (some played via Usenet newsgroups) and writing, historical information on women in the Surrealism movement, and much more of a playful and absurdist nature.
Type: WWW
Address: **pharmdec.wustl.edu/juju/surr/surrealism.html**
Region: Europe, World

Survival Research Laboratories

Fire! Explosions! Robots on the rampage! Awesome machines! This is my kind of "performance art." They're San Francisco-based, but they perform around the world. This site includes awesome photos from gigs past and advance information on SRL's 1995 show, which will be at an industrial site in Glasgow, Scotland.

Type: WWW
Address: **http://robotics.eecs.berkeley.edu/~paulos/SRL/**
Region: U.S., Scotland, World

Tandanya National Aboriginal Cultural Institutes

This online gallery shows gorgeous stuff—including landscapes and objects—from Aboriginal artists. The styles are a blend of traditional and modern techniques.
Type: WWW
Address: **http://chopper.macmedia.com.au/Tandanya.html**
Region: Australia

Whit Blauvelt's Grandpa on Art

Whit set up this site in New York City to publish online the diary kept by his grandfather on his visit to Japan. It is an idyllic travelogue about Japanese art and culture (until it is disrupted by the cataclysmic Tokyo Earthquake and Fire).
Type: WWW
Address: **http://www.dorsai.org/~whitfb/chas.html**
Region: Japan

World Art Resources

A wonderful resource, this site connects to hundreds of art galleries, online exhibits, and commercial/governmental/private art-related lnks. It's an alphabetical list that includes many sites in Eastern and Western Europe, Japan, Singapore, the Caribbean, Israel, Australia, and the U.S.
Type: WWW
Address: **http://www.cgrg.ohio-state.edu/Newark/galleries.html**
Region: World

World Art Treasures

World Art Treasures is based in France, but its clickable map of art treasures currently features images with a meditative or spiritual quality from the Middle East to the Far East. The beautiful images are accompanied by a brief French text.

Type: WWW
Address: http://sgwww.epfl.ch/BERGER/
Region: France, World

z.mag@zine

z.mag@zine (no relation to the American *Z Magazine*) is a monthly Swedish multimedia product on paper—*très* arty. "Compare us to *Wired* if you like. We would be flattered," they say. It has a great look, but the text is in Swedish. Which means it is also as hard to read as *Wired*!

Type: WWW
Address: http://www.everyday.se/hem/ zcentral/zhome.html
Region: Sweden

AVIATION

This category encompasses flying, aircraft, and aircraft design. It gets a surprising amount of space online, with some of the best pages around. And since flying and travel go hand in hand, many sites include efforts to network with like-minded individuals around the world.

Aerospace Engineering

Aviation Theory is a mailing list for those with a serious interest in how planes are designed and built. More for pros than amateurs.

Type: Mailing list
Address: aviation-theory-request@mc.lcs .mit.edu
Address: aviation-theory@mc.lcs.mit.edu
Region: U.S., World

Aircraft Discussion

This mailing list is for those with a burning desire to know all about the world's aircraft. Significant international participation.

Type: Mailing list
Addresses: listserv@grearm.bitnet aircraft@grearn.bitnet
Region: World

Airplane Clubs

A mailing list for the discussion of all matters relating to the management of groups operating aircraft.

Type: Mailing list
Address: airplane-clubs-request@dg- rtp.dg.com
Region: World

Aviation Community Online

This is a moderated newsgroup for pilots, designers, trainees, and flyboys of all sorts, based in Australia.

Type: Usenet newsgroup
Address: aus.aviation
Region: Australia, World

Aviation FAQs

A complete collection of frequently asked questions about aviation is available through this moderated newsgroup.

Type: Usenet newsgroup
Address: rec.aviation.answers
Region: World

Aviation Products

Here's the right spot to post about, peruse, review, and discuss products useful to pilots and plane-builders.

Type: Usenet newsgroup
Address: rec.aviation.products
Region: World

Aviation Stories

Sharing anecdotes of flight experiences is the subject of this moderated newsgroup.

Type: Usenet newsgroup
Address: rec.aviation.stories
Region: World

Aviation Questions?

A moderated newsgroup for asking questions about aviation topics and getting informed answers.

Type: Usenet newsgroup
Address: rec.aviation.questions
Region: World

Aviation Week Online

McGraw-Hill's *Aviation Week* is the world's most authoritative source of aviation/aerospace information. It features stories on the latest technological advances, new products, and the inside scoop on the manufacturers, and you can see some here.

Type: Gopher
Address: datapro.mgh.com:71/
Region: World

Charlie Alpha's Aviation Site

Says its own blurb: "The aim of this site is to bring together all things about private flying with an emphasis on Europe and the U.K. in particular. Although as with many things on the Net much of the information will come from the U.S."

Type: WWW
**Address: http://www.hiway.co.uk/
            aviation/aviation.html**
Region: England, France, Germany, Western
           Europe, U.S.

Cyberspace's Aviation Archive

Images, documents, and everything else. U.S.-based, but the archives are definitive and global in scope.

Type: WWW
**Address: http://www.cyberspace.com/
            mbrunk/aviation.html**
Region: World

Delft Aeroplane Pictures

JPEG and GIF images of planes for downloading, including lots of U.S. and European models.

Type: Gopher
Address: olt.et.tudelft.nl:1251/11/planes
Region: Holland, U.S., World

European WWW Aviation Server

Run by an amateur pilot in the Czech Republic, this site provides images of airplanes, stories of his exciting flying experiences, and information on aviation in Middle Europe (Czech Republic, Slovakia, and environs).

Type: WWW
**Address: http://www.math.ethz.ch/~zari/
            zari.html**
Region: Czech Republic, Slovakia

Flight Simulators

Wheee! Flight simulation is as close as I'd like to get to the controls of an airplane in flight, thank you. Many people in this newsgroup can compare both experiences. All levels of flight simulators are discussed here, from cheapie desktop software to the Air Force's latest.

Type: Usenet newsgroup
Address: rec.aviation.simulators
Region: World

Fly with Us

Like to fly a MiG-21, MiG-25, MiG-29, or other super-fast Soviet aircraft? It costs over $10 grand, but if you really want the chance to pull 9 Gs with a trained Russian co-pilot by your side, this is probably the best place to seek those thrills. Information on the planes and pilots is here, too.

Type: WWW
Address: http://www.intnet.net/mig29/
Region: Russia

French Aviation Archive

There's lots and lots of stuff to be checked out here. Images, documents, up-to-date weather information, all of it in French.

Type: WWW
**Address: http://eerie.eerie.fr/~janaudy/
            Aviation.html**
Region: France

Frequent Flyer's Friend

If it seems like you are always traveling on business, use your laptop to subscribe to this chatty group about airlines, airline food, airline service, and money-saving tips.

Type: Usenet newsgroup
Address: rec.travel.air
Region: World

General Aviation Server

Choix d'Éditeur

Awesome! Info on clubs, schools, research, and more, with a worldwide directory of hotlinked aviation-related Web pages. Includes gliders, blimps, hang-gliders, and other ways to fly, plus manufacturers' and airlines' Web pages.

Type: WWW
**Address: http://adswww.harvard.edu/
            GA/ga_servers.html**
Region: World

Homebuilt Planes

Selecting, designing, building, and restoring aircraft. This is a hobby for the careful and highly skilled (I hope).

Type: Usenet newsgroup
Address: rec.aviation.homebuilt
Region: World

Instrument Flight Rules and You

Flying under Instrument Flight Rules: what you need to know, and how to do it properly.

Type: Usenet newsgroup
Address: rec.aviation.ifr
Region: World

Military Aviation

Here's a place to talk about military aircraft of the past, present, and future. Sort of like the Discovery Channel online—only chattier. How do the latest models work? What's next in Stealth technology?

Type: Usenet newsgroup
Address: rec.aviation.military
Region: World

Miscellaneous Topics in Aviation

If your question or interest doesn't fit one of the other newsgroups listed, try this one.

Type: Usenet newsgroup
Address: rec.aviation.misc
Region: World

More Airplane Pix

Images of aircraft from around the world in GIF and JPEG formats, offered by Utrecht University. Not the same as the Delft Aeroplane Pictures archive, even though both collections are from Holland.

Type: FTP
Address: ftp.cs.ruu.nl:/pub/
            AIRCRAFT-IMAGES/
Region: Netherlands, U.S., World

Own Your Own Plane

Information on owning airplanes. Hint: It's right up there with owning boats or horses as a way to look rich, but be broke.

Type: Usenet newsgroup
Address: rec.aviation.owning
Region: World

Pilot Talk

This is a general discussion group for aviators and trainees.

Type: Usenet newsgroup
Address: rec.aviation.piloting
Region: World

The RAF: Looking for a Few Good People

This makes sense: If you want to recruit high-tech people, recruit online. This Web page from England's Royal Air Force is the first recruiting station I've seen in cyberspace. I don't know if their motto will inspire many to sign up though: "Just like any other job, but with wings."

Type: WWW
Address: http://www.open.gov.uk/raf/
            rafhome.htm
Region: England

Soaring above the Rest

A discussion group about all aspects of sailplanes, gliders, and hang-gliders.

Type: Usenet newsgroup
Address: rec.aviation.
Region: World

Student Aviation

Learning to fly: It's a challenge, but what a payoff! Find support and encouragement here, along with some helpful hints about flying instructors, flying schools, and logging those required air-hours.

Type: Usenet newsgroup
Address: rec.aviation.student
Region: World

Ultralights in Flight

Light and ultralight aircraft in general are the thing here, but all related topics come in for discussion.

Type: Usenet newsgroup
Address: rec.aviation.ultralight
Region: World

BUSINESS

See also Economics page 196; Financial Data page 266

Doing business on the Net was once a no-no; now it seems to be taking over. That's because the National Science Foundation's acceptable use policy, which banned commercial activity, no longer applies to private parts of the Internet. The private side has been claimed by CIX, the Commercial Internet Exchange, a collection of regional networks that now route business traffic among themselves without encroaching on NSF's turf. Most of CIX's members are U.S.-based, although it includes Demon INTERnet in the U.K., DCI in Taiwan, EUnet in Europe, Hong Kong Supernet, IIJ in Japan, Canada's HookupNet, and a few more.

There is still a great deal of confusion over what CIX can and can't do. In the meantime, business information on the Net is alive and well. From small businesses using the World Wide Web as a cheap advertising tool, to full-scale online business enterprises and for-fee services, growth in this area will be exponential. And for those with some interest in international trade, tariffs, markets, and more, getting information online is much faster and cheaper than ordering by mail. Here are just a few of the thousands of business-related sites available.

ACCESS e-journal

An electronic digest of *ACCESS Czech Republic Business Bulletin,* which covers business and stocks in the Czech Republic.

Type: E-serial
Address: hewes@traveller.cz
Region: Czech Republic

BISNIS Bulletin

This is a U.S. Department of Commerce newsletter on doing business in the former Soviet Union, including tips, leads, and info on financing.

Type: Gopher
**Address: sunny.stat-usa.gov/11/
            STAT-USA/NTDB/Bisbul**
Region: Russia, C.I.S., U.S.

The Branch Mall

This was the first online shopping center, and its site will give you an idea of the possibilities for online shopping. It has now been joined by several more "malls." Offerings include everything from contemporary Russian art to flowers, chocolates, and imported coffee. Supports PGP-encrypted ordering with credit cards.

Type: WWW
Address: http://branch.com:1080/
Region: U.S., Canada, World

Business Practices in Africa

This FAQ covers much of what a businessperson needs to know when dealing with his or her African counterparts, including common procedures and important cultural issues.

Type: Gopher
**Address: umslvma.umsl.edu/11/LIBRARY/
            GOVDOCS/IBPA/IBPF**
Region: Africa

DataStar

Trade and business data, updated daily, is available from DataStar, a rather pricey database that requires a subscription. It's like Nexus in the United States, but with a European emphasis. Text is available in French, German, and Italian as well as English. It includes links with Tradstats, a word-trade statistics service; and FIZ Technik, a German engineering and management information provider.

Type: WWW

Address: http://www.rs.ch/www/rs/datastar.html

Region: U.S., Italy, Germany, England, France, World

DEVLINE: DEVelopment Information Service OnLINE

Sponsored by the British Library for Development Studies, DEVLINE's resources cover the economic and social relations between rich and poor nations. Includes publications, library databases, information on teaching, and resources programs.

Type: Telnet

Address: LIB.IDS.SUSX.AC.UK (or 139.184.17.254)

Region: England, World

Dun & Bradstreet Information Services

This company maintains a database of businesses around the world, which you can share for a fee. To bring you into the fold, they've provided this site, with information on marketing your business globally, predicting which customers will be slow to pay, and other useful topics.

Type: WWW

Address: http://www.dbisna.com/

Region: England, World

ECONINFORM

Sponsored by the Central Library of Budapest University of Economics, this site offers business information databases in German, Hungarian, and English.

Type: Telnet

Address: pernix.bke.hu

Region: Hungary, Romania

The Economist

This site includes an archive of past articles plus samples from the current issue. This is on the Electronic Newsstand and is intended to entice you to subscribe to *The Economist* magazine, which is easily the most erudite and amusing (really!) of business magazines.

Type: Gopher

Address: gopher.enews.com:2100/11/business/pubs/international/economist

Region: U.K.

EEBICnet: Central and Eastern Europe Business Information Center Online

A project of the U.S. Department of Commerce, this site offers all kinds of information on doing business in Eastern Europe, Russia, and the Commonwealth of Independent States. Includes links to home pages sponsored by governments or universities. Coming soon: Albania!

Type: WWW

Address: http://www.itaiep.doc.gov/eebic/ceebic.html

Region: Russia, Romania, C.I.S., Lithuania, Czech Republic, Slovakia

European Commission Host Organization

This group archives business-related databases in eight European languages.

Type: Telnet
Address: echo.lu
Login: echo
Region: Europe

Far East Economic Review

This archive, based in Hong Kong, featurs news and trends from the nations of the Far East. Pulling no punches in its analysis, the *Review* has a strong slant toward the European investor, but it is widely read throughout Asia as well. This archive of past and current articles is on the Electronic Newsstand; the idea is to get you to subscribe.

Type: Gopher
**Address: gopher.enews.com:2100/11/
           business/pubs/international/feer**
Region: Hong Kong, Taiwan, China, Japan,
           Vietnam, World

Finance and Currency News

At this Gopher site maintained by the Federal Reserve Bank of New York, daily reports are available, including the latest statistics on European currencies.

Type: Gopher
**Address: una.hh.lib.umich.edu/00/ebb/
           monetary/tenfx.frb**
Region: U.S., Europe

Foreign Statistics and Research Index

This is an index to trade information, including studies by the International Monetary Fund and the World Bank, items related to the GATT treaty, and information on international trade carried out in each U.S. state.

Type: WWW
**Address: http://www.einet.net/galaxy/
           Business-and-Commerce/
           Business-General-Resources/
           Foreign-Statistics-and-Trends.html**
Region: World

German Development Institute Gopher

Papers on aspects of business and development worldwide are available at this site, created by a non-profit German think tank. The GDI does research and sponsors educational outreach efforts and development projects.

Type: Gopher
**Address: csf.colorado.edu/11/ipe/
           Thematic_Archive/documents/
           german_development_institute**
Region: Brazil, Kenya, Albania, Zimbabwe,
           India, Germany, World

Global Recycling Network

This Internet-based information service is set up to give out trade leads worldwide for recyclables, including raw materials, industrial byproducts, used merchandise, and more. Archives include a newsletter and databases accessible by Telnet.

Type: WWW
Address: http://grn.com/grn/
Region: World

How to Do Business in Mexico FAQ

This very well-written FAQ on Mexican business customs and procedures is aimed primarily at Americans.

Type: WWW
Address: http://daisy.uwaterloo.ca/~ alopez-o/busfaq.html
Region: Mexico

IndiaOnline

This site offers shipping and import/export information, joint ventures leads, Indian telecommunications information, and news on Indian business. There's also a section of online requests for bids, such as, "A major buyer needs 300,000 tons of sugar."

Type: WWW
Address: http://IndiaOnline.com/
Region: India

IndiaWorld Business

This site provides business data and publications from the booming subcontinent of India, including daily and weekly newspapers, the India Business Directory, and the business magazine *India Today*. It may be a subscription-only service by the time you read this, but it seems that anyone with investments or business interests in India would find subscribing worthwhile.

Type: WWW
Address: http://www.indiaworld.com/
Region: India

InfoMarket Server

Sponsored by the Institute for Commercial Engineering, this server holds data on Russian securities (riskier than bungee jumping), privatization efforts, financial markets, and stock quotes. Much of the information is available in both Russian and English. Has a Libertarian bent, but clients include major U.S. finance companies.

Type: WWW
Address: http://www.fe.msk.ru/info market/ewelcome.html
Region: Russia

International Trade Network

A service for advertising international import and export opportunities, distributed weekly via e-mail and posted at the Gopher/FTP site as well. Sections for the Americas, Europe, and Asia.

Type: Gopher
Address: ftp.std.com/11/vendors/ IntlTrade-Network
Type: FTP
Address: ftp.std.com/ftp/vendors/Intl Trade-Network
Type: E-mail
Address: USA@world.std.com
Region: U.S., World

Internet Business Journal

It's not an electronic 'zine, but sample stories are available here. *IBJ* covers business online, from getting on the Net to electronic advertising techniques. A good source of the latest information on this growing sector of the Internet.

Type: WWW
Address: http://www.phoenix.ca:80/sie/ ibj-home.html
Type: E-mail
Address: Subscriptions@Strangelove.Com
Region: Canada

Israeli Research and Development

This official government site offers information on the state of Israeli high-tech research and development.

Type: WWW

Address: http://www.israel.org/israel-info /facts3/science/research.html

Region: Israel

NAFTANET, AMERICASNET, and the Free Trade Network

FTN is a project intended to foster international trade within the current and future free-trade zones of the the Americas. Information is available on opportunities opened by the NAFTA agreement, and on its extension southward. They use an interesting "online village" metaphor to present information and foster communication. There is a charge for membership and full access.

Type: Gopher

Address: gopher.gate.com

Region: U.S., Mexico, Canada, South and Central America

Nogales Foreign Trade Zone Information

Thinking of starting a Mexican maquiladora? This Gopher site offers leads to information about the advantages and drawbacks of these facilities, including seemingly dubious items like how to relabel goods not actually made in Mexico for entry into the United States as "Hecho en Mexico."

Type: Gopher

Address: econ.tucson.az.us/00/biz/.nogo /NOGOFTZ.TXT

Region: Mexico, U.S.

Nijenrode University School of Business Gopher

Some areas on this server were not in operation when I visited, but here's what is there: statistics; information on GATT, NAFTA, and other international trade pacts; efforts to stem the flow of counterfeit goods; and more. Includes links to many other business-related resources in Scandinavia and the rest of Europe.

Type: Gopher

Address: zeus.nijenrode.nl/11/Business/ International

Region: Holland, World

NYSERNet

This archive includes a textbook on export business, *Commerce Business Daily,* defense conversion information, an international business practices guide, and a FAQ on advertising on the Internet, among many other valuable items.

Type: Gopher

Address: nysernet.org:70/11/Special%20 Collections%3A%20Business%20 and%20Economic%20 Development

Region: U.S., World

Pacific Rim Business Info

Simon Fraser University's David See-Chai Lam Centre for International Communications in Vancouver, B.C. offers degrees and unique educational programs in business communications, management, and marketing in a cross-cultural context. Look here for information on Asian language, culture, and communication styles for the businessperson.

Type: Gopher
**Address: hoshi.cic.sfu.ca:70/11/dlam/
           business**
Region: China, Japan, Korea, Vietnam, Canada

Singapore Online™

Business information on Singapore is available via this glitzy site.
Type: WWW
Address: http://www.singapore.com
Region: Singapore

Surfing the Internet for Trading Jewels

A tutorial on getting financial data online, which includes several hotlinks to excellent archives.
Type: WWW
**Address: http://galaxy.einet.net/galaxy/
           Business-and-Commerce/
           Investment-Sources/federico-
           brown/stocks.html#FEDERICO**
Region: U.S., World

COMICS AND CARTOONS

See also Film page 259; Music page 390

In this section you will see the words "anime" and "manga" mentioned often, because these Japanese styles have taken the world by storm—especially the part of it that confers by Internet. If you've seen TV favorites like Ultraman and Speed Racer, you've seen an older video version of the immensely popular anime—anime is Japanese for animation. Manga are comic books, many of which are more similar to what U.S. fans would call "graphic novels." Although many anime and manga are for kids,

a high percentage are violent and/or sexually oriented, and suitable for adults only.

Anime are a multimedia thing—comic books, videos, films, and toys—but I included them here for the sake of convenience.

Of course, if you collect obscure foreign comics, the Net could be a superb resource for making that essential trading connection with overseas fans. The same can be said if you are interested in networking with comic artists, especially if it's the latest animation and cartooning techniques you're after.

Unfortunately, I had little luck in finding sites about comics from south of the border. They are such an important part of popular media there, particularly in Mexico, Brazil, and Argentina, that this was most puzzling. Someone should rectify this Net oversight, and soon!

Ah! My Goddess WWW Page

"Ah! My Goddess" is an anime series well-loved around the world. Here you can find movie clips and images from the series, as well as a FAQ with lots of information about the characters, actors, artists, plot, and so forth.
Type: WWW
**Address: http://bookweb.cwis.uci.edu:80
           42/Anime/AMG/intro.html**
Region: Japan

Alternative Comics

"Weird comics you know are bad for you" are the subject of this newsgroup, according to one online review. That means unknown artists, filthy plots, strange drawing styles, the new underground.

Type: Usenet newsgroup
Address: alt.comics.alternative
Region: World

Animation 2000

Sponsored by the Institut National de l'Audiovisual in France, this project is an outreach to artists working in 2D animation around the world. The Animation 2000 working group now includes French, Spanish, and German animators, visual artists, and researchers, working together to create "a global solution for producing 2D animation" with computer software.

Type: WWW
Address: http://www.ina.fr/Ina/Recherche/Anim2D/A2000/
Region: France, Spain, Germany

Anime Club Directory 1/2

Want to find an anime club in your area? Just look at this list, organized conveniently by location. Addresses and phone numbers are provided.

Type: WWW
Address: http://web.mit.edu/afs/athena/user/d/g/dgaxiola/www/acd1.html
Region: World

Anime Discussion

A very active discussion group for fans of anime. One member writes, "Am I the only one who's seen Armored Trooper Votoms?" With this group, probably not.

Type: Usenet newsgroup
Address: rec.arts.anime
Region: Japan, World

Anime Discussion, Part II

More discussion of anime, with emphasis on individual episodes and summaries.

Type: Usenet newsgroup
Address: rec.arts.anime.info
Region: Japan, World

Anime/Erotica

Like its cousin, alt.binaries.pictures.erotica, this newsgroup is something of a pariah: You may not be able to get it at your site. If you can, though, you will find hentai (Japanese for sexual anime and manga) here.

Type: Usenet newsgroup
Address: alt.binaries.pictures.erotica.anime
Region: Japan, World

Anime FAQ WWW Page

Answers to lots of your questions about anime. Includes an "anime primer" with lists of films by genre; a directory of anime-related BBSes; a list of anime conventions you can attend; and a resource list with addresses for ordering films and scripts, as well as Internet resources.

Type: WWW
Address: http://www.cis.ohio-state.edu/hypertext/faq/usenet/anime/top.html
Region: Japan, U.S., World

Anime Germany Mailing List

This is a German mailing list for fans of anime and manga, conducted in German, of course.

Type: Mailing list

Address: Send e-mail message with body: subscribe AnimeGer majordomo@brewhq.swb.de

Region: Japan, Germany

Anime Gopher Site

Lots of files, songs, synopses of shows, images. Also a list of anime on laserdisc.

Type: Gopher

Address: gopher.stolaf.edu/11/Internet%2 0Resources/St.%20Olaf%20Spon sored%20Mailing%20Lists

Region: Japan, U.S.

Anime.Guide 1.6

A nice HTML guide to various anime information: title listings, episode guides, and a bibliography.

Type: WWW

Address:

http://www.lysator.liu.se:7500/ anime/anime.guide.main

Region: Japan, Sweden

#anime! Home Page

If you can't stop talking on the IRC channel #anime!, you might try wandering over here during a break in the conversation. There is a list of #anime! personalities with extensive bios and some pictures, and pointers to other anime resources.

Type: WWW

Address: http://joyce.eng.yale.edu/ anime-irc.html

Region: Japan, World

The Anime Home Page

A pleasant Web page on anime, maintained by the Anime Film Society in St. John's, Newfoundland. You can find anime pictures, dictionaries of anime terms (in both English and Japanese), a list of anime series, and a guide to renting anime in St. John's.

Type: WWW

Address: http://www.cs.mun.ca/~anime/ afs/welcome.html

Region: Canada, Japan

Anime Internet Resource List

This site offers a listing of many Internet resources relating to anime.

Type: WWW

Address: http://csclub.uwaterloo.ca/u/ mlvanbie/anime-list/

Region: Japan

#anime! Live Chat

Talk to people live about anime! Using IRC, you type /join #anime! (remember the exclamation point) and you are there. For a guide to #anime! with pointers to information on IRC, try the Web site.

Type: IRC

Address: #anime

Type: WWW

Address: http://web.mit.edu/afs/athena/ user/d/g/dgaxiola/www/irc_ anime.html

Region: Japan, World

Anime Marketplace

Anime is hard to find in the U.S. To see your favorite show, you have to 1) go to Japan, 2) attend a club meeting in your town, or 3) buy it yourself. This group is for selling and trading anime. I strongly advise reading the FAQ before buying or selling on this group, since the deals are sometimes confusing (the titles are often in Japanese, and the items are sometimes offered for auction instead of a straight sale). As with any buying/selling on Usenet, it is possible to get scammed.

Type: Usenet newsgroup
Address: rec.arts.anime.marketplace
Region: Japan, U.S.

Anime Pictures

If you want to see the latest anime pictures as they come out, this is where to look. Beware copyright violations....

Type: Usenet newsgroup
Address: alt.binaries.pictures.anime
Region: Japan

Anime Pocket Guide

A searchable database on anime. Type the word "Macross," and you see a new page with details about the Macross series and links to more information. You can search by title, voice actor, or genre. The author also rates the films for you.

Type: WWW
**Address: http://venice.mps.ohio-state.
            edu/~adam/pocket-guide.html**
Region: Japan, U.S.

Anime Shops in San Francisco

A thorough listing, with capsule comments, of shops in SF that sell anime-related products. Several of these stores do mail-order and cater to an international market. You can get comic books, videos, animation cels, toys depicting the brave big-eyed warriors who populate this genre, T-shirts—whatever tie-in merchandise your anime-loving heart desires.

Type: Gopher
**Address: gopher.stolaf.edu/0R0-9536-
            /Internet%20Resources/St.%20
            Olaf%20Sponsored%20Mailing
            %20Lists/Omni-Cultural-
            Academic-Resource/Fine-Arts/
            Art/Japanese-Animation/anime.
            sanfran.shops**
Region: Japan, U.S.

Anime Stuff 'n' More

A major site for anime information, including issues of *Anime Stuff* magazine. The subtitle says that this 'zine is for "Reviews and Information on Japanese Animation Software," but there is much more here: gossip about upcoming films, interviews with industry folks, inside information on drawing methods, and filming techniques. You'll also find sound samples, pictures, games, software, and MPEG movies of anime action here.

Type: FTP
**Address: venice.tcp.com/pub/
            anime-manga/anime.stuff**
Type: WWW
**Address: http://www.tcp.com/pub/
            anime-manga/sorted/**
Region: Japan

Arctic Animation

This is a fan subtitling group in Vancouver, B.C., Canada: They put English subtitles on anime films so non-Japanese-speakers can follow the plot. You can examine their list of films and find out how to get copies from them.

Type: WWW
**Address: http://www.cs.ubc.ca/spider/ed
            monds/anime/arctic.html**
Region: Japan, Canada

Benoit's Anime Page

It's in French, but it has lots of pretty pictures.

Type: WWW

Address: http://alpha.univ-lille1.fr:28080/~gi097/Anime.html

Region: Japan, France

Best of Victor Bogorad

Russia's top topical cartoonist, Bogorad regularly uploads new cartoons here. These are very *New Yorker*-esque: nice style, pointed political and social commentary.

Type: WWW

Address: http://www.spb.su/victor/index.html

Region: Russia

Bubble Gum Crisis

Discussion of the extraordinarily popular (and oddly named) anime series *Bubble Gum Crisis*.

Type: Usenet newsgroup

Address: alt.fan.bgcrisis

Region: Japan, World

The Capricous KOR Home Page

A page for fans of "Kimagure Orange Road," an anime series. You can find a list of characters and places, story synopses, a guide to episodes, and scripts of the shows.

Type: WWW

Address: http://ghost.pc.cc.cmu.edu/kor/

Region: World

Cartoon Arts Network Page

This organization for cartoonists, based in England, is now on the Web with leads to education, tools, internships, and more for would-be pros.

Type: WWW

Address: http://prinny.pavilion.co.uk/cartoonet

Region: England, World

Cartoon Heaven

Next time you're in Melbourne, Australia, stop by Cartoon Heaven, a cartoon and animation store with tapes, pictures, cels, and more. What? You're thousands of miles from Melbourne? Well, try this Web page: the store delivers all over the world.

Type: WWW

Address: http://symphony.ucc.ie/~niall/cheaven.html

Region: Australia

Collecting Comics

This is a newsgroup for buying and selling collectable comics.

Type: Usenet newsgroup

Address: rec.arts.comics.marketplace

Region: World

Comic Books Mailing List

Worldwide comics discussion takes place here.

Type: Mailing list

Address: majordomo@world.std.com

Send e-mail message with body:
subscribe comix
comix@world.std.com

Region: World

Comics Conventions, Happenings, and News

Announcements about comics-world happenings are posted and discussed here.

Type: Usenet newsgroup

Address: rec.arts.comics.info

Region: World

Comics 'n' Stuff

This is a searchable Web page that helps you find comics and comic strips on the Net, including Norwegian, German, Finnish, English, and U.S. titles.

Type: WWW
Address: http://www.phlab.missouri.edu/ HOMES/c617145_www/comix.ht ml
Region: World

Comics Resource Center

Links to various comics archives and Web pages are here—from Disney to adult stuff to Jack Chick's comic-style religious tracts. Also offers Animation Newswire, information on conferences and conventions, and an exhaustive listings of strips and books online, including Korean, Greek, Italian, and Canadian titles.

Type: WWW
Address: http://www.yahoo.com/ Entertainment/Comics
Region: World

Comics Reviews from the Forbidden Planet

This chain of comics, science fiction, fantasy, and horror shops maintains a Web presence that offers blunt and amusing reviews of the latest titles, commercial, adult, and underground. Good use of graphics here, too.

Type: WWW
Address: http://www.maths.tcd.ie/mmm/ ReviewsFromTheForbiddenPlanet. html
Region: Ireland, England, Wales, Scotland, U.S.

Comic Writing Workshop

Would-be comics writers may subscribe to this discussion group. Peer review of work is required.

Type: Mailing list
Address: listserv@UNLVM.UNL.EDU
Region: World

De Rovers van Clwyd-Rhan

The name means "The Thieves of Clwyd-Rhan," and this Dutch comic by Reinder Dijkhus is a strange amalgam of the Furry Freak Brothers and Dungeons & Dragons. Go figure. The series is posted online; you use an arrow button to click through the panels. The comic is in Dutch; there's an English summary but it made no more sense to me than the Dutch....

Type: WWW
Address: http://www.let.rug.nl/dist/a_stuf f/roversuk.htm
Region: Holland

ElfQuest Discussion

This newsgroup likes chatting about elfish doings in this alternative comic that mixes Tolkein-style story lines with modern preoccupations.

Type: Usenet newsgroup
Address: alt.comics.elfquest
Region: World

ElfQuest Fans Mailing List

If you can't get enough elf action through the newsgroup, join this list.

Type: Mailing list
Address: listserv@PSUVM.PSU.EDU
Region: World

English-Japanese Translation Tables

Titles of many anime series, in English and Japanese side-by-side, are here. Your Web browser must be able to display Japanese characters.

Type: WWW
Address: http://www.phys.titech.ac.jp/uja /Anime/Translation_Tables/index .html
Region: Japan, U.S.

EpitAime—Le Club de la Japanimation

It's in French, and it has pictures, translations of scripts, and FAQs.

Type: WWW
Address: http://www.epita.fr:5000/~ epitanim/
Region: France, Japan

Eppo Archive

Eppo is a popular Dutch comic magazine. This archive, in Dutch, catalogs the various issues and has information about the cartoons and cartoonists who appeared in each.

Type: WWW
Address: http://www.cs.rulimburg.nl/~ wiesman/eppoinde/
Region: Holland

European Comics on the Net

"Tintin," "Spirou," "Bob and Bobette"—the whole gang's here. Primarily French, Belgian, and Dutch comics, most aimed at teens and adults, are the target of this searchable page—with tons of links to comics all around the Net.

Type: WWW
Address: http://grid.let.rug.nl/~erikt/ .Comics/welcome.html
Region: Belgium, France, Holland

Fan Subtitlers List

This is a thorough list of anime fan subtitling organizations in North America. Doesn't use much HTML, but still useful.

Type: WWW
Address: http://www.imsa.edu/~leda/ani me/fansub.html
Region: Japan

<<fin>>

In French, by Greek comic artist Lydia Venieri, this online story, illustrated in white-on-black, is very mysterious and artistic.

Type: WWW
Address: http://www.way.com/~tarcl/ Lydia/Lydia.html
Region: Greece, France

French Anime FTP Site

Scripts, files, and other stuff relating to various anime series.

Type: FTP
Address: ftp.emn.fr/pub/anime
Region: France, Japan

French Anime Images

Many anime images in GIF and JPEG format. I can't speak to the copyright status of these, so, downloader beware.

Type: WWW
Address: http://www.cica.fr/~bouton/ anime.html
Region: France, Japan

French Anime Mailing List

A mailing list about/for French-speaking fans of Japanese anime. In France, anime are regularly broadcast on television, so the fans have more access to the episodes.

Type: Mailing list
Address: listserv@centre.univ-orleans.fr
Send e-mail message with body: SUB anime-fr
Region: France, Japan

Gaston Lagaffe Index

This Belgian comic by André Franquin is a Euro-slacker classic. Information, including an index to the series, is available here in Dutch, French, German, English, and other languages.

Type: WWW
Address: http://grid.Let.rug.nl/~erikt/ .GuustIndex/
Region: Belgium

Independent Comix

European and U.S. alternative comics, most from small comics publishers, are the subject here. Harvey Pekar, Lynda Barry, and many less well-known names are linked in to this comprehensive Web page.

Type: WWW
Address: http://bronze.ucs.indiana.edu/ ~mfragass/altcom.html
Region: U.S., World

Hitoshi Doi's Anime Page

Pointers to several anime resources: character/series home pages, mailing lists, and so forth.

Type: WWW
Address: http://www.tcp.com/doi/anime 2.html
Region: Japan

Japanese Animation Fans of Western Australia

This is the home page of JAFWA, an anime fan club in Western Australia. You can find out about their screenings of anime films, learn about upcoming club events, and find pointers to other sources of anime information.

Type: WWW
Address: http://iinet.com.au/~gmb/jafwa. html
Region: Australia, Japan

Japanese Animation Infospace Project

Currently under construction. The goal of those creating this Gopher archive (the Anime Club of the University of Texas) is to create a "one-stop info space" for anime information.

Type: Gopher
Address: actlab.rtf.utexas.edu/11/art_and _tech/JapAnimation
Region: Japan, World

Japanese Anime Page

To use parts of this site properly, you should have a Web browser that can display Japanese text. This page is mostly pointers to other pages about specific topics and shows, many in Japan (and in Japanese).

Type: WWW
Address: http://www.ipl.t.u-tokyo.ac.jp/~ kusano/anime.html
Region: Japan

Johann's Comics Page

Leads to comics pages, including commercial and alternative titles, comics-related newsgroups, and mailing lists.

Type: WWW
Address: http://www.cen.uiuc.edu/~jb256 1/comic.html
Region: World

KISS Home Page

Kisekae is the Japanese word for "changing clothes." A KISS program shows you a picture of a character from anime and lets you dress and undress them—it's sort of like playing with dolls, electronically. Here you can find answers to many questions about KISS, plus pointers to KISS data sets (characters for you to play with) and where to get the program itself.

Type: WWW
Address: http://net.cs.utexas.edu/users/ mcurley/kiss/kiss.html
Region: Japan

KISS Mailing List

Subscribe here to join a mailing list of people interested in KISS.

Type: Mailing list
Address: himechan@usagi.jrd.dec.com
Region: Japan

La Pagina de Mafalda

"Mafalda" seems to be the Argentinean equivalent of "Peanuts" or "Calvin and Hobbes": a comic strip for kids whose themes appeal to adults. Mafalda herself is a saucy little girl who questions authority—very cute and funny. A few strips, in Spanish, are archived here by a (homesick?) professor.

Type: WWW
Address: http://arcadia.informatik. uni-muenchen.de/rec/argentina/ mafalda.html
Region: Argentina

Lum Home Page, France

This English-language Web page in France focuses on the anime character Lum. Some pictures and pointers to anime information on the Continent.

Type: WWW
Address: http://web.univ-orleans.fr/html_ lum/
Region: France, Japan

Magic Knight Rayearth

Guides to characters, episodes, books, and tapes of this anime series are linked in here. Some entries are in Japanese, so you'll need an appropriate browser to read it.

Type: WWW
Address: http://madeira.cc.hokudai.ac.jp/ RD/take/rayearth/rayearth.html
Region: Japan

Maison Ikkoku QuickTime Movies

Look here for an archive of movies taken from the "Maison Ikkoku" anime series, including both opening and closing themes. Warning: these are very large files, and you must have a program that lets you view QuickTime files.

Type: WWW
Address: http://www.engr.csulb.edu/~gka wano/web/mi.movies.html
Region: Japan

Manga Discussion

This newsgroup is for talking about manga, Japan's favorite time-waster.

Type: Usenet newsgroup
Address: rec.arts.manga
Region: Japan

Manga Discussion, Part II

This group chats about some of the more "adult" manga, and about non-mainstream manga books.

Type: Usenet newsgroup
Address: alt.manga
Region: Japan

Panji Koming

Proving once again that comics are an international language, these Indonesian comics made me laugh even though I didn't understand a word. The strip lampoons village life with universal wit.

Type: WWW
**Address: http://www.engin.umich.edu/
~asiregar/PanjiKoming.html**
Region: Indonesia

Pig's Anime Homepage

Pointers to home pages on various anime series are available at this site, partially in Japanese.

Type: WWW
**Address: http://www.on.cs.keio.ac.jp/shu
/anime.html**
Region: Japan

Ranma 1/2 Expanded Home Page

Ranma 1/2 is a martial arts comedy featuring a boy who changes into a girl when splashed with water (hence the 1/2). This page has information on the voice actors, addresses for tapes and books, and links to a R1/2 mailing list and other net resources.

Type: WWW
**Address: http://www.coe.uncc.edu/~
tecardwe/ranma.html**
Region: Japan, World

rec.arts.comics

"r.a.c." is the granddaddy of all fanboy and fangirl discussion groups. Talk is about mostly mainstream and commercial titles, mostly U.S., but it's essential reading for the serious fan. Archived at the Web site listed.

Type: Usenet newsgroup
Address: rec.arts.comics
Region: World

Robotech

Discussion of the anime series "Robotech," which has been occasionally broadcast on U.S. TV. All I know about it is that some of the spin-off merchandise is really neat.

Type: Usenet newsgroup
Address: alt.tv.robotech
Region: Japan, U.S., World

Rutgers Anime FTP

Includes translations of song lyrics, some pictures, and synopses of anime films and episodes.

Type: FTP
Address: remus.rutgers.edu/pub/anime
Region: Japan, World

Seiyuu Database

Seiyuu is Japanese for "voice actor." If you loved a character in a series, you might want to find out who did his or her voice, and this is where to find out. There are interviews with the seiyuu, pointers to books and CD-ROMs, and a database of seiyuu games.

Type: WWW
Address: http://www.tcp.com/doi/seiyuu/ seiyuu.html
Region: Japan

Servidor de Humor

This server at the University of Guadelajara presents "Chabela y Gorgoro," a cute comic about love, plus a weekly single-panel cartoon—both by Güitròn.

Type: WWW
Address: http://udgftp.cencar.udg.mx/ caricatura.html
Region: Mexico

Skuld Shrine

Skuld is a character in the anime series "Aa Megamisama," and here you can find over 300 screen shots of her, listen to songs, and join the mailing list about her.

Type: WWW
Address: http://server.berkeley.edu/~ joepet/skuld_shrine.html
Region: World

Subbed and Dubbed in U.S. List

It's hard for English-speakers to follow the plot of anime films, since they are written in Japanese (then there's the plots themselves—but I digress…). If you don't want to learn Japanese, look at this list, which tells you how to find subtitled and dubbed versions of most major anime releases. Updated monthly.

Type: Gopher
Address: wiretap.spies.com/00/Library/ Media/Anime/subbed.lis
Region: Japan, U.S.

Sweden Anime-Manga FTP

A Swedish FTP site for all sorts of anime and manga files. Pictures, lyrics, fan fiction, audio files of anime theme songs, digests of anime magazines, and more.

Type: FTP
Address: ftp.sunet.se/pub/comics/ anime-manga
Region: Sweden, Japan

Tank Girl (Official)

This U.K. alternative comic with an outrageous punky heroine appears in *Deadline* magazine and in the glossier *Details*. Now MGM has done a movie version—fans of the comic may enjoy this, but will probably prefer the site below.

Type: WWW
Address: http://www.tankgirl.mgmua. com
Region: England, Australia

Tank Girl (Unofficial)

At this "unofficial" site there's pictures, plots, info on books and strips, a lead-in to the alt.fan.tank-girl Usenet group, and more. Less slickness, more sickness.

Type: WWW
Address: http://www.dcs.qmw.ac.uk/~ bob/stuff/tg/index.html
Region: World

Texas A&M Comics and Anime Gopher

Pointers to a number of comics sites, mostly anime, are maintained here.

Type: Gopher
**Address: gopher.tamu.edu/11/.dir/comics.
dir**
Region: Japan, U.S., World

University of California—Irvine's Anime WWW Page

The University of California at Irvine Bookstore will sell you all kinds of anime products—and you can order from home! You can also find pointers here to other anime resources.

Type: WWW
**Address: http://bookweb.cwis.uci.edu:
8042/anime.html**
Region: Japan, U.S.

Unofficial List of Anime FTP Sites Names and Addresses

Here's a list of anime-related FTP sites: just click on the one you want to examine. After a brief version of the list comes an expanded version, with maintainer addresses and descriptions.

Type: WWW
**Address: http://www.mit.edu:8001/
people/dgaxiola/anime.ftp.html**
Region: Japan, U.S

Vampire Miyu Home Page

"Vampire Miyu" is an anime series drawn by a Japanese woman. Here you can find images, sound files, script translations, information on how to order tapes, and more.

Type: WWW
**Address: http://csclub.uwaterloo.ca/u/
mlvanbie/miyu/miyu.html**
Region: Japan

Video Girl Ai

Manga and anime versions of this popular series are featured here: you can find translations, a manga database, scripts, a cast list, a FAQ list, sound files, and pointers to a mailing list.

Type: WWW
**Address: http://www.eecs.umich.edu/~
warrenf/vgai.html**
Region: Japan

West Australian Anime and Manga Page

Pointers to Australian anime resources are available here, as well as a link to the maintainers' FTP site with lots of pictures.

Type: WWW
**Address: http://www.tower.com.au/
~akira/anime.html**
Region: Australia, Japan

Where the Buffalo Roam

Fans of this satirical PostScript comic strip, which is released online weekly, gather here. The newsgroup is also archived at the Web site below.

Type: Usenet newsgroup
Address: alt.comics.buffalo-roam
Type: WWW
Address: http://plaza.xor.com/wtbr/
Region: World

Wildcat

In the "images" section of the Spunk Press online catalog, you can download pictures from Donald Rooum's "Wildcat" series of British anarchist comics.

Type: WWW
Address: http://www.cwi.nl/cwi/people/ Jack.Jansen/spunk/catalogs/Cat _us.html
Region: England

Writing Comics

This is a discussion group for would-be comic artists and scripters.

Type: Usenet newsgroup
Address: rec.arts.comics.creative
Region: World

COMPUTERS

See also Encryption and Privacy Issues page 228; Internet Resources Online page 349

If you love computers, would rather learn Fortran than French, and live to learn about the latest hack for your machine, you don't need me to tell you that the Internet is the place to be. This section merely scratches the surface of what's available in computing resources. Please take the time to check out the myriad of U.S.-based resources, for example, the umpteen "alt.comp" and "comp." Usenet newsgroups.

I've tried to concentrate here on a few sites that cover the basics—such as overseas contacts and sites offering information on foreign computers—should you be so afflicted as to own, say, a Sinclair "portable." These listings could prove especially useful to anyone who works with computers and is considering looking for work overseas.

Technical universities are almost always online, no matter what country you're seeking information from. These are also excellent resources, and frequently have software and file archives on their systems. There are far too many to list here, but they can be easily found through any major online Internet index to Gopher servers, FTP servers, or WWW servers.

This book's "Encryption and Privacy Issues" listings include contact information for groups around the world dedicated to preserving and extending access and safety in cyberspace.

Atari ST Virus Alert

This group provides fast and efficient help where infection with computer viruses is concerned, for Atari ST/TT/Falcon machines only. It's also the electronic helpline for registered users of the Ultimate Virus Killer program. Questions about virus symptoms or any other general questions of Atari 16/32 bit viral nature may be directed here.

Type: Mailing list
Address: r.c.karsmakers@stud.let.ruu.nl
Region: Netherlands, World

Assembly Programming on the Amiga

The devpac list is for assembly programmers on the Amiga Platform, with discussions relating to assembly language programming open to everyone. The list is run under emailurl, and there is provision for establishing a large file library.

Type: Mailing list
Address: emailurl@flevel.demon.co.uk
**Send e-mail message with body: subscribe
            devpac <Your E-mail Address>**
Contact: devpaclist@flevel.demon.co.uk
Region: England, World

Australia Access Point

This Pasadena, California server mirrors an Australia site with archives of computer-related information for Asian and English computers.
Type: FTP
Address: cobalt.cco.caltech.edu/
Region: Australia, England

Australian Computer Chat

Here's a few of the Australian computer-related newsgroups. Aussies are in a unique position, since they import computers from the U.S., Europe, and Asia, and discussion is still in English (or a reasonable facsimile thereof). These groups might be useful if you're looking for information on obscure aspects of the subject they cover, or just to chat with your professional or hobbyist counterparts Down Under.
Type: Usenet newsgroups
Address: aus.computers (General computer chat)
           aus.computers.ai (Artificial Intelligence)
           aus.computers.amiga (Amiga computers)
           aus.computers.cdrom (CD-ROMs and computers)
           aus.computers.logic-prog (Logic programming)
           aus.computers.ibm-pc (Chat about Big Blue PCs)

aus.computers.linux (Linux and Unix)
aus.computers.mac (Mac chat)
aus.computers.os2 (OS/2 operating system chat)
aus.computers.sun (Sun workstations)
aus.computers.tex (Texas Instruments computers)
Region: Australia, World

Brazilian Software Search

This search system in Portuguese will scour major software repositories for what you need. Most are outside Brazil.
Type: WWW
**Address: http://www.cr-df.rnp.br/
            hipertextos/cr-df/meta-index.
            html/#SOFT**
Region: Brazil, World

C-IBM-370

The "C on IBM Mainframes" mailing list is a place to discuss aspects of using the C programming language on s/370-architecture computers—especially under IBM's operating systems for that environment.
Type: Mailing list
Address: majordomo@pooh.com
**Send e-mail message with blank Subject
            line and body: subscribe c-ibm-
            370**
**Contact: listserv@research.canon.oz.au,
            david@pooh.com (David
            Wolfskill)**
Region: Australia

C and C++ Parsing

Here you can discuss Graham Stoney's c2man program, which parses comments from C and C++ programs, and produces documentation for man pages, information files, and so forth. This list is archived.

Type: Mailing list
Address: listserv@research.canon.oz.au
Region: Australia, World

Compilers

The mailing list compil-l addresses the topics of compilers in particular, and programming language design and implementation in general. Recent topics have included optimization techniques, language design issues, announcements of new compiler tools, and book reviews. The material is exactly the same as the Usenet group comp.compilers. If you have Usenet access, please read it that way.

Type: Usenet newsgroup
Address: comp.compilers
Type: Mailing list
Address: listserv@american.edu
**Send e-mail mesage with body: sub
           compil-l <Firstname Lastname>**
**Contact address: compilers-server@iecc.com
           or compilers-request@iecc.com
           (John Levine)**
Region: World

Comp.Sys.Amiga.Announce

This mailing list has been created for those folks who have no access to Usenet, providing a gate between the Usenet newsgroup C.S.A.A. and mail. This group distributes announcements of importance to people using the Commodore Amiga. Announcements generally deal with new products, disk library releases, software updates, reports of major bugs or dangerous viruses, notices of meetings or upcoming events, and so forth. A large proportion of posts announce the upload of software packages to anonymous FTP archive sites.

Type: Mailing list
Address: announce-request@cs.ucdavis.edu
Send e-mail message
**Contact: announce-request@cs.ucdavis.edu
           (Carlos Amezaga)**
Region: World

Computer Underground Digest (CuD)

CuD is a weekly e-journal of debates, news, research, and discussion on legal, social, and other issues related to computer culture. The home page has links to other Web pages and newsletters that are in a similar vein.

Type: E-journal
Address: listserv@vmd.cso.uiuc.edu
**Send e-mail message with one-line body:
           SUB CUDIGEST**
Type: WWW
           **http://sun.soci.niu.edu/~
           cudigest/**
Region: U.S.

Cubase and MIDI

The cubase-users list is for discussion, suggestions, and moaning about Cubase. Cubase is one of the most well-known MIDI sequencers on the market, supported on the Atari, PC, and Mac platforms, and supplied by the German company Steinberg Software und Hardware GMBH. Several Steinberg programmers are members of the list, which includes both beginners and professional musicians. The newsgroup alt.steinberg.cubase is gatewayed to this mailing list; cubase-users is also archived at the FTP site listed below, along with Mixer Maps and other useful items.

Type: Mailing list
Address: Majordomo@mcc.ac.uk
Send e-mail message with body: subscribe cubase-users <Your E-mail Address>
Type: FTP
Address: ftp.mcc.ac.uk:pub/cubase
Region: England, Germany, World

Dice C

Discussion of Dice C Programming techniques for Amiga Computers happens here, to provide mutual support for Dice C users and information of value to Amiga C programmers. The listserver system also provides registered Dice C users with access to a file exchange system of benefit to all C programmers.

Type: Mailing list
Address: emailurl@flevel.demon.co.uk
Send e-mail message with body: subscribe dice <Your E-mail Address> end
Contact: diceclist@flevel.demon.co.uk
Region: England, World

Fortran Computing

The comp-fortran-90 list covers all aspects of Fortran 90 and HPF, the new standard(s) for Fortran, with an emphasis on the new features of Fortran 90. It welcomes contributions from people who write Fortran 90 applications, teach it in courses, want to port programs, and use it on (super)computers.

Type: Mailing list
Address: mailbase@mailbase.ac.uk
Send e-mail message with body: join comp-fortran-90 <Firstname Lastname>
Region: England, World

Funet FTP Site

A simply humongous site, with lots of freeware and shareware programs for the downloading.

Type: FTP
Address: ftp.funet.fi
Region: Finland, World

German Computer Info

This site catalogs information and software available from the archives of German technical universities, of which there are dozens.

Type: WWW
Address: http://www.rz.uni-karlsruhe.de/ Outerspace/VirtualLibrary/004. en.html
Region: Germany

German Chat about emTeX

The emtex-userlist concerns emTeX, an implementation of TeX for MS-DOS and OS2. This list is meant for everyone who wants to discuss problems concerning installation and/or use of the emTeX package, and offers information about bugs, fixes, and new releases (in English, not German).

Type: Mailing list
Address: emtex-user-request@chemie. fu-berlin.de
Contact: emtex@chemie.fu-berlin.de (Vera Heinau & Heiko Schlichting)
Region: Germany

GNU to You

The crossgcc list is for discussion about the GNU environment for cross-compilation. This includes compiling for "embedded systems." Note: There's also a whole series of gnu. newsgroups for your perusal.

Type: Mailing list
Address: majordomo@first.gmd.de
Send e-mail message with body: subscribe
          crossgcc <Your E-mail Address>
Contact address: gt@first.gmd.de (Gerd
          Truschinski)
Region: Germany, World

Guida

Written in Croatian, Guida ("Guide") covers the Croatian BBS and Internet scene; programming in C, assembly language, Pascal, and BASIC; and buying and selling computer hardware.
Type: FTP
Address: aris.ffk.hr/pub/guida/
Contact: dkezele@oleh.srce.hr(Dalibor S.
          Kezele)
Region: Croatia

Guide to Japanese Computing

Although in the United States, this site is of especial interest to Japanese users (and users of Japanese computers). Tons of good stuff, from programs and software to resources for families.
Type: WWW
Address: http://www.uwtc.washington.
          edu/Computing/Japanese/
          JapaneseResources.html
Region: Japan

The Hack Report

The hack-l list is a vehicle for distributing the monthly Hack Report, an informational newsletter which warns of hacked, hoax, Trojan Horse, and pirated files that have been seen posted on BBSs worldwide. The Hack Report is very biased towards MS-DOS programs and is also readily available through Fidonet or via anonymous FTP. If you are a sysop or run a corporate network, you should be getting this!
Type: Mailing list
Address: majordomo@alive.ersys.
          edmonton.ab.ca
Send e-mail message with body: subscribe
          hack-l
Contact: hack@alive.ersys.edmonton.ab.ca
          (Marc Slemko)
Region: Canada, World

Insoft

Internationalization of software relates to two subjects: software that is written so a user can easily change the language of the interface, and versions of software adjusted to work with different language and cultural systems, such as Czech WordPerfect, whose interface language differs from the original product. Topics discussed on this moderated list include techniques for developing new software, techniques for converting existing software, internationalization tools, announcements of internationalized public domain software, announcements of foreign-language versions of commercial software, calls for papers, conference announcements, and references to documentation related to the internationalization of software.
Type: Mailing list
Address: majordomo@trans2.b30.ingr.com
Send e-mail message with body: subscribe
          insoft-l <Your E-mail Address>
Contact: insoft-l-owner@trans2.b30.
          ingr.com *or* insoft-l-request@
          trans2.b30.ingr.com
Region: World

Interface Magazine

This Canadian magazine is about how people are using technology to create art, invent games, and further the cause of science. It's not so much a hardware/software review magazine as a computer-oriented general-interest one. Also published on paper.

Type: WWW
Address: http://vvv.com/interface/
Region: Canada

International FTP Sites List

If you are looking for a non-U.S. program, it makes sense to look in its country of origin. This long list of FTP servers for PC software and files is organized by country.

Type: WWW
Address: http://proper.com:70/pc/files
Region: Poland, Russia, Finland, Germany, Switzerland, England, Hong Kong, Korea, Taiwan, Thailand, South Africa, U.S.

Internet Computer Index

ICI provides indices to WWW servers that have data or software for Macs, PCs, or Unix machines. The leads include information on Usenet groups, FAQs, mailing lists, online publications (including many overseas), and FTP and Gopher sites for software. Very complete listings make this an invaluable resource.

Type: WWW
Address: http://ici.proper.com/
Region: World

Linux Activists

This list is about Linux operating system hacking, with discussions centering mostly on development versions. It's archived at the FTP site below.

Type: Mailing list
Address: linux-activists-request@ niksula.hut.fi (Ari Lemmke)
Type: FTP
Address: ftp.funet.fi/pub/OS/Linux/doc/
Region: World

Logo Pals

Discussion of the Logo computer language is the topic of this list.

Type: Mailing list
Address: logo-friends-request@aiai.ed.ac.uk
Region: England, World

London PC User Group

Interact with your British PC-using counterparts.

Type: WWW
Address: http://www.ibmpcug.co.uk/
Region: England

MacShareNews

This is a free electronic publication reporting fast and up-to-date information about shareware and freeware programs for the Macintosh and the Newton.

Type: Mailing list
Address: steg@dircon.co.uk
Send e-mail message with Subject <MSN-request> and body: SUBSCRIBE MSN <Firstname Lastname>
Region: England, World

Media Global Monitor

This online computer magazine from Ottawa, Canada, has local BBS listings, software and hardware reviews, feature stories, users group news, and more. Nicely done!

Type: WWW
Address: http://gate.globalx.net:80/ monitor/
Region: Canada

Melbourne PC User Group

For pointers to local software, PC User Groups are the best places to begin your hunt. Interface here with PC fans in Australia.

Type: WWW
Address: http://www.melbpc.org.au/
Region: Australia

OFOGH: The Journal of Computer Science and Engineering

This Iranian computer magazine, produced by Iranian students abroad, is currently published out of Australia. It has well-written articles on highly technical subjects, such as "Single Layer Multi Output Network for Pattern Association in Electrical Capacitance Tomography."

Type: WWW
Address: http://www.w3.org/hypertext/ DataSources/News/Groups/ relcom.html
Region: Iran

Russian Computer Discussion

There are several computer-oriented newsgroups carried on the Russian network Relcomp under the general banner of "relcom.comp," including relcom.comp.binaries and relcom.os.windows. If your provider carries them, check them out. If not, you may be able to access archived posts from the Web page or FTP sites below.

Type: Relcom newsgroup
Address: relcom.comp (see current Relcom listing for titles)
Type: WWW
Address: http://info.cern.ch/hypertext/ DataSources/News/Groups/ relcom.html
Type: FTP
Address: infomeiseter.osc.edu/pub/central _easterm_europe/russian/ relcom
Region: Russia

Shareware Library Site

This is a library of more than 5,000 shareware programs around the world, and a very cool site indeed. Not very graphical, but it has tons of programs you can download and test.

Type: WWW
Address: http://www.fagg.uni-lj.si/ SHASE/
Region: World

SIL Computer Resources

Here you can find a computing dictionary for those mystery terms, links to major U.S. software archives, and primarily U.S. resources—including Microsoft, DEC, VMS, Sun, and Apple information. If you're working on a U.S.-made machine, this is a good place to look for software and tips.

Type: WWW
Address: http://www.sil.org/computing/ computing.html
Region: U.S.

Sunet Shareware

This simply humongous site has thousands of shareware programs that you can download and try.

Type: FTP
Address: ftp.sunet.se/
Region: Sweden, World

Tokyo PC User Group

Make Japanese PC friends and get the low-down on the latest Japanese software for the PC here.

Type: WWW
Address: http://shrine.cyber.ad.jp/~jwt/ tpc.html
Region: Japan

Vancouver PC User Group

Chat up Canadian PC users and see what's up "Up North" at this Web page.

Type: WWW
Address: http://www.wimsey.com/~ infinity/vpcus/vpcus_hp.html
Region: Canada

The WWW Virtual Library: Computing

The computing site to end all computing sites (and it's international!): Its information is categorized by subject, including computer systems, manufacturers, software, and universities. There are massive amounts of stuff. Everyone can find something they like in this site (if they like computers, that is).

Type: WWW
Address: http://src.doc.ic.ac.uk/bySubject /Computing/Overview.html
Region: England, World

World Wide Web Issues Worldwide

Commercial sites have their own issues with using World Wide Web technology. Companies' concerns range from liability when using free software and finding solid or simply commercial solutions, through deciding how to deploy an infrastructure. This list is for discussion of these issues, and for sharing solutions that have worked.

Type: Mailing list
Address: majordomo@qiclab.scn.rain.com
Send e-mail message: subscribe www-sites <Firstname Lastname> <Your E-mail Address>
Contact: www-sites-approval@qiclab. scn.rain.comm
Region: World

Word-Mac

Word-Mac is a mailing list dedicated to serving users of the Microsoft Word package in its various versions on the Apple Macintosh platform. The list is available in digest form, and archives of all digests are available on the FTP and Gopher servers below.

Type: Mailing list
Address: Send e-mail message with body: subscribe word-mac <Firstname Lastname> www-sites listproc@alsvid.une.edu.au
Type: FTP
Address: ftp.scu.edu.au/lists/ word-mac/digests
Type: Gopher
Address: gopher.scu.edu.au (port 70)
Region: Australia, World

CONSPIRACY

See also Paranormal page 402; Politics page 409

They really are out to get you. Well, if not you personally, they're definitely out to get somebody. There are so many conspiracy theories rolling around on the Net that you could get thoroughly confused. My best advice is to keep repeating to yourself, "It's only a newsgroup, it's only a newsgroup…." No doubt paranoia can be as dangerous to your health as the bad guys—and you may well end up on alt.support.paranoia if you hang out in the vicinity of these sites too long.

Ad Busters

This Vancouver, B.C.-based magazine takes on one of the real conspiracies—the effort to brainwash us all through advertising and mass media. Ad Busters deconstructs ads, does hilarious ad spoofs, and prints research into tricks of the advertising trade, like subliminal and overt suggestion. This site also includes the raucous "Culture Jammer's Manifesto," an essay on how to deal with the barrage of obnoxious messages.

Type: Gopher
**Address: gopher.well.sf.ca.us:70/00/
           Publicat ions/online-zines/
           Ad_Busters**
Region: Canada, U.S.

Activism and Conspiracy

Political activists of every conceivable persuasion, from all parts of the spectrum (and from outside the spectrum entirely) opine, rebut, and compare techniques here between vicious attacks and pleas for civility. Usenet makes for strange bedfellows; stranger bedfellows than this bunch are hard to find.

Debate ranges from the meticulous scholarship of serious researchers to the infantile knee-jerks of the over-educated and under-informed.
Type: Usenet newsgroup
Address: alt.activism
Region: World

Alternative Theories of Health and Longevity

This is a catalog of books on medical conspiracies and conspiracies against health from A-Albionic Research (who also sell books alleging that the British royal family and their cohorts are the root of all evil).
Type: WWW
**Address: http://garnet.msen.com:70/
           vendor/a-albionic/health**
Region: World

Conspiracy Discussion

The people who post to alt.conspiracy range from diligent scholars in pursuit of the truth about our history, to full-bore bull-goose loonies in search of an ear (any ear) to bend. Some encrypt their messages. Some post anonymously. One, Sergar Argic, is widely believed to be an Artificial Intelligence. They are always amusing and often informative. Take with a grain of salt.
Type: Usenet newsgroup
Address: alt.conspiracy
Region: World

Conspiracy Nation

This newsletter is usually not much more than transcripts from a wild conspiracy-theory radio show. Some of the interview subjects seem to have a tenuous relationship with the concept of reality, but there are occasional gems of either information or unintentional humor.

Type: E-zine
Address: bigxc@prairienet.org
Region: U.S., World

Conspiracy—NHS

This newsgroup was apparently started as a joke. If so, some people don't get it. Others seem to be having splendid fun. It's not about the National Honor Society or "<GLORIOU.S. SPAM>."
Type: Usenet newsgroup
Address: alt.conspiracy.nhs
Region: World

Conspiracy Zines A-Go-Go

A variety of self-published paranoid rags are archived here.
Type: FTP
**Address: red.css.itd.umich.edu/pub/
            Politics/**
Address: red.css.itd.umich.edu/pub/Zines/
Region: U.S., World

Counter-Revolution

Today's thriving neo-fascist community plans ahead for when they get to take over the reins of power from the leftist establishment (a reality in Europe, if not so much in the U.S.) via this newsgroup. They are not truly conspiring, which would of course be kept secret, since they feel confidant enough to plan in public. The denizens of this group tend toward three-digit IQs.
Type: Usenet newsgroup
Address: alt.revolution.counter
Region: World

Coup Coverage

This is an archive of what passed over Russia's Relcom net, without being impeded by oblivious official censors, during the Russian coups of 1991 and 1993. With a spot that says "This place is reserved for another coup (just in case)." Mostly in Russian, which will require support for Cyrillic in your browser. Also here is the online Soviet Archive.
Type: WWW
**Address: http://www.kiae.su/www/wtr/
            arts.html**
Region: Russia

Cyberspace Rebels

The place to be on planet three if what you want most from this life is to meet net cops in drag, and sell them your warez. They're plotting behind your back even now, d00dz. They probably read even anonymous e-mail. Here is where you can learn where to send it. When that wears thin you can always count on a good laugh watching the undergraduate speed-freaks nurture carpal tunnel syndrome in an ongoing, marathon dis fest. Some can even spell.
Type: Usenet newsgroup
Address: alt.cyberspace.rebels
Region: World

Fifty Greatest Conspiracies of All Time

This site is a promo, more or less, for a book by Jonathan Varkin and John Whalen. Very interesting excerpts and regular "hot news" updates regarding evidence and theory on Lyndon LaRouche, JFK, Jonestown, the French Priory of Zion, the recent Mexican assassinations, international terrorism, and much more. Links to more sites, some of which are extremely wacko and entertaining.

Type: WWW

Address: http://www.webcom.com/~ conspire/

Region: U.S., World

Guns

This group is focused on guns themselves, gun owners, and gun sports. However, paranoia and conspiracy theories creep into any discussion of guns today. A certain degree of topic drift, impelled by contemporary politics, gives rec.guns some of this flavor. They try to keep it to a minimum.

Type: Usenet newsgroup

Address: rec.guns

Region: U.S., World

Illuminati Among Us

That secret societies are among the engines that drive society is incontrovertible. That they are all fronts for One Big Conspiracy is highly debatable. Discussion here ranges from the ridiculous to the sublime; the ridiculous is easier to confront.

Type: Usenet newsgroup

Address: alt.illuminati

Region: World

IllumiNet Press

Purveyors of paranoid lit extraordinaire, IllumiNet publishes and sells books on the UFO "conspiracy," FEMA and those dreaded Black Helicopters, JFK, and much more. Fun fun fun.

Type: WWW

Address: http://www.illuminet.com/~ron/ inet.html

Region: U.S.

JFK Conspiracy

This is where JFK buffs display their mastery of the esoteric detail as well as make serious inquiry into America's quintessential UFO—the so-called "Single Bullet." Far more focused than alt.conspiracy, this group is also far more scholarly and down to earth. The real question for many is not who, but why? (For others, the question is "why bother?")

Type: Usenet newsgroup

Address: alt.conspiracy.jfk

Region: World

Masonic Demolay

Some people believe these folks are a subsidiary of a vast, ancient, and insidious conspiracy against all human liberty. They are clearly also the well-meaning, if sometimes misdirected, do-gooders and pillars of their communities that they say they are. They have also developed an admirable networking matrix, now partly silicon.

Type: Usenet newsgroup

Address: alt.masonic.demolay

Region: World

Masonic Youth

One would think that a newsgroup with a name like alt.masonic.youth would either be concerned with dire warnings about an insidious plot by a major Illuminati front to enslave youth, or be peons to the righteous civic-mindedness of the organization's members. But noooo....

Type: Usenet newsgroup

Address: alt.masonic.youth

Region: World

Microsoft Must Die

"Flamefest" doesn't adequately portray the nasty tone of "conversation" on this newsgroup. Microsoft-haters go to town, painting the software industry leader as an evil force that's conspiring to kill its competition through nefarious means, with the goal of MS-DOS/Windows world domination. High volume, in both senses of the word.

Type: Usenet newsgroup
Address: alt.destroy.microsoft
Region: World

Mind Control

"Thanks to my biographer Manuel de Mosa you can read (in German language) a report on my life and my problems caused by innovative mind-control-techniques," says Lukas Servatius Derenbold. Stasi (East German) secret police and mind manipulation allegations.

Type: FTP
**Address: ftp.ira.uka.de/pub/doc/BRDStasi
            .roman**
Region: Germany

Mind Control Redux

If you have ever considered that those voices you're hearing might be being projected into your brain by way of a tight beam of modulated microwaves, but then were inexplicably tempted to dismiss the notion as "paranoia," don't be so hasty. Read up on MK-ULTRA, Project Artichoke, Project Paperclip, neural implants, subliminal messages, implanted memories, and the search for the real "Manchurian Candidate." Paranoia will take on a whole new meaning.

Type: Usenet newsgroup
Address: alt.mindcontrol
Region: World

MossadWatch

Inside poop on the Israeli spy guys, from a former officer. Methods, recruitment, "evil deeds."

Type: WWW
**Address: http://www.Phoenix.CA:80/mos
            sad/**
Region: Israel, Palestine, Syria, U.S., Africa,
            Europe

Revisionism

In this newsgroup, the rewriting of history is hotly contested and vigorously defended. Have you heard that the Holocaust is Zionist propaganda, or that it was the Armenians who slaughtered the Turks at the end of WW I? Have you ever wondered why? You are not alone. Various conspiracy theories can be found here.

Type: Usenet newsgroup
Address: alt.revisionism
Region: World

Skeleton Key to the Gemstone File

In pre-Glasnost Russia, they called banned publications that were copied by hand and shared amongst the underground "samizdat." *The Gemstone File* is probably the oldest, strangest American samizdat. It purports to be a secret history of, to put it in overly simplistic terms, how the U.S. government was bought and taken over by hostile forces. Much of the information is tied in with the Kennedy assassination, but it goes much deeper than that—right up to Ollie North's alleged "secret team," if you want to trace certain names that appear in it forward to the present day. Kinda wacky, kinda wild, kinda…scary. This is an annotated version from the mid-1970s.

Type: Gopher
Address: **wiretap.spies.com/00/Library/ Fringe/Conspiry/gemstone.txt**
Region: U.S.

Skinheads

Yet another youth cult with its own newsgroup, skinheads stand out for their radical politics. Many are violent racists and fascists who are even now being actively recruited to serve as the new brownshirts of the neo-fascist movement. Others are just as violently anti-racist and anti-fascist. Many can actually read and write. Some conspire here, while others talk about the Big Conspiracy of the moment.
Type: Usenet newsgroup
Address: **alt.skinheads**
Region: World

Sumeria—Politics

Sumeria's an all-purpose source for banned ideas. Information here on Nazis and the occult; eugenics and the New World Order; Trilateral skullduggery; CIA baddies, drugs, shady banks, and a fallen government in Australia; JFK; the coming economic collapse…you get the picture.
Type: WWW
Address: **http://werple.mira.net.au/ sumeria/politics.html**
Region: World

Sumeria—Free Energy

The theory is that we're being held hostage by corporations and their governments, who are supressing discoveries that would provide free energy to release us from our lives of toil. Hey, it could happen. Nicolai Tesla and more.

Type: WWW
Address: **http://werple.mira.net.au/ sumeria/free.html**
Region: World

Usenet Cabal

Certain "forces," some apparently believe, are attempting to control the Internet and use it to advance their own political agenda. Tangential contemporary events like the rise of the populist militias also crop up in discussions here.
Type: Usenet newsgroup
Address: **alt.conspiracy.usenet-cabal**
Region: World

UFO—Paranet

If you want to go beyond analyzing individual UFO "incidents" and theorizing in the scientific manner (or otherwise), here's where unanswered questions collide with unquestioned answers. Strange particles are seen to whirl and careen in the wake of their collision. And those cattle don't mutilate themselves. Or do they? You go figure. Maybe "The X-Files" really is "their" way of breaking it to us gently. That's what some in this group think.
Type: Usenet newsgroup
Address: **alt.paranet.ufo**
Region: World

UFO Reports

But are they reporting a single kind of phenomenon or many? Are they all hoaxes? If so, by whom? And why? The cover-up, alone, is reason enough for suspicion. Let's start with the witnesses. Then we can deduce and speculate to our heart's content. Here's the place, reportedly lurked by the Men in Black, and posted to by a very broad range of individuals. Draw your own conclusions, everyone else does. Watch the skies—and your back.

The second group listed focuses in on an alleged secret UFO base maintained by the U.S. government.

Type: Usenet newsgroup

Addresses: alt.ufo.reports
alt.conspiracy.area51

Region: World

Web of Conspiracy

"Channeled" hoo-ha about underground alien cities and abductions. The "good" aliens set up appointments telepathically, they say—how convenient!—allowing you to tell them from the "bad" ones. Very long, very amusing.

Type: Gopher

Address: wiretap.spies.com/00/Library/
Fringe/Ufo/web.txt

Region: World

X-Files Chat Live

Fans of this popular television show gather here and the conversation often turns to (allegedly) real-life alien abductions, government conspiracies, and paranormal events.

Type: IRC

Address: #XF

Region: World

CONVERSATION AND FRIENDSHIP

Of course, Usenet and other newsgroups are terrific for fostering friendships, and so are mailing lists. A new online resource for getting to know new people is the explosion of personal Web pages (see

below for places to find indexes to these). It's fun to see what people's hobbies and lives are like; in many cases you can leave messages via e-mail at the page.

There's a section further on in this book about MUDs and other interactive games. We also mention them here, because there's a move on to take the online conversation and "action" tools designed for games and use them for more "real-world" interaction online. Several of the "chat" systems (also known as "talkers") listed here use MUD-style tools for talking.

Also important to furthering online conversation is Internet Relay Chat. There are several hundred IRC channels where you can hop on anytime and chat away with whoever else is there. This system depends on telnet, so make sure your web browser is suitably equipped. Many of these systems now have WWW interface for easier access. Entire books are available about IRS, so I've included a couple of samples and resources for getting started.

Last, but not least, you can get a pen-pal online. Most of the arrangements mentioned in this chapter are for writing by e-mail, but some also have a "snail mail" option. There are some special pen-pal resources for kids and classrooms in Appendix C.

Abwenzi African Studies

A registered nonprofit corporation promoting friendships between Americans and Africans,

Abwenzi African Studies sets up pen-pal contacts between both kids and adults.

Type: WWW
Address: http://infosphere.com/clients/ smallworks/abwenzi/abwenzi .html
Region: Africa

#blaklife

This IRC channel is for chat amongst black folks (although a few participants are Asian, Indian, and Middle Eastern), especially college students and young professionals. The conversational tone is very friendly and fun, with lots of flirting going on. It's mostly a social channel, although conversations sometimes do turn to more serious issues. The Web page offers a peek at who's online and what's happening with offline events.

Type: IRC
Address: #blaklife
Type: WWW
Address: http://ww.engin.umich.edu/ ~atb/umich.pub/blaklife.html
Region: U.S., World

cafe.net

You can chat online with the habitués of a Vancouver, B.C. online "café" (actually an Internet service provider that uses a café metaphor for its services). Unfortunately, they can't send espresso over the wire. They plan to open an actual café someday, they say.

Type: WWW
Address: http://espresso.cafe.net/ Welcome.html
Region: Canada

The Complete Home Page Directory

Also known as Who's Who on the Internet, this England-based directory is an attempt to compile the largest, most complete collection of personal WWW home pages online.

Type: WWW
Address: http://web.city.ac.uk/citylive/ pages.html
Region: World

CityLive! WWWChat

At this site, mostly European folks are leaving messages for each other, many of them seeking pen pals. Some messages are in languages other than English.

Type: WWW
Address: http://web.city.ac.uk/citylive/ wwwchat/wwwchat.html
Region: England, World

Cyberia

Here's the online interface to Cyberia, London's first café to offer good lattes and Internet access, now with a branch in Edinburgh. (If you've ever had English coffee, you know which half of that combo is most amazing.) There's also a guide to "cybercafés" around the world.

Type: WWW
Address: http://www.easynet.co.uk/page s/cafe/cafe.htm
Region: England, Scotland

Doug's WWW Chat Server

This real-time chat system offers multiple forums for online discussion, or you can create one yourself on the subject of your choice.

Type: WWW
Address: http://www.ohiocap.com/Chat/
Region: World

EGOWEB

Everything you wanted to know about IRCs is linked in here. There's nothing that's specifically for international online chatting, but it is a good jumping-off point. It's got a clean design and a nice rainbow thing going on with links to Usenet groups, GIFs of IRC "denizens," and guides, tips, and libraries for those seeking knowledge.
Type: WWW
Address: http://edb518ea.edb.utexas.edu /html/irc.html
Region: World

The E-mail Pen Pal Connection

Fill out the form here and they'll match you up with someone who has similar interests and characteristics. Many participants in this exchange are here to practice their written English.
Type: WWW
Address: http://www.interport.net/~come nius/penpal.html
Region: World

#England (The Friendly Channel)

This home page for the #England IRC channel is a good place to start if you know nothing about Internet Relay Chat but have a decent Web reader. You'll find lots of people from around the world (not just England, as they'll remind you) as well as software to download and other hints and tips for chatting with them. The best part is the pictures. Unfortunately, they aren't sorted by attractiveness or

goofiness, but you can pretty much tell what kind of person you might be chatting with based on the visuals they provide (everything from semi-nude cheesecake to cartoon representation to boring black-and-white mug shots).
Type: IRC
Address: #England
Type: WWW
Address: http://www.fer.uni-lj.si/~ iztok/england.html
Address: http://deeptht.armory.com/~ nick ie/england.html
Region: England, World

Friends and Partners

This site is dedicated to U.S./Russian friendship. You can browse classifieds and files but, more importantly, you can also join in online discussions in their "interactive coffee house." There's also information on exchange opportunities here.
Type: WWW
Address: http://solar.rtd.utk.edu/friends/ home.html
Region: U.S., Russia

Fury's Talker Page

Here's a guide to all sorts of interactive multiuser Internet activities, including "Talkers," chat programs, IRCs, and MUDs. Among the various lists linked in here, there must be at least 100 talkers alone!
Type: WWW
Address: http://spacely.dfci.harvard.edu/ Fury/talkers.html
Region: World

German Chat Groups

The de.talk.chat archive at this site can clue you in about talk systems where the language is Deutch, and how they work. Includes IRC and BITNET Relay groups.

Type: WWW
**Address: http://www.uni-karlsruhe.de/
            ~ig25/de-talk-chat-faq-html**
Region: Germany

Getting to Know IRC

From a Singapore Internet provider, this is an introduction to IRC. It includes the IRC Primer manual, FAQs, lists of IRC channels and related newsgroups, and a list of essential IRC commands to get you started. The linked-channel lists include IRCs that are conducted in German, Slovakian, Danish, Esperanto, Hindi, and other languages in addition to English.

Type: WWW
**Address: http://merlion.singnet.com.sg/pu
            blic/IRC/**
Region: Singapore, World

Home Page Directories List

This page has links to 15 personal home page collections. It also offers phone-book-style ways to find a particular person online.

Type: WWW
**Address: http://www.rpi.edu/Internet/
            Gui des/decemj/icmc/
            culture-people-lists.html**
Region: World

The ICB Home Page

ICB stands for Internet Citizens Band, and you can "breaker, breaker, good buddy" here. This site contains FAQs, ICB server lists, a users guide, and a way to see who's on ICB at the moment.

Type: WWW
**Address: http://web.sjsu.edu/~kzin/icb.ht
            ml**
Region: World

Interactive Applications

A long list of links to chat systems around the world is available here, including MUDs, MOOs, and IVC (see below).

Type: WWW
**Address: http://www.clark.net/pub/
            global/interact.html**
Region: World

Interactive Theatre

And now for something completely different (in the words of Monty Python). At this site an experiment is beginning on using cyberspace as a stage for topical or mythic drama. Check out the idea and process, and give it a whirl.

Type: WWW
**Address: http://www.rit.com/Whats_IT.
            html**
Region: U.S., World

Internet Relay Chat Channels

This is a simple list, but effective. It includes links for romance, computer geeks, and other specific interest-related IRCs. You can chat with people in German, you can check out the Czechs, you can talk to Danes, Brits, and Indians. This link will even lead to a bar in Tahiti.

Type: WWW
**Address: http://www.funet.fi:80/~irc/
            channels.html**
Region: World

Internet Relay Chat FAQ

A Q&A Web site on IRC. Again, not a very international-specific Web page, but it does mention Moscow and Finland in the opening paragraph. Basically, this is a very well-organized guide to IRCs and how to get going if you want to make some new cyberpals. Warning: I tried a few of the Mac FTP links off this page and got nowhere. Maybe the links are current, maybe not, but at least the information is good.

Type: WWW
Address: **http://www.kei.com/irc.html**
Region: World

Internet VoiceChat

Here's the application that's going to really get the phone companies riled up when they figure it out. Using IVC on your PC (no Mac version yet), you can use the Internet to make two-way voice calls. In other words, if you have an unlimited-time account you can use it to give yourself free long-distance service. Of course, the person you want to talk to must have IVC also. They're working on a system for conference calls also. Find out about the software and procedures here.

Type: WWW
Address: **http://futures.wharton.upenn .edu:80/~ahrens26/ivc.html**
Type: Usenet newsgroup
Address: **alt.winsock.ivc**
Type: IRC
Address: **#IVC Channel**
Region: World

Link Everything Online

Argv has to be one of the most fashionable people I've ever seen. The white legs with the black socks and brown suede shoes really show a certain je ne sais quoi that can only be found in Stuttgart, or parts of southwest Washington in the U.S. His picture is here because he's connected to a chat line nearby. The "leo" in the FTP address stands for "Link Everything Online," out of Munich, Germany. I tried to connect to the English-language WWW home page to chat with Argv, but the connection took forever. If you get through, tell Argv to wear long pants in the future!

Type: FTP
Address: **ftp.leo.org/pub/comp/ networking/irc/RP/stuttgart/ viviane/argv.jpg**
Type: WWW
Address: **http://www.leo.org/leo_e.html**
Region: Germany

Lintilla

Lintilla uses the conventions of a MUD, but for "real-life," real-time interaction. At last visit, port 5000 was for general chat, 5001 was a women's group, 5002 was just for men, 5003 was rather sexual. There are over a dozen groups going at any one time. When you log in, see port 2000 for a FAQ on the latest groups.

Type: Telnet
Address: **130.235.88.95**
Region: England, World

Matchmaker Electronic Pen-Pal Network

U.S.-based, but with some international participation, this pen-pal club is romantically inclined. There are 30,000 active users in their "date-a-base," they say. Fill out a questionnaire and they'll see if they can hook you up automatically by matching your characteristics to those of other callers. Dating by e-mail—what a concept!

Type: WWW
Address: http://www.email.net/
Region: U.S., World

MUD Connection

This site's links concentrate on MUDs and MOOs, making it a jumping-off point into the sea of interactive MUDness. Try BOB's MOOGate for a link to MOO Français or the Global Village—both of which have an international flavor.

Type: WWW
**Address: http://www.yahoo.com/
Entertainment/Games/MUDs_
MUSHes_MUSEs_MOOs_etc_/**
Region: World

Multi-User Dungeons (MUDs)

Multi-User Dungeons (MUDs), the MUD FAQ, MOOs, links to MOOs, other MUD Pages, home pages for Specific MUDs, MUD lists. MUD newsgroups on Usenet: It's all here. It's a nice place to start, with lots of helpful info on MUDs—without a lot of download-slowing graphics.

Type: WWW
**Address: http://draco.centerline.com:
8080/~franl/mud.html**
Region: World

The Nemeton Bar

Not open at press time, but its programmers say The Nemeton Bar will be a real-time Telnet gathering place with an optional WWW interface. It'll be largely for the rave/techno crowd, and may host organized lectures or discussions as well as plain old chat.

Type: WWW
**Address: http://www.demon.co.uk/drci/
shamen/bar.html**
Type: Telnet
Address: bungle.derby.ac.uk
Region: England, World

Oslo Net

The virtual English language "café" here is the place in cyberspace to discuss avant-garde art. BYO espresso.

Type: WWW
**Address: http://www.oslonett.no/home/
atelier/**
Region: Norway, World

Pen Pal Connection

Register yourself, fill out the questionnaire, and this Web server will automatically search its database for a good pen-pal match.

Type: WWW
**Address: http://www.start.com/start/
penpal2.html**
Region: World

Pen Pals

Links to other pen-pal clubs are available here, as well as e-mail and "snail mail" pen-pal lists. Services include personals, romance, and sex; the latter had by far the most participation.

Type: WWW
**Address: http://www.yahoo.com/
Society_and_Culture/Friendship/
Pen_Pals/**
Region: U.S., World

Pen Pals by Usenet

Leave information here in your search for a pen-pal, and check out other peoples' requests.
Type: Usenet newsgroup
Address: soc.penpals
Region: World

Talker

This is a real-time chat application from InfiNet: Check it out. You register yourself and choose a cartoon or other icon to represent you online, then talk away in several "rooms." When I dropped in it was full of Australians and New Zealanders, many of whom seemed to be regulars.
Type: WWW
Address: http://www2.infi.net:80/talker/
Region: World

Techno3

Now here's a twist: an interactive soap opera featuring the adventures of three Latina super-hackers and their boss, "a diabolical cyber-terrorist." Reader participation in determining the plot line is encouraged. There's text, plus photos and sound that carry the story along—it's lots of fun. Note: This New York-based and Hispanic-run site is also working on an interactive chat application to be called The Slosh Factory Bar, which may be up by the time you read this.

Type: WWW
**Address: http://bluepearl.com/bluepearl
/entertainment/entertainment.ht
ml**
Region: U.S.

W³ Interactive Talk

WIT is an experimental WWW-based chat system, with some potential advantages over other ones out there. Check on a topic to join in, or set up your own.
Type: WWW
**Address: http://www.w3.org/hypertext
/WWW/Discussion**
Region: World

The Webchattery

Part of a larger site that includes some MUDs, but this area is accessible to nonplayers. See what kinds of wacky things denizens are "emoting" (saying) and join in the conversation.
Type: WWW
**Address: http://sensemedia.net/sprawl/
32545/interactive**
Region: World

CRAFT

See also Art page 100; Hobbies page 333

"Craft" is usually distinguished from "art" by whether there is some sort of utilitarian purpose for the object created. Often, this means that anything not purely for display in a gallery is called craft, including items that I would consider the finest of art: totem poles, masks, art quilts, and sculptures intended for religious use, for example. Often this designation has some negative Eurocentric or sexist motives behind it. My own labeling here follows the same rather arbitrary utilitarian rule, so be sure to see the Art and Hobbies sections, among others, for related entries.

Bonsai

This forum covers all aspects of Bonsai, the Asian art of miniaturizing trees and plants into unnatural or windswept forms. The FAQ sheet available here is practically a Bonsai how-to-book.

Type: Usenet newsgroup
Address: rec.arts.bonsai
Region: Japan

Bookbinding

Richard Minsky is a master bookbinder and artist. This page has links to information about this craft, including links to the Center for Book Arts' WWW page.

Type: WWW
Address: http://www.avsi.com/minsky/
Region: U.S., World

Crafts Galore

General discussion of crafting occurs here on everything from calligraphy, to matting, to basket-weaving. For the universally creative, or those looking to try something new.

Type: Usenet newsgroup
Address: rec.crafts.misc
Region: World

Crafts of Malaysia

This marvellous online display called Crafts of Malaysia comes from two coffee-table books by Éditions Didier Millet, one of Asia's leading publishers of illustrated books. It's part of a Web site established by Silk Route, the company that did Singapore's fab Digital Media Centre.

Type: WWW
Address: http://silkroute.com/silkroute/ EDM/
Region: Malaysia

Folk Art and Craft Exchange

This online shop offers crafts from the Americas, especially those made by Native or indigenous peoples. Toys, decorative items, blankets, and pottery are just some of the items for sale, and beautifully presented. The site also includes information about craft and folk art museums.

Type: WWW
Address: http://www.folkart.com
Region: U.S., Mexico, Guatemala, Central America, South America, Canada

Historical Costuming

Information on designing and sewing the right outfits for plays, Society of Creative Anachronism tournaments, historical reinactments, and so forth.

Type: FTP
Address: grasp1.univ-lyon1.fr/pub/faq/ crafts-historical-costuming
Address: rzun2.informatik.uni-hamburg. de/pub/doc/news.answers/ crafts-historical-costuming
Address: svin02.info.win.tue.nl/pub/ usenet/news.answers/crafts/ historical-costuming
Region: World

Internet Center of Arts and Crafts Specialty Gift Shop

Here's a collection of places to buy arts and crafts products. You can also set up your own shop on their site. Includes jewelry from the American Southwest, and much more.

Type: WWW
**Address: http://www.xmission.com:80/
~arts/**
Region: World

Javanese Masks

This page offers a lovely display of Javanese masks in full color, with historical data.

Type: WWW
**Address: http://rs6000.bvis.uic.edu/
museum/javamask/Javamask.
html**
Region: Indonesia

Jewelry

Everything from gems to beads enters into the wide discussion of jewelry-making on this newsgroup. Join and be able to say "I made them!" when friends admire your cufflinks or necklace.

Type: Usenet newsgroup
Address: rec.crafts.jewelry
Region: World

Koorie Art and Craft

The Cann River Cooperative Group maintains a number of Web pages devoted to aboriginal life and issues. This one shows off traditional boomerangs, throwing sticks, and other objects decorative and useful. The items are available for sale. Be prepared for large graphics files at this site.

Type: WWW
**Address: http://webnet.com.au/koori/
artpage1.html**
Region: Australia

Marrakesh Express

This is an online shop where you can examine and purchase Moroccan rugs, pillows, and textiles. The color images of woven fabrics are detailed and lovely, and the pages include some history and information about the weaving processes used.

Type: WWW
Address: http://uslink.net/ddavis/
Region: Morocco

Mathers Museum: Textile Collections

There's just a snippet on this page about this museum's textile collection, which includes items from Africa, South America, the Middle East, Asia, and Tibet, as well as Native American works. It appears from the text that a more comprehensive online display is in the works.

Type: WWW
**Address: http://www.indiana.edu/~
mathers/textile.html**
Region: World

Metalworking

Interested in working with metal? Whether you're looking for a sword to go with a costume, or interested in blacksmithing your way through life—this is the spot.

Type: Usenet newsgroup
Address: rec.crafts.metalworking
Region: World

Motherland Artworks Gallery

This site claims to offer the Internet's largest selection of authentic hand-crafted African sculptures, jewelry, masks, musical instruments, and clothing, with 24-hour ordering. The images of the art were not the close-ups I would need to assess quality, but they look intriguing.

Type: WWW
Address: http://www.inmet.com/~dscott/ mlaw/mlaw.html
Region: Africa

Needlework

Have a lot of patience, time, and skill? Try your hand at needlework, and your family may be wearing lumpy socks forever.

Type: Usenet newsgroup
Address: rec.crafts.textiles.needlework
Region: World

New Mexican Crafts

In this archive are several articles on Mexican-American crafts, including colcha embroidery and woodcarving.

Type: Gopher
Address: latino.sscnet.ucla.edu:70/11/ Community/Cultural%20Customs
Region: U.S.

ORIGAMI-L

This very active conference is for discussion of all facets of origami, the Japanese art of paper folding. Learn a dozen ways to fold your paper. Any question will get dozens of answers here.

Type: Mailing list
Address: ORIGAMI-L
Region: Japan

Prince Edward Island Crafts Council

A goldmine of craft information, this Web page has links to many, many craft-related resources. Want to make a kite? Maybe do some metalworking? What about cross-stitching? It's all here. The Gopher site has a searchable database with references to over 5,000 craft product suppliers, plus a large number of FAQs, tutorials, and links to other spots on the Internet.

Type: WWW
Address: http://www.crafts-council.pe.ca/ craftsinfo/index.html
Type: Gopher
Address: gopher.crafts-council.pe.ca
Region: Canada

Quilting

Quilts and related topics are talked about here in excess, including where to order better fabrics, composing an artistic quilt, competitions, and bees. Quilting's not an "old ladies" craft anymore: U.S. and Japanese fabric artists are using this age-old craft technique to turn out artworks meant for hanging rather than sleeping under.

Type: Usenet newsgroup
Address: rec.crafts.quilting
Region: World

Textiles

General discussion of textiles goes on here: where to buy, how to make, and how to use.

Type: Usenet newsgroup
Address: rec.crafts.textiles
Region: World

Textiles for Quilting

Quilting textiles, all you can eat, are the subject of this newsgroup.

Type: Usenet newsgroup
Address: rec.crafts.textiles.quilting
Region: World

Textiles for Sewing

Sewing textiles, if you enjoy that sort of thing are discussed here. Learn all about the latest miracle fibers. There are some really interesting new fabrics out that make professional-looking garments easier to sew.

Type: Usenet newsgroup
Address: rec.crafts.textiles.sewing
Region: World

Yarn

Yarn! What a wonderful thing. Come and extoll its virtues with others. No matter if you knit, crochet, or make your own yarn, you'll like this.

Type: Usenet newsgroup
Address: rec.crafts.textiles.yarn
Region: World

World-Wide Quilting Page

This page is a lead-in to how-tos, guilds, and history, and includes international information.

Type: WWW
Address: http://ttsw.com/mainquilting page.html
Region: U.S., World

CYBERPUNK

What is cyberpunk? Well, it's a style of science fiction that's more Dashiell Hammett or Mickey Spillane than Isaac Asimov. It takes a generally dark view of the future in its scenarios, with tough, punky lead characters. Prominent writers in the genre include William Gibson, Bruce Sterling, and John Shirley.

The reason it's in its own section instead of with the rest of the literature is that cyberpunk is also a worldview of sorts, adopted by cyberspace's Dead-End Kids and embracing brain and body enhancement through science, fun with cryptography, emulation of and admiration for the computer hacker subculture, and a certain amount of overlap with the rave/techno world. A lifestyle for the fin de siècle decade.

Cyberpunk Page

A fairly generic-looking cyberpunk home page in the wilds of Idaho. Has a good definition of cyberpunk, both as a literary style and a social movement, plus links to other places—including Usenet groups and their FAQs. Almost no graphics.

Type: WWW
Address: http://www.cs.uidaho.edu/lal/ cyberspace/cyberpunk/cyber punk.html
Region: U.S., World

Cyberpunk and the New Edge

A number of nicely spread-out links are included on this attractive page, which has a table of contents. Slanted toward Sterling over Gibson.

Type: WWW
Address: http://phenom.physics.wisc.edu/ ~shalizi/hyper-weird/new-edge. html
Region: U.S., World

Cyberkind

This Web publication offers prose and poetics for a wired world. *Cyberkind* has nonfiction, fiction, poetry, and art and is updated often. Also, there is information here on how to submit articles for publication, on the notification mailing list, and more.

Type: WWW
Address: http://sunsite.unc.edu/ckind/ title.html/
Region: World

Cybermind

Cybermind mailing list, cybermind text, articles in theme, and links to related resources are here, as are archives from the mailing list and information on subscribing.

Type: WWW
Address: http://www.uio.no:80/~mwatz/ cybermind/
Type: Mailing list
Address: Majordomo@jefferson.village. virginia.edu cybermind@jefferson.village. virginia.edu
Region: World

Cyberpunk

Discussion of "High-Tech Low-Life" topics happens in this newsgroup. There's quite a bit of traffic.

Type: Usenet newsgroup
Address: alt.cyberpunk
Region: World

Cyberpunk

The "Chatsubo" stories are literary virtual reality in cyberpunk style and are posted here. There are not many messages.

Type: Usenet newsgroup
Address: alt.cyberpunk.chatsubo
Region: World

Cyberpunk

Discussion of the "Chatsubo" stories happens here.

Type: Usenet newsgroup
Address: alt.cyberpunk.chatsubo.d
Region: World

Cyberpunk as a Social/Political Movement

These people are talking about the cyberpunk "movement": It's pretty interesting stuff, but there's not much of it.

Type: Usenet newsgroup
Address: alt.cyberpunk.movement
Region: World

Cyberpunk Tech

Chat about cyberpunk technology is the topic here. Again, worth joining.

Type: Usenet newsgroup
Address: alt.cyberpunk.tech
Region: World

Cyberspace

Cyberspace and how it should work comes in for scrutiny in this newsgroup. Not exactly cyberpunk, even if the whole construct does get touted as William Gibson's idea, but still interesting.

Type: Usenet newsgroup
Address: alt.cyberspace
Region: World

E-Serials at CICnet

A large selection of electronic magazines, including *Phrack, Phirst Amendment,* and other cyberpunk periodicals for the nascent hacker or those who just want to know how to talk (or write) the talk are archived here.

Type: Gopher
Address: gopher.cic.net:2000/11/e-serials
Region: U.S.

Future Culture Mailing List

This is a low-flame newsgroup that features a lot of far-ranging discussions. I think it's cyberpunk enough to qualify.

Type: Mailing list
Address: LISTSERV@UAFSYSB.UARK.EDU
Region: World

The Internet Underground

The Internet Underground, which is a bold statement as a name, is a pretty good Web page. The owner mentions at the top that he's not responsible for what you might do with the information you find here, and claims he's not encouraging you. Instead he says "Think of this as a guide of what _not_ to do."

Type: WWW
**Address: http://www.engin.umich.edu/
            ~jgotts/underground.html**
Region: World

The Internet Wiretap

This page has a lot of good information, although there are few links. The Online Library has a whole section catering to Cyberpunk, and the Cyberpunk reading list is in there under SciFi.

Type: Gopher
Address: wiretap.spies.com/
Type: FTP
Address: ftp.spies.com/
Region: World

LOpht Heavy Industries

Great techno/rave-inspired graphics, home pages for the LOpht "residents," excellent file archives, and many links to intriguing data are here. LHI is a U.S. Internet provider with a strong orientation toward freedom of information.

Type: WWW
**Address: http://www.lOpht.com/archives.
            html**
Region: U.S., World

Randy King's Home Page

Randy King, aka Taran King, has quite a nice cyberpunk-related home page, with pictures from various conventions, links to FAQs, and so on. If viewed graphically, there is a large scanned-in picture at the top, so be warned.

Type: WWW
**Address: http://www.phantom.com:80/
            ~king/**
Region: World

Travels in Hypermedia

Choix d'Éditeur

Subtitled "A Snapshot of the Techno Subculture," this site has well-done, but quite large, graphics. Lots of cyberpunk/hacker links, a link to back issues of Computer Underground Digest, and a page of beginning Internet user stuff, including a searchable "Big Dummy's Guide to the Internet."

Type: WWW
Address: http://www.york.ac.uk/~jjrk1/
Region: England, World

The Uebercracker's Security Web

Lots of links to hacking and security-related information here, including online hacking publications and details of the latest hackers' conventions.

Type: WWW
Address: http://underground.org/
Region: World

Unofficial Cyberpunk Home Page

This is a very good cyberpunk page: although it doesn't have much information itself, it has links to anything you might want to see regarding cyberpunk. It also has a list of sites linked to its own with mucho good stuff.

Type: WWW
**Address: http://rohan.sdsu.edu/home/
          vanzoest/www/cyberpunk/**
Region: World

Whole Earth 'Lectronic Link

The WELL has Agrippa, William Gibson's electronic-only self-destructing novella (online in the Poetry section), as well as a whole area called "Cyberpunk and Postmodern Culture" with more interesting items in it.

Type: Gopher
Address: gopher.well.sf.ca.us/
Region: U.S., World

DANCE

Dancers are the world's most social humans, so naturally they're networking online in great numbers. It seems that the Internet has become an important tool for hooking up devotees of dance styles unusual in their home countries: the tango in Germany, Cajun dance in London, bellydancing in Sweden, to name just a few.

Also included are a few leads to scholarly dance sites; you might also try Web pages for colleges that have dance programs for information about specific degrees, courses, or instructors.

as-Sayf

This troupe specializes in dances from the Middle East and North Africa, including Classical Oriental Dance ("bellydancing"). Information is available here in English, Swedish, and French about the group, its schedule, and how to arrange a performance in your town. There are also pictures of the troupe, sound and text files, and links to other archives of interest on Middle East and North African issues and culture.

Type: WWW
**Address: http://www.pi.se/as-sayf/
          englishindex.html**
Region: Sweden, Middle East, North Africa

Ballet Discussion

Here's where to talk about the art of ballet dance, dancers, dance companies, and learning to dance.

Type: Usenet newsgroup
Address: alt.arts.ballet
Region: World

Cajun Home Page

From the bayous of Louisiana to the wilds of Big Ben, the dance steps of the Acadian people have gone world-wide. But the real question is, can they get honest-to-gosh mud bugs and 'gator in Camden?

Type: WWW
**Address: http://www.net-shopper.co.uk/
dance/cajun/index.htm**
Region: U.S., England

DANCE-HC

This is the mailing list for the scholarly world in folk dance from the Dance Heritage Coalition. Documentation, history, and upcoming events are what it's all about here.
Type: Mailing list
Address: LISTSERV@CUNYVM.CUNY.EDU
Region: World

Dancer's Archive

Here is a listing of files on everything from dance shoes, to the e-zine *The International Electronic Newsletter of Folk Dancing,* to files on dances from Africa, Asia, Europe (including the Commonwealth of Independent States), Oceania, and the Americas. Most of the Web links are European, but there are plans to expand.
Type: WWW
**Address: http://www.net-shopper.co.uk/
dance/archive.htm**
Type: FTP
Address: ftp.std.com/nonprofits/dance/
Type: Gopher
**Address: ftp.std.com:70/11/FTP/
world/nonprofits/dance**
Region: World

Ernesto's Flamenco Page

"Ernesto" (actually Ernst from Germany) has a Tango page, too. Lots of good links, including one to a Spanish flamenco page; a bibliography on Flamenco

dance, music, and guitar; and a videography. These dances from Spain and South America must help heat up that Stuttgart winter.
Type: WWW
**Address: http://www.ims.uni-stuttgart.de/
phonetik/ernst/flamenco/
ebflamenco.html**
Region: Germany, Spain, Argentina

European Ballet Page

This page includes photos, online polls, news, tour schedules, and more about the great ballet companies of Europe. Lots of resources are here for both dancers and fans.
Type: WWW
**Address: http://www.ens-lyon.fr/~
esouche/danse/dance.html**
Region: France, England, Germany, Russia

Finnish Dance Server

You'll find everything you ever wanted to know about recreational dancing in Finland here, and the page is also available in Finnish for really adventurous fans.
Type: WWW
**Address: http://www.utu.fi/harrastus/
tanssi/english/index.html**
Region: Finland

Folk and Traditional Dance

This mailing list covers folk dancing and other forms of traditional dance from an academic standpoint.
Type: Mailing list
Address: listserv@hearn.nic.surfnet.nl
Contact: dance-l@hearn.nic.surfnet.nl
Region: World

Frankfurt's Tango Home Page

This site provides information in German and English on the German tango scene, which is apparently pretty hot. CD lists, sound files, and links to several other sites in Germany, Austria, Switzerland, Argentina, and Uruguay are included.

Type: WWW
Address: http://www.uni-frankfurt.de/~garrit/tango/tango.html
Region: Germany, Austria, Switzerland, Argentina, Uruguay

Highlands and Islands Society of London

Here's a home page for those individuals who want to have a manly dance with a manly man in a kilt. About once a month this society sponsors traditional Ceilidhs in the central London area. (A Ceilidh is an evening of informal Scottish dancing.)

Type: WWW
Address: http://www.net-shopper.co.uk/dance/ceilidh/index.htm
Region: England, Scotland, Ireland

International Tap Association

Tap dancers, choreographers, and fans will find information on venues, movies, Internet resources, worldwide event listings, and tour schedules, all about tap or its Appalachian country cousin, clogging.

Type: WWW
Address: http://www.hahnemann.edu/tap/ITAhome.htm
Region: World

Internet Shopper European Dance Server

This is a free service for dancers, listing events and resources for the following dance styles: Cajun, Ceilidh, Lindy Hop, Western Square Dancing, Tap Dancing, Round Dance, and Ballet.

Type: WWW
Address: http://www.net-shopper.co.uk/dance/index.htm
Region: England, Scotland, Ireland, Wales, Finland, France, Germany, Hungary, Holland, Sweden, U.S.

Israeli Folk Dance Home Page

This page is mainly about Israeli folk dancing in the U.S., and is also useful for its archive of Israeli folk dances.

Type: WWW
Address: http://ftp.bellcore.com/pub/ernie/israeli/homepage.html
Type: FTP
Address: ftp.bellcore.com/pub/ernie/israeli/
Region: Israel, U.S.

Lindy Hop in Stockholm

The Lindy Hop is alive and well in Stockholm, and if you want to a be a better Lindy dancer, this page can hook you up with the appropriate resources.

Type: WWW
Address: http://www.fysik4.kth.se/lindy/intl-index.html
Region: Sweden

Other Dance Servers

This page includes pointers to information on a long list of dance-related topics, including dance directories, tango dance notation, ballroom dance, UNWMBDA and USDSC rulebooks, and more.

Type: WWW
Address: http://bighorn.terra.net/menlo/dance/other.html
Region: U.S., World

The Rhythm Hot Shots/The Herräng Dance Camp Home Page

The Rhythm Hot Shots are a professional dance troupe specializing in Afro-American dances, while The Herräng Dance Camp is a place to learn the ever-popular Lindy Hop.

Type: WWW
Address: http://www.fysik4.kth.se/lindy/ trhs.html
Region: Sweden

Salsa in London Home Page

If you ever wanted to salsa in swinging London, this page will tell you when and where. It has listings of events and clubs from Kings Cross to Brixton and beyond.

Type: WWW
Address: http://www.net-shopper.co.uk/ dance/uk/salsa.htm
Region: England

Society for Creative Anachronism Music and Dance Home Page

Here's a fun-filled resource for Renaissance and medieval dance, including both European and Middle Eastern styles. Lists of recordings, a newsletter, and Morris dancing "cheat sheets" are among the offerings.

Type: WWW
Address: http://fermi.clas.virginia.edu/ ~gl8f/music_and_dance.html
Region: England, France, Europe, Middle East

Usenet Dance Resources

There are several dance-related groups on Usenet. Two of the most popular are listed here; these can lead you to others.

Type: Usenet newsgroup
**Addresses: rec.arts.dance
            rec.folk-dancing**
Region: World

The Vancouver Morris Men

This is a semi-professional Morris dancing troupe that tours Canada and England. Information on this flashy, theatrical, and ancient English dance style, rooted in the pagan past, is here as well as tour schedules, photos, reports, and the like.

Type: WWW
Address: http://www.info-mine.com/ vmm/
Region: England, Canada

Victor Eijkhout Home Page

Victor works with supercomputers, and has written a book on TeX. He's also a musician and dance fiend who offers lists of songs that go well with particular dance styles. You may find the idea of doing the Hustle to the Clash's "Rock The Casbah," well…both unlikely and very amusing. But it just might work!

Type: WWW
Address: http://www.netlib.org/utk/ people/VictorEijkhout.html
Region: U.S., World

WWW Virtual Library Dance Index

This is a good starting point for dance resources. It includes academic dance resources, calendars, links to other dance servers, and more.

Type: WWW
Address: http://bighorn.terra.net/menlo/ dance/
Region: World

Zoots and Spangles

The Zoots and Spangles are a British professional dance company that tours Europe and puts on demonstrations, cabarets, performances, and workshops.

Type: WWW
**Address: http://www.net-shopper.co.uk/
            dance/troupes/zoots/index.htm**
Region: England

DIGITAL MEDIA: NEWS AND CURRENT EVENTS

See also Business page 111; Environmental Data and Issues page 243; Internet Resources Online page 349; Journalism and the Media page 356; Politics page 409

Have a hunger for international news that hasn't been filtered, reinterpreted, and squeezed to fit into some tiny spot on Page 23 of your local daily? On the Internet, you can get free (usually), regular home delivery of over 100 foreign newspapers and newsletters. You can find news sources that fit your interests—papers covering changes in the former Soviet Union; publications with a liberal, moderate, conservative, or radical slant; news that takes you back to the nation of your birth or your favorite vacation spot. Many of the publications listed are in English: If not, I've indicated the language.

Publications that are delivered via the World Wide Web will often be in full color, with huge photos, blaring headlines, and a look that puts the oh-so-gray *New York Times* to shame. Some publishers are experimenting with totally new ways to deliver news online, ways that go far beyond duplicating the look of a printed page. For example, a multimedia news "paper" could potentially include spoken-word segments, like the Austrian *APAnet* below, or video segments, like those in *L'Unione Sarda* of Italy.

Africa Information Network

This site provides an archive of articles on or from many African nations, from Angola to Zaire. Most are in English, some in French or other languages.

Type: Gopher
**Address: //csf.Colorado.EDU:70/11/ipe/
            Thematic_Archive/newsletters/
            africa_information_afriq_net**
Region: Africa

APAnet

APAnet is an Austrian newspaper constructed as a set of clickable image maps. These maps lead the visitor to German-language text and graphics describing Austrian current events and news. The site is easy to navigate, but the stark graphics get old quickly.

Type: WWW
Address: http://www.apa.co.at/
Region: Austria

Brazilian News

Text here is in Portuguese, and the connection is extremely slow.

Type: Gopher
**Address: uspif.if.usp.br/11gopher_root_1
            %3a%5bnews%5d**
Region: Brazil

The Bulgarian News Archive

This archive contains articles from diverse sources relating in one way or another to Bulgaria. It opens with a disclaimer about the accuracy and potentially controversial nature of some of the files. In the true Internet spirit, "These documents are made available in the interest of freedom of communication, information, and viewpoint," they say. Most of the news is in English.

Type: WWW
**Address: http://ASUdesign.eas.asu.edu/
          places/Bulgaria/news/**
Region: Bulgaria

Canada-L

Keep abreast of the latest developments in Canadian politics and society through this mailing list.
Type: Mailing list
Address: listserv@mcgill1.bitnet
Contact: canada-l@mcgill.bitnet
Region: Canada

Carolina

This mailing list will bring you the weekly newsletter *Carolina*, with news from the Czech Republic in English.
Type: Mailing list
Address: car-eng@csearn.bitnet
Region: Czech Republic

CBC Radio Trial

You can grab Canadian Broadcasting Corporation (CBC) radio programs here; they're stored as audio files in several formats.
Type: WWW
Address: http://radioworks.cbc.ca/
Type: FTP
Address: debra.dbgt.doc.ca/
Type: Gopher
Address: debra.dbgt.doc.ca/
Region: Canada

Central Europe Today

CET On-Line is the product of a daily news service providing information on Eastern Europe. Articles are mainly current events–related, but each issue has some cultural and entertainment news as well. Devoid of graphics, the well-written and balanced articles read like wire service copy (in fact, several of the correspondents are also with Reuters). If you're looking for up-to-the-minute information on the Ukraine, Poland, and other Eastern European countries, then this site is for you.
Type: Gopher
**Address: gopher.eunet.cz/11/Journals/
          cet-online/**
Region: Czech Republic, Poland, Ukraine,
          C.I.S., Eastern Europe

Choong-ang Daily News

Find out the latest from South Korea's most popular newspaper, in Korean.
Type: WWW
Address: http://www.joongang.co.kr/
Region: South Korea

China Times News

Your browser must support Chinese characters to check out this archive of articles from Taiwan's leading newspaper. Full-text versions of selected articles are available, without graphics.
Type: Gopher
**Address: gopher.nsysu.edu.tw/11/
          infotimes**
Region: Taiwan

ClariNet Communications Corp.

This service packs up Reuters newsfeeds into news briefs delivered via ClariNet newsgroups. Check in here for a sample of their world news service, and for information available elsewhere about the hundreds of specific ClariNet services available.

Type:　　WWW
**Address:　http://www.clarinet.com/
　　　　　Samples/reutworld.html**
Region:　World

CNN Headline News

That's right, you can download the very same scripts that the on-air talent reads. They're automatically distributed on the Net.

Type:　　Gopher
**Address:　info.umd.edu:925/11/Todays
　　　　　_News**
Region:　U.S., World

Copesa Diario Electronico

This Spanish-language site, which contains weekly news from Chile, is incredible in scope and impressive in layout. The introductory page is relatively empty, but venture into the archive and you find a tasteful mix of short news articles and well-placed graphics. *Copesa Diario Electronico* reports on a wide range of topics, both local and international. The archive currently covers a two-month period.

Type:　　WWW
**Address:　http://huelen.reuna.cl/copesa/
　　　　　index.html**
Region:　Chile

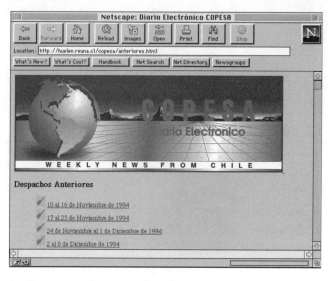

Daily News from Iceland

This news service posts stories from the monthly paper *News from Iceland*. You can also check out travel and business news from Iceland at this site, which has a fun design.

Type:　　WWW
Address:　http://www.centrum.is/icerev/
Region:　Iceland

The Electronic Telegraph

Registration and a graphical browser are required to access this daily English paper, which has a generally conservative viewpoint.

Type:　　WWW
Address:　http://www.telegraph.co.uk/
Region:　England

French Language Press Review

This site contains almost-daily summaries of news that has appeared in the French press, in English.

Type:　　Gopher
**Address:　burrow.cl.msu.edu:70/11/news/
　　　　　news/general/french_language**
Region:　France

Haberler

The Turkish text of the newspaper *Haberler* is posted here daily. You can also read the monthly magazine *Onceki Aylar*.

Type: Gopher
Address: gopher.metu.edu.tr/11/haberler
Region: Turkey

IndiaWorld

The English text and some graphics from *India Daily, India Weekly,* and *India Today* can be browsed here. The IndiaWorld service may be limited to subscribers soon.

Type: WWW
**Address: http://www.indiaworld.com/
open/news/index.html**
Region: India

InTV

Updates on the news, weather, sports, and stock quotes from Singapore TV, mostly in English. The graphic interface is very difficult to navigate.

Type: WWW
**Address: http://www.technet.sg/
cgi-bin/intv-form?5+100**
Region: Singapore

The Irish Times

This site includes excerpts from the day's paper, with some graphics.

Type: WWW
**Address: http://www.ireland.net/market
place/irish-times/**
Region: Ireland

Islamic World News

The electronic publication *IMNET* is issued twice per week, and provides news updates, analysis, book reviews, essays, and opinions from readers. Published by the International Muslim Student Union in Seattle, Washington, it covers all parts of the Islamic world and news of interest to followers of Islam everywhere.

Type: E-zine
Address: imnet2@max.u.washington.edu
Region: World

Israeline

This Gopher site provides daily news from Israel, including selections from a number of major newspapers, official government statements and policies from press releases, and some features, weather, and sports information as well. Everything I looked at was in English.

Type: Gopher
Address: israel-info.gov.il/11/new
Region: Israel

Kyodo Cyber Express

This is a Japanese newsmagazine that's dominated by lots of big color photos. In Japanese and English.

Type: WWW
Address: http://www.toppan.co.jp/
Region: Japan

Mercury Center

This is the electronic version of the *San Jose Mercury News,* and is the premier U.S. online newspaper. It's best known for its excellent coverage of the computer industry and related Silicon Valley issues, but there's national and international news here as well.

Type: WWW
Address: http://www.sjmercury.com/
Region: U.S., World

News from the Former Yugoslavia

There's an entire selection of electronic newsletters here—daily, weekly and monthly—from and/or about the republics that were once Yugoslavia. Mostly in local languages.

Type: Gopher
Address: znanost.mz.hr.:70/11/eng/ lokalni-info/djelatnosti/ostale-us luge/enews
Region: Yugoslavia, Croatia, Bosnia-Hercegovina, Serbia, Slovenia

The New South Polar Times

My partner Steve has wanted to live in Antarctica ever since spending an interlude on sub-Antarctic Stewart Island off New Zealand. He'll enjoy this; you may also. *The New South Polar Times* is a biweekly newsletter written by one of the staff at the Amundsen-Scott South Pole Station on Antarctica. The site includes current and back issues, as well as some ideas about using the newsletter as a learning tool in the classroom. There are lots of stories about exploration and, yes, weather.

Type: WWW
Address: http://www.deakin.edu.au/edu/ MSEE/GENII/NSPT/NSPThome Page.html
Region: Antarctica

Nicanet Hotline

This page contains news from Nicaragua: What's up with business, the economy, and politics. In English.

Type: WWW
Address: http://www.ualr.edu/~ degonzalez/nicanet.txt
Region: Nicaragua

Non-U.S. Newspapers on the Internet

It seems like this site hits every continent: Roma, Mexico City, Madras, Israel, London, Singapore, Poland, and more. The site encompasses more than 50 links to newspapers outside the U.S., some free and some available only via paid subscription, all online.

Type: WWW
Address: http://marketplace.com/ e-papers.list.www/e-papers .home.page.html
Region: World

El Norte

This is a special Internet edition of the influential daily paper for the fast-growing Monterrey region of Mexico. You can view the Spanish text using your Web browser, or see it onscreen just as it was printed with Adobe Acrobat.

Type: WWW
Address: http://www2.infosel.com.mx/ pub/elnorte.htm
Region: Mexico

The Omnivore

If you are an outright news junkie, you'll think this is heaven. Daily global news updates in brief are instantly available here, or you can choose to view news by region. There are also links to a selection of online publications of interest to news nuts.

Type: WWW
Address: http://history.cc.ukans.edu/ carrie/news_main.html
Region: World

Public Radio News

Presented by the University of Queensland Department of Journalism, Public Radio News is an Internet news server that provides hourly bulletins to Australian community radio broadcasters. PRN's stated aim is to "help create an international syndicated network of radio news." One very cool feature of their home page is its archive of downloadable sound bites relating to each short news clip.

Type: WWW
Address: http://www.uq.oz.au/jrn/rad .html
Region: Australia

Radio Free Europe/Liberty Research Institute Reports

News from Russia, Central Asia, and Eastern and Central Europe is available here in English, with a conservative point of view.

Type: FTP
Address: poniecki.berkeley.edu/pub/ polish/publications/RFE-RL/
Type: Gopher
Address: gopher.lib.umich.edu:4320/ 1nntp%20ls%20misc.news. east-europe.rferl
Type: Mailing list
Address: listserv@ubvm.cc.buffalo.edu
Contact: rferl-1@ubvm.cc.buffalo.edu
Region: Russia

Recent Bangladesh News

This site includes daily links from Bangladesh-related newsgroups, wire services, and newspapers. Also has pointers to newsletters and other sources. Everything here is in English.

Type: WWW
Address: http://www.asel.udel.edu/~ kazi/bangladesh/bdnews.html
Region: Bangladesh

Reforma

This is a special Internet edition of the largest Mexico City paper, in Spanish. Adobe Acrobat will let you see the full document in color, or you can see just the text with your Web browser.

Type: WWW
Address: http://www2.infosel.com.mx/ pub/reformae.htm
Region: Mexico

St. Petersburg Press

At this site you can read the English-language, business-oriented weekly from this Russian city, in a very attractive format.

Type: WWW
Address: http://www.spb.su/sppress/ index.html
Region: Russia

Severo-Zapad

Daily news updates from northwest Russia are available on this Web page, some in English.

Type: WWW
Address: http://www.spb.su/sev-zap/ index.html
Region: Russia

Somalia News Update

This irregularly published newletter is devoted to critical discussion of events in Somalia. Back issues are archived at the FTP site below.

Type: E-zine
Address: antbh@strix.udac.uu.se
Type: FTP
**Address: ftp.uu.net/doc/politics/
          umich-poli/SNU**
Region: Somalia

South Africa Weekly Mail and South Africa Free Press

These two papers can be found archived at this site.
Type: FTP
Address: ftp.misanet.org/pub/
Region: South Africa

Der Standard On-Line

The Austrian newspaper *Der Standard* comes to the Net as more of an archive than an e-zine. *Der Standard On-Line* offers recent articles in German on the news, politics, and culture of Austria and the world. The site is notable for its lack of graphics, with one exception: You can download a GIF file of the front page.
Type: WWW
**Address: http://www.derstandard.co.at/
          DerStandard/**
Region: Austria

L'Unione Sarda

This is one of the most thorough and informative electronic news sites on the Internet. For starters, there is a full-text version of each day's newspaper in Italian. Links within each article point to other relevant stories and sites worldwide. Next, there are video clips available for downloading and an advertisement section (sorry, no coupons). You can even search the entire archive by key words. A great deal of hard work and innovative thinking is evident on every page.

Type: WWW
**Address: http://www.vol.it/UNIONE/
          unione.html**
Region: Italy

The Victoria Age

Still hauling itself into the computer world, the *Age* now offers an online archive of its back issues. It's a good source for news on not just Australia and New Zealand, but Asia–Pacific issues as well.
Type: WWW
**Address: http://www.vicnet.net.au/vicnet/
          age/compage.htm**
Region: Australia

Weekly Update on the Americas

This newsletter with a left/liberal slant covers the latest news from Central America, South America, and the Caribbean, including many stories you won't find elsewhere. Their motto: "All the news that didn't fit."
Type: WWW
**Address: http://www.ualr.edu/~
          degonzalez/update.txt**
Region: Central America, South America,
          Caribbean

The Weekly Mail and Guardian

The Weekly Mail and Guardian bills itself as South Africa's leading independent newspaper, and maintains this site to provide better access to African news to students around the world. *The Weekly e-Mail*, its primary service, is a full-text version of the paper delivered to your computer each Friday. The service costs $100 per year through electronic subscription. A six-month archive of South African news is accessible for free.

Type: WWW
**Address: http://www.is.co.za/services/
            wmail/wmail.html**
Region: South Africa

Winnipeg Free Press

The *Winnipeg Free Press* takes a graphical approach to news reporting. Just check out the front page of the paper, click on any headlines that sound interesting, and away you go. Full-length news stories augmented by images and sound clips combine to form a well-rounded multimedia presentation. Topics range from politics to entertainment news. Unfortunately, the site is still under construction, and some of the links yield little content.

Type: WWW
**Address: http://www.mbnet.mb.ca:80/
            freepress/March9front.html**
Region: Canada

Winnipeg Today

This is a weekly news roundup that's a supplement to the *Winnipeg Free Press*. Includes headlines, features, local events, and weather updates.

Type: WWW
**Address: http://www.umanitoba.ca/win
            today.html**
Region: Canada

Women's Web

This site was brand-new when I checked in, but it's already providing U.S. and international news stories with an eye toward "women's issues," broadly defined to include everything from population problems to crime to the "glass ceiling" effect in business. It also offers a link to women's organizations and woman-oriented resources online. It's a project of the Women's Wire commercial online service.

Type: WWW
**Address: http://sfgate.com/examiner/
            womensweb.html**
Region: U.S., World

Yahoo's International News Roundup

Once again, the Yahoo service at Stanford provides a useful front-end to the Net. Follow the links here to find news from the country of your choice.

Type: WWW
**Address: http://www.yahoo.com/News/
            International/**
Region: World

DIGITAL MEDIA: ONLINE PUBLICATIONS FOR THE NETHEAD

See also Literature page 372

These listings are for publications devoted to something other than hard news, specifically Internet-related topics or single topics that fit easily into one of the other categories. That includes 'zines ("homemade" publications), general-interest online magazines, and other fun publications that are distributed or archived online with regularity.

There seems to be a growing interest in online publishing, fueled by the ease of creating and distributing documents with graphics and color on the World Wide Web. With major desktop publishing applications now adding the ability to convert any document to HTML format, this niche is most likely about to explode.

For some reason, Canada appears to be at the forefront of this movement, producing some of the most highly developed, most creative online 'zines. Must be the Marshall McLuhan influence (you do remember that he was Canadian, don't you?). On the other hand, I searched endlessly for titles from Africa, South America, and Central America, and came up almost empty-handed. I suspect that they're out there but have yet to be catalogued and indexed in English, or are archived on the mostly technical university Gopher and FTP sites in the South.

The Beat

This Australian online magazine is your typical urban lifestyle publication, thriving on local events, film and music reviews, arts, comedy, clubbing, and dancing around Melbourne, Sydney, and other cities in Oz.

Type: WWW
Address: http://www.ozonline.com.au/ beat/
Region: Australia

The "Bobby" Chronicles

This is a personal 'zine from twentysomethings in rural New Brunswick, Canada. From the writer's own description: "'Bobby' has several meanings, including 'redneck.' This 'zine is not written from a redneck's point of view. A stop on one of the dirt roads feeding into the info highway."

Type: E-mail
Address: merriman@nbnet.nb.ca
Region: Canada

Chinese Magazines Online

Over a dozen Chinese-language magazines are archived at this site, as is information on configuring your Web browser to handle Chinese characters. Some of these are of general interest, while others are news or computer-related.

Type: WWW
Address: http://meena.cc.uregina.ca/ ~liushus/chn-mag.html
Region: China, Taiwan

City Live!

This is an online student magazine from City University of London. It includes news, reviews, games, and things to do around town. The interface is still a bit amateurish, but it's a unique effort.

Type: WWW
Address: http://web.city.ac.uk/~cb157/ citylive.html
Region: England

CTHEORY

This is an international, monthly electronic review of books on theory, technology, and culture. Big-name contributors include Kathy Acker, Jean Baudrillard, Bruce Sterling, Arthur and Marilouise Kroker, and Deena and Michael Weinstein. Articles tend to be long-winded, with heavy-duty verbiage and post-postmodern analysis. Archived at the WWW site below.

Type: E-zine
Address: LISTSERV@VM1.MCGILL.CA
Send e-mail message with body:
SUBSCRIBE CTHEORY <Firstname Lastname>

Type: WWW
Address: **http://english-server.hss.cmu
.edu/ctheory/ctheory.html**
Region: Canada, World

The Electronic Newsstand

This is what the name implies, a place where you can browse magazines online. All sorts of popular, glossy, and mostly American titles are available here in digest style: It's intended to induce you to subscribe. Everything from *Time* to fashion magazines and medical titles.

Type: Gopher
Address: **gopher.enews.com:2100/**
Region: U.S.

eye WEEKLY

Like New York's *Village Voice*, the *eye* is a big-circulation, big-city arts-and-news weekly. This electronic version has everything that's in the print version, including full-color cover graphics. Alternatively, you can read it as straight text. Very nice! Published online every Thursday.

Type: WWW
Address: **http://www.interlog.com/eye**
Type: Gopher
Address: **interlog.com**
Region: Canada

Euphony

This is a local online magazine, with feature stories and coverage of arts, music, movies, comics, and politics in British Columbia. The funky interface looks nothing like any printed page you've ever seen. Kinda neat.

Type: WWW
Address: **http://euphony.com/euphony**
Region: Canada

Exclaim!

Mostly but not exclusively about alternative rock, the online monthly *Exclaim!* also features some surreal techno/hip-hop-inspired digital art, a wild and creative interface, regular columns, and fiction.

Type: WWW
Address: **http://www.inforamp.net/pw
casual/exclaim/index.html**
Region: World

Factsheet Five Electronic

This is the first place you should look for information on 'zines, those kitchen-table creations that let average folks publish and circulate their thoughts on just about any topic. *Factsheet Five* is a quarterly magazine of nothing but 'zine reviews; *F5 Electronic* is its online counterpart. The reviews themselves are well worth reading just for entertainment value—always lots of funny, ascerbic, and occasionally vicious commentary here. *F5* includes listings for 'zines on all types of music, science fiction, poetry, politics, street fashion, pets, collecting, travel, and many more categories; plus many "perzines," personal 'zines where a single writer spills his or her guts on a number of subjects. The latter are sometimes the most interesting of the lot. *F5* also reviews independent music releases and small-press comics, plus mail art projects and the occasional event or T-shirt. Back issues through Spring 1994 are archived at the Web sites below, but this project seems to have come to a standstill.

Type: WWW
Address: **http://kzsu.stanford.edu/uwi/
f5e/f5e.html**
Address: **http://www.well.com/www/
jerod23/**

**http://www.nitv.net/~mech/F5/
f5index.html**

Type: Gopher
Address: gopher.well.sf.ca.us/Publications
**Address: gopher.etext.org:70/11/
Factsheet.Five**
**Address: gopher.well.sf.ca.us:70/11/
Publications/F5/Reviews**
Type: FTP
**Address: ftp.etext.org: /pub/
Factsheet.Five/**
Type: WAIS
Address: nigel.msen.com
Region: U.S., World

The Fashion Page

An online rag mag from New York City, *The Fashion
Page* covers the latest styles and, more importantly,
the fashion scene—designers, shows, collections, and
so on. See the spring collections and have fun with
this irreverent magazine.
Type: WWW
**Address: http://www.charm.net:80/~
jakec/**
Region: U.S., World

FiX

FiX is a London-based style and culture monthly that
features interviews, news, reviews, and features on
sex, drugs, politics, music, art, and football—all
written in a cheeky, slangy London street style.
Type: WWW
**Address: http://www.easynet.co.uk/fix/
fix.htm**
Region: England

Friday

Friday is the most popular weekly lifestyle magazine
in Japan. Right now this site offers just a tantalizing
promise of an online version "coming soon," in
English and Japanese. When it does arrive, it'll be
heavily designed with lots and lots of photos and
graphics, like its print predecessor.
Type: WWW
Address: http://www.toppan.co.jp/
Region: Japan

Frogmag

"The e-zine of the French community abroad," this
reader-written magazine carries general-interest sto-
ries—always in French—on art, science, literature,
history, and more.
Type: WWW
**Address: http://www.princeton.edu/
Frogmag/**
Type: Mailing list
Address: listproc@list.cren.net
**Send e-mail message with body: subscribe
frognet <Firstname_Lastname>**
Contact: dhaussy@cnam.fr
Region: France

Geekgirl

This is a cool quarterly fanzine for cyberchicks. The
editors interview interesting people, Australian and
otherwise, and chat about everything from tapioca to
cryptography.
Type: WWW
**Address: http://www.next.com.au/spy
food/geekgirl/**
Type: E-mail
Address: spyfood@next.com.au
Region: Australia

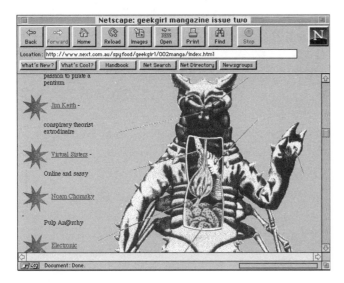

hip webzine

The name may be lowercase, but this 'zine's hardly lowkey. Based in British Columbia, *hip* is an online 'zine with lots of articles on art happenings, music, and more. It's fun to read, with a colorful, kicky interface and an "alternative" orientation.

Type: WWW
Address: http://www.hip.com/
Region: Canada

Hot Wired

This is the online adjunct of *Wired* magazine, that cyberbible of all that's hip and cool. You'll find articles on computers, games, music, books, social movements (particularly those involving computers), and more, including interactive discussions.

Type: WWW
Address: http://www.hotwired.com/
Region: U.S., World

Ideas DIGest Online

This online magazine is devoted to entrepreneurship and inventing, with an eye on the small business market. Issues offer feature stories, editorials, regular departments, and resource directories.

Type: WWW
Address: http://www.ideas.wis.net//
Region: Canada

International TeleTimes

This bimonthly electronic magazine with a global staff has features with an international angle, plus columns on photography, wine, Central American issues, and more. Both text and HTML-with-graphics versions are available, in English or French.

Type: WWW
Address: http://www.wimsey.com/tele times/teletimes_home_page .html
Address: http://www.acns.nwu.edu/ ezines/teletimes/
Type: Gopher
Address: gopher.etext.org:70/11/Zines/ Intl_Teletimes
Type: FTP
Address: ftp.etext.org/Zines/Intl_Tele times/
Address: sumex-aim.stanford.edu/ info-mac/per/tele/
Region: Canada

I/O/D

I/O/D is an interactive multimedia e-zine that is mailed in compressed format. When uncompressed on your drive, it gives you animations, QuickTime movies, strange sounds, and stranger text. In bin-hexed, self-extracting MacroMind Director format.

Type: E-mail
Address: ifgraphics@gn.apc.org
Region: U.S., World

John Labovitz's E-Zine List

Regularly updated, this long list of e-zines is lots of fun to read, even more fun to use as a guide to some of the Net's most interesting publications.

Type: WWW
Address: **http://www.ora.com:8080/johnl /e-zine-list/e-zine-list.txt**
Type: FTP
Address: **ftp.etext.org/pub/Zines**
Type: Gopher
Address: **ftp.etext.org/pub/Zines**
Region: World

Lian Yi Tong-Xun (LYTX)

A comprehensive Chinese journal published by the Ottawa Chinese Students and Scholars Association, this monthly is available both online and on paper. Entirely in Chinese, *LYTX* includes articles on literature, poems, science, and technology; topics of general interest; and CSSP (Chinese Students, Scholars, and Professionals) activities. E-mail versions are available in more than one format, depending on how you prefer to read Chinese characters. A document at the FTP site has more complete directions in English on how to subscribe to each, or you can use the brief instructions below.

Type: E-mail (GB format)
Address: **listserv@vm1.mcgill.ca**
Send e-mail message with body: sub lytx <Firstname Lastname>
Type: E-mail (HZ format)
Address: **listserv@ucalgary.ca**
Send e-mail message with body: subscribe cssads-l <Firstname Lastname>
Type: E-mail (BIG5 format)

Address: **simon@sg2.chem.nrc.ca**
Type: WWW
Address: **http://uwalpha.uwinnipeg .ca:8001/lytxindex.html**
Type: FTP
Address: **ftp.met.kth.se/pub/LYTX/**
Type: Gopher
Address: **sunrise.cc.mcgill.ca:70**
Region: China, World

Metlice

This humor rag is from Prague, is written in Czech, and is oriented toward college-age (but not necessarily sophomoric) humor.

Type: WWW
Address: **http://www.cuni.cz/cucc/metlice /metlice.html**
Region: Czech Republic

MillieniuM

This Dutch art and literature magazine has an interesting interface and worthwhile content, too. In Dutch.

Type: WWW
Address: **http://www.dds.nl/kiosk/ millennium/**
Region: Holland

Le Mondo Diplomatique

Very attractively produced electronic magazine on politics, economics, and social movements in France and in other nations. In French.

Type: WWW
Address: **http://www.ina.fr/CP/Monde Diplo/mondediplo.fr.html**
Region: France

Newsletters, Journals, and 'Zines on the Internet

In French and English, this is an exhaustive list of the above, including many European titles.

Type: WWW
Address: http://www.loria.fr/~charoy/ zines.html
Region: France, World

NWHQ

This is a hypermedia magazine of art and literature that's becoming a network of novel-length literature. *NWHQ* has a really lovely techno-baroque look.

Type: WWW
Address: http://www.knosso.com/ NWHQ/
Region: Canada

OneEurope

Printed and distributed three times a year at 170 European universities, *OneEurope* is the product of an international students' organization, AEGEE. This is the online version, available in both French and English. Each issue has several features on a large theme, such as "The Power of Symbols," with various national and political viewpoints represented. There are also contributions relating to culture, student life, and AEGEE itself.

Type: WWW
Address: http://www.informatik. rwth-aachen.de/AEGEE/one Europe/
Type: FTP
Address: ftp.ask.uni-karlsruhe.de:/pub/ aegee/papers/
Region: Europe

Pete and Bernie's Philosophical Steakhouse

This is a humorous, and frequently offensive, monthly 'zine. It's archived at the Gopher and FTP sites below.

Type: E-mail
Address: DL@CATES.DEMON.CO.UK
Send e-mail message with body: Subscribe <Your E-mail Address> PAB
Type: Gopher
Address: gopher.etext.org:70/11/Zines/ PAB
Type: FTP
Address: ftp.etext.org/pub/Zines/PAB/
Region: England

Schroedinger's Radio

All ASCII, all the time, this 'zine includes history, research, rants, and conspiracy theories, most of them anti-Dominant Paradigm.

Type: WWW
Address: http://www.io.org/~pwcasual/ shroder.txt
Region: U.S.

SEMA

SEMA is the yearly undergraduate journal for the University of Toronto Semiotics department (semiotics is the study of the sign or of the nature of representation). It offers stories on art theory, post-structuralism, linguistics, anthropology, philosophy, film theory, feminist theory, and more, written by students and faculty.

Type: Gopher
Address: gopher.etext.org:70/11/Zines/ SEMA
Type: FTP
Address: ftp.etext.org/pub/Zines/SEMA/
Region: Canada, World

Singapore

This is an official online city magazine for Singapore, and like the city, it's at the same time cosmopolitan and puritanical. Nice use of graphics.

Type: WWW
**Address: http://www.ncb.gov.sg/sif/
issues.html**
Region: Singapore

Spojrzenia

This is a magazine covering chiefly—but not exclusively—various aspects of Polish culture, history, politics, and so on.

Type: Gopher
**Address: poniecki.haas.Berkeley.EDU:70/
11/archives/polish.archives/
Publications/**
**Contact: spojrz@k-vector.chem.
washington.edu**
Region: Poland

Strobe

This is an independent magazine about new music and modern culture. *Strobe* includes music reviews, art files, links to sites of interest, and a slick interface.

Type: WWW
Address: http://www.iuma.com/Strobe/
Region: U.S., England

Tango Online

This is an Internet supplement to the German magazine *Tango,* published weekly in Berlin. Mostly in German, it covers news, lifestyles, music, and events.

Type: WWW
Address: http://www.tango.de/
Region: Germany

The Underground Review

This is a generally conservative online 'zine with radical-right tendencies. It has articles on subjects like avoiding taxes, beating the IRS in court, constitutionalism, the unorganized militia movement in the U.S., and so on. Their site has some Web links as well.

Type: WWW
Address: http://www.ionet.net/~ordway/
Region: U.S.

The "umich" Archive

This is a comprehensive storehouse of online 'zines, ranging from the tacky and offensive to the tame and thoughtful. Browse and enjoy.

Type: FTP
**Address: etext.archive.umich.edu/pub/
Zines/**
Region: U.S., World

Voices from the Net

An experiment in "net-ethnography," this electronic magazine presents interviews with cyberspace celebrities and notables.

Type: E-mail
Address: voices-request@andy.bgsu.edu
**Send e-mail message with the subject
Voices and body: subscribe**
Type: FTP
**Address: ftp://etext.archive.umich.edu/
pub/Zines/**
Region: U.S., World

DISABILITIES
See also Health and Medicine page 310; Politics page 409

Researching this section was both interesting and personally rewarding. Computers can open up new avenues for communication and education for the handicapped, and the best of the resources they find there are empowering. I hope that you, too, find useful information and contacts online.

I was particularly impressed with disabled-advocacy efforts online in Singapore and Australia—the sites created by groups there should be held up as a model for others to emulate.

A quick word about terminology: Like everyone else, I'm not particularly fond of the terms "disabled" and "handicapped," with their messages of limitation and dependency. But the few "politically correct" alternatives are rather cumbersome, and it didn't seem prudent to employ any of the self-deprecating and humorous terms, such as "wheelies," that many of my disabled friends and colleagues use. So I've used the most universally understood terms, and I hope that no one will be offended by that choice.

Reviews of just some of the support groups available are included. There are many, and they are incredibly valuable to disabled people, especially to families with disabled children, who can talk online to adults who have made it despite their physical or mental limitations, as well as to other parents and professionals. These newsgroups are also conduits for medical help, including the latest treatments, information about physicians and hospitals with innovative programs, and information about local in-person support groups and resources. See the Usenet newsgroup news.answers or the first listing below to find a group for a particular disability, if it isn't one of the few listed here.

Access Foundation for the Disabled
Send e-mail to this group for a list of e-mail addresses and Internet sites for support groups for those with various handicaps.
Type: E-mail
Address: danyaon@savvy.com
Region: U.S., World

alt.support.spina-bifida
Here is where people who suffer from spina bifida, as well as their friends, loved ones, and others who care, can share advice and medical information.
Type: Usenet newsgroup
Address: alt.support.spina-bifida
Region: World

alt.support.mult-sclerosis
People with multiple sclerosis and their families can network with each other here, and find out about the latest medical treatments and adaptive technologies.
Type: Usenet newsgroup
Address: alt.support.mult-sclerosis
Region: World

alt.support.musc-dystrophy
Muscular dystrophy and how to deal with it is the subject of this newsgroup.
Type: Usenet newsgroup
Address: alt.support.musc-dystrophy
Region: World

alt.support.learning-disab

Learning disabilities, including attention deficit disorder and hyperactivity, are discussed here. There are also special groups for individual learning disabilities, and this is a good place to find out about them.

Type: Usenet newsgroup
Address: alt.support.learning-disab
Region: World

alt.support.epilepsy

Epilepsy is still poorly understood by many, but the people in this newsgroup have first-hand experience with the many forms it takes and how it affects quality of life and medical condition.

Type: Usenet newsgroup
Address: alt.support.epilepsy
Region: World

alt.support.dwarfism

Dwarfism is a hereditary growth disorder, and here's where dwarves and their families can meet to discuss the medical problems that sometimes accompany it, as well as issues of societal acceptance, careers, adaptive equipment, and more.

Type: Usenet newsgroup
Address: alt.support.dwarfism
Region: World

alt.support.cerebral-palsy

Cerebral palsy and related brain-body disorders are the subject of discussion in this newsgroup.

Type: Usenet newsgroup
Address: alt.support.cerebral-palsy
Region: World

The Black Bag Medical List

For a list of Internet sites and e-mail addresses for information on many disabilities, send a message to this address. You'll receive a regularly updated list.

Type: E-mail
Address: list@blackbag.com
Region: World

BLIND-L

This mailing list covers issues surrounding blind and visually impaired computer usage. There's relatively low traffic here.

Type: Mailing list
Address: listserv@uafsysb.uark.edu
Contact: blind-l@uafsysb.uark.edu
Region: U.S.

Blind News Digest

This is a digest of posts to the Blind News mailing list. Participants discuss aspects of being partially or totally blind. There is some discussion of experiences and anecdotes, and also medical and technical information. It is moderated.

Type: Mailing list
Address: listserv@ndsuvm1.bitnet
**Send e-mail message with body: subscribe
            bit.listserv.blindnws**
Contact: blindnws@ndsuvm1.bitnet
Region: World

BRAILLE

This is a discussion forum for the blind, carried out in Czech and English.

Type: Mailing list
Address: braille@csearn.bitnet
Region: U.S., Czech Republic, World

Canine Companions for Independence

This group trains dogs to assist people with disabilities other than blindness. These smart dogs can help people with everyday tasks like opening doors and pushing wheelchairs (they can learn up to 65 tasks!), give them signals, and be daily companions. There's lots of information about the program and how they train the dogs, plus pictures and a children's story.

Type: WWW
Address: http://grunt.berkeley.edu:80/cci /cci.html
Region: U.S.

Le Centre de Résources Technologique pour Personnes Handicapées

This site in Luxemburg has links with resources for handicapped individuals in this tiny European country, including adaptive technologies and groups. Of special interest is a project called EUROTALK, which is developing computer-based communications devices for the disabled. Some information in French and English.

Type: WWW
Address: http://www.crpht.lu/HANDITEL/ home.html
Region: Luxemburg

The CHATBACK Trust

This project began as a way to connect 100 English schools, most of them "special schools" for children with physical, mental, or emotional disabilities. It has since become an international program. See some of their ongoing work here, and learn more about the program.

Type: WWW
Address: http://www.tcns.co.uk/chatback/
Region: England, World

Cornucopia of Disability Information

This Gopher archive offers files and links to databases, demographic data, publications, legal information, and much more. Most, but not all, is U.S.-specific.

Type: Gopher
Address: val-dor.cc.buffalo.edu/1
Region: U.S.

The Deaf Magazine

This home page gives you access to current and back issue of *The Deaf Magazine*, which is also archived at the FTP and Gopher sites. It can also be delivered by fax to almost anywhere in the world.

Type: WWW
Address: http://deaf-magazine.org/~ guardian/deafmag.html
Type: FTP
Address: FTP.Deaf-Magazine.org/pub/ deaf.magazine
Region: U.S., World

The Disability Directory

This Gopher provides adaptive computing information, publications, events announcements, and data about U.S. government programs for the disabled. The document "internet-sites" is particularly useful: It has an extensive list of Usenet and BITNET discussion groups, mailing lists, and Internet sites related to various disabilities.

Type: Gopher
Address: gopher.inforM.umd.edu:70/11/ EdRes/Topic/Disability
Region: U.S.

Disability Information Archive

A large archive with information about disabilities, the Disability Information Archive includes digests, computing information, legal issues, college guides, government documents, employment, a directory of Assisted Living Centers, and a link to the National Rehabilitation Information Center.

Type: Gopher
Address: val-dor.cc.buffalo.edu
Region: U.S.

Disability International

Published by Disabled Peoples' International, a group that serves people of all abilities, *Disability International* follows world trends toward accessibility, disabled rights issues, and more with, of course, an international perspective. Available online, including the full-color covers.

Type: WWW
Address: http://darwin.technet.sg/dpa/ publication/dpi.html
Region: Canada, World

Disability Resources from Evan Kent Associates

This company sells adaptive equipment, and has created an online mall for such offerings. These items include vans, wheelchairs, devices, and so on—it's a good place to check out pricing and features without making a special trip to a medical-supplies store. There are also links here to EKA's *One Step Ahead* newsletter and other disability-related resources.

Type: WWW
Address: http://disability.com/
Region: U.S.

disABILITY Resources on the Internet

This page includes links to research programs, adaptive equipment information, handicapped advocacy groups, and more. U.S. readers may find the information about the Social Security Administration's programs for financial support especially useful.

Type: WWW
Address: http://www.eskimo.com/~ jlubin/disabled.html
Region: U.S.

DO-IT Disability Program

This University of Washington program offers access to mailing lists, newsletters, newsgroups, and Gopher sites: There is lots of interesting information for the disabled and caretakers here.

Type: Gopher
Address: hawking.u.washington.edu
Region: U.S.

ENABLEnet

This huge compendium of resources was placed online by the Disabled Peoples' Association of Singapore. Many of its offerings are specific to that city, including an excellent guide to accessibility in Singapore, but there are links to information worldwide. You can also find your way to *The Integrator*, the DPA's well-written and informative online newsletter.

Type: WWW
Address: http://www.technet.sg/dpa/
Region: Singapore, World

Gallaudet University

The world's only liberal arts university for the deaf, Gallaudet has an international reputation as a center for "deaf culture" and for research into deaf issues. This excellent site includes information on the school and its programs, as well as Gallaudet's Gopher server with many useful files and a link to the archives of its National Information Center on Deafness.

Type: WWW
Address: http://www.gallaudet.edu/
Region: U.S., World

Handicap News

This site provides material that originated on the Handicap News BBS. Topics include medical, educational and legal issues, technological aids, and the handicapped in society; the archives also include free software.

Type: Usenet newsgroup
Address: misc.handicap
Contact: wtm@bunker.shel.isc-br.com
Type: FTP
Address: handicap.shel.isc-br.com/pub/
Type: Gopher
Address: SJUVM.STJOHNS.EDU:70/11/
disabled/rrc-ftp/handicap
Region: World

Handicap Information Resources

This Japanese personal home page includes links to resources in Japan and beyond. Available in Japanese or English, these include Braille fonts, accessibility guides, leads to adaptive software, and information about disabled peoples' access to the Internet.

Type: WWW
Address: http://www.dais.is.tohoku.ac.jp/
~iwan/index_eng.html
Region: Japan, World

Independent Living Center of Western Australia

The ILC concept is more like a movement that advocates self-help for the disabled. I'm most familiar with the Berkeley, California center, which was infamous for having a "secret network" of wheelchair mechanics who could turn a slow-mo electric wheelchair into a law-breaking speed demon! I'm glad to see this concept is expanding. The Western Australia IRC provides invaluable information about special equipment and accessibility issues; advice and counseling about many issues, including careers and parenthood; and links to other IRCs in Australia and related resources. Many of their offerings have global appeal, such as a paper on how to deal with "wandering" (a common problem among those with neurological disorders), information on incontinence, and a publication on helping rural and isolated handicapped individuals.

Type: WWW
Address: http://www.iinet.com.au/~ilcwa
/ilc.html
Region: Australia

Information Technology and Disabilities

This is a moderated journal devoted to the practical and theoretical issues surrounding the development and effective use of new and emerging technologies by computer users with disabilities. Founded by EASI (Equal Access to Software and Information), "Information Technology and Disabilities" features articles on issues affecting educators, librarians, adaptive technology trainers, rehabilitation counselors, human resources professionals, and developers of adaptive computer hardware and software products.

Type: E-journal

Address: listserv@sjuvm.stjohns.edu

Send e-mail message with body: subscribe itd-jnl

Type: Gopher

Address: sjuvm.stjohns.edu

Contact: mcnulty@acfcluster.nyu.edu

Region: U.S., World

International Exchange of Experts and Information in Rehabilitation

This project of the National Institute for Disability and Rehabilitation Research in Austria helps specialists in rehabilitation network with each other. Their publications, monographs, and many files are archived here; unfortunately, this Gopher is very unreliable and frequently out of commission.

Type: Gopher

Address: ieeir.unh.edu/

Region: World

International Wheelchair Aviators

There's lots of information here about flying, gliding, parasailing, hang-gliding, and so on for those who normally get around on wheels, including links to information about where to get special hand controls, and how various countries handle the flight licensing procedure when you are disabled.

Type: WWW

Address: http://www.dsg.cs.tcd.ie/dsg_pe ople/sloubtin/IWA.html

Region: Ireland, France, World

Media Access

This mailing list is dedicated to closed-captioning, audio description, and other media access issues for the disabled. It's a forum for reporting particularly skillful or inept captioning, reporting "captioning outrages," discussing the merits of a captioning company's style, and so on. It covers TV, film, and new media, including computer games and virtual reality.

Type: Mailing list

Address: listmanager@hookup.net

Send e-mail message with body: subscribe access

Contact: owner-access@hookup.net

Region: Canada, World

Mission Handicap

Using the latest technology, the University of Lyons is trying to make disabled students welcome on campus and enhance their educational experience. Learn about their innovative program here, mostly in French, with some English translations available.

Type: WWW

Address: http://handy.univ-lyon1.fr/eng/home.html

Region: France

MS Direct

Links to U.S. and international resources regarding multiple sclerosis, including the alt.support.mult-sclerosis newsgroup, databases, and several Web sites.

Type: WWW

Address: http://www.aquila.com/dean.sporleder/ms_home/

Region: U.S., World

Neil Squire Foundation

This foundation helps those with severe disabilities through technology, including its Computer

Comfort program, which gets nursing-home residents and housebound disabled persons basic computer training and Internet access, education, needs assessment, and advocacy. There's lots here about its innovative and compassionate programs.

Type: WWW
Address: **http://mindlink.bc.ca/nsf/**
Region: Canada

Net Connections for Communications Disorders and Sciences

This file offers a long list of places to hunt down information about specific communications disorders, as well as general scientific and medical information about their causes. It's aimed at the professional or educator, but is of equal interest to those with such disorders and their families. The list includes dozens of Usenet, BITNET, and other newsgroups, as well as several mailing lists and file archives. It also offers many resources for the deaf, blind, and others whose handicaps may have an effect on speech.

Type: Gopher
Address: **una.hh.lib.umich.edu/00/inetdirs stacks/commdis%3Akuster**
Region: U.S.

Olivetti Archive for the Hearing Impaired

This site contains files about sign language, related graphics files, and more.

Type: FTP
Address: **handicap.afd.olivetti.com/pub/ hearing/**
Region: Italy, World

Project HIIT: Internet for the Hearing Impaired

Resources and databases for the deaf and hearing-impaired are linked in here, with a special emphasis on Internet access.

Type: WWW
Address: **http://biomed.nus.sg/DF/ databases.html**
Region: Singapore

Rehab Resources

There's lots of information about the Working Group on Rehabilitation Engineering at the Institute of Electronics of Vienna University of Technology, which is working on new designs for adaptive equipment and other aids for the disabled and elderly. Part of their mission is advocacy and activism as well, to bring disabled persons into the mainstream. It includes information about designing accessible WWW pages and about papers and publications on enabling technologies and design in Europe, too.

Type: WWW
Address: **http://sun4.iaee.tuwien.ac.at/ e359.3/abtb/abtb.html**
Region: Austria, World

St. John's University Electronic Rehabilitation Resource Center

This Gopher site has a huge amount of information, including publications, disability-specific files, a parent's guide to helping preschool kids with disabilities, autism, repetitive stress injury, chronic fatigue syndrome, and brain-injury information. The Equal Access to Software and Information archive is housed here, as is the WIDLIST archive, with information about several dozen mailing lists about specific acquired or congenital handicaps.

Type: Gopher
Address: **SJUVM.STJOHNS.EDU:70/11/ disabled**
Region: U.S., World

Web Server for the Visually Handicapped

This page has leads to medical data, treatment information, and enabling resources for the visually disabled or blind, including information on how blind people can access the Net.

Type:　　WWW
Address:　http://biomed.nus.sg/vh/vh.html
Region:　Singapore, World

The White Cane

A fascinating look into the world of the blind and disabled in Singapore, this online publication has photos and text about programs of the White Cane Club for the blind and their supporters, and related groups. Projects include job training in areas such as hydroponic farming, traditional Chinese massage, and foot reflexology. There are many ideas here that would work well anywhere.

Type:　　WWW
Address:　http://darwin.technet.sg/dpa/
**　　　　　publication/savh.html**
Region:　Singapore

Yellow Dream Machine Home Page

This site contains information and links relating to the rights of the disabled and disabled activism. It includes scary information about the potential impact on the disabled of the Republican "Contract with America," which will be of interest to U.S. readers.

Type:　　WWW
Address:　http://www.realtime.net/~
**　　　　　cyanosis/**
Region:　U.S., World

See also Disabilities page 173; Health and Medicine page 310; Sexuality and Gender Issues page 450

Cyberspace is the place for making the human connections you need to get over rough patches, whether it's making it through drug-use recovery or coping with illness. Most of the resources listed here are online discussion groups that bring people together via Usenet. There are also a few information sources and Web sites that exist to help and maintain people in recovery. Incidentally, despite the huge size of this section, it's hardly all-inclusive: There are probably another 100 or 200 alt.support and related groups (see the listing below for the Psychology and Support Newsgroups Pointer, which is a complete list).

Al-Anon and Alateen

These Al-Anon Family Groups are a fellowship of relatives and friends of alcoholics who believe alcoholism is a family disease, and that practicing the 12 steps can aid in recovery. Al-Anon has but one purpose: to help families of alcoholics by giving understanding and encouragement to the alcoholic. The Al-Anon list and related Web site offers information, including an international contacts list.

Type:　　Mailing list
Address:　listproc@solar.rtd.utk.edu
Send e-mail message with blank Subject
**　　　　　line and body: subscribe Al-Anon**
**　　　　　<Firstname Lastname>**
Type:　　WWW
Address:　http://solar.rtd.utk.edu/~alanon/
Region:　World

The Alcoholism and Other Drug Addictions Home Page

Some alternative views on alcoholism and its causes are available here, particularly regarding the biogenic (physical addiction) model.

Type: WWW
Address: http://hookomo.aloha.net/ ~robert/
Region: U.S.

alt.abuse.recovery

This is a very touchy issue. Emotion runs high, even when it's still below the surface. Just talking about this stuff has been known to spark violence. Here's a place where you can speak freely.

Type: Usenet newsgroup
Address: alt.abuse.recovery
Region: World

alt.irc.recovery

Internet Relay Chat (IRC) is a highly addictive way to communicate onlne interactively. "Abandon hope, all ye who <enter> here" is the message of this brand-new support group for those who'd like to quit, but can't.

Type: Usenet newsgroup
Address: alt.irc.recovery
Region: World

alt.recovery.na

Unlike alt.recovery.aa, where everyone has basically the same problem (whatever its roots) because they like the same drug, the people who post to alt.recovery.na have different problems because they like different drugs. This can result in misunderstandings and "flame wars," but the support is useful all the same.

Type: Usenet newsgroup
Address: alt.recovery.na
Region: World

alt.sexual.abuse.recovery

Just in case you thought that alt.recovery.abuse wasn't a touchy enough topic, here's where it gets really specific.

Type: Usenet newsgroup
Address: alt.sexual.abuse.recovery
Region: World

alt.support

This is the general topic of all alt.support groups. If you can't find a group that is specific enough, post here. Occasionally a thread will drift into the sociopolitical basis of some personal problem, but mostly this is just people sharing their knowledge, experiences, and good wishes. Some advice is sounder than others, but most is given in good faith.

Type: Usenet newsgroup
Address: alt.support
Region: World

alt.support.abuse-partners

Here is where people with abusive partners, as well as well as their friends, loved ones, and others who care, can share, enquire, advise, and generally commiserate in a supportive, nonthreatening, and empathetic environment with others like themselves.

Type: Usenet newsgroup
Address: alt.support.abuse-partners
Region: World

alt.support.anxiety-panic

This is a group for people who suffer from anxiety and panic attacks, as well as their significant others. It's reassuring to know you always have a place to drop in for a reality check.

Type: Usenet newsgroup
Address: alt.support.anxiety-panic
Region: World

alt.support.arthritis

This is for people who suffer from arthritis. Information about research, treatments, and physical therapy often comes through here.

Type: Usenet newsgroup
Address: alt.support.arthritis
Region: World

alt.support.asthma

Asthmatics and their families are online here, talking about this all-too-common and potentially deadly condition.

Type: Usenet newsgroup
Address: alt.support.asthma
Region: World

alt.support.cancer

Here is where people who suffer from cancer, as well as their friends, loved ones, and others who care, can find friendly and experienced voices to discuss treatment options and fears.

Type: Usenet newsgroup
Address: alt.support.cancer
Region: World

alt.support.cancer.prostate

Men with prostate cancer and their families chat here about operations, treatments, medications, and life afterwards.

Type: Usenet newsgroup
Address: alt.support.cancer.prostate
Region: World

alt.support.diabetes.kids

People who suffer from childhood-onset diabetes, as well as their parents and friends, talk here. This is an extra-valuable resource for rural diabetic kids, who may not have the benefit of a hospital-run support group.

Type: Usenet newsgroup
Address: alt.support.diabetes.kids
Region: World

alt.support.dissociation

Here is where people who dissociate, and occasionally their friends and loved ones, commiserate and express themselves in their inimitable way. It's ASCII to rivet the eye. This group is a must-read for any serious student of the psyche, not to mention of the disorder. The writing varies, but some fairly soars. The subject matter lends itself to description.

Type: Usenet newsgroup
Address: alt.support.dissociation
Region: World

alt.support.divorce

How do divorce laws vary from state to state? Where's the best deal? Can your ex's lawyer be reasoned with? How do you tell the kids? Does anybody out there ever actually see their child-support money? When will those awful phone calls stop? Are you in physical danger, or was that just the liquor talking? Here's the place to ask the experts.

Type: Usenet newsgroup
Address: alt.support.divorce
Region: World

alt.support.eating-disord

If you have an eating disorder, or think you might, or are worried that your child, friend, or relative does, here's a place to talk about it.

Type: Usenet newsgroup
Address: alt.support.eating-disord
Region: World

alt.support.ex-cult

People who have broken free from the the psychic grip of various cults (Aum Shinriko, Amway, or Jehovah's Witnesses, among others) share their experiences here. These experiences bear remarkable similarity to one another. Read and learn how to defend yourself.

Type: Usenet newsgroup
Address: alt.support.ex-cult
Region: World

alt.support.foster-parents

Here is a place where foster parents can pool their brainpower to solve those problems that are both unique to the foster-parenting relationship and common enough that no one ever has to go through it alone. Any foster parent can learn something here, make friends, and have fun. For the new foster parent this site is practically a necessity.

Type: Usenet newsgroup
Address: alt.support.foster-parents
Region: World

alt.support.grief

The will to console runs deep in the human soul. We have always reached out in times of grief, now we can reach out to the ends of the earth with a single finger.

Type: Usenet newsgroup
Address: alt.support.grief
Region: World

alt.support.headaches.migraine

Are migraine headaches really getting to you? If they are, it's easier to commiserate in silence than to have to actually talk. Find out about promising new treatments here.

Type: Usenet newsgroup
Address: alt.support.headaches.migraine
Region: World

alt.support.menopause

Women going through menopause can share words of hope here ("It's only a phase, really!"), and talk.

Type: Usenet newsgroup
Address: alt.support.menopause
Region: World

alt.support.nutty.as.a.fruitcake

This is where you'll end up if you spend too much of your life hanging around in the alt.support groups!

Type: Usenet newsgroup
Address: alt.support.nutty.as.a.fruitcake
Region: World

alt.support.obesity

For some, obesity can become a threat to health and well-being, and not everyone can shed pounds easily or safely. This is a group where these troubles are well known and solutions may be found.

Type: Usenet newsgroup
Address: alt.support.obesity
Region: World

alt.support.ostomy

People with colostomies and oleostomies have some special problems to deal with as a result of injury or illness. This is a good place to meet people who understand.

Type: Usenet newsgroup
Address: alt.support.ostomy
Region: World

alt.support.personality

Some of us have one and some of us don't. We've known that all along. But some people have extra personalities. As personalities are wont to do, they sometimes take on a life of their own, and this can be disconcerting and dangerous. Here "multiples" can meet other online, and seek help together.

Type: Usenet newsgroup
Address: alt.support.personality
Region: World

alt.support.post-polio

Here is where people who have had polio and their family members can get together and talk about the after-effects as well as new treatments and strengthening strategies.

Type: Usenet newsgroup
Address: alt.support.post-polio
Region: World

alt.support.schizophrenia

Schizophrenia as an illness is finally getting the attention it deserves, with some breakthrough drugs finally making relief possible for many without the "zombification" effects that old-line drugs like Thorazine can bring. In this support group, schizophrenics and their concerned families and friends have a chance to talk in an accepting environment.

Type: Usenet newsgroup
Address: alt.support.schizophrenia
Region: World

alt.support.short

Here's where short people and their families can discuss the current growth-hormones-for-short-kids scandal and other issues of interest. In cyberspace, we're all the same size.

Type: Usenet newsgroup
Address: alt.support.short
Region: World

alt.support.single-parents

Though demonized and scapegoated by the rhetoric of ambitious politicians, and beset with many problems (often legal) unique to them alone, single parents persevere. But they're there for each other—they have to be. These days, they're here for each other, too.

Type: Usenet newsgroup
Address: alt.support.single-parents
Region: World

alt.support.sleep-disorder

Here is where people who suffer from various sleep disorders can spend time trying to get relief. Insomniacs, in particular, are prevalent on the Internet, and not just in this group.

Type: Usenet newsgroup
Address: alt.support.sleep-disorder
Region: World

alt.support.step-parents

Though nowhere near the magnitude of those of single parents, the unique problems facing the step-parent are no cakewalk, either. Like all problems, they are the hardest if you have to figure them out by yourself. Here's where you can get some help.

Type: Usenet newsgroup
Address: alt.support.step-parents
Region: World

alt.support.stuttering

Treatment of stuttering has come a long way in just the last few years. Here's a good place to find out the latest for self-help, or for working with your kids or students.

Type: Usenet newsgroup
Address: alt.support.stuttering
Region: World

alt.support.tall

Here is where tall people, as well as their friends, can talk in a supportive and empathetic environment with others like themselves.

Type: Usenet newsgroup
Address: alt.support.tall
Region: World

alt.support.telecommute

People who telecommute can get together "at home," after work, to discuss their unique lifestyle, its unique problems, and undeniable benefits; and during work, to kill a little time at the virtual water cooler while the "boss" picks up the tab for the phone.

Type: Usenet newsgroup
Address: alt.support.telecommute
Region: World

alt.support.tinnitus

Tinnitus sufferers can chat in this group, without that annoying ringing in their ears drowning out the conversation.

Type: Usenet newsgroup
Address: alt.support.tinnitus
Region: World

alt.support.tourette

Here is where people with Tourette's Syndrome hang out and compare experiences. And what do their neighbors think? Their friends check in with fascinating tales of Tourette life, and every once in a while somebody realizes that he or she, too, has Tourette's.

Type: Usenet newsgroup
Address: alt.support.tourette
Region: World

alt.sysadmin.recovery

In the highly addictive world of computers, as in the world of illegal drugs, the people at the end of the marketing chain are known as "users." The role of the sysop is much like that of the dealer. Users pester you at all hours with their silly questions. They annoy you with their inane antics. They insult your intelligence with their lame, and often bizarre, excuses. Worse, the boss always wants results immediately—yesterday would be better—and just like Lou Reed said, "The first thing you learn is you always gotta wait." It's a rough life but at least the money's good. Commiserate here at this humor-filled online sysadmin convention.

Type: Usenet newsgroup
Address: alt.sysadmin.recovery
Region: World

The Big Book

This is the text on which AA is based. The version here is the Third Edition.

Type: WWW

Address: http://uts.cc.utexas.edu/~clyde/ BillW/BB_Introduction.html

Region: U.S.

Big Gals Unite

Look here for information on combating bad attitudes about fat folk. It includes empowering images and resources galore, including local organizations and links to the newsgroups alt.support.big-folks and soc.support.fat.acceptance.

Type: WWW

Address: http://www.lm.com/~lmann/ feminist/sizism.html

Region: World

Blain Nelson's Abuse Pages

Here you'll find domestic abuse resources especially for men: How to stop abusing, what to do if you or a friend is being abused, how to support battered women and men, and how to find help for abusers who want to change.

Type: WWW

Address: http://www.az.com/~blainn/dv

Region: U.S.

Diabetic

This list is a forum for diabetics to exchange ideas, comments, gripes, fears, even recipes, related to their condition. It has evolved into a kind of support group for people with diabetes, but welcomes other interested people.

Type: Mailing list

Address: listserv@lehigh.edu

Send e-mail message with body: subscribe: diabetic <Firstname Lastname>

Region: World

Facts for Families

This is a U.S. government series of texts on issues of interest to troubled parents—anorexia, depression, and divorce are just a few of the subjects covered. There's also information about recognizing symptoms in your children or yourself and getting help.

Type: WWW

Address: http://www.med.umich.edu/ aacap/facts.index.html

Region: U.S.

immune

The support group immune is for people with immune-system breakdowns or their symptoms, such as Chronic Fatigue Syndrome, Lupus, Candida, Hypoglycemia, multiple allergies, and some learning disabilities; and for their families, medical caretakers, and so on. The group is open to anyone anywhere in the world. Archives are available at the FTP site. Also of interest to those with HIV/AIDS, although not specifically so.

Type: Mailing list

Address: immune-request@weber.ucsd.edu

Type: FTP

Address: weber.ucsd.edu/pub/immune

Region: World

Karra's Korner

This is a general page for bringing together recovery resources, particularly around abuse issues.

Type: WWW
Address: http://www.xroads.com/ rainbow/karra.html
Region: U.S.

Medical Web

This site leads to more AA, Narcotics Anonymous, and Alateen information, including Europe- and Australia-specific sites.

Type: WWW
Address: http://www.gov.nb.ca/hotlist/ medical.htm
Region: U.S., Australia, Canada, Sweden, England, Scotland

Parent Guide to Drug Abuse

This site is about recognizing drug abuse in your kids and deciding what to do. Sponsored by Brooks Pharmaceuticals.

Type: WWW
Address: http://www.clark.net/pub/ murple/local/
Region: England

Prisoner Support

This site offers many resources for prisoners, ex-prisoners, and their friends and familes. Includes archived text of prison magazines, prisoners' writing, news, and activism information.

Type: WWW
Address: http://www.cs.oberlin.edu/ students/pjaques/prison/home .html
Region: U.S., World

Psychology and Support Newsgroups Pointer

This Web page and Gopher more than likely have leads to a Usenet newsgroup on your specific issue, including many of the groups listed here. The Pointer is also regularly updated and posted to the alt.support newsgroup.

Type: WWW
Address: http://chat.carleton.ca/~tscholbe /psych.html
Type: Gopher
Address: owl.nstn.ns.ca
Type: Usenet newsgroup
Address: alt.support
Region: World

The Recovery Home Page

This page is U.S.-based, but since these groups are worldwide, it is of interest to many. It contains lots of information about Alcoholics Anonymous, Al-Anon, Alateen, Cocaine Anonymous, and related 12-step programs.

Type: WWW
Address: http://www.shore.net/~tcfraser/ recovery.html
Region: U.S.

SafetyNet

This page is for bringing together domestic violence resources: statistics, where to get help, support groups, and more.

Type: WWW
Address: http://www.interport.net/~ asherman/dv.html
Region: U.S.

SANDS

SANDS is an Australian support group for parents who have experienced the loss of a child due to miscarriage, stillbirth, or Sudden Infant Death Syndrome. Many of the materials and texts they use are stored here, and there are also ways to make contact.

Type: WWW
Address: http://www.vicnet.net.au/vicnet/ community/sands.htm
Region: Australia

recovery

The recovery list is intended as a forum and support group for survivors of childhood sexual abuse/incest and/or their significant others. Postings are published in digest format, and contributors may post anonymously. The emphasis is on healing and recovery through the use of the 12 Steps of Alcoholics Anonymous, as adapted for this purpose.

Type: Mailing list
Address: recovery@wvnvm.wvnet.edu
Region: World

The Rainbow Connection

This is a support group for people in long-distance relationships (LDRs), and provides a forum for discussion and debate on all aspects of being in an LDR.

Type: Mailing list
Address: rainbow-request@rmit.edu.au
Region: Australia

suicide-prevention

This list is an international forum for people interested in or working in the fields of suicide prevention and crisis counseling on or off the Internet. Mental health professionals, volunteers, and Net users are all welcome to contribute to the discussion. Relevant topics include suicidal thoughts, self-injury attempts, completed suicide deaths or survivals, and education related to preventing these types of problems. It is suggested that people seeking emotional support would find one of the support-oriented mailing lists or the alt.support newsgroup hierarchy more helpful.

Type: Mailing list
Address: listserv@research.canon.oz.au
Send e-mail message with body: subscribe suicide-prevention <Firstname Lastname>
Region: Australia, World

ThisIsCrazy-L

ThisIsCrazy is an electronic action and information letter for people who experience mood swings, fright, voices, and visions. ThisIsCrazy is an electronic forum and distribution device for exchanging ways to change political systems and for distributing any information and resources that might be useful. A basic premise of science and research is also a value of ThisIsCrazy: to share your findings with others.

Type: Mailing list
Address: majordomo@netcom.com
Region: World

Unplanned Pregnancy

This pro-life site has links to resources in your area for those personally opposed to abortion but in need of help with an unplanned pregnancy. I was unable to find a similar pro-choice site, but contacting your nearest Planned Parenthood should also put you in touch with counseling, health-care, adoption, and abortion services.

Type: WWW
Address: http://copper.ucs.indiana.edu/~ ljray/lifelink.html
Region: U.S.

walkers-in-darkness

The walkers-in-darkness list is intended for sufferers from depression or bipolar disorder, as well as affected friends. This includes both "novices" and those who have learned to cope. It is not a place to get data for research or for journalism. Members should respect the privacy and the copyrights of the other members.

Type: Mailing list
Address: majordomo@world.std.com
Send e-mail message with body: info.
          walkers
Contact: dmh@world.std.com (David
          Harmon)
Region: World

DRUGS

Most of the information on illegal drugs and drug use available on the Internet is antiprohibition. Put it down to a general antigovernment stance, or to having blinders on about the ill effects of drug abuse, but it's nonetheless the simple fact of it.

I've tried to balance out this somewhat by including a few government sites that provide drug abuse statistics, information on adverse effects, and data on international antidrug efforts. This list also includes a few items relating to legal drugs and pharmaceuticals.

Alien DreamTime

Psychedelics researcher Terrence McKenna's latest video, "Alien DreamTime," is showcased here. Includes sound samples and a little info on McKenna.

Type: WWW
Address: http://organic.com/Music/City
          .o.tribes/Alien.dreamtime/index
          .html
Region: U.S., World

alt.drugs

alt.drugs is a forum where people interested in the use of mind-altering substances—not necessarily illegal ones—get together to share information and swap stories. If you are against drug use and post about it, be prepared to have lots of references and solid information on hand, since otherwise you will be flamed. alt.drugs is subdivided into a number of groups. In addition to alt.drugs, which covers everything—substances from caffeine to psychedelics have their own subgroups.

Type: Usenet newsgroup
Address: alt.drugs
Region: World

The alt.drugs FAQ List

The disclaimer for this newsgroup says that irresponsible illegal drug use should not be encouraged. That said, the majority of people who read alt.drugs do generally condone legal or illegal drug use—at length, and often at four o'clock in the morning. Their FAQs are a good source of information: some of it scientific, some wild-eyed.

Type: Usenet newsgroup
Address: alt.drugs
(FAQ list is also posted weekly to alt.answers and news.answers)
Type: FTP/Gopher
Address: ftp.bhp.com.au/internet/alt.
          drugs/drugs/alt-drugs-FAQ

Type: E-mail
Address: gnosis@brahman.nullnet.fi
Region: World

Australia and New Zealand NORML

The National Organization for the Reform of Marijuana Laws has a branch at Adelaide University. If you'd like to brainstorm the politics of marijuana law reform with them, they're only a keystroke away.

Type: E-mail (Australia)
**Address: groo@smug.student.adelaide
.edu.au
daroussy@teaching.cs.adelaide
.edu.au**
Type: E-mail (New Zealand)
Address: gkerde@genix.equinox.gen.nz
Region: Australia, New Zealand

Australian National Clearinghouse on Drug Development

Participants in this mailing list discuss pharmaceutical drug research in Australia.

Type: Mailing list
Address: listserv@cc.utas.edu.au
Contact: anchodd@cc.utas.edu.au
Region: Australia

Beer for Breakfast

Though many in alt.recovery.aa and alt.recovery.co-dependency would strongly disagree, beer is believed by many to be a form of food, or food substitute. Rich in essential carbohydrates and brimming with wholesome B vitamins, this staple of the world's diet stokes many a short-lived relationship, as well as exercising the liver and freshening the breath.

Type: Usenet newsgroup
Address: rec.food.drink.beer
Region: World

Canadian Centre on Substance Abuse

This group works to limit harm from tobacco, alcohol, and illegal drugs in Canada. Its site includes information on Canada's drug policies and prevention efforts. Text is available in English or French.

Type: WWW
Address: http://www.ccsa.ca/
Region: Canada

Canadian Hemp Activists

Yet another Canadian marijuana law reform organization, HEMP BC, has gone online in its never-ending, and perhaps futile, quest for justice.

Type: E-mail
Address: marc_emery@mindlink.bc.ca
Region: Canada

Coffee Addicts Unite

How does one make espresso in a microwave? Does coffee interfere with nutrition? What's the best method of extracting the active ingredient alone? What happens if you smoke caffeine on foil? Exactly how much caffeine does it take to actually kill you? If you read this group, you'll know.

Type: Usenet newsgroup
Address: alt.drugs.caffeine
Region: World

Commission on Narcotic Drugs

This is the home page for the UN-sponsored CND, an international drug research and scheduling authority.

Type: WWW
Address: http://www.undcp.org/cnd.html
Region: World

Consciousness Research

Before you start altering yours, why not check out the latest research on just what "consciousness" is? This mailing list is a scientific and academic attempt to understand and discuss what physical—and, yes, even spiritual—phenomena make up what we call consciousness, unconsciousness, and states in between. Serious research into the effects of psychedelic drugs has played no small part in this quest.

Type: Mailing list
Address: LISTSERV@NKI.BITNET
**Address: LISTSERV%NKI.BITNET@CUNYVM
            .CUNY.EDU**
**Send e-mail message with body:
            SUBSCRIBE PSYCHE-D <Firstname
            Lastname>**
Type: Gopher
**Address: frontier.unl.edu.:2009/11/
            psyche-l**
Type: FTP
Address: ftp.cs.monash.edu.au/psyche
Region: World

Crime and the Drug War

This is an article on the effect of alcohol and drug prohibition on the U.S. crime rate.

Type: WWW
**Address: http://w3.ag.uiuc.edu/Liberty/
            Tales/CrimeAndDrugWar.Html**
Region: U.S.

The Deoxyribonucleac Hyperdimension

This site includes Timothy Leary's update of the *Tibetan Book of the Dead,* psyche-apocalyptic mumbo-jumbo, Robert Anton Wilson, Terrance McKenna, and more.

Type: WWW
**Address: http://www.intac.com/~dimitri/
            dh/deoxy.html**
Region: World (including other worlds…)

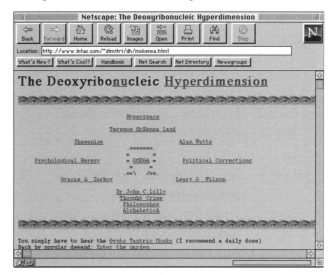

The Drug Culture Chats

Here the overwhelmingly dominant topic is the reform of marijuana laws, though to a certain degree Usenet's ubiquitous flirting and flaming creeps in, sometimes in the same post. (Some customs are held in common by all cultures.)

Type: Usenet newsgroup
Address: alt.drugs.culture
Region: World

Drug Info Library

This Gopher site has files on all sorts of drugs, from the text of LSD inventor Albert Hoffman's *LSD: My Problem Child* to information on natural cancer treatments.

Type: Gopher
**Address: wiretap.spies.com/11/Library/
            Fringe/Pharm**
Region: World

The Drug Price Project Report

Of use to buyers, sellers, and law enforcers, this information has been collected through e-mail from a number of helpful contributors. It is posted every month on alt.drugs, alt.drugs.psychedelics, alt.-drugs.pot, and alt.drugs.hard.

Type: Usenet newsgroup
Address: rich@weeds.xs4all.nl
Type: WWW
**Address: http://www.paranoia.com/
            drugs/**
Type: FTP
**Address: hyperreal.com:/drugs/misc/
            price.report.non-us**
**Address: hyperreal.com:/drugs/misc/
            price.report.us**
Type: Mailing list
Address: report@weeds.xs4all.nl
**Send e-mail message with body: S <Your
            E-mail Address>**
Region: Holland, U.S., World

Drug Abuse in Canada

Here's a place to get the most recent statistics on drug use in the Great White North, plus studies on causes and effects.

Type: WWW
Address: http://www.ccsa.ca/stats.htm
Region: Canada

Drunks Online

They're abusers of ethanol. How could they do such a thing to themselves? Why, the very idea! It's embalming fluid they're drinking, that's what it is.

Type: Usenet newsgroup
Address: alt.drunken.bastards
Region: World

The Finnish Cannabis Society

The home page of Suomen Kannabisyhdistys is available in Finnish, Swedish, and English. It has by far the most amusing and informative set of links to drug-related material on the Internet.

Type: WWW
Address: http://katto.kaapeli.fi/~sky/
Region: Finland

German Cops for Drug-Law Reform

Bundesarbeitsgemeinschaft Kritischer Polizistinnen und Polizsten is an organization of German police officers who favor drug law reform. They discuss their ideas here, in German.

Type: E-mail
Address: R.Borchers@cl-hh.comlink.de
Region: Germany

The Growing of the Green

George Washington did it. So did Thomas Jefferson. The ancient and venerable tradition has in no way died out. Au contraire, now that marijuana is worth more than gold, everyone wants in on the act. See alt.drugs.pot.cultivation for the latest techniques and warnings.

Type: Usenet newsgroup
Address: alt.drugs.pot.cultivation
Region: World

Hard Drug Discussion

Here's where the hard-core drug users hang out, get down, and pass on the lore of their tribe. Cotton fever got you down? Think that lump on your neck might be AIDS? Check in here. If the stuff was legal you'd never steal another computer, but as long as you have it around, you might as well use it.

Type: Usenet newsgroup
Address: alt.drugs.hard
Region: World

Hemp Is Not (Necessarily) a Drug

This is the place for in-depth discussions about various other uses of the plant, with a focus on industrial use.
Type: Usenet newsgroup
Address: alt.hemp
Region: World

High Times Online

This Gopher archives the American druggie magazine *High Times,* for all those articles you were maybe too zonked to actually read.
Type: Gopher
Address: echonyc.com/11/Pub/HighTimes
Region: U.S.

Homeopathic Drugs

Homeopathy works on the principle that a miniscule amount of what produces your symptoms could produce a vaccinelike boost to your immune system, and a cure. Does it work? See the research here in the FAQ on homeopathic drugs.
Type: WWW
**Address: http://community.net/~neils/faq
hom.html**
Region: World

Hooked on the Internet!

It's the most addictive drug of all! Started as a joke (and still funny) this group is a place where computer addicts bemoan their carpal tunnel syndrome at 60 words per minute. They don't call people with computers "users" for nothing.
Type: Usenet newsgroup
Address: alt.drugs.usenet
Region: World

HyperReal

As a public service to the rave scene, this page offers information on drugs frequently used in that mileau, such as Ecstacy and LSD, including warnings and cautionary tales. It also features Lamont Granquist's list of links to informtion on psychedelics.
Type: FTP
Address: ftp.hyperreal.com/drugs/
Type: WWW
**Address: http://www.hyperreal.com/
drugs/**
Region: World

International Narcotics Control Board

The United Nations Drug Control Programme supports the International Narcotics Control Board, which endeavors to halt international drug trafficking and the diversion of chemicals that could be used to make drugs from legit manufacturing use. Text is available in French, Spanish, and English.
Type: WWW
**Address: http://www.undcp.org/en_incb
home.html**
Region: World

Italian Anti-Prohibitionists

CORA, Coordinamento Radicale Antiproibizionista, is part of the Transnational Radical Party, which organizes primarily online. Take the Internet straight to their BBS, and check out Conference Drugs and News CORA for information on CORA activities.

Type: Telnet
Address: telnet agora.stm.it
Sign in as "walk"
Region: Italy

Libertarian Alliance

The Libertarian Alliance supports drug law reform, as well as all other aspects of personal freedom in general.

Type: E-mail
Address: liberty@capital.demon.co.uk
Region: England

Liberty Activist List

So you're sick of the War on (some) Drugs, are you? You're not alone. Here's an international list of over 200 organizations that support drug law reform. Although most of them are in the U.S., the list stretches from Sydney, Australia, where it was compiled, to Youngstorget, Norway, by way of Ljubljana, Slovenia and Ucluelet, British Columbia. It's posted monthly to the newsgroups listed below.

Type: Usenet newsgroups
Addresses: alt.activism
alt.drug
talk.politics.drugs
alt.answers
talk.answers
news.answers
Contact: aldis@zeta.org.au
Region: Australia, World

Mind-L

Mind-L is a discussion group for people interested in mind-altering techniques in general, and mind machines (light and sound, TENS/CES, electromagnetic pulse, floatation) and biofeedback equipment in particular. Related topics covered here include smart nutrients, hypnosis, relaxation techniques, and subliminal tapes and videos. Conversation ranges from serious research to home electronics to amateur personal observations. This group does not cover hallucinatory drugs. It's archived at the Gopher site.

Type: Mailing list
Address: listproc@gate.net
Send e-mail message with body: subscribe
mind-l <Firstname Lastname>
Region: World

Mizuno Pharmacies Home Page

How come you can't buy Tylenol at the drugstore in Japan? One of Japan's big pharmaceutical companies provides answers to the Internet public in English at this site. It covers over the counter (OTC) drugs and pharmacies in Japan—what's available, how to get it, how the Japanese pharmacy systems works. Also has info on Mizuno's staff, theses of master pharmacy students, and other information.

Type: WWW
Address: http://www.drug.com/Welcome
.html
Region: Japan

National Clearinghouse for Alcohol and Drug Information

NCADI is a service center for substance abuse prevention sponsored by the Substance Abuse and Mental Health Services Administration of the U.S. Public Health Service. It's also the world's largest resource for drug information and abuse-prevention materials for health professionals, educators, businesses, and individuals. Some educational materials are available in Spanish and other languages.

Type: WWW
Address: http://www.health.org
Region: U.S.

Outreach to Addicts

ADUN, the Injecting Drug User Group Network, promotes drug law reform, harm reduction, education, outreach, and research.

Type: E-mail
Address: spike@bazza.ak.planet.co.nz
Region: New Zealand

Paranoia on Drugs

This site contains all sorts of drug information, with a generally "pro" standpoint—news, medical data, drug testing, and more are included.

Type: WWW
**Address: http://www.paranoia.com/
            drugs/**
Region: World

Pharmaceutical Drugs

The sci.med.pharmacy group is a good place for technical discussions about pharmaceutical drugs and the profession of pharmacy, but this group is in no way devoid of humor. While it's not a Physicians Desk Reference online, where else can you learn what possible side effects chromium picolinate might have on a diabetic and hear requests for EMU oil on the same day?

Type: Usenet newsgroup
Address: sci.med.pharmacy
Region: World

Psychedelics Discussion

Who needs a color monitor, anyhow?

Type: Usenet newsgroup
Address: alt.drugs.psychedelics
Region: World

Scientific Discussion of "Smart Drugs"

The alt.psychoactives newsgroup deals primarily with nootropics—"smart drugs." This group is for serious "scientific" discussion by mostly laypersons on the reputed benefits of the stuff.

Type: Usenet newsgroup
Address: alt.psychoactives
Region: World

The "Smart Drugs" File Archive

They're called nootropics. They don't get you high, but they are said to heighten cognitive abilities in a number of ways, primarily by being rich in nutrients that contain the natural precursors of vital neurotransmitters. Read the FAQs and decide for yourself.

Type: FTP
**Address: ftp.hyperreal.com:/drugs/
            nootropics**
Region: World

Smoking: The Legal Addiction

A place for those addicted to the government-subsidized drug, whose lethal swath is what keeps Social Security solvent. But is it the tobacco itself that kills you? Or is it the additives? Opinions vary. Discuss the evidence here.

Type: Usenet newsgroup
Address: alt.smokers
Region: World

This Is Your Brain on Drugs, Personified

Hemp is the answer…uh…what was the question?

Type: Usenet newsgroup
Address: alt.drugs.pot
Region: World

Underground Chemistry

This is the home of the ASCII molecules, the straight-edge flamers, and the underground chef. Here the furtive and free but frustrated egos get to show off their chops in front of the world. Content ranges from the highly technical and arcane to totally silly, sometimes in the same post. Some of these guys are good at what they do. Others are poisoning your children for profit.

Type: Usenet newsgroup
Address: alt.drugs.chemistry
Region: World

World Wide Drugs

This site's a front end that helps you search the Internet for pharmaceutical info. It's maintained by a practicing pharmacist, professionally oriented, and includes archives of journals and research data as well as international pharmaceutical database links.

Type: WWW
Address: http://community.net/~neils/ new.html
Region: World

ECONOMICS

1) *causing gloom or misery; depressing; 2) dark and gloomy; bleak; dreary; 3) depressed; miserable.* That's the Webster's dictionary definition of the word "dismal." Economics has long been described as "the dismal science," and for good reason. The statistics economists must crunch are often the data of misery and poverty. This section presents a number of resources for obtaining, analyzing and discussing those numbers—and some economics jokes for when you, too, begin to feel dismal.

alt.politics.economics

This newsgroup is where economists and other pundits hold forth on war, poverty, and other political facts of life that impact economics.

Type: Usenet newsgroup
Address: alt.politics.economics
Region: World

Asian Development Bank

The Asian Development Bank, a development finance institution consisting of 55 members, is engaged in promoting the economic and social progress of its developing member countries in the Asian and Pacific region. Its site includes information about new and ongoing projects, Asian Development Outlook online, news releases, and links to many other development and economics sites.

Type: WWW
Address: http://www.asiandevbank.org/
Region: Asia

Berkelely Roundtable on Economics

BRIE is a think tank that pursues focused research in areas ranging from international trade and investment to technology development and conversion. These individual projects then inform BRIE's wider theoretical formulations about economic dynamics, trends, industrial structures, and their implications for political relations.

Type: WWW
Address: http://server.berkeley.edu/BRIE/
Region: World

Bill Goff's Resources for Economists List

As its title implies, this site collects together many mostly academic links to economic data, files, papers, and tools. It's well worth checking into.

Type: WWW
Address: http://econwpa.wustl.edu/other econ.html
Region: World

Centre d'Études et de Recherches Économiques et Sociales (CERES)

Find out here about this Tunisian school's educational and research programs, which includes research projects into markets, poverty, and the role of women in economic development. There are also a number of projects underway here in cooperation with European nations, especially regarding the cause of outmigration from Tunisia to Europe. Some documents are in French, some in English.

Type: Gopher
Address: gopher.rnrt.tn:70/00c%3A/ organise/ceres.txt
Region: Tunisia

CERRO-L

This is the electronic newsletter of the Central European Regional Research Organization, a joint initiative of the University of Economics and Business Administration in Vienna, the Slovak Academy of Sciences, and the University of North Carolina at Chapel Hill. Issues of economic development in Eastern and Central Europe are the subject.

Type: Mailing list
Address: cerro-l@aearn.bitnet
Region: Slovakia, Eastern Europe, Central Europe

clari.biz.economy.world

Economy-related stories that cover the international spectrum are collected and mailed to you via this newsgroup.

Type: ClariNet newsgroup
Address: clari.biz.economy.world
Region: World

CoombsPaper Archive

This Asian/Pacific Studies site's files include extensive studies of the economies of Asian and Pacific nations.

Type: FTP
Address: coombs.anu.edu.au
Region: Australia, Asia

Data Research Africa

DRA is a private South African economics and marketing research firm. It charges for specific services, but can provide some information and analysis on the nations of southern Africa.

Type: WWW
Address: http://www.cstat.co.za:80/ dradata/index.html
Region: South Africa

E-EUROPE

This mailing list is home to lively discussions on doing business in Eastern Europe, and on the transition of Eastern European countries to market economies.

Type: Mailing list
Address: e-europe@ncsuvm.cc.ncsu.edu
Region: Eastern Europe

econ-dev

This mailing list is for those who want to share information and network with professionals in economic development.

Type: Mailing list
Address: majordomo@pipeline.csn.net
Send e-mail message with body: subscribe econ-dev
Contact: majordomo@lists.csn.net
Region: World

econ-soc-devt

This multidisciplinary mailing list is for academic discussion of national economic and social development, especially for developing countries and countries in transition.

Type: Mailing list
Address: mailbase@mailbase.ac.uk
Send e-mail message with body: Subscribe econ-soc-devt <Firstname Lastname>
Region: World

economic-growth

This discussion list about economic growth is aimed at all researchers who are working in the field of economic growth, and at those who export concepts and/or methodology from that field to their own. Everyone with an interesting suggestion, new approach, problem, abstract, data set, or announcement is invited to submit it to this list.

Type: Mailing list
Address: majordomo@ufsia.ac.be
Send e-mail message with body: HELPINFO economic-growth END
Contact: DSE.VANHOUDT.P@ALPHA.UFSIA. AC.BE (Patrick Vanhoudt)
Region: World

Economics Gopher Server

This is a database of economists and how to contact them, and also includes all sorts of archives, calls for papers, and other items. It's aimed mainly at academics and serious researchers. Includes much information on Europe and Asia, international trade, and NAFTA.

Type: Gopher
Address: niord.shsu.edu:70/11gopher_root %3a%5b_DATA.ECONOMICS%5d
Region: World

Economics Journals on the Net

A huge archive of online economic journals, from A (Agricultural Economics) to T (Theory and Decision). Most are in English. Among the non-U.S. titles are the *Pacific-Basin Finance Journal*, *Labour Economics* (U.K.), the *Indian Economic and Social History Review*, and the *European Economic Review*. This archive is invaluable for any student of economics and economic theory, as well as those interested in how economics impacts on the political and social worlds.

Type: WWW
Address: http://www.hkkk.fi/~tormaleh/ journals.html
Region: Finland, World

Economics Schools Online

This page, maintained at the University of Victoria, contains leads to most other Economics departments online. It's a long, long list, with entries for Australia, New Zealand, most European countries, Japan, and the U.S. Hardly complete, of course, as it virtually ignores the non-European nations of the Southern Hemisphere, as well as Eastern Europe and most of Asia.

Type: WWW
Address: http://sol.uvic.ca/econ/depts .html
Region: Europe, New Zealand, Australia, Philippines, Japan, Canada, U.S.

Economics Working Papers Archive

Provides access to working papers on all areas of economics that have been posted online. Subjects range from game theory to international trade; it also includes crunchable data sets and economics software. The archive is searchable by keyword, author, and title, and has links to other economics resources.

Type: WWW
Address: http://econwpa.wustl.edu/
Type: Gopher
Address: econwpa.wustl.edu/
Type: FTP
Address: econwpa.wustl.edu/econ-wp/
Region: World

Economics WWW Page at Helsinki

Extensive guide to online economics resources, including statistics, newsgroups, mailing lists, publications, economics departments at universities worldwide, databases, and more.

Type: WWW
Address: http://www.helsinki.fi/~lsaarine /econ.html
Region: Finland, World

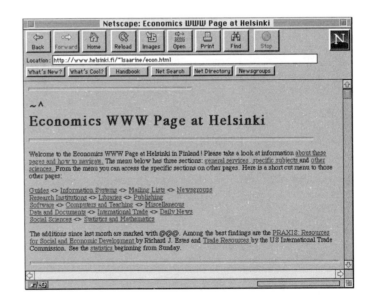

ECONOMY

This discussion list is focused on the problems of emerging economies in the Third World.

Type: Mailing list
Address: economy@tecmtyvm.bitnet
Send e-mail message with body: subscribe ECONOMY
Region: World

E-EUROPE

This discussion list is focused on the economies of Eastern Europe.

Type: Mailing list
Address: listserv@pucc.princeton.edu
Send e-mail message with body: sub E-EUROPE
Contact: info-request@tradent.wimsey .bc.ca
Region: Eastern Europe

A Guide to Statistical Computing Resources on the Internet

Lots of pointers toward software, data sets, and other resources for those using computers as statistical tools for dissecting economics can be found here. Includes many resources for the statistical programs SAS and SPSS, as well as BMDP, S, LISREL, and others.

Type: WWW
Address: http://asa.ugl.lib.umich.edu/ch docs/statistics/stat_guide_home .html
Type: Gopher
Address: una.hh.lib.umich.edu/00/inetdirs stacks/statistics%3avarnweise
Region: World

International Trade and Commerce

This list is for discussions of international trade, commerce, and the global economy, including posting company profiles, trade leads, and topics pertaining to entrepreneurial ventures.

Type: Mailing list
Address: info-request@tradent.wimsey.bc.ca
Region: World

Jokes about Economists and Economics

If reading all those depressing statistics about the world economy is starting to make you lose your sense of humor, stop in here.

Type: WWW
Address: http://www.etla.fi/pkm/joke .html
Region: World

Manchester Information Datasets and Associated Services

MIDAS provides a National Datasets Service to universities throughout the U.K. (and to you), utilizing the talents of a huge Cray supercomputer to analyze and interpret census, socio-economic, and other data sets.

Type: WWW
Address: http://netec.mcc.ac.uk:80/
Region: England, Scotland, Wales, Northern Ireland

MERCOSUL

This is the Gopher to go to for Brazilian economic and development information, in Portuguese.

Type: Gopher
Address: gopher.cr-df.rf.rnp.br:70/11/ assunto/mercosul
Region: Brazil

Ministry of the Economy and Public Works and Services of Argentina

This well-organized and attractively designed government site brings together economic statistics, information about research programs, and public economic development projects in one place. At least some information is available in English; most original data is in Spanish.

Type: WWW
Address: http://www.mecon.ar/default .htm
Region: Argentina

Murdoch University

A small section of journals on economics can be found here, along with a little Australia-specific information.

Type: FTP
Address: infolib.murdoch.edu.au
Region: Australia

National Centre for Social and Economic Modelling

This Canberra server is dedicated to articles about micro-simulation and tools for economic research.

Type: FTP
Address: natsem.canberra.edu.au
Region: Australia

The NetEc Project

NetEc is a volunteer effort to improve communication about research in economics via electronic media. It consists of information on printed working papers, links to full-text electronic working papers, and the Code for Economics and Econometrics, all with a common search system.

Type: WWW
Address: http://cs6400.mcc.ac.uk/NetEc .html
Region: England

Nova Scotia Economic Data

This coastal Canadian province has put all its current economic data online.

Type: WWW
Address: http://www.cfn.cs.dal.ca/ Govern ment/NovaScotia/ DoF-Statistics/index.html
Region: Canada

Pacific Region Forum on Business and Management Communication

The Gopher server of a conference on Pacific nations trade, this site offers current data and analysis from experts.

Type: Gopher
Address: hoshi.cic.sfu.ca/11/dlam/ business/forum
Region: Asia, Australia, U.S.

Penn World Economic Tables

The Penn World Tables are currently comprised of data for 152 countries and 29 subjects. It's fundamental and invaluable data for students, researchers, and writers, as well as those with a casual interest in economics.

Type: WWW
Address: http://cansim.epas.utoronto.ca: 5680/pwt/pwt.html
Region: World

Post-Keynesian Thought Archive

Catch up on the latest economic theories here. Environment and Game Theory, the new Growth Theory, and more.

Type: Gopher
Address: gopher://csf.colorado.edu:70/11/econ
Region: World

Queen's University, Kingston, Ontario, Economics Department

Another economics department on the Internet, this Canadian school's archive specializes in estimation and inference in econometrics.

Type: FTP
Address: qed.econ.queensu.ca
Region: Canada

The Russian Economy Resource Center

This Seattle-based resource pulls together all sorts of statistical, demographic, and socio-economic information on Russia. It's very thorough.

Type: WWW
Address: http://www.eskimo.com:80/~bwest/rerc.html
Region: Russia

Service de Prestations Informatique

This site, maintained by the École Normale Supérieure, has a small section of data dealing with primarily French economics.

Type: FTP
Address: ftp.ens.fr
Region: France

sci.econ

General discussion on economics for professionals and students takes place here.

Type: Usenet newsgroup
Address: sci.econ
Region: World

sci.econ.research

Research in all fields of economics and the latest scientific tools for understanding trends and predicting patterns is discussed on this moderated mailing list. It's archived at the Web site.

Type: Usenet newsgroup
Address: sci.econ.research
Type: WWW
Address: http://walras.econ.duke.edu/
Region: World

Social Sciences Data Center and Geographic Information Systems Lab

The University of Virginia lab has developed a forms interface for access to data from the Regional Economic Information System (REIS) CD-ROM, now available via the World Wide Web. You can analyze data from the U.S., or specific regions, states, counties, or MSAs; or select variables from REIS income and employment data, and specify years to be displayed.

Type: WWW
Address: http://www.lib.virginia.edu/socsci/
Region: U.S.

The World Bank

The World Bank Group is the International Bank for Reconstruction and Development (IBRD), the International Development Association (IDA), the International Finance Corporation (IFC), and the Multilateral Investment Guarantee Agency (MIGA). IBRD is the main lending arm of the World Bank. IDA is the World Bank affiliate that lends to the poorest countries. IFC finances private-sector projects, and advises businesses and governments on investment issues. MIGA promotes foreign direct investment through guarantees, policy advice, and promotional services. Since the World Bank literally runs the economies of many impoverished nations through its demands for hard-currency payments on loans to government elites, it's an important source for information.

Type: WWW
Address: http://www.worldbank.org/
Region: World

Yahoo's Guide to Economics Online

Yahoo's index of pointers to foreign development groups and other economics-related sites includes both U.S.-based and global sites.

Type: WWW
**Address: http://www.yahoo.com/
Economy/Organizations/
International_Development/**
Region: U.S., World

EDUCATION

See also Appendix C

The Net is a great resource for teachers, school administrators, counselors, and, of course, students. Since universities are an integral part of the Net, you have access to materials and course information from education departments at colleges around the world. There are also a number of other Net-based resources such as classroom exchange programs, professional newsletters, and courseware.

Homeschooling students and rural classrooms can gain access to the resources of large institutions, and even attend classes online.

Academic Software

Here's an archive of academic software for sharing, including European Academic Software Association award winners.

Type: WWW
**Address: http://askhp.ask.uni-karlsruhe
.de/welcome.html**
Region: Germany, Europe

Adam und der Rechenriese

One of the neatest benefits of the Net is that it lets you share learning materials with teachers and students worldwide. This will be especially useful for ESL and foreign-language teachers. Here's an example (loosely translated, the title means "Adam and the Learning Journey"). You can get a playable demo of this German MS-DOS program for first-grade mathematics on this page, as well as some digitized videos of the program.

Type: WWW
**Address: http://trevaris.uni.trier.de/~
mausz/ariese.html**
Region: Germany

African Educational Research Network

AERN brings together educators from African and North American universities to share reports of research studies and to consider developmental issues.

Type: Gopher
**Address: ra.cs.ohiou.edu/11/dept.servers/
            aern/**
Region: Africa, U.S., Canada

Alternative Education

Look here for leads to sites covering alternative education systems, including Waldorf schools, Montessori schools, and homeschooling.

Type: WWW
**Address: http://www.yahoo.com/
            Education/Alternative/**
Region: U.S., Canada, Russia, Norway, World

Association for Experiential Education Home Page

The AEE is an international professional organization that believes the best way to learn is by doing. It sponsors conferences, has a newsletter (available online here), and fosters contacts between its members around the world. Many AEE members are involved in wilderness or environmental training programs.

Type: WWW
**Address: http://www.princeton.edu/~
            rcurtis/aee.html**
Region: U.S., Canada, Costa Rica, Germany,
            Netherlands, New Zealand, South
            Africa

Chinese Academic Link

This project, carried on primarily by overseas Chinese academics, sets up lecture series, exchange programs, cooperative research projects, and assistance programs for educators, schools, and students in China. This site also has links to CREN, China's academic network on the Internet.

Type: WWW
**Address: http://www.ifcss.org:8001/
            www/pub/org/cal-aeic/.index
            .html**
Region: China

The Commonwealth of Learning

The Commonwealth of Learning provides teaching materials, educational resources, and more to schools and teachers in the mostly English-speaking nations of the (British) Commonwealth in Africa, Asia, Southeast Asia, the Caribbean, the Pacific, Europe, Canada, and the U.K. Programs include fellowships, scholarships, and developmental programs, especially in capacity building and distance learning. Includes links to universities and large file archives.

Type: WWW
**Address: http://www.col.org/0/html/
            col.htm**
Type: FTP
Address: ftp.COL.org/pub/
Region: World

Cyberspace Middle School

This Web page features resources and special programs for seventh, eighth, and ninth graders who are using the Net to get an education. Links include Surf City, an amalgam of hot links, Virtual Bus Stops, links with middle school classes online, and resources for teachers.

Type: WWW
**Address: http://www.scri.fsu.edu/~
            dennisl/CMS.html**
Region: World

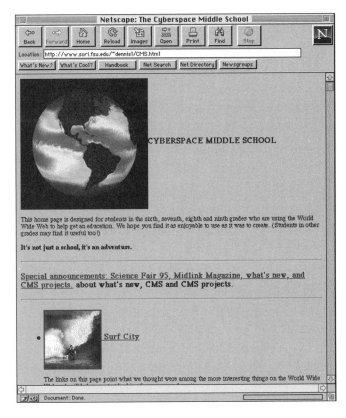

EDNET Guide to Usenet Newsgroups

These sites offer a list of education-related Usenet newsgroups, updated fairly regularly.
Type: WWW
**Address: http://netspace.students.brown
            .edu/eos/usenet_plain.html**
Type: FTP
Address: nic.umass.edu/pub/ednet
Region: World

Educating International Students

Working with international students and exchange students is the subject of the INT-ED mailing list.
Type: Mailing list
Address: listserv@msu
**Send e-mail message with body:
            SUBSCRIBE INT-ED**
Region: World

Education in Ethiopia

Need to know about the education system in the home country of a new student? Here's an example of what's available online. This is a well-written history of the Ethiopian education system, with illustrations and information about changes that have occurred since the 1970s, and their results.
Type: WWW
Address: http://rs6.loc.gov/et_02_07.html
Region: Ethiopia

Education Journals

Electronic access to education journals online, most from the U.S. but including *Education, Research and Perspectives* from Australia, *Revista Electronica de Investigacion y Evaluacion Educativa* from Spain, some English titles, and a few other education resources.
Type: Gopher
**Address: info.asu.edu/11/asu-cwis/
            education/journals**
Region: U.S., Spain, Australia, England

Education Mailing Lists

A list of education-related mailing lists, ordered by subject, is archived at this site. It includes hundreds of titles, from the Brazilian Students networking list to the Dead Teachers Society list, where teacher "burnout" and how to survive is the topic.

Type: FTP
Address: nic.umass.edu/pub/ednet/
           educatrs.lst
Region: U.S., World

Education Network Resources

This Gopher site is full of files, including newsletters, online and distance learning information, multimedia and graphics files for educators, and the Project Gutenberg electronic books archive.

Type: Gopher
Address: digital.cosn.org/11/Resources%
           20on%20the%20Network/
           Network%20Resources%
Region: U.S., World

Education Resource Leads

Leads to all aspects of education on the Net, including K–12 education, journals for teachers, literacy programs, special education, guidance resources, grant programs, and so forth.

Type: WWW
Address: http://www.yahoo.com/
           Education/
Region: U.S., World

Educational Technology

TECFA (Technologies de Formation et Apprentissage) is a teaching and research unit within the School of Psychology and Education at the University of Geneva. This site includes information about TECFA courses and research, and links to many more education-related sites.

Type: WWW
Address: http://tecfa.unige.ch/
Region: Switzerland

Educators Helping the World

This site offers links to home pages of charitable or missionary groups who specialize in educational services where they're most needed worldwide.

Type: WWW
Address: http://www.netmarket.com/isa/
           html/education.html
Region: World

The EdWeb Project

This is a central gathering place for Internet information on education. It includes links to discussion groups, resources, and files—most but not all U.S.-based.

Type: WWW
Address: http://edweb.cnidr.org:90/
Region: U.S., World

European Schools Project

The name is a bit of a misnomer, as participants in this project have grown to include schools in Asia and the Americas. Over 350 schools are doing education and telecommunications experiments here, and this site in the Netherlands serves as a support system for their efforts.

Type: WWW
Address: http://www.educ.uva.nl/ESP/
Region: Europe, Canada, Chile, Iceland, Japan,
           Russia, Ukraine, U.S.

The Global Classroom

Chat on the GLOBALED list about processes and resources for international education.

Type: Mailing list
Address: listserv@unmvm
Send e-mail message with body:
           SUBSCRIBE GLOBALED
Region: World

Global Educational Networking Discussion

Get on the GNET list to find out about computer communication in developing countries—and how it could be that Net access is better in many Third World schools than in South Central Los Angeles.

Type: Mailing list
Address: listserv@gnet_request@dhvx20 .csudh.edu
Region: World

Global Schoolhouse

Global Schoolhouse is an experiment in connecting K–12 schools via the Internet, both nationally and globally. An archive of supporting material is stored at this Gopher site.

Type: Gopher
Address: vinca.cnidr.org/
Region: World

Homeschooling Discussion

Two major newsgroups are devoted to chatting about homeschooling issues, problems, and curricula. The first is especially for Christian homeschooling families, the second for those taking a secular approach.

Type: Usenet newsgroup
Address: misc.education.home-school .christian
Address: misc.education.homeschool.misc
Region: World

The Incomplete Guide to the Internet

Especially for K–12 teachers and students, this document is a resource guide and how-to manual for using the Internet and other telecommunications options in the classroom.

Type: FTP
Address: ftp.ncsa.uiuc.edu/Education/ Education_Resources/Incomplete_ Guide
Region: U.S.

Informatica y Computacion en Educacion

The Spanish-language IEDUCOM concentrates on the use of computers and networking technologies to enhance the classroom experience.

Type: Mailing list
Address: listserv@usachvm1
Send e-mail message with body:
SUBSCRIBE IEDUCOM
Region: World

Information for Educators

This site presents a long list of resources for teachers, mostly U.S.-based but with some multicultural and international content. Items range from the San Francisco Exploratorium's science offerings to a directory of educational researchers.

Type: Gopher
Address: info.asu.edu:70/11/asu-cwis/ education/other/select
Region: U.S., World

International Development Exchange

This nonprofit social change organization sponsors the School Partnership Program, which partners educators or entire schools with an overseas community. The Partners prepare educational presentations and projects that the overseas community has requested.

Type: WWW
Address: http://www.digimark.net/idex/ school-prog.html
Region: U.S., World

International Student Organizations

Here's a list with many hotlinks to student organizations worldwide, mostly for college and graduate students.

Type: WWW
Address: http://www.informatik .rwth-aachen.de/AEGEE/orgas/ imiso.html
Region: World

JANET Network

JANET is an education and research network in the U.K., administered currently by British Telecom. At this site there are archives of JANET-related news and user group activities, access to other education Gopher sites in U.K., address lists, and more.

Type: Gopher
Address: news.janet.ac.uk
Region: England, Scotland, Wales, Ireland

Jon's Home-Schooling Page

This page is oriented more to the Christian home-schooling community but it has links to resources of interest to all homeschooling families. It includes links to homeschooling kids' own Web pages.

Type: WWW
Address: http://www.armory.com/~jon/ hs/HomeSchool.html#
Region: U.S., World

The Journey North

A good example of the Net's educational possibilities, this site is a collaboration between three U.S. colleges and an international team of explorers who went on a research expedition through the Canadian Arctic in 1994. The Inuit legends and science presented here mix well, as the scientists made their research available online and sweetened it with photos, weather information, and anthropological data.

Type: WWW
Address: http://ics.soe.umich.edu/ed712/ IAPIntro.html
Region: Canada

K–12 African Studies Materials

All sorts of African and African-American curriculum materials are stored here, on subjects like dance, science, music, and literature.

Type: WWW
Address: http://www.sas.upenn.edu/ African_Studies/K-12/menu_ K-12.html
Region: Africa, U.S.

K–12 Resource Index

There are tons of resources listed here for teachers and students, from where to access weather data for classroom use to full online schools. Includes a link to the World Wide Web Digital Library for Schoolkids, as well as an electronic textbook archive.

Type: WWW
Address: http://www.yahoo.com/ Educa tion/K_12
Region: World

Kids from Kanata

This is a learning project under development in Canada to help teachers and students use computer learning tools to better understand native Canadians ("Indians") and Canadian history. It's a good example of multimedia research that can be used in the classroom.

Type: WWW
Address: http://schoolnet.carleton.ca/ demo/elijah/html/kanata.html
Region: Canada

Kidsphere

Kidsphere is an international mailing list that promotes networking among K–12 teachers and other educational personnel involved in globally oriented education.

Type: Mailing list
Address: kidsphere-request@vms.cis.pitt .edu
Contact: kidsphere@vms.cis.pitt.edu
Region: World

Linking with Ireland

This mailing list is intended to foster joint research, collaboration, and contacts between educators in Ireland and the rest of the world.

Type: Mailing list
Address: IRL-NET
listserv@irlearn
Region: Ireland, World

MayaQuest

Ever wished your classroom had access to the resources at the nation's finest universities? This project is a step in the direction of that kind of cooperation. Sponsored by the state of Minnesota and private-industry partners, it encourages kids to get involved in supporting a real Mayan archeological expedition. Lots of online activities, from scavenger hunts to experts who'll answer your questions.

Type: WWW
Address: http://mayaquest.mecc.com/
Region: Mexico, Guatemala, U.S.

National Council for Educational Technology

This site provides access to educational and networking software, info on using it, and help with networking. You can download the software here.

Type: WWW
Address: http://ncet.csv.warwick.ac.uk/
Region: England

Online Education

Sponsored by Scotland's University of Paisley, this is a Hong Kong-based program that uses live teleconferencing, closed and open discussion forums, and e-mail to give students in Hong Kong a way to earn an overseas college degree. The program includes an online library and tutoring. Several universities now offer "distance learning" options, but this is probably the best-developed and most extensive I've seen.

Type: WWW
Address: http://www.online.edu/
Region: Hong Kong

The Pharmacology Higher Education Network

Here's a home page by folks interested in unifying the teaching of pharmacology in England. It's mostly a text document on PHEN, with a few links.

Type: WWW
Address: http://cblmsu.leeds.ac.uk/WWW /Lprojcts/pharml/www3.html
Region: England

SchoolNet

SchoolNet is intended to equip high schools across Canada with the necessary technology to connect to the electronic information and communications resources. Partners in the project include Industry and Science Canada, Canadian universities and colleges, provincial ministries of education, telecommunications carriers, Canadian high-technology companies, and the schools themselves. All information is available in French and English. The site includes special events announcements, information on using the Internet, leads to education resources arranged by subject (these are especially good), a chat function, an education-related MOO, and links to an electronic classroom newspaper sponsored by the *Toronto Globe and Mail* that's delivered via the Internet.

Type: WWW
Address: http://schoolnet.carleton.ca/
Type: Gopher
Address: gopher.schoolnet.carleton.ca
Type: FTP
Address: schoolnet.carleton.ca:70/1ftp%3 Aschoolnet.carleton.ca@/pub/ schoolnet/
Region: Canada

SOS Children's Villages Association of South Africa

SOS Children's Villages is an international organization dedicated to the well-being of children. In South Africa's Mamelodi township they run a Computer Training Centre for kids, which you can find out about here.

Type: WWW
Address: http://ekhaya.sos.pta.school.za/ welcome.html
Region: South Africa

Teacher Education Internet Server

A joint project of the University of Virginia and University of Houston, this server was established to explore ways in which the Internet could benefit teacher education programs around the world. It offers lesson plans, information on educational technology, special education programs, science education, networking and telecommunications, math education, and international education.

Type: WWW
Address: http://curry.edschool.virginia.edu /teis/
Type: Gopher
Address: teach.virginia.edu
Region: U.S., World

Teacher's Guide to the Internet

Put together under the auspices of NASA's K–12 Initiative program, this page is a basic guide to the Internet and how it can be used in the classroom, for continuing education and for research. An invaluable resource!

Type: WWW
Address: http://quest.arc.nasa.gov/
Region: U.S.

Teaching in Prison

Serving that fastest-growing of all worldwide growth industries, this list is for discussion among education professionals working in the penal system.

Type: Mailing list
Address: PRISON-L listserv@dartcms1
Region: U.S., World

Teaching with Independent Learning Technologies

TILT is a program for educators at the University of Glasgow that endeavors to make learning more productive and efficient through applied technology, particularly multimedia software. The results of their research and their software are available here. It has apparently been quite successful, and some alumni are off to take jobs with major U.S. software companies that are eyeing the education/edutainment market.

Type: WWW
**Address: http://www.elec.gla.ac.uk/TILT/
TILT.html**
Region: Scotland

Times Higher Education Supplement

This online version of *The London Times'* supplement
is invaluable to any teacher or professor seeking work
overseas or interested in the doings of their English
counterparts. Includes worldwide job ads.
Type: WWW
**Address: http://www.timeshigher.newsint
.co.uk/**
Region: England, World

The UK Teacher Education Page

This page collects resources for teachers-in-training
and education instructors, including grants; job
opportunities; licensing and union information; and
courses, workshops, and seminars for skill-building.
Type: WWW
**Address: http://weblife.bangor.ac.uk/
teached.html**
Region: England, Scotland, Wales, Ireland

Using WWW as a Teaching Tool

In English and Italian, this site has backing documentation plus actual examples of Web-based
courseware you can link over to, including classes in
computer science, physics, and education.
Type: WWW
**Address: http://www.dsi.unimi.it/Users/
aprile/Didattica.html**
Region: · Italy, World

Virtual Reality Classroom

This page has lots of data about using MUD technol-
ogy for learning. Workshops, potential mentors,
actual learning-oriented MUDs, and newsgroups are
just some of what's here.
Type: WWW
**Address: http://tecfa.unige.ch/edu-comp/
WWW-VL/eduVR-page.html**
Region: World

Vose School Education Resources Page

Want to get started looking for education resources
online? This page was thoughtfully created by an
Oregon teacher to help you begin. Includes links to a
vast array of search resources, schools, and subject-
specific file libraries.
Type: WWW
**Address: http://www.teleport.com/~
vincer/starter.html**
Region: U.S., World

WWW Virtual Library—Education List

Based in Australia, this site is a one-stop spot for lectures and tutorials, books, software, journals, and
other resources aimed at educators.
Type: WWW
**Address: http://www.csu.edu.au/
education/library.html**
Region: World

Yamanashi University

Links to the University's Center for Education Research and its experimental elementary school can be accessed here. The elementary school has its own Web site, which includes a student newspaper, curricula, items created by the kids, and so forth. Documents are available in Japanese and some English.

Type: WWW
Address: http://peach.kjb.yamanashi.ac .jp/home_e.html
Region: Japan

ELECTRONIC CASH AND DIGITAL BANKING

Welcome to one of the biggest controversies in cyberspace: digital money and digital banking.

Of course, now that you can use ATM cards and credit cards for almost any purpose, it may seem as though "digital money" is a daily reality. The difference is that your current plastic shuffles around funds that—at least hypothetically—can be exchanged for hard currency: the kind that's backed by a government. The new digital money is backed largely by the companies issuing and controlling it.

It all started with online games. Rather than winning and using actual money (which would contravene laws against gambling in some countries), players of online games agreed to use virtual play money. It could be exchanged for online time, building up your character's virtual arsenal—that sort of thing. But the acceptance of this digital cash started some people to thinking about the possibility of creating another type of electronic money.

There are now several serious players in the electronic money game. Their funds can be used to purchase items sold online, from comic books to Macintosh computers—I've included listings for several such merchants here.

Controversy remains, particularly concerning the security of the scrip's value and of information about transactions made with it online. Then there's the "Swiss bank" wrinkle: This type of cash, particularly when issued by companies that shield transactions from view, could be used as a tax-free form of money. It could even be secreted away in digital banks that behave like like those of Switzerland or the Cayman Islands, allowing people to avoid government scrutiny of their financial transactions. Once banked, it might even be instantly transferable to cash via an ATM-style card, allowing for worry-free money laundering.

There are those who say that such a system could topple the banking and government system as we know it. And among the strongest proponents of digital cash are many who say, "So what?"

It would be wise to consult a financial advisor before making a substantial investment in any form of electronic cash.

Berlin E-cash Shopping

Benjamin Pannier of Berlin, whose home page is here, has an e-cash shop in the works. Maybe it'll be open by the time you read this.

Type: WWW
Address: http://www.artcom.de/~karo/
Region: Germany

Business and E-Cash

Premenos Corporation, a company that specializes in electronic commerce systems for business, offers a Guide to Electronic Commerce online here. It has information on corporate use of e-cash systems, and an introduction to TemplarNet, Premenos' experimental virtual Electronic Commerce Network. TemplarNet will use encryption to allow organizations to conduct business securely over public e-mail networks, including the Internet.

Type: WWW
Address: http://www.premenos.com/
Region: World

Bytown Electronic Marketplace

This online e-cash mall is a project of Ottawa, Canada–based Global-X-Change. At press time, the only store online was a souvenir shop. They take DigiCash.

Type: WWW
Address: http://www.globalx.net/digicash
Region: Canada

Claude Lecommandeur's E-cash Shop

I think Claude sells graphics, but I couldn't get pictures to come up when I tried. Maybe he's still working out some bugs in his system.

Type: WWW
Address: http://slhp1.epfl.ch/ecash.html
Region: France

Cypherpunks Mailing List

Encryption is the nominal subject matter here, but participants on this list have a burning interest in digital cash and banking systems. They want financial transactions online to be safe, which requires encryption systems. They also want them to be anonymous. List volume is extremely heavy, as much as 50 to 60 messages per day. The list and related files are archived at the WWW and FTP sites below.

Type: Mailing list
Address: majordomo@toad.com
Send e-mail message with body: subscribe
            cypherpunks
Type: WWW
Address: http://www.hks.net/cpunks/
            index.html
Type: FTP
Address: ftp.csua.berkeley.edu
Region: World

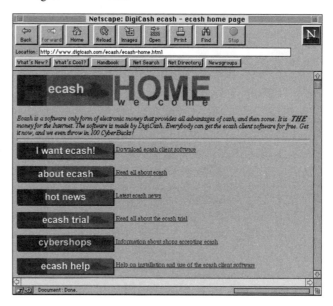

Digicash Home Page

Digicash is a Dutch company pushing for anonymous, international electronic cash. Its management feels that spending e-cash should be just like spending paper money: No one should be using your spending habits to collect information for files on you to use for marketing (or taxation). They are doing so well that at press time they had several urgent job openings listed. This home page has leads to lots of information on how their system works; it also offers a great deal of general information about digital cash, and a lead-in to the CAFE e-cash project in Europe.

Type: WWW
Address: **http://www.digicash.com/ecash/ ecash-home.html**
Region: Holland, World

Eccosys Shop

Eccosys is a Japanese Internet service provider. They also run an online store through this Web page. It offers Japanese music videos, Mac software and hardware, and other goodies for DigiCash.

Type: WWW
Address: **http://www.eccosys.com/ E-SHOP/**
Region: Japan

Electronic Cash, Tokens, and Payments in the National Information Infrastructure

Check in here for the current U.S. government position on e-cash. It's pushing audit trails on transactions, biometric signatures (fingerprint IDs) for e-cash, and, of course, taxation and quite possibly some kind of official bank in charge.

Type: WWW
Address: **http://www.cnri.reston.va.us: 3000/XIWT/documents/dig_cash _doc/ToC.html**
Region: U.S.

Electronic Commerce Info

Information on online commerce strategies, related conferences and other events, recent surveys, and other data of interest to e-cash researchers.

Type: WWW
Address: **http://www.einet.net/galaxy/ Business-and-Commerce/ Electronic-Commerce.html**
Region: U.S., World

NetBill Electronic Commerce Project

The NetBill project at CMU's Information Networking Institute is designing the protocols and software to support charging for network-based goods and services delivered over the Internet. NetBill acts as a third party to provide authentication, account management, transaction processing, billing, and reporting services for clients and users. This site includes downloadable information on other digital cash protocols as well.

Type: WWW
Address: **http://www.ini.emu.edu/netbill/**
Region: U.S., World

NetCash

Issued by the NetBank (the "First National Bank of Cyberspace"), NetCash is intended for small online transactions. You can exchange NetCash coupons for goods or services, and vendors can set up NetCash merchant accounts that allow for converting NetCash into hard currency for a 2 percent fee. Transactions can be encrypted using PGP. This site includes a list of merchants who accept NetCash for items like magazine subscriptions, Internet service, or prepaid calling cards. Information is also available by e-mail at the address below.

Type: WWW
Address: **http://www.teleport.com:80/~ netcash/**
Type: E-mail
Address: **netbank-info@agents.com**
Region: U.S.

NetCheque

This Internet payment system was developed at the University of Southern California. It requires an account, and could be useful for institutions, businesses, and individuals. They're also developing an anonymous payment system.

Type: WWW

Address: http://nii-server.isi.edu/info/ NetCheque/

Region: U.S.

NetChex

This service lets you write and send secure electronic checks that draw on your regular checking account. U.S.-based, personal and merchant accounts are available.

Type: WWW

Address: http://www.PrimeNet.Com/~ rhm/

Region: U.S.

The Phantom Exchange

This "cyberbank" issues an online scrip called GhostMarks. It's based on a client/server program for handling financial transactions automatically, developed by a cypherpunk known as Product Cypher. People can use GhostMarks to buy goods, pay consulting fees, or place bets over the net, instantly—without ever having to exchange paper. Information and leads to necessary software are here for anyone who wants to set up a client account.

You can also finger phantom@stein.u.washington .edu for list of people willing to exchange GhostMarks for products or services

Type: FTP

Address: ftp.u.washington.edu/public/ phantom/cpunk/mgmny.html

Region: U.S., World

SICS Electronic Store

This shop, run by the Swedish Institute of Computer Science, sells software for DigiCash.

Type: WWW

Address: http://www.sics.se/adi-bin/ sicseshop

Region: Sweden

Tim May's Cyphernomicon Page

This page has a long list of questions and answers under the heading Digital Cash. Why isn't digital cash already happening in a big way? Why is the U.S. government worried? What are the merits and demerits of various systems? They're all well-answered here, by someone who's put a lot of research into the matter.

Type: WWW

Address: http://asylum.sf.ca.us/pub/u/ nelson/bin.cgi/splitout

Region: World

VBShop

More software is for sale here, this time utilities for Windows and Visual Basic tools. DigiCash accepted.

Type: WWW

Address: http://www.helsinki.fi/~salste/ eshop.html

Region: Finland

World Trade Clearinghouse

World Trade Clearinghouse says it offers a completely gold-backed electronic currency. I would be careful, because the hyperbole level in their online ads is high and there appears to be a pyramid structure to the plan.

Type: WWW

Address: http://netmar.com/mall/shops/ success/wtc.html

Region: World

Yahoo Index to E-cash Resources

There are lots of links here to businesses developing e-cash solutions, plus papers, research, and more on the subject.

Type: WWW
Address: http://www.yahoo.com/Business /Electronic_Commerce/
Region: World

ELECTRONICS

Whether electronics is your vocation or your hobby, you should find some good information here. Robotics, computer design, communications, itty-bitty gadgets—it's all covered. There is an especially rich selection of sites related to short-wave and amateur radio included here—not least of which are those concerning Internet Radio, a totally new way to send and receive information, news, and music over "virtual airwaves."

Arrick Robotics Home Page

This U.S. company is into building industrial robots in a big way. This page includes information on their research and products, plus lots of resources for the do-it-yourselfer and links to other robotics resources on the Net.

Type: WWW
Address: http://robotics.com/index.html
Region: U.S.

Automate Your Home!

This site links you into databases, FAQs, and standards that will let you design and install home-automation devices. This is the stuff that turns on your coffeepot before you wake up, turns the lights on and off while you're gone, adjusts the thermostat automatically—that sort of thing. Includes a link to the comp.home.automation Usenet newsgroup.

Type: WWW
Address: http://web.cs.ualberta.ca:80/~ wade/HyperHome/
Region: Canada, World

Cambridge University Engineering Department

Information on programs, faculty, and research at this famous university. Including electrical engineering, robotics, communications, and more.

Type: WWW
Address: http://www.eng.cam.ac.uk/
Region: England

Cardiff's Video Game Database Browser

This U.K.-based Web page has the latest news on video game software and hardware. Also linked to this site are numerous newsgroups dealing with specific games or gaming systems, FAQs on the same subjects, and a guide to other resources, such as magazines and software archives.

Type: WWW
Address: http://www.cm.cf.ac.uk/Games/ index.html
Region: England, World

Centro de Pesquisa e Desenvolvimento em Engenharia Elétrica

This site is a guide to the electrical engineering program at this center, with links to file archives and other related sites in Brazil.

Type: WWW
Address: http://www.cpdee.ufmg.br/
Region: Brazil

Circuit Cookbook Archive

Provided by the University of Alberta, this site has all sorts of files for designed circuits, including software, information on optics, FAQs, and much more.

Type: FTP
Address: ftp.ee.ualberta.ca/pub/cookbook/
Region: Canada

Cool Electronics Stuff

Here's a long list, with no visible organizing principle, that links you into a wide variety of electronics resources online. Subjects include wireless communications, circuit design, and much more.

Type: WWW
**Address: http://pasture.ecn.purdue.edu/
~laird/Electronics/index.html**
Region: U.S., World

Daewoo Electronics Home Page

This company is involved in designing and building high-tech multimedia communications devices, including satellite equipment, antennas, displays, and ISDN items. Most specific information here is in Korean, so you'll need a Web browser that can support Korean characters. It's mainly a list of the company's most important products and technologies.

Type: WWW
Address: http://parrot.dwe.co.kr/
Region: Korea

Delft University Circuits and Systems group

This home page of a group that's working on electrical engineering and network theory offers research, publications, software, student proposals, and even a map of their building. Includes a pointer to Delft University of Technology, and is in English with some Dutch.

Type: WWW
Address: http://olt.et.tudelft.nl/index.html
Region: Netherlands

Department of Electrical Engineering at Dresden University of Technology

Some limited information on programs and faculty is available at this site, which appears to be under construction. Includes documents on precision engineering, electronic systems technology, circuits, and systems, some in German only.

Type: WWW
**Address: http://eietu2.et.tu-dresden.de/
ET-en.html**
Region: Germany

EE-Times Interactive

Electronic Engineering Times is the top commercial news publication in the U.S. for electronics, with lots of articles on components, new technologies, and the electronics business. This online version offers the current issue and a WAIS search engine that can find previous stories on the topic of your choice from this and several other publications.

Type: WWW
**Address: http://wais.wais.com:80/eet/
current/**
Region: U.S.

Electronic Advances List

Frequented by the electrical engineering community, this e-mail discussion list covers the cutting edge of electrical design.

Type: Mailing list
Address: LISTSERV@UTFSM
**To receive an index of available files, send
e-mail message with body: INDEX**
Region: U.S.

Electronic African News

A list of reports on just about every major radio news service in Africa can be found here, from Arson at Senegal Radio to Burkina Faso's STN. Get your international news directly from the source!

Type: WWW
**Address: http://www.sas.upenn.edu/
African_Studies/Electronic/menu_
Electronic.html**
Region: Africa

Electronic Engineering at the University of Kent

This page is all about the latest electronics research at this British university. Subjects include radio astronomy and robotics.

Type: WWW
**Address: http://stork.ukc.ac.uk/electronics
/research/index.html**
Region: England

Electronics Humor

When you're knee-deep in trying to hook up a stupid computer that won't work, or find yourself in the middle of a hopeless "home improvement" project gone bad, stop by here for some comic relief. Most of it's in the "politically incorrect" vein, but it's still funny.

Type: WWW
**Address: http://www.paranoia.com/
~filipg/HTML/FAQ/BODY/Humor
.html**
Region: U.S.

EXACT

EXACT is a group working on the exchange of electronic component technology between nations, independent of business interests. You can find reports on new developments and a directory of test equipment, and find out how to get EXACT reports on CD-ROM. There are even some pictures from the lab.

Type: WWW
Address: http://exact.fmv.se/
Region: Sweden, England, World

Hitachi Home Page

At the home page of the Japanese technology company, you can find information on new products, research and development, and pointers to various Hitachi labs. In English or Japanese.

Type: WWW
Address: http://www.hitachi.co.jp/
Region: Japan

HUT Circuit Theory Laboratory

This home page covers courses, research, and faculty at this lab at the Helsinki University of Technology, plus publications and information about the circuit design program APLAC. In English and Finnish.

Type: WWW
Address: http://picea.hut.fi/
Region: Finland

Laserdisc Users in Europe

The Europe-LD mailing list discusses the use of laserdisc technology in Europe and other PAL countries. It discusses both hardware and software matters, and related issues about home cinema systems. both PAL and NTSC software are covered, as the majority of European LD players are dual-standard. It's archived at the WWW site.

Type: Mailing list
Address: europe-ld-request@ee.surrey.ac.uk
Type: WWW
Address: http://www.ee.surrey.ac.uk/ Personal/EuropeLD/
Region: England, Europe

Life in Dave's Flat

"Welcome to the home page of a sad Elec Eng student at the Uni. of Warwick" is the opening line here. It's a true roommate soap opera, with 11 personalities from several countries thrown together in one tiny campus flat, and a couple of hidden links to some electronics information. Give Dave and his mates a visit; it's a funny time-waster.
Type: WWW
Address: http://www.csv.warwick.ac.uk/ ~esufl/
Region: England

Linkoping University's Department of Applied Electronics Engineering

Find out about the electronics programs at Sweden's premier technology university, including ongoing research, courses, and its students' thesis projects.
Type: WWW
Address: http://lin.isy.liu.se/
Region: Sweden

The Living City's Electronics Page

Check here for dozens of links to more Internet sites with electronics-related information, including online newsletters, CAD information, data on massively parallel systems, IEEE and neural networks. Absolutely huge.

Type: WWW
Address: http://www.cadvision.com/guide /science/electron/electron.html
Region: Canada, World

Mobile and Wireless Computing

Not just about computers, this site includes links to files and conference information and proceedings, regarding wireless devices: pagers, radios, computers, communications equipment, telephone systems, and so on, from all over the world.
Type: WWW
Address: http://snapple.cs.washington .edu:600/mobile/mobile.html
Region: World

NEC Research and Development

This is an archive of the technical research newsletter of Japanese electronics giant NEC. Lots of research papers on electronics from NEC's fine staff are presented here, on subjects that include films, chips, screens, and various components for computers and other devices. This version is in English; it's also available in Japanese.
Type: WWW
Address: http://www.nec.co.jp/english/ r_and_d/techrep/r_and_d/list .html
Region: Japan

"Numbers Stations" on Shortwave

Ever turned on your shortwave radio and heard mysterious voices repeating a sequence of five numbers? There are many theories about these mysterious broadcasts, which are most likely top-secret spy transmissions. Check out the link here to ENIGMA, a group of around 200 people who monitor the "numbers stations" for clues.

Type: WWW
Address: **http://itre.uncecs.edu/radio/ numbers.html**
Region: World

Penworld Online

Everything you need to know about the cutting edge of pen-based computers, video and video game technology, personal organization computers, and interactive multimedia systems is provided at this home page. This includes back and current issues of *Personal Electronics News,* which contains reviews of personal electronics products, trade show reviews, and the like, as well as pointers for ordering components or items. The page is linked to several other sites, including the British Cardiff Video Game Database Browser and Compendium, the personal electronics industry sourcebook. Some links here were under construction when I checked in.

Type: WWW
Address: **http://www.penworld.com/ newcont.htm**
Region: U.S.

Radio JAPAN

Radio JAPAN is an international shortwave radio broadcast program carried out by NHK (Japan Broadcasting Corporation). It provides up-to-the-minute news from Japan and Asia.

Type: WWW
Address: **http://www.ntt.jp/japan/NHK/**
Region: Japan

Radio on the Internet

You can get general information about Internet Talk Radio and Internet Radio at this site—one the most exciting applications yet for the Net! You can listen to these radio programs most effectively by finding a server close to you, as sound travels at a rate of 30MB per hour.

Type: WWW
Address: **http://town.hall.org/radio/**
Region: World

sci.electronics

This is the primary Usenet newsgroup dedicated to the discussion of amateur and professional electronics, covering both design and construction aspects of the field. The FAQs for this group can be found at the FTP and WWW sites below (the WWW site has more resources than the former). The FAQs are absolutely essential: not just internal newsgroup info, but things like lists of electronics books for the beginner and the basics of circuit design are covered as well.

Type: Usenet newsgroup
Address: **sci.electronics**
Type: WWW
Address: **http://www.paranoia.com/~ filipg/HTML/FAQ/Index21.html**
Type: FTP
Address: **rtfm.mit.edu/pub/usenet/sci .electronics.**
Region: World

Science Hobby Page

Here's electronics and science fun for smart kids and playful grownups. Tons of links to information about building electronic devices, getting parts, designing circuits and boards, and science museums—plus many "just for kicks" listings.

Type: WWW
Address: **http://www.eskimo.com/~billb/**
Region: World

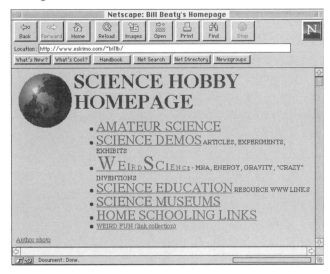

Shortwave/Radio Catalog

This document provides shortwave and radio hobbyists with informative and timely links to services and information related to Shortwave Listening (SWL), satellite radio, and other topics on or about radio. Seems to have it all.

Type: WWW
Address: **http://itre.uncecs.edu/radio/**
Region: World

Shortwave Radio Frequently Asked Questions

This WWW archive is searchable and has links for both the amateur and the expert. Move up the hierarchy here for more information on ham radio.

Type: WWW
Address: **http://www.acs.ncsu.edu/Ham Radio/FAQ/FAQ_Shortwave.html**
Region: World

Sony Stuff

Not an official Sony site by any means (although it does have a hotlink to Sony On-Line, which is), this archive includes much raw information about Sony's electronic products, links to related Usenet newsgroups, and a pointer to the American Society of Reverse Engineers.

Type: WWW
Address: **http://pasture.ecn.purdue.edu/ ~laird/Sony/index.html**
Region: U.S., Japan, World

Surplus Electronic Sources

This is a list of U.S. companies that carry new, refurbished, and used components. It's a good resource if you are building a robot, computer, or other device and need a piece that can't be obtained locally.

Type: WWW
Address: **http://robotics.com/surplus.html**
Region: U.S.

Tesla Coil Info

Some people say Nicolai Tesla invented devices that actually produced "free" energy (of course, his findings were suppressed by Big Business, they add). What's certain is that he came up with many brilliant ideas regarding electronics and electromagnetism. This page has information about the Tesla Coil and other unique inventions, plus links to newsgroups, mailing lists, and related sites. Fascinating stuff to check out, if you have an interest in the fringe side of electronics.

Type: WWW
Address: **http://www.eskimo.com/~billb/ tesla/tesla.html**
Region: World

Video, Audio, and Photography

This page has a bunch of links for those who like to tinker with latest stereo and video equipment, including info on set-top boxes (a new type of computer/TV/video-game player hybrid), HDTV (High-Definition TV), and other consumer electronics.

Type: WWW
Address: http://www.newspage.com/
          NEWSPAGE/cgi-bin/walk.cgi/
          NEWSPAGE/info/d12/d1/
Region: U.S., World

The Waseda Humanoid Project

This fascinating set of pages covers the ultimate feat of engineering: the creation of a truly "humanoid" robot. It's going on at Waseda University, and data is available in Japanese and English. Includes links to other sites on robotics and engineering.

Type: WWW
Address: http://www.shirai.info.waseda
          .ac.jp/humanoid/index.html
Region: Japan

What's on Shortwave?

This is a guide to who's broadcasting what, and at what time. There's lots to see at this experimental site, but it's poorly organized.

Type: WWW
Address: http://itre.uncecs.edu/radio/
          whatson.html
Region: World

**EMERGENCIES AND
DISASTER RESPONSE**

See also Health and Medicine page 310

Hurricanes, floods, mud slides, tornadoes, tsunamis, earthquakes, wildfires, riots, war, and famine: The past few years seem to have had more than their share, or at least CNN brings them to us so immediately that it's impossible not to notice. Although there are many people in the world whose sole job is to plan for such emergencies, their plans generally are carried out by volunteers in the end. So whether you're one of the pros, or just an average person who wants to know how to help, this section has some pointers for you.

1995 South Hyogo Earthquake: List of the Deceased

A spartan and very moving page devoted to listing the names of victims of the Kobe Quake.

Type: WWW
Address: http://www.ntt.jp/QUAKE/index
          .html
Region: Japan

alt.disasters.planning

A newsgroup for disaster-planning professionals.

Type: Usenet newsgroup
Address: alt.disasters.planning
Region: World

alt.med.ems

This newsgroup is for discussion, support, and mutual commiseration between Emergency Medical Services personnel worldwide.

Type: Usenet newsgroup
Address: alt.med.ems
Region: World

Asian Disaster Preparedness Center

The ADPC was designed to help coordinate disaster preparedness and relief efforts throughout Asia and the Far East. Information here revolves around the development of policy-level disaster response mechanisms, and includes a list of forthcoming international disaster-related events.

Type: Gopher
**Address: emailhost.ait.ac.th:70/00/ait/
            GenInfo/ADPC/**
Region: Thailand

Australian Disaster Management Information Network Gopher

A heady technical site with information on Australia's preparedness for various natural disasters. Interestingly, it also houses a folder full of IBM antivirus software intended, no doubt, to combat virtual as well as natural disasters.

Type: Gopher
Address: gopher.vifp.monash.edu.au
Region: Australia

Christian Emergency Relief Team

This religious humanitarian organization is there in times of need, and also brings medical, dental, and other services to impoverished areas where "emergency" is an ongoing fact of life. They go everywhere—even remote islands in the Philippine archipelago, even Iraq. Learn more about their mission here.

Type: WWW
Address: http://www.li.net/~jmc/cert.html
Region: World

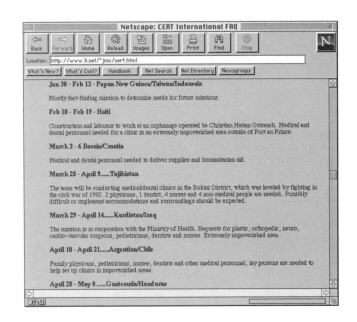

The City of Kobe Home Page

The City of Kobe home page greets you with this understatement: "We had a severe earthquake." The authors of this page almost seem more concerned about the condition of their marginally damaged Web server than they do about their city, but there are plenty of images of the devastated city as well as information on how to volunteer for the relief effort.

Type: WWW
**Address: http://www.kobe-cufs.ac.jp/
            kobe-city/**
Region: Japan

Disaster Group Discussion Information Forum

The Gopher site below is an archival supplement to this group of mailing lists from England, which were formed to engage in supportive discussion of personal experiences in disasters of all kinds. The primary focus is on Third World countries. The disaster-all list includes all the others.

Type: Mailing list
Addresses: disaster-all
              disaster-news
              disaster-3rd-world-dev
              disaster-teaching-software
              disaster-sdss
              mailbase@mailbase.ac.uk
Type: Gopher
Address: nisp.ncl.ac.uk:70/11/lists/
              disaster-all
Region: World

EMED-L

This mailing list is for health-care professionals who work in an in emergency-services capacity.
Type: Mailing list
Address: majordomo@itsa.ucsf.edu
Send e-mail message with body:
              SUBSCRIBE EMED-L@itsa.ucsf.edu
              <Your E-mail Address>
Contact: EMED-L@itsa.ucsf.edu
Region: World

Emergency Management/Planning Newsletter

This journal is used to discuss events in the emergency management and planning community. Past issues have focused on programs being used in various areas. The journal has an international distribution, including Japan, Australia, the U.S., Canada, Mexico, Norway, the Czech Republic, and Russia.
Type: E-mail
Address: kanecki@cs.uwp.edu
Region: U.S., World

Emergency Medicine Educators List

This list is intended to foster communication between educators in the field of emergency medicine.
Type: Mailing list
Address: Listserv@informatics.sunysb.edu
Send e-mail message with body:
              SUBSCRIBE EMS-EDU-L <Firstname
              Lastname>
Region: World

Emergency Preparedness Information eXchange

EPIX is a research organization that tries to facilitate the exchange of ideas and information among Canadian and international public and private sector organizations about the prevention of, preparation for, recovery from, and mitigation of risk associated with natural and socio-technological disasters. Their Gopher site offers information about current and recent disasters, posts about upcoming meetings, and links to similar sites worldwide.
Type: Gopher
Address: hoshi.cic.sfu.ca:5555/11/epix
Region: Canada, World

EMERGENCY-PSYCHIATRY

This list covers issues involved in emergency psychiatric care.
Type: Mailing list
Address: MAILBASE@MAILBASE.AC.UK
Send e-mail message with body: JOIN
              EMERGENCY-PSYCHIATRY
              <Firstname Lastname>
Region: World

EMERG-L

This Canada-based mailing list covers emergency services and emergency medicine.

Type: Mailing list
Address: **listserv@vm.marist.edu**
Send e-mail message with body:
                SUBSCRIBE EMERG-L <Firstname Lastname>
Region: World

Federal Emergency Management Network

Look here for the official public relations page from FEMA, the U.S. agency that's supposed to help in case of natural disaster. In the past decade or so it has spent a great deal of its time and at least one-fourth of its money preparing plans for martial law instead (although you'll find nothing explicit about that here…you might try http://www.mojones.com/JF94 /fema.html for the tip of the iceberg, though). What you will find is quite a few online pamphlets on subjects like dealing with extreme heat, earthquake preparedness, and building up an emergency food supply. Interesting reading that could come in handy.

Type: WWW
Address: **http://www.fema.gov/**
Region: U.S.

Fire/Rescue/EMS/Emergency Sites

Here's a page from Alaska that's devoted to collecting and presenting all known emergency-services sites, from the prosaic (the Boulder, Colorado Police Emergency Squad) to the profound (Godiva Chocolates). Many international links.

Type: WWW
Address: **http://gilligan.uafadm.alaska .edu/WWW_911.HTM**
Region: U.S., World

Greater Horn Information Exchange

Hopefully this will not remain the temporary project that it appears to be, because it's a very good resource. The idea is to provide varied information in one place on the problems and situations at the root of ongoing difficulties in the Greater Horn of Africa area, which includes Ethiopia, Somalia, Sudan, Rwanda, and Eritrea. There's data here on refugees, war, food production, disease, and international aid.

Type: WWW
Address: **http://www.intac.com/ PubService/rwanda/HORN/**
Region: Ethiopia, Somalia, Sudan, Rwanda, Eritrea

International Service Agencies Page

Here you'll find a list of international relief organizations that provide help in times of natural disaster and wartime, with links to their home pages. You'll find information about CARE, Oxfam, refugee assistance, and more.

Type: WWW
Address: **http://www.netmarket.com/isa/ html/disaster.html**
Region: World

Japan/Kobe Earthquake Images

This page contains links to stark images of Kobe on fire, captured from Japanese news broadcasts. It became quite well known immediately after the earthquake as one of the first Web servers to provide coverage of the event, and has links to related pages in Japan. Find out here about the maintainer's efforts to create an ongoing current-events presence on the Net.

Type: WWW
Address: **http://www.niksula.cs.hut.fi/ ~haa/kobe.html**
Region: Japan

misc.emerg-services

This newsgroup is for questions or discussions about emergency services that may not fit into one of the more tightly focused newsgroups.

Type: Usenet newsgroup

Address: misc.emerg-services

Region: World

The Natural Hazards Mitigation Group

Based at the University of Geneva, this group provides a great deal of information about volcanoes, earthquakes, floods, and other natural disasters. It also has links to information about Swiss disaster-relief organizations and efforts.

Type: WWW

Address: http://www.unige.ch/hazards/

Region: Switzerland, World

New Zealand Search and Rescue

They've only just begun, but New Zealand SAR has already put together a nice page with a good set of links. Offerings include search and rescue manuals, plus information on rescue equipment, training, and procedures. The page also has a link to the Amateur Radio Emergency Corps in New Zealand, which plays an essential part in almost every search they do.

Type: WWW

Address: http://www.vuw.ac.nz/~ szymanik/SAR.html

Region: New Zealand

North American Center for Emergency Communications

This volunteer group provides communications services to nonprofits that help people in times of disaster. They also offer communications assistance for military families.

Type: WWW

Address: http://www.winternet.com/ ~nacec/index.html

Region: U.S., Canada, Mexico

Observatario Vulcanologico y Sismologico de Pasto

The staff here is monitoring the very active volcanic range in Colombia. Volcanic history, with regular updates, in Spanish.

Type: WWW

Address: http://www.univalle.edu.co.:80/ ~ovp/

Region: Colombia

Provincial Emergency Program

This series of pages covers emergency preparedness in British Columbia—including earthquake and tsunami response plans.

Type: WWW

Address: http://hoshi.cic.sfu.ca/~pep/

Region: Canada

The Relief Rock Home Page

This shamelessly commercial page suffers from the "Live-Aid" syndrome: Under the auspices of humanitarian goals, record companies hawk their chattels online. You can choose to make a pledge to your favorite organization (Oxfam America, CARE, YMCA, and Doctors Without Borders are among the possible recipients) and download some tasty sound samples. At least this is an inexpensive alternative to mounting "benefit concerts" that cost a bundle and leave less for charity.

Type: WWW

Address: http://www.reliefnet.org:2805/ reliefrock.html

Type: Gopher
Address: gopher.earthweb.com:2801/11/
           rrock
Contact: info@earthweb.com
Region: World

Rwanda Crisis Web

This is an incredibly well-written site with exhaustive information on the Rwandan civil war. This page contains links to such diverse things as image maps, the World Health Organization, various disaster relief sites, and even a list of job openings in Burundi.

Type: WWW
Address: http://www.intac.com/Pub
           Service/rwanda/index.html
Region: Africa

The Unofficial Disaster Management Home Page

This page is a well-done public service. Maintained in Iceland, there are lots of links here related to emergency preparedness, disaster management, risk assessment, and emergency medical services resources. The management is also experimenting with providing an online disaster-management text-book and a database of related documents.

Type: WWW
Address: http://rvik.ismennt.is/~gro/
           dislist.html
Region: Iceland, World

Victoria State Emergency Service

This "unofficial" page sports images of Australians in bright yellow slickers giving aid to victims of natural and human-caused disasters. Be sure to check out the severe storms link, which has some scary images of serious weather-related property damage.

Type: WWW
Address: http://144.110.160.105:9000/
           ~jck/vicses/vicses.html
Region: Australia

VolcanoWorld

Using images and data from NASA's satellites and the space shuttle, this site offers lots of information about volcanoes, the history of volcanic eruptions, and the likelihood of future events. It includes an excellent segment about the volcano that I can see on the occasional clear day—Mount St. Helens. This is an especially good site for kids with an interest in things that go BOOM!

Type: WWW
Address: http://volcano.und.nodak.edu/
Region: U.S., World

Volunteers in Technical Assistance

This group provides a database of up-to-date disaster information. As this book was being written, its concentration was on the aftermath of the Kobe earthquake in Japan and the worsening crisis in the Rwandan refugee camps. Includes links to emergency assistance organizations and personnel.

Type: Gopher
Address: gopher.vita.org:70/11/disaster
Region: World

World Conservation Monitoring Centre

Based in England, this organization maintains a page that provides information about emergency conservation efforts in case of natural or man-made disasters. Events covered at publication time include an oil spill in the Russian Arctic and fires on the Galapagos Islands.

Type: WWW
**Address: http://www.wcmc.org.uk/
             infoserv/is_emap.html**
Region: England, World

The World Health Organization

This site contains press releases and other general information on WHO and its activities world wide. It also has some valuable links to other health-related resources. If you are planning a trip abroad to the site of an emergency, this site will tell you what painful vaccinations you'll need before you go.

Type: WWW
Address: http://www.who.ch/
Type: Gopher
Address: gopher.who.org
Region: World

World-Wide Earthquake Locator

This very interesting resource is provided by the Department of Geography at the University of Edinburgh. It leads you through a hierarchy of image maps showing the epicenters of earthquakes around the world. It even rates the quakes as either poor, fair, or good (which may mean something different to scientists and victims).

Type: WWW
**Address: http://www.geo.ed.ac.uk/
             quakes/quakes.html**
Region: Japan

One downside of the Internet is the vulnerability of e-mail and software as it travels across the wires. Personal records and letters can be fairly easily intercepted. There's also the problem of malicious hackers seeking to gain unauthorized access to computers and resources. All of these issues are being actively addressed by many organizations and archive providers. In this section you can get access to information about security, encryption, and privacy, and tools to provide it for personal or business computers and networks.

Associazione per la Liberta' nella Comunicazione Elettronica Interattiva

ALCEI/EF-Italy is an association of people dedicated to affirm and protect constitutional rights for "electronic citizens" in Italy as new communications technologies emerge. It offers a mailing list and related files, and will soon be opening up a discussion forum on the new Italia Online service.

Type: Mailing list
Address: majordomo@inet.it
**Send e-mail message with body: subscribe
             alcei**
Type: WWW
Address: http://www.nexus.it/alcei.html
**Address: http://www.eff.org/pub/Groups
             /EF-Italy/**
Type: Gopher
Address: gopher.eff.org, 1/Groups/EF-Italy
Type: FTP
Address: ftp.eff.org, /pub/Groups/EF-Italy/
Contact: alcei@mailbox.iunet.it
Region: Italy

Cliff Stoll's Performance Art Theatre and Networking Security Review

Fun recap of a lecture from Cliff Stoll, author of the hacker-tracking bestseller *The Cuckoo's Egg*, about how he caught German hacker/spies. Includes a soundbyte from Stoll, who is much in demand for his amusing and fact-filled speeches on security issues.

Type: WWW
Address: http://town.hall.org/university/ security/stoll/cliff.html
Region: U.S., Germany

CommUnity

Also known as the Computer Communicators' Association, this group represents the interests of the U.K. online community. It has worked against BBS licensing threats, responds to smear campaigns in the popular press, and has even launched its own investigation into computer pornography. Subscribe to its electronic magazine, *CommUnicator*, for regular updates.

Type: Mailing list
Address: mail-server@nowster.demon.co .uk
Send e-mail message with body:
        SUBSCRIBE COMMUNICATOR
        <Firstname Lastname>
Contact: mjb@mavericks.bt.co.uk
Type: FTP
Address: ftp.demon.co.uk/pub/archives /community/
Address: ftp.eff.org/pub/Groups/ CommUnity/

Type: Gopher
Address: gopher.eff.org:1/Groups/ CommUnity
Type: WWW
Address: http://www.demon.co.uk/ community/index.html
Type: Usenet newsgroup
Address: uk.org.community
Region: England, Scotland, Wales, Northern Ireland

Computer Emergency Response Team

CERT puts out the word whenever there's a significant threat to computer security. Subscribe to their mailing list or check out the newsgroup for the latest warnings and news.

Type: Usenet newsgroup
Address: comp.security.announce
Type: Mailing list
Address: cert-advisory-request@cert.org
Contact: cert@cert.org
Region: World

Computer and Network Security Reference

Maintained by Telecom Australia, this nicely designed page offers all sorts of security-related FAQs, network firewalling tools, info on commercial security products, links to FTP, Gopher, and WWW sites, and links to newsgroups and mailing lists.

Type: WWW
Address: http://www.telstra.com.au/ info/security.html
Region: Australia

Computer Professionals for Social Responsibility

CPSR's mission is providing the public and policy-makers with realistic assessments of the power, promise, and problems of information technology. Its current projects include the U.S. government's National Information Infrastructure project, furthering the cause of civil liberties and privacy online, and several projects related to computers in the workplace—including computer-based workplace surveillance and safety issues. At this main site, one can find information on these projects, information about and archives of their mailing list, membership information, and more information about CPSR.

Type: WWW
Address: http://cpsr.org/cpsr
Type: Gopher
Address: gopher.cpsr.org, ftp.cpsr.org
Region: U.S.

Computer Professionals for Social Responsibility Usenet Groups

Dedicated to the discussion of social issues involved with computing, information exchange, and the Internet, these newsgroups were started by the CPSR to provide a public forum for these topics outside of their extensive mailing-list network. The comp.org .cpsr.talk group is designated for discussion of topics relevant to the activities or interests of the CPSR. The comp.org.cpsr.announce newsgroup is a moderated group which provides organizational announcements, relevant news items, and postings from other organizations or the general public as the moderators see fit. Items are gatewayed to this group from the e-mail list of the same title, which has over 5,600 subscribers.

Type: Usenet newsgroups
Addresses: comp.org.cpsr.talk
            comp.org.cpsr.announce
Region: U.S.

CPSR Listserver

Computer Professionals for Social Responsibility hosts some 50 lists, all available via their listserver. These mailing lists are archived at CPSR's FTP server below.

Type: Mailing list
Address: listserv@cpsr.org
To receive a complete list of their lists including the CPSR Announcement list regional lists, administrative lists, and the CyberRights mailing list, send an e-mail message with blank Subject line and body: LIST
To receive information about a specific list, send a one-line e-mail message with body: REVIEW <name of the list>
Type: FTP
Address: ftp.cpsr.org:/cpsr/lists/listserv_ archives
Region: U.S.

Cryptography and Security Page

There are lots of links here to many other resources online, including how-tos, software, information about security procedures and hardware, people in the crypto scene, and leads to commercial firms and consultants who specialize in setting up security for computer networks and companies.

Type: WWW
Address: http://theory.lcs.mit.edu/~rivest/ crypto-security.html
Region: U.S., World

Cryptography Export Control Archives

Cypherpunk John Gilmore maintains this site, where you can find the most current news on the NSA's (losing) battle to restrict the export of cryptography technologies and software.

Type: WWW
Address: http://www.cygnus.com/~gnu/ export.html
Region: U.S., World

Cryptography Newsgroup

I hope you've got a degree in computer science or math, because discussion in this newsgroup runs to the very technical. News about cryptography issues, on and off the Internet (that is, various countries trying to ban certain encryption programs, new breakthroughs in decryption, and so on), are covered, as well as crypto specs.

Type: Usenet newsgroup
Address: sci.crypt
Region: U.S.

Cryptography, Privacy, and PGP

This site's a rich trove of information, links, and online tools. The Cryptography section has links to online articles and bibliographic resources, including several different FAQs on computer cryptography, mathematical cryptographic theory, links to major online works on cryptography such as *Applied Cryptography* by Bruce Schneier and *Cryptography Theory and Practice* by Douglas Stinson, and information about DigiCash. There are also links to cryptography utilities, information about current legal

standards and struggles regarding encryption, and the archives for the newsgroup sci.crypt. The PGP section has, of course, links to sites that provide PGP, plenty of documentation, and some background on the program's creator, Phillip Zimmerman. There is also an access point and archive for the newsgroup alt.security.pgp. The Privacy section is certainly the most interactive and interesting. It includes the latest word on computer privacy issues, struggles and pitfalls, plus a host of notes about and links to anonymous remailer services, and to sites that offer anonymous remailing. These remailing services offered include chain remailing systems and PGP-based encryption remailing systems.

Type: WWW
Address: http://draco.centerline.com: 8080/~franl/crypto.html
Region: U.S., World

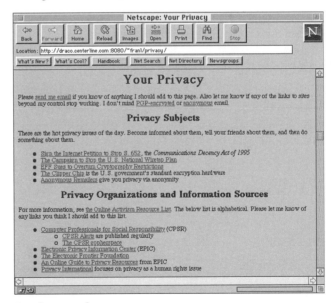

Cypherpunks

This group's home page provides anonymous remailing services; news on cryptography issues, the Clipper Chip, and related topics; and a number of excellent texts on Cyber-Anarchy, including "From

Crossbows to Cryptography," "The Cypherpunk's Manifesto," and "The Crypto Anarchist Manifesto." Their mailing list is an extremely high-traffic conduit for technical and political information. It's archived at the FTP sites listed, which are also accessible through their Web page.

Type: WWW
Address: http://www.csua.berkeley.edu/ cypherpunks/Home.html

Type: FTP
Address: ftp.csua.berkeley.edu/pub/ cypherpunks/

Type: Mailing list
Address: majordomo@toad.com
Send e-mail message with body: subscribe cypherpunks
Contact: hughes@toad.com
Region: U.S., World

Datenschutz-Informationen

In German and some English, this page has a great deal of data on privacy, security, and encryption ("datenschutz"). Most of the actual documents linked are in German, and there are links to a number of other German archives and sites here, as well as official European Union reports on the subject.

Type: WWW
Address: http://www.rewi.hu-berlin.de/ Datenschutz/
Region: Germany

Digital Citizens' Movement of the Netherlands

According to the DB.NL (Digital Burgerbeweging Nederland) introduction, they are striving for digital democracy: civil liberties for computer-network communications, such as freedom of expression and protection of privacy, publicly useful applications of information and communications technology, and an accessible and user-friendly public digital network. To this end, their Web page provides a link to their mailing list (which is conducted primarily in Dutch). Several information resource sections dealing mainly with European privacy, civil rights, and freedom of information exchange issues; and a very full set of links to PGP proliferation sites, general cryptography information, and remailer information.

Type: WWW
Address: http://www.xs4all.nl/~db.nl/ english/ (In English)
Address: http://www.xs4all.nl/~db.nl/ (In Dutch)

Type: Gopher
Address: gopher.eff.org.1/Groups/DB.NL/
Type: FTP
Address: ftp.eff.org/pub/Groups/DB.NL/
Region: Netherlands

Electronic Frontier Foundation (EFF)

The EFF has fought since 1990 to see that Constitutional rights are protected for emerging information technologies in the U.S., and has encouraged similar efforts worldwide. They are a nonprofit civil-liberties organization. Membership in EFF includes subscription to their twice-monthly online journal, The *EFFector,* and to their quarterly printed newsletter, as well as online alerts and bulletins dealing with EFF concerns and projects, and, most importantly, online response mechanisms for giving input on, and acting in regards to, pressing issues like the Clipper chip and the Decency in Communications Act. Also available at this site are EFF's online file and document libraries, current and back issues of The EFFector, the latest edition of the excellent EFF guide to the Internet, and links to EFF chapters all over the U.S. and similar organizations in Japan, France, Canada, New Zealand, Australia, Spain, Italy, and many other countries.

Type: WWW
Address: http://www.eff.org/
Type: Gopher
Address: gopher.eff.org, ftp.eff.org
Region: U.S., World

Electronic Frontier Foundation Usenet Discussion Groups

There are two EFF-oriented Usenet groups: comp.org.eff.news is a moderated newsgroup providing news of EFF projects, current information on restrictive legislation, EFF announcements and press releases, and public input that the moderators chose to include; comp.org.eff.talk is a public forum for discussion of EFF activities, events, and issues. They are also available in mailing-list form, and are archived at EFF's Web and Gopher servers below.

Type: Usenet newsgroups
Addresses: comp.org.eff.news
            comp.org.eff.talk
Type: Mailing list
Address: listserv@eff.org
Send e-mail message with blank Subject
            line and body: subscribe <name
            of list>
Contacts: info@eff.org (infobot)
            eff@eff.org (human)
Type: WWW
Address: http://www.eff.org/
Type: Gopher
Address: gopher.eff.org
Type: FTP
Address: ftp.eff.org
Region: U.S., World

Electronic Frontiers Australia

Join the EF-Australia newsgroup or subscribe to their mailing list to find out the latest on communications and networking restrictions in that continent. They even have their own MOO set up for real-time discussions.

Type: Usenet newsgroup
Address: aus.org.efa
Type: Mailing list
Address: efa-request@efa.iinet.com.au
Send e-mail message with Subject and
            body: subscribe
            Fidonet Echo:EFA
Contact: ask@efa.iinet.com.au
Type: FTP
Address: ftp.eff.org, /pub/Groups/
            EF-Australia/
Type: Gopher
Address: gopher.eff.org, 1/Groups/
            EF-Australia
Type: WWW
Address: http://www.efa.org.au/EFA/
Type: MOO
Address: EFA-MOO - telnet://cleese.apana
            .org.au:7777
Region: Australia

Electronic Frontiers Japan

This mailing list discusses computer security and privacy issues in English and Japanese, including the role of governmental organizations in the formation of the Japanese side of the Internet.

Type: Mailing list
Address: efj-request@twics.com
Send the e-mail message with body:
            subscribe <Firstname Lastname>
Contact: efj-admin@twics.com.
Region: Japan

European Symposium on Research in Computer Security

This organization sponsors symposia on security issues, especially as they affect European users and networks. Find out about upcoming and past meetings here, including proceedings.

Type: WWW
Address: http://www.laas.fr/~esorics/
Region: Europe

Firewalls Mailing List

Firewalls are security systems that protect computers or file libraries connected to the Internet from unauthorized use or abuse. This list is for discussions of Internet firewalling systems and related issues. It is an outgrowth of the Firewalls BOF session at the Third UNIX Security Symposium in Baltimore on September 15, 1992, and it's archived at the WWW site below.

Type: Mailing list
Address: Majordomo@GreatCircle.COM
Address: Firewalls-request@GreatCircle .COM
Send e-mail message with body: subscribe firewalls
Contact: Firewalls@GreatCircle.COM
Type: WWW
Address: http://www.telstra.com.au/ hypermail/firewalls/
Region: World

Forum for Rights to Electronic Expression

This computing rights group in India recently formed in response to huge government fees (U.S. $50,000 yearly to run a BBS, more for e-mail systems) levied on would-be online service providers, plus roadblocks to freedom of speech online and outright censorship. The Indian government won't even allow private satellite uplinks. These users are fighting back—find out more here.

Type: WWW
Address: http://www.eff.org/pub/Groups /FREE/
Type: Gopher
Address: mahavir.doe.ernet.in:70/11/ telecom/free
Address: gopher.eff.org/1/Groups/FREE
Type: FTP
Address: ftp.eff.org/pub/Groups/FREE/
FidoNet Echo: FREE
Contact: free@arbornet.org
Region: India

German Encryption and Privacy Newsgroups

These groups each discuss slightly different aspects of security/encryption issues and techniques. All are conducted in German.

Type: De, Cl and Zer.z-netz newsgroups
Addresses: de.soc.datenschutz
cl.datenschutz.aktionen
cl.datenschutz.allgemein
cl.datenschutz.diskussion
cl.datenschutz.g10
cl.datenschutz.isdn
zer.z-netz.datenschutz.allgemein
zer.z-netz.datenschutz.g10
zer.z-netz.datenschutz.spionage
Region: Germany

Info-PGP

Discussion of Phil Zimmerman & Co.'s Pretty Good Privacy (PGP) public-key encryption program for MS-DOS, UNIX, SPARC, VMS, Atari, Amiga, and other platforms takes place here. The list also mirrors the alt.security.pgp newsgroup and includes related articles culled from the sci.crypt newsgroup.

Type: Mailing list
Address: info-pgp-request@lucpul.it.luc.edu
Region: World

International Association for Cryptological Research

Find out about the annual meetings sponsored by this group, including the AsiaCrypt meeting. You can also read their electronic journal.

Type: WWW
Address: http://www.swcp.com:80/~iacr/
Region: World

Mixmaster Remailer Page

This page provides anonymous remailing for enhanced e-mail privacy through a couple of new remailing systems.

Type: WWW
**Address: http://obscura.com/~loki/
             Welcome.html**
Region: U.S., World

Mukund Mohan's Cryptography Home Page

Another page with many links, in this case including a good selection of vendor-sponsored and unofficial security pages for safeguarding hardware or your operating system. Especially important information for the network manager or individual computer user.

Type: WWW
**Address: http://obscura.com/~loki/
             Welcome.html**
Region: U.S., World

Privacy Forum Digest

Sort of a mailing list, sort of an e-journal, Privacy Forum Digest publishes the best submissions received on the subject of personal and collective privacy issues on the Internet on a semiweekly basis. Supported in part by the Association for Computing Machinery's Committee on Computers and Public Policy, and the Data Services Division of MCI Communications Corp., the list/journal is moderated, and is archived on the Vortex Technology home page listed below.

Type: E-Journal
Address: listserv@vortex.com
Contact: privacy@vortex.com
Type: WWW
**Address: http://www.vortex.com/
             privacy.html**
Region: U.S.

Privacy International

Privacy International is an NGO founded in 1990 to take on issues of invasion of privacy by governments around the globe. Issues of interest to PI include gathering and exchange of personal data on individuals by governmental, economic, and political institutions; military surveillance; and national ID systems. They have waged successful campaigns in Europe, Asia, and North America, and have an active system for members to input new cases for consideration. Besides general organizational information, this site contains back issues of the PI newsletter, which monitors ongoing cases, provides international privacy law information, and reviews the record of various governments on these issues.

Type: WWW
**Address: http://cpsr.org/cpsr/privacy/
             privacy_international**
Region: World

Privacy Issues Newsgroup

The primary Usenet newsgroup for discussion of issues regarding free Internet information exchange and social/political privacy and individual rights is alt.privacy. It's very active.

Type: Usenet newsgroup

Address: alt.privacy

Region: U.S., World

Privacy Issues Newsgroup, II

Topics discussed in this group range from free information exchange and Internet issues to items of a more social or political bent, such as drug testing, governmental information gathering and surveillance, and the ever-terrifying National ID Card.

Type: Usenet newsgroup

Address: comp.society.privacy

Region: U.S.

Raph Levien Remailer Page

This is an automatically generated list of remailing sites with a 12-day history of reliability and usage provided to help guide the process of choosing one.

Type: WWW

**Address: http://www.csu.berkeley.edu/
~raph/remailer-list.html**

Region: U.S., World

Security-related Newsgroups

There are a burgeoning number of Usenet newsgroups related to computer security and privacy, network security, and related issues. Here are a few that you might want to check out.

Type: Usenet newsgroups

Address: alt.security
(alternate security measures)

Address: alt.security.index
(an index of the measures discussed in alt.security)

Address: comp.security.misc
(security issues of computers and networks)

Address: comp.security.unix
(discussion of UNIX security)

Address: misc.security
(miscellaneous security topic)

Address: comp.risks
(risks to the public from computers and users)

Address: comp.virus
(computer viruses and security)

Address: alt.security.pgp
(Pretty Good Privacy discussion)

Address: alt.security.ripem
(information about Privacy Enhanced Mail)

Region: World

Sirene's Security and Cryptography Page

This page is an excellent archive of deep information on cryptography and other security measures—especially if you use UNIX. Access to tools, security teams worldwide, non-U.S. libraries of cryptography software, alert sites on the Net, and much more.

Type: WWW

**Address: http://www.zurich.ibm.ch/
Technology/Security/sirene/
outsideworld/security.html**

Region: Switzerland, World

talk.politics.crypto

Just as one would expect, this newsgroup provides a forum for the discussion of legal, social, and political issues regarding the use (or restriction of the use) of encryption tools and software.

Type: Usenet newsgroup

Address: talk.politics.crypto

Region: U.S.

ENGINEERING

See also Electronics page 216

This section includes resources on chemical, water, waste water, civil, and environmental engineering, plus bioengineering and a few other specialties. Most of the resources relating to electrical engineering are in the Electronics section, although you'll find a few pointers here as well. Most of these sites are academic, because that's where most public engineering research goes on. In some cases these universities also have private-side partners, who may provide some material for their file libraries.

Acoustical Imaging Symposium

Here's a home page with information on this symposium, to be held in Florence, Italy in fall 1995. You can find a list of papers to be read at the conference, with abstracts, and find out how to sign up.

Type: WWW
Address: http://www.area.fi.cnr.it/acoima /home.htm
Region: Italy, World

alt.engr.explosives

Here's where demolitions pros trade techniques.

Type: Usenet newsgroup
Address: alt.engr.explosives
Region: World

Asian Institute of Technology

Various documents on the programs of this university are available here, including water and waste-water engineering and food process engineering.

Type: Gopher
Address: emailhost.ait.ac.th/1m/ait/ GenInfo/serd/fields
Region: Thailand

Association of Consulting Engineers of Manitoba

The home page of ACEM, an advocacy group for private engineers in Manitoba, Canada serves up their press releases about government regulation, an events calendar, and information about their committees.

Type: WWW
Address: http://www.mbnet.mb.ca:80/ acem/
Region: Canada

Beijing University of Chemical Technology

The home page of the university has information on the school, pointers to its departments, and a "science salon" with pointers to other sites. In both Chinese and English, and with lots of pictures that take quite a while to load.

Type: WWW
Address: **http://www.buct.edu.cn/**
Region: China

Chemical Engineering URL Directory

Pointers to hundreds of chemical engineering sites around the world, organized by country, are online here.
Type: WWW
Address: **http://mv70.rz.uni-karlsruhe.de/ ~ig32/chem-eng.html**
Region: Germany

Chulalongkorn University

Programs and faculty of this university, including the faculty of engineering, are listed here. Not a very good interface, but it's interesting to see what's there.
Type: WWW
Address: **http://www.chula.ac.th:80/ college/**
Region: Thailand

Civil and Environmental Engineering at Carleton University

This department's home page includes info on faculty, staff, research, student groups, etc. Some pictures and text about student projects, including one on the Tacoma Narrows Bridge, are available.
Type: WWW
Address: **http://www.civeng.carleton.ca/**
Region: Canada

comp.cad.pro-engineer

This newsgroup is for discussion of Pro-Engineer, a CAD program. It's echoed in the mailing list pro-engineer.

Type: Usenet newsgroup
Address: **comp.cad.pro-engineer**
Type: Mailing list
Address: **majordom@caesun6.epg.harris .com**
Send e-mail message with body: subscribe pro-engineer
Region: World

Department of Biomedical Physics and Technology

This biomedical engineering department in the Netherlands provides publications, research projects, and information about the faculty of the school online.
Type: WWW
Address: **http://www.eur.nl/FGG/BNT/ index.html**
Region: Netherlands

Department of Machine Elements and Engineering Design

The Technical University of Darmstadt offers the usual faculty and course information here, along with a directory of components available over the Internet and a catalog. Much of this site is in German.
Type: WWW
Address: **http://www.muk.maschinenbau .th-darmstadt.de/englishhome .html**
Region: Germany

Edinburgh Chemical Engineering WWW Home Page

Faculty, students, and programs of this department of the University of Edinburgh are listed here, including course materials and some FTP-able documents.

Type: WWW
Address: http://www.chemeng.ed.ac.uk/
Type: FTP
Address: ftp.chemeng.ed.ac.uk/
Region: Scotland

Eindhoven University of Technology, Department of Chemical Process Engineering

A directory of this department is here, with pointers to faculty members and their research. Also includes a modest FTP server. Available in Dutch, with some English.

Type: WWW
Address: http://www.tcp.chem.tue.nl/
Region: Holland

EINet Engineering and Technology

Thousands of pointers to engineering and technology sites around the world are on this Web page, which is easily searchable.

Type: WWW
**Address: http://galaxy.einet.net/galaxy/.
            /Engineering-and-
            Technology.html**
Region: World

Electronics Research Group of the University of Aberdeen

This group is working on neural webs and other computer engineering projects. You can get archives of several journals, updates on projects, and copies of papers.

Type: WWW
Address: http://www.erg.abdn.ac.uk/
Region: Scotland

Engineering Usenet Groups

There are many engineering-related Usenet newsgroups with the sci.engr prefix. Here are quite a few; see any complete list of newsgroups for more.

Type: Usenet newsgroup
**Addresses: sci.engr
            sci.engr.advanced-tv
            sci.engr.biomed
            sci.engr.chem
            sci.engr.civil
            sci.engr.control
            sci.engr.geomechanics
            sci.engr.manufacturing
            sci.engr.marine.hydrodynamics
            sci.engr.mech
            sci.engr.metallurgy
            sci.engr.safety
            sci.engr.semiconductor
            sci.engr.lighting**
Region: World

G.A.U.S.

This is the home page of an acoustics research group at the University of Sherbrooke in Canada. You can find information on their history, current research and papers, and technical resources. In English and French.

Type: WWW
**Address: http://www-gaus.gme.usherb.ca
            /gaus_ang.html**
Region: Canada

Gunma University

History and some FTP-able documents from this university and its faculty of engineering, in both English and Japanese, are linked here.

Type: WWW

Address: http://www.la.gunma-u.ac.jp/

Region: Japan

Hong Kong University of Science and Technology Home Page

Here's a document on this university, with a few pictures and information on its history and programs. Includes information on the faculty of engineering and has a link to SunSITE Hong Kong's archive.

Type: WWW

Address: http://www.ust.hk/

Region: Hong Kong

Hyperactive Molecules Using Chemical MIME

An HTML-format paper on this chemical engineering subject, this site includes many images and some video animations. Turn off automatic image loading before going to this page if you need to conserve bandwidth—there are a lot of big images.

Type: WWW

Address: http://www.ch.ic.ac.uk/

Region: England

Ingenioeren/net

Ingenioeren is the weekly engineering publication of Denmark. This home page is mostly in Danish, but has a brief English guide. You can subscribe to the paper edition through this site.

Type: WWW

**Address: http://www.ingenioeren.dk/
index.html**

Region: Denmark

Institute for Machine Tools and Industrial Management

This is a department of the Munich University of Technology. Includes information on robotics, manufacturing equipment, and optimizing production systems.

Type: WWW

**Address: http://www.iwb.mw.
tu-muenchen.de/welcome-e.html**

Region: Germany

Institute of Mechanics

Projects, lectures, and staff of this institute in Zurich, including some in German, are available here. It has links to a FTP site and other resources.

Type: WWW

Address: http://www.ifm.mavt.ethz.ch/

Region: Switzerland

International Center for Genetic Engineering and Biotech

The ICGEBnet Gopher has lots of pointers to biological engineering and genetic engineering information around the world.

Type: Gopher

Address: genes.icgeb.trieste.it/1

Region: Italy

ISSO MicroSpace Network

The International Small Satellite Organization (ISSO) is interested in low-cost space exploration, particularly for commercial use. At its home page, you can find launch reports with details of almost all international satellite launches. There are also updates on technology breakthroughs, and pointers to aerospace companies working on space technology.

Type: WWW
Address: http://www.isso.org/
Region: U.S., World

Japanese Engineering Program for Americans

There's info here about several programs that help American technical specialists get training and cross-cultural experience in Japan.
Type: WWW
Address: http://www.doc.gov/JTP.Mosaic.
Materials/JTP/iss24.html
Region: Japan, U.S.

Korea Advanced Institute of Science and Technology

The home page of this university includes its schools of mechanical engineering, industrial engineering, applied engineering, and electrical engineering.
Type: WWW
Address: http://cair-archive.kaist.ac.kr/
kaist/dept.html
Region: Korea

Mechanical Engineering Department at University of Pohang

There's an introduction to the faculty and research programs of the university in English here, along with a prospectus and annual reports in Korean.
Type: WWW
Address: http://firefox.postech.ac.kr/
Region: Korea

Ny Teknik

This is the home page of a Swedish technical newspaper, from which some current stories are available online. It's a very nicely designed page in Swedish, with links to subscription forms and lots of enjoyable and entertaining Internet sites.

Type: WWW
Address: http://www.et.se/nyteknik
Region: Sweden

Rheinland-Westphalen Technical High School

This is the home page of a technical hochschule in western Germany. A hochschule is roughly equivalent to an American high school, but this school looks more like a college, with a faculty of Elektrotechnik and a program in mechanical engineering. In German. Take a look at the kind of preparation these kids will have going into university.
Type: WWW
Address: http://www.informatik.
rwth-aachen.de/RWTH/index
.html
Region: Germany

Singapore Biotechnology Database

Pointers to all kinds of biotechnology resources in Singapore are online at this archive.
Type: Gopher
Address: biomed.nus.sg/11/biotechdb
Region: Singapore

STEP Home Page, Ikeda Lab

STEP stands for Standard for the Exchange of Product Model Data. This is the home page of this ISO project to develop standards for computer models of products, so a company in, say, Taiwan, can easily get product specifications from a German firm without an undue need for translation. You can find all kinds of news and data about the project here.
Type: WWW
Address: http://www.hike.te.chiba-u.ac.jp
/ikeda/documentation/STEP.html
Region: Japan, World

Technical University of Chemnitz

The home page of this university has pointers to information about their programs, faculty, and projects. Items include publications like Mechanical Engineering and Process Technology and information on the Institute of Mechatronics. Mostly in German, but with an English index.

Type: WWW
Address: **http://www.tu-chemnitz.de /index-e.html**
Region: Germany

Technical University of Denmark

Here's a directory of home pages for various institutes within the university, including material physics, computers, fluid mechanics, and electronics. In Danish, but they say they'll have an English version soon.

Type: WWW
Address: **http://www.dtu.dk/dtu/dtu.html**
Region: Denmark

The Technion

The Technion is a technical university in Israel, and here you'll find pointers to information about the various faculty members and programs of its departments. You also can get to local Gopher, FTP, and Archie resources with pointers to more information.

Type: WWW
Address: **http://www.technion.ac.il/**
Region: Israel

Universidad de Costa Rica

This Gopher provides a modest archive of information on the university, which includes programs in civil, electrical, industrial, mechanical, and chemical engineering. The interface is not so hot, and most of the departments have simply a description and a document or two. But then again, they are just getting started.

Type: Gopher
Address: **gopher.ucr.ac.cr/11/Facultades/ Ingenieria**
Region: Costa Rica

University of Auckland Engineering Department

This site is very limited at the moment, with only a few pointers within the department. However, the maintainers plan to expand soon to provide engineering file libraries to the public.

Type: WWW
Address: **http://www.auckland.ac.nz/esc/**
Region: New Zealand

University of Leeds Institute for Transport Studies

Check here for the home page of civil engineers working on planning and operation of roads, bridges, and other land transport infrastructure. There are pointers to staff and research, as well as a paper on traffic-network analysis programs.

Type: WWW
Address: **http://its02.leeds.ac.uk/**
Region: England

University of Ljubljana Faculty of Civil Engineering and Geodesy

The home page of this Slovenian civil engineering department provides faculty and student projects, plus home pages and information on programs of study. The emphasis is on CAD. In English with some Slovene.

Type: WWW
Address: **http://www.fagg.uni-lj.si/**
Region: Slovenia

University of Manitoba Department of Civil and Geological Engineering

Here's a home page for the department, which includes programs in geological engineering, geotechnical engineering, and transportation engineering. Details of programs and pointers to other resources are among its contents.

Type: WWW
Address: **http://www.ce.umanitoba.ca/ homepage.html**
Region: Canada

University of Portsmouth School of Civil Engineering

Research, faculty, and programs of this school of civil engineering are online, including fascinating engineering information about the Kobe earthquake and texts for courses at the university.

Type: WWW
Address: **http://www.civl.port.ac.uk/ index.html**
Region: England

University of Tasmania Department of Civil and Mechanical Engineering

This engineering department's home page has data on its faculty, courses, and research projects, as well as information on an upcoming conference on mechanics.

Type: WWW
Address: **http://info.utas.edu.au/docs/ beasley/civenghp.htm**
Region: Australia

Virtual Library: Engineering

This is the WWW Virtual Library section on engineering, a comprehensive list of engineering resources around the world. Includes many sublists.

Type: WWW
Address: **http://epims1.gsfc.nasa.gov/ engineering/engineering.html**
Region: U.S.

Water Resources Engineering

Programs, research, and faculty of this program at the University of Alberta are available here. Copies of publications and technical reports are provided, as well as computer programs.

Type: WWW
Address: **http://maligne.civil.ualberta.ca/**
Region: Canada

ENVIRONMENTAL DATA AND ISSUES

Environmental activists of all sorts have taken to the Internet like salmon to a swift-running stream. And so have environmental researchers with governments, think tanks, and private organizations. If you want to know about endangered wildlife, pollution, efforts to halt the use of dangerous pesticides and other chemicals, and projects that promote biodiversity, the sites below are just the beginning.

40 Tips to Go Green

This is a flyer distributed by the Jalan Hijau ("Go Green" in Malay) Environmental Action Group during Earth Day 1992 in Singapore. It's basic advice—nicely and simply illustrated.

Type: WWW
Address: **http://www.ncb.gov.sg:80/jkj/ env/greentips.html**
Region: Malaysia

alt.pave.the.earth

Here's where to hang out if your personal environmental preference is concrete gray.

Type: Usenet newsgroup
Address: **alt.pave.the.earth**
Region: World

Base de Dados Tropical Web

The Base de Dados Tropical (Tropical Database) is a department within the Fundacao Tropical de Pesquisas e Tecnologia Andre Tosello, a Brazilian non-profit private foundation. It provides a database of information on tropical issues from biological control to zoology. The database is available in Portuguese and English.

Type: WWW
Address: **http://www.ftpt.br/**
Region: Brazil

BioDeisel Information

Information in German about fossil fuels and ecology.

Type: WWW
Address: **http://www.phil.uni-sb .de/oeko/**
Region: Germany, World

Biodiversidad, Taxonomia, Conservacion

This publication of the Instituto de Ecologia in Mexico covers the topics of biodiversity, wildlife preservation, and conservation, in Spanish.

Type: WWW
Address: **http://dell.ieco.conacyt.mx/ biodiver.htm**
Region: Mexico

Bioline Publications

Bioline Publications is an electronic publishing service for bioscientists. In collaboration with scientific publishers, newsletter editors, and authors of reports, it makes scientific material available more easily and more cheaply. The service is provided by Bioline Publications in association with the Base de Dados Tropical.

Type: WWW
Address: **http://www.ftpt.br/cgi-bin/ bioline/bioline**
Region: Brazil

Brazilian Bioinformatics Resource Center

BBRC is a Gopher site for biological information on various topics ranging biodiversity to plant parasites, with a wonderful search function so you to can find your favorite nematode.

Type: Gopher
Address: **gopher://asparagin.cenargen .embrapa.br/1**
Region: Brazil

Center for Earth Observation

A joint project of the European Space Agency and the European Commission, the CEO is the centerpiece of a coordinated,

decentralized Earth observation network called the European Earth Observation System. See current clips of the Earth, data on climate and conditions, and supporting documents here.

Type: WWW
Address: http://ceo-www.jrc.it/
Region: Europe, World

The Center for Ocean-Land-Atmosphere Studies

This U.S.-based group maintains an informative site on the Web that includes software, research results, and constantly updated weather and climate forecasts.

Type: WWW
Address: http://grads.iges.org/home.html
Region: U.S., World

Central European Environmental Data Request Facility

CEDAR offers access to environmental data for Austria, Poland, and nearby countries, including UN documentation and newsletters that cover small local environmental projects. Files are available in English, German, and some Eastern European languages as well. This site includes the excellent Gopher site of the Regional Environmental Centre for Central and Eastern Europe, and leads to many other environmental data providers and advocacy groups in Eastern and Central Europe.

Type: WWW
Address: http://pan.cedar.univie.ac.at/
Region: Austria, Poland, Slovakia, the Czech Republic, Ukraine, Hungary, World

The Earth Council Home Page

The Earth Council, based in Costa Rica, provides information to the sustainable development community through this Web server. The text is available in both Spanish and English.

Type: WWW
Address: http://terra.ecouncil.ac.cr/ecweb .htm
Region: Costa Rica

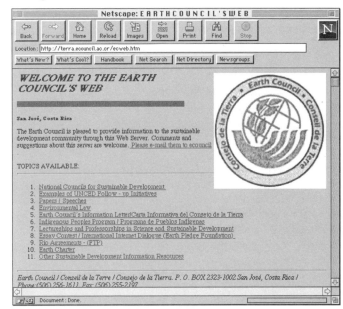

Eco-Chronice

This is a biweekly online magazine on the Russian environment and its problems, including the horrific Soviet environmental legacy.

Type: WWW
Address: http://www.spb.su/eco-chro/ index.html
Region: Russia

EcoGopher

This ongoing project provides libraries of environmental data, publications, and leads to environmental organizations worldwide. It's searchable, has an environmental chat area online, and has a built-in hypertext access mechanism via Lynx.

Type: Gopher
Address: ecosys.drdr.virginia.edu/
Region: U.S., World

Ecology Action Centre: Environmental Internet Resources

This is quite possibly the best source for finding international environmental contacts. The Ecology Action Centre pages are simple, useful, and user-friendly.

Type: WWW
**Address: http://www.cfn.cs.dal.ca/
            Environment/EAC/eac-
            internet-resources.html**
Region: World

ECOSERV

ECOSERV is an independent research and consulting company that provides technical environmental consulting services. It offers data on African environmental problems, and works on high-tech solutions.

Type: WWW
Address: http://www.iaccess.za/ecoserv/
Region: South Africa

Environment Pollution Prevention Project

Tunisia's EPPP seeks to head off environmental disasters in this fast-developing North African nation before they occur, and find ways to deal with emergencies that may crop up along the way. Its offerings online include case studies on the environmental impact of local industries, including textile dyeing and olive oil production. Some information is in French, some in English.

Type: Gopher
Address: alyssa.rsinet.tn.:70/11/
Region: Tunisia

Environmental Action Centre

The Environmental Action Centre is Nova Scotia's oldest environmental group. Their page is nicely designed, although of course it's Nova Scotia-specific. It has quite a few good links to more eco-info on the Net.

Type: WWW
**Address: http://www.cfn.cs.dal.ca/
            Environment/EAC/EAC-Home
            .html**
Region: Canada

Environmental Resources Information Network

ERIN has an easy-to-use interface that gets you to information about air, land, water, humans, and land and marine life in Australia. Government and private environmental efforts are discussed, and they also get report cards. Links to databases, Gopher servers, and other resources are here as well.

Type: WWW
Address: http://kaos.erin.gov.au/erin.html
Region: Australia

Environmental Sites on the Internet

Here's another starting point with dozens of links, including many online ecology journals from Europe.

Type: WWW
Address: http://www.lib.kth.se/lg.html
Region: Sweden, World

EnviroWeb

This project of the EnviroLink Network is comprised of the Virtual Environmental Library, the Environmental Education Network, the Progressive Mailing List Archive, EnviroArts Gallery, the EnviroForum, and many more resources. The project attempts to provide a comprehensive list of all environmental information services that provide important resources to the public. It also includes the Internet Green Marketplace, with listings for environmentally friendly ("green") products and services.

Type: WWW
Address: http://envirolink.org/
Region: World

Friends of the Earth Home Page

Friends of the Earth is the largest international network of environmental groups, is represented in 52 countries, and is one of the leading environmental pressure groups in the U.K. with its unique network of local campaigning groups in England, Wales, and Northern Ireland. Mostly funded by its supporters, this site includes an online magazine. Its report screaming "Mahogany Is Murder!" is enough to make your average do-it-yourselfer give up that weekend paneling project.

Type: WWW
Address: http://www.foe.co.uk/
Region: England, Wales, Northern Ireland, World

Gateway to Antarctica Home Page

The International Antarctic Centre, based in Christchurch, New Zealand, is the biggest and best academic research center for Antarctic environment studies. Their page includes information on all aspects of Antarctica, including tourism, treaties, and newspapers. The news is also available in Spanish.

Type: WWW
Address: http://icair.iac.org.nz/
Region: Antarctica

Geomatics International

Geomatics International is a consulting firm based in Canada with offices in the United States, Germany, the Czech Republic, Poland, and Nigeria. It offers various services related to ecology, geoscience, information management, and systems development. Through the extensive use of Geographic Information Systems (GIS) and Remote Sensing, GI provides you with the ability to download current GIF or JPEG images of Africa and a full-resolution window of Tibesti, Chad, and Libya accurate enough to make Moammar Quaddafi and the CIA shake in their sandals and black Florsheim wingtips, respectively.

Type: WWW
Address: http://www.geomatics.com/
Region: Canada, World

Green League of Finland

The Finnish Green League is part of the European Green Coordination, and is a party split about joining the European Economic Union. Look here for information on Green politics in Finland and around Europe.

Type: WWW
Address: http://www.kaapeli.fi/~vihreat/ engl.html
Region: Finland

Greenpeace International

This the home page for the environmental action group Greenpeace, based at its Amsterdam headquarters. It has many subpages, access to Gophers, information on the group's international campaigns, and so forth.

Type: WWW
Address: http://www.greenpeace.org/
Region: World

A Guide to Environmental Resources on the Internet

This site is old by WWW standards, meaning that it was last updated in October 1994, but is does include indexes for FTP, Gopher, Telnet, and World Wide Web resources, plus many mailing lists. A good starting point for further research.

Type: WWW
Address: **http://www.cfn.cs.dal.ca/ Environment/EAC/ briggs-murphy-toc.html**
Region: World

Hiraiso Solar Terrestrial Research Center

There are lots of places online where you can find out whether the rain will fall in Spain tomorrow. This is one of the few where you can get an environmental quality reading for outer space. Information about solar flares, plus scientific results and reviews in solar-terrestrial physics (solar, interplanetary, magnetospheric, ionospheric, and atmospheric) with a special emphasis placed on improving predictions is available here. Data is nearly real-time.

Type: WWW
Address: **http://hiraiso.crl.go.jp/**
Region: Japan, World

Instituto de Ecología, A.C.

Located in the city of Xalapa (Jalapa), this site gives special attention to the ecology in Latin American countries, in three languages. Documents on plant geography in Veracruz are here, as are electronic books on biotechnology, links to other information on biodiversity, plus species preservation and conservation in Mexico and in the rest of the world. This site also offers *Interciencia*, a fine Spanish-language magazine from Venezuela on science and technology.

Type: WWW
Address: **http://dell.ieco.conacyt.mx/ default.htm**
Region: Mexico

Inter Natura

Inter Natura is a Spanish clearing house for environmental topics. Information is available in mostly Spanish, but there are some English articles. The site also has a list of ecology groups in the Canary Islands.

Type: WWW
Address: **http://llevant.uji.es/~bort/index .html**
Region: Spain, Canary Islands

NativeNet/Native Web

This page provides information about issues relating to indigenous people around the world, and current threats to their cultures and habitats (for example, the rainforests). Lots of discussion about problems and solutions.

Type: WWW
Address: **http://kuhttp.cc.ukans.edu/~marc**
Type: Mailing list
Address: **gst@gnosys.svle.ma.us (Gary S. Trujillo)**
Region: World

Pagina Principal de INBio

Instituto de Nacional de Biodiversidad is a Costa Rica–based private organization that promotes Costa Rica's use of biodiversity management techniques. Available in both Spanish and English.

Type: WWW
Address: **http://www.inbio.ac.cr/**
Region: Costa Rica

The Progressive Directory

Several dozen environmental groups ranging in attitude from Earth First! to the Sierra Club, and in interests from protecting small local ecosystems to monitoring conditions on all the world's rivers, are linked into this directory. It's an excellent place to hook up with activists on issues you are passionate about. You can also find out about EcoNet—the environmentalists' online network—on a linked page.

Type: WWW
**Address: http://www.igc.apc.org/igc/
              people.html**
Region: World

specieslist

The specieslist is a mailing list for contacting those interested in information regarding the World Species List (WSL). The WSL is a free world-species database.

Type: WWW
Address: http://envirolink.org/species/
Region: World

Tiempo

The online version of this English journal on the effects of global warming on the Third World is a real eye-opener. Stories cover Vietnam, Ethiopia, India, and many other nations, as well as both international and self-help efforts.

Type: WWW
**Address: http://www.cru.uea.ac.uk/cru/
              tiempo/index.htm**
Region: World

ToxList

This mailing list was created to generate discussions and disseminate information in the discipline of toxicology. Discussions related to the fields of drug, pesticide, or hazardous waste toxicology, risk assessment and management, analytical toxicology, immunotoxicology, and other areas related to the study of the effects of toxins on man or the environment are welcome.

Type: Mailing list
**Address: listserv@cornell.edu
Send e-mail message with body: SUB
              ToxList <Firstname Lastname>**
Region: World

WELL Environmental Archive

There's a small archive of articles here on environmental issues, including a well-written piece on pesticide dumping in Eastern Europe. There's a also a Telnet link to the Classroom Earth BBS.

Type: Gopher
**Address: gopher.well.sf.ca.us:70/11/
              Environment**
Region: U.S., World

Wildlife Rehabilitation Mailing List

The WLREHAB list exists to serve the needs of wildlife rehabilitators and those interested in wildlife. It's open to discussion of all areas of the care of injured and orphaned wildlife with the ultimate goal of releasing healthy animals back into the wild. Through this list discussion, support, and information-gathering can be accomplished by wildlife rehabilitators, as well as by other interested individuals.

Type: Mailing list
**Addresses: listserv@VM1.nodak.edu
              listserv@NDSUVM1.bitnet**

Send e-mail message with blank Subject line and body: SUBSCRIBE WLREHAB <Firstname Lastname>

Region: World

Wildnet

This list is concerned with computing and statistical issues in fisheries, and with wildlife biological research and management. Relevant topics include GIS, ecological modelling, conferences, and so on.

Type: Mailing list

Address: wildnet-request@tribune.usask.ca

Region: Canada

World Conservation Monitoring Centre

WCMC provides information services on the conservation and sustainable use of species and ecosystems, and supports others in the development of their own information management systems. It offers a great deal of data about threatened animals.

Type: WWW

Address: http://www.wcmc.org.uk/index .html

Region: World

FANDOM INTERNATIONAL

See also Comics and Cartoons page 116; Film page 259; Literature page 372; Sports page 463; Television page 470

"Fandom" has a specific meaning to many people; being a science fiction fan or a Trekker, for example, can be very much a way of life. These fans are people who spend a lot of time and money on costumes, videotapes, books, collectables, and bumper stickers. They may meet their closest friends and future spouses without leaving the "fannish" (an adjective favored by fans) world, with its hierarchical clubs and yearly round of "Cons" (conventions). But who am I to criticize? It harms no one, and it's all in good fun.

Sports fans can be just as consumed by their obsessions, as can those who wax fanatic about popular singers, bands, actors, or TV shows. But the sci-fi universe has certainly gone the farthest—heck, some fannish people even speak Klingon!

I've concentrated on sci-fi resources here because I know how popular they are, particularly on the Net. But I've included a smattering of other fan clubs to provide a glimpse of what else—and who else—is out there.

In addition to the Usenet newsgroups reviewed separately below, there are many, many others in the group with the rec.arts.sf prefix. See any list of current Usenet groups for a complete run-down.

AEK Supporters and Fans

Athlitiki Enosis Konstantinoupoleos (Athletic Union Constantinople) is a Greek soccer club. This page is kept by rabid fans, the kind who refer to the team's manager as "the god." Includes game schedules, statistics, news, and more.

Type: WWW

Address: http://www.lpac.qmw.ac.uk/ SEL-HPC/People/Dimitris/AEK/ enosis.html

Region: England, Greece

alt.fan Newsgroups

There are many newsgroups devoted to fawning worship of various idols. See this or any other repository of newsgroup information to see if there's one for you.

Type: WWW
**Address: http://src.doc.ic.ac.uk/usenet/
            news-faqs/**
Region: World

Anime Fan Club Directory

Here's an online list of anime fan clubs worldwide, with expanded information on each after the listings.

Type: WWW
**Address: http://web.mit.edu/afs/athena/
            user/d/g/dgaxiola/www/
            acd2.html**
Region: U.S., Netherlands, Australia, Canada,
            Singapore, Japan

Ansible

Oh-so-English and snide, this science fiction fandom newsletter and gossip sheet has been around since the early 1980s. It's archived here, and is a most entertaining read.

Type: E-zine
ansible-request@dcs.gla.ac.uk
Send e-mail message with body:
            SUBSCRIBE
Type: FTP
**Address: ftp.dcs.gla.ac.uk. cd
            /pub/Ansible**
Type: Gopher
**Address: gopher.dcs.gla.ac.uk:70/11/pub/
            SF-Archives/Ansible**
Region: England

Bamboleo: The Gypsy Kings Home Page

All you need to know about this enjoyable French band, who play their own unique variation on traditional Gypsy music.

Type: WWW
**Address: http://www.dur.ac.uk/~d22ukn/
            Gypsy_Kings/**
Region: France

Cancrelas Fan Club

In French, this page supports the band Cancrelas, who appear to play in a style called "le comic Metal." This could be amusing, maybe even good.

Type: WWW
Address: http://timb.imag.fr/~promayon/
Region: France

Clouds

This Aussie band's page offers some song samples, album covers, and a discography.

Type: WWW
Address: http://www.nbn.com/aaj/clouds/
Region: Australia

COMSTAAReast

This is a general science fiction and fantasy fan club at Acadia University, in Wolfville, Nova Scotia. The club also has connections to the Kingcon Society, a nonprofit sci-fi group in New Brunswick.

Type: WWW
**Address: http://dragon.acadiau.ca/
            ~860473m/comseast.html**
Region: Canada

The Convention Scene

These newsgroups will keep you up to date on the dates, locations, and plans for the many, many science fiction and related conventions.

Type: Usenet newsgroup
Address: rec.arts.sf.announce
Address: alt.fandom.cons
Region: U.S., World

Country Music Fans Unite!

The keepers of this page hope it will be linked to just about everything country real soon now, including show reviews, tour schedules, fan-club lists, and places to go to enjoy country music. Country is huge worldwide, and especially so in England and Australia, so you'll find lots of international content here.

Type: WWW
Address: http://www.einet.net/EINet/staff/ wayne/country/country.html
Region: U.S., World

Cyberspace Vanguard

This 'zine contains lots of news and opinions about science fiction films, TV shows, and fiction, with more emphasis on film and video than some other publications. It's also available on CD-ROM.

Type: Gopher
Address: gopher.etext.org:70/11/Zines/ Cyberspace.Vanguard
Address: gopher.well.sf.ca.us: Publications
Address: gopher.cic.net: e-serials/ alphabetic/c/cyberspace-vanguard
Type: FTP
Address: ftp.etext.org/pub/Zines/ Cyberspace.Vanguard/
Address: ftp.cic.net/pub/e-serials/ archive/alphabetic/c/ cyberspace-vanguard/E-mail
Type: E-mail
Address: cn577@cleveland.freenet.edu
Address: Cyberspace Vanguard@1:157/564 (FidoNet)
Address: tj@phantom.com
Region: U.S., World

DargonZine—The Magazine of the Dargon Project

DargonZine is an electronic magazine printing stories written for the Dargon Project, a shared-world anthology similar to (and inspired by) Robert Asprin's *Thieves' World* anthologies. The Dargon Project centers around a medieval-style duchy called Dargon in the far reaches of the Kingdom of Baranur on a world named Makdiar, and contains stories in the fantasy fiction/swords-and-sorcery vein.

Type: Gopher
Address: gopher.etext.org:70/11/Zines/ DargonZine
Type: FTP
Address: ftp.etext.org: /pub/Zines/ DargonZine/
Type: Usenet newsgroup
Address: rec.mag.dargon
Type: E-mail
Address: dargon@wonky.jjm.com
Region: World

Derby County Football Club

In this site that contains lots of information for supporters of this English soccer team, most of the game reviews follow the pattern of this one: "We were absolutely awful." You have to hand it to supporters so loyal as to stand behind their team—whether they win or lose.

Type: WWW
Address: **http://lard.sel.cam.ac.uk/
derby_county/**
Region: England

Diana Ross Fan Club

Created by Dutch fans of the diva, this semi-official page offers a quarterly newsletter, photos, and concert information.

Type: WWW
Address: **http://www.knoware.nl/music/
diana/ross1.htm**
Region: Holland, World

EastEnders Fan Page

I was once addicted to this working-class British soap myself, so I understand the fascination, at least a little. Aimed primarily at U.S. and Canadian "EastEnders" fans, the Web page covers what stations are carrying the show, links to a big map of the Walford neighborhood where the show takes place and to EE trivia, and information on EE chat groups on several commercial online services (Prodigy, Delphi, and so on).

Type: WWW
Address: **http://found.cs.nyu.edu/beads/
eastenders.html**
Region: England

Fan Fiction

No, I don't mean those abysmally bad sci-fi stories by amateurs that appear all too often in fanzines. This is an archive of wishful TV-show scripts written by fans. They might be just as bad, but at least it's something different!

Type: WWW
Address: **http://src.doc.ic.ac.uk/public/
media/tv/collections/tardis/html/
fiction.html**
Region: World

Finnish Science-Fiction Societies

In Finnish, this site includes lots of links to science fiction clubs in Finland, mailing lists and newsgroups about sci-fi topics that are carried out in Finnish, and Finnish SF archives. "Spock" apparently is the same in any language.

Type: WWW
Address: **http://www.jyu.fi/~jtv/
42-rest.html**
Region: Finland

Forces of the Empire

These fans like to dress up as their favorite *Star Wars* characters and do battle. I'll bet it's fun, too.

Type: WWW
Address: **http://maniac.deathstar.org/user/
pfurlong/FoE.html**
Region: World

Gaia: Olivia Newton-John Home Page

This site has lots of information on the varied career of this perky Australian export.

Type: WWW
Address: **http://www-leland.stanford.edu/
~clem/**
Region: U.S., Australia

Hayashibara Megumi Internet Fan Club

Megumi is a cute, bubbly *seiyuu* (voiceover actress for anime cartoons). She has even been the voice of Hello Kitty, the girl-cat with no visible mouth. Find out her shoe size and blood type here.

Type: WWW

Address: http://www.tcp.com/doi/seiyuu/ hayashibara-megumi.html

Region: Japan

The Hong Kong Bridge

Find GIFs and information here about pop idols from Hong Kong, Japan, and other parts of Asia. If you've been there, you know these regional superstars get adulation from their fans that's the equivalent of the devotion of Elvis fans or Beatlemania in its prime. Includes fan polls that result in a Net HK hit parade.

Type: WWW

Address: http://www.mdstud.chalmers .se/hkmovie/

Region: Hong Kong, Japan, Taiwan

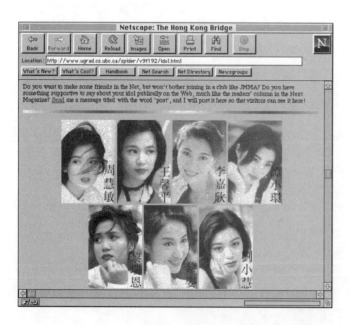

International Roxette Fan Club

Yup, the two-piece rock band with the bleached-blond singer. It's got photos plus links to (this scares me) several more Roxette sites online.

Type: WWW

Address: http://www.wirehub.nl/~introxfc/

Region: Netherlands

International Star Trek Conventions

In the immortal words of William Shatner, "get a life!" I suppose you could get one here, if a Trekker life is the kind you really like!

Type: WWW

Address: http://www.wwcd.com/shows/ strekconv.html/

Region: World

J.R.R. Tolkien Fan Archive

Here is where to check in on serious discussion of the "languages" Tolkien invented for his fantasy series *The Lord of the Rings*, along with the formation and doings of Tolkien societies and games based on the author's works.

Type: FTP

Address: ftp.math.uni-hamburg.de/pub/ misc/tolkien/

Region: World

The Junior Ganymede Fan Club Book

The Web page contains the FAQ for the alt.fan.wodehouse Usenet newsgroup, for fans of the British mystery writer.

Type: WWW

Address: http://ickenham.isu.edu/pgw.html

Type: Usenet newsgroup

Address: alt.fan.wodehouse

Region: England, World

The Lila Feng Fan Club

Ms. Feng is the attractive anchorperson on Canada's The Weather Network. Feng has a following that's more interested in her charms than the chance of precipitation on Tuesday. Here's their fan club FAQ. Discussions happen on the Usenet newsgroup.

Type: WWW
Address: http://itre.uncecs.edu/misc/ lila.faq.html
Type: Usenet newsgroup
Address: alt.fan.lila-feng
Region: Canada

The Linkoping SF and F Archive

One of the world's largest online collections of science-fiction and fantasy ephemera is held on this server. Includes an archive of Swedish fanzines, in addition to huge amounts of material on books, stories, movies, TV shows, conventions, and fannish activities. There are also bibliographies of the Russian sci-fi writers Stanislaw Lem, Arkadii Strugatskii, and Boris Strugatskii.

Type: WWW
Address: http://www.lysator.liu.se/ sf_archive/sf_main.html
Region: Sweden, Russia, World

The Lion Online

This is the online version of *The Lion Sleeps*, a print fanzine for fans of the Canadian professional figure skater Brian Orser. Published since 1989, it contains news and information on Brian Orser's career, where he is performing and can be seen on television, as well as reviews of live and televised shows, interviews with Brian, Brian-related stuff for sale, and a pen-pal/e-mail pal column. The e-zine includes everything but the photos.

Type: E-mail
Address: tamcmp@rit.edu
Region: Canada

Pern Fans

The newsgroup alt.fan.pern is for devotees of the *Dragonriders of Pern* science-fiction series by Anne McCaffrey. Their FAQ is at this Web page.

Type: WWW
Address: http://www.lib.ox.ac.uk/ internet/news/faq/archive/ pern-intro.part1.html
Type: Usenet newsgroup
Address: alt.fan.pern
Region: England, World

Pet Shop Boys Info

This English duo create amusing music: danceable beats with slyly subversive and smart lyrics. Who else would mention Che Guevara and Claude Debussy in the same pop song? Their fans will enjoy this FAQ.

Type: WWW
Address: http://www.dsv.su.se/~mats-bjo/ psbfaq.html
Region: England

Quanta

Quanta is an online-only magazine of science fiction and fantasy. Each issue features fiction from amateur and professional authors from around the world. Available in both PostScript and ASCII text versions.

Type: WWW
Address: http://www.etext.org/Zines/ Quanta/
Type: Gopher
Address: gopher.etext.org:70/11/Zines/ Quanta

Address: gopher.contrib.andrew.cmu.edu/
11/magazines/quanta

Type: FTP

Address: ftp.etext.org/pub/Zines/Quanta/

Address: lth.se:/pub/documents/quanta/

Address: ftp.cic.net:/pub/e-serials/
archive/alphabetic/q/quanta/

Type: E-mail

Address: listserv@netcom.com

**For ASCII text version, send e-mail
message with body: subscribe
quanta-ascii**

**For PostScript version, send e-mail
message with body: subscribe
quanta-postscript**

**To receive a notice by e-mail when a new
issue comes out, so you can
retrieve it by FTP or other means,
send e-mail message with body:
subscribe quanta-notice**

Region: U.S., World

rec.arts.sf.fandom

This is the largest, most mainstream, and most complete group for the fandom side of science fiction. It includes conventions, clubs, personal bickering, and lots of fun.

Type: Usenet newsgroup

Address: rec.arts.sf.fandom

Region: World

Red Dwarf Fan Club

The Web page holds the FAQ for this discussion group about the extremely low-budget English science-fiction TV show, just in case you needed to know what *smeg* means.

Type: Usenet newsgroup

Address: alt.tv.red-dwarf

Type: WWW

Address: http://www.cis.ohio-state.edu/
hypertext/faq/usenet/red_dwarf
-faq/faq.html

Region: England

The Sandy Lam Home Page

This Chinese chanteuse has recorded in Cantonese, Mandarin, Japanese, and now English. She sings pop, light rock, and country, and has millions of fans by the look of this page, which is in English.

Type: WWW

Address: http://www.tezcat.com/
~sleepy/sandy/

Region: Japan

Sarko

Someone once accused *Sarko* of being "weird Gothic Chinese Cyberpunk," and I think this description fits. It's a fiction 'zine with a very stream-of-consciousness feel to it—good writing, too. In English.

Type: Gopher

Address: gopher.etext.org:70/11/Zines/
Sarko

Type: FTP

Address: ftp.etext.org: /Zines/Sarko/

Type: E-mail

Address: sarko-request@mach.hk.super.net

**To be added to the announcement list, send
e-mail message with Subject:
Sarko-Announce**

**To receive each issue by mail, send e-mail
message with Subject:
Sarko-Distribution**

If you want to be mailed a specific issue, send e-mail message with Subject: Sarko-Request X.X

Region: Hong Kong

Science Fiction Archives

Several science fiction 'zines are archived at this site. Browse around the Wiretap hierarchy and you'll find other items of a fannish nature as well.

Type: FTP
Address: **ftp.spies.com/Library/Zines/**
Type: Gopher
Address: **wiretap.spies.com:70/11/ Library/Zines**
Region: U.S., World

Science Fiction Archives in Slovenia

There's too much information here for anyone but a fan. This archive is organized according to author, and the authors include many English and a few European writers. I only see one name from Eastern Europe, though, and that's a shame—science fiction is incredibly popular in Russia and its environs, and it'd be interesting to find out more about these largely unknown-in-the-West writers.

Type: Gopher
Address: **sk2eu.eunet.sk:70/11/sf/authors**
Region: Slovakia, World

Science Fiction Lovers Headquarters

The mailing list sf-lovers was the first known Internet mailing list on anything other than a work-related topic. It's still going strong. It's archived at the FTP and Web sites below; the Web page also has links to all sorts of related sites, including other archives, bibli-ographies, bookstores, publishers, science-fiction and fantasy role-playing games, 'zines, and more.

Type: Mailing list
Address: **sf-lovers-request@rutgers.edu**
Contact: **sf-lovers@rutgers.edu**
Type: FTP
Address: **gandalf.rutgers.edu/pub/sfl**
Type: WWW
Address: **http://rschp2.anu.edu.au:8080/ sfres.html**
Region: World

The Slan Shack: Science Fiction and Fact Pages

There are several links here to specifically fannish pages and convention information.

Type: WWW
Address: **http://www.lm.com/~lmann/hot/ sf.html#sffen**
Region: World

Starfleet: The International Star Trek Fan Association

This is a worldwide fan organization, which sponsors conventions and has hundred of chapters from Azerbaijan to Australia. It has its own Usenet newsgroup for internal use.

Type: Usenet newsgroup
Address: **alt.org.starfleet**
Type: WWW
Address: **http://www.halcyon.com/dyar/ strfleet.html**
Region: U.S., World

Star Trek Home Page in Graz, Austria

This page is where members of other "Star Trek" fan clubs around the world can drop in add their club to the growing list. If you're looking for an offline club in your area, this is a good place to start.

Type: WWW
**Address: http://fvkma.tu-graz.ac.at/
            star-trek/fanaddr.html**
Region: Austria, World

Star Trek: WWW

This page offers leads to all "Star Trek" pages on the Internet, say its creators. (I wouldn't be so confident, folks.)

Type: WWW
**Address: http://www-iwi.unisg.ch/
            ~sambucci/scifi/startrek/
            st-www.html**
Region: World

The Timebinders Home Page

This is a project of the Society for the Preservation of the History of Science Fiction Fandom, and was founded at the similarly themed 1994 convention, Fan Historicon I. Find out here about the group and its mission, as well as specific historic items and addresses they're looking for.

Type: WWW
**Address: http://www.lm.com/~lmann/
            timebinders/tbstart.html**
Region: World

Tomorrow People Fans

This English science-fiction show for kids is just now being shown on the Nickleodeon cable-TV channel, so it's picking up fans stateside as well. This is a fannish FAQ, with script synopses and cast lists.

Type: WWW
**Address: http://www.cs.mcgill.ca/
            ~timelord/Tomorrow_People/
            tomorrow-people.faq**
Region: England, Canada, U.S.

University Science Fiction Association

Located at the University of Western Australia, it includes fans of science fiction, fantasy, horror, graphic novels, "Monty Python," "The Goon Show," "Calvin and Hobbes," anime, and Hong Kong cinema (as well as Coca-Cola, chocolate, and caffeine, they admit). They not only lounge about and talk shop, but also get out in the sunshine for some soccer and badminton.

Type: WWW
**Address: http://www.gu.uwa.edu.au/
            unisfa/**
Region: Australia

UK SF Fandom Archives

Along with the *Ansible* archive reviewed above, this site has many other documents and fannish items relating to the British scene.

Type: Gopher
**Address: gopher.dcs.gla.ac.uk/11/pub/
            SF-Archives**
Region: England

Vivian Lai Home Page

GIFs, discography, and much breathless hyperbole about this Hong Kong–based pop singer.

Type: WWW
**Address: http://www.csua.berkeley.edu/
            ~ngocle/vivian.html**
Region: Hong Kong

Wolverhampton Wanderers F.C.

Unofficial home page for the Brit soccer team from Wolverhampton, a rather posh area near London. Includes *A Load of Bull*, the club's fanzine.

Type: WWW
Address: http://www.wlv.ac.uk/~cm6618/ wolves/
Region: England

FILM

See also Comics and Cartoons page 116; Fandom International page 250

Even ignoring all the commercial advertising pages put up by big film studios (which I did—you'll have no trouble at all finding these on your own; they're ubiquitous!) there's an amazing variety of material on film online. The arrival of a visual organizing method with the World Wide Web has added a new dimension to these archives, with many offering movie stills, film clips, sounds, movie posters, and publicity shots of favorite actors and directors.

African Films and Filmmakers

This file is an attempt at a filmography of recent African cinema. It's by no means complete.

Type: WWW
Address: http://www.sas.upenn.edu/ African_Studies/Audio_Visual/ African_Film_10050.html
Region: Africa

AMIA List

AMIA is an organization concerned with the preservation of old, valuable, or rare films and videos. This list is intended for members of AMIA, as well as archivists or librarians dealing with such films. As well as medium-volume discussion, there are news postings, job opportunities, conferences, and so on.

Type: Mailing list
Address: listserv@ukcc.bitnet
Region: World

Anime

A casual discussion list relating to animation, manga, and other Japanese animedia subjects, it is at times highly specific—there are requests for particular collectors items and such. But it also includes more general discussion about animators, artists, soundtracks, legends, and availability. High volume and high noise.

Type: Mailing list
Address: LISTSERV@VTVM1.BITNET
Region: Japan

Asia Film/Cinema Page

This page was still under construction when I looked in. It will have links to information on Chinese, Japanese, and Korean films, but for now only the Japanese section is up. However, it has links not found elsewhere, including Japanese filmographies in English and directories of Japanese film collections.

Type: WWW
Address: http://pears.lib.ohio-state.edu/ AsiaSub/asiafilm.html
Region: China, Japan, Korea

Asian Movies Home Page

There is a page full of pictures and information on Asian pop celebrities—film directors, actors, actresses, pop stars, and comedians. It includes some introductory files for people new to the subject. Unfortunately, it's rather high on celebrity adoration and low on content.

Type: WWW
**Address: http://www.seas.upenn.edu/
            ~luwang/lu.html**
Region: Asia

Cardiff Movie Database

This searchable database has information from the earliest silents to the latest films, even some that haven't made it to the theaters yet. It includes biographies and filmographies of actors, too, as well as French films and many other foreign-language films.

Type: WWW
**Address: http://www.cm.cf.ac.uk/Movies/
            moviequery.html**
Region: World

CINEMA

This mailing list is conducted in French, and is for discussion on both classic and recent films. The archives are at the Web site.

Type: Mailing list
**Address: cinema-request@email.enst.fr.
Send e-mail message with body: subscribe**
Type: WWW
**Address: http://autan.enst.fr/~tardieu/
            mailarchive/cinema/**
Region: France

Cinema-L

This is a more informal list devoted to all aspects and forms of cinema. Participants come from a wide variety of backgrounds; there are people from within the industry, as well as film buffs and people who use film in their work. There is a very high volume of postings, and many are informal to the point of irrelevance.

Type: Mailing list
Address: listserv@auvm.auvm.edu
Region: World

CineMedia

This Australian site provides resources to those interested in cinema and the media. There is very little original material, but hundreds of links to other resources. It covers a broad spectrum of interests, from professionals to students to the casual filmgoer. There are many image, movie, and sound clips.

Type: WWW
**Address: http://www.gu.edu.au/gwis/
            cinemedia/CineMedia.HOME.HTML**
Region: Australia, World

Cuban Cinema

A few documents are here from the Instituto Cubano de Arte e Industria Cinematografica, and are about the latest Cuban films and the state of movie-making in that island nation.

Type: Gopher
**Address: makenda.edu.uy:70/11/
            otros-gophers/cuba/cine**
Region: Cuba

The Cult Page

Devoted to directors, filmmakers, and movies that have a rabid cult following—Quentin Tarantino, Ed Wood, that kind of stuff. It also links to many horror and vampire and things-that-go-slash-in-the-night sites.

Type: WWW
**Address: http://www.public.iastate.
             edu:80/~abormann/**
Region: U.S., World

Experimental Film and Video

This archive is for and about experimental art films and filmmakers. The Gopher contains mostly papers about film, postings of requests for films, and information from the Prelinger archives. These hold the transcripts of documentaries that cover the history of the visual media—a key source for the art side of filmmaking

Type: Gopher
**Address: gopher.well.sf.ca.us/11/Art/
             Experimental.Film.and.Video**
Region: World

Film and Video Sources for Educators

This resource is a bibliography of sources for educators selecting and ordering videos and films. It is located on the Vanderbilt University Gopher; consequently, the list is of resources at Vanderbilt University. However, most of them are widely available elsewhere. Although the list is quite small, the bibliography does include other directories, instructional resources, and indexes.

Type: Gopher
**Address: vuinfo.vanderbilt.edu/00/
             library/guides/video**
Region: World

Film Feature Forum

This newsletter contains digests and abstracts of articles published in European film magazines. There are articles in most major European languages, including stories from *Blimp, Filmbulletin, Film a Doba, Skrien, Kinovedcheskie,* and others. The site is chiefly of interest to editors of festival catalogues and magazines. There are contact addresses and numbers for the publications featured, so you can get the complete articles.

Type: WWW
**Address: http://gewi.kfunigraz.ac.at/
             ~puntigam/FFF/**
Region: Europe

Film-Historia

This journal of film in English, Spanish, and Catalan is published regularly by the University of Barcelona. Information about it is available here.

Type: WWW
**Address: http://www.swcp.com/~cmora/
             historia.html**
Region: Spain

Filmographies from the University of Michigan Film and Video Library

This is a collection of lists of films in minority or fringe areas. Subject areas covered include Asian Americans, African-American studies, gay and lesbian studies, Hispanics/Latinos/Latinas, and racism/race relations. Some of the lists are just titles; others are annotated. Both documentary and feature films are covered. Some of the lists include useful ordering information (distributors, and so on).

Type: Gopher
**Address: una.hh.lib.umich.edu:70/11/
             humanities/fvlexp/fvllocal/
             filmogs/diversity**
Region: World

Flicker

This site is for aficionados of alternative and avant garde film. It includes information about new films and their makers, including experimental shorts and many foreign titles. It also has information about alternative film, video showcases, and other events.

Type: WWW
Address: http://www.sirius.com/~sstark/
Region: U.S., World

Gay Paree

Here's a surprisingly long list of French films with a gay theme. This is part of a larger list of gay films.

Type: WWW
**Address: http://acacia.ens.fr:8080/home/
            delmas/fqrd/culture/movies.html**
Region: France

Hong Kong Movies

Reviews and a searchable database of Hong Kong movie actors, filmographies, alternative names, and pictures, with links to many related sites. You can search and display text in English, Cantonese, and Mandarin. There is a picture library, MPEG movie clips, and a wealth of information on everyone from John Woo to "female action stars" to Jackie Chan.

Type: WWW
**Address: http://www.mdstad.chalmers.se/
            hkmovie/**
Type: FTP
**Address: ftp.u.washington.edu/pub/
            user-supported/magritte**
Region: Hong Kong

Horror-ListA

This is a discussion list for both fans and students of the genre. Subjects include natural and supernatural horror in legends, films, and fiction. Classical and modern horror films are covered, as well as speculation about future trends. There is a certain Stephen King bias.

Type: Mailing list
Address: LISTSERV@PACEVM.BITNET
Region: World

The Independent Film and Video Makers Resource Guide

This is a hypertext reference to resources for the independent film and video community. There is information on new technological developments—multimedia, CD-ROM, computer animation, and more. Also, there are up-to-date announcements, events, and news. A lot of links, but rather U.S.-centered.

Type: WWW
**Address: http://www.echonyc.com/
            ~mvidal/Indi-Film+Video.html**
Region: U.S., World

Indian Film Essay

This essay on Tamil film director Mani Rathnam has a great deal of background information on Indian cinema—it's the world's most prolific movie industry, you know, famous for its huge epics and for both historical and modern romances.

Type: WWW
**Address: http://www.public.iastate.edu/
            ~chari/chute.html**
Region: India

Indian Film Humor

Standard Hindi film dialogs are presented in cartoon form here—a nice touch for making Indian humor more accessible to non-Hindi speakers.

Type: WWW
Address: http://menger.eecs.stevens-tech .edu/~sahirns/india.html
Region: India

Indian Film Info

This site has synopses and bibliographies on Indian film from the 1950s through today.

Type: WWW
Address: http://www.ids.net/picpal/ indhome.html
Region: India

Internet Film Institute

This site offers links to mostly academic film resources online: film schools, film researchers, film groups, and societies. It also has a Reading Room with online publications.

Type: WWW
Address: http://Penny.ibmPCUG.CO.UK:80/ ~scrfin/ifi/ifi.htm
Region: England, World

Internet Movie Database

This huge searchable database covers over 40,000 films, and also offers indexes of actors and industry figures. You can search titles by country, genre, production company, and more. It includes some technical data, but is mainly of interest to the movie buff. There are some sound and movie clips, a trivia quiz, and a form to vote for your favorite movies.

Type: WWW
Address: http://www.cm.cf.ac.uk/Movies/ welcome.html
Address: http://www.leo.org/Movies/ welcome.html
Address: http://www.msstate.edu/ Movies/welcome.html
Address: http://ballet.cit.gu.edu.au/ Movies/welcome.html
Address: http://www.csl.sony.co.jp/ Movies/welcome.html
Region: England

John Woo Central

This home page is devoted to Hong Kong action director John Woo, director of rock 'em shock 'em epics that make most Hollywood "action" films look like a slow ride around the roller-skating rink. Lots of photos and a filmography.

Type: WWW
Address: http://trill.pc.cc.cmu.edu/~jkoga/ jw_gallery.html
Region: Hong Kong

Mongolian Movies

Information at this site concerns Mongolian cinema (heavy on the epics), and on images of Mongolia and Mongolians in movies made elsewhere.

Type: Gopher
Address: gate1.zedat.fu-berlin.de:70/11/ mongolei/films
Region: Mongolia

Monty Python Scripts

A site for devoted Monty Python fans. Here there are scripts for the three Monty Python films: *The Life of Brian*, *The Holy Grail*, and *The Meaning of Life*. Note: I had some trouble accessing this site.

Type: FTP

Address: **quartz.rutgers.edu/pub/humor/ Python**

Region: England

Movie Resources

This exhaustive listing of film-related Web sites includes pages devoted to individual directors (Kurusawa, Tarantino, and so forth), actors, and production companies.

Type: WWW

Address: **http://www.maths.tcd.ie/pub/ films/movie_hypdocs.html**

Region: Ireland, World

Movie Trivia

You'll find in-jokes, cameos, and signatures in this regularly updated site of movie trivia. It's full of little-known facts about directors, films, and actors, as well as stories and anecdotes about filming.

Type: Gopher

Address: **jupiter.sun.csd.unb.ca/00/FAQ/ rec/tv/news.answers.00521**

Region: World

Picture Palace Home Page

This hypertext film information site has a definite "trash movies" orientation. It includes anime, Hong Kong action movies, Indian films, and directors like Russ Meyer.

Type: WWW

Address: **http://www.ids.net/picpal/ homeindx.html**

Region: World

Rogue Cinema

This page is for anyone who wants to be the next John Waters: it's all about low-budget, personal, and independent filmmaking. It includes file archives, a book on screenwriting, links to Usenet newsgroups, and more.

Type: WWW

Address: **http://www.netins.net/showcase/ rogue/**

Region: U.S.

Science Fiction Movie Reviews

This is a collection of about 100 science fiction and fantasy film reviews, based at Linkoping University in Sweden. More reviews are added periodically, so it is reasonably up-to-date. A broad range of films is covered, from the mainstream to cult classics.

Type: Gopher

Address: **gopher.lysator.liu.se:70/11/ lysator-Science_Fiction_Archive/ .sf-texts/movies**

Region: Sweden, World

Screen Finance

So you want to make a movie, huh? Find out how to get the cash here. It concentrates on U.S. and U.K. filming with information on production companies, money sources, and more. There are also links to lots of other film resources and databases.

Type: WWW

Address: **http://www.ibmpcug.co.uk/ ~scrfin/**

Region: England

Screen-L

This high-volume list is intended for professional users of film—teachers, researchers, and filmmakers. Topics covered include film criticism, history, theory, and production. The discussion is generally scholarly, with very little noise.

Type: Mailing list
Address: listserv@ua1vm.ua.edu
Region: World

The Script Emporium

This site contains the screenplays to (mostly Hollywood) films. They are indexed by genre. The purpose of the site is to let you download and print the script you want, so it is direct and down to earth, with no graphics. It's not yet very comprehensive.

Type: WWW
**Address: http://www.cs.tufts.edu/
~katwell/**
Region: World

Scrnwrit

The Scrnwrit list is open to professional, amateur, and aspiring screenwriters. Topics cover the challenges of writing for films and TV. They include formats, story ideas, dialogue, characters, agents, producers, directors, and so forth. It's a very friendly and open forum, so a lot of the messages tend to be rather chatty, and not directly related to screenwriting.

Type: Mailing list
Address: listserv@tamvm1.tamu.edu
Region: World

Sinema Uzerine Tartisma Listesi

SINEMA-L is a discussion group on films in Turkish; the discussion here is in Turkish as well.

Type: Mailing list
Address: listserv@tritu.bitnet
Region: Turkey

Soundtrack Web

This is the Web page of the rec.music.movies newsgroup. There is a FAQ and a searchable database of soundtrack information, lists, and soundtrack reviews. There are also links to other resources, including Cardiff's Internet Movie Database.

Type: WWW
**Address: http://www.uib.no/People/midi/
soundtrackweb/**
Region: World

Study Cinema in Barcelona!

At this site you can get information on filmmaking and film-studies programs at the University of Barcelona, incubator of many filmmakers in the Spanish new wave.

Type: WWW
**Address: http://www.cm.cf.ac.uk/Movies/
moviequery.html**
Region: Spain

Transient Images

This weekly e-zine covers film and TV news.

Type: WWW
**Address: http://www.cais.com/jpadgett/
www/home.html**
Region: U.S.

Turku Cinema and Television Studies

This is the Gopher of the department of Cinema and Television Studies at the University of Turku in Finland. The information is of relevance to similar departments around the world. There is material in both English and Finnish. There is a small resources section, but of most interest is their journal *Lahikuva*—with articles arranged thematically so the information is easy to find.

Type: Gopher
**Address: gopher.utu.fi/11/
             tdk_ja_laitoksia/**
Region: Finland

Video and Movie Review Database

This site is a collection of general movie reviews. The database is searchable in many ways, including title, MPA rating, quality rating, cast, year of release, keywords, and so on. Anyone can add to the database, so the reviews are of varying quality. Mostly mainstream films.

Type: Gopher
**Address: isumvs.iastate.edu/
             1%7edb.VIDEO**
Region: World

Video Laserdiscs

This site contains about 25 articles covering selection, purchase, and maintenance of both laserdiscs and players. It would be useful for both consumers and retailers. Some of the articles are rather long, but they are very comprehensive, covering all the technical information in a very readable way. Some of them may well be out of date by now.

Type: Gopher
**Address: chop.isca.uiowa.edu:8337/11/
             laserdisc**
Region: World

Watmedia AV Materials Database

This Gopher site containing detailed information on a wide variety of audio-visual materials is especially useful for film librarians. It is a database searchable by academic level (for example, undergraduate), geographical area, subject, title, name, and more. There are over 40,000 titles in the database.

Type: Gopher
**Address: watdcs.uwaterloo.ca:3000/
             1%7edb.WATMEDIA**
Region: World

FINANCIAL DATA

See also Business page 111; Economics page 196

If you asked my personal advice on what to do with your excess money (and you didn't), I'd suggest investing it in the first company that develops a foolproof, uncrackable system for paying for things over the Internet. On the other hand, there are people with much more experience at giving this sort of advice than I have.

You can find some of them at the sites listed here, either dispensing the data, or listening on the sidelines and laughing up their sleeves at how easily the proverbial fool and his money are parted. As with any type of investment, be sure to check the legality and worth of any securities, precious metals, investment property, and so on that you are offered online. Never buy without having received and read a printed prospectus beforehand, preferably with approval from your lawyer and financial advisor. I have tried to include only the most reputable of sites here, but there are no guarantees.

It's much safer to use the informational tools available online: instant stock quotes, fast ways to check the differences between currencies, leisurely methods for investigating companies before you buy their stock. Here are a few places to peruse for money-saving and money-making opportunities.

Austrian Stock Market

See how The Boerse in Vienna is faring—reports are in German.

Type: Telnet
Address: fiivs01.tu-graz.ac.at
Login: boerse
Region: Austria

Banking on the Net

This list of links assembled by Wall Street Direct will take you to banking resources worldwide, including banks that advertise or provide some services online, such as investment advice; and to actual bank-by-Internet services, which are still in the fledgeling stages due to continuing security concerns. Bank listings are an international mix, including firms in the U.S., Austria, Ecuador, Ireland, Scotland, England, Germany, Canada, and other nations.

Type: WWW
Address: http://www.cts.com/~wallst/ w_banks.htm
Region: World

The Canadian Investment Jump Station

As the name implies, this site tries to help you choose your investments up North more wisely. The Jump Station has links to Canadian and American stock quotes, information on Canadian public companies, and profiles of Canadian mutual funds. It's the pet project of an enthusiastic commerce student, Rich McCue.

Type: WWW
Address: http://islandnet.com/~rmccue/ invest.html
Region: Canada

Canadian Investment News

This Canada-specific newsgroup provides a forum for the discussion of investments of all kinds. Stock tips and market quotes make up the bulk of the posts. This is a good place to find out how healthy that Canadian company you invested in really is.

Type: Usenet newsgroup
Address: misc.invest.canada
Region: Canada

ClariNet Newsgroups

These subscription-only newsgroups are based on wire-service reports, and many concern international finance and business. They're a good source for up-to-the-minute breaking news on money markets, stock markets, and related issues. Check here for a list of current newsgroups and information about how to access them via the World Wide Web, if your service provider does not offer them directly.

Type: WWW
Address: http://wwwhost.cc.utexas.edu/ ftp/pub/cc-training/w3times/ clarinet.html
Region: World

Daily Financial News

In Russian, from the business consulting agency Finmarket, this online newsletter covers the latest in Russian stocks and commodities. It requires a Web browser that supports Cyrillic type.

Type: WWW
**Address: http://www.fe.msk.ru/
            infomarket/finmarket/daily.html**
Region: Russia

DowVision

It's still being tested, but this would be a service worth either paying for or slogging through ads to see (as I'm sure you someday will have to). It lets you do a WAIS-based search of the complete *Wall Street Journal*, the daily Dow Jones News Service, Global Business Reports, and the Press Release Wires.

Type: WWW
Address: http://dowvision.wais.net/
Region: U.S., World

The Electronic Banker

This is an excellent source of information for bankers and finance pros, but average people who want to learn how financial markets, banking, and big money games work can also learn a great deal here. It includes links to financial newsletters, a finance dictionary to explain those difficult terms, an encyclopedia of financial products that explains how various types of investments work, and much more.

Type: WWW
**Address: http://www.euro.net/
            innovation/FinanceHP.html**
Region: World

Experimental Stock Market Data

MIT goes the big boys one better with an easy-to-use stock quote system. They don't guarantee it to be the fastest or most accurate, but it is incredibly simple to check on the status of your favorite companies here. It currently seems to be limited to the U.S. stock exchanges, and it does not carry every company.

Type: WWW
**Address: http://www.ai.mit.edu/
            stocks.html**
Region: U.S.

Finance and Economics Gopher

There are more file folders bulging with data here than can be described. From reports on the Asian markets to an archive of the FEDTAX-L mailing list to risk-assessment data—you could spend a week just browsing. Essential.

Type: Gopher
**Address: Niord.SHSU.edu:70/11gopher_
            root%3A%5B_DATA.ECONOMICS
            %5D**
Region: U.S., World

FinanceNet

This site is aimed primarily at finance experts in government. It brings together a huge number of resources, including databases, mailing lists, and more, to help them exercise fiscal responsibility. Includes a link to government asset sales, which can provide consumers and small-business people with an opportunity to save cash as well.

Type: WWW
Address: http://www.financenet.gov/
Region: U.S., World

Financial Economics Network

This site is home to the electronic version of the *Journal of Financial Abstracts.*

Type: WWW

Address: http://www.crimson.com/ssep/ ssephome.html

Region: World

Ghana Stocks

Although updates are irregular, Ghana's stock exchange is now online. Wouldn't a few shares of Kumasi Brewery add some caché (and maybe even some cash) to your portfolio?

Type: WWW

Address: http://www.uta.fi/~csfraw/ ghana/gh_gse.html

Region: Ghana

Global and Ethical Financial Advice

Ready to put your money where your mouth is? Check in with GÆIA to find profitable investments that don't involve your funds in supporting dictators, testing on bunnies, or polluting the environment. This company specializes in "socially conscious" investing.

Type: WWW

Address: http://www.u-net.com/~gaeia/ gaeia.htm

Region: World

Goethe Investment

This German firm provides information for investors, in German and English, and also has an online stocks, bonds, and currencies service for the European and Asian markets with current and past quotes. In addition, it has an excellent selection of financial prediction resources for investors, such as business cycle indicators and risk data. There's also a teletext link to Singapore that will get you in touch with the Asian-Pacific markets—this requires special software, also available here.

Type: WWW

Address: http://www.wiwi.uni-frankfurt. de/AG/JWGI/

Region: Germany, U.S., Netherlands, Austria, Italy, Norway, Hong Kong

High Finance in Ecuador

Here's information about the Banco del Pacifico, the Ecuadoran consumer price index, and finance laws and customs for Ecuador. In Spanish.

Type: Gopher

Address: mia.lac.net.:70/11/ee/ financiera/Ecuador

Region: Ecuador

Huang Weekly Futures Reports

See how various currencies and commodities are faring on the Taiwan stock market, one of Asia's most active trading floors. Chart trends by going through back issues.

Type: Gopher

Address: wuecon.wust1.edu:671/11/holt/ weekfut

Region: Taiwan

Institutional Investor's Guide to Russia

Find out here about Russian laws regarding foreign investment, finding a broker in Russia, customs and relationships, taxation, currency exchange issues, and more, including what kinds of instruments are traded.

Type: WWW

Address: http://www.fe.msk.ru/ infomarket/rinacoplus/guide.html

Region: Russia

International Exchange Rates

The Koblas Currency Converter is a nifty application that lets you know the current rates for world currencies against the dollar. It's essential for investors and those playing the money markets.

Type: WWW
Address: http://gnn.com/cgi-bin/gnn/currency
Region: World

Investment Funds News

Pssst…don't tell anyone, but have I got a tip for you! Take the investment advice you get here with a grain of salt and remember, always consider the source. This newsgroup is a forum for discussing investment, and the level of expertise of the posters varies wildly.

Type: Usenet newsgroup
Address: misc.invest.funds
Region: World

Investment Guide to Trinidad and Tobago

You'll find everything you ever wanted to know about the economic environment in Trinidad and Tobago here—from energy, manufacturing, and construction to the culture, history, and government of this island nation. If you plan on investing in the Caribbean, make sure you check this site out.

Type: WWW
Address: http://www.mit.edu:8001/afs/ athena.mit.edu/user/b/o/boofus/ www/inv-gid/inv-htm.html
Region: Trinidad and Tobago

Investment News

Keeping up with the high volume of posts to this group can be a daunting task in of itself, let alone narrowing your focus to articles relevant to a specific geographic location. For worldwide investment tips, this site is pure gold. Be aware, however, that pyramid scams abound here.

Type: Usenet newsgroup
Address: misc.invest
Region: World

Investment News Online

i-no is a slick, brightly colored online magazine for the investor. There's enough raw data here to bake one pie chart or 40. The Global Exchange News section will be of special interest to the international investor: It gives the day's readings for just about every futures market from China to Chile, with contact information to boot. It also offers links to a number of international investment newsletters, such as the *Australian Market Exchange*.

Type: WWW
Address: http://inorfg.com/
Region: World

Investment Stocks News

This is the counterpart of the funds investment newsgroup. Stock tips abound and—as with the funds group—skepticism should rule the day. It's easy to get bogged down in the get-rich-quick schemes, so you must use a sharp eye to find valuable information. There really is some here.

Type: Usenet newsgroup
Address: misc.invest.stocks
Region: World

Joe Bozzi's Finance and Economic Information

This enthusiastic home page has leads to lots of useful investment information online.

Type: WWW
**Address: http://turnpike.net:80/metro/
           Biff/joepage.html**
Region: U.S., World

Journal of Finance

This is the publication of the American Finance Association, the trade association for financiers.

Type: WWW
**Address: http://www.cob.ohio-state.edu/
           dept/fin/jof.htm**
Region: U.S.

Kiwi Club Finance Server

I think the Kiwi Club is associated with the University of Texas School of Finance. In any case, there is information from their finance classes here, plus a truly impressive set of links to information worldwide on finance and economics.

Type: WWW
**Address: http://kiwiclub.bus.utexas.edu/
           finance/kiwiserver/
           kiwiserver.html**
Region: U.S., World

The London International Financial Futures and Options Exchange

This new service is in the process of being enhanced to allow users to access summary trading data, LIFFE publications, and other relevant information for investors. At present, offerings include daily futures statistics, financial options data, equity options statistics, SPAN Files, and some special datasets available to subscribers only.

Type: WWW
Address: http://www.liffe.com/
Region: England, World

misc.entrepreneurs

While a forum for budding entrepreneurs sounds like a great idea, this one is all too often home to the worst of the Internet "get.rich.quick" scams. For amusement value only.

Type: Usenet newsgroup
Address: misc.entrepreneurs
Region: World

Ozzie Jurok's Real Estate Server

Want to make a killing in real estate? Try booming British Columbia, much loved by savvy Hong Kong investors, among others. This company offers real-estate informtion, prices, and predictions, plus links to other real-estate servers and data.

Type: WWW
Address: http://www.jurock.com/
Region: Canada

PAWWS

This site offers portfolio-management tools and its own brokerage services. There are some free services here as well, including the PAWWS Portfolio Management Challenge.

Type: WWW
Address: http://pawws.secapl.com/
Region: U.S., World

Personal Financial Resources on the Internet

This FAQ is a regularly updated compendium of sources for personal financial data online. It is very worthwhile: It includes reviews of Usenet newsgroups like those in the misc.consumers series (these offer home-buying, credit-card information, and the like), relevant mailing lists, leads for finding financial software, and pointers to FTP, Gopher, and Web resources for financial advice, data, and more. This should be one of your first stops, as it will help make your search for information much easier.

Type: Gopher
Address: Niord.SHSU.edu:70/00gopher_root%3A%5B_DATA.ECONOMICS.INFO%5DPERSFIN.INFO
Region: U.S., Canada, World

Polish Stock Exchange Online

This Gopher has quotes and data from the Polish Stock Exchange, both current and archival. In Polish, it includes charts of economic activity and markets (*wykresy*).

Type: Gopher
Address: infomeister.osc.edu:74/11/polish/gielda
Region: Poland

QuoteCom

This is a subscription-only service, although they do have some free services for the Netting public. You can check up on the Canadian and overseas markets, get daily and historical reports, and more. Weather and news of interest to commodity investors is also available here. It has a nice interface with buttons, too.

Type: Telnet
Address: quote.com
Type: WWW
Address: http://www.quote.com/
Region: Canada, World

Rabobank WWW Services Home Page

Find out here in English or in Dutch about the services for banking and investing at Rabobank. The offerings include a biweekly survey of the Dutch economy. (One question: Is the name *Engels* in their URL someone's name, or is there a communist mole loose in the Rabobank computing department?)

Type: WWW
Address: http://rabobank.info.nl/Engels/default.htm
Region: Netherlands

Security APL Market Watch

Updated every three minutes, this page brings you the latest virtual ticker-tape from the Dow Jones, Standard & Poor's, and NASDAQ exchanges in the U.S. It also has current figures from the Canadian Exchange and several major financial indexes, including the Euro Top 100 and the Japan Index.

Type: WWW
Address: http://www.secapl.com/secapl/quoteserver/mw.html
Region: U.S., World

Sharenet

South African financial information, including real-time quotes from the Johannesburg Stock Exchange (JSE) and SA Futures Exchange (SAFEX), can be found at this site.

Type: WWW
Address: http://www.nis.za
Region: South Africa

SimTel Finance Index

Using SimTel is like visiting a free financial software shopping mall. Among the best goodies it can find for you are the AmortizeIt loan-amortization program, without which I would never have figured out my mortgage; Bank Account Manager 3.61; BondCalc, a bond value and yield calculator; software for setting up a family budget and investment plan, and for calculating those capital gains; and a financial planning package for kids. The SimTel search engine, which pulls from FTP sites worldwide, is available through the Virtual Shareware Library here. Many localized and foreign-language software packages are available, if you use the right search terms.

Type: WWW
**Address: http://www.acs.oakland.edu/
cgi-bin/shase/About/simtel**
Type: FTP
Address: oak.oakland.edu/SimTel/msdos
Region: World

Taxing Times

This site will be useful only for U.S. and Canadian citizens, and for foreign nationals who pay income tax in these nations—but to these, it's *very* useful. Tax forms online, tax advice, some tax software, the latest updates on our ever-changing federal tax codes, leads to related newsgroups and mailing lists are included. Wheee!

Type: WWW
**Address: http://inept.scubed.com:8001/
tax/tax.html**
Region: U.S., Canada

Technical Investment News

The questions posed in this newsgroup can be complex, as it caters to professional investors. Don't despair, though, amateur investors can get some good tips here if they know what to look for.

Type: Usenet newsgroup
Address: misc.invest.technical
Region: World

Tel Aviv Stock Exchange

Check here for daily report on closing numbers for the Tel Aviv stock exchange, in English. It comes with the currency exchange rate against the U.S. dollar, plus weather and sports news.

Type: Gopher
**Address: israel-info.gov.il:70/
0R7786-9518-/new/brief1**
Region: Israel

World Real Estate Listings

Billing itself as an international resource, this fledgling site attempts to list real estate information worldwide. Unfortunately, most of the items are U.S.-based (646 listings for the U.S. as opposed to 31 for all of western Europe). You can find some interesting ads though. Have you ever entertained the idea of owning a restaurant in Rome? For $420,000, it's yours.

Type: WWW
**Address: http://interchange.idc.uvic.ca/
wrels/ITA_Roma/796521455
.5376.html**
Region: World

Yanoff's Business/Economics/Financial List

Part of a much larger list of good Internet resources, this list includes leads to many financial service providers. There are also pointers to Mammon and Gigabucks—stock-market simulation games that'll let you test your skills without risking anything but your ego. You'll need a Telnet application in your Web browser to check into these.

Type: WWW
Address: http://www.uwm.edu/Mirror/ inet.services.html
Region: World

Zagreb Stock Exchange

Recent cultural reforms in the former Soviet Union have caused a sea change in how we view our former enemies and in how they view themselves. This fascinating site documents a part of that change. As Croatia moves towards a free market economy, this document attempts to provide guide posts for potential investors. Stock quotes, updated daily, are supplemented with a wealth of information on banking and finance in Croatia.

Type: WWW
Address: http://ksaver208.zse.com.hr/
Region: Croatia

FOLKLORE AND MYTHOLOGY

See also Anthropology page 81; History page 324; Paranormal page 402; Religion and Spirituality page 420

"Myth is what we call other people's religion," said Joseph Campbell, the modern collector of myths. And much of what you'll find here relates to what were once religious beliefs but have since become fairy tales, legends, and stories of times gone by. It's important to note that some of this material is still part of a living religious tradition and would not be considered "myth" by those who believe. And who knows, what we call "religion" today could be the "myth" of tomorrow.

alt.folklore

There are several groups in this category, including collegiate and military folklore. See alt.folklore.urban and alt.folklore.suburban below, and also check out the complete list with links to FAQs at this Web site.

Type: WWW
Address: http://www.lib.ox.ac.uk/ internet/news/alt.folklore.html
Region: World

alt.folklore.suburban

The modern era is not without its myths. There's the UFO abduction mythos, for example (that *is* a myth, isn't it?). The Usenet newsgroup alt.folklore.suburban is a serious attempt to discuss such tales. Its FAQ can be found at the Web site below. Unlike alt.folklore.urban, which covers much the same ground, this is a moderated newsgroup.

Type: Usenet newsgroup
Address: alt.folklore.suburban
Type: WWW
Address: http://www.lib.ox.ac.uk/ internet/news/faq/archive/ folklore.afs-faq.html
Region: World

alt.folklore.urban

Yes, this is the repository of all those crazy urban legends like the story of the little old lady innocently trying to dry her pet poodle in the microwave, someone bringing home a chihuahua from Mexico only to discover that it's actually a giant rat, ghostly hitchhikers, and so on. The alt.folklore.urban newsgroup is very active—around a hundred postings a day—so be prepared to sort through a lot to find what you want. The FAQ is available in four parts at the FTP site below, while the Web site is the "official" Frequently Posted Legends page.

Type: Usenet newsgroup
Address: alt.folklore.urban
Type: FTP
Address: ftp.cathouse.org/pub/cathouse/ urban.legends/cache
Type: WWW
Address: http://www.dsg.cs.tcd.ie:/ dsg_people/afcondon/AFU/
Region: World

alt.mythology

The mythology discussions here include a wide range of myths, both geographically and temporally. Some related FAQs are stored in the archive below.

Type: Usenet newsgroup
Address: alt.mythology
Type: WWW
Address: http://src.doc.ic.ac.uk/usenet/ news-faqs/alt.mythology
Region: World

The Ancient World

This is a very interesting and informative site. The maintainer of this Web page is attempting to bring together all sorts of information sources on the ancient world, including archaeology, anthropology, history, art, and myth.

Type: WWW
Address: http://atlantic.evsc.virginia.edu/ julia/AncientWorld.html
Region: World

Animal Mythology

This group is for the whimsical and imaginative, as well as for the student of literature and folklore. If you've ever wanted to discuss pegacats with someone from the Society for Creative Anachronism, search no more.

Type: Usenet newsgroup
Address: alt.mythology.mythic-animals
Region: World

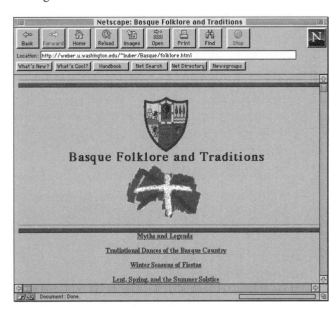

Basque Folklore and Traditions

This archive holds a relatively well written and interesting series of articles on Basque culture.

Type: WWW
Address: http://weber.u.washington.edu/ ~buber/Basque/folklore.html
Region: France, Spain

The Bermuda Triangle

The page states that the Bermuda Triangle's reputation as an unearthly graveyard for ships and planes is a myth, and offers lots of supporting data.

Type: WWW
Address: **http://tigger.cc.uic.edu/~toby-g/ tri.html**
Region: Caribbean

Bigfoot and His Brothers

These newsgroups can lead you to scientific or "other" information, while the Yahoo archive can lead you to lots of information about this perhaps mythical creature from the Pacific Northwest, and similar humanoid "animals" from elsewhere. Did you know they have Bigfeet in Siberia and other parts of the former Soviet Union? They do. The alt.bigfoot newsgroup has a high net.loon quotient (see the alt.bigfoot.die.die.die group for some heated opinions on that), while the alt.bigfoot.research is a more scientific moderated group.

Type: Usenet newsgroup
Address: **alt.bigfoot**
Address: **alt.bigfoot.die.die.die**
Address: **alt.bigfoot.research**
Type: WWW
Address: **http://www.yahoo.com/Society_ and_Culture/Folklore/Bigfoot/**
Region: U.S., World

Creatures of Philippine Lower Mythology

This compendium of the creatures of Filipino mythology is also a great source for information about other aspects of Filipino culture.

Type: WWW
Address: **http://www.pitt.edu/~filipina/ mythology.html**
Region: Philippines

Dazhdbog in Russian Mythology

This is a modern interpretation of the tale of Dazhdbog, the myth of the origins of the Russian people.

Type: WWW
Address: **http://sunsite.unc.edu/sergei/ Dazhdbog.html**
Region: Russia

Department of Slavic and East European Studies

This Web page is a good general resource for Slavic and East European Studies, and they have some information about the myths and legends of the region here as well.

Type: WWW
Address: **http://gpu.srv.ualberta.ca/ ~lfowler/slavic.html**
Region: Eastern Europe, Slovenia, Slovakia, Croatia, Bosnia-Herzegovina, Serbia

Egyptian Book of the Dead

This is Budge's translation, not the best as his cultural biases show through. But it's still one of the few complete translations of the basic Egyptian mythos available and, as far as I know, the only one online.

Type: WWW
Address: **http://www.sas.upenn.edu/ African_Studies/Books/ Papyrus_Ani.html**
Region: Egypt

Egyptian Mythology FAQ

This is a long document on the gods and goddesses of ancient Egypt, with leads to other sources of information. Fascinating stuff.

Type: WWW
**Address: http://www.the-wire.com/
            culture/mythology/egyptian.txt**
Region: Egypt

Flood Myths

Almost every culture has one: a story about a great flood and divine intervention. Perhaps it could be called an archetypal myth. Here's a text file with a rundown of many of them.

Type: WWW
**Address: http://www.the-wire.com/
            culture/mythology/floodmyt.txt**
Region: World

Folklore Archive

The Anthropology Department at the University of California in Berkeley has over 350,000 items in their folklore archive. Learn more about what's available here.

Type: WWW
**Address: http://www.mip.berkeley.edu/
            mip/collections/folklore.html**
Region: World

Folklore Discussion List

Folklore is a mailing list devoted to discussing folklore from around the world.

Type: Mailing list
Address: listserv@tamvm1.tamu.edu
Region: World

The Gnosis Archive

This is a good resource on gnosticism—the religious doctrine that holds that the truth lies in hidden processes and doctrines that lead believers to intense

spiritual knowledge. Many of these processes are based on the use of myth, archetype, and legend.

Type: WWW
**Address: http://www.webcom.com/
            ~gnosis/**
Region: World

Greek Mythology

This site is a "who's who and what's what" of Greek mythology.

Type: WWW
**Address: http://info.desy.de/gna/
            interpedia/greek_myth/greek_
            myth.html**
Region: Greece

Guinness Beer FAQt and Folklore

Mother's milk—sorry, I mean Guinness: What the beer and the myth are made of, and everything you could possibly want to know about the stuff. I got thirsty just reading about it.

Type: WWW
Address: http://www.pi.se/guinness.html
Region: Ireland

Hacker Folklore

A Web page on the folklore of the computer hacking, with some very funny stories and a link to the Hacker's Jargon dictionary, this site includes the tale of the "magic/more magic" switch at MIT and other yarns.

Type: WWW
**Address: http://www.denken.or.jp/local/
            misc/JARGON/app-a.html**
Region: World

Haitian Proverbs, Riddles, Jokes, and Folktales

Tales of Voudoun, politics, and just plain silliness, this site is evidence of a fine sense of dry and subtle humor, which must be helpful in difficult times.

Type: WWW
Address: http://www.PrimeNet.Com:80/
            ~rafreid/prov.html
Region: Haiti

INDKNOW

INDKNOW is an e-mail discussion list concerned with the traditions and folkloric knowledge of indigenous societies around the world, such as household and family traditions, traditional inter-community relations, folk cures, and the like.

Type: Mailing list
Address: listserv@u.washington.edu
Send e-mail message with blank Subject
            line and one-line body:
            subscribe INDKNOW <Your
            E-mail Address>
Region: World

Irish Myth Concordance

This is a survey of sources and stories related to the ancient Irish myth cycle.

Type: WWW
Address: http://www.the-wire.com/
            culture/mythology/irishcon.txt
Region: Ireland

Legends of King Arthur

These stories are more than old myths, they include echoes of the ancient religious beliefs of Britain. This regularly updated FAQ covers Arthurian scholarship and publishing.

Type: FTP
Address: rtfm.mit.edu/pub/usenet/
            news.answers/books/arthurian
Region: England

The Lilith Myth

An article on the Lilith myth, an ancient Jewish story of a frightening female figure that goes back to the pre-Judaic religions of the Middle East.

Type: WWW
Address: http://www.webcom.com/
            ~gnosis/lillith.html
Region: Israel

Lycanthropy

If you think (or know) you're a werewolf, you're not alone. Included here are stories of human-to-animal transformations from many cultures.

Type: WWW
Address: http://www.csh.rit.edu/~dylan/
            weres.htm
Region: World

Mexico: Arte, Cultura y Folklore

This Web page about Mexican art, culture, and folklore is in Spanish. The section on traditions and fiestas has a little about the myths behind the processions and other goings-on.

Type: WWW
Address: http://mexico.udg.mx/
            Tradiciones/Tradicion.html
Region: Mexico

Middle Eastern Folklore

This archive includes a sound file, "Fairuz," and some Arabic folk tales called "QomKolthoum."

Type: FTP

Address: ftp.cs.sunysb.edu/pub/EN/lib/ folklore/

Region: Middle East

Myth Archive

Here's an archive of various mythological and historical bibliographies, mostly concerning Northern European myths.

Type: WWW

Address: http://www.the-wire.com/ culture/mythology/mythbibl.html

Region: World

Mythology in Western Art

A source of GIFs of the various Greek gods as they have been portrayed through history. It's interesting to see how images of and ideas about these figures in Western mythology reflect the changing times.

Type: WWW

Address: http://www-lib.haifa.ac.il/ www/art/MYTHOLOGY _WESTART.HTML

Region: Greece

Myths and Legends of Indigenous Peoples

This Web page has myths from around the world, including Australia and Africa. This is aimed at elementary-school children, but adults will enjoy it too.

Type: WWW

Address: http://www.ozemail.com.au/ ~reed/global/mythstor.html

Region: World

Multicultural Cosmology World Wide Web Page

This page relates myth to astronomy, which makes good sense since many mythic systems are based on trying to recognize and explain the forces that govern the sun, moon, planets, and other forces of nature. They plan to have information available on six different societies of the ancient Americas. For now, you can access data about the Mayans, Aztecs, and Inuits (Eskimos).

Type: WWW

Address: http://arcturus.pomona. claremont.edu

Region: North America, Central America, South America

Norse Myth

A bibliography of Norse paganism, with both New Age and scholarly works included.

Type: WWW

Address: http://www.the-wire.com/ culture/mythology/bibnorse.txt

Region: Denmark, Norway

The Organ Snatchers: A Report

This site is a report to the United Nations on the "organ snatching" myths that have become prevalent in many parts of the world, leading to some scary scenes for Western tourists who have been mistaken for illicit organ harvesters. No, *Coma* isn't alive and well in Central America. At least we hope not.

Type: WWW

Address: http://www.ualr.edu/ ~degonzalez/uninfo.txt

Region: World

Pagan Mythology

A guide to neo-pagan mythology online, including texts, prayers, and many links, this site includes Celtic, Scandinavian, shamanistic, and other traditions.

Type: WWW
Address: http://www.netspace.org/ ~athomps/pagan/paganres.html
Region: World

Poteen

This is an article on myths and legends that swirl around that infamous Irish moonshine. If you drink some, you'll believe.

Type: WWW
Address: http://celtic.stanford.edu/pub/ post/Dec/Poteen
Region: Ireland

Project Runeberg

Project Runeberg is a three-year-old open and voluntary initiative to create and collect free electronic editions of classic Nordic literature and art. You can find myths and sagas digitized here in Danish, Norwegian, Icelandic, and Finnish.

Type: WWW
Address: http://www.lysator.liu.se/ runeberg/Main.html
Region: Denmark, Norway, Iceland, Finland

The Rough and Ready Guide to the Gods

A starting-off point for investigating myths, folklore and magic, this site has links to everything from *Bullfinch's Mythology* to the Koran.

Type: WWW
Address: http://www.the-wire.com/ culture/mythology/mythtext.html
Region: World

Russian Mythology

This Gopher site is a treasure trove of files relating to Russian mythology.

Type: Gopher
Address: president.oit.unc.edu/11/.pub/ academic/russian-studies/Myth
Region: Russia

A Select Bibliography of the Oral Tradition of Oceana: Fiji

Everything you ever wanted to know about Fijian myths, which sometimes combine entirely local themes with more modern Islamic tales, is available here.

Type: WWW
Address: http://www.upei.ca/~meincke/ fijimyth.htm
Region: Fiji

Social Context and the Limits on Symbolic Meanings

This is an academic paper on signs and symbols in a cultural context, in this case, of the Cook Islands. But instead of being dry and footnote laden, it's a fresh, easy to read work that combines history, folklore, customs, and sociology.

Type: WWW
Address: http://lucy.ukc.ac.uk/Tradition/ Vaka.html
Region: Cook Islands

Springtime in Iraq

In Bet-Nahrain (present-day Iraq), the inhabitants celebrated the new year annually on the first day of Nissan (April), with a festival of revival and renewal of nature. This was one of the most important religious and national celebrations held in Bet-Nahrain. Learn here about the myths and traditions behind it.

Type: WWW
Address: **http://www.cs.toronto.edu/ ~jatou/nissan.txt**
Region: Iraq

StoryWeb

An attempt at an interactive page on myths and stories, this page includes some folktales and some interactive and hypertext fiction with mythic overtones.

Type: WWW
Address: **http://www.sccs.swarthmore. edu:80/~csunami1/Story/**
Region: World

The Trickster Archetype

This article is about the trickster as a common mythic figure in many parts of the world, including his or her role in the pantheon and in human thought.

Type: WWW
Address: **http://www.the-wire.com/ culture/mythology/ridltrik.txt**
Region: World

Vampires in Folklore

It's just so goth, it's to die for: tales of vampirism from around the world and links to those who like to play vampire in real life are the topics here.

Type: WWW
Address: **http://www.yahoo.com/Society_ and_Culture/Folklore/Vampires/**
Region: World

Vikings

A WWW page for Viking lore and resources on the Net, this includes links to similar places online and to museum exhibits about the real-life Vikings.

Type: WWW
Address: **http://control.chalmers.se/ vikings/viking.html**
Region: Denmark, Norway, Sweden, Russia, Iceland

FOOD AND DRINK

They say that computers are taking people away from everyday, hands-on activities…. Here's proof that in some cases computers can enhance them. Look here for recipes from many lands and information about food, drinks, and restaurants.

Al Miller's Recipes for Trout and Salmon

Sponsored by the University of Wisconsin's Sea Grant Advisory Services, this little archive contains some 60 different recipes gathered from Great Lakes anglers, appropriate to salmon, trout, or other fatty fishes. In an attempt to be health-conscious, priority and prominence are given to recipes for grilled or steamed fish preparation, and the categories of the archive are organized by cooking style for easy access to healthful recipes. All categories are indexed.

Type: Gopher
Address: **thorplus.lib.purdue.edu:70/11/ databases/AquaNIC/publicat/ recipe/**
Region: U.S.

alt.coffee

In the primary Usenet newsgroup devoted to coffee-lovers and connoisseurs, one can find the recipe for the newest trendy coffee drink, advice on care and acquisition of coffee machines, and tidbits of coffee culture in all its varieties. Alt.coffee shares a FAQ document with the other three Usenet coffee newsgroups. That document, "Coffee and Caffeine's Frequently Asked Questions" by Alex Lopez-Ortiz, is archived at the FTP site below.

Type: Usenet newsgroup
Address: alt.coffee
Type: FTP
**Address: rtfm.mit.edu/pub/usenet/
            alt.coffee**
Region: U.S.

alt.food.coffee

Discussed in this coffee newsgroup are the subtleties of this roast versus another, and how lousy such and such restaurant's coffee is compared to some other eating establishment's.

Type: Usenet newsgroup
Address: alt.food.coffee
Region: U.S.

American Wine on the Web

The premier issue of this wine aficionado's Web magazine debuted in April 1995. It contains a half-dozen feature articles and interviews, as well as a group of regional reports on wineries around the states. Like its sister journal *The Electronic Gourmet Guide*, this publication is very well organized and has an easy-on-the-eye design.

Type: WWW
**Address: http://www.2way.com:80/food/
            wine**
Region: U.S.

Bangladesh: Food and Recipes

Besides recipes of incredible kababs, basmati rice dishes, desserts, and very complex fish dishes (this site is certainly not stingy on quantity either, each category having a fair number of dishes and excellent directions), there is also a list and a guide to the various restaurants of Dhaka, the Bangladesh capital.

Type: WWW
**Address: http://axe.asel.udel.edu/~kazi/
            bangladesh/bdfruits.html**
Region: Bangladesh

Beer-related Usenet Groups

The mighty subject of beer, the breakfast of champions, is covered in several Usenet news groups. Two out of the three are primarily concerned with the differentiation between different types of beer, beer venues such as local microbreweries, and the consumption and enjoyment of fermented malt beverages. These two newsgroups would be alt.beer and rec.food.beer, whereas the third group, rec.crafts.brewing, focuses on the home production of beers, ales, and other fermented malt beverages, including information on special brewing techniques, equipment and original recipes. The FAQs for these groups are available in the FTP site below.

Type: Usenet newsgroup
Address: alt.beer
Address   rec.food.drink.beer
Address   rec.crafts.brewing
Type: FTP
**Address: rtfm.mit.edu/pub/
            usenet-by-hierarchy/**
Region: World

Beyond Milk and Honey: Traditional Israeli Recipes

The diaspora of the Jewish nation has brought many cultural traditions into what are considered "Jewish" customs, and this international flavor has certainly impacted the food of the nation of Israel as the return of the Jewish people brings all these cultural strains together. This assortment of about 35 recipes includes such Middle Eastern standards as baba ghanouj, hummus, and Turkish coffee; traditional European Jewish dishes like blintzes and latkes; and items from other cultural strains, including an interesting looking chicken curry recipe. There is also a good introduction from the Israeli embassy in Washington, D.C. regarding Israeli eating and meal customs, and a little about the Jewish dietary (kosher, or *kashrut*) laws.

Type: Gopher
Address: israel-info.gov.il:70/00/tour/recipe/950101.rec
Region: Israel

Boat Drinks

"The Parrotthead Madness Boat Drink Mixer" is the name of this page, and it's a bartender's guide to tropical beers, ales, wines and, most importantly, "boat drinks." Think Trader Vic's, with Jimmy Buffet playing in the background.

Type: WWW
Address: http://www.prz.tu-berlin.de/~nicolai/topics/meal/drinks.html
Region: Caribbean

Bug Cuisine

I just included this one to "bug" the squeamish among you. Tasty insect recipes: All one can say is, "Mmmm, mmmm, good!"

Type: Gopher
Address: gopher.ent.iastate.edu:70:/00ftp %3AThomomys%3AEntoGopher %3ATasty%20Insect%20Recipes
Region: World

Caribbean Recipes

In Spanish, this site currently features a Guatemalan chicken dish and tasty Cuban tropical desserts.

Type: WWW
Address: http://www.nando.net/prof/caribe/recipes.html
Region: Caribbean

La Cocina Mexicana Pagina

This very colorful Web page is part of the "Mexico" Web documents located at the University of Guadalajara, which portray the history and culture of the Mexican people. The page includes two very traditional and popular recipes for posole and birrias, and a brief history of Mexican cuisine. The page is available in Spanish or English.

Type: WWW
Address: http://mexico.udg.mx/Cocina/menu.html
Region: Mexico

The Creole and Cajun Recipe Page

This page has a wide variety of Cajun recipes, some background on Cajun cooking techniques and the unique ingredients used, and pointers on where to find some of the more obscure ingredients outside of the bayous of Louisiana. Spicy hot!

Type: WWW
Address: http://www.webcom.com/~gumbo/recipe-page.html
Region: U.S.

The Electronic Gourmet Guide

Billing itself as the first food and cooking magazine of the Internet, this biweekly publication provides not only recipes and cooking tips, but also food news, guides to upcoming product releases, and a food trivia game. Very nicely organized, it makes it possible to get a main table of contents or an index of recipes, and at the top of every page is a series of buttons that allow you to directly zip to any feature article or regular column. It's certainly worth the time if you're planning that big dinner party, as the recipes are very unusual and international in scope.

Type: WWW

Address: **http://www.2way.com/food/ egg/index.html**

Region: World

Fat-Free Indian Recipe Archive

Containing just over 50 recipes, this site covers all those wonderful mysterious Indian dishes that boggle the mind and tantalize the palate: vindaloo, dahl dishes, curries of all sorts, tandoori paste recipes, and even a couple of recipes to help you make your own garam-masala spice mixture.

Type: FTP

Address: **ftp.halcyon.com/pub/recipes/ indian**

Region: India

Homebrew Digest List

Homebrew Digest provides a forum to share all those palate-pleasing, mind-crunching homebrew recipes, tricks, and secrets.

Type: Mailing list

Address: **homebrew-request@hpfcmi.fc .hp.com**

Region: World

Hungarian Cuisine Page

Heavily laden with paprika, the spicy cuisine of Hungary stands out as one of the more distinctive of European cuisines. This colorful page provide information on and recipes for many of the traditional foods and drinks of Hungary, including goulash (of course!), lecss, and paprika chicken.

Type: WWW

Address: **http://www.fsz.bme.hu/ hungary/cuisine/foods.html**

Region: Hungary

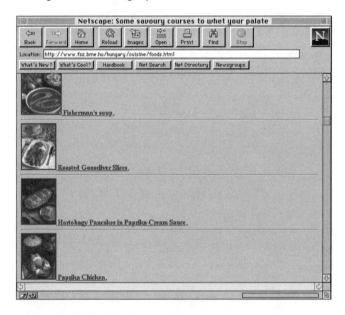

IndiaOnline Recipes

This site includes recipes, a guide to Indian food, and a guide to Indian restaurants worldwide, including vegetarian restaurants.

Type: WWW

Address: **http://IndiaOnline.com/ food.html**

Region: India

Indonesian Delights

Mix coconut milk with equal parts Asian and Indian cuisine, and you get the fab recipes on this page. There's also a guide to Indonesian restaurants worldwide.

Type: WWW
Address: http://www.umanitoba.ca/ indonesian/food.html
Region: Indonesia

Institute for Nuclear Chemistry Recipe Page

From the Universitdt Mainz, this offers a couple dozen mostly German recipes of very high caliber (none of which involve any nuclear chemistry, thank goodness.) The page is in English, but it is also available in German.

Type: WWW
Address: http://dkcmzc.chemie.uni-mainz .de/~FRANZ/recipes.html
Region: Germany

International Recipe Archive

This huge archive of international recipes has everything from African stews to advokaat (is that a recipe for lawyer?), and onward.

Type: Gopher
Address: gopher.dcs.gla.ac.uk:70/11/ pub/recipes/Recipes
Region: World

IRC Beer Tastings

Every first and third Tuesday of the month (and even the fifth, when there is one!) at 10 p.m. U.S. Eastern Time, there is a beer-tasting and discussion on Internet Relay Chat. For more information, contact the organizer of this virtual event at the e-mail address below.

Type: IRC
Address: #tasting
Contact: harupa@new-orleans.neosoft.com
Region: World

Mexican Cuisine and Recipes

Included online here are gastronomical treats from the author's family cookbook and the cookbooks of his friends. The recipes abound, and the dishes range from a basic mole sauce, guacamole, enchiladas, and quesadillas, to very exotic dishes from deep in the heart of *la cultura Mexicana*.

Type: WWW
Address: http://csgwww.uwaterloo.ca/ users/dmg/mexico/cocina/ cocina.html
Region: Mexico

Mexican Recipes

Something over one hundred recipes make this a formidable compendium of the cuisine of Mexico. Intentionally drawn from every region of Mexico, this site will make a great start for any *cocina* to build a strong Mexican recipe base.

Type: Gopher
Address: unicornio.cencar.udg.mx/11/ cultfolk/cocina
Region: Mexico

Over the Coffee

"Serving the Online Coffee Community" is the mission of the Over the Coffee Web resource page, and considering what a late-night, espresso-sippin' crowd Netsurfers tend to be, that is quite a mission. The site includes links to both retail and wholesale coffee distributors, coffee machinery manufacturers and distributors, links to a long list of coffee-oriented Web pages, and a file archive of FAQs, resource lists, and reviews.

Type: WWW
Address: http://www.netins.net/ showcase/coffee/
Region: U.S.

Persian Recipes

In this archive from the Iranian Cultural Information Center, there are about a half-dozen solid Persian recipes. They sound delicious.

Type: WWW
Address: http://tehran.stanford.edu/ Recipes/recipes.html
Region: Iran

rec.crafts.winemaking

This is the stomping grounds for producers and consumers of homemade wines on the Net, making it a good place to post questions or suggestions on technique, supplies, and recipes for those special homespun vintages. There's also some discussion of wine-related issues that don't necessarily focus on home production.

Type: Usenet newsgroup
Address: rec.crafts.winemaking
Region: World

rec.food Groups

Within the Usenet hierarchy "rec.food." there are at least 11 different groups focusing on various subtopics, such as vegetarian dietary and cooking information, sourdough baking, foods of past historical periods and civilizations, and so on. The primary groups are rec.food.cooking, which covers the most general cooking related topics, and rec.food.recipes, which serves as a cyber-community

recipe bulletin board. The FAQs for the major groups in this hierarchy are archived at the FTP site below.

Type: Usenet newsgroup
Address: rec.food.cooking
Address: rec.food.drink
Address: rec.food.drink.beer
Address: rec.food.historic
Address: rec.food.preserving
Address: rec.food.recipes (moderated)
Address: rec.food.restaurants
Address: rec.food.sourdough
Address: rec.food.veg
Address: rec.food.veg.cooking (moderated)
Type: FTP
Address: rtfm.mit.edu/pub/ usenet-by-hierarchy/rec/food/
Region: U.S.

Rolling Your Own Sushi

Ever wanted to skip the extreme pricing at those lovely little sushi bars? Well, this site will give you all the information you need, including recipes, technique, and what equipment to buy.

Type: WWW
Address: http://www.rain.org/~hutch/ sushi.html
Region: Japan

Serbian Food

Lots of yummy recipes with an Eastern European flair are available here.

Type: WWW
Address: http://www.umiacs.umd.edu/ research/lpv/YU/HTML/food.html
Region: Serbia

Shandy!

The national drink of Trinidad-Tobago—and a perennial favorite in England as well—has a site on the Web. There's even a big photo of a tall, cool bottle.

Type: WWW
**Address: http://www.ugcs.caltech.edu/
~benedett/trinidad/shandy.html**
Region: Trinidad and Tobago

Slovene Food

This site includes recipes, information about Slovene wines, and a most intriguing text file about wild mushrooms—one of Slovenia's favorite local delicacies.

Type: WWW
**Address: http://www.ijs.si/slo/
resources-by-subject**
Region: Slovenia

Turkish Cuisine

Turkish-style dolmas, pepper kebabs, baklava, and even a handy assortment of very interesting egg dishes grace this page with a dozen or so recipe categories. Also included is a brief guide to Turkish cuisine in general.

Type: WWW
**Address: http://www.metu.edu.tr:80/
~melih/recipes.html**
Region: Turkey

University of Minnesota Recipe Archive

This small recipe archive is located on the University of Minnesota Gopher, though it is not clear from where the recipes originate. Nevertheless, a cursory glance will reveal some real gems among the items populating the two dozen menu categories. This site also contains, most importantly, the archives of the Usenet newsgroup rec.food.recipes.

Type: Gopher
**Address: spinaltap.micro.umn.edu/11/
fun/Recipes**
Region: U.S., World

University of Victoria Faculty and Staff Recipe Archive

Favorites of the faculty and staff of the University of Victoria in Canada are featured in this Gopher archive. The categories are, as is typical, broken up into side dishes, soups, salads, deserts, and main courses, but this is where the typicality vanishes, as the recipes contained here vary greatly in international origin and complexity. The site excels in quantity as well as variety, but if one can't find enough to please here, there is a link to another archive at the University of Michigan.

Type: Gopher
Address: kafka.uvic.ca:70/11//recipes
Region: Canada

VEGAN-L

Providing a forum on the Net for those devoted to eliminating the exploitation of animals for food, clothing or any other reason, VEGAN-L offers vegan recipes, plus nutritional and cultural information pertinent to that lifestyle.

Type: Mailing list
Address: LISTSERV@VM.TEMPLE.EDU
Region: World

VegLife

The VegLife discussion list helps to disseminate information about the vegetarian diet and lifestyle including recipes, food content information, and information on the impact of the meat industry to the planet. Digests of this list's recent activity are archived at the Gopher site in the next listing.

Type: Mailing list
Address: listserv@vtvm1.cc.vt.edu
Region: World

VegLife FTP Archive

Quite a voluminous archive, this site is organized by those who take care of the VegLife mailing list. It contains a list of other discussion lists on vegetarianism, guides to vegetarian organizations, environmental information regarding the global impact of meat consumption and production, and a host of other vegetarian-related issues.

Type: Gopher
**Address: cadadmin.cadlab.vt.edu/
            11ftp%3aBanshee%3a
            FTParchives%3aveglife%3a**
Region: World

WWW Virtual Library Beer and Brewing Index

Certainly this web site falls into the "be all, end all" category. If it's beer that needs to be found, this is the site to start from: a comprehensive list of Web beer sites, beer-related personal Web pages, commercial brewers, microbrew festival sites, and a variety of different types of pointers to Web resources on beer brewing and enjoying.

Type: WWW
**Address: http://www.mindspring.com/
            ~jlock/wwwbeer.html**
Region: World

Yugoslavian Recipe Pages

The rugged terrain of the area which was the former Yugoslavia, as well as an influx of invaders, settlers, and immigrants, led to pockets of separate cultural and ethnic traditions within the small region over the centuries. This diversity is reflected in the wonderful recipes displayed on this Web page. Especially interesting are the appetizers and desserts, the main dishes being very heavy on the beef. Not exactly a health stop, but a treat nonetheless.

Type: WWW
**Address: http://www.umiacs.umd.edu/
            research/lpv/YU/HTML/food.html**
Region: Slovenia, Bosnia-Herzegovina, Serbia,
           Montenegro, Croatia, Macedonia

FORTUNETELLING

People want to know what the future will bring, and throughout history they've employed all sorts of means to find out—from praying for the desired results to visiting fortunetellers. Personally, I don't put much stock in astrology and card-reading and such, but it's a pleasant diversion. And if you do happen to take it seriously, you'll have plenty of company online.

I have noticed a trend toward for-pay services in this category—I'm sure Personal Psychic pages will be the next online trend to go for your credit card. Even if I believed in fortunetelling, I would be leery of such services, particularly considering the potential for fraud when you give out your credit-card number. Also remember that any "psychic" who starts telling you to send him or her money as a "sacrifice" to lift an alleged curse is working an age-old scam—beware!

alt.astrology

Here's the newsgroup for people who want to discuss astrology. Participants range from True Believers, who will believe anything, to diehard skeptics, who wouldn't believe their own eyes if what they saw contradicted their prior assumptions. Content ranges from the arcane and technical (often in obtuse jargon), to the inane and simplistic (but often in surprisingly fluent gibberish). Sort according to your own taste. It's archived at the FTP site below.

Type: Usenet newsgroup
Address: alt.astrology
Type: WWW
**Address: http://www.cis.ohio-state.edu/
          hypertext/faq/usenet/astrology-
          faq/top.html**
Region: World

alt.divination

This newsgroup is a place for discussing divination techniques (for example, I Ching, Tarot cards, runes, throwing the bones, examining sheep's entrails, and what have you) from around the world. What are they? Do they work?

Type: Usenet newsgroup
Address: alt.divination
Region: World

Asian Astrology

Choix d'Éditeur

This Web page is a great place to start for information on Asian fortunetelling systems: It's an amazing resource, and the information is presented in full cultural context.

Type: WWW
**Address: http://www.deltanet.com/users/
          wcassidy/astroindex.html**
Region: India, Tibet, China, Vietnam

Asian Astrology and Divination Bibliography

This site offers a bibliography of works on many forms of astrology and other divination methods from Asian countries.

Type: WWW
**Address: http://www.deltanet.com/users/
          wcassidy/astrobiblio.html**
Region: India, Tibet, China, Vietnam

Ask Mr. Puddy

Actually, Mr. Puddy is an advice cat, not a feline psychic. But he will answer any question, and the answers are pretty good, too. Questions are accepted from cats and their human owners. Smarter than your average oracle—and with better fur.

Type: WWW
**Address: http://www.sils.umich.edu/
          ~nscherer/AskPuddy.html**
Region: U.S.

Astrolog

This is a birth charts program for Western astrology (which is really a misnomer, since "European" astrology has its roots in Africa, Asia, and the Near East). It's just one of the astrology-related items in this archive.

Type: FTP
**Address: ftp.stolaf.edu/gopher/Internet%20
          Resources/FTP%20 Sites/Astrology**
Region: World

Astrology Basics

Here's an astrology page with a sense of humor and a hip sensibility.

Type: WWW
**Address: http://cyborganic.com/~justin/
          astrol/**
Region: World

Astrology Chatline

To chat about astrology and related topics in real-time, check out this rather popular IRC channel.

Type: IRC
Address: #Astrology
Region: World

AwareNET

AwareNET aims to "expand your consciousness" by providing this online astrological service. There is a free service in English, German, and Dutch, and in the future there will be a paid service (billed to your credit card) in 13 languages. At the time of this writing, AwareNET's site still looked very much under construction, even though it had been going for a year—maybe it will be more comprehensive in the future.

Type: Gopher
Address: awarenet.com:8104/1
Region: U.S.

Biorhythm Bonanza for Amigas

If you remember disco, you'll remember biorhythms. If you forgot how long it's been since you had one of those "special" days, your problems are over. If you use an Amiga, look here for programs and information on this "scientific" method for deciding whether it's a propitious day or one you should stay in bed for.

Type: FTP
**Address: ftp.freebsd.cdrom.com/pub/
            aminet/util/misc/**
Type: Gopher
**Address: caramba.cs.tu-berlin.de:70/11/
            pub/CD-ROM/AmiNet/Aminet/
            util/misc**
Region: U.S., World

Biorhythm Bonanza for Macs

If you have a Mac, look for biorhythm software here.

Type: FTP
**Address: ftp.freebsd.cdrom.com/.13/
            mac/umich/game/board/**
Type: WWW
**Address: http://www.umich.edu/~archive
            /mac/game/board/**
Region: U.S., World

Divination Web

Visit the Divination Web and see what's up with others who share your interests.

Type: Telnet
Address: bill.math.uconn.edu 9393
Region: World

Feng Shui FAQ

This is a FAQ on the Chinese art of correct placement and construction to assure good luck: feng shui. It'll explain why you see red doors on many Chinese homes, why there are sometimes oddly placed mirrors in Chinese restaurants, and why the Bank of America building in San Francisco has been plagued with bad luck.

Type: WWW
**Address: http://www.deltanet.com/users/
            wcassidy/fengshuifaq.html**
Region: China

Fortunetelling File-o-Rama

This site has a number of files that you may find interesting. They include an astrology FAQ list as well as files on Tarot and biorhythms and a HyperCard astrology clock.

Type: FTP
Address: ftp.freebsd.cdrom.com
Region: World

Frequently Asked Questions about the Tarot

Here's where you can find out about these strangely decorated cards, whose heritage goes back into European and Eastern antiquity. There's also a folder of information about the Celtic Tarot here.

Type: WWW
**Address: http://cad.ucla.edu/repository/
          useful/**
Region: Europe, World

Hong Kong Fortune Cookie

Way down at the end of this introductory page for Hong Kong SuperNet (the HK Internet), there's a place where you can click on the words *fortune cookie*. Do it, and get the traditional one-liner.

Type: WWW
Address: http://www.hk.net/
Region: Hong Kong

Horoscopes

These are like the kind you read in the newspaper, only a little better written and longer. Updated weekly.

Type: WWW
**Address: http://www.dircon.co.uk/
          networks/stars.html**
Region: England, World

HyperBiorhythm

This is a HyperCard-based application for charting biorhythms on a Mac.

Type: WWW
**Address: http://www.umich.edu/~archive/
          mac/hypercard/fun/hyper
          biorhythm1.0.sit**
Region: U.S.

Interactive Astrology Chart

Using this forms-based Web page, still in the experimental stage, you can generate an astrological chart for yourself or a loved one. You'll need to know the date, time, and place of birth; an online map will help you find the latitude and longitude readings needed. It's fun!

Type: WWW
**Address: http://spirit.satelnet.org/Spirit/
          Astro/astro-chart.html**
Region: World

The Magic 8-Ball Knows All

I know you might not think this fortunetelling scheme is as valid the others, but I beg to differ. There isn't much science behind any of them, in my opinion— and besides, the Magic 8-Ball is a valid folk tradition.

Type: WWW
**Address: http://www.studentservices.com:
          3001/cgi-bin/8-ball.cgi**
Region: U.S.

The Nostradamus Gopher

All the prophecies of the ancient European seer Nostradamus have been digitized and put online here. This is the guy who supposedly foretold of the rise of Hitler (if you twist his actual words around enough to fit this presupposition).

Type: Gopher
**Address: skynet.usask.ca:70/
          1nostradamus/nostradamus.70**
Region: France

Rosicrucian Astrology

Those mysterious Rosicrucians are heavily into things Egyptian. Find out here about their astrology system.

Type: Gopher

**Address: locust.cic.net:70/11/Religious.
            Texts/Rosicrucian/astrology**

Region: Egypt, World

RuneCaster

An interactive program to cast the runes for divination, this application also includes a guide to runes (the ancient writing system of Scandinavia) and their meanings.

Type: WWW

**Address: http://antioch.acns.nwu.edu/
            ~jacker/runecaster/**

Region: Scandinavia

Tarot

A randomly generated Tarot reading is available here, as are Tarot FAQs. There are three-card and full Celtic readings, with interpretive text. Nice graphics, too.

Type: WWW

**Address: http://cad.ucla.edu/repository/
            useful/tarot.html**

Region: Europe

Tell Your Own Fortune

Here's a site that offers Tarot, biorhythm, and I Ching files for IBM, Amiga, Mac, UNIX computers, and even a few more. Things you're likely to find include astrological charting programs, biorhythm charting programs, and Tarot software and images. Incidentally, checking the major FTP and Gopher archives will turn up similar goodies almost every time.

Type: WWW

**Address: http://www.lysator.liu.se/ftp/
            pub/religion/neopagan/
            Astrology/**

**Address: http://www.lysator.liu.se/ftp/
            pub/religion/neopagan/Tarot/**

Region: World

The Uselessness of Fortune Telling

A wonderful, totally scathing attack on all aspects of fortunetelling—no one's safe! Truly inspired, and a needed antidote to the rest of this section.

Type: WWW

**Address: http://www.primus.com/staff/
            paulp/useless/fortune-telling.html**

Region: World

The Usenet Oracle

Grovel sufficiently and the infamous Usenet Oracle may deign to answer your query—although it may require a small service in return…. Its pronouncements are known as "Oracularities." See the Usenet groups and check out the Oracle's Web page for a FAQ, archives, and more about this amusing Net tradition.

Type: Usenet newsgroup

Address: rec.humor.oracle

Address: rec.humor.oracle.d

Type: WWW
**Address: http://www.pcnet.com/~stenor/
            oracle/**
Region: World

Vedic Astrology

You can learn the basics of the Indian Zodiac here, and how it is applied. There are also links to other interesting pages at this site.
Type: WWW
**Address: http://www.protree.com/kiwi/
            Spirit/Astro/astro-basics.html**
Region: India

Web-o-Rhythm

Here's a page that provides your biorhythms as a graph, rather than a stuffy old list of data. The color charts look pretty good.
Type: WWW
**Address: http://qns1.qns.com/html/
            weborhythm/**
Region: U.S.

The World™ Guide to Biorythm

This is a commercial service. Since some companies love to milk New Age saps for their dough, I would be cautious about leaving my e-mail address here as requested.
Type: WWW
**Address: http://www.theworld.com/
            HEALTH/BIORYTHM/SUBJECT.HTM**
Region: U.S.

World-Wide I-Ching

Check in here for a randomly generated I-Ching "throw" created with a computer program. It will interpret the strokes for you in the traditional elliptical style.

Type: WWW
Address: http://cad.ucla.edu:8001/iching
Region: China

World Wide Web Ouija

This online Ouija board lets the spirits talk through your mouse. The final instruction, "Don't take this seriously!" is good advice.
Type: WWW
**Address: http://www.math.unh.edu/
            ~black/cgi-bin/ouija.cgi**
Region: U.S.

GAMES AND GAMBLING

The workday is over, and it's time for some fun. Naturally, computer games are the big story on the Internet. Some are especially popular online, because you can play them interactively or with teams. There are also lots of chat groups about favorite games and other recreational activities—see any Usenet newsgroup list and check the many entries in the alt.games and rec.games categories.

Role-playing games (RPGs) and wargames are a favorite here. These can be played with dice and paper, or with figurines and a sand table, entirely online, or in full vampire get-up in the alleys of London at 2 a.m. In a way, MUDs are a type of RPG, but there are so many of them they get their own chapter. And other sorts of games, from crossword puzzles to tiddlywinks, also have their advocates on the Net.

And then there's gambling, which is shaping up as a Net controversy to beat all but computer porn. With encryption and the right software, it would be fairly easy to set up a virtual casino, with your servers based in a country that allows gambling. As you'll see in the listings, the first "real" online gambling den is slated to go online in the fall of 1995. Obviously, there are some legal issues to grapple with for those who live in nations that strictly control or outlaw gambling. There's also a legitimate reason to worry about underage gamblers taking advantage of the Net's anonymity, and about increasing the rate of gambling addiction. So be careful out there, eh? You can have just as good of a time without losing your shirt.

Active XPilot Servers

XPilot is another popular online game. Check in at this page and see who's playing where around the world. When I last peeked, there were tons of Scandinavians, the French and Germans were doing battle, and the English team at St. Andrews had been joined by a player from Uganda.

Type: WWW
**Address: http://rs560.cl.msu.edu/misc/
          xpilot.html**
Region: World

BattleTech

This is an RPG in which giant robots battle until one is reduced to a pile of spare parts. This is done with a hex board and dice, not actual giant robots. Find out more here, including strategy tips.

Type: WWW
**Address: http://www.physics.adelaide
          .edu.au/~dlow/btech.html**
Region: Australia, World

Bolo

This is an Internet game for Macs, based on tank warfare. It can be played by huge international teams for hours and hours and hours. Find out more from this FAQ, then track down a game to join.

Type: WWW
**Address: http://www.cis.ohio-state.edu/
          hypertext/faq/usenet/bolo-faq/
          faq.html**
Region: U.S., World

Bradford University Role-Play Society

The B.U.R.P.S play Mage: the Ascension, Masquerade, WereWolf: The Apocalypse, Call of Cthulhu, and Ars Magica, all of which are complicated, almost theatrical, role-playing games. They've put all sorts of information online to share with other players here.

Type: WWW
**Address: http://www.brad.ac.uk/
          ~thoskiso/rps.html**
Region: England, World

Bridge on the Web

The Web page for the world's most popular card game has information about bridge clubs, bridge games via Telnet, tournaments, and so on.

Type: WWW
**Address: http://www.cs.vu.nl/~sater/
          bridge/bridge-on-the-web.html**
Region: Netherlands, World

China-Japan Super Go Matches

Go is the Japanese strategy game with the deceptively simple appearance. Maintained by a Go fanatic, this page features all of the China-Japan Super Go Matches in SmartGame format, as well as other important matches. Serious Go players can study the moves and get better.

Type: WWW

**Address: http://nobi.ethz.ch/martin/
            games.html**

Region: China, Japan

.coNsOle .wORlD

Yes, that's how it's written. This is an internationally popular site for video gamers, based in Cardiff, Wales. It has a large archive of video game information for Sega, Nintendo, Amiga, Atari, and 3DO, with the promise that 32X and 3-Di are coming soon. Material ranges from the most basic lists of games to files on programming your own. Also here are links to video gaming clubs, newsletters, and other related stuff. Of course, this site also has information on the Internet's favorite bloody shoot 'em-up, Doom.

Type: WWW

Address: http://www.cm.cf.ac.uk/Games/

Region: Wales, World

Crambo's Place: The Word Games Page

This is the place for those silly word games that people all over the world know and love. The ones played here are the English and American ones, such as Crambo, Stinky Pinky, and Clarihew. There are also links to other word-games pages, including ones that cover crosswords, acrostics, and other word puzzles.

Type: WWW

**Address: http://www.primenet.com/
            ~crambo/**

Region: World

Dan's Poker Dictionary

This dictionary of poker has almost everything for the serious player, but doesn't include some of the more obscure stuff. For instance, he omitted the world's stupidest poker game, Indian Head Poker.

Type: WWW

**Address: http://www.universe.digex.net/
            ~kimberg/pokerdict.html**

Region: U.S., World

DoomGate

Doom is an addictive, extremely violent 3-D computer game from id software. The general rule is, kill everything. Understandably, this strikes a chord with many (and the graphics really are out of this world). DoomGate is a gateway to an interlocked series of pages with a common theme, "Doom: How to Play," tricks and tips, local clubs, servers that run the online version, and all the rest.

Type: WWW

Address: http://doomgate.cs.buffalo.edu/

Region: U.S., World

Fantasy Role Playing Games

This is the best site I found for information on RPGs like Advanced Dungeons & Dragons, Star Trek, and the Web-based Heavy Ordinance. Includes links to free RPG stuff online and other fantasy RPGs. Some MUD info, too.

Type: WWW

**Address: http://www.fcaglp.unlp.edu.ar/
            ~spaoli/games.html**

Region: Argentina, World

The Fascist Game

Fascist is a variation on a game called Nomic, which was invented by Peter Suber in 1980 and described by Douglas Hofstadter in his "Metamagical Themas" column in *Scientific American* in June 1982. It is a game about rule-making and legislation, and is very precise. The newsgroup is for discussion of Nomic and related games in general, the mailing list is for discussion about playing Fascist, and the Web page explains how to play Fascist, including archives of previous games.

Type: Usenet newsgroup
Address: alt.games.nomic
Type: Mailing List
Address: listserv@cs.vu.nl
Send e-mail message with body:
     SUB FASCIST
Type: WWW
Address: http://wombat.doc.ic.ac.uk/ fascist/fascist.html
Region: England

Foosball Arcade Archive

A site for foosball, full of lore, rules, and the strategy of the game. What's a "snake shot"? Find out here.

Type: FTP
Address: conrad.harvard.edu/pub/ foosball/
Region: U.S., England

French-Language Role-Playing Games—The List

There are quite a few RPG companies in France, and some of their games sound pretty fun. I especially liked the one with the futuristic theme in which the Catholic Church has complete control of the world. There's also information about some Swiss games here. Includes contact information for the RPG companies and hotlinks to detailed game information.

Type: WWW
Address: http://io.com/user/crgeneva/ French_games.html
Region: France, Switzerland

Game Links

A page that links you directly to game companies, most for computer games. You can get some shareware games through here, for example, I found the site to download the game Heretic.

Type: WWW
Address: http://www.ifi.uio.no/~jankr/@/ www_links.game.html
Region: Norway

Game Magazines

The FutureNet online service offers several on- and offline magazines about video games, including *Sega Power* and *Edge*, plus the week's current Gallup Games Charts.

Type: WWW
Address: http://www.futurenet.co.uk/ games/superplay.html
Region: England

The Game Room

The Game Room is for information regarding tabletop games, including computer games; miniatures, role-playing, and war games; and a really interesting selection of obscure games from Asia. Learn here about Jungle, Xian Qui (Chinese Chess), Korean Chess, Shogi (Japanese Chess), Backgammon, Russian card cames, variations on Go and Chess that you've never heard of, Swedish games, and more.

Includes copious links to more board-game and war-game pages.

Type: WWW

Address: http://cs.weber.edu/home/val/ www/games/gamespage.html

Region: U.S., China, Korea, Japan, England, Russia, Sweden, World

Games and Puzzles on the Internet

You'll find on this page links to games and puzzles sites on the Internet, some information about events and clubs in the U.K., and eventually some more specific information about puzzles, especially the mechanical variety.

Type: WWW

Address: http://www.dcs.qmw.ac.uk/ ~steed/GandP.html

Region: England, World

GamesNet

Shareware games, hints and tips on favorite video and computer games, and the Australian site for Internet Doom, too.

Type: WWW

Address: http://www.next.com.au/ games/

Region: Australia

Global Casino

Global Casino will open in the fall of 1995, if it can get around the legal obstacles that various governments would like to throw in its way. Operating out of Antigua in the Caribbean, it will offer online versions of craps, roulette, slots, mini-baccarat, video poker, seven other types of poker, Pai Gow, and other ways to lose your money. You can go ahead and open an account with them here if you must.

Type: WWW

Address: http://www.netaxs.com/ people/sportbet/casino.htm

Region: Antigua, World

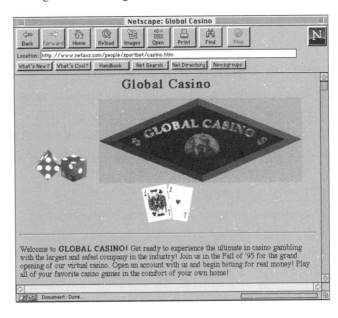

Go Rules

This page has The American Go Association Rules of Go, and several other documents that should make learning and playing Go easier.

Type: WWW

Address: http://www.cs.cmu.edu/afs/cs/ user/wjh/public/go/ Rules.AGA.html

Region: U.S., Japan

Illuminati New World Order

No, not the secret cabal behind the United Nations or Robert Anton Wilson, but apparently an outgrowth of the old role-playing game Illuminati from Steve Jackson Games, the company made famous when it was mistakenly raided during the "Operation Sundevil" hacker crackdown. Now there are a bunch of Illuminati trading cards and card decks to collect, and games to play with them.

Type: WWW
Address: http://www.io.com/sjgames/ inwo/
Region: U.S., World

Intelligent Gamer Online

Choix d'Éditeur

This is an online, biweekly journal for "the mature gaming community." In other words, not for force-feeding Sega ad copy to the little kiddies. The articles actually have content, the layout is attractive, and if you enjoy video games, you'll like it.

Type: WWW
Address: http://igonline.escape.com/ igograph.html
Region: World

Internet Chess Library

A good archive of chess-related software, text, and games. It has info on GNU chess, too.

Type: WWW
Address: http://caissa.onenet.net/chess/
Region: World

Internet Slot Machine

Enter your name and e-mail address, and pull the lever to see what happens. What makes me think that the real winner is the company, which gets to add you to their database for free? Call me a cynic....

Type: WWW
Address: http://www.datawave.net/ slotmachine/register.html
Region: World

IRCbot for Poker

Yes, you can play poker using Internet Relay Chat as your mode of communication. IRCbot is a program that does the dealing. The Web page lays out the rules and procedures; there are several IRC channels to choose from, such as #holdem.

Type: WWW
Address: http://www.cs.cmu.edu/afs/cs/ user/mummert/public/www/ ircbot.html
Region: U.S., World

The Journal of the PK Institute for Information Engineering

This quarterly gaming 'zine is dedicated mostly to GURPS (Generic Universal Role Paying System) games.

Type: WWW
Address: http://http2.sils.umich.edu/~ superman/jpkinst.html
Region: World

Ken's Go Page

Information about the page maintainer's Go idol, Wu Qing Yuan, and about famous Go matches. Emphasis is on strategy and improving your game. Although the URL indicates China, the guy who runs the page is an Asian-Canadian currently living in Switzerland. Lots of links here to Go clubs and resources worldwide.

Type: WWW
Address: http://ltiwww.epfl.ch/~warkent/ go/
Region: China, Japan, World

Kirk's List of Interactive Games on the Web

This is a British link to other games played on the Net. It's extensive and varied, and includes a film trivia quiz, tic-tac-toe, and the always-fun Pop Culture Internet Scavenger Hunt.

Type: WWW
**Address: http://web.city.ac.uk/~cb157/
            game.html**
Region: England, World

Lucky Number

Check here for information on playing international lotteries, like Spain's El Gordo ("The Big One," the world's largest), by mail or phone—and no doubt soon by Internet; and for links to lottery-number software.

Type: WWW
**Address: http://www.yahoo.com/Business/
            Products_and_Services/
            Get_Rich_Quick_/Lotteries/**
Region: World

Magic: The Gathering

This page offers an overview of Magic: The Gathering for the beginner. Magic is probably the hottest game for younger players in the U.S. right now (if you have kids, I'm sure this is not news). Players use decks of cards to "throw spells" at each other, and use other cards to ward off their opponents' spells. There are over 450 cards in this complex game, and they are highly collectable and avidly traded (see the Hobbies listings for more on this aspect).

Type: WWW
**Address: http://marvin.macc.wisc.edu/
            deckmaster/magic/overview.html**
Region: U.S., World

The Miniatures Page

The Miniatures Page is an online magazine dedicated to miniature wargaming in all periods: historical, fantasy, science fiction, and silly; ground or naval; all figure scales; from grand-tactical to skirmish level. Includes articles, graphics of well-done new miniatures, and information about new miniatures games.

Type: WWW
**Address: http://biochem.dental.upenn.edu/
            Mosaic/bill/tmp.html**
Region: World

More Magic on the Net

Everything you ever wanted to know about Magic, the trading cards and games. Lots of rabid collecting is going on here.

Type: WWW
**Address: http://marvin.macc.wisc.edu/
            deckmaster/magic/
            other.www.html**
Region: World

Netrek

It's like Star Trek, only you play it on the Internet. A space-based wargame so addictive that it has been banned on some college campuses. This page includes links to related archives, rules, FAQs, information for beginners and advanced players, and leads to Netrek servers. The FTP sites hold much the same information, for those without Web access, and the Usenet groups are for ongoing discussion of Netrek.

Type: WWW
**Address: http://www.cs.cmu.edu/Web/
            People/jch/netrek/README.html**
Type: FTP
**Address: grind.isca.uiowa.edu
            (128.255.21.233)**

Address: **ftp.risc.uni-linz.ac.at (193.170.33.112)**
Address: **infant2.sphs.indiana.edu/**
Type: Usenet newsgroups
Address: **alt.games.xtrek**
Address: **rec.games.netrek**
Region: World

The Nexus

This page was designed with the computer game developer, both novice and expert, in mind. Comprehensive information for the program-it-yourselfer.
Type: WWW
Address: **http://wcl-rs.bham.ac.uk/Games Domain/gamedev/gprog.html**
Region: England, World

1995 World Series of Poker

This is where the high rollers play—the jackpot is a cool million. And the game is played for keeps. If you haven't ever seen a "real" poker game, check one out on one of the sporting networks, or peek in here: It's more intimidating than a Scientology personality test.
Type: WWW
Address: **http://www.conjelco.com/ wsop.html**
Region: U.S.

Pachinko—Japan's Pinball

Every year the Japanese drop over $300 billion U.S. into pachinko machines! These incredible machines combine colorful art, mechanical animation, and top-flight electronics in a small, tabletop package. This page includes playing information and a bit of pachinko history.

Type: WWW
Address: **http://www.resultsdirect.com/ pachinko.htm**
Region: Japan

Paintball

Paintball is a game where you dress up and play soldier, but instead of bullets you use a gun that shoots little round balls filled with paint. You get splattered, you're a goner. It looks like a kick! This page has rules and a lot of links to paintball groups.
Type: WWW
Address: **http://warpig.cati.csufresno.edu/ other_pages.html**
Region: U.S.

Philippine Traditional Games

These sound like great fun. Games for children, although I think we grownups should try some silly things like this sometimes. Even the names sound great: Banog-Banog, Gagamba, Habulan Estatwa, and many more. They are traditional circle, chase, and tag games, and most are very active. Includes some stuff little boys will love—like spider fights.
Type: WWW
Address: **http://www.pitt.edu/~filipina/ games.html**
Region: Philippines

Pinball Wizards

Pin-Wizard Archive is the best Web page to find out about different pinball machines, link up with players' associations, and find links to other pinball resources online. The newsgroup is for ongoing pinball chat. Tommy, can you hear me?

Type: WWW
Address: http://www.glue.umd.edu/ %7Edstewart/pinball/
Type: Usenet newsgroup
Address: rec.games.pinball
Region: U.S.

Play by E-Mail

If you'd like to try some play-by-electronic-mail games, check out *PBEM*, an e-zine with reviews, game openings, and more information.

Type: WWW
Address: http://fermi.clas.virginia.edu/ ~gl8f/pbem_magazine.html
Type: FTP
Address: ftp.erg.sri.com/pub/pbm/ magazines/
Address: ftp.funet.fi/pub/doc/games/ play-by-mail/magazines/
Type: Usenet
Address: rec.games.pbm
Region: World

Puzzle Archive

The Web page archives puzzles and brain teasers from the newsgroup rec.puzzles. They're categorized by subject, and both the puzzles and their solutions are given.

Type: WWW
Address: http://alpha.acast.nova.edu/ puzzles.html
Type: Usenet newsgroup
Address: rec.puzzles
Region: World

Railroad Games Home Page

These games were first developed by Francis Tresham, and they involve similar rules for running virtual railroad companies from their earliest beginnings into the twentieth century.

Type: WWW
Address: http://ntia.its.bldrdoc.gov/ ~bing/mayf2.html
Region: England

rec.gambling

This is the newsgroup for those who enjoy trips to Vegas, Reno, Monaco, and other gambling hotspots. Lately it's been consumed by talk about virtual casinos. The Web page includes FAQs and links to other gambling resources online.

Type: Usenet newsgroup
Address: rec.gambling
Type: WWW
Address: http://www.conjelco.com/r_g/ las_vegas/r.g.html
Region: World

Roleplaying and Storyteller Game Archive

Player sheets, stories and other supporting materials for these games in English, German, and occasionally other languages. Offerings include Masquerade, Elric: The Eternal Hero (based on the books of Michael Moorcock), Call of Cthulhu, Runequest, Cyberpunk 2020, and many more, plus the freeware Fudge gaming engine, and a selection of fantasy, science fiction, and mythology books from the Gutenberg Project's archive for online inspiration.

Type: WWW
Address: http://www.uni-passau.de/ archive/WW/archive/
Region: Germany, World

Role-Playing Game Internet Resource Guide

A good link to information about RPGs, with a Danish and German mirror, and links to other RPG sites.

Type: WWW
Address: **http://falcon.cc.ukans.edu/~heresy/rpg/**
Region: England

RPG Organizations

Groups available here range from the famous MIT Assassins Guild to Britain By Night, the Daughters of Twilight, and a long list of U.S. and European RPG clubs. If you are looking for people to play with, chances are some of the links here will eventually lead to what you're searching for.

Type: WWW
Address: **http://wwwpub.utdallas.edu/~kalxen/gaming.html**
Region: World

The Scottish Tiddlywinks Association

Although it sounds like something out of a twisted Monty Python sketch, this is real. You too can learn all about the complexities of tiddlywinks here, and it has links to the Oxford University Tiddlywinks Society's page, the Cambridge University Tiddlywinks Club, the St. Andrews University Tiddlywinks Society, and the alt.games.tiddlywinks newsgroup. Makes you wonder.

Type: WWW
Address: **http://www-groups.dcs.st-and.ac.uk:80/~ben/tiddlywinks/**
Region: England, Scotland

Shebuté

This is a "serious" video game that involves world-systems simulation. The idea is to create a simple model of how economics and other systems work to illustrate how sustainable systems might be created—like SimCity on a global scale—and to have fun at the same time.

Type: WWW
Address: **http://shebute.com/Home.HTML**
Region: World

The TCP/IP Internet Doomer's FAQ

A how-to article on playing Internet Doom.

Type: WWW
Address: **http://www.cee.hw.ac.uk/~mapleson/doom/helpdocs/inetdoom.html**
Region: World

Um Die Welt (Around the World)

This is a World Wide Web game, currently in German but soon to be playable in English.

Type: WWW
Address: **http://ds1.wu-wien.ac.at/~derbuch/**
Region: Austria

Universal Access Inc. Blackjack Server

This is a simple online blackjack game—just click on "play blackjack!" and go.

Type: WWW
Address: **http://www.ua.com/blackjack/bj.html**
Region: U.S.

URouLette

In this "game," you gamble that the randomly chosen Web page you're sent to from this gateway will turn out to be really cool. Check it out!

Type: WWW
Address: http://kuhttp.cc.ukans.edu/cwis/organizations/kucia/uroulette/uroulette.html
Region: World

Vampire: The Masquerade

This is a real-world role-playing game, where you become a vampire for a night. Played in some night-clubs as well as at Masquerade parties and online. Popular with the gothic crowd, of course—just try to look very hip, very cool, and very very very undead!

Type: WWW
Address: http://acacia.ens.fr:8080/home/granboul/Vampire/
Region: France, World

The Virtual Vegas Home Page

Exactly what it sounds like, with a perfectly tacky American sensibility and sense of aesthetics. Showgirls, casino games, blackjack games, and real-time chat in their MUD are available, and it even has its own background theme music. Some information is in Japanese as well as English.

Type: WWW
Address: http://www.virtualvegas.com/
Region: U.S.

The World Wide Web Virtual Library: Games and Recreation

The best Net source for anything to do with games, this page has information on all aspects of games and gaming.

Type: WWW
Address: http://www.cis.ufl.edu/~thoth/library/recreation.html
Region: World

Zarf's List of Interactive Games on the Web

A wonderful Web site with links to a large list of games and puzzles you can play on the Net—everything from tic-tac-toe to MUDs.

Type: WWW
Address: http://www.cs.cmu.edu/afs/andrew/org/kgb/www/zarf/games.html
Region: World

Zylwee's WWW Page

Zylwee is a mail or e-mail multi-player wargame. Each player tries to conquer cities. You can download the rules and join in here.

Type: WWW
Address: http://dico.unice.fr/~berthon/zylwee.html
Region: France

GENEALOGY

Computer databases have given an incredible boost to genealogy. The power they provide, and the ability to store huge amounts of information, offer individuals new ways to trace their family tree.

The Internet's contribution is shaping up to be making these resources more accessible. Interactive surname searches, and global access to library catalogs and public records will make it possible to do your research without traveling around the world.

And personal contacts made through newsgroups and mailing lists are not to be discounted: Often it's that chance encounter with someone who "looks like family" that provides the missing piece of your family tree, and the Internet makes these serendipitous meetings even more likely.

Afrigeneas

This is a mailing list for discussing and sharing information about African genealogy. It was formerly known as the AAGENE-L mailing list.

Type: Mailing list
Address: afrigeneas@drum.nscs.com
Region: Africa

Australian Family History Compendium

Sponsored by Coherent Software Australia Pty Ltd., suppliers of genealogy software and services, this site features information about important resource centers for genealogy information in Australia, such as Public Record Offices and State Libraries. It also has a list of Australian genealogical societies. Were your ancestors among the "transported" poor and incarcerated? In Australia, it's now fashionable, not shameful, to declare it to the world.

Type: WWW
Address: http://www.ozemail.com.au/ ~coherent/
Region: Australia

BANAT

This moderated mailing list was created specifically for those doing research into ancestors from the Banat region of what was formerly Hungary.

Type: Mailing list
Address: majordomo@sierra.net

Send e-mail message with body:
SUBSCRIBE BANAT
Contact: madler@sierra.net
Region: Hungary

BBANNOUNCE-L

This mailing list will bring you 10 to 15 product announcements per year from Banner Blue, the popular genealogy software vendor.

Type: Mailing list
Address: majordomo@best.com
Send e-mail message with blank Subject line and body: subscribe bbannounce-l
Region: World

BK5-L

This is a moderated mailing list for the discussion of a genealogy program called Brother's Keeper. The author of BK, John Steed, is a subscriber and contributor to this list.

Type: Mailing list
Address: bk5-l-request@genealogy. emcee.com
Send an e-mail message with Subject:
SUBSCRIBE
Region: World

British Isles Genealogy and Beyond

Here's a fabulous guide, located in England, to getting started on searching for ancestors in the United Kingdom. Includes information about where records are kept and how to get them, guides to libraries with genealogical data, and so much more. There's also information here on researching your roots in other parts of the world, general genealogy procedures, and doing research from abroad.

Type: WWW

Address: **http://cs6400.mcc.ac.uk:80/**
          ~zzassps/genuki/

Region: England, Ireland, Northern Ireland,
          Wales, Scotland, Channel Islands, Isle
          of Man, World

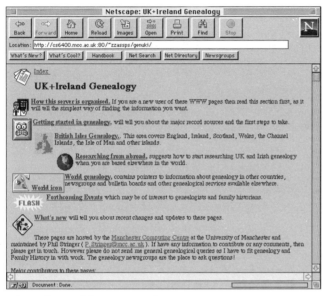

Churchyard/Orr Family Museum

Over 360 different family names and 835 different individuals are indexed here. The main regions of origin are England, Quebec/France, Germany, Northern Ireland, colonial and post-revolutionary New England, New York, and the middle states of the U.S.

Type: WWW

Address: **http://uts.cc.utexas.edu/**
          ~churchh/genealgy.html

Region: U.S.,World

David Walker's Genealogy Page

This page lets you browse a list of surnames; see if yours is here. There are also links to other genealogy resources.

Type: WWW

Address: **http://www.epm.ornl.gov/**
          ~walker/genealogy/

Region: U.S., World

Everton Publishers Home Page

This family-history information service is based in Utah. Little actual archival data is online, but this agency is a supplier of genealogical microfilms and equipment to other libraries. An abbreviated online version of the *Everton Genealogical Helper* periodical is provided, along with an impressive offering of up-to-date, interactive information.

Type: WWW

Address: **http://www.xmission.com/**
          ~jayhall/index.html

Region: U.S., World

Family Trees Made Easy

This is the home page of Vitarbor Graphics, which produces attractive supplies for the genealogy buff.

Type: WWW

Address: **http://www.teleport.com/**
          ~jcrunch/vitarbor.html

Region: U.S.

FTMTECH-L

This list is a forum for Banner Blue users and the company's staff to discuss its Family Tree Maker software and Family Archive CDs. Technical questions posted to this list will be answered by company employees.

Type: Mailing list

Address: **majordomo@best.com**

**Send e-mail message with blank Subject
          line and body: subscribe ftm
          tech-l**

Contact: **ftmtech-l@best.com**
Region: U.S., World

Genealogical Research in Ireland

This page or some part of the path to it was down at this writing, but this is one of the main Irish genealogical resources online.
Type: WWW
**Address: http://www.bess.tcd.ie/
             roots_ie.html**
Region: World

Genealogy Archive

This FTP site has software, how-to texts, information about specific families and regions, and many more sources for the family researcher.
Type: FTP
Address: ftp.cac.psu.edu/pub/genealogy/
Region: World

Genealogy FAQs

At this page, you can find a list of Frequently Asked Questions documents from the U.S. Census Bureau. Excellent basic information about government archives, pointers to the Church of Latter-day Saints' huge private collection of genealogical data, the largest in the world. U.S. Census Bureau data is not available online, but is available on microfilm at many libraries, colleges, and government offices. Some of the indexes for historic censuses are now available on CD-ROM from private companies. You can find out more about these resources here.
Type: WWW
**Address: http://www.census.gov/
             genealogy/genealogy.faq.draft**
Region: U.S.

Genealogy Home Page

Possibly the most thorough and useful site in America for the pursuit of genealogy, this page's contents are presented in a simple, friendly format, with a great many avenues of inquiry possible. There is a good level of feedback and exchange by users at this site.
Type: WWW
**Address: http://ftp.cac.psu.edu/~saw/
             genealogy.html**
Region: U.S., World

Genealogy Links

An ever-growing list of links to genealogical information online is maintained here.
Type: WWW
**Address: http://www.infi.net/~cwt/
             gen-oln.html**
Region: World

Helm's Genealogy Toolbox

This is a truly remarkable attempt to offer access to all recorded knowledge of human family relations, with an obvious emphasis on the ability to utilize developing information resources. Includes information on Native American and African-American genealogy, as well as many other ethnic groups. Without a doubt, this type of comprehensive information service is an impressive technological achievement, and clearly advancing the state of large information base technology.
Type: WWW
**Address: http://lcweb.loc.gov/
             homepage/lchp.html**
Region: U.S., World

Helm's Genealogy Toolbox Introduction Page

The result of work by a University of Illinois information science student, this page serves as an introduction to the source of genealogy information listed above. Online information about a few hundred surnames is offered, among many other experimental and cutting-edge services. This seems to be a showcase for only newer things, such as graphic images of historic civil documents and American Civil War information.

Type: WWW
**Address: http://ux1.cso.uiuc.edu/
            ~al-helm/genealogy.html**
Region: U.S., World

How to Use Maps in Genealogy

Information is online here from the U.S. Geological Survey on using maps to help trace your family tree.

Type: WWW
**Address: http://info.er.usgs.gov/
            factsheets/genealogy/index.html**
Region: U.S.

Jewish Genealogy Home Page

One would be hard-pressed to find better online resources concerning Jewish genealogy. Much of it references general public archives not specific to Judaic heritage, and a significant portion of the data referred to appears to be directly online. Created by the "Dallas Virtual Jewish Community," this site is an invaluable index to high-quality general information sites that are probably not well known.

Type: WWW
**Address: http://dc.smu.edu/dvjcc/dvjcc.
            genealogy.html**
Region: U.S., World

The Linkages Project

This project is attempting to bring together datasets relating to family relationships in many parts of the world. It includes the genealogical backgrounds of U.S. presidents, Old Testament patriarchs, and Javanese elders, among others. This is anthropological data with a tangential relationships to genealogy per se—good as background.

Type: WWW
**Address: http://eclectic.ss.uci.edu/
            linkages/linkages.html**
Region: World

Mindspring Genealogy Resources

Lots of information on birth and death records, building family histories, and software for genealogy activities is archived here.

Type: WWW
**Address: http://www.mindspring.com/
            ~sledet/genealogy/**
Region: U.S., World

Mine Interesser

This is a personal page ("My Interests") belonging to a Norwegian individual, with some interesting Usenet and other newsgroup indexes pertaining to genealogy. In Norwegian.

Type: WWW
**Address: http://www.uio.no/~achristo/
            alfchr.html**
Region: Norway, World

New Brunswick Genealogical Information Page

This is a nicely done online guide to genealogical resources and information concerning the region of New Brunswick, Canada. Like other sites, most archival data is not online, but the page seems to be an excellent candidate for future expansion of online services.

Type: WWW
Address: http://www.bess.tcd.ie/ roots_ie.html
Region: Canada, World

The North of Ireland Family History Society

Here's one of the main Internet sites for Northern Irish heritage information. Not much actual data is online yet, but it refers to all useful historical documentation concerning genealogy in Northern Ireland, and provides contacts for additional assistance.

Type: WWW
Address: http://www.os.qub.ac.uk/nifhs/
Region: Northern Ireland

no.slekt

This is a Norwegian site for genealogy information and for cultural news of genealogical interest, in Norwegian.

Type: No newsgroup
Address: no.slekt
Region: Norway

Odessa

A unique source of genealogy information about the so-called "Germans from Russia" in America, this site seems to have been created entirely by individuals communicating through the Net. It's a small archive, but user-maintained and supported, and it's a source of online transcriptions by users of family and civil documents.

Type: FTP
Address: pixel.cs.vt.edu
Region: Russia, Germany, U.S.

RAND Genealogy Club Home Page

This is a simple, well-thought-out, and extremely powerful all-purpose genealogical resource. Included is the "Roots Surname List," an address list of persons currently researching any name requested, along with the time period and geographic region they are focusing on.

Type: WWW
Address: http://www.rand.org/personal/ Genea/
Region: U.S., World

soc.genealogy.computing

This newsgroup is for discussing genealogy software, Net use, and general tech-related questions.

Type: Usenet newsgroup
Address: soc.genealogy.computing
Region: World

soc.genealogy.misc

This newsgroup for genealogy is probably the main resource for online information, all of it user-generated. Archives and FAQs are linked to the Web page.

Type: Usenet newsgroup
Address: soc.genealogy.misc
Type: WWW
Address: http://ftp.cac.psu.edu/~saw/ charters.html
Region: U.S., World

Tiny Tafel

Genealogy Online's fully automated e-mail server lets you conduct e-mail searches and retrievals for names and other family data. For instructions and other details about accessing the server, send e-mail to the address below, or see gateways at the FTP, Telnet, and WWW sites.

Type: Mailing list
Address: tt-info@genealogy.emcee.com
Address: info@genealogy.emcee.com (for general information)
Address: 1880@genealogy.emcee.com (for 1% 1880 Census Info)
Type: FTP
Address: genealogy.emcee.com
Type: Telnet
Address: genealogy.emcee.com
Type: WWW
Address: http://genealogy.emcee.com
Region: U.S., World

University of New Mexico LIBROS Online Library System

The UNM Internet site is generally impressive and easy to use. There is an online catalog of unusual archival books of genealogical interest in the main library. Check this out as an example of the resources available at university and public libraries worldwide.
Type: Telnet
Address: library@library.unm.edu:23
Region: U.S., World

Vicki's Home Page

This is a personal page about genealogical research with references to little-known sites and subscription services related to specific countries or surnames.
Type: WWW
Address: http://www.eskimo.com/ ~chance/
Region: U.S., World

Wales

Look here for general information on Wales, with recommendations on genealogy research avenues.

Type: WWW
Address: http://cs6400.mcc.ac.uk/ genuki/big/wal/
Region: Wales

What's New with the Genealogy Home Page

This document summarizes recent changes and additions to genealogical information available through the WWW Genealogy Home Page. The small collection of WWW documents here points to many resources spread throughout the world.
Type: WWW
Address: http://ftp.cac.psu.edu/~saw/ whats_new.html
Region: World

WW-Person

This is a small, free lookup service for tracing German nobility. The genealogy of German nobility seems to be its own popular subcategory, with quite a few dedicated resources.
Type: WWW
Address: http://faui80.informatik. uni-erlangen.de/html/ ww-person.html
Region: Germany

WWW Genealogy Databases

A number of people are experimenting with using WWW and HTML to present the results of their genealogical research. Several of these efforts are showcased here, including links to family data from Germany, Holland, Syria, England, France, and more.
Type: WWW
Address: http://ftp.cac.psu.edu/~saw/ genwww.html
Region: World

Yahoo's Genealogy Resources

There are lots of links here, and the list is sure to grow rapidly. One of the more intriguing resources is to lists of inmates and victims associated with Newgate Prison in England.

Type: WWW
**Address: http://www.yahoo.com/Science/
            Genealogy/**
Region: World

HEALTH AND MEDICINE

See also Discussion and Support Groups page 180

The Internet and medicine are gradually being shaped into an entity known as *telemedicine* or *distance medicine*. The Net's resources allow medical personnel to communicate quickly and to share files and high-resolution images that can help them solve medical puzzles.

As a result, there are many sources for mainstream medical information online. There are also a great many alternative medicine sites.

If discussion's your thing, dozens of Usenet newsgroups are available: See subjects and names with the prefix sci.med, alt.med, and alt.health on any list of Usenet groups. There are also many groups devoted to discussing particular illnesses; most of these are support groups for sufferers and their families.

Academic Press Journals

This is a guide to various journals published by the English company Academic Press, including many medical journals.

Type: Gopher
**Address: ukoln.bath.ac.uk:7070/11/Link/
            Tree/Publishing/AcademicPress/
            APJournals**
Region: England

act-up

This mailing list was set up for the discussion of the work being done by the various ACT-UP chapters worldwide, to announce events, to exchange ideas related to AIDS activism, and, more broadly, to discuss the politics of AIDS and health care.

Type: Mailing list
Address: act-up-request@world.std.com
Region: World

AIDS

AIDS is a mailing list mirror of the newsgroup sci.med.aids. It covers medical, political, and social issues of AIDS and HIV. Several newsletters, including the CDC Daily Summary (for those who trust the government) and AIDS Treatment News (for the rest of us), are carried. Postings to the AIDS list are only considered confidential by those who believe an anonymous server can't be hacked. The average number of postings is between 10 and 20 per day, including some large articles. This is a moderated mailing list.

Type: Mailing list
Address: listserv@rutvm1.rutgers.edu
**Send e-mail message with body: subscribe
            AIDS**
Type: Usenet newsgroup
Address: sci.med.aids
Region: World

Archives of Quackery

You can grab a bibliography of essays on all sorts of unproven "cures," from the humorous to the down-right scary, at this site.

Type: WWW
Address: http://www.public.iastate.edu/ ~edis/skeptic/quackery.html
Region: U.S., Germany, England

Atlanta Reproductive Health Clinic

This is a very valuable site for women and their part-ners. Factual information about fertility problems, PMS, contraception, adoption, breast cancer, cervical cancer, eating disorders, and many other health con-cerns are included.

Type: WWW
Address: http://www.mindspring.com/ ~mperloe/index.html
Region: U.S.

Biometry Home Page

This is the home page for a mailing list on biometry. It includes information on subscribing and an archive, as well as calls for papers, information on the International Biometric Society, and pointers to biometric information on the Internet. Also includ-ed is a very comprehensive list of general medical information on the Net.

Type: WWW
Address: http://www.AMS.Medizin. Uni-Goettingen.DE/~rhilger/ biometry.html
Region: Germany

BITNET Medical Newsgroups

If your provider offers BITNET newsgroups, these are among those that have significant international participation on medical subjects. See a list of more at the Web page below, along with several Usenet groups and mailing lists.

Type: BITNET newsgroup
Address: bit.listserv.medforum
Address: bit.listserv.mednews
Type: WWW
Address: http://umt.umt.edu:700/1/ internet/News
Region: World

Brain Scans

This could be your brain on the Internet. Various images (magnetic resonance, CAT scan, and so on) of brain scans are stored here for examination and comparison.

Type: WWW
Address: http://www-ipg.umds.ac.uk/ archive/heads.html
Region: England

Brain 3-D Reconstruction

This is just what it says, although waiting for the image to take form takes a long, long time.

Type: Gopher
Address: gopher.austin.unimelb.edu.au/ l9/images/petimages/ brain_3D_recon
Region: Australia

Calcium Imaging Site

This is a brief HTML-format paper on *in vivio* calcium imaging, including an MPEG movie and a nice image.

Type: WWW
Address: http://wwwfml.mpib-tuebingen .mpg.de/borst/work/projects/ calcium/imaging.htm
Region: Germany

Canadian Health Network

Lots of information on the Canadian health system is available here: pesticide reports, nutrition data, pointers to health care providers and organizations, links to sites on specific topics from AIDS to women's health, funding programs, and more.

Type: WWW
Address: http://hpb1.hwc.ca/
Region: Canada

China Medical College

This semibilingual Chinese/English server provides medical information, especially on both traditional and modern Chinese medicine.

Type: WWW
Address: http://cmc.cmc.edu.tw/ cmcstart.html
Region: Taiwan

The Chiropractic Page

For practitioners, students, and interested laypeople, this site offers images, documents, and links to related Web and Gopher sites, as well as newsgroups, BBSs, mailing lists, and nutrition information.

Type: WWW
Address: http://www.mbnet.mb.ca/ ~jwiens/chiro.html
Region: Canada, U.S., World

Communicable Disease Surveillance Centre

This is the British analogue of the familiar CDC in the U.S.; here you can find out what diseases they are following and what the current rates of infection are, as well as lots of other information. Also, issues of the "Communicable Disease Report" published by the center are available, which you'll need a copy of Adobe Acrobat Reader to view.

Type: WWW
Address: http://www.open.gov.uk/cdsc/ cdschome.htm
Region: England, Scotland, Wales, Northern Ireland

CROMED-L

This list covers current events in Croatia, particularly in medicine. It's also used as a tool to gather medical and humanitarian help.

Type: Mailing list
Address: cromed-l@aearn.bitnet
Region: Croatia

Department of Orthopædic Research and Biomechanics

Information on research and staff at the University of Ulm is available here. You can also find publications and a map of the university, or find out about job openings in the lab. The address below is for the English version; German pages are also available.

Type: WWW
Address: http://lyra.medizin.uni-ulm.de/ ufb.html/ufb-home.html
Region: Germany

Department of Psychology at McMaster University

A faculty directory and research undertakings at the psychology department of one of Canada's larger universities are available here.

Type: WWW
Address: http://www.science.mcmaster.ca/ Psychology/psych.html
Region: Canada

Dermatology WWW-Server

The University of Erlangen in Germany has provided lots of information here on dermatology. Includes case reports, course outlines, an address book, and an image atlas.

Type: WWW
Address: http://www.rrze.uni-erlangen.de/ docs/FAU/fakultaet/med/kli/ derma/
Region: Germany

Directory of Medical Information

This is a general directory of medical information online. It's mostly U.S. stuff, but there's some non-U.S.-related information as well, particularly Japanese. In English.

Type: WWW
Address: http://synap.neuro.sfc.keio.ac.jp/ medical/medical.html
 Region: Japan

European Molecular Biology Laboratory

This lab is in Heidelberg, Germany, and here you can find information on courses and workshops, scientific programs, and other projects of the center. If

you download special software from this site, you can talk by voice to others using the site.

Type: WWW
Address: http://www.embl-heidelberg.de/
Region: Germany

First Aid

In Portuguese, this page provides basic information on dealing with medical emergencies.

Type: WWW
Address: http://sweet.ua.pt/~helder/pt/ sos.htm
Region: Portugal

French Flu Map

Yes, this is a map of the spread of the flu in France, maintained by the French Communicable Disease Network. It appears that Paris in the springtime can have you carrying about a bouquet of handkerchiefs rather than flowers. *Quel dommage*!

Type: WWW
Address: http://www.b3e.jussieu.fr/ carte_grippe_eng.html
Region: France

Gallery of Medical Imaging Movies at CRS4

This page contains eight movies of medical imaging, including CAT scans and Magnetic Resonance Imaging (MRI).

Type: WWW
Address: http://www.crs4.it/Animate/ Animations_med.html
Region: Italy

GenomeNet WWW Server

Lots of information on genome research, specifically the Human Genome Project, can be found here. Includes papers and other documents, pointers to those working on HGP in Japan, and a searchable index of genome resources.

Type: WWW
Address: http://www.genome.ad.jp/
Region: Japan

German Cancer Research Center

Various departments of the center maintain home pages here. These pages are mostly just telephone numbers and brief information about researchers there.

Type: WWW
Address: http://www.dkfz-heidelberg.de/
Region: Germany

German Newsgroups

German medical personnel use these groups to discuss a variety of subjects. If you would enjoy participating (and have a good command of the language), see if any of these lists share your interests.

Type: Zer.t-netz and other newsgroups
Address: zer.t-netz.med.allgemein
Address: zer.t-netz.med.notfall
Address: zer.t-netz.med.pflege
Address: zer.t-netz.med.studenten
Address: zer.t-netz.med.therapie
Address: cl.gentechnik.medizin
Address: fido.ger.medizin
Region: Germany

Health and Longevity

This text-only monthly newsletter available in Spanish or English focuses on wellness and health-promoting lifestyles. Written by a naturopath.

Type: WWW
**Address: http://www.sims.net/
organizations/naturopath/
naturopath.html**
Type: E-zine
Address: naturopath@sc.net
Region: U.S., World

Health in Chile

At this Gopher site maintained by Chile's Ministry of Health, you can find disease statistics, information about government health and wellness programs, and links to other medicine-related Gophers in South America and elsewhere.

Type: Gopher
**Address: huelen.reuna.cl:70/11/gopher/
reuna/minsal**
Region: Chile

Health Informatics in Africa

This is an archive of HELINA-L, a moderated mailing list about computer and communications support for health care in Africa. A subscription form is available in this archive.

Type: Gopher
**Address: trout.ab.umd.edu:152/11/
pointers/helina-l**
Contact: Mikko.Korpela@uku.fi
Region: Africa

HealthNet

This page is a directory of health-care resources on the Internet. It's searchable, and it also has lots of documents and examples of how to use the Internet to find health-care resources.

Type: WWW

Address: http://www.hwc.ca/healthnet/

Region: Canada

Homeopathy Home Page

This one looks especially useful to practitioners: bibliographies, schools, conferences, U.S. and U.K. contacts.

Type: WWW

Address: http://www.dungeon.com/ home/cam/homeo.html

Region: U.S., England

Interactive Anatomy Programs

What you'll find here is lots of graphics files that will let you view various parts of the human anatomy when downloaded.

Type: FTP

Address: ftp.monash.edu.au/pub/ medical/

Region: Australia

Interactive BodyMind Information System

IBIS is a software reference tool that contains homeopathic and other complementary therapeutics. Produced by AMR'TA, a nonprofit medical research and teaching association, it gives doctors who enter a patient's condition information about therapies that include physical medicine, nutrition, Western botanicals, Chinese herbals, traditional Chinese acupuncture, homeopathy, vibrational therapies, and psychospiritual approaches. Includes the homeopathic Materia Medica and much more. You can get information about the software and how to order it here.

Type: WWW

Address: http://www.teleport.com/~ibis/

Region: England, China, U.S., World

International Health News

Check out a sample issue of *International Health News* here. It gathers together short articles and research abstracts from doctors around the world for your perusal. It looks interesting—especially for medical practitioners and students.

Type: WWW

Address: http://vvv.com/HealthNews/ abstract.html

Region: World

Internet World Congress on Biomedical Science

Mie University in Japan held this conference in December of 1994; this site is based on a CD-ROM of the papers and speeches of the conference. Searchable, and in English.

Type: WWW

Address: http://www.medic.mie-u.ac.jp/

Region: Japan

Japanese AIDS Patents

Various information about patents relating to AIDS and AIDS treatment in Japan is available here, organized by month of submission.

Type: WWW

Address: http://www.netaxs.com/ ~aengel/JapanAIDSPatents/

Region: Japan

Japanese National Cancer Center

You'll find documents from and information about the NCC here. Some are in HTML format, others are text documents available via linked Gopher sites.

Type: WWW
Address: http://www.ncc.go.jp/
Region: Japan

Lee Hancock's Health Resource List

This page offers a list of health resources on the Internet, including many non-U.S. sites.

Type: WWW
**Address: http://www.hwc.ca/healthnet/
            lhlist/hancock.html**
Region: U.S., World

McConnell Brain Imaging Centre

This center is working on computer images of brains, and they provide information on their research and faculty here as well as some demo movies of brain scans.

Type: WWW
Address: http://www.mni.mcgill.ca/
Region: Canada

Medical Emergency Assistants

Ready to give your talents to the world? Here you'll find links to groups who provide medical help in impoverished areas, from Africare to Médecins Sans Frontières.

Type: WWW
**Address: http://www.netmarket.com/isa/
            html/medcare.html**
Region: World

Medical School of Rennes

This site offers data on research projects underway at the school, and pointers to other sites.

Type: WWW
**Address: http://www.med.univ-rennes1.fr/
            index_an.html**
Region: France

Medical Web

Medical Web includes support and information for People With AIDS, data from the Arthritis Foundation, and much more.

Type: WWW
**Address: http://www.gov.nb.ca/hotlist/
            medical.htm**
Region: U.S., Australia, Canada, Sweden,
            England, Scotland

Medicine in Japan

You can find all the Web servers in Japan related to medical sites here: hospitals, universities, and research firms. These should give you access to many medical Gopher sites as well.

Type: WWW
**Address: http://www.med.nagoya-u.ac.jp/
            pathy/medicine.html**
Region: Japan

MedLink Home Page

This is a central information distribution point for Swedish doctors; the maintainers hope to share news and information with all 40,000 physicians in Sweden. It's only in Swedish now, but most items should be available in English as well by the time you read this. Also includes address lists, mail, and more.

Type: WWW
**Address: http://www.ls.se/medlink_eng/
            homepage.html**
Region: Sweden

MedNews

MedNews, the Health Info-Com Newsletter on recent developments in medicine, is distributed worldwide via the Internet. Here are several places you can find it.

Type: WWW
**Address: http://biomed.nus.sg/
            MEDNEWS/welcome.html**
            (Asia/Pacific)
**Address: http://cancer.med.upenn.
            edu:3000/** (Americas)
**Address: http://www.dmu.ac.uk/0/
            departments/pharmacy/archive/
            www/MEDNEWS/welcome.html**
            (Europe)
Type: Gopher
Address: cucc.ruk.cuni.cz:70/11/MedNews
Region: World

Med Student Discussion

This mailing list is devoted to networking and discussion among medical students worldwide.

Type: Mailing list
Address: listserv@unmvm
**Send e-mail message with body:
            SUBSCRIBE MEDSTU-L**
Region: World

Midwifery and Homebirth

Contacts, books, texts, and magazine articles from the U.S.-based professional journal *Midwifery Today* are just some of what you can find here. Includes many international resources and leads.

Type: WWW
**Address: http://www.efn.org/~djz/birth/
            birthindex.html**
Region: U.S., World

Monkey Head

MRI images of a monkey's head, with text files in English or Japanese are what you'll find here.

Type: FTP
**Address: ftp.nc.nihon-u.ac.jp/pub/
            data/MRIMonkeyHead**
Region: Japan

Neurosciences Internet Resource Guide

The University of Michigan maintains this thorough list of neuroscience resources, many outside the U.S.

Type: WWW
**Address: http://http2.sils.umich.edu/
            Public/nirg/nirg1.html**
Region: U.S., World

Numeric Imaging Unit

This page is for a team at the University Hospital of Geneva that's working on improvements to their image storage and processing procedures. Includes information on their projects and pointers to other sites.

Type: WWW
**Address: http://expasy.hcuge.ch/www/
            UIN/UIN.html**
Region: Switzerland

Nurse Gopher

This Gopher has lots of information for nurses: education resources, conferences, job openings, and pointers to other nursing sites.

Type: Gopher
Address: nurse.csv.warwick.ac.uk/1
Region: England

The Politics of Medicine

This active newsgroup talks about how government policy, the media and the court of public opinion affect medical practice. Recent topics have included the French abortion pill controversy and health-care reform.

Type: Usenet newsgroup
Address: talk.politics.medicine
Region: U.S., World

PSI PET Program

This is the home page of an institute working on Position Emission Tomography; it includes a directory of research projects and staff.

Type: WWW
Address: http://pss023.psi.ch/
Region: Switzerland

Psychiatry On-Line

This is an electronic journal on psychiatry. It includes letters (write one yourself!), articles, and news.

Type: WWW
Address: http://www.cityscape.co.uk/ users/ad88/psych.htm
Region: England

Red Cross/Red Crescent

Reports, news, and documents on world health disasters and the work of these organizations to take care of the victims is some of what you'll find here.

Type: WWW
Address: http://www.ifrc.org/
Region: World

Royal Australian Flying Doctor Service

In Australia, it only takes 90 minutes to bring a doctor to your door for an emergency housecall, no matter how remote your home is. Learn about this innovative public health program here.

Type: WWW
Address: http://www.csu.edu.au/ australia/defat/flydoc.html
Region: Australia

Rural Health Support, Education, and Training Program

RHSETnet provides remote health workers in Australia with immediate and easy access to information, training programs, and computer-assisted learning programs. It encourages competency in the use of new and emergent technologies in a cost-effective manner. This site includes online catalogs, links to health information databases, software, electronic courses for rural health workers, and more. It's a must-see if you'd like to find out how the Internet can be used to improve access to essential knowledge.

Type: WWW
Address: http://tei-cal.tei.uq.oz.au/ RHSETNET/Index.html
Region: Australia

Sapporo Medical University

Lots of information on medicine in Japan is available here: the state exam for medicine, a catalog of medical books, a gateway to the library of medicine, even how to donate a body to the university!

Type: WWW
Address: http://www.sapmed.ac.jp/
Region: Japan

Serveur Multimedia de la Radiologie Française

The Collège des Enseignants de Radiologie de France maintains this multimedia server for radiology information, in French. It includes images and related files.

Type: WWW
Address: http://www.med.univ-rennes1.fr/ cerf/cerf.html
Region: France

Skull Base Surgery Planning Project

This Web page is a brief paper, with nice pictures, on imaging for skull base surgery.

Type: WWW
Address: http://nothung.umds.ac.uk/ www/skullbase/skullbase.html
Region: England

Sound Photosynthesis Archive

Audio tapes are available here related to research into the practice of shamanistic alternative healing, with an emphasis on psychotherapy and mental health applications. Listings include many cultural traditions.

Type: WWW
Address: http://www.photosynthesis.com/ SoundPhotosynthesis/html/sham anism.html
Region: Nigeria, Mexico, Brazil, Peru, U.S.

Sumeria's Alternative Health Section

This "alternative information" service in Australia has loads of leads to information on alternative medicine, including new and traditional medical theories and practices. Subjects include oxygen therapy, many items related to AIDS and other immune-system disorders, midwifery, cancer, and more.

Type: WWW
Address: http://werple.mira.net.au/ sumeria/
Region: Australia, World

The Swedish Association for the Electrically or VDT Injured

Sweden is just about the only country to recognize that computers and electricity can have harmful effects on the body. It was the first to set up emissions standards for computer terminals, for example. This is the *only* information I have ever seen about electrical sensitivity syndrome, even though I suspect it's more common that we think. Learn here about this little-known illness, and possible ways to prevent and treat it.

Type: WWW
Address: http://www.isy.liu.se/~tegen/ feb_info.html
Region: Sweden

Synapse Root Page

An archive of demonstration medical documents, all in a nice style, is what you'll find here, along with pointers to other resources.

Type: WWW
Address: http://synapse.uah.ualberta.ca/ root/root.htm
Region: Canada

Theoretical Neurobiology Index

This is the home page of a lab at the University of Antwerp, Belgium. It offers a directory of researchers, publications, and research files, including information on the neural simulation software they are writing and how to order it.

Type: WWW
Address: **http://bbf-www.uia.ac.be/**
Region: Belgium

TRAMIL

TRAMIL, the Traditional Medicine Island List, is concerned with the study, preservation, and practice of folk or traditional medical and healing techniques, with a focus on the Caribbean. This is primarily a Spanish-language list.

Type: Mailing list
Address: **listserv@conicit.ve**
Send e-mail message with one line body:
subscribe TRAMIL <Firstname Lastname>
Region: Caribbean

Tropical Disease Research Scientist Network

This mailing list on tropical diseases is sponsored by the World Health Organization, the United Nation's health authority.

Type: Mailing list
Address: **tdr-scientists-REQUEST@who.ch**
Contact: **tdr-Scientists@who.ch**
Region: World

UMDS Image Processing Group, London

This image processing and computer vision lab is working on medical uses for technology. Their page includes a directory of staff, research archives, conference information, images from their work, and an audio file about them.

Type: WWW
Address: **http://nothung.umds.ac.uk/ index.html**
Region: England

UMIN

This is a central server with pointers to various Japanese medical schools and departments, in both English and Japanese.

Type: WWW
Address: **http://cc.umin.u-tokyo.ac.jp/**
Region: Japan

University of Bonn Medical Center

This is the server of the Institute of Medical Statistics, Documentation and Data Processing at the university. It has many pointers to useful medical data worldwide, some of it in German. It includes a link to CancerNet, announcements of topical and medical events, and information on the medical center itself.

Type: WWW
Address: **http://imsdd.meb.uni-bonn.de/ welcome.en.html**
Region: Germany

The Virtual Hospital

This extremely educational site for medical professionals and laypeople alike includes multimedia medical textbooks and teaching files, "patient simulations," guidelines, courses, an online history of medicine, publications, and many medical links. There's also a whole section of information for patients, such as "Helping Children Cope with the Intensive Care Unit."

Type: WWW
Address: **http://indy.radiology.uiowa.edu/**
Region: U.S., World

The Virtual Medical Center

Hospitals and medical schools online, information about and demos of telemedicine, medical texts and multimedia files, and lots of WWW and Gopher links is some of what you'll find here. Very comprehensive!

Type: WWW

Address: http://www-sci.lib.uci.edu/ ~martindale/Medical.html

Region: U.S., World

Virus Gopher

This Gopher contains lots of documents on viruses affecting living things, both plant and animal, in Australia.

Type: Gopher

Address: life.anu.edu.au/11/viruses

Region: Australia

World Health Organization

Various documents from WHO are archived here.

Type: FTP

Address: ftp.who.ch/

Region: World

Zen Hospice Center

You'll find resources on death and dying, including multicultural information and AIDS-specific data at this site. From the San Francisco Zen Center's hospice.

Type: WWW

Address: http://www.well.com/user/ devaraja/index.html

Region: U.S., World

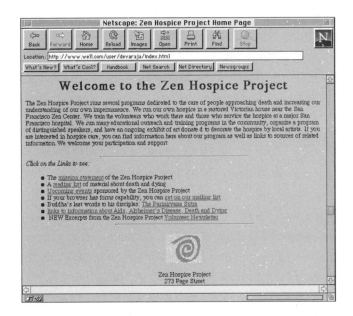

HISTORICAL DOCUMENTS

It might not be as sexy as alt.devilbunnies or as colorful as an online art museum, but text documents are still what a lot of people are looking for on the Internet. In response, a number of universities and organizations have created archives for historical documents, such as national constitutions and major treaties. These are of great interest to students, historians, and average citizens who haven't had a chance to read the full text of these important papers before.

If you don't find what you're looking for through this list, why not volunteer to create an electronic version yourself? Just make sure it is not subject to copyright restrictions.

African National Congress Archive

Pronouncements, newsletters, and internal documents of the ANC are stored here.

Type: Gopher
Address: wn.apc.org:70/11/anc/history
Region: South Africa

Alcuin: A Database of Internet Resources

If you know a snippet of the title or a phrase that appears in the document you seek, try this search engine. It includes the ALEX database of electronic texts, and seems to do an excellent job of turning up e-texts from Internet archives around the world.

Type: WWW
Address: http://library.ncsu.edu/drabin/ alcuin
Region: World

Argentine Constitution

This is a very thorough constitution indeed, which outlaws slavery but institutes Catholicism as the official religion. In Spanish.

Type: Gopher
Address: gopher.recyt.net:70/11/ argentina
Region: Argentina

Black American History

This archive includes many documents, from slave narratives to the Emancipation Proclamation to twentieth century works on the Black experience in the United States.

Type: Gopher
Address: UMSLVMA.UMSL.EDU:70/11/ LIBRARY/SUBJECTS/BLACKSTU/ BLACKHIS
Region: U.S.

Canadian Historic Document Archive

This archive includes the Canadian Charter of Rights and Freedoms, Canada's 1867 Constitution, the Meech Lake Accord, and much more. These items are also available in French.

Type: WWW
Address: http://WWW.Screen.COM/ CPACf/program/resources/ English/hist.html#FED
Region: Canada

Chinese Democracy Movement

Here are the documents of the Chinese democracy movement, some of them smuggled out, others published before the crackdown of Tienanmien Square, still more from the pens of exiles.

Type: WWW
Address: http://darkwing.uoregon.edu/ ~felsing/cstuff/history.html
Region: China

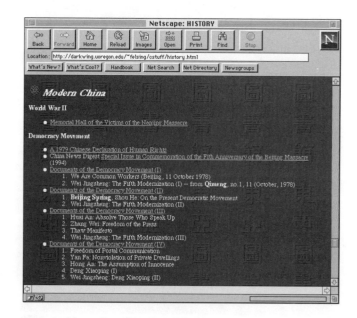

Chinese Documents

This site leads to many links for Chinese texts, both historical and literary.

Type: WWW
Address: **http://www.c3.lanl.gov/~cim/ chtxtsrc.html**
Region: China

Declaration of the Rights of Man and of the Citizen

An English translation of the seminal document of the French Revolution, which was an important milestone in the history of democratic ideals, can be found here.

Type: FTP
Address: **nptn.org/pub/e.texts/freedom .shrine/french**
Region: France

Fourth World Documentation Project

Focused primarily on sovereignty and survival issues, this archive is a repository of calls to action, speeches, declarations, and other documents from the nations of the Fourth World: "Nations" that are politically unrecognized, such as Native American tribes and other indigenous peoples.

Type: WWW
Address: **http://www.halcyon.com/FWDP/ fwdp.html**
Region: World

Freedom Shrine

This is a collection of mostly political and governmental documents concerning the idea and development of democracy. It's mostly U.S. items, but there's more here if you look carefully.

Type: FTP
Address: **nptn.org/pub/e.texts/freedom. shrine/**
Region: U.S., World

Government Documents A-go-go

The Wiretap archive is the place to go for government documents—not just U.S.-related, but also Canadian, Australian, European, and a few others. Treaties, laws, bills before Congress, it's mostly here. Especially interesting is Wiretap's collection of constitutions of the world, many of them in their original languages.

Type: Gopher
Address: **gopher://wiretap.spies.com:70/ 11/Gov**
Region: World

Hawaiian Nation

Several recent laws and proclamations regarding Hawaiian nationhood and sovereignty, as opposed to statehood, are available here. Includes new Hawaiian National Constitution.

Type: WWW
Address: **http://www.halcyon.com/FWDP/ melpac.html**
Region: U.S.

History FTP Site

This site includes links to a wide variety of sources for documents, including pointers to several FTP sites for historians; texts of major documents like the Atlantic Charter, Cairo Conference Agreement, and Japanese surrender from World War II; directories of information dealing with U.S. military history, especially Vietnam and World Wars I and II; and a woefully empty women's history archive.

Type: FTP
Address: byrd.mu.wvnet.edu
Region: U.S., World

Human Rights Documents

Labor movement, child protection, women's rights, and racial equality decrees and conventions are stored at these mirrored sites—access them from the one closest to you. Includes the 1948 Universal Declaration of Human Rights.

Type: Gopher
Address: libaccess.essex.ac.uk:70/11/ plus/law/Human%20Rights% 20%20documents%20and%20 conventions
Address: gopher.law.cornell.edu:70/11/ foreign/fletcher-cat/h
Region: World

Israeli Government Information

All sorts of official documents from the Israeli government, from the state's founding to the modern-day Arab-Israeli peace process are at this Gopher. Most are in English, and many are also available in French and Spanish; presumably they could also be accessed in Hebrew.

Type: Gopher
Address: israel-info.gov.il:70/1
Region: Israel

Italian Politics

Several documents related to modern Italian politics are stored here, in Italian.

Type: Gopher
Address: italia.hum.utah.edu:70/11ftp%3 Altalia%3Agopher%3A02.%20 Italia%3A07.%20Politica%3A
Region: Italy

NAFTA

Read the treaty that your Congressional representative probably didn't. If you are Canadian or Mexican, you may want to read it and weep. Americans who catch the subtext of the treaty for environment and labor issues may want to join them.

Type: Gopher
Address: Niord.SHSU.edu:70/11gopher_ root%3A%5B_DATA.NAFTA%5D
Region: U.S., Canada, Mexico

HISTORY

See also Anthropology page 81; Archeology page 90; Historical Documents page 321

History is one of the most subjective of academic disciplines: An Armenian history of Turkey and a Turkish history of Armenia will no doubt take totally opposite tracks. One of the Net's advantages is that you can easily seek out opposing points of view and place them side by side; make links between historical and other information, such as modern culture or anthropology; and discuss controversial topics online with others who share your interest. For those who study the history of other nations, it's relatively easy to find natives online who can tell it to you from their point of view.

Some of the resources below are mailing lists, some of which maintain related archives for files and images. Many of these are aimed at a scholarly audience and expect a certain level of knowledge from participants. Quiet readers who are there to learn will cause no trouble, but be careful about asking elementary questions of busy experts—they can get testy.

alt.history.what-if

Ever wondered aloud about how things might have been different if, say, the Indians had eaten Columbus and his crew for dinner instead of greeting them with open arms? Historical speculation of that sort is the stock in trade here. It's all archived on the Web page.

Type: Usenet newsgroup
Address: alt.history.what-if
Type: WWW
**Address: http://www.lib.ox.ac.uk/
            internet/news/faq/alt.history.
            what-if.html**
Region: World

Ancien-L

This mailing list is a debate forum for issues related to ancient history.

Type: Mailing list
**Address: listserv@ulkyvm.louisville.edu
Send e-mail message with body: SUB
            ANCIEN-L <Firstname Lastname>**
Region: World

The Annual Bibliography of Portuguese History

This is a publication of the History Group of the Faculty of Letters of the University of Coimbra in Portugal. It's in Portuguese or English.

Type: WWW
Address: http://auc2.uc.pt/
Region: Portugal

Asian Studies: WWW Virtual Library

This is the definitive Asian Studies page. You can click on any country in the list and see pretty much everything available on the World Wide Web that relates. It's updated more frequently than most similar sites, too.

Type: WWW
**Address: http://coombs.anu.edu.au/
            WWWVL-AsianStudies.html**
Region: Australia

Atatürk

Most history is made up of thousands of small actions by many "small" people, but occasionally someone comes along who completely changes the course of things, for better or worse. In the history of Turkey, Atatürk was such a man. From the way Turkish people now dress, to the modern Turkish language, to the level of literacy among women, he had a profound influence, and is revered to this day. Find out more here.

Type: WWW
**Address: http://www.cs.umd.edu/
            ~kandogan/FTA/Ataturk/
            ataturk.html**
Region: Turkey

Australian History

The Australia/New Zealand history archive here is fully searchable. Also at this site are archives of *CLIONET: Australian Electronic Journal of History*, and of History-Link, a bulletin board for Australian historians.

Type: Gopher
Address: cheops.anu.edu.au/11/ ResearchFacilities/HISTORY/ AUSHISTORY
Region: Australia

BIRON Archive System

Biron is a retrieval system for a collection of 3,000 datasets covering most areas of social and economic life in the United Kingdom. It can be searched by name, date, geographical area, or research methodology.

Type: Telnet
Address: dasun.essex.ac.uk (155.245.96.2)
Login: biron
Password: norib
Region: England, Scotland, Wales, Northern Ireland

Canadian History in Pictures

Hundreds of downloadable images from Canada's history tell stories that words sometimes can't. Be sure to see the rest of this site, too: It's meant for Canadian schoolchildren but holds plenty of interest for their elders.

Type: WWW
Address: http://SchoolNet.Carleton.ca/ schoolnet/english/canadisk.html
Region: Canada

Center for Armenian Studies

Based at the University of Michigan at Dearborn, this site currently offers brief histories related to the Armenian genocide, and is in the process of putting its entire archives of historical and cultural material online.

Type: WWW
Address: http://www.umd.umich.edu:80/ dept/armenian/
Region: Armenia

Chinese Studies

If you know your Ming from your Tang, here's a place to learn even more and share your knowledge with others.

Type: Mailing list
Address: CHINA@PUCC
Region: China

Colombia: A Daring Synthesis of Character

Available in Spanish or English, this is a very basic but highly readable introduction to modern Columbia through its history.

Type: WWW
Address: http://www.univalle.edu.co/ ~servinfo/colombia.ca.en.html
Region: Colombia

De Re Militari History Server

This is an archive of military history, from medieval to modern. Includes archives of several military-history mailing lists.

Type: WWW
Address: http://history.cc.ukans.edu/ history/deremil/deremain.html
Region: World

Discussion Lists for Historians

This is a list of Internet special-interest lists on all sorts of topics in or related to history.

Type: WWW
Address: http://neal.ctstateu.edu/history/ world_history/histlist.html
Region: World

EHN: Economic History Newsletter

Written by grad students at the prestigious London School of Economics and the European University Institute in Florence, Italy, this newsletter is aimed at academics in the field. Find out here about conferences and seminars, job openings, and grants for research. They also include book reviews and information on using computerized research tools. Subscribers to the newsletter automatically join a related discussion group.

Type: Mailing list
Address: MAILBASE@MAILBASE.AC.UK
**Send e-mail message with one-line body:
           JOIN history-econ <Firstname
           Lastname>**
Region: World

Electronic Sources for History

A list of Gophers, FTP sites, mailing lists and other Internet-based sources for historical data and discussion are available here.

Type: WWW
Address: http://www.the-wire.com/ culture/mythology/elechist.txt
Region: World

Electronic Sources for West European History and Culture

This guide tries to take a cross-disciplinary approach to varied electronic sources directly related to Western European history. It includes historical information about related disciplines, such as literature, culture, art, and music.

Type: Gopher
Address: una.hh.lib.umich.edu:70/00/ inetdirsstacks/eurhistcult:welsch
Region: Europe

Espora-L

This is a forum for discussing history of the Iberian Peninsula (Portugal and Spain). Postings are in English, Spanish, Portuguese, and Catalan.

Type: Mailing list
Address: listserv@ukanvm.bitnet
**Send e-mail message with body: SUB
           ESPORA-L <Firstname Lastname>**
Region: Spain, Portugal

FICINO

This list covers the European Renaissance and Reformation. It is moderated, and you must fill out a questionnaire to join.

Type: Mailing list
Address: listserv@utoronto.bitnet
**Send e-mail message with body: SUB
           FICINO <Firstname Lastname>**
Contact: FINICO@utoronto
Region: Europe

Flags of the World

This list's purpose is to create a worldwide, real-time, regularly updated database of all kinds of flags: (inter)national, (un)official, ethnic, political, religious and more. Topics discussed herein include symbols and colors used on flags and information about flags' history.

Type: Mailing list
Address: bottasini@cesi.it (Giuseppe Bottasini)
Region: World

German History Forum

All subjects and periods relating to German history are discussed here, although particularly specialized discussions may be referred to a more appropriate forum, if one exists.

Type: Mailing list
**Address: GRMNHIST@DGOGWDG1.
           GRMNHIST@USCVM**
Region: Germany

Haitian History

There's just a little here via the links to the unofficial Haitian Home Page and other resources, but that's more than most people know. With Haiti in the news (and in trouble), you should make a stop. Some parts are available in French and Creole as well as in English.

Type: WWW
**Address: http://lanic.utexas.edu/la/ca/
           haiti/**
Region: Haiti

The Hellenic Discussion List

This list covers all aspects of ancient Greek culture. It is preferred that posts be in Greek, but written with latin characters.

Type: Mailing list
Address: HELLAS@AUVM
Region: Greece

H-ETHNIC

This mailing list from the University of Illinois at Chicago is dedicated to ethnic and immigrant history in the United States.

Type: Mailing list
Address: listserv@uicvm.uic.edu
**Send e-mail message with body:
           subscribe H-ETHNIC**
Region: U.S., World

Histnews

If you are an academic historian, this'll be useful. It's an online academic journal, with calls for papers, jobs available, and news about programs in history education around the world. It's archived at the FTP and Gopher sites below.

Type: Mailing list
Address: listserv@ukanvm.bitnet
Address: listserv@ukanvm.cc.ukans.edu
Type: FTP
**Address: byrd.mu.wvnet.edu:/pub/
           history/internet/hist_news**
Type: Gopher
**Address: nwoca7.nwoca.ohio.gov:72/0ftp
           %3Abyrd.mu.wvnet.edu@/pub/
           history/internet/hist_news/**
Region: World

Historian's Resources

Some good historical information is presented in a chatty and highly accessible way on this Web page.

Type: WWW

Address: http://www.arts.gla.ac.uk/www /ctich/histlinks.html

Region: Canada

History of the Gaúchos and Rio Grande do Sul

This southern state in Brazil is the home of the Gaúcho people, and was an independent country (the Republic of Piratiny) for ten years. The Gaúchos are known for their sympathy and bravery. This page includes historical anecdotes and a cool photo of modern Gaùchos relaxing with their favorite beverage.

Type: WWW

Address: http://sfbox.vt.edu:10021/V/ vkern/rgs.html

Region: Brazil

H-JUDAIC

This University of Illinois at Chicago mailing list focuses on Jewish cultural history, with an international flavor.

Type: Mailing list

Address: listserv@uicvm.uic.edu

**Send e-mail message with body:
        subscribe H-JUDAIC**

Region: U.S., World

Holocaust Archives

Tons of documentation from the Nazi era, most regarding the Jewish victims of the Holocaust, are available in one part of this site. Other offerings include information on current cases of anti-Semitic activity and trials of alleged war criminals.

Type: Gopher

Address: israel-info.gov.il:70/11/hol

Region: Israel, Germany, Poland, Europe

Holocaust Research List

The Holocaust Research List is devoted to Holocaust research and the refutation of those who deny the event. Subscriptions to the list are available by invitation, and are limited to those with useful research, editing or writing skills. The list is published as a moderated digest. To automatically receive a guide to the needs of the list group, include the word *HLIST-SUB* in the Subject field of your message.

Type: Mailing list

Address: kmcvay@oneb.almanac.bc.ca

Region: Canada

H-WOMEN

This mailing list is a place to discuss women's history, something that is frequently forgotten in the rush to document great men and "great" wars.

Type: Mailing list

Address: H-WOMEN@UICVM

Region: World

Ireland's Historic Science Center

This site documents Irish scientific activities and discoveries in County Offaly. It's an interesting approach to both science and history, and an attempt to prove that Ireland is more than "an island of poets."

Type: WWW

Address: http://itdsrv1.ul.ie/Information/ Birr/bshc.html

Region: Ireland

Japanese History

This page has links to a few papers on Japanese history, plus related Internet sites.

Type: WWW
Address: http://darkwing.uoregon.edu/ ~felsing/jstuff/history.html
Region: Japan

The Korean War Project

What began as a family history project by the son of a Korean War vet has expanded to fill volumes online. More than rah-rah military history, it's an examination of causes and effects of the war.

Type: WWW
Address: http://www.onramp.net:80/ ~hbarker/
Region: Korea, U.S.

Kurdish History

Heavy on the propaganda, but considering current events it's hard to blame them. Includes historical information about the Kurdish people, language, and territory.

Type: WWW
Address: http://nucst11.neep.wisc.edu/
Region: Turkey, Iraq, Iran

Latin American History Archive

Bibliographies, papers, and journals on the history of Central and South America. One especially large section covers the United States/Mexican border and its special history.

Type: Gopher
Address: gopher.uic.edu:70/11/research/ history/hnetxx/40227007
Region: Central America, South America

Latin American Studies Discussion

Topics of conversation on this list include not just history, but sociology, economics, and other related disciplines as they interrelate in Latin America.

Type: Mailing list
Address: LASNET@EMX.UTEXAS.EDU
Region: South America

LT-ANTIQ

Utilizing information and analysis from many academic disciplines, LT-ANTIQ participants discuss the history of European and Middle Eastern societies of the Late Antiquity (A.D. 260–640).

Type: Mailing list
Address: listserv@univscvm.csd.scarolina. edu
Send e-mail message with one-line body: subscribe LT-ANTIQ <Firstname Lastname>
Region: Europe, Middle East

Medieval Women's Studies

This list is an open forum for feminist scholarship in the realm of medieval history. Topics related to feminist, women's, and gay and lesbian issues are welcome.

Type: Mailing list
Address: MEDFEM-L@INDYCMS
Address: MEDFEM-L@INDYCMS.IUPUI.EDU
Region: World

MEDIEV-L

This list is a forum for scholars and students of the medieval period (defined for this list as A.D. 283 to 1500). It and related materials are archived at the FTP site.

Type: Mailing list
Address: MEDIEV-L@UKANVM
Type: FTP
Address: kuhub.cc.ukans.edu
Region: World

Mexican History

This survey of Mexican history is presented as an expanded timeline from prehistory to today, with a few hotlinks to related texts and sites.
Type: WWW
Address: http://mexico.udg.mx/ingles.html
Region: Mexico

Milestones in the History of the ANC

If you've been curious about the roots of the African National Congress, whose leader Nelson Mandela, is now president of South Africa after years of struggle and imprisonment, here is an official history. It starts with an African women's anti-pass campaign in 1918 and goes up to 1948, when the European Nationalist Party took power and instituted Apartheid.
Type: Gopher
Address: wn.apc.org:70/00/anc/history/ milestn.48
Region: South Africa

Postmodern Culture

This electronic journal of interdisciplinary studies covers topics in history, sometimes in unusual and nonlinear ways. If you've always wondered what "PoMo" is all about, here's a place to check it out. The e-zine is archived at the WWW site. Most interesting of all, the Postmodern Culture gang has set up an experimental MOO for real-time postmodern chats (or pickups).

Type: E-zine
Address: listserv@ncsuvm
Send e-mail message with body: sub pmc-list <Firstname Lastname>
Type: WWW
Address: http://jefferson.village.virginia. edu/pmc/contents.all.html
Type: MOO
Address: http://jefferson.village.virginia. edu/pmc/pmc-moo.html
Region: World

Recent Tibetan History

Most of it's not too pretty, although I'm certain that life with the huge religious bureaucracy that preceded the Chinese military dictatorship was no picnic for the common person either. I guess the most important difference is that the religious bureaucracy was theirs. In any case, learn about the invasion, the destruction of the monasteries, the flight of the Dalai Lama and more in this archive.
Type: FTP
Address: coombs.anu.edu.au/coomb spapers/otherarchives/ asian-studies-archives/ tibetan-archives/ tibet-recent-history/
Region: Tibet

Singapore and Malaysia

This nicely laid out set of pages covers the basics of the history of Singapore proper and, later on, the Malaysian federation.
Type: WWW
Address: http://www.technet.sg/InfoWEB/ history/welcome.html
Region: Malaysia, Singapore

Southeast Asia Studies

If you are interested in the history of Vietnam, Cambodia, Laos, and Thailand, here is where it is discussed.

Type: Mailing list
Address: SEASIA-L@MSU
Region: Vietnam, Cambodia, Laos, Thailand

Spojrzenia

A weekly e-journal, devoted to Polish culture, history and politics, is available here, in Polish.

Type: E-journal
Address: spojrz@k-vector.chem. washington.edu
Region: Poland

Tito Home Page

This homage to the late dictator seems somehow tongue-in-cheek. It includes Tito's most famous speeches, pictures of Tito with everyone from Idi Amin to his German shepherd dog, and photos of Yugoslavs crying at his funeral.

Type: WWW
Address: http://www.fer.uni-lj.si/tito/ tito-eng.html
Region: Slovenia

University of Kansas World History Index

This is the motherlode, if you're looking for links to history-related sites, regularly updated and worldwide. Strangely, when I visited some URLs had been switched, leading to odd events like getting a page about Appalachian history when I had asked for Bolivia. But it's still an absolutely essential resource for the history buff.

Type: WWW
Address: http://history.cc.ukans.edu/ history/index.html
Region: U.S., World

Victorian Studies

This list is for discussing the history and culture of Victorian England.

Type: Mailing list
Address: VICTORIA@IUBVM
Address: VICTORIA@IUBVM.UCS.INDIANA. EDU
Region: England

Vietnam War History

For many, it still seems too recent to be "history." But there is a growing body of scholarship about the Vietnam War. Make your contribution here.

Type: Mailing list
Address: VWAR-L@UBVM
Region: Vietnam, U.S., France, Cambodia, Laos, Russia

The Viking Expeditions from Central Sweden

This amazing doctoral thesis is done in hypertext style, and covers the era from A.D. 700 to 1000.

Type: WWW
Address: http://www.css.itd.umich.edu/ users/lars/thesis.html
Region: Sweden

Women's History Collaborative Page

Intended as a celebration of Women's History Month, this page is collecting short biographies of famous and/or important women in history. You're invited to contribute to this page, which will remain online indefinitely as a women's history resource especially for primary and secondary students.

Type: WWW
**Address: http://www.teleport.com/
             ~megaines/women.html**
Region: U.S., World

World History Page

This site has an excellent collection of links to foreign sites that deal with history and related materials.

Type: WWW
**Address: http://neal.ctstateu.edu:80/
             history/world_history/
             world_history.html**
Region: U.S., World

World War II Discussion

The WWII-L list is dedicated to the discussion of World War II. Tactical, strategic, technological, and political discussions are welcome.

Type: Mailing list
Address: WWII-L@UBVM
Region: World

WPA Life Histories Home Page

WPA Life Histories came out of a Depression-era make-work project. The intention was to document American folklore; the result was an immense body of work that is finally reaching the Internet, and so perhaps will become better known. This archive is searchable by region, state, and keyword.

Type: WWW
**Address: http://lcweb2.loc.gov/wpaintro/
             wpahome.html**
Region: U.S.

Hobbies: all the stuff we do that's not "real work." Many popular hobbies are covered in other sections of this book, including Animals, Comics and Cartoons, Crafts, Dance, Electronics, Food and Drink, Film, Literature, Music, Sports, and Television. That leaves just a few avocations, such as collecting all sorts of things from dolls to stamps, photography, trainspotting, and a grab-bag of other activities. Dive in—perhaps you'll find a lead to one of your favorites.

alt.collecting.barbies

This location is for those with a mania for the Girl in Pink.

Type: Usenet newsgroup
Address: alt.collecting.barbies
Region: World

alt.collecting.autographs

Serious autograph hounds will do anything to get that prized signature. Learn their techniques and hear about their big scores here.

Type: Usenet newsgroup
Address: alt.collecting.autographs
Region: World

alt.history.living

This newsgroup is a forum for discussing the hobby of living history, such as historical reinactments of great battles or events.

Type: Usenet newsgroup
Address: alt.history.living
Region: World

Amateur Drama in the UK

There is a lot of local and national amateur drama in the United Kingdom, which they've affectionately shortened to "Am Dram." Amateur means unpaid, but it doesn't necessarily mean awful. Find out here about local companies, productions, and schedules.

Type: WWW
Address: http://www.nag.co.uk:70/0/ Homes/Robertl/Amateur.html
Region: England

Ancient and Medieval Coins

This Web page for ancient (Roman) and medieval (English and Italian) coins has a link to a Numismatic Identification Database for Roman coins and other useful resources.

Type: WWW
Address: http://www_wwrc.uwyo.edu/ coinnet/coinnet.html
Region: England, Italy

Australian Alan Arnold Stamp Collecting Sub Page

Look at a GIF of the ever-coveted and impossible to find misprint of a U.S. mail plane on 24-cent stamp. That's probably the closest you'll ever get to it, too! Lots of other information is available here for philatelists.

Type: WWW
Address: http://apamac.ch.adfa.oz.au/ OzChemNet/ChemDept/staff/ apa/stamps.html
Region: Australia, U.S., World

Books Buy/Sell/Trade

This is a classified ads archive for book collectors, mostly mainstream collectable/antiquarian stuff.

Type: FTP
Address: ftp.netcom.com/pub/co/ collector/BOOKS.TXT
Region: World

Camping in the Netherlands

Find a spot to pitch a tent in Friesland here. Americans aren't the only ones who like to rough it, although some of the camping in more heavily populated Europe and Asia is pretty posh by U.S. standards.

Type: WWW
Address: http://www.xxlink.nl/nbt/ camping/
Region: Holland

China Stamp Album

An advertisement for a comprehensive CD-ROM catalog of Chinese stamps from 1878 to 1993. Philatelists have had a tough time getting these, so it's exciting stuff.

Type: WWW
Address: http://sunsite.nus.sg/bibdb/pub/ asiainfo/asiainfo010.html
Region: China

C.H.U.N.K. DCLXCVI

This is the unlikely name of a self-styled "chopper bicycle gang" that operates on a college campus not far from where I live. They modify their bikes to ride low and look funky. It's art, it's attitude, it's silly. Enjoy.

Type: WWW
Address: http://www.reed.edu/~karl/ chunk/chunk.html
Region: U.S.

```
Netscape: Chunk Operations.
Back  Forward  Home  Reload  Images  Open  Print  Find  Stop
Location: http://www.reed.edu/~karl/chunk/meet.html
What's New?  What's Cool?  Handbook  Net Search  Net Directory  Newsgroups
```

The Support Vehicle.

Chunk missions require quite a lot of supplies. The usual bicycle tools must be supplemented with a hammer, long pipe for bending things, anaesthetic and first aid, and weapons to fend off marauders. Even with these precautions, there is quite an attrition rate on every Chunk excursion, and our route can often be traced by the trail of disabled bicycles locked up along the route. We look forward to this weeding-out process as an opportunity to pick up some cool scabs. Transportation is maintained with the help of padded racks, towed skateboards, and huge banana seats; however, chunklings have had to resort to taking the bus at times.

77% of 99K (at 436 bytes/sec, 53 secs remaining)

CigarNet

More like a personal page than anything semipro, this is a fun intro to smoking with the big boys (really, I should have put this in Drugs!). Where to buy cigars online, a cigar database, information on buying or building a good humidor, cigar-smoking celebs, advice on cigars and marriage from Rudyard Kipling, and tales of smuggling Cuban contraband. Fun—especially so if you like stogies.

Type: WWW
**Address: http://astro.ocis.temple.edu/
            ~joejohn/cigarnet.html**
Region: U.S., Cuba, Dominican Republic, World

Coin Collecting FAQs

The basics of the coin collecting life are covered in this selection.

Type: WWW
**Address: http://turnpike.net/emporium/
            M/mikec/gold3.htm**
Region: World

The Coin Collector's Home Page

The Cline Group was formed in 1982 to service the needs of the coin collecting hobby, this says. In other words, to trade the hobbyist's modern money for the old kind. Along with the ads there's good links here for the numismatics nut.

Type: WWW
**Address: http://turnpike.net/emporium/
            M/mikec/index.htm**
Region: World

The Collectors Network

This network for collectors is a mandatory stopping point for all hopeless compulsives. Their Web site's offerings range from Star Wars paraphernalia to phone cards.

Type: WWW
**Address: http://www.xmission.com/
            ~patco/collect.html**
Region: World

The Colt Woodsman Pocket Guide

This is a compilation of Woodsman lore, oriented toward the collector, with an interest in the details and variations through the 62 years of regular production of the Colt .22 Automatic.

Type: WWW
**Address: http://www.eskimo.com/
            ~rayburn/woodsman/**
Region: U.S.

Creative Retirement Manitoba—Stamp Club

This is an online stamp collecting e-zine for the geriatric set.

Type: WWW
**Address: http://www.mbnet.mb.ca/crm/
            lifestyl/stampclb.html**
Region: Canada

The European Train List

Trainspotting is the activity of making special trips to see trains and train stations, often with a side habit of collecting railway paraphernalia. It's so popular in England that the term "trainspotter" has become a popular British euphemism for "nerd." That said, if you wear the name as a badge of honor, you'll enjoy this page. It contains data on locomotives, shunters, EMUs, and DMUs of European railways. The final goal is to describe all European railways and their rolling stock here.

Type: WWW
**Address: http://mercurio.iet.unipi.it/
europe.html**
Region: Italy, Europe

GardenNet's Guide to Internet Garden Resources

This is a catch-all for gardening information on the Net, including sources for seeds and tools, and gardening groups online.

Type: WWW
**Address: http://www.olympus.net/
gardens/point1.htm**
Region: World

The Gilbert and Sullivan Society of Nova Scotia

This is one of many of Gilbert and Sullivan Societies. Do light opera and cod go together? You could definitely find out from this crew. This page has links to Gilbert and Sullivan societies in Britain as well.

Type: WWW
**Address: http://www.cfn.cs.dal.ca/cfn/
Culture/GS-Society/GS-Home.html**
Region: Canada

Guide to Internet Firearms Information Resources

Jeff Chan has done a great job of collecting gun information on the Net. This page has everything from FTP sites to Web sites linked in, including pro-gun and anti-gun political information and collectors' links. An amazing resource!

Type: WWW
**Address: http://www.portal.com/~chan/
firearms.faq.html**
Region: World

Hunt for Peking Man

In 1941, the celebrated Peking Man fragments were sent to New York City—but never arrived. Now there's a $25,000 reward and an Internet treasure hunt is on. I guess the real question is, will they only pay for a dead specimen? Because I think I could find a man from Peking in New York without too much trouble.

Type: WWW
**Address: http://www.treasure.com/
reward.htm**
Region: U.S., China

International Paperweight Society

No, it's not a joke! People will collect anything, from the little paper circles inside milk-bottle caps (*pogs*) to barbed wire. And some paperweights really are beautiful works of art. Network with other collectors here.

Type: WWW
**Address: http://www.armory.com/~larry/
other.html**
Region: World

International Treasure Hunters Exchange

This is a forum for treasure hunters to freely exchange information, research, and treasure-hunting information. A clearinghouse for the big boys like Ballard as well as the mom-and-pop metal-detector types.

Type: WWW
Address: http://www.treasure.com/ index.htm
Region: World

Introduction to Phone Cards

In many places throughout the world, you can buy "smart cards" to use in phone boxes instead of cash. Now these cards have become collectible, thanks to the cool graphics and the limited-edition nature of some designs.

Type: WWW
Address: http://www.funet.fi/pub/doc/ telecom/phonecard/
Region: World

Joseph Luft's Philatelic Resources on the Web

The page for stamp collectors seems to have it all for the philatelist, including the new (Groucho) Marx and (John) Lennon stamp from the former Soviet republic of Abkhazia.

Type: WWW
Address: http://www.execpc.com/ ~joeluft/resource.html
Region: U.S., Abkhazia, Switzerland, Canada, Japan, England, Bangladesh, Holland, Thailand, World

LEGONET: The Internet Lego Enthusiasts Organization

This is a call for members for a new Lego building club aimed at Net-savvy adults. I confess, one of the best parts about having a four-year-old is getting to build big Lego things without shame. These guys are obviously beyond me, trumpeting to the world that they love those little plastic building blocks.

Type: WWW
Address: http://legowww.itek.norut.no/ info/legonet.html
Region: World

Model Horse Web Page

It seems every girl falls in love with horses in the later stage of childhood, usually as a precursor to boys. This stage involves collecting realistic models of horses and playing virtual-riding games. Some people just never grow out of it.

Type: WWW
Address: http://www.metronet.com/ ~kira/model-horse/
Region: U.S.

MONEYCARD Collector Magazine

Moneycards include phone cards, but also other types of cards that can be used in place of cash. And yes, some folks do collect them in a big way—and not just ladies who hang out on Rodeo Drive a lot.

Type: WWW
Address: http://www.hmt.com/ phonecards/moneycard/ index.html
Region: World

Motorcycle Coming Events in Australia

There's not a thing here about racing, just rallies, runs, and other fun events that the average biker can participate in and enjoy. Nicely designed page with color photos, too.

Type: WWW
Address: http://ledoux.arbld.unimelb. edu.au/~mtc/motorbike/ comingup.html
Region: Australia

Natural Resources Canada

Find out about camping, hiking, fly-fishing, and other activities in Canada's extensive system of parks and preserves. In French and English.

Type: WWW
Address: http://www.emr.ca/
Region: Canada

North Cape R/C Model Flyers

Learn about flying radio-controlled model planes on the northernmost tip of Norway. It has links to more model-airplane and actual airplane pages, and pictures of finished models.

Type: WWW
Address: http://www.oslonett.no/home/ tkholst/ncmf.html
Region: Norway

Nude and Online

People do poke fun at naturists and nudists, but they're usually quite nice. This page has links to many groups in the United States that enjoy innocent clothing-free outings, including camping and boating (The Camping Bares), swimming, sunbathing, and socializing. There are also links to special interest groups for nudists, including one for amateur radio enthusiasts (yes, they sometimes broadcast in the altogether) and another for Christian nudists. A tasteful page.

Type: WWW
Address: http://www.realtime.net/~kr4ah/
Region: U.S.

Numismatics Home Page

This is another good Web page with links building up to interesting resources, but it's still under construction. Coin collectors may find something of interest here.

Type: WWW
Address: http://www.cs.vu.nl/~fjjunge/ numis.html
Region: World

The Original Motor Scooter Page

Choix d'Éditeur

I couldn't look at the gorgeous pictures of Italian scooters on this page for too long; it reminded me of those younger, freer days when I tooled around the hills of San Francisco on a battered but beautiful Vespa P-200. One of these days I'll get another one…one with a better carburetor, I hope. Anyway, this page is linked to a huge number of national scooter enthusiast pages and will be a real thrill to any fan of these most perfect vehicles.

Type: WWW
Address: http://weber.u.washington.edu: 80/~shortwav/
Region: U.S., Argentina, Europe, Russia, Taiwan

Photography Newsgroups

There are several newsgroups under the "rec.photo" rubric for amateur and some professional photographers. See the FAQ at the FTP site about what is appropriate for each group, as they underwent a reorganization not long ago.

Type: Usenet newsgroup
Address: rec.photo.marketplace
Address: rec.photo.darkroom
Address: rec.photo.advanced
Address: rec.photo.help
Address: rec.photo.misc
Type: FTP
**Address: moink.nmsu.edu/rec.photo/
               charters_guides**
Region: World

The Plastic Princess Collector's Page

At last, a Web site devoted to the world's most famous anatomically incorrect doll, Barbie. I always preferred her more tomboyish friend Midge, and she's here too, along with the controversial Earring Magic Ken, his predecessor Mod Ken (of the hip detachable sideburns and beard), and the new jazz-goatee Ken, who can switch from smoothy to fashionable stubble in a jiff. It's as interesting to students of popular culture as to for-real collectors—if only I hadn't cut all the hair off my Barbies and wrecked them playing cowboys-and-Indians games, I could be rich now!

Type: WWW
**Address: http://d.armory.com/~zenugirl/
               barbie.html**
Region: U.S., World

Postal Code Formats of the World

This is a breakdown of the rhyme and reason behind the world's postal codes. Helpful for philatelists and other mail-related hobbyists.

Type: WWW
**Address: http://www.io.org/~djcl/
               postcd.txt**
Region: World

Rallying Links Page

Fun with cars in the U.K. and beyond: car clubs devoted to various makes (Minis, TVRs), get-togethers, shows, and drives.

Type: WWW
**Address: http://www.chem.rdg.ac.uk/
               g50/mmrg/john/rallying.html**
Region: England, Scotland, Wales, Northern
               Ireland, Finland, U.S.

rec.arts.books.marketplace

This Usenet group for book collectors is like a virtual swap meet with a wide range of books on offer. Related information is available through the Web page.

Type: Usenet newsgroup
Address: rec.arts.books.marketplace
Type: WWW
**Address: http://ecsdg.lu.se/cgi-bin/
               wwwnntp?rec.arts.books.
               marketplace**
Region: World

rec.models.scale

This newsgroup is for the serious model builder—the kind that does something more than slop a little Testor's Cement between snap-together plastic pieces and pronounce it done. It's supported by the Web page, which includes the best models FAQs and links to other model-building pages.

Type: Usenet newsgroup

Address: rec.models.scale

Type: WWW

Address: http://meteor.anu.edu.au/~dfk/ scale_model.html

Region: World

Scouting around the World

Every kid's favorite hobby, and one that Scout leaders also enjoy, is the subject of this Web page. Links from here lead to Scout and Guide organizations around the world (mostly in the United States, Canada, and Europe).

Type: WWW

Address: http://skypoint.com/members/ srtobin/sc-links.html

Region: World

The Society for Creative Anachronism

This is a page for that semimythical place where grown-ups go to play good knight and bad knight. As much fun as you can have in tights and a codpiece, guaranteed.

Type: WWW

Address: http://mac9.ucc.nau.edu/sca.html

Region: World

The Toy Train Company and Reference Valve Guides

Not very complete, this has mostly Lionel train sets and a little on Marx train sets. But this appears to be the first train-collectors page on the Net (and the fact that it's there proves once again that dads are really buying those trains for themselves, not Junior).

Type: WWW

Address: http://www.mountain.net/ttc/

Region: U.S.

Treasure Hunting Shopping Mall

There's gold in them thar hills! And this online shopping mall for every type of treasure hunter has poop sheets on the metal detectors that can help you find it. They even have affordable production submarines (mass-produced mini-submarines).

Type: WWW

Address: http://www.treasure.com/ mall.htm

Region: World

Tuan's Photography Page

This Berkeley, California student has put together a nice photography page, with information about lens testing, large-format photography, and more. There is also an excellent selection of links to other pages that have even more in-depth technical and artistic information.

Type: WWW

Address: http://robotics.eecs.berkeley.edu/ ~qtluong/photography.html

Region: U.S., World

The World Guide to Photography

This commercial effort hasn't quite fulfilled its global ambitions. It *does* have links to some German photography institutes, however, plus the Gopher site for Black Star—the famous photography agency in New York.

Type: WWW

Address: http://www.theworld.com/ SPECIALI/PHOTOGRA/ SUBJECT.HTM

Region: World

World Wide Collector Digest Home Page

This is a good starting-off point for card, comic book, figurine, and toy collectors. It seems to have a worldwide assortment of information, including items from sporting events like the Tour de France, rugby matches, and so on.

Type: WWW
Address: http://www.wwcd.com/
Region: World

The WWW Bicycle Lane

There are lots of bike links here from all over the world—mountain biking, recumbent biking, cyber-biking, neat stuff to put on your bike, and lots of ways to make contact with bicyclists in your area. This is for the recreational cyclist more than the "serious" bike racer, although there are some racing links. See the Sport section if that's more your bag.

Type: WWW
Address: http://www.cs.purdue.edu/ homes/dole/bike.html
Region: World

Yahoo! It's Motorcycles!

The usual huge selection of links at Yahoo's archive of motorcycle-related sites covers the German BMW, Bultaco and other Spanish bikes, Motoguzzi and similar Italian lovelies, British motorcycles, motorcycle clubs and publications, and motorbiking Usenet groups.

Type: WWW
Address: http://www.yahoo.com/ Entertainment/Motorcycles/
Region: World

Zach "The Lego Maniac" Benz Lego Page

Wow! Teenage Zach has photos here of his incredible Lego creations, including a huge castle with highly detailed rooms (we're talking tapestries here) that open up. This guy is destined for a career in design or engineering for sure. Lots of links to other Lego pages, too.

Type: WWW
Address: http://jawbox.st.hmc.edu/
Region: U.S.

INTERNATIONAL LAW

Finding out about legal issues in your own country can be hard enough, since law libraries have traditionally been difficult to access for the layperson. The Net is changing all that: Case law and legislation are both finding their way online all over the world, making citizen access and international research easier. These sites should provide you with a starting point for either personal or professional legal projects.

African Law

There are lots of legal research resources here, including a database of laws sorted by geographic region, South African legal databases, and a link to Amnesty International.

Type: WWW
Address: http://www.sas.upenn.edu/ African_Studies/Home_Page/ WWW_Links.html#Law
Region: South Africa, Africa, World

Australian Legal Gopher

Directories, discussion lists, pointers, and databases related to Australia's laws are online here. Look under "Electronic Journals, Newsletters—Law," and you will find two electronic legal journals, *The Murdoch E-Journal of Law* and *Legal Bytes*.

Type: Gopher
**Address: infolib.murdoch.edu.au/11/.ftp/
            pub/subj/law/**
Region: Australia

Bibliography of British and Irish Legal History

It's just what it says it is: a Gopher database of the legal history of the two nations.

Type: Gopher
**Address: gopher.aber.ac.uk:71/11/uwares
            /lawsubj**
Region: Ireland

Brazilian Patents—INPI

Here you can access a searchable database of Brazilian patents, in Portuguese.

Type: WWW
Address: http://www.bdt.org.br/inpi/
Region: Brazil

Canadian Law Resources

The University of Montreal has a number of resources at this site: a directory of Canadian law professors, a mailing list, many Quebeçois legal documents (in French, of course), and more.

Type: WWW
**Address: http://www.droit.umontreal.ca/
            english.html**
Region: Canada

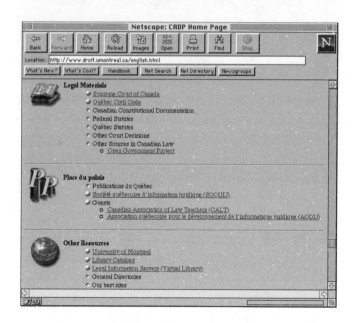

Canadian Supreme Court Rulings

Thanks to the University of Montreal, you can look up any Canadian Supreme Court ruling since 1993, in a variety of formats, or search the database for topics.

Type: WWW
**Address: http://www.droit.umontreal.ca/
            CSC.html**
Region: Canada

Center for the Study of Constitutionalism in Eastern Europe

This is an institute at the University of Chicago Law School. Here you can find information on the programs, faculty, and students of the law school, as well as papers and publications of the institute.

Type: Gopher

Address: lawnext.uchicago.edu/1

Type: WWW

Address: http://lawnext.uchicago.edu/ hh/.web/index.html

Region: Eastern Europe

Computer Law

Information about computer-related law, such as laws related to hacking, electronic communications, and cryptography, can be found here. Includes both U.S. and worldwide items.

Type: FTP

Address: ftp.eff.org/pub/cud/law/

Region: U.S., World

The Constitutional Court of the Slovak Republic

Decisions, texts, organization, and lots more about the Supreme Court of the Slovak Republic are located here.

Type: WWW

Address: http://www.tuzvo.sk/court/

Region: Slovak Republic

Constitutional Materials from Peru and Other Countries

A Spanish-language directory to a number of Peruvian Constitution-related materials is available here, as are legal materials from several other nations.

Type: Gopher

Address: ulima.edu.pe/11/ccpp

Region: Peru

Constitutions

In the Government Documents folder, under World Constitutions, you can find constitutions of most of the major nations. There are also a few other legal documents on this site.

Type: Gopher

Address: wiretap.spies.com

Region: World

Copyright Law in Japan

If your browser can handle Japanese characters, there's information here about Japanese copyright laws and enforcement.

Type: WWW

Address: http://www.ntt.jp/japan/misc/ copyright.html

Region: Japan

Cornell Legal Gopher

Here are lots and lots of pointers: a directory of law schools, a thorough list of discussion lists (some of which are archived here), and pointers to much more.

Type: Gopher

Address: gopher.law.cornell.edu/

Region: U.S., World

E-Law

E-Law is an electronic law journal from Australia.

Type: Mailing list

Address: Majordomo@cleo.murdoch.edu.au

Send e-mail message with body: subscribe elaw-j

Region: Australia

European Law Students Association

Information on meetings, minutes, and programs, plus information on the laws of member countries, is online at the ELSA page.

Type: WWW
Address: **http://129.240.178.157/WWW/ elsa/homepage.html**
Region: Belgium, Europe

The Faculty of Law, University of Auckland

This site has a prospectus and directory of faculty, as well as how to enroll; it also includes a list of e-mail addresses for lawyers in New Zealand, and a directory of current New Zealand legislation.

Type: WWW
Address: **http://130.216.73.108/**
Region: New Zealand

fj.soc.law

Law discussions with a Japanese focus are the topic of this newsgroup.

Type: Fj newsgroup
Address: **fj.soc.law**
Region: Japan

GARANT-SERVICE Russian Law Database

A commercial site, this page provides updates on Russian law changes in both Russian and English. To use this database fully you need to sign an agreement and pay a subscription fee.

Type: WWW
Address: **http://garant.msu.ru/3index.html**
Region: Russia

Gateway to Antarctica—Antarctic Treaty System

Look here for information on the treaties maintaining Antarctica as an international scientific and exploration zone.

Type: WWW
Address: **http://icair.iac.org.nz/treaty/ treaty.html**
Region: Antarctica

GATT 1994

Love it or leave it, here is the whole text of the General Agreement on Tariffs and Trade.

Type: WWW
Address: **http://ananse.irv.uit.no/trade_ law/gatt/nav/toc.html**
Region: World

German Laws

Lots of copies of various German laws, mostly in German, are online here, in .gz (gnuzip) format.

Type: FTP
Address: **info2.rus.uni-stuttgart.de/pub/ doc/law/german**
Region: Germany

Global Legal Studies Journal

This is an electronic version of the paper magazine, which covers legal matters around the world with an academic slant. You can read each of the papers published in the current issue and back issues, or find out how to subscribe to the paper version.

Type: WWW
Address: **http://www.law.indiana.edu/ glsj/glsj.html**
Region: World

GSU College of Law Legal Research Meta-Index

A meta-index of various searchable legal indexes: You pick an index and instead of having to go to that WWW page, you can do the searching directly from the meta-index. Seems slanted toward U.S. stuff, but you should be able to find non-U.S. items as well.

Type: WWW
Address: http://130.216.73.108/Lawform .html
Region: U.S., World

Hawaiian Sovereignty

It's not a foreign country yet, but these folks want Hawaii to secede from the U.S., and they seem to have a good quantity of international law on their side. They've archived that law here along with arguments for secession.

Type: WWW
Address: http://hinc.hinc.hawaii.gov/ sovereignty/sov.html
Region: Hawaii (U.S.)

InfoSel Legal Database

This appears to be similar to the Lexis database used in the U.S. It's a compendium of Mexican court cases and proceedings, in Spanish, as well as some state and federal laws. There is a fee for some types of access.

Type: WWW
Address: http://www2.infosel.com.mx/ infosel/infosel.htm
Region: Mexico

International Association of Constitutional Law

This is an international association of constitutional scholars. You can find out here how to join the IACL, read about their congresses, and browse through world constitutions.

Type: WWW
Address: http://www.eur.nl/iacl/index. html
Region: Holland, World

International Law Gophers

Directory of various legal Gophers around the world. From here you should be able to find most any law that's online in archived text form.

Type: Gopher
Address: honor.uc.wlu.edu:1020/1%201/ ty%20%23jx/cl
Region: World

IrishLaw

This list for discussion of the laws of both Ireland and British-controlled Northern Ireland is archived, along with related documents on Irish laws and the Irish Constitution, at the Web site.

Type: Mailing list
Address: listserv@irlearn.ucd.ie
Send e-mail message with body: subscribe irishlaw <Firstname Lastname>
Type: WWW
Address: http://www.maths.tcd.ie/pub/ IrishLaw/jurweb-irl.html
Region: Ireland

Italian Legal Materials

Documents and pointers to legal Gopher sites, in Italian, are available here.

Type: Gopher
Address: risc.idg.fi.cnr.it/
Region: Italy

Japanese Law and Regulation Information Guide

Here are pointers to several Japanese sites, with courses, Japanese copyright laws, and the Japanese Constitution.

Type: WWW
Address: http://fuji.stanford.edu/Guide/ japan_legal_info.html
Region: Japan

Jurweb

A guide to worldwide legal information maintained by the University of Bayreuth, Jurweb includes a Gopher site and several indices, including an index of mailing lists. It's available in German and English, and provides pages on many African and South American countries.

Type: WWW
Address: http://www.uni-bayreuth.de/ students/elsa/elsa-home-english .html#jurweb
Type: Gopher
Address: gopher.uni-bayreuth.de/11/ Studenten/ELSA/info-engl/ jurgopher-engl
Region: Germany, World

Law Faculty of the University of Tromso

Faculty and programs, as well as a number of legal documents and an archive of international trade law materials, are accessible here via the Web.

Type: WWW
Address: http://ananse.irv.uit.no/law/nav /hp.html
Region: Norway

Law Lists Directory

This is a list of law-related mailing lists. Mostly, but not all, American.

Type: FTP
Address: 129.194.70.1/pub/dbelsa/law lists.txt
Region: U.S.

Law-Related Internet Project

The University of Saarland has archived many legal documents at this page, mostly in German but some in English or with English summaries. The German Federal Constitution, Roman law, and news bulletins of German courts are among the offerings.

Type: WWW
Address: http://www.jura.uni-sb.de/index engl.html
Region: Germany

Legal Discussion Groups

Discussions of legal issues in Canada, Australia, and the U.K. take place via these forums.

Type: Can, Aus, and U.K. newsgroups
Address: can.legal
Address: aus.legal
Address: uk.legal
Region: Canada, Australia, England, Scotland, Wales, Northern Ireland

Legal Discussion Lists

This page is a list of law-related mailing lists on the Internet, with brief reviews and information on how to subscribe.

Type: WWW
Address: http://www.kentlaw.edu/ cgi-bin/ldn_news/-G+law.listserv
Region: U.S., World

The Legal List

A large file containing thousands of pointers to Internet legal resources, this list is full of sites, including many outside the U.S.

Type: FTP
**Address: ftp.midnight.com/pub/LegalList/
            legallist.txt**
Region: U.S., World

Lund University Law Menu

A seemingly random sampling of legal documents can be found at this Swedish site, including several on Australian law and one folder of Finnish laws.

Type: Gopher
**Address: munin.ub2.lu.se/11/resources/
            bysubject/social/law**
Region: Sweden, Finland, Australia, World

Luxembourg Legislation

Not just the home of pretty postage stamps, the tiny European country of Luxembourg actually passes laws, and you can find some of them (in French) here. It has a terrible interface, though, with no clue as to what you are looking at.

Type: WWW
Address: http://www.men.lu/legislation/
Region: Luxembourg

misc.legal. Newsgroups

Lots of legal discussions, with several subgroups take place here. It's mostly U.S.-related but some international issues are covered as well. See this newsgroup for pointers to the rest.

Type: Usenet newsgroup
Address: misc.legal
Region: U.S.

Multilaterals Project

Want to find the latest international treaties on human rights or the "rules" of warfare? This is where to look: The database includes the texts of many of these multilateral conventions, organized by subject and searchable.

Type: WWW
**Address: http://www.tufts.edu/
            departments/fletcher/
            multilaterals.html**
Region: U.S.

New Zealand Government Web Pages

This site stores political news, government documents, and historical information from the New Zealand government.

Type: WWW
Address: http://www.govt.nz/
Region: New Zealand

Resources

This is an archive of recent issues of this Canadian law journal, dealing with environmental and resource law. It's a Gopher with a WWW front end.

Type: WWW
**Address: http://www2.waikato.ac.nz/
            law/resource.html**
Type: Gopher
**Address: acs6.acs.ucalgary.ca/11/library/
            serials/journals/**
Region: Canada

Rules and Regulations in Russia

Various decrees and lists from the Russian government, courtesy of the *Russian Business Law Journal,* can be found here.

Type: WWW

Address: http://www.spb.su/rulesreg/ index.html

Region: Russia

The School of Law at Queen's University, Belfast

Here you can access a directory of staff and find out how to apply to the college. The page also includes a database on states of emergency in various countries, and publications and documents on law in Ireland and Northern Ireland.

Type: WWW

Address: http://143.117.33.25/default. htm

Region: Northern Ireland, Ireland

The Trade Law Home Page

Sounds dry—but check it out. You'll find nifty buttons that take you everywhere you would want to go, a searchable WAIS database, and even a neat little green map of the world. It's quite graphic for a law page.

Type: WWW

Address: http://ananse.irv.uit.no/trade_ law/nav/trade.html

Region: World

UN Criminal Justice Information Network

All kinds of information on crime and criminal justice from around the world is here: country profiles, the World Criminal Justice Library Network, documents, and information on individual nations.

Type: Gopher

Address: uacsc2.albany.edu/11/newman

Region: World

University of Alberta Faculty of Law

Faculty, admission information, and courses of the university are online here, and you can also sign up for law courses on the Web or look up property law in Alberta.

Type: WWW

Address: http://gpu.srv.ualberta.ca/ ~bpoohkay/law.html

Region: Canada

University of Oslo Law School

In Norwegian, this is the usual student and faculty directory with research pointers.

Type: Gopher

Address: jusit.uio.no/1

Region: Norway

University of Warwick Gopher

This site offers information on programs at this English university, as well as a directory of British law schools and pointers to other legal resources.

Type: Gopher

Address: gopher.law.warwick.ac.uk/1

Region: England

Waikato Law School Home Page

Courses, faculty, and other information on the school, plus an index to Internet resources and a law-library home page are available at this site.

Type: WWW

Address: http://www2.waikato.ac.nz/law /homepage.html

Region: New Zealand

Web Journal of Current Legal Issues

This is an electronic legal journal in hypertext format.

Type: WWW

Address: http://www.ncl.ac.uk/~nlaw www/

Region: England

INTERNET RESOURCES ONLINE

Here's a long list of sites and services on the Internet that may make your Netsurfing experience more enjoyable. I've tried to include as many general sites with an international orientation as possible: In fact, this list includes all of my personal "bookmarks" for finding international information online.

There are also many items on this list that will help you learn more about the Internet itself, and how to make better use of its resources.

Art McGee's List of Black/African Related Resources

This is a list of online information storage sites (FTP, Gopher, Telnet, WWW, BBSs, databases, and so on) that contain a significant amount of information relating to or of concern to Black or African people. It's an impressive effort that succeeds in bringing together information that's hard to find elsewhere.

Type: WWW

Address: http://www.sas.upenn.edu/ Afric an_Studies/Home_Page/ mcgee.html

Region: U.S., Africa, Brazil, Caribbean, World

Brent's Internet Jumpstation

This part of one very nifty site is an online introduction to the World Wide Web, with a built-in interactive tutorial. Try it, you'll like it.

Type: WWW

Address: http://www.catalog.com/ bhunte r/demo.htm

Region: World

Central List of Canadian WWW Servers

Sorted by province and topic, this is the first place to stop if you're looking for Canadiana. Available in French and English.

Type: WWW

Address: http://www.csr.ists.ca/w3can/ Welcome.html

Region: Canada

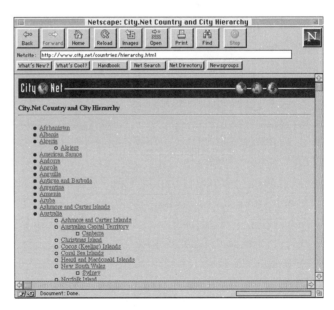

City.Net

This indispensable international Internet resource claims to be the most comprehensive international guide to communities around the world. City.Net is updated each day to provide easy and timely access to information on travel, entertainment, and local business, plus government and community services for all regions of the world. It's got links to maps, indexes, and more.

Type: WWW
Address: http://www.city.net/
Region: World

Clearinghouse for Subject-Oriented Internet Resource Guides

The semi-official Internet Resource Discovery Project was behind the founding of this Clearinghouse and many of the guides included in it. These efforts have evolved into a course designed specifically for guide builders: Internet Resource Discovery, Organization, and Design, offered by the School of Information and Library Studies at the University of Michigan. Their own pages are among the best for Web users.

Type: WWW
Address: http://http2.sils.umich.edu/~lou/ chhome.html
Region: World

CLNET Diversity Page

Diversity is this page's middle name, and with good reason. It includes mailing lists, Gopher and FTP sites, WWW resources, newsgroups, and more international resources, all broken down by continent, with an eye toward non-Eurocentric sites.

Type: WWW
Address: http://latino.sscnet.ucla.edu/ diversity1.html
Region: World

Connectivity around the World

This document from Net pioneer Randy Bush is regularly updated to show how each region is connected to the Net. This site also contains dozens of related service provider lists and information about getting online from most anywhere.

Type: Gopher
Address: gopher.psg.com:70/11/networks /connect
Region: World

Coombspapers Archive

The Coombs Social Sciences Research Data Bank at the Australian National University in Canberra houses documents collected by ANU's Research Schools of Social Sciences and Pacific and Asian Studies. It is a fabulous and extremely complete source of information about all aspects of life and history in Australia, Asia, and the nations of the Pacific Rim.

Type: WWW
Address: http://coombs.anu.edu.au/
Type: Gopher
Address: coombs.anu.edu.au/
Type: FTP
Address: coombs.anu.edu.au/
Region: Australia, New Zealand, Asia, Pacific Islands

CPMCnet: It's a Big World!

This resource for documenting Net diversity has links to the Philippines, LatinoNet, the Fourth World Documentation Project, and more.

Type: WWW
Address: http://cpmcnet.columbia.edu/ internet/misc/diversity.html
Region: World

Directory of Organizations

This is a list that just goes and goes, with plenty of international and multinational organizations listed. These are all groups that have a connection with IGC, a public-service Internet network with a commitment to social justice, so there's everything from the International Arctic Project and the Latin American Database, to Physicians for Human Rights. A bookmark must for the well-traveled cybersurfer.

Type: WWW
**Address: http://www.igc.apc.org/igc/
            people.html**
Region: World

EINet Galaxy

This site has over 130,000 hypertext-linked titles. They are listed by subject, with a nice format that's easy to read and pleasing to the eye.

Type: WWW
Address: http://www.einet.net/
Region: World

FedWorld

For Americans, this is an essential link. This site was set up to provide one-stop shopping for government information. If you need to check out Social Security regulations on extra income or find out who to call about your missing pension check, here's where to start looking.

Type: WWW
Address: http://www.fedworld.gov/
Region: U.S.

FTP Cornucopia

This document is a regularly updated list of FTP sites worldwide. If you are searching for software or files available by FTP, grab it.

Type: FTP
**Address: rtfm.mit.edu/pub/usenet/news.
            answers/ftp-list/sitelist**
Region: World

Gopher Bookmarks

The comp-gopher-diffs list is a place to distribute and discuss bookmarks to new Gopher material. If you want to hear about the latest goodies, join the list.

Type: Mailing list
Address: listserv@eff.org
**Send e-mail message with blank Subject
            line and body: subscribe
            comp-gopher-diffs**
Contact Address: eff@eff.org
Region: World

Gopher Jewels

This site catalogs many of the best Gopher sites by subject.

Type: WWW
**Address: http://galaxy.einet.net/GJ/index
            .html**
Region: World

IANWeb—International Affairs Network Home Pages

This site is cited as a link just about everywhere that you might be looking for international flavor. The International Affairs Network (IAN) is a three-year project designed to enhance the institutional capacity of schools of International Affairs in East and Central

Europe. It includes lists of think tanks, associations, and independent research facilities; universities; political groups, and much more.

Type: WWW
Address: http://www.pitt.edu/~ian/index. html
Region: World

IGC's African American Facts and Resources

Here's another site brought to you by the good people at IGC. It's updated on a regular basis, and a gold mine of African- and African-American-oriented links.

Type: WWW
Address: http://www.igc.apc.org/igc/ www.africanam.html
Region: Africa

International Gopher Sites

It's the mother of all international-resource Gopher lists—no easy feat. It's also clear and to the point: just the FAQs.

Type: Gopher
Address: marvel.loc.gov/11/federal/intl
Region: World

Internet by E-mail Information

If your Internet access is occasionally limited to an e-mail connection (perhaps during work hours), you can still get documents and software from FTP, Gopher, WWW, and other sites using special e-mail commands. Order this file by e-mail to learn how.

Type: E-mail
Address: MAILBASE@mailbase.ac.uk
Send e-mail message with blank Subject line and body: send lis-iis e-access-iet.txt
Region: World

Internet Help Desk

Are you still confused by some Internet services or terms? Okay, take a deep breath and stop in here. The commercial service GNN has organized all of the basic information you could possibly need about the Internet in one place. It includes guides to getting online, like EFF's popular "Big Dummy's Guide to the Internet," freeware and shareware for Internet navigation, a guide to places in your area that offer classes on using the Net, and a long list of Internet service providers.

Type: WWW
Address: http://gnn.digital.com/gnn/help desk/index.html
Region: World

Internet Information Resources

This is another international Internet page that can take you to Asia, Europe, Latin America, and beyond.

Type: WWW
Address: http://www.rahul.net/lai/ inetres.html
Region: World

Internet Meta-References

Like it says, it's a meta-reference from A to Z, a link to links sorted according to the Dewey Decimal system. It sure gives the library a run for its money.

Type: WWW
Address: http://www.slac.stanford.edu/ ~clancey/metarefs.html
Region: World

Japan Edge

This site wants to be your window on the Japanese underground: music, fashion, culture, and politics from Japan's Generation Xers.

Type: WWW
**Address: http://www.ces.kyutech.ac.jp/
            student/JapanEdge/e-index.html**
Region: Japan

Mailing List List

The file interest-groups provides a list of mailing lists that are available to Internet e-mail users.

Type: Mailing list
Address: mail-server@sri.com
**Send e-mail message with body: send
            interest-groups**
Type: FTP
Address: crvax.sri.com/netinfo
Region: World

The Mother-of-All-BBS

Internet resources are listed here, from Accounting to Zynet (whatever that is). Find out—talk to your mother.

Type: WWW
**Address: http://www.cs.colorado.edu/
            homes/mcbryan/public_html/bb/
            summary.html**
Region: World

News of the Web

This site has daily updates on news about the Internet: what's new online, what technologies are emerging to change the Net, which countries are passing laws that affect it.

Type: WWW
**Address: http://www.w3.org/hypertext/
            WWW/News/9305.html**
Region: World

The Political Science List of Lists

This list includes just about any mailing-list address you would ever need that deals with international and political issues, including everything from arms proliferation issues to British and Irish history.

Type: Gopher
**Address: rs6000.cmp.ilstu.edu:70/00/
            depts/polisci/listof**
Region: World

PRAXIS: Resources for Social and Economic Development

PRAXIS is the international-development home page of Richard J. Estes, a professor at the University of Pennsylvania. It provides access to a vast array of archival resources on international and comparative social development.

Type: WWW
**Address: http://caster.ssw.upenn.edu/
            ~res tes/praxis.html**
Region: World

Resources on International and Comparative Politics

Call up this site to see what's going on with Amnesty International, the UN, or Voice of America. There are lots of choices here in the arena of international issues, human rights, and politics. Compare and contrast, find out what works, and where conflicts are occurring.

Type: WWW
**Address: http://www.anu.edu.au/polsci/
            austpol/int/int.html**
Region: World

Scott Yanoff's Special Internet Connections List

This is Mr. Yanoff's extensive list of the "best" sites in many categories. He has excellent taste, too. Looking here can save you a lot of time and trouble.

Type: WWW
Address: http://www.uwm.edu/Mirror/ inet.services.html
Region: World

Search the Web

This Web page provides absolutely everything you need to search the World Wide Web, including links to Web crawlers, search engines, and other resources of all sorts.

Type: WWW
Address: http://info1.vub.ac.be:8080/ search_tools/index.html
Region: World

Silk Route

The organizers of this site call their contribution to the Net the Digital Silk Route of the twenty-first century, and I believe it. It has everything you might want from a virtual trip to Asia: shopping links, information services, convention services, travel services, business services—and all with neat little icons that just scream "click me."

Type: WWW
Address: http://silkroute.com/silkroute/
Region: World

University of Tokyo

Files available here include Chinese and Japanese software, games, Linux, communications software, and much more.

Type: FTP
Address: azabu.tkl.iis.u-tokyo.ac.jp/
Region: Japan, China

Usenet Newsgroups

Want to know if there's a newsgroup about your pet subject, and what it's like? Check these sites and documents for complete lists of what's online, access to Frequently Asked Questions files, and more.

Type: Usenet newsgroup
Address: news.answers
Type: FTP
Address: rtfm.mit.edu/pub/usenet/news .lists
Type: Gopher
Address: rtfm.umich.edu/pub/usenet/ news.answers/
Type: WWW
Address: http://www.lib.ox.ac.uk/internet /news/alt.html
Region: World

Virtual Shareware Library

This library has a humongous compilation of practically every shareware application available, with over 90,000 offerings for every use and every personal computer. Includes links to FTPable software archives in all corners of the globe.

Type: WWW
Address: http://www.acs.oakland.edu/ cgi-bin/shase
Region: World

The Virtual Tourist

This virtual tourist map of the world is a clickable interface for sites on every continent. Put this site on your bookmark list and you'll never get lost again.

Type: WWW
Address: http://wings.buffalo.edu/world/
Region: Europe

W3 Servers

This is a list of registered WWW servers organized alphabetically by continent, country, and state. It's so large that it takes a long time to download to your screen.

Type: WWW
Address: http://www.w3.org/hypertext/ DataSources/WWW/ Geographical.html
Region: World

WebFax

This service can be used to obtain any WWW documents from any fax machine. Very interesting!

Type: WWW
Address: http://www.datawave.net/
Region: World

The Weird, the Wild, and the Wonderful on WWW

Wacky and wicked apply to the offerings at this Web page as well.

Type: WWW
Address: http://www.wired.com/Staff/ justin/dox/www.html
Region: World

The Whole Internet Catalog and GNN

This site has corporate funding and curious investors wondering whether you'll stop in for some cyber commercials. Well, if you do, you'll also get to see what the GNN (Global Network Navigator) can do for you, and why they were able to attract sponsors in the first place. It's an online resource with links organized by subject, neatly laid out in a logical fashion, and with pleasing graphics.

Type: WWW
Address: http://nearnet.gnn.com/wic/ newrescat.toc.html
Region: World

WWW Servers in Mexico

Listed by state, this is a compendium of the Internet in Mexico, and it's growing daily. There's a spot where you can find out what's new, too.

Type: WWW
Address: http://info.pue.udlap.mx/mexico .html
Region: Mexico

WWW Virtual Library

The WWW Virtual Library is a set of subject-oriented guides to the Internet, each maintained at a different site around the world.

Type: WWW
Address: http://www.w3.org/hypertext/ DataSources/bySubject/ Overview.html
Region: World

Yahoo

Talk about a fun name for a resource site. They're also a major search engine (maybe the biggest) with over 36,000 entries, and growing exponentially by the minute. If you want to find something, just say "Yahoo!"

Type: WWW
Address: http://www.yahoo.com/
Region: World

JOURNALISM AND THE MEDIA

See also Digital Media: News and Current Events page 158; Digital Media: Online Publications for the Nethead page 165; Electronics page 216

If you are a professional journalist, writer, or photographer, here some sites in both the "fun" and "essential reading" categories. Media consumers can also find a great deal that's of interest here: In this era of much debate about "balance" in journalism, the most important filter for information is your own mind. Read up to see how journalists think, how topics are chosen, and how news gets written and published. It'll put you ahead in the information game.

alt.fan.art-bell

Most folks will find Art Bell's extreme-right politics absolutely reprehensible, but most of the time the man is talking about UFOs and ghosts, so who cares? The absolute best in overnight talk radio, Art may not please you all the time but he's sure to entertain. This newsgroup is host to Art's biggest fans, along with many GIFs of UFOs and aliens, Gordon Michael Scallion interviews, and the like. Art himself, a big advocate of the Internet and information technology, can also be heard from here occasionally. It includes station listings for his weekday overnight show, "Coast to Coast AM with Art Bell," and "DreamLand," his Sunday evening show focusing on afterlife/past life, supernatural, and alien/UFO issues. Alternative journalism with a twist.

Type: Usenet newsgroup
Address: alt.fan.art-bell
Region: U.S.

alt.radio.networks.npr

The focus of this Usenet newsgroup is discussion of the American National Public Radio network.

Type: Usenet newsgroup
Address: alt.radio.networks.npr
Region: U.S.

alt.radio.pirate

This Usenet discussion group deals with low-power and surreptitious radio broadcasting. A FAQ is available at the FTP archive.

Type: Usenet newsgroup
Address: alt.pirate.radio
Type: FTP
Address: rtfm.mit.edu/pub/usenet-by-hierarchy/alt/radio/pirate
Region: U.S.

alt.radio.talk

Talk radio and its use as a tool of social and political organizing is a fascinating topic. Dominated by the radical right, with radio personalities like Rush Limbaugh leading, it is emerging as a social and political force to be reckoned with in the U.S. Now the left is joining in, with spokespersons like Texas populist Jim Hightower. This Usenet newsgroup focuses its discussion on this most controversial of radio formats.

Type: Usenet newsgroup
Address: alt.radio.talk
Region: U.S.

AlterNet/Institute for Alternative Journalism

AlterNet is an independent, left-leaning information service providing subscribers with news, views, information, and ideas from alternative media and public interest organization sources. Formerly available only via subscription on CompuServe, this Web page allows access to their latest projects, including "Culture Wars"—a critique of the Religious Right and their influence on the public-issues debate in the U.S.

Type: WWW
Address: http://www.igc.apc.org/an/
Region: U.S.

American Journalism Review Home Page

Available at the home page of one of the best journalism-oriented periodicals in the U.S. is a selection of articles from the latest issue of the *AJR*, subscription and feedback information, and a link to the Electronic Newsstand for a selection of archived articles from previous issues. Don't miss the Grants, Awards, and Fellowships section; it contains a list of some 70 or so ongoing grant possibilities for professional journalists.

Type: WWW
**Address: http://jnews.umd.edu/ajr/
          home.html**
Region: U.S.

Arab-Press List

Based in Israel, this list was formed from a monthly newsletter of Arab press research, and consists primarily of unedited excerpts from press sources throughout the Arab world.

Type: Mailing list
**Address: arab-press-request@jerusalem1.
          datasrv.co.il**
**Contact: arab-press@jerusalem1.datasrv
          .co.il**
Region: Israel, Palestine, Middle East

Bowling Green State Department of Telecommunications Home Page

The BGSU TCOM Department home page provides links to a tremendous amount of background information, including hypertext and cable/broadcast television resources and an excellent list of broadcast media on the Web.

Type: WWW
**Address: http://www.bgsu.edu/
          Departments/tcom/**
Region: U.S.

CARA-L

The e-mail discussion list CARA-L was started to facilitate communication between working journalists in any media, journalism educators, news librarians, and researchers. The topic is focused on the use of computers in journalism, not general journalism. Topics range from text-processing and graphics to online database searching, computer communications and investigative reporting.

Type: Mailing list
Address: LISTSERV@ULKYVM.LOUISVILLE.EDU
Region: World

Convergence: The New Media Journal

Devoted to entertainment in the age of the information superhighway, this journal is not about hardware but information itself, including film, laserdisc, audio CD, CD-ROM, online magazines, and other forms. Includes reviews of electronic media, essays, profiles, and product information.

Type: E-zine
**Address: aenigma@netcom.com (Glenn
          Peters)**
Region: World

Covington's Homeless

This is a photojournalist's documentary, a beautifully shot and sensitive exploration of real people and their lives. Not many papers or magazines do this kind of journalism anymore. It's a good example of the kinds of opportunities for personal, issues-oriented reporting that the Net can provide. Follow the links to the photographer's other project: a documentary about carnival workers.

Type: WWW
Address: **http://www.iia.org/~deckerj/ index.html**
Region: U.S.

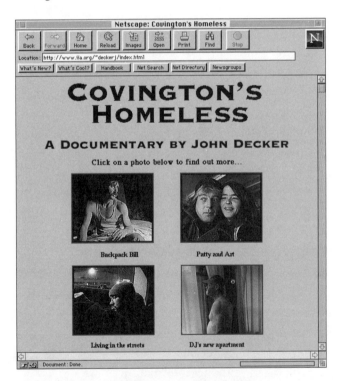

Culture Communication and the Media in Israel

This history of the Israeli press includes information about current media outlets in Israel and Voice of Israel shortwave broadcasts.

Type: Gopher
Address: **israel-info.gov.il:70/11/cul/ media**
Region: Israel

East European Media Studies

This site features a group of extremely well-researched student projects on the state of the media in several Eastern European countries. Subjects include censorship, government-supported media, electronic media, and more.

Type: WWW
Address: **http://www.utexas.edu/ftp/pub/ eems/main.html**
Region: Czech Republic, Bulgaria, Estonia, Latvia, U.S.

Expert Rolodex Project

Organized by the Institute for Alternative Journalism, the Expert Rolodex Project is an attempt to broaden the scope of who the mainstream media considers "experts." Provided are a subject index of individuals who excel in their given areas of expertise—yet are typically overlooked—and a contact list for those people. Some examples are Jim Hightower (radio talk-show host and chair of an alliance of consumer, church, labor, farmer, and consumer groups opposing the S&L and banking bailouts), James Zogby (president of the American Arab Institute), and Marjorie Heins (director and staff counsel of the ACLU Arts Censorship Project).

Type: Gopher
Address: **gopher.igc.apc.org/11/orgs/ alternet/expert**
Region: U.S.

FAIR Media Resources List

FAIR—Fairness and Accuracy in Reporting—is by far the strongest and hardest-hitting progressive media-watch/resource organization. The FAIR Media Resources List is a bibliography of alternative news sources, corporate media critiques, and critical journalistic background reading. A must-read.

Type: Gopher
Address: wiretap.spies.com/00/Library/ Media/Misc/fair.lis
Region: U.S.

FAIR Web Pages

FAIR's Web pages provide access to partial present and back issues of *EXTRA!*, their monthly media-watch journal; an archive of selected FAIR special reports; information about the "Counter Spin" radio show, including station listings; and FAIR's "Media Bias Detector" and media contact lists.

Type: WWW
Address: http://www.igc.org/fair/
Type: Gopher
Address: gopher.igc.apc.org:70/1
Region: U.S.

FOI-L

Discussion on this list centers around freedom of information and freedom of speech issues. The list is coordinated by the National Freedom of Information Coalition.

Type: Mailing list
Address: listserv@suvm.syr.edu
Region: U.S.

Freedom Forum

A pro-First Amendment/free speech group for journalists, professors, and students, the Freedom Forum sponsors this set of pages with information on media around the world—status, contacts, censorship, and so on.

Type: WWW
Address: http://www.nando.net/prof/ freedom/1994/freedom.html
Region: U.S., World

GlasNews

GlasNews is a quarterly publication on East-West contacts in communications, including journalism, telecommunications, advertising, and public relations. This Web page provides excerpts from the most recent issues of the publication. Back issues, supplementary material about the C.I.S., and news bits from GlasNet are available at the FTP site.

Type: WWW
Address: http://solar.rtd.utk.edu/friends/ news/glasnews/master.html
Type: FTP
Address: ftp.eskimo.com/GlasNews
Region: U.S.

Hypertext Reading as Practical Action

Subtitled "Notes on Technology, Objectivation, and Knowledge," this long, scholarly hypertext "essay" discusses and investigates the changing nature of knowledge and information exchange as effected by hypertextual media. Seriously intense, this is very dense reading.

Type: WWW
Address: http://www.nta.no/telektronikk/ 4.93.dir/Rasmussen_T.html
Region: Norway

IRE-L

Organized by the professional organization Investigative Reporters and Editors, this list centers on the discussion of investigative journalism and the techniques of the trade.

Type: Mailing list
Address: LISTSERV@MIZZOU1.MISSOURI.EDU
Region: U.S.

The Journalism List

Tons of related resources, Gopher and FTP sites, Usenet groups, and mailing lists for journalists are linked into this Web page.

Type: WWW
**Address: http://www.jou.ufl.edu/commres/
           jlist.HTM#Discussion Groups—
           Mailing Lists**
Region: World

Lemming's Photography and Photojournalism Page

This photojournalist's page includes links to photography, photojournalism, news media, and some just-plain-fun sites as well. He also has his portfolio online.

Type: WWW
**Address: http://www.yahoo.com/Art/
           Photography/Photojournalism/**
Region: U.S.

Media 3

This is a media education resource magazine from Melbourne's Deakin University Rusden Campus, and is published twice a year.

Type: WWW
**Address: http://www.deakin.edu.au/arts/
           VPMA/Media3.html**

Contact: greenp@deakin.edu.au
Region: Australia

MISA Free Press

Media Institute of Southern Africa (MISA), based in Namibia, covers press freedom and media issues in Southern Africa. There is a small charge to subscribe to the e-mail version, but you can see sample issues for free at the FTP site.

Type: E-mail
Address: dlush@misa.alt.na
Type: FTP
**Address: wmail.misanet.org or ftp.
           misanet.org/pub/FreePress**
Region: Namibia, South Africa, Southern Africa

Missouri School of Journalism

One of the United States' best-known journalism schools is on the Net. Their site includes lots of media, new-media, and journalism information, plus a real-time discussion forum for journalists and students using MUD methodology, J-MUSH.

Type: WWW
**Address: http://www.missouri.edu/
           ~jscho ol/index.html**
Region: U.S., World

National Public Radio Home Page

For almost two decades NPR has delivered a wide variety of radio programming to audiences all over the United States. Their news programs "All Things Considered" and "Morning Edition" are staple informational programming for college and public radio stations across the nation, but NPR also provides excellent talk programming, current affairs programming, radio drama and comedy, and music shows. Station listings, program lists, and soon, news transcripts grace the Web and Gopher sites for NPR, as well as comment forms to voice feedback about their services.

Type: WWW
Address: http://www.npr.org/
Type: Gopher
Address: gopher.npr.org/
Region: U.S.

Online Journalism Collection

Hosted by the Journalism and Mass Communications department of the University of Tampere in Vostok, Finland, this well-linked Web site provides excellent information on online journalism with a European bent. There are three primary information menus, as well as a guide to the journalism program at the University of Tampere. Within the "Texts about Journalism" section are several general but strong articles about online journalism and journalistic views of the Internet, linked e-zine and online newspaper listings, and a brief history of hypertext. The "Net Medias" menu provides a gateway to online television and radio "broadcasts," and links to more resources. The "Journalism and Media Information Sources" contains lists of and links to online general journalism resources and links to the major Usenet journalism newsgroups; this makes an excellent start-ing point on a hunt for Internet resources on this subject. All sections are available in Finnish and English.

Type: WWW
**Address: http://www.uta.fi/jarjestot/
           vostok/ojc/ojceng.html**
Region: Finland, Europe, World

Pirate Radio List

Shiver me timbers, laddies! The PRL e-mail list focuses on the shady world of small pirate broadcasters, exchanging technical information, tall radio tales, and reports on pirate stations picked up in the wee hours of the night.

Type: Mailing list
Address: brewer@ace.enet.dec.com
Region: U.S., World

PROG-PUBS List

This discussion list is for those interested in progressive publications, radio, and television.

Type: Mailing list
**Address: prog-pubs-request@fuggles.acc.
           virginia.edu**
Region: U.S.

RadioSpace Home Page

Billed as the "home of radio on the Internet," this home page provides contact information for radio networks and organizations, online audio resources and guides, and audio news clips available for broadcast. The North American Network, a broadcast agency that provides news and programming services to radio stations and organizations, runs the page, which includes audio news releases, radio media tours, and public service programming. Programming in RadioSpace is sponsored by a variety of commercial and not-for-profit organizations.

Type: WWW
Address: http://www.radiospace.com/welcome.html
Region: Canada

rec.radio.broadcasting

This Usenet discussion group deals with the medium of broadcast radio. It's also available in mailing list format.

Type: Usenet newsgroup
Address: rec.radio.broadcasting
Type: Mailing list
Address: subscribe@airwaves.chi.il.us
Send e-mail message with subject:
SUBSCRIBE AIRWAVES <Firstname Lastname>
Region: World

rec.radio.noncomm

The focus of this Usenet newsgroup is discussion of noncommercial and public radio broadcasters. A FAQ is available at the FTP site below.

Type: Usenet newsgroup
Address: rec.radio.noncomm
Type: FTP
Address: rtfm.mit.edu/pub/usenet-by-hierarchy/rec/radio/noncomm
Region: World

rec.video.cable-tv

This Usenet newsgroup centers on cable-television technology and social and regulatory issues. It has a FAQ available at the FTP archive below.

Type: Usenet newsgroup
Address: rec.video.cable-tv

Type: FTP
Address: rtfm.mit.edu/pub/usenet-by-hierarchy/rec/video/cable-tv
Region: U.S.

SDS Media Digest

The Slovakian Document Store Media Digest is a news digest put together by the Center for Independent Journalism in Bratislava and OMRI, the Open Media Research Institute. Besides straight news items on the Balkans, the Commonwealth of Independent States, and the rest of Eastern Europe, the *SDS Media Digest* covers a healthy range of journalism and information-exchange issues.

Type: WWW
Address: http://www.eunet.sk/media/media.html
Region: Slovakia

Self-Censorship and the Mexican Press

By Jeffrey Stoub, a former editor and reporter for the *Mexico City News*, this is a very well-written essay on the problems of the Mexican press and its lapsed role as a government and business watchdog during a period of extreme corruption at the top.

Type: WWW
Address: http://daisy.uwaterloo.ca/~alopez-o/politics/selfcens.html
Region: Mexico

SPJ-ONLINE

This fairly new e-mail discussion list covers general journalistic topics and information and is organized by the Society of Professional Journalists.

Type: Mailing list
Address: listserv@netcom.com
Region: U.S.

University of Iowa Communications and Mass Communications Resources

As part of the Information Arcade Gopher system at the University of Iowa, the Communications and Mass Communications Gopher provides a wide variety of links to Gopher sites around the world in an attempt to increase information exchange. Found amongst the many links are everything from lists of e-mail discussion groups to media- and communication-related FAQs, Internet resource guides on mass communications, and links to many e-journals, e-zines, and other online news sources on a wide variety of topics.

Type: Gopher
Address: iam41.arcade.uiowa.edu:2270/
Region: U.S., World

The University of Queensland Journalism Department Home Page

Besides the usual course and staff information for their Journalism department, there are also quite a number of online resources here. Some of these include *The Weekend Independent*, a fortnightly newspaper produced by students; an online style book; abstracts of the quarterly interdisciplinary scholarly journal *Australian Studies in Journalism*, and a linked list of online journalism resources.

Type: WWW
**Address: http://www.uq.oz.au/jrn/
           home.html**
Region: Australia

LANGUAGE STUDIES
See also Conversation and Friendship page 141

Studying languages online can take many forms. Some may want to simply download instructional software, or check out foreign-language dictionaries for that elusive definition. Others may want to try online lessons, some of which use hypertext, audio, and even video files. And for practice, there are always foreign-language mailing lists and BIT-NET, Usenet, and other newsgroups—see listings in other sections to find groups that interest you. IRC and related interactive chat services are also a good place to test your skills.

Aboriginal Language Resources

The Australian Institute of Aboriginal and Torres Strait Islander Studies at Coombs University provides language libraries for some of the many Aboriginal languages and dialects here.

Type: WWW
**Address: http://coombs.anu.edu.au/
           SpecialProj/ASEDA/ASEDA.html**
Region: Australia

The Abyssinia CyberSpace Gateway

This great-looking page is the first of a swiftly building series on Ethiopian culture. It includes some Amharic software and fonts, plus related information.

Type: WWW
**Address: http://www.cs.indiana.edu/
           hyplan/dmulholl/acg.html**
Region: Ethiopia

African-Related Software and Information

It's mostly language-specific items in this archive, including special fonts and word processing software as well as language-learning aids. Tongues represented include Arabic, Amharic (Ethiopian), Sabaen, and more.

Type: WWW

Address: http://www.sas.upenn.edu/ African_Studies/Software/menu_ Software.html

Region: Africa

Afrikaans Home Page

This page includes lessons in Afrikaans, the language of the Dutch settlers in South Africa.

Type: WWW

Address: http://www.sun.ac.za/local/ library/home.html

Region: South Africa

Catalan Pages

One of my favorite languages, Catalan, is the subject of a growing group of pages here that may include online lessons by the time you read this.

Type: WWW

Address: http://www.willamette.edu/ ~tjones/languages/Catalan/ webcat7.html

Region: Spain, Andorra, France, Sardinia (Italy)

Chinese Chatlines

IRC channels #Hanzi and #Shanghai have a Web-page interface here, making them easier to use. Test out your Chinese with native speakers online, interactively!

Type: IRC

Addresses: #Hanzi
#Shanghai

Type: WWW

Address: http://odin.pat.dcu.ie:8080/ irc.html

Region: China

The Chinese-Language-Related Page

This is the best place to start online if you want to learn Chinese. Places to read and hear Chinese on the Net, FTP archives with Chinese text files and related software, language course links, and much more are available here.

Type: WWW

Address: http://www.c3.lanl.gov/~cim/ chinese.html

Region: China

Esperanto: La Internacia Lingvo

Remember Esperanto, the deliberately created international language? Well, it's back, and might even come in handy online, what with all this cross-cultural communication going on. This page links to FAQs, an Esperanto IRC channel, a hypertext Esperanto course, translators, software, mailing lists, and more.

Type: WWW

Address: http://wwwtios.cs.utwente.nl/ esperanto/

Region: World

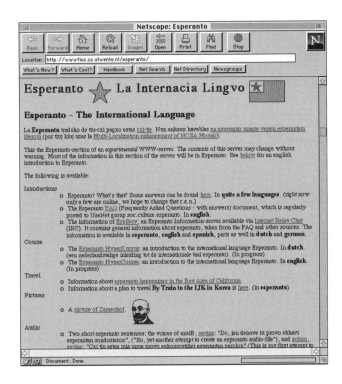

Ethnologue Database

Get access here to a database of about 6,500 known world languages and dialects, with information on their relationships and roots. There are also world language maps here.

Type: WWW

Address: http://www-ala.doc.ic.ac.uk/ ~rap/Ethnologue/

Region: World

Foreign Language and Culture

This is your basic page with massive amounts of links to foreign-language resources.

Type: WWW

Address: http://www.speakeasy.org/ ~dbrick/Hot/foreign.html

Region: World

Foreign Languages for Travelers

Just need those few essential words and phrases ("Otra cerveza, por favor" and "¿Donde es el baño?," for example) to get through a brief visit to a foreign country? Check in here for basic vocabulary lessons in English, Hungarian, Russian, Spanish, Portuguese, French, and Turkish, with sound files for proper pronunciation. Silent refresher courses are also available in many other languages, and the page has a huge list of links.

Type: WWW

Address: http://insti.physics.sunysb.edu/ ~mmartin/languages/ languages.html

Region: World

FrenchTalk

This mailing list is for discussion in French, and has a multinational membership. If your Web browser supports forms, you can subscribe via the Web page, which also includes emulation software for Minitel, the French chat-line system—another good place to practice. FrenchTalk is archived at the Gopher site below.

Type: Mailing list

Address: listproc@list.cren.net

Send e-mail message with body: subscribe frenchtalk <Firstname Lastname>

Type: WWW

Address: http://www.limsi.fr/~krus/ frenchtalk/

Type: Gopher

Address: list.cren.net:70/11/archives/ french-embassy/frenchtalk

Region: France

Gaelic Language Resources
This page includes information about the Irish, Scottish, and Manx variants of Gaelic, including links with a Gaelic college, Irish newspapers and literature, a couple of Gopher and FTP sites with Gaelic materials, and a collection of Gaelic Web pages.
Type: WWW
Address: http://futon.sfsu.edu/%7Ejtm/ Gaelic/
Region: Ireland, Scotland, Isle of Man (England)

Gesture-L Archives
This searchable WAIS database, provided within the massive Australian National University system, has information for those interested in the study and documentation of gestures, gesture systems, and alternate sign languages. Subscription and posting privileges to the list are by invite only, but if you are interested enter *subscribe* into the search field and you will get the address to apply to the list.
Type: WAIS
Address: Gesture-L
Type: Gopher
Address: cheops.anu.edu.au/7waissrc%3a/ Coombs-db/ANU-Gesture-L.src
Region: Australia, World

Hacker's Dictionary
Yes, it sure is a different language. This version was placed online by students from Korea, who no doubt found it a puzzling cultural artifact worthy of serious study.
Type: WWW
Address: http://venus.hanyang.ac.kr/ jargon/WelcomHackers Jargon.html
Region: World

Hapax: French Resources on the Web
Resources for teachers and students of French, including language-related stuff, cultural sites and publications, are what you'll find here.
Type: WWW
Address: http://hapax.be.sbc.edu/
Region: France

Hawai'ian Language Resources
The native Hawaiian language is making a comeback with a new generation of islanders, just in time to prevent its disappearance. Learn how to speak it here, haoles and natives. It's mostly in Hawaiian, with some pages translated for English speakers.
Type: WWW
Address: http://www.olelo.hawaii.edu/
Region: Hawaii (U.S.)

Hebrew: A Living Language
This Israeli site offers grammar and vocabulary lessons, as well as the Hebrew alphabet and numbers. There's also an interesting history of modern Hebrew, which says that a Hebrew-language comedy troupe had an important effect on revitalizing the language. You learn something new everyday, and this is a good place to do so.
Type: WWW
Address: http://www.macom.co.il/ hebrew/
Region: Israel

Hindi Program
Set up by Pennsylvania University, this page offers some basic Hindi lessons, including audio files, and information about Penn's Hindi language program.

Type: WWW
**Address: http://philae.sas.upenn.edu/
           Hindi/hindi.html**
Region: India

Honyaku Mailing List

Have a Japanese-English translation problem? Here's the place to get answers. It's archived at the FTP site below, while the Web page has FAQs, announcements, and related links.

Type: Mailing list
Address: listserv@netcom.com
**Send e-mail message with body: subscribe
           honyaku**
Type: FTP
**Address: ftp.netcom.com/pub/ho/
           honyaku/**
Type: WWW
**Address: http://www.realtime.net/
           ~adamrice/**
Region: Japan

The Human-Languages Page

The plan behind this page is to create a single central site for information on all languages of the world—is that ambitious or what? They are collecting and digitizing noncopyrighted translation dictionaries and other materials, and doing an admirable job of adding links. This page is available in English, Dutch, German, French, Portuguese, Finnish, Norwegian, Spanish, Afrikaans, and Russian.

Type: WWW
**Address: http://www.willamette.edu/
           ~tjones/Language-Page.html**
Region: World

Immersion Language Schools

New Horizons runs language immersion schools in 25 countries. Check here for programs to learn the language you want in countries where it is spoken daily.

Type: WWW
**Address: http://www.execpc.com/~nrcsa/
           toc_nh.html**
Region: World

Indonesian Home Pages

Drop someone a line in Indonesian (or in English, if they're trying to learn it). This is a long list of Indonesian personal home pages.

Type: WWW
**Address: http://www.umanitoba.ca/
           indonesian/persons.html**
Region: Indonesia

Institute of the Estonian Language

Brief contact information from the Institute, itself based in Finland, is available here, along with online Estonian dictionaries.

Type: WWW
**Address: http://muhu.helsinki.fi/By_
           Subject/Language/eki/**
Region: Estonia

Internet Relay Chat (IRC) FAQ Page

IRC is one of the best ways to practice your languages online. Channels exist for conversing in many languages other than English, including Finnish, German, Japanese, Dutch, and Esperanto. Check here for basic information, IRC client software, and links to IRC manuals.

Type: WWW
**Address: http://mistral.enst.fr/~pioch/IRC/
           ircfaq.html**
Region: World

Iranian Cultural and Information Center

Links to Farsi software, including TeX and internationalized Mosiac, and Iranian texts are accesible at this site.

Type: WWW
Address: http://tehran.stanford.edu
Region: Iran

Italian Lessons

You can download these as PostScript files and work at your own pace, or jump right into them online. Basic Italian words, phrases, and grammar are covered.

Type: WWW
**Address: http://www.willamette.edu/
~tjones/languages/Italian/
Italian-lesson.html**
Region: Italy

Japanese Chat

Practice your Japanese and learn about Japanese culture on the #Nippon Internet Relay Chat channel.

Type: IRC
Address: #Nippon
Region: Japan

Kamusi/Internet Living Swahili Dictionary Project

Swahili is primarily a trade language, and as such is widely spoken in many areas of Africa. This Gopher archive includes FAQs and files relating to this project for creating a new, up-to-date Swahili dictionary using the resources of the Internet. The effort itself is taking place through the Kamusi-L mailing list.

Type: Gopher
Address: yaleinfo.yale.edu:7702/1
Type: Mailing list

Address: kamusi-l@yalevm.cis.yale.edu
**Send e-mail message with body: subscribe
KAMUSI-L <Firstname Lastname>**
Region: Africa

Kurdish Information Network

Kurdish language lessons and a backgrounder on the Kurdish language accompany patriotic propaganda on this home page for one of the world's most embattled minorities, whose land has been divided by nations that allow them little autonomy.

Type: WWW
Address: http://nucst11.neep.wisc.edu/
Region: Turkey, Iraq

Less Commonly Taught Languages Gopher

From Early Welsh to Cherokee to Lao, there are 250 languages represented here. This Gopher lists institutions and instructors where specific "Less Commonly Taught Languages" are taught. Its creators' goal is to eventually have names, addresses, and phone numbers of a contact person for each language.

Type: Gopher
Address: lctl.acad.umn.edu
Region: U.S.

Let's Learn Arabic

This is a hypertext education program for Arabic. This page also has links to Arab cultural resources, and information about obtaining Arabic software.

Type: WWW
**Address: http://philae.sas.upenn.edu/
Arabic/arabic.html**
Region: Middle East

Lojban—The Logical Language

Lojban is less well known than Esperanto, but it too is a constructed modern language intended as an international substitute for all our divisive and difficult little dialects. Find out more here.

Type: WWW
Address: http://xiron.pc.helsinki.fi/lojban/
Region: World

The Maori Language

If you want to sound tough, learn Maori: They are probably the biggest, baddest folks on the planet. This site includes a small selection of vocabulary words, texts, and other resources.

Type: WWW
**Address: http://www.cs.cmu.edu/afs/cs
            .cmu.edu/Web/People/mjw/NZ/
            Maori/MainPage.html**
Region: New Zealand

Mayan Epigraphic Data Project

Living languages aren't the only ones being studied online. This is an attempt to use computers to continue the process of cracking the "code" of the Mayan hieroglyphics found at ancient Mesoamerican sites. It includes links to databases and researchers.

Type: WWW
**Address: http://jefferson.village.virginia
            .edu/med/medwww.html**
Region: Mexico, Guatemala

Native American Languages

After two generations of forced English, particularly for those tribes whose children were forced into boarding schools, many Native Americans are trying to recover their languages. This site from the NativeNet network profiles efforts in North and Central America to preserve and relearn.

Type: WWW
**Address: http://kuhttp.cc.ukans.edu/
            ~marc/language/language.html**
Region: U.S., Canada, Guyana

Ohio University CALL Page

Choix
d'Éditeur

CALL stands for *Computer-Assisted Language Learning*, and this page is a great idea! Leads to WWW resources on languages taught at OSU are provided, plus you can check out special learning projects developed for students. The languages include Arabic, Chinese, English (ESL), French, German, Greek, Indonesian, Italian, Japanese, Klingon (they don't actually teach it, but it's here), Latin, Russian, Spanish, and Swahili. Typical resources include language lessons from simple to intermediate, foreign-language sites and publications to check out, and places to practice your new skills, perhaps on Internet Relay Chat.

Type: WWW
**Address: http://www.tcom.ohiou.edu/
            OU_Language/OU_Language.html**
Region: World

The Quick and Dirty Guide to Japanese Grammar

All the basics are here, in a breezy text file.

Type: FTP
**Address: ftp.spies.com:/Library/Article/
            Language/grammar.jap**
Region: Japan

Russian and Related Languages at REESweb

Many resources for the learner are here for Russian, Ukrainian, Polish, Serbo-Croatian, Czech, Hungarian, and various Slavic languages, including software, dictionaries, and the very valuable Russian Obscenities file.

Type: WWW
Address: http://www.pitt.edu/~cjp/ rslang.html
Region: Russia, Ukraine, Croatia, Estonia, Serbia, Ukraine, Poland, Slovakia, Bulgaria, Finland, Hungary, Czech Republic

Russian IRC

Talk with Russian expatriates, students of Russian, and others here. The Web page has personality profiles of some frequent IRCers and information about protocols for chatting on this friendly channel.

Type: IRC
Address: #russian
Type: WWW
Address: http://www.cs.umd.edu/users/ fms/RussianIRC.html
Region: Russia

Simple Serbian

It really is simple to learn to read, write, and speak Serbian, because in the modern era the language was changed to be more logical. It can be written in the Latin or Cyrillic alphabet, and when it's in Cyrillic each letter has only one sound. Compare *that* to English. This site includes basic vocabulary lessons and some audio files.

Type: WWW
Address: http://www.umiacs.umd.edu/ research/lpv/YU/HTML/jezik.html
Region: Serbia

Slovene Language Learning Materials

Geared toward English speakers, this archive holds dictionaries, texts, and lessons for learning Slovenian.

Type: WWW
Address: http://www.ijs.si/ slo-language-learning.html
Region: Slovenia

Spanish Lessons

Here are basic Spanish lessons, with an accent on Mexican Spanish. (This is important: I learned the Costa Rican variety and was considered most amusing when I tried to speak in New Mexico. And I've seen some terrible online flamefests between Spanish and Mexican speakers over correct usage.) You can download the PostScript files and work at your leisure, or take your lessons online.

Type: WWW
Address: http://www.willamette.edu/ ~tjones/Spanish/Spanish-main. html
Region: Mexico

Spanish Newsgroups

Find out here about newsgroups that are conducted in Spanish on a variety of subjects.

Type: WWW
Address: http://latoso.cheme.cornell.edu/ Spain/News/
Region: Spain, World

Swahili-L

Persons interested in communicating in Swahili can subscribe to the African Studies Outreach Program's conversation list, Swahili-L.

Type: Mailing list
Address: listserver@relay.adp.wisc.edu
Send e-mail message with Subject:
 subscribe swahili-l
Region: Africa

The Tagalog Home Page

A friendly Filipino tutor takes you on a beginner's tour of the Tagalog language. This language page would be even more fun if a program was set up that gave each visitor one of those great Filipino nicknames on request.

Type: WWW
Address: http://www.halcyon.com/dizon/
 welcome.html
Region: Philippines

UT Foreign Language Bookmarks

You'll find about a hundred language and culture leads here, with an especially extensive collection of links to French resources.

Type: WWW
Address: http://131.183.82.151/
 Bookmarks.html
Region: World

WebChat

This is a relatively new WWW-based interactive chat application. This site tells about the WebChat project, and the "Hotlist of Sites Running WebChat" takes you to a list of WebChat links. You can hop right in using your browser. International options include Japan, Canada, England, and an Islamic chatspace.

Type: WWW
Address: http://www.irsociety.com/
 webchat.html
Region: U.S., World

Yiddish Culture and Language Page: The Virtual Shtetl

That's virtual "village" in Yiddish, the language spoken for generations by Jews living in Eastern Europe. It's a blend of Hebrew, German, and Slavic languages, with many unique and colorful phrases. You probably already know a few words, some of them a bit slangy: oy vay, shtick, schlemiel, chutzpah. Learn more here.

Type: WWW
Address: http://calypso.oit.unc.edu/
 yiddish/shtetl.html
Region: Eastern Europe

The Yuen Ruen Society

This linguistics society is devoted to field work and research on the various dialects of China (you didn't really think that one billion people could speak a language the same way, did you?). This page has a fresh, somewhat irreverent attitude toward a rather specialized topic, and lots of links to Chinese-related items online.

Type: WWW
Address: http://weber.u.washington.edu/
 ~yuenren/Circular.html
Region: China

LITERATURE

See also Digital Media page 158; Fandom International page 250; Folklore and Mythology page 274

I still like books better than I like computers. They're tactile, more visual, and when you carry them with you, you don't have to ask if you can use an electrical outlet. Here are lots of Internet resources that cover books, literature of many nations, and writing.

Algunos Poemas

You'll find 39 poems in Spanish here, from Octavio Paz, Pablo Neruda, Jose Luis Borges, and other writers of the Americas.

Type: WWW
Address: http://csgwww.uwaterloo.ca/ users/dmg/literatura/poesia.html
Region: Mexico, Central America, Argentina, Chile, South America

alt.books.reviews

Talk about books you love and books you hate here.

Type: Usenet newsgroup
Address: alt.books.reviews
Region: World

Angstkultur

This Norwegian literature site, with the accent on modern works with a dark outlook, looks like it could be fun if you know Norwegian.

Type: WWW
Address: http://www.ifi.uio.no/ ~hermunda/lyrikk/angstkat.html
Region: Norway

Antologia della Letteratura Italiana

If you know Italian, you can read such classics as Dante's *La Divina Commedia* and *La Vita Nuova* in the original. This is a small but growing archive.

Type: WWW
Address: http://www.crs4.it/HTML/ Literature.html
Region: Italy

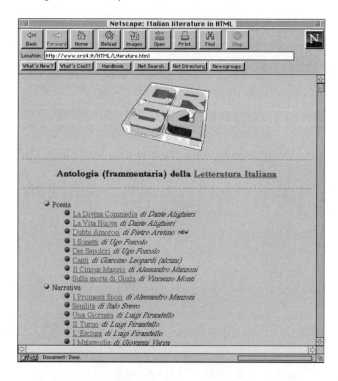

Appalachian State University: Literary Texts

HyperBooks from Homer, Plato, Kant, Descartes, Leibniz, Sun Tzu, Nietzche—all the big boys and their big books are listed here with links to their Gopher sites. Happy reading.

Type: WWW
Address: http://www.acs.appstate.edu/ ~griffinw/lit_texts.html
Region: World

Arachne: A Great Books Server

This site is dedicated to discussing the Great Books of Western Civilization online, from the Greek Classics and the Hindu Vedas to modern and scientific works. It also has information about this kind of classical, intensive liberal-arts education. It's a new effort that will no doubt bear interesting fruit.

Type: WWW

Address: **http://altair.stmarys-ca.edu:70/
           0/studwork/integral/integral.html**

Region: World

Banned Books Online

This page has excerpts and background on books banned around the world. It's an illustrious list, including Chaucer, Voltaire, and Walt Whitman. There's a lot here—you'll want to add this site to your Web browser's bookmarks and keep coming back.

Type: WWW

Address: **http://www.cs.cmu.edu/Web/
           People/spok/banned-books.html**

Region: World

Biblioteca Virtual de Literatura

The home page is available in English or Portuguese, but the archive itself is a collection of texts in Portuguese, most of them from Brazil. You can search it using WAIS as well from here.

Type: WWW

Address: **http://www.cr-sp.rnp.br/
           literatura/index.html**

Region: Brazil

Book Publishers and Retailers On-line

I had one of the first bookstores to go online, and now it's gone—but there are oh so many more now. This page has links to dozens in every category, from alternative to scientific.

Type: WWW

Address: **http://thule.mt.cs.cmu.edu:8001/
           bookstores**

Region: World

Caribbean Literature Online

Two nonfiction books are all that's here for now, hopefully with more to come.

Type: WWW

Address: **http://www.mrl.uiuc.edu/~stuart/
           car3.html**

Region: Caribbean

Chiba University, Japan

Everything here is in Japanese. It's an online archive of Japanese literature.

Type: WWW

Address: **http://www.ll.chiba-u.ac.jp/**

Region: Japan

Contes per a Extraterrestres

This e-zine is devoted to short stories and related matters, such as reviews and literary features. The text is written in Catalan, Spanish, and English.

Type: WWW

Address: **http://www.uji.es/CPE/**

Type: E-mail

Address: **extraterrestres@guest.uji.es**

Region: Spain

The CURIA Project

This digitization project is bringing medieval Irish texts online, with a search feature and accompanying documents. They are in Gaelic and other ancient and modern languages of Ireland.

Type: WWW
Address: http://curia.ucc.ie/curia/ menu.html
Type: FTP
Address: curia.ucc.ie/pub/curia/
Region: Ireland

Digital Freedom Net

An archive of excerpts from banned books worldwide, including currently embattled titles from Pakistan and Egypt, is available here.

Type: Gopher
Address: gopher.iia.org/11/Banned
Region: World

Directory of Book-Related Usenet Groups

They're all here, from the mainstream rec.arts.books to the fawning alt.fan.rush.limbaugh.

Type: WWW
Address: http://sunsite.unc.edu/ibic/ IBIC-Newsgroups.html
Region: World

Electronic Text Centres, Text Archives, and Literature

This English page is a good starting point for finding books, especially if you are searching for a particular author or title. It has a list of search mechanisms hotlinked in, plus many basic resources.

Type: WWW
Address: http://sable.ox.ac.uk/ departments/humanities/ele.html
Region: England, World

The English Server

The English Server is run by a cooperative that has been publishing texts to the Internet since 1990. You can read about the server, browse new items, use FTP and Gopher archives, attend meetings or classes on the English Server conference line, search for a word or phrase, or send comments and contributions to the editors. You can also read about the Web and browse other CMU servers or collections worldwide by topic or location. Its collection includes a huge list of classic books and shorter literary works.

Type: WWW
Address: http://english-www.hss.cmu.edu/
Type: Gopher
Address: 128.2.19.107/
Type: FTP
Address: 128.2.19.107/
Region: World

EROFILE: Electronic Reviews of French and Italian Literary Essays

EROFILE disseminates solicited and unsolicited reviews of works of interest to scholars in the fields of French and Italian studies, and welcomes submissions and proposals for reviews from qualified individuals. It also provides an open forum for comments on previously published reviews.

Type: Gopher
Address: 155.47.1.127/1D-1%3a1530% 3aEroFile
Region: France, Italy

French Lit 101

Classic French literary selections from Rousseau, Balzac, Moliére and more are available here, in French. It's a very nice little online library.

Type: WWW

Address: http://web.cnam.fr/ABU/ principal/bibABU.html

Region: France

The Future Fantasy Bookstore

Says *Wave* magazine, the *Wired* of Holland: "Spijtig genoeg is het nog niet mogelik om de boeken on-line te bestsellen." Yup. English-speaking Netizens just know that this is a great place to find out about the latest science fiction and fantasy titles, as well as hard-to-find collectables in that genre.

Type: WWW

Address: http://www.commerce.digital .com:80/palo-alto/FutureFantasy /home.html

Region: U.S., World

The German Collection at UVA

Here's a bunch of books by Germans, or in German: Kafka, Wittgenstein, and the ever-popular "Various Authors."

Type: WWW

Address: http://etext.lib.virginia.edu/ german.browse.html

Region: Germany

German Stories

Here's where to find *Rumpelstilzchen* and *Der Froschkönig (The Frog King)* by the Brothers Grimm, as well as works by Heinrich Hoffmann and Wilhem Busch. Did you know that Mark Twain translated *Der Struwwelpeter* into English? You can read both the German and English versions right here.

Type: WWW

Address: http://www.fln.vcu.edu/ menu.html

Region: Germany

JATE University Library Special Collections

Hungarian literature: the impressive reading room of old books on the first floor stores a very valuable part of the University Library. The collection consists of books ranging from sixteenth century Hungarian texts to eighteenth- or nineteenth-century books published in, or relating to, Hungary. There's also a good selection of non-Hungarian Baroque literature. Takes awhile to download, but where else are you going to go for sixteenth-century Hungarian literature online?

Type: WWW

Address: http://www.bibl.u-szeged.hu/ bibl/specials.html

Region: Hungary

Kurdish Literature

Kurdish literature and poetry can be found here, much of it political.

Type: WWW

Address: http://nucst11.neep.wisc.edu/

Region: Turkey, Iraq, Iran

Library Information Servers via WWW

It's Libweb—and you wouldn't want your own library to be left off this list. My favorites are the international listings (of course). You can start here and go to the dustiest, dankest library on any of the continents.

Type: WWW

Address: http://www.lib.washington.edu/ ~tdowling/libweb.html

Region: World

Literary Kicks

As American as a beat-up Chevy, this one. It's a Web page and associated archive devoted to the poetry and literature of the Beat Generation: Kerouac, Ginsberg, Snyder, and so on. My only question: Where are diPrima and the other Beat women?

Type: WWW
Address: http://www.charm.net/ ~brooklyn/LitKicks.html
Region: U.S.

Literature Peruana

You'll find Peruvian literature here, in Spanish. There's a very large selection from the province of Pacasmayo, but the entire spectrum of modern and older Peruvian writing is covered here.

Type: WWW
Address: http://tfnet.ils.unc.edu/~felipe/
Region: Peru

Literature and Writing Resources on WWW

Choix d'Éditeur

For the aspiring writer and those especially interested in how hypertext could change literature, this is the place. Lots of links to literature ancient and modern, conventional and unusual, including surrealist writing, literary journals, writer's groups and resources, e-text collections, and much more.

Type: WWW
Address: http://www.itp.berkeley.edu/ ~david/LitITP.html
Region: World

Literaturo en Esperanto

This is an archive of writings in the international language Esperanto.

Type: FTP
Address: ftp.netcom.com/pub/do/donh/ literaturo.html
Region: World

Loompanics Unlimited

Not "great books," but weird books, banned books, and fun books can be found here. Loompanics's catalog of offbeat titles on such topics as dirty tricks and revenge, starting your own independant island nation, James Bond-style weaponry, and wacky home businesses like worm farming for fun and profit is an underground classic in its own right. The entire catalog is available as a text file at this Gopher, but they take orders by phone or mail only. Readers with an interest in computer security might want to check out one of the company's most recent releases, the uncharacteristically large and glossy-covered *Secrets of a Superhacker*. They ship worldwide.

Type: Gopher
Address: gopher.well.sf.ca.us/00/ Business/catalog.asc
Region: U.S.

NativeLit-L (Native American Literature)

This is a place for the discussion of Native American Literature. For the purposes of this list, "native" refers to autochthonous peoples of the North Americas (the U.S., Canada, and Mexico) and neighboring islands, including Hawaii. Discussions in this list are open to any aspect of native literature. While different points of view are always welcome, flamers will be deleted from the subscription list without notice.

Type: Mailing list
Address: listserv@cornell.edu
**Send e-mail message with body: SUBSCRIBE
             NativeLit-L <Firstname Lastname>**
**Contact: idoy@crux2.cit.cornell.edu
             (Michael Wilson)**
Region: U.S.

El Nocturno

Mauricio-José Schwarz—better known as "El Nocturno," the "All-Nighter"—has been writing for over 20 years, mainly in the areas of science fiction, horror, crime fiction, and journalism, as well as being a translator, consultant, and creative writer. His work as a journalist has appeared in the most important Mexican newspapers, including *Excélsior*, *El Universal*, and *Reforma*. He has received several awards, including the Mexican "Puebla" prize. Find out more about Schwarz and his work on this, his very own home page.

Type: WWW
**Address: http://www.spin.com.mx/
            usuarios/mschwarz/nocturno.html**
Region: Mexico

The On-line Books Page

This Web page can take you to hundreds of books stored online as digital files, in many languages.

Type: WWW
**Address: http://www.cs.cmu.edu/afs/cs/
            misc/mosaic/common/omega/
            Web/books.html**
Region: World

ORTRAD-L

ORTRAD-L is an e-mail discussion list dealing with the topic of oral traditions in literature, culture, and history. This includes the world's living oral traditions, as well as literature rooted in ancient oral traditions such as *The Iliad*, *The Odyssey*, *Beowulf*, and the Bible.

Type: Mailing list
**Addresses: listserv@mizzou1.missouri.edu
             listserv@mizzou1.bitnet**
**Send e-mail message with blank Subject
             line and one-line body: subscribe
             ORTRAD-L <Firstname Lastname>**
Region: World

Persian Literature

This page includes biographies, reviews of recent book from or about Iran, and poetry. I'm told that Khomeini himself was known as quite a racy poet in his earlier years, but I'll bet that none of his youthful work will be found here!

Type: WWW
**Address: http://tehran.stanford.edu/
            Literature/literature.html**
Region: Iran

The Poetry and Prose of Maria Gummeson

This contemporary Swedish writer's work combines poetic, lyrical language with modern topics like technology. It's very original and critically acclaimed. In Swedish.

Type: WWW
**Address: http://www.luth.se/depts/lib/
            poetry/gummesson.html**
Region: Sweden

Prasowska

This is an electronic journal of modern Polish poetry and literature.

Type: WWW
Address: **http://www.uci.agh.edu.pl/pub/e-press/prasowka/**
Region: Poland

The Project Gutenberg E-Text Home Page

The premise on which Michael Hart based Project Gutenberg was that anything that can be entered into a computer can be reproduced indefinitely, which he called the concept of Replicator Technology. In other words, once a book or any other item (including pictures, sounds, and even 3-D items) has been stored in a computer, then any number of copies can and will be available. Everyone in the world can have a copy of the hundreds of classic, noncopyrighted books that have been lovingly typed in by their fans as part of this project, which never fails to remind me of the classic Ray Bradbury story *Fahrenheit 451*.

Type: WWW
Address: **http://jg.cso.uiuc.edu/PG/welcome.html**
Region: World

Project Runeburg

Project Runeberg, founded in December 1992, is an open and voluntary initiative to create and collect free electronic editions of classic Nordic literature and art. The Project's site also features a pack of links and information about related mailing lists, FTP sites, Gopher sites, and other electronic text projects.

Type: WWW
Address: **http://www.lysator.liu.se/runeberg/**
Region: Sweden, Norway, Finland

rec.arts.books

This group discusses books of all genres, and the publishing industry. Its FAQs are available through the Web page.

Type: Usenet newsgroup
Address: **rec.arts.books**
Type: WWW
Address: **http://www.io.com/user/tittle/books/homepage.html**
Region: World

rec.arts.books.reviews

This is a moderated forum for book reviews.

Type: Usenet newsgroup
Address: **rec.arts.books.reviews**
Region: World

The Shiki Internet Haiku Salon

Wow, what fun—and I don't even like poetry very much. But this site may get me to like haiku. Its layout is simple yet elegant, with cool graphics and an eye for tasteful placement. It's inspired by Shiki Masaoka, a haiku poet born in Matsuyama in 1867. Shiki is well known in Japan for introducing a new style of haiku, a short poetic form, and for enhancing the arts.

Type: WWW
Address: **http://mikan.cc.matsuyama-u.ac.jp:80/~shiki/**
Region: Japan

Technical University of Darmstadt: Literature

A very simple and understated page (as the one-word name implies), this one has links to libraries and "New Literature" preprints from around the world.

Type: WWW
Address: **http://www.physik.th-darmstadt.de/htdocs/literatur.html**
Region: Germany

Turkish Poetry Home Page

This is an attempt to put together Turkish poems posted in various places over a period of time. It may seem obscure now, but soon everyone will have a link to the Turkish Poetry Home Page!

Type: WWW
Address: http://www.cs.umd.edu/~sibel/ poetry/poetry.html
Region: Turkey

University of Texas: Literature

This project is an attempt to digitize Russian and American literature, as is being done with the Gutenberg project and similar efforts. The server may also become the home of an electronic publication of contemporary literature. For now, they have some good ideas and some classics by Tolstoy and Dostoevsky.

Type: WWW
Address: http://solar.rtd.utk.edu/friends/ literature/literature.html
Region: Russia

The Vatican Library: Books for Popes and Scholars

I don't know how many Popes there are out there, but they'd better bring their library card when they come. If you're just a scholar like me, however, this site doesn't offer links to great works of literature. It is designed as part of a virtual tour of the Vatican. Still, it's nice to be able to pop in for a bit and look around in a fabulous library that most of us can never see in reality.

Type: WWW
Address: http://sunsite.unc.edu/expo/ vatican.exhibit/exhibit/a-vatican_ lib/Vatican_lib.html
Region: Italy

WWW Virtual Library: Literature

Find all sorts of bookish links here, including reviews of current bestsellers and pointers to archives of ancient volumes turned into electronic text. It includes information about book awards and competitions, bookstores, and more.

Type: WWW
Address: http://sunsite.unc.edu/ibic/ IBIC-homepage.html
Region: World

The Zhaoming Wenxuan Project

The Zhaoming Wenxuan is the oldest extant "Collection of Refined Literature" in China. No other culture in the world was able to preserve such a vast selection of different poetic and prosaic writing forms. This project intends to convert the Lishan Commentary edition (woodprint) into computer-readable format. (I'm carving this in a tree now, son, but some day it will be digital.)

Type: WWW
Address: http://www.pristine.com.tw/ wenxuan/wx01.html
Region: China

MUDS AND MORE: ONLINE INTERNATIONAL COMMUNITIES
See also Games and Gambling page 293

MUD is variously defined as Multi-User Dungeon or Multi-User Dimension. It's the simplest type of interactive online game. New ideas about these games have spawned many variations, including MOOs (MUD, Object Oriented) and MUSEs (Multi-User Simulated [or Simulation] Environment), and MUSHes (Multi-User Shared Hallucination). MU* is a term commonly used to refer to all of these and any similar systems. Games are further defined by the type of software used to build them, and the theme of the game itself.

If you have ever played a wargame or role-playing game, such as Dungeons & Dragons, think about playing such games in a virtual environment and you'll have a good grasp of what a MUD is. If you haven't, think of signing on to a computer over the Internet as a virtual representation of yourself—either as literally "yourself" or as an alternate personality you've dreamed up. This online character, which is sometimes called an *avatar*, can move around in a text and/or graphics-based environment created by others, talk to other avatars, fight, have pie fights, play tricks, and eventually, with a bit of programming expertise and the right software, extend the environment. Your avatar might build a device, such as a record player that only plays "Clair de la Lune" off key; or a tiki bar room; or an entire new world to play in.

These interactive role-playing games are highly addictive. In fact, they're banned from the public Internet in Australia (although some exist there on private servers—and perhaps hidden away on the public side as well). People have married who met through MUDs, in cyberspace-only weddings or real ones. Others have feuded violently, or simply made new friends.

Popular themes include warfare, original space and science fiction situations, "furry" games populated by animals with human characteristics, games based on various fantasy or science fiction books, supernatural plotlines with vampires or magicians, and historic recreations, such as Vikings in Norway or the Middle Ages in France.

In identifying the "location" of these games I have included the nation where the game is set wherever possible, as well as the location of the server and/or most of the players.

alt.mud

Subscribe to the alt.mud newsgroup for a rapid introduction to the world of MUDs. There are several other newsgroups in the alt.mud hierarchy, including alt.mud.german for German-language games.

Type: Usenet newsgroup
Address: alt.mud
Region: World

alt.sex.bestiality

Not what you think: This newsgroup is a bit of a joke, most frequently used by FurryMuck fans. After all, they are playing beasties, and I'm afraid there is an awful lot of sex in the Furry world…. It's archived at the Web site.

Type: Usenet newsgroup
Address: alt.sex.bestiality
Type: WWW
**Address: http://web.syr.edu/~pjkappes/
          zoolunch.txt**
Region: World

Amberyl's Almost-Complete List of MUSHes

This long list lets you know what's going on in the world of MUSHes and related game environments. It includes descriptions of current MUSHes (and doesn't disregard the controversies and problems in some of them, either). If you are interested in the many MUSHes based on Anne McCaffrey's *Dragonriders of Pern* books, this list has several to choose from—

along with medieval, vampire, science fiction, and other themes.

Type: WWW
Address: http://www.cis.upenn.edu/~lwl/ muds.html
Region: World

The Arctic MUD Centre

A pair of servers at this site run several MUDs, most with a "Northern" flair, including Midnight Sun and Northern Lights. See the Web page below for information and hot links to all of them.

Type: WWW
Address: http://mud.ludd.luth.se/
Region: Sweden

BioMOO

BioMOO is a virtual meeting place for professional biology researchers, and is connected to the Globewide Network Academy. The main physical part of the BioMOO is located at the BioInformatics Unit of the Weizmann Institute of Science in Israel. Here you can meet colleagues in biology studies and related fields from around the world for brainstorming sessions, colloquia and conferences, or just bio-chat. You need to register before you can participate—see the FAQ first for procedures and rules. It's available via the Web page below, as is a multimedia interface for the MOO.

Type: Telnet
Address: bioinfo.weizmann.ac.il 8888 (132.76.55.12 8888)
Type: WWW
Address: http://bioinfo.weizmann.ac.il:70 /1s/biomoo
Region: Israel, World

Bloodletting: Dublin by Night

This MUSH uses the StoryTeller system, but isn't too heavy on statistics and rules. It has vampires and other supernatural characters, and emphasizes a "realistic" approach to the city of Dublin, where the action occurs.

Type: Telnet
Address: piaget.psych.mun.ca 4991
Region: Ireland, World

Brazilian Dreams MUCK

This "furry" MUCK has anthropomorphic animal characters cavorting in several interesting environments, including a Brazilian rainforest, the Aztec civilization of Tenochtitlan (modern Mexico City) around the year 1450 A.D., the Taoist/Confucian Eastern Realm, and an anything-goes "unthemed" area. Small and friendly, and a very enjoyable set of games.

Type: Telnet
Address: brazil.tbyte.com 8888, (198.211.131.13 8888)
Type: WWW
Address: http://cs.weber.edu/home/ holmbeck/brazil.html
Region: Brazil, World

ChristianMUSH

This is a social MUSH for Christians, rather than a "game" per se. Lots of conversation—more like an IRC channel than a MUD.

Type: Telnet
Address: cyberearth.mscl.msstate.edu 6250
Region: U.S., World

Conspiracy!

This MUSH has a psuedo-historical medieval theme, with activities set in the mythical European kingdom of Cardas.

Type: Telnet
Address: almond.enmu.edu 1066
Type: WWW
Address: http://www.uunet.ca/~kris/ cons.html
Region: Canada, World

CSUWEB MUDlist

This may be the most frequently updated list of MUDs, MUSHes, and even some "chat spaces" online. It divides the games according to the game system used (diku, mare, and so forth) and has hot links to the Telnet nodes where the games take place. It includes many MUDs set or located outside the U.S., including some conducted in German.

Type: WWW
Address: http://csugrad.cs.vt.edu/soc/ dorans.html
Region: World

Daedalus MOO

This university-run MOO is part of the Online Writery project, and is open to all writers: student, amateur, or professional. It's fun and possibly even educational to meet up with other writers here, where you can discuss writing, computer tools for writing, Internet resources for writers, and more.

Type: Telnet
Address: logos.daedalus.com 7777
Type: WWW
Address: http://www.missouri.edu/ ~wleric/writery.html
Region: U.S., World

Danse Macabre

This World of Darkness MUSH is set in Paris, in 1356 A.D. Because it's intended to be historically accurate, Society of Creative Anachronism types and medievalists will find it especially fun. The affiliated Web site is an excellent compendium of information on the medieval era. This game uses the White Wolf system, which requires dice; you might want to check in with the Web page for some instruction before Telnetting in if you're not familiar with this gaming method.

Type: Telnet
Address: OMEGA.ACUSD.EDU 9999 (192.195.155.207 9999)
Type: WWW
Address: http://where.com/Danse/
Region: France, World

Das MorgenGrauen

This German-language MUD features a bar, a sauna, elves, and other elements of a Germanic fantasy environment.

Type: Telnet
Address: mud.uni-muenster.de 4711
Type: WWW
Address: http://www.cis.upenn.edu/~lwl/ mhome.html
Region: Germany

Diversity University

This is a MOO for educators around the world. It uses the metaphor of a university campus, and offerings have included lectures and historical simulation projects, along with the presentation of research.

Type: Telnet
Address: moo.du.org 8888

Type: WWW
**Address: http://148.100.176.70/1/
duwww.htm**
Region: World

ElendorMush Home Page

ElendorMush is the premiere J.R.R. Tolkien–based MUSH (yes, there are others), with over 500 users and almost 3,500 rooms. Founded in March 1993, Elendor enjoys a wide range of players from all backgrounds and a well-designed world. Its setting is ten years before the events chronicled in Tolkien's *Lord of the Rings* trilogy, so the outcome is uncertain. Maybe *you* will find the Ring and create a new myth here.

Type: Telnet
Address: dana.ucc.nau.edu 1892
Type: WWW
**Address: http://where.com/Elendor/
Welcome.html**
Region: World

Encyclopedia of MU*s

This "encyclopedia" has many MUD terms nicely defined. However, the odd layout makes it difficult to read, even on a computer with a large screen.

Type: WWW
**Address: http://weber.u.washington.edu/
mcdaniel/mud/dict.html**
Region: World

EnsemMUD

This MUD, based in France, is an adventure-and-battle game with several different environments to choose from. Characters include ninjas, samurai, Highland warriors, knights in armor, and more.

Type: Telnet
Address: oldensun.imag.fr 4000
Type: WWW
**Address: http://www.neurosci.tufts.edu/
~rlee1/ensem.html**
Region: France, World

Eon

An experiment in virtual education, Eon is a MOO run by Mesa Community College. Credit and non-credit courses are available online here. Supporting documents and logs can be seen at the Web, Gopher, and FTP sites below.

Type: Telnet
Address: mcmuse.mc.maricopa.edu 23
Type: WWW
Address: http://mcmuse.mc.maricopa.edu/
Type: Gopher/FTP
Address: mcmuse.mc.maricopa.edu
Region: U.S.

FringeWeb: Virtual Edinburgh

Created with the LambdaMOO software, Virtual Edinburgh is a MOO for the annual "Edinburgh Fringe" arts festival.

Type: Telnet
Address: pfeiffer.ues.unipalm.co.uk 7777
Type: WWW
**Address: http://www.gold.net/lynx/
fringe/moo/moo.html**
Region: Scotland

Furry Chat

The newsgroup alt.fan.furry is for those with a thing for anthropomorphic critters in all their permutations: comic-book and cartoon characters, for example, or furry characters used in role-playing games. The alt.fan.furry.muck newsgroup is more specifically for role-playing game aficionados who like the "furry" games. These lists have a surprising amount of traffic. The Web page includes a brief FAQ for alt.fan.furry.

Type: Usenet newsgroups
Addresses: alt.fan.furry
           alt.fan.furry.muck
Type: WWW
Address: http://www.lib.ox.ac.uk/ internet/news/faq/archive/ furry.faq.html
Region: World

Furry MUCK

This is the oldest and biggest of the "furry" games. The Web page serves as a good introduction, while the FTP archive is a source for guides (including a beginner's guide), and FAQs.

Type: Telnet
Address: sncils.snc.edu 8888 (138.74.0.10 8888)
Type: WWW
Address: http://www.furry.com/
Type: FTP
Address: avatar.snc.edu/pub/furry/mud/ furrymuck/
Region: World

Furry MU*s

Descriptions of various "furry" MUCKs and MUSHes can be found here, some of them quite elaborate. Links to the games themselves are included, as are links to Web pages and FTP archives for the games listed.

Type: WWW
Address: http://web.syr.edu/~pjkappes/ furry/
Region: England, World

GarouMUSH

This MUSH is based on a game from White Wolf, Werewolf: The Apocalypse. The use of dice in this game is rare; it relies more on social interaction and role-playing to move the story along. A player's guide is available at the Web and FTP sites below.

Type: Telnet
Address: cesium.clock.org 7000
Type: WWW
Address: http://www.best.com/~hine/ primer.html
Type: FTP
Address: ftp.best.com/pub/hine/ garoumush.guide.txt
Region: World

GlobalMUSH

A MUSH with a global "theme," where almost anything goes. Create worlds that are international in scope—perhaps even in the same room!

Type: Telnet
Address: lancelot.cif.rochester.edu 4201
Region: World

Guardians MUSH

Guardians MUSH is a themed role-play environment with four time periods and settings to choose from: post-Civil War Montana, a medieval European port town, a small Roman city in 8 B.C., or a mining and space-exploration ship in the mid-2020s. A player's guide is available via the Web site.

Type: Telnet
Address: jitter.rahul.net 4205
Type: WWW
Address: http://www.missouri.edu/ ~jourkma/guardians/ guardians.html
Region: U.S., Italy, France, Outer Space

Heroes of the Lance

Created in Singapore but conducted in English, this MUD is a fantasy adventure game, complete with fierce dragons and champions who slay them bare-handed.

Type: Telnet
Address: mud.technet.sg 4040
Region: Singapore, World

HyperMUDs

If you're already wondering how advanced MUDs could get, read this paper about marrying Telnet-based MUD technology to World Wide Web sounds and visuals. The author proposes that this combination will not only make game-playing online more fun, it could have interesting commercial implications. For example, you could create a virtual store where potential customers could pick up, examine, and ask questions about the merchandise, with salespeople on hand to help.

Type: WWW
**Address: http://wwwseti.cs.utwente.nl/
~stan/HMUD/HyperMUD.html**
Region: Netherlands

Imbris MUSH

This is a German-language MUSH with a conversational, social tone.

Type: Telnet
Address: sun1.lrz-muenchen.de 6250
Region: Germany

An Introduction to MU*s

This page has links to lots of documents interesting to potential MU* programmers.

Type: WWW
**Address: http://www.vuw.ac.nz/who/
Jamie.Norrish/mud/mud.html**
Region: World

LambdaMOO

LambdaMOO is a MOO that encourages exploration and extension of the environment. It has one of the most unusual assemblages of characters online. It's also where the infamous and widely reported "cyber-rape" occurred. Learn more from a *Village Voice* article linked to the Web page.

Type: Telnet
Address: lambda.xerox.com 8888
Type: WWW
**Address: http://www.lightside.com/
SpecialInterest/Places/
LambdaMOODesc.html**
Region: U.S., World

MC-MUD

This fantasy MUD's environment is inspired by the first Roman empire. It's conducted in Italian.

Type: Telnet
Address: mclmud.mclink.it 4000
Type: WWW
Address: http://www.mclink.it/gioco1.htm
Region: Italy

MediaMOO

This MOO is connected to the famous Media Lab at MIT, and includes both "fun" parts and sections that are used as an online adjunct to scientific and academic conferences.

Type: Telnet
Address: purple-crayon.media.mit.edu
Region: U.S.

Miami MOO

This educational MOO is a collaborative project from Miami University in Ohio that brings together research from the school's Classics, Education, Educational Psychology, Art, and Architecture departments and students and faculty from its Classics, Archaeology, English, and History departments (along with other callers). Two pilot environments are under construction for learners to explore: Greek and Roman sanctuaries, and a South Asian pilgrimage experience that includes India, Nepal, and nearby regions. You can participate via Telnet or WWW.

Type: Telnet
Address: moo.cas.muohio.edu 7777
Type: WWW
**Address: http://moo.cas.muohio.edu/
          ~moo/**
Type: FTP
Address: moo.cas.muohio.edu/pub/moo/
Region: U.S., Italy, India, Nepal, Asia

MOO: A Collaborative Networked Project Forum

This site brings together a number of MOO-related links, including MOO software, links to home pages, and the results of a recent InfoSeek search on "MOO" that will provide you with links to the latest MOOs and MOO information.

Type: WWW
**Address: http://topaz.sensor.com/work/
          lang/moo/index.html**
Region: World

MOO/MU* Document Library

This library is a catch-all for information on MOO/MU*s—with everything from how-to manuals to dissertations.

Type: WWW
**Address: http://lucien.berkeley.edu/
          moo.html**
Region: World

The MUD Archive

Documents here on the history of MUDs have this to say: "MUD software is still evolving. Computer interaction, where identities are fluid and the division between word and deed is nonexistent, presents new and unique problems that may never be solved." This page gives a nice historical perspective on MUDs. It's only as accurate as the authors cited, and gives fair warning on offensive language or dreadful spelling.

Type: WWW
**Address: http://www.ccs.neu.edu/home/
          lpb/muddex.html**
Region: World

MUD Home Page Links

This is a collection of links to MUD home pages, classified by type and color-coded.

Type: WWW
**Address: http://www.cis.upenn.edu/~lwl/
          mhome.html**
Region: World

MUD Info

A veritable glossary of MUDdom, this site has links to MU*s of various sorts, as well as many useful files on subjects like "Approaches to Handling Deviant Behavior in Virtual Communities" and "Serious Uses of MUDs."

Type: WWW
**Address: http://lydia.bradley.edu/
          interlabs/391/mud.html**
Region: World

The MUD Resource Collection

This page is a list of links to many useful sources of MUD information. There is a particular emphasis on MUSHes, along with plenty of general information.

Type: WWW

Address: http://www.cis.upenn.edu/~lwl/ mudinfo.html

Region: World

MUDs at Lysator

Several MUDs are run off this Swedish university server, including Svenskmud, the world's first Swedish-language MUD.

Type: WWW

Address: http://www.lysator.liu.se:7500/ mud/main.html

Region: Sweden

MUD Stuff

This FTP archive is the place to look for MUD client software, FAQs, and other files related to MUDding and MUCKing about.

Type: FTP

Address: ftp.math.okstate.edu/pub/muds/

Region: World

Multi-User Dungeons (MUDs)

This page has MUD FAQs, links to MOOs and to other MUD pages, MUD lists, and MUD newsgroups on Usenet, making it a nice place to start.

Type: WWW

Address: http://draco.centerline.com:8080/ ~franl/mud.html

Region: World

NarniaGolden

This site is based on C.S. Lewis' *Chronicles of Narnia* novels, and is a bit strict about the plot rules, players say. Some "desert" areas of this MUSH have an Arabian theme.

Type: Telnet

Address: dobest.lib.virginia.edu 6250 (128.143.166.52 6250)

Region: England, Middle East, World

Navigating MOOs

How-tos for MOOs are available at this pair of linked sites.

Type: WWW

Address: http://www.missouri.edu/ ~wleric/moohelp.html

Type: Gopher

Address: logos.daedalus.com/11/Alliance %20for%20Computers%20and %20Writing/NETORIC

Region: World

Ragnarok

This MUD is a medieval Nordic fantasy, with lots of magic and supernatural goings on along with battles.

Type: Telnet

Address: rag.com 2222

Type: WWW

Address: http://www.rag.com/

Region: Norway, World

RealTime MUSH

"RealTime" is an "alternative" radio show on the Canadian CBC network. This MUSH is a place for listeners to hang out and chat, mostly during the show.

Type: Telnet

Address: realtime.pci.on.ca 6125

Type: WWW

**Address: http://www.pci.on.ca/~dgilbert/
RealTime.html**

Region: Canada

rec.games.mud

This is the basic newsgroup in the rec.games hierarchy; there are many more, for administrators, players, and programmers. Subscribe to rec.games.mud or see the Web page to find the one that's right for your interests.

Type: Usenet newsgroup

Address: rec.games.mud

Type: WWW

**Address: http://www.yahoo.com/
Entertainment/Games/MUDs_
MUSHes_MUSEs_MOOs_etc_/
Usenet/**

Region: World

Requiem

This MUSH is a cyberpunkish future adventure with supernatural overtones. Mega-corporate vampire execs and monsters battle it out in chrome-and-glass canyons.

Type: WWW

**Address: http://www.best.com/~wyldefyr/
requiem.html**

Region: World

RiffRaff's Unofficial List of Diku MUD Home Pages

Diku MUDs are beloved by those who enjoy shoot 'em ups and war games. They tend to be fast-paced, battle-heavy adventure games for the testosterone-enhanced. This page has links to many such games worldwide.

Type: WWW

**Address: http://www.daimi.aau.dk/
~shadow/anothermud/
diku.homepage**

Region: World

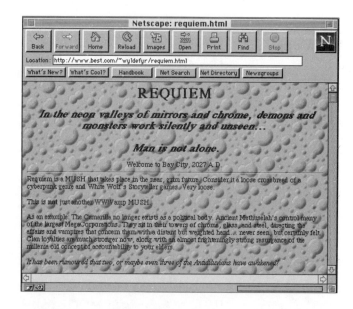

SeaMOO's World

SeaMOO is an education-oriented MOO, with the research emphasis on building online models of sea and space colonies. There are games and purely social interactions here also, though. The first thing you see is a smiling cow and the state of Hawaii. The next thing you see is the answer to the first question you probably have about this site (What is SeaMOO?). Overall, a very clean and happy place to MOO about.

Type: WWW
**Address: http://www.soc.hawaii.edu/con/
           com/misc/SeaMOO.html#Wat**
Region: U.S.

Sociopolitical Ramifications

This "furry" game is a spin-off from FurryMUCK.
The home page has information about "SPR" itself,
as well as links to six more German MUDs.
Type: Telnet
**Address: tigerden.com 4711
           (198.30.162.2 4711)**
Type: WWW
**Address: http://www.uni-karlsruhe.de/
           ~ukjp/spr.html**
Region: Germany, World

Spirit of Anime MUCK

If you're an anime (Japanese animation) fan, you
might get a kick out of this MUCK. Everyone here is
an anime character.
Type: Telnet
Address: spirit.com.au anime
Type: WWW
**Address: http://spirit.com.au/spiritmuck/
           anime.html**
Region: Australia, Japan

The Sprawl

This site includes many interlocking worlds, which are
constantly being extended by the players. You might
see a live Aerosmith concert in the arena, visit a brothel, or join the French Club. It's a large and fairly tight-
knit community here, with its own news media.
Type: WWW
Address: http://sensemedia.net/sprawl
Region: World

Stonia

In English and Estonian, this is a Tolkienesque fantasy,
adventure, and war game.
Type: WWW
Address: http://www.cs.ut.ee/mud/
Region: Estonia, World

Types of MUDs

This site gives a quick description of the various
types of MUDs and other online role-playing games.
Type: WWW
**Address: http://csugrad.cs.vt.edu/soc/
           mud_types.html**
Region: World

Varjuorg

This MUD, conducted in Estonian, is among the few
MUDs in Eastern Europe.
Type: Telnet
Address: kaktus.edu.ee 5555
Type: WWW
Address: http://www.edu.ee/explorer.html
Region: Estonia

VikingMUD

This MUD tends more toward the duel-to-the-death
sort of plotline, with a population of mighty Vikings
and Norse gods.
Type: Telnet
**Address: viking.pvv.unit.no 2001
           (129.241.190.14 2001)**
Type: WWW
Address: http://www.pvv.unit.no/viking/
Region: Norway

WaxWeb

This MOO/Web combo is a hypertext version of the 1991 independent film *WAX, or the Discovery of Television among the Bees*. Callers can add interactively to the story.

Type: WWW
Address: http://bug.village.virginia.edu/
Region: U.S., World

WriteMUSH

A MUSH for the teaching of writing. Documentation is available from its FTP archive.

Type: Telnet
Address: palmer.sacc.colostate.edu 6250
Type: FTP
Address: ftp.netcom.com/pub/marcia
Region: U.S., World

Yahoo's Real Big Page on MU*s

Loads of links to the games and to related sites.

Type: WWW
**Address: http://www.yahoo.com/
           Entertainment/Games/MUDs__
           MUSHes__MUSEs__MOOs__etc__**
Region: World

ZenMOO—The Meditation Hall

The Buddha Nature says, "Gopher is not the path to enlightenment." The Buddha Nature says, "IRC is not the path to enlightenment." Perhaps the virtual meditation hall in this MOO is. Or perhaps not.

Type: Telnet
Address: cheshire.oxy.edu 7777
Type: FTP
Address: pc4.math.oxy.edu/html/pc4.html
Region: Japan, World

See also Fandom International page 250

Talking about music is fun, and the set of Usenet newsgroups for that purpose is large and growing daily. Under the alt.music prefix, they stretch from alt.music.enya to alt.rock-n-roll.metal, and the list under the rec.music prefix is similarly long. But even better is hearing music, which you can do through many of the sites in this section; making music, which you can get more resources to do online; and seeing music played live, which you can now also do on the Internet as some sites sponsor online concerts.

3 Mustapha 3 World Headquarters

This is the Web site for 3 Mustapha 3, an English band with great chops, Middle-Eastern stylings, and an excellent sense of humor. Better yet, this page has links to all kinds of other world-music pages and archives. From here, you can go "forward in all directions," as their motto says.

Type: WWW
**Address: http://www.nwu.edu/music/
           3m3/**
Region: England, World

alt.music.world

This newsgroup is for discussing mostly traditional music from around the globe, and for discussing groups that incorporate these sounds into more modern hybrids.

Type: Usenet newsgroup
Address: alt.music.world
Region: World

Anime CD List

Songs are a big part of many anime episodes (see the "Comics and Cartoons" section to find out more about anime), and the songs are released on CD in Japan. This is a seemingly exhaustive list of anime CDs.

Type: Gopher
Address: wiretap.spies.com/00/Library/ Media/Anime/anime.cd
Region: Japan

Asian Pops Information

Here you can find all the latest on Asia's hottest pop superstars, including photos, announcements of upcoming records and tours, CD reviews, and links to other pop-music pages in Japan. In English or Japanese.

Type: WWW
Address: http://frig.mt.cs.keio.ac.jp/ person/hosokawa/ asian_pops_e.html
Region: Japan, Hong Kong, Taiwan

The Bhangra Page

Who would have thought that discos would be throbbing to the beat of Bhangra, a type of Punjabi dance music? But they are, now that it has fused with reggae rhythms and the danceable rhythms of disco, techno, house, rap, and more. It's hot stuff. Check out the list of radio shows, records, TV shows, and sound samples here.

Type: WWW
Address: http://yucc.yorku.ca/home/ sanraj/bhangra.html
Region: India, World

Canadian Music Discussion

Canada has more to offer than Anne Murray and Québeçois folk tunes. Check in here to see what's on the air and on CD.

Type: Usenet newsgroup
Address: alt.music.canada
Region: Canada

Caribbean Music

Merengue, Salsa, Reggae, Calypso, Son, Boleros, Bachata, Perico Ripiao: There's lots of information here about the many styles of Caribbean and Latin music, in Spanish.

Type: WWW
Address: http://www.nando.net/prof/ caribe/Caribbean_Music.html
Region: Caribbean

Ceolas: Celtic Music on the Internet

This archive has links to pretty much everything having to do with Celtic music online—song lyrics, concert schedules, discographies, mailing lists, newsletters, and the online editions of popular folk magazines like *The Living Tradition*, *Dirty Linen*, *Folk Roots*, and *Hot Press*.

Type: WWW
Address: http://celtic.stanford.edu/ ceolas.html
Region: Ireland, Scotland, France, U.S., World

Chinese Music

Huge index to Chinese music, from the Beijing opera to pop. Includes audio files.

Type: WWW
Address: http://sunsite.unc.edu:80/pub/ multimedia/chinese-music/
Region: China

Classical Indian Music

FAQs on classical Indian music, including groups, styles, ragas, instruments, and schools.

Type: WWW

Address: **http://www.cis.ohio-state.edu/ ~sundar/rmic/**

Region: India

Countdown: An Online Opera

You can find and play back the opera *Countdown* here, a modern work by composer Christopher Yavelow with a post-nuclear theme and high-tech execution.

Type: WWW

Address: **http://www.xs4all.nl/~yavelow/ docs/CnDnIntro.html**

Region: U.S.

Cuban Music Page

Sound samples, song lyrics in Spanish and English, and audio files of actual station IDs and sign-offs from Cuban radio. Lots of information about enjoyable, high-intensity music that U.S. listeners are rarely able to hear due to the trade ban.

Type: WWW

Address: **http://itre.uncecs.edu/music/ cuban-music.html**

Region: Cuba

Digital Biscuit

"This is *DIGITAL BISCUIT* from Tokyo underground. Please bite and taste it. Low fat + digestive, electronic + healthful." This WWW e-zine covers the techno, house, and hip-hop scene in Tokyo, with some information on other parts of Japan as well.

Type: WWW

Address: **http://www.ces.kyutech.ac.jp/ student/JapanEdge/DIGIBI/ digibi.html**

Region: Japan

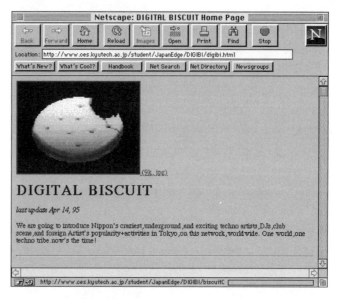

The Digital Tradition

You can download the Digital Tradition database of folk song lyrics here, for use on your own computer.

Type: FTP

Address: **parcftp.xerox.com/pub/music/ digital_tradition**

Region: World

EARLYM-L

This discussion group is a forum for exchanging news and views about medieval, Renaissance, and baroque music. The mailing list echoes the Usenet newsgroup.

Type: Usenet newsgroup

Address: **rec.music.early**

Type: Mailing list

Address: **earlym-l@aearn.bitnet**

Region: Europe, Middle East

The Eden Matrix: Music

The sponsor of these Web pages provides band profiles (including audio and sometimes video clips, plus graphics), concert information, and occasionally live online performances.

Type: WWW
Address: http://www.eden.com/music/ music.html
Region: World

Edinburgh Samba School Newsletter

This is a quarterly newsletter devoted to the music and culture of samba, to Brazilian carnival music, and to the activities of the Edinburgh Samba School.

Type: E-mail
Address: ekya07@castle.ed.ac.uk
Region: Brazil, Scotland

El Camino Silica

This multilingual, multinational site supports electronic music in the Americas. You can find information organized by country or group here, and there's lots of networking going on.

Type: WWW
Address: http://www-crca.ucsd.edu/ bobw/camino.html
Region: U.S., Mexico, Brazil, Argentina, Venezuela

EthnoFORUM/hypermedia

This is a new, World Wide Web-based, peer-reviewed journal about ethnomusicology. Includes articles, dissertation abstracts, multimedia offerings, and links to ethnomusicology resources on the Net.

Type: WWW
Address: http://umbc7.umbc.edu/~signell/ efhm/index.html
Region: World

Ethnomusicology Research Digest

This is a somewhat sparse e-journal following activities in the discipline of ethnomusicology for professionals and students. Issues are archived at the sites below, back to the beginnings of the journal in December 1989 and up to the present day.

Type: Mailing list
Address: ETHMUS-L
Type: WWW
Address: http://www.inform.umd.edu/ Educational_Resources/ ReadingRoom/Newsletters/ EthnoMusicology
Type: FTP
Address: ftp.uwp.edu/pub/music/folk/
Type: Gopher
Address: gopher.inform.umd.edu:70/11/ Educational_Resources/ ReadingRoom/Newsletters/ EthnoMusicology/Digest
Region: World

El Factoria del Ritmo

This is a fanzine about all sorts of music popular in Spain, including rock and roll, heavy metal, rap, flamenco, punk, and experimental arty stuff. In Spanish.

Type: WWW
Address: http://www1.uniovi.es/musica3/
Region: Spain

Folk Music Discussion

You can talk with other fans of folk music here.

Type: Usenet newsgroup
Address: rec.music.folk
Region: World

The Fractured Mirror

This fortnightly magazine is devoted to electronic "Head Music," ranging from surreal ambient excursions to thumping techno, and everything in between. Reviews, interviews, competitions, reader submissions, and more are featured.

Type: E-mail
Address: ambinet@vick.demon.co.uk
Type: Usenet newsgroup
Address: alt.music.techno
Type: WWW
**Address: http://www.demon.co.uk/drci/
           fractured/index.html**
Region: World

Gamelan and Indonesian Music

This is an excellent page on Indonesian music, including gamelan. Links to lyrics, plus information on popular singers and musicians are online here.

Type: WWW
**Address: http://www.umanitoba.ca/
           indonesian/music.html**
Region: Indonesia

Get Funky

You can talk here about all kinds of music that's got the funk: rhythm and blues, rap, soul, dance music, and more.

Type: Usenet newsgroup
Address: rec.music.funky
Region: World

HardC.O.R.E.

A monthly electronic magazine of hip-hop music and culture, HardC.O.R.E. includes links, rap lyrics, and sound files of the latest tunes from KBLK "online radio."

Type: E-mail
Address: listserv@vnet.net
**Send e-mail message with body: subscribe
            hardcore-l <Your E-mail Address>**
Type: WWW
**Address: http://library.uncc.edu/people/
            chris/**
Type: Gopher
Address: gopher.etext.org:Zines/HardCORE
Type: FTP
**Address: ftp.etext.org:70/11/pub/Zines/
            HardCORE/**
Region: U.S., World

The Harmony List

This page is a clearinghouse for links to artist-specific sites. There are over 100 bands listed, including both extremely obscure groups and those on top of the pop, rock, easy listening, urban, and dance charts. The list includes mostly U.S., Australian, and European groups or solo artists.

Type: WWW
**Address: http://orpheus.ucsd.edu/
            webmaster/artists.html**
Region: World

HIBI-R

HIBI-R is a noisy cover band from Japan that three guys have created as a hobby. The photos here are funny, and so is the music.

Type: WWW
**Address: http://pckiso3.cs.shinshu-u.ac.jp/
            hobby/music/index-e.html**
Region: Japan

HyperReal

The online home of ravers and techno/ambient music, HyperReal is a visual treat and a window into a world that most of us can't stay up late enough to see in person. It includes links to all sorts of related music archives, a Global Rave Calendar, do-it-yourself information, lots of publications, drugs information, and rave reviews. The calendar is browseable and includes the lowdown on raves from an interracial thang in South Africa to a wild party in Denver, Colorado, some with full-color online reproductions of those neat rave circulars that are used as surreptitious street ads.

Type: WWW
Address: http://hyperreal.com/
Region: World

The Indie-List Digest

This twice-weekly digest of writing related to the world of independent music (that is, stuff generally not found on major labels or commercial radio) includes record reviews, show reviews, and commentary. It's archived at the FTP and WWW sites.

Type: E-mail
Address: grumpy@access.digex.net
Type: FTP
Address: ftp.uwp.edu:/music/lists/indie/
Type: WWW
**Address: http://www.wit.com:/mirrors/
           music/lists/indie/**
Region: U.S., World

InterMusic Australia

This online music newsletter covers the Australian music scene, with both Aussie bands and imports getting attention. I was sad to see nothing about This Is Serious Mum, my favorite wackos from down under, but Brisbane's Custard looks promising. Interviews, reviews, news, and gossip, including stuff from *The Buzz*, a suburban music tabloid for 20- and 30-somethings.

Type: WWW
**Address: http://www.ozonline.com.au/
           TotalNode/AIMC/**
Region: Australia

The International Library of African Music

The Web page offers a little information about ILAM, a research institution devoted to the scientific study of music and the oral arts in Africa. ILAM has a journal and has also put together a 213-LP set of Southern and Central African music, as well as a large archive of other recordings. You can contact ILAM for more specific information at the e-mail address below.

Type: E-mail
**Address: ILLK@hippo.ru.ac.za (Ms. L.M.G.
           Kekana)**
Type: WWW
Address: http://www.ru.ac.za/ilam.html
Region: South Africa, Southern Africa, Central
           Africa

Internet Underground Music Archive

This extremely popular site has actual sound files of all sorts of music—alternative rock, punk, blues, and much more. Super graphics too, if you want them; a text-only version is also available, and considerably faster.

Type: WWW
Address: http://www.iuma.com/IUMA/
Region: U.S., Canada, Europe

Iranian Songs

Iranian songs, including some in Kurdish, are on the bill here. Includes sound files with some history of the musical styles.

Type: WWW
Address: http://tehran.stanford.edu/ audio.html
Region: Iran

IRCAM—Centre de George Pompidou

This is the musicology arm of the museum, and their Web page includes information about its worldwide research projects. Parts are in French only, but much is in French or English.

Type: WWW
Address: http://www.ircam.fr/equipes/ equipes-e.html
Region: France, World

Jammin Reggae Home Page

Articles, catalogs, lyrics, clubs, discographies, and even how to understand Jamaican patois are all available here.

Type: WWW
Address: http://www-cse.ucsd.edu/users/ ddiplock/jammin.html
Region: Jamaica

Jazz Improvisation Primer

Dive in for a thorough lesson on how to play jazz, including theory and practice.

Type: FTP
Address: ftp.njit.edu/pub/jazz-primer/
Region: U.S., World

Katice

The female vocal group Katice sings in the old Slovenian style. This site includes information about the chorus and sound samples.

Type: WWW
Address: http://www2.ijs.si/~bostjan/ katprop.html
Region: Slovenia

LEO Music Archive

If you've just gotta know the lyrics to "Sounds Like Teen Spirit," check the vocal music section here—ditto for hundreds of other songs old and new. You can search alphabetical folders until you find the band or singer you're interested in. There's also information on bass, guitar, and MIDI scores for your favorites.

Type: FTP
Address: ftp.informatik.tu-muenchen.de/ pub/rec/music/
Region: Germany, World

The Mammoth Music Meta-List

A huge compendium of music info on the Net, now associated with *Vibe* magazine's online offerings. Browse through it according to your tastes for lyrics, discographies, specific instruments, your favorite genres, and artists.

Type: WWW
Address: http://www.pathfinder.com/ @@pyT2qAAAAAAAAMHr/vibe/ mmm/music.html
Region: World

Middle Eastern Music List

The MIDDLE-EASTERN-MUSIC mailing list is for discussing all aspects of music in the Middle East.

Type: Mailing list

Address: middle-eastern-music-request@nic.funet.fi

Region: Middle East

MIZIK

"Warning! On this server you may find music you have not heard before!" That's the opening line here, and how true it is. The collection here includes music from Africa, the French Antilles, Latin America, and the Caribbean. The site includes brief discographies for some featured artists, too.

Type: WWW

Address: http://www.unik.no/~robert/mizik/

Region: World

Modern Medieval Music

Altramar is an Indiana medieval music ensemble with a sense of humor and a Web page. The site includes funny tour tales, information about mostly European medieval music, and links to pages about other groups with a similar interest.

Type: WWW

Address: http://silver.ucs.indiana.edu/~smithcj/althome.html

Region: Europe

Mongolian Folk Music

If you have not heard the strange and beautiful sounds that the folk singers of Tuva make, you must. Somehow these traditional musicians have learned to produce two or three vocal lines at once, creating a low bagpipe-like drone, the sounds of steppe birds, and more. This site has information on Tuvan and other Mongolian music, discography, singers, and groups. Most information in English, some available in German.

Type: Gopher

Address: gate1.zedat.fu-berlin.de:70/11/mongolei/music

Region: Mongolia

Musica Peruana

Traditional and more modern songs of the Andes, including audio files, are archived here. There's also a link to some recordings of classical music, including Bach and Carl Orff.

Type: WWW

Address: http://www.rcp.net.pe/snd/snd.html

Region: Peru

Musica Regional del Estado de Sinaloa

Sound files here are of local songs, representative of Sinaloa's popular folk-music stylings.

Type: WWW

Address: http://docs.ccs.conacyt.mx/musica.html

Region: Mexico

Musician's Web

Based in the Netherlands and available in Dutch and English, this site combines information from musicians themselves, and from musical instrument and equipment manufacturers. Within this site are news, Drummer's Web, Guitar & Bass Web, MIDI Web for electronic/computer musicians, and a huge selection of links worldwide that are of interest to musicians.

Type: WWW
Address: http://valley.interact.nl/av/
           musweb/home.html
Region: Netherlands, World

Music Mags Online

Check here for leads to music magazines: some available online, some just advertised there, via the Electronic Newsstand. The selection ranges from *Classical PULSE!* to *Spin*.
Type: Gopher
Address: gopher.enews.com:2100/11/
           entertainment/music
Region: World

Music Mailing Lists

Wonder if there's a mailing list available that covers your favorite style of music or musical specialty? Read this document, which is updated frequently, to find out. You can obtain it via e-mail or by raiding one of the servers below.
Type: E-mail
Address: mkwong@sdcc13.ucsd.edu
Send e-mail message with body: List of
           Music Mailing Lists
Type: FTP
Address: server.berkeley.edu/pub/misc/
           lomml
Address: ftp.wwa.com/pub/dattier/lomml
           /2.1-950220.gz
Address: ftp.uwp.edu/pub/incoming/
           misc.music.files/lomml
Address: ftp.uwp.edu/pub/music/misc/
           mail.lists.music
Type: WWW
Address: http://server.berkeley.edu/
           ~ayukawa/lomml.html
Region: World

Natty Dread Server

Based in Japan, this site contains a listing of Caribbean clubs, events relevant to the Caribbean community as well as events being put on by Caribbean clubs. Graphics, sound files, lyrics of many popular artists and songs, and Caribbean news are also included. Created by Michio "Rankin'" Ogata in an act of supreme cultural crosspollination. Very nifty.
Type: WWW
Address: http://WSOGATA.CC.
           U-TOKAI.AC.JP/
Region: Jamaica

Nemeton

Lots of bands have their own home pages. This one, from the English rave group The Shamen, is an example of how complex and creative they can be. It includes not just the expected photos of the band, tour schedules, discography, and sound samples, but an interactive discussion room, political and religious files, information about the band's musical and cultural side projects, and more. Cool graphics, too.
Type: WWW
Address: http://www.demon.co.uk/drci/
           shamen/nemeton.html
Region: England

New Zealand Symphony Orchestra

The first symphony on the Web, they claim, and one that weighs in with a page that includes information about musicians and administrators, their schedule and history, and a sound file of the symphony playing the New Zealand national anthem. It also has dozens of links related to orchestral and classical music, and to musicians (such as the FAQ on tinnitus).

Type: WWW
Address: http://www.actrix.gen.nz/users/ dgold/nzso.html
Region: New Zealand

Norwegian Music Information Centre

Address guide, information on new and current bands, and the latest music news out of Norway are found here.

Type: WWW
Address: http://www.notam.uio.no/nmi/ index.html
Region: Norway

oo zoo may news

This is a publication from the Uzume Taiko Drum Group Society of Vancouver, Canada. Taiko is a Japanese drumming style that borders on dance or martial arts—very physical and precise relays of drummers take their turns at banging out the rhythms on a series of drums and other percussion devices.

Type: WWW
Address: http://www.wimsey.com/~tneel/ oozoomay/index.html
Region: Japan, Canada

The Opera Schedule Server

See where specific companies and operas are being performed—perhaps somewhere near you! It also brings together the largest collection of opera-related links online, from Web pages to mailing lists.

Type: WWW
Address: http://www.fsz.bme.hu/opera/
Region: Hungary, World

Punk List

If you like punk rock, and do not pay by the message for your e-mail, join up here. High adolescent quotient, high volume of mail, and worldwide participation.

Type: Mailing list
Address: punk-list-request@cs.tut.fi>
Region: World

rec.music Newsgroups

There are tons of newsgroups under the rec.music umbrella, from rec.music.a-cappella on up. See the group rec.music.info for the details about current and new groups, and see the rec.music.info FAQ at the Web site below. This Web page also has FAQs on many of the music-related Usenet newsgroups, from rec.music.a-cappella to rec.music.XTC. There's even one dedicated to the charming and multitalented Poi Dog Pondering.

Type: Usenet newsgroup
Address: rec.music.info
Type: WWW
Address: http://www.cis.ohio-state.edu/ hypertext/faq/usenet/music/ rec-music-info/top.html
Region: World

rec.music.reviews

You can post your reviews of music to this moderated newsgroup. That's all that's allowed. Its FAQ is available at the Web page.

Type: Usenet newsgroup
Address: rec.music.reviews
Type: WWW
Address: http://www.cis.ohio-state.edu/ hypertext/faq/usenet/music/ music-reviews-faq/faq.html
Region: World

Reverb

This "Techno/Hip Hop Digizine" is a monthly stand-alone application for Macintosh or Windows. You can check out back issues at the Web address, or send e-mail about getting a subscription. It's based in Detroit, but covers the world electronic music scene.

Type: E-zine
Address: reverb@hyperreal.com
Type: WWW
Address: http://hyperreal.com:70/1/zines /reverb/
Region: U.S., World

RockStar On Line

A rock-music idol-worship magazine, in Italian.

Lifestyles of the jaded and famous, reviews, interviews. Includes a list of links related to music videos, many in Italian, and music sites elsewhere.

Type: WWW
Address: http://www.videomusic.com/ edicola/rockstar/rockhome.html
Region: Italy, World

Russian Pop

Lyrics of romantic Russian ballads and the latest bands (The Aquarium Band, Alexander Malinen, and so on), from the "Little Russia in San Antonio, Texas" pages. Some sections include sound and video files, and there's "where to buy" information too.

Type: WWW
Address: http://mars.uthscsa.edu/Russia/ Music/
Region: Russia

Screams of Abel

This weekly e-zine serves up the latest information on Christian metal and thrash, including new releases, tours, lineup changes, and any other points of interest. Current and back issues are available through the sites below. The 'zine also sponsors a related discussion group; joining up will also bring you the 'zine via e-mail.

Type: Mailing list
Address: listserv@music.acu.edu
Send e-mail message with blank Subject line and body: sub Soae <Firstname Lastname> <Your E-mail Address>
Type: WWW
Address: http://music.acu.edu/www/jr/ metal/soae.html
Type: Gopher
Address: gopher.etext.org: Zines/ Screams.of.Abel
Type: FTP
Address: locust.cic.net
Address: music.acu.edu/www/jr/metal/ archive/
Contact: metalhed@cap.gwu.edu
Region: U.S.

Smoke Signals

This page is dedicated to Juan Luis Guerra and bachata music, a popular Latin style that is related somewhat to merengue. Some parts in Spanish only, others in Spanish or English. Includes lyrics and discographies.

Type: WWW
Address: http://www.math.fu-berlin.de/ ~stolting/JLG/hacha.html
Region: Dominican Republic, South America

Soukous Info

This new site may eventually include many more "world music" resources. For now, it's concentrating on providing an introduction to Soukous, the irresistible pan-African dance music that's very popular both within and outside of Africa. Includes a brief discography and history. There are also some other music-related links here.

Type: WWW
**Address: http://www.interport.net/
          ~laronson/WorldBeat.html**
Region: Zaire, Congo, Africa, World

Spike Your Leg-Hairs Page

Show announcements for the Toronto area, information about Punkfest '95 (like Woodstock, only louder), and links to punk/underground record-label pages.

Type: WWW
**Address: http://www.interlog.com/
          ~kovcvc/sylhp.htm**
Region: Canada

Streetsound

This is a street-level DJ-written music e-zine, which covers the "techno rap house rock reggae acid jazz dancehall freestyle industrial bhangra soul funk alternative r&b latin hi-nrg jungle ambient" scene, as they themselves put it. Offerings include information on media and hardware for DJs and musicians, equipment classifieds, street style, and more. They also publish comments from their telephone hotline and from online readers, too.

Type: WWW
**Address: http://www.phantom.com:80/
          ~street**
Region: World

The Tejano Page

Tejano is a Tex-Mex musical blend that combines traditional Mexican pop forms like cumbia with country and dance sounds. Here you can find out about the Tejano Music Awards, see pictures of Tejano stars, and hear song samples.

Type: WWW
**Address: http://ra.oc.com:2157/tejano/
          tejano.html**
Region: U.S., Mexico

World Power Systems

This page and Gopher are associated with a "business" owned by my old friend Tom Jennings, who is also the guy who invented FidoNet. The page links to the Gopher site, which includes among its archives punk zines, stories about the infamous Shred of Dignity warehouse/flophouse in San Francisco (home to the nation's premiere skateboarders' union), and lots of music-related weird stuff. Oh, and then there's Tom's plans for converting your car to run on propane. Cool.

Type: WWW
Address: http://wps.com/
Type: Gopher
Address: wps.com
Region: U.S.

PARANORMAL

See also Fortunetelling page 288; Religion and Spirituality page 420

What's "paranormal"? It's the unexplained, the strange, the unusual phenomena that keep us all guessing. Bigfoot, Nessie, and other odd beasties; UFOs and their alien drivers; extrasensory perception and other supposed superhuman powers—all that fun stuff that makes for good "Twilight Zone" episodes and edge-of-the-seat stories to tell late at night.

#ufo

Real-time discussions of UFO sightings and theories happen here on Internet Relay Chat.

Type: IRC
Address: #ufo
Region: World

alt.alien Discussions

Discussions of aliens, abductions, UFOs, and related topics are what's on in these newsgroups.

Type: Usenet newsgroup
Addresses: alt.alien.research
            alt.alien.visitors
Region: World

alt.paranet Newsgroups

Various discussions of paranormal topics are the order of the day in this special collection of newsgroups. Lots of traffic and good information can be found.

Type: Usenet newsgroup
Addresses: alt.paranet.abduct
            alt.paranet.metaphysics
            alt.paranet.paranormal
            alt.paranet.psi
            alt.paranet.science
            alt.paranet.skeptic
            alt.paranet.ufo
Region: World

alt.paranormal and Friends

The first newsgroup is for discussion of general "paranormality," from ghosts to crop circles to telekinesis. The other two in the group cover special topics: channeling and "forteana" (weird scientific events à la *Fortean Times*, about which more later).

Type: Usenet newsgroup
Addresses: alt.paranormal
            alt.paranormal.channeling
            alt.paranormal.forteana
Region: World

alt.ufo.reports

This is the place to post if you see a UFO. It's supposed to be for reporting and discussing current news of such sightings, but there's lots of noise here to get in the way.

Type: Usenet newsgroup
Address: alt.ufo.reports
Region: World

Anders Magick Page

This page is a thorough index of magic, mysticism, and related subjects.

Type: WWW
**Address: http://www.nada.kth.se/
            ~nv91-asa/magick.html**
Region: Sweden

Archive X

This may have moved by the time you read this. It's a collection of information on the paranormal and the supernatural, including ghost stories, the TV show *The X Files*, and UFOs. It includes the Archive X Ghost Hunter's Guide to documenting ghosts and similar phenomena.

Type: WWW

Address: http://www.declab.usu.edu: 8080/X/

Region: World

The Bigfoot Research Project

This site is for a relatively scientific-minded project in cryptozoology—the study of unknown animals on Earth—as it relates to the famous hairy hominid that is occasionally sighted from Northern California to Northern Canada (similar critters are alleged to exist in Siberia's forests as well, incidentally). Call me credulous, but I've spent enough time in the deep woods of the Pacific Northwest to believe that something eight feet tall and hairy could very well be in there and yet be rarely seen by humans. I hope they find one! The Web page is based in Mt. Hood, Oregon, one of Bigfoot's frequent haunts, and the mailing list and moderated newsgroup carry related information for Sasquatch hunters.

Type: WWW

Address: http://www.teleport.com/~tbrp/

Type: Mailing list

Address: majordomo@teleport.com

Send e-mail message with body: subscribe bigfoot

Type: Usenet newsgroup

Address: alt.bigfoot.research

Contact: tbrp@teleport.com

Region: U.S., Canada

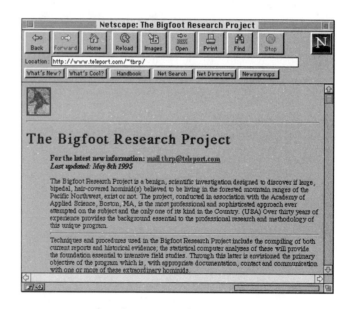

Committee for the Scientific Investigation of Claims of the Paranormal

CSICOP's pages are seriously designed, but hidden amongst the sober-minded articles about examining and (generally) debunking ESP, spoon-bending and similar claims are links to all sorts of—can I say this without offending?—wacko stuff, from Jack Chick's religious tracts (which often target occultism and belief in the non-Christian paranormal), various Web and Gopher sites, *American Psychic* magazine, and the like. You can also subscribe to the mailing list for the latest news on paranormal claims and their unravelling.

Type: WWW

Address: http://iquest.com/~fitz/csicop/ paranorm.html

Type: Mailing list

Address: aa538@freenet.buffalo.edu

Send e-mail message with body that includes the word: CSICOP

Region: U.S., World

Cryptozoology SIG

Bigfoot, Yeti, and the Jelly Glob all are topics of articles found on this special interest group of the National Capital Freenet.

Type: Telnet

Address: 134.117.1.25

At Login prompt, type: guest

At Your Choice prompt, type: crypt-zoo

Region: U.S.

Dreamers

This page is a collection of dreams: dreams of prophecy, love, fear, change, whatever, in the form of text, audio, and pictures. It's sort of an art project, but at the same time sort of a "paranormal" thing in that many of the contributors have a strong belief in the power of dreams in the real world. Very interesting.

Type: WWW

Address: http://ziris.syr.edu/dj/dj.dreamers/dreamers.html

Region: World

Electromagnetics

These folks believe they have made new discoveries in electricity and magnetics that have been ignored by "mainstream" physicists: antigravity, perpetual motion, and more. You can find various text documents on these ideas archived here.

Type: WWW

Address: http://nucleus.ibg.uu.se:80/elektromagnum/

Region: Sweden

Extraterrestrials Discussion List

This discussion group covers UFOs, the search for extraterrestrials, and related topics. The FAQ is available at the Web site below.

Type: Mailing list

Address: mailbase@mailbase.ac.uk

Send e-mail message with body: join extraterrestrials <Firstname Lastname>

Type: WWW

Address: http://www.cs.bgsu.edu/~jzawodn/ufo/etlist.html

Region: England, World

Faking UFOs

If you want to ruin everyone's fun, look here for specific and amusing instructions on how to make fake UFOs. It includes information on past fakes, and also provides detailed instructions and photos on how to make hoax crop circles.

Type: WWW

Address: http://www.strw.leidenuniv.nl/~vdmeulen/UFOfake.html

Region: Netherlands

Fortean Times

This British magazine collects bizarre occurrences from around the world, in the tradition of "weird science" writer Charles Fort: raining frogs, strange coincidences, and more. You can learn about their UnConvention 95 conference here, or find out how to subscribe to the magazine.

Type: WWW

Address: http://alpha.mic.dundee.ac.uk/ft/conv95.html

Region: England, World

The Fringes of Reason

Oh my, this site is rich with entertaining possibilities. The wackiest of the New Age and cult culture comes in for a drubbing here; those sorts of sites are listed along with many UFO, cryptozoology, ESP, parapsychology, altered consciousness, astral projection, and other things Cosmic, man. Check here early and often. Includes links to some sites in Europe.

Type: WWW

Address: http://phenom.physics.wisc.edu/ ~shalizi/hyper-weird/fringe.html

Region: World

Ghost Stories

Yahoo's search site for ghost stories online has links to FTP sites and to the Usenet newsgroup alt. folklore.ghost-stories. Get some new ones to spook out everyone on your next camping trip!

Type: WWW

Address: http://www.yahoo.com/Society_ and_Culture/Folklore/Ghost_ Stories/

Region: World

Internet UFO Group

Mass volumes of files, links to related sites, the Roswell Declaration, UFOs in the media, and much more can be found here. There's also a link to a list of online 'zines for UFO fans and for those interested in parapsychology and other strange phenomena.

Type: WWW

Address: http://erau.db.erau.edu/~elston/ iufog.html

Region: World

Jarmo's UFO-links

This is a fun Finnish page with links to UFO, paranormal, *and* skeptic sites.

Type: WWW

Address: http://weikko.tky.hut.fi/ufo.html

Region: Finland

Magick

You'll find lots of documents here, mostly on Aleister Crowley's work. You can also get your Tarot or I Ching read.

Type: WWW

Address: http://www.uib.no/zoo/wolf/ bjorn/magick.html

Region: Norway

Magick Directory

Various documents with information on magical sites and people around the world are here: Golden Dawn Society, Knights Templar, and more.

Type: FTP

Address: lysita.lysator.liu.se/pub/magick/ Community

Region: Sweden, World

Mind and Body

This is a nicely laid out index of various paranormal and alternative sites around the world.

Type: WWW

Address: http://www.stud.unit.no/~olavb /mindbody.html

Region: Norway, World

Nessie on the Net!

This page is about the Loch Ness Monster and the area surrounding the loch where it supposedly lives.

Type: WWW

Address: http://www.scotnet.co.uk/ highland/index.html

Region: Scotland

Occult Archive

Look here for magic, the infamous *Necronomicon*, and other text files related to the paranormal and occult.

Type: WWW
Address: http://www.funet.fi/pub/doc/ religion/occult/
Region: Finland, World

PAIC Mailing Lists

This is a directory of several mailing lists on "alternative topics," including UFOs and "lightwork."

Type: WWW
Address: http://www.protree.com/ mailing-list.html
Region: U.S.

ParaNet Information Services

See the sites below for information about this group, which sponsors a newsletter, radio show, and BBS, and is involved with the organization MICAP (Multinational Investigations Cooperative on Aerial Phenomena). Much of these informational offerings is archived at the FTP site.

Type: FTP
Address: grind.isca.uiowa.edu/info/ paranet/infopara
Type: WWW
Address: http://www.duke.edu/~dpk/ paranet.html
Type: E-mail
Address: mcorbin@paranet.org
Region: World

Paranormal Links and Sources

This nifty and colorful site has links to many more, covering UFOs, vampires, strange physics, and more.

Type: WWW
Address: http://www.abdn.ac.uk/ ~u01rpr/para.html
Region: England, World

SCHWA

My personal favorite among UFO sites, SCHWA could be construed as an art project that taps into the paranoia about UFOs and aliens. You can use their "protective devices" to find out if the aliens are out to get you—or if they already have! Great graphics, and lots of fun.

Type: WWW
Address: http://fringeware.com/ SchwaRoot/Schwa.html
Region: U.S.

SKEPTIC

SKEPTIC is a mailing list devoted to critical discussion of extraordinary claims. Among the paranormal topics that are commonly examined are parapsychology and psychic claims, creationism, cult archeology, UFOs and cryptozoology. It's echoed in the newsgroup, and the FAQ and an extensive bibliography on various topics is available at the Web page.

Type: Mailing list
Address: listserv@jhuvm.hcf.jhu.edu
Address: listserv@jhuvm.bitnet
Send e-mail message with body: sub skeptic <Firstname Lastname>
Type: BITNET newsgroup
Address: bit.listserv.skeptic
Type: WWW
Address: http://www.public.iastate.edu/ ~edis/skeptic/
Region: U.S., World

The Skeptic

Don't believe this stuff? Read *The Skeptic*, the magazine that takes shots at UFOs and other paranormal phenomena. You can get a free sample issue, read selections from the magazine, and find out how to subscribe.

Type: WWW
Address: http://www.cs.man.ac.uk/aig/
staff/toby/skeptic.html
Region: England, World

Skeptical Gopher

Pointers and documents from a skeptical viewpoint are what you'll find on this Gopher site. A Web interface makes finding things easier.

Type: Mailing list
Address: LISTSERV@JHUVM.HCF.JHU.EDU
Address: LISTSERV@JHUVM.BITNET
Send e-mail message with body: get
skeptic faq
Type: WWW
Address: http://gopher.lysator.liu.se:70/
information/Skeptical/
Type: FTP
Address: jhuvm.hcf.jhu.edu
Log on with the name <skeptic> and use
any password, then get
skeptic.faq
Contact: OWNER-SKEPTIC@jhuvm.hcf.jhu
.edu
Region: Sweden

The Skeptics' Page

This page mostly has links to other skeptics' pages.

Type: WWW
Address: http://dragon.acadiau.ca/
~860099w/skeptic/skeptic.html
Region: Canada

Society for Scientific Exploration

This is the site for an association of scientists and others researching UFOs and other "fringe" topics. It includes information on the *Journal of Scientific Exploration*, the magazine of the society. This group tries to take an objective look at claims of paranormal phenomena.

Type: WWW
Address: http://valley.interact.nl/av/
kiosk/sse/
Region: Netherlands

Spirit WWW

Here you'll find information on channelings, healing methods, Mayan prophecies, crystals, UFOs, yoga, and more. Documents on all these topics, as well as images, movies, sound clips, and an archive of various newsgroups are included. There are also pointers to other sites. It's mostly U.S.-based, but there's some information on non-U.S. issues.

Type: WWW
Address: http://www.protree.com/
Spirit.html
Region: U.S., World

Starbuilders

This is the home page of a couple of (channeled?) aliens named Azlor and Azina, who would love to tell you all about their worlds and energy technologies, and give you an issue of their magazine, the *Federation Flash* (electronically or physically, but not telepathically).

Type: WWW
Address: http://zeta.cs.adfa.oz.au/Spirit/ starbuilders.html
Region: Australia, Outer Space

Suomen Ufotutkijat Ry

This is a UFO site with information in Finnish.

Type: WWW
Address: http://weikko.tky.hut.fi/ufo tutkijat/SuomenUfotutkijat.html
Region: Finland

UFO and Space Pictures

Lots of pictures of UFOs, aliens, and space scenes are here for your downloading pleasure.

Type: FTP
Address: phoenix.oulu.fi/pub/ufo_and_ space_pics
Region: Finland

UFO Gopher

This site is a repository for various documents on abductions, crop circles, the Roswell incident, and other topics of interest to UFOnauts and fans of the paranormal.

Type: Gopher
Address: bubo.vslib.cz/11/pub/mirrors/ OBI/UFO
Region: Czech Republic

UFO Info

A few pictures and a history of UFOs, plus some film clips are available here.

Type: WWW
Address: http://nucleus.ibg.uu.se/ elektromagnum/ufo/
Region: Sweden

UFO Virtual Library

Look here for tons of links to documents online on UFOs, alien abductions, secret bases, what the astronauts have said about UFOs, and all sorts of similar stuff.

Type: WWW
Address: http://ernie.bgsu.edu/~ jzawodn/ufo/
Region: World

The Voodoo Server

This page has documents and a bibliography on this Afro-Caribbean religion. Spirit possession is a central tenet of Voodoo (or Voudoun), so I've included it here as well as in the Religion listings. There's also the issue of zombies…and that's tangentially related to Voodoo as well.

Type:WWW
Address: http://www.nando.net/prof/ caribe/voodoo.html
Region: Haiti

Will of Nature

An e-zine on spirituality, virtual reality, and magic, *Will of Nature* has some pictures, some music, and links to databases. One issue features some interesting articles on tattooing as a metaphysical art.

Type: WWW
Address: http://erg.ucd.ie/won.html
Region: Ireland, World

Wiretap Fringe Directory

Documents on the occult, UFOs, and "weird" stuff are available at this FTP site.

Type: FTP
Address: wiretap.spies.com/Library/Fringe
Region: U.S., World

The World Wide Web Virtual Library: Sumeria

All kinds of alternative science information and pointers can be found on this Web page.

Type: WWW
**Address: http://werple.mira.net.au/
           sumeria/**
Region: Australia, World

POLITICS

From left to right and way off the scale, political discussion, news, and organizing are what it's all about on much of the Internet. You can instantly check up on your political allies and enemies, join in heated arguments over IRC or in newsgroups, and even put up a server with your own personal political views, should you so desire.

This list includes some extremely controversial fringe political movements, plus many closer-to-the-mainstream left/liberal and conservative/right sites—but not much for moderates. Why? Perhaps moderates feel their views are so sensible that they needn't bother to convince the rest of the world. Perhaps they know their practical, everyday, logical thoughts just don't have the sheer entertainment value of the competition. Whatever it is, the voices of moderation are truly hard to find online.

That said, here's a collection of links that are sure to inform and, in many cases, amuse and/or horrify.

Abortion and Reproductive Rights Internet Resources Page

Maintained by a California Abortion Rights Action League activist, this page provides links to Web, Gopher, and FTP sites on both sides of this controversial issue. These resources include information as well as organizational contact and update pages for some of the major players in the ongoing reproductive rights debate.

Type: WWW
**Address: http://www.matisse.net/~kathy/
           caral/abortion.html**
Region: U.S.

ACT

This forum for discussions on conspiracies, the "New World Order," conservative values and other political issues attracts the usual suspects.

Type: Mailing list
Address: majordomo@fc.net
**Send e-mail message with body: subscribe
           ACT**
Region: World

ACTIvism ONline

The ACTION Internet mailing list exists to serve as a tightly focused, self-moderated forum and resource for online activists, both professional and volunteer. The Electronic Frontier Foundation (EFF) hosts this conference, though it is open to all. The list hosts both news announcements and relevant discussion. ACTION is not intended as a debate area or general chat forum, being geared toward networking among activists, planning and strategy, sharing information, and coordinating efforts.

Type: Mailing list
Address: listserv@eff.org
Send e-mail message with body: ADD action
Region: World

ACTIV-L

This list is for discussion of peace, empowerment, justice, and environmental issues.

Type: Mailing list
Address: listserv@mizzou1.missouri.edu
Send e-mail message with body: SUB
          ACTIV-L subscribers_name
Region: World

alt.individualism

Here one may debate the relative virtues of the philosophies of Ayn Rand and Max Stirner, affirm the validity of one's belief in the necessity of self reliance, and extol the superior wisdom of the self-educated in that rarest of company, one's peers.

Type: Usenet newsgroup
Address: alt.individualism
Region: World

alt.politics

If you enjoy fanning the flames of political discourse, this Usenet hierarchy is for you. I've listed only a few of the newsgroups in the alt.politics family, just enough to give you a picture of what's out there. See any complete list of Usenet newsgroups to learn more.

Type: Usenet newsgroup
Addresses: alt.politics
          alt.politics.british
          alt.politics.democrats (Moderated)
          alt.politics.ec (European Community)
          alt.politics.economics
          alt.politics.elections
          alt.politics.europe.misc
          alt.politics.greens
          alt.politics.india.communist

alt.politics.india.progressive
alt.politics.italy
alt.politics.libertarian
alt.politics.media
alt.politics.org.batf (U.S. Bureau of Alcohol, Tobacco and Firearms)
alt.politics.org.covert
alt.politics.org.suopo (Finland's security police)
alt.politics.org.un (United Nations)
alt.politics.perot
alt.politics.reform
alt.politics.socialism.trotsky
alt.politics.usa.constitution (Constitutionalism)
alt.politics.usa.newt-gingrich
alt.politics.usa.republican
alt.politics.vietnamese
alt.politics.white-power
Region: U.S., World

alt.society.anarchy

This Usenet forum is for the discussion of anarchist social and political ideas. It leans more towards the Libertarian or anarcho-capitalist side rather than anarcho-socialist or syndicalist thought.

Type: Usenet newsgroup
Address: alt.society.anarchy
Region: World

alt.discrimination

This is a discussion forum for political issues regarding discrimination (race, gender, and so on) and ways to deal with and organize against it.

Type: Usenet newsgroup
Address: alt.discrimination
Region: U.S.

Alternative Institutions

AltInst is for proposing and critiquing alternative institutions for various walks of life. Alternative ways to run conversations, countries, households, markets, offices, romances, schools, and so on are all fair game. AltInst is open to folks from any political persuasion, but general political flaming/discussion is forbidden. Skip the theory and just tell your vision of how something could be different and how that would work, just as if you had a say in the matter.

Type: Mailing list
Address: Altinst-request@cco.caltech.edu
Region: World

alt.prisons

With the advent of the War on Drugs and new sentencing guidelines, more people in the U.S. are going to jail these days than in the past, and they're staying there longer. England is one of the few other nations following its lead, at least in the First World. Prison labor is becoming more of a profit-oriented venture, and private prisons are springing up around the nation. Along with these changes comes a host of controversial issues and activists, inside and out of the joint, willing to tackle them head on in the name of justice. This newsgroup provides just such a forum.

Type: Usenet newsgroup
Address: alt.prisons
Region: U.S.

Amnesty International Home Page

Recognized as probably the most effective and important nongovernmental human rights organization in the world, Amnesty International provides information to activists involved in fighting injustice and governmental or other human rights abuses on every continent, and has carried on campaigns to safeguard the freedom and lives of tens of thousands of individuals across the globe. This Web page is rich with resources, giving the Net public access to campaign materials, news on current events, and more.

Type: WWW
Address: http://www.io.org/amnesty/
Region: UK, World

Australian Politics FAQ

This is a brief look at Australia's curious political system, without reference to the economic arrangement that underlies it—other than the inclusion of information about the Australian Republican movement, which seeks to sever ties to the English crown. The version at the Gopher is part of a much larger (quite unwieldy, actually) document.

Type: WWW
**Address: http://155.187.10.12:80/oz/
            faq-politics.html**
Type: Gopher
**Address: megasun.bch.umontreal.ca:70/
            00/Australiana/OzFAQ**
Region: Australia

Bad Subjects

The journal *Bad Subjects: Political Education for Everyday Life* is a forum for the rethinking of the basic tenets of "leftist" or "progressive" politics. At the site is a full collection of current and back issues of the journal, a manifesto for the group and journal, and samples from the most recent several days on their mailing list, which you can subscribe to at the address below.

Type: Mailing list
**Address: badsubjects-request
            @uclink.berkeley.edu**

Type: WWW
**Address: http://english.hss.cmu.edu/BS/
BadSubjects.html**
Region: U.S.

Chiapas/Zapatista Mailing List

Find out more about what's going on in the Mexican province of Chiapas, where a revolution seems to be building steam. Mostly conducted in Spanish, this list includes eyewitness and participant accounts.

Type: Mailing list
Address: ellokal@pangea.upc.es
Region: Mexico

CIA World Factbook

This is what the Central Intelligence Agency is supposed to do: collect intelligence so the U.S. government won't be caught by surprise. Its yearly World Factbook is a survey of the nations of the world, including political systems, political problems, and potential for unrest. Versions from several different years are floating around online; the one at the Web page below is from 1994, while the Gopher version is from 1992.

Type: WWW
Address: http://www.odci.gov/
Type: Gopher
**Address: wiretap.spies.com:70/00/Library
/Classic/world92.txt**
Type: WAIS
Address: world-factbook
Region: World

civil-liberty-index

This list exists to distribute indexes of "newsy" civil-liberties articles. Now is a very good time to read up on civil liberties; if it ever gets to be too late, you won't get a chance.

Type: Mailing list
Address: listserv@eff.org
**Send e-mail message with blank Subject
        line and body: subscribe civil-
        liberty-index**
Contact: eff@eff.org
Region: World

Criminal Justice Act Information

The Internet has become a rallying point for activists against England's Criminal Justice Act. Passed in late 1994, the CJA repeals many civil rights for British citizens, including the right to silence at arrest, the right to assemble (making virtual gatherings more necessary), even the "right" to dance and enjoy music without approval from the State. Find out about civil disobedience at these Web sites.

Type: WWW
Address: http://hyperreal.com/cjb/
**Address: http://www.quipu.com/~elliot
            /cja/**
Region: England, Scotland

Critical Mass

This group is active in campaigning against the "car culture," which they like to do by riding their bikes en masse—occasionally during rush hour—among other things. Chapters have been active in the U.S. and U.K. for awhile and are now starting to spring up elsewhere.

Type: WWW
**Address: http://www.chu.cam.ac.uk/
          home/tgs1001/cm.html**
Region: U.S., England, World

Democratic Party Activists Home Page

This is an official U.S. Democrats page, with news about current candidates and races around the nation, local Democrat clubs, and information on getting involved with elections and other party activities.

Type: WWW
Address: http://www.webcom.com/ ~digitals/
Region: U.S.

The Democratic Party of the Left

This Italian social-democratic party maintains a Web presence. Its respected paper, *L'Unita* (founded by Antonio Gramsci) is available at the second Web address.

Type: WWW
Address: http://www.pds.it
Address: http://www.mclink.it/unita/ index.html
Region: Italy

Democratic Socialists of America

This is the United States's version of the social-democratic parties that are popular in Europe and South America. They have a nice site here, with some history, and links to other related pages and to a list of affiliated parties around the world.

Type: WWW
Address: http://ccme-mac4.bsd.uchicago .edu/DSA.html
Region: U.S.

East Timor Net

Since the 1975 Indonesian occupation of East Timor, some 200,000 Timorese have been killed. Educational controls, forced birth control, and Indonesian migration have done the rest. The East Timor Net Web page contains political and historical documents in reference to the invasion, as well as contacts for East Timor solidarity groups.

Type: WWW
Address: http://www.uc.pt/Timor/Timor Net.html
Region: East Timor, Indonesia

Ecuador/Peru Conflict

This is a small archive of information about the ongoing border war between Peru and Ecuador, including photos, newsgroup archives, and links to other related data.

Type: WWW
Address: http://www.seas.upenn.edu/ ~leer/ecuador/peru/
Region: Peru, Ecuador

EDIN Directory of Issues

This page is just a list of links, but it's quite useful. Some of the pages are linked to particular issues with political overtones, such as trade or human rights. There's also a page of mostly U.S. left-wing/liberal links, and a matching set of right-wing links.

Type: WWW
Address: http://garnet.berkeley.edu:3333 /EDINlist/EDINlist.html
Region: World

Extropy

Extropians may be roughly described as those simultaneously interested in anarchocapitalist politics, cryonics (and other life-extension techniques), the technological extension of human intelligence and perception, nanotechnology, spontaneous orders, and a number of other related ideas. If you are an Extropian (or suspect you might be), the concept that these are all related topics will seem natural. The online newsletter *Extropy* costs $14 per year at this writing, but there's a 30-day free trial.

Type: Mailing list
Address: exi-info@extropy.org
Region: World

EZLN Page

Look for information in English and Spanish on the Zapatistas, and on Chiapas and the other embattled provinces of Mexico from which they draw their support. The sympathetic paper *La Jornada* is linked in here, as are all past and current EZLN communiques.

Type: WWW
**Address: http://raptor.swarthmore.edu/
            ~justin/Docs/ezln/ezln.html**
Region: Mexico

Firearms Politics

This list provides a forum for firearms-rights activists to freely discuss tactics, techniques, and other issues of concern without the distraction of anti-gun rhetoric.

Type: Mailing list
Address: majordomo@world.std.com
**Send e-mail message with body: subscribe
            fap**
Region: World

Forza Italia

Forza Italia is the main right-wing party in Italy, led by Silvio Berlusconi. Their pages are in Italian, with some English.

Type: WWW
**Address: http://www.iunet.it:8988/~
            forza-it/**
Region: Italy

Internet Conservative Resources Network

This is a compendium of mainstream conservative political resources, plus some a bit further to the right. Included are a Conservative Calendar (updated monthly), organizational contacts, informational resources like the C-News conservative news service, archival documentation of U.S. conservative organizations, home pages of famous North American right-wingers (Jesse Helms, Rush Limbaugh, Newt Gingrich), and online right-wing journals and magazines.

Type: WWW
Address: http://world.std.com/~icrn/
Region: U.S.

Journalist's Toolbox: Government Resources

Part of a resource collection of journalistic leads on the Internet, the Government Resources page of the Journalist's Toolbox provides a hopping-off point for a number of lists of U.S. government sites, as well as resources from other countries such as Israel, Japan, Canada, and a list of African countries. There are about three dozen links on this site, some of which have literally hundreds of sites within them.

Type: WWW
**Address: http://www.jou.ufl.edu/
            commres/tbgovt.htm**
Region: U.S.

The Kurdish Experience

This page, with color photos, is an exploration of current Kurdish nationalist politics.

Type: WWW
**Address: http://nucst11.neep.wisc.edu/
            html/kurdish_ex.html**
Region: Iraq, Turkey

Left-Wing/Progressive Politics Chat

These two very active newsgroups are the places to find discussion on and up-to-the-minute news about left-wing and progressive politics, including parties and specific issues. Misc.activism.progressive tends to be more news and activist oriented, while alt.politics.radical-left leans towards more theoretical discussions.

Type: Usenet newsgroup
**Addresses: misc.activism.progressive
            alt.politics.radical-left**
Region: U.S.

Links for the Conservative Generation X

More militant than some for older conservatives, this page has links to conservative and far-far-right think tanks, lots of college Republican clubs, and Republican Party sites, and…The Brady Bunch Home Page. I always thought those Brady kids looked like Reagan Youth! Now I know for sure.

Type: WWW
**Address: http://www.teleport.com/
            ~pcllgn/links.html**
Region: U.S.

Love and Rage/Amor y Rabia

This anarchist group is active in the U.S. and Mexico, and provides their newspaper and other material here in both English and Spanish.

Type: WWW
Address: http://thales.nmia.com/~bright/
Region: U.S., Mexico, World

Il Manifesto

Founded by dissident members of the Italian Communist Party, this is one of the better leftist papers in Europe—not least because of the hilarious satirical art in the "Vignetta di Vauro" section. In Italian.

Type: WWW
Address: http://www.mir.it
Region: Italy

Marxism Page

Not *quite* dead, despite being battered and rather moldy, Marxism has found a home at this small corner of the Net. There's even an audio clip of "L'Internationale," the Communist anthem.

Type: WWW
**Address: http://online.anu.edu.au/polsci/
            marx/marx.html**
Region: World

New Democrat Party

This Canadian progressive party apparently hopes that using the Net in a major way will give it an edge over its stodgier competition. Here at their official party site you can find convention notes; an online version of their party paper, *The Democrat*; and information on upcoming activities and elections.

Type: WWW
Address: http://www.bc.ndp.ca/
Region: Canada

Non Serviam

Non Serviam is an electronic newsletter centered on the philosophy of Max Stirner, author of *The Ego and Its Own (Der Einzige und Sein Eigentum)*, and his dialectical egoism. The contents, however, are decided by the individual contributors, and the eye of the editor. The aim is to have somewhat more elaborate and carefully reasoned articles than are usually found on newsgroups and mailing lists. Stirner's thought has appeal to individualist elements of both the right and the left. It's archived at the Gopher site.

Type: E-zine
Address: solan@math.uio.no
Type: Gopher
**Address: gopher.etext.org:70/11/Politics/
            Non.Serviam**
Region: Norway, World

Papers on Mexican Politics

This is a large archive of papers on current Mexican politics, in both English and Spanish. The title that seemed to best sum up the precarious situation there was an essay from Carlos Fuentes: "La hora del Alka-Seltzer."

Type: WWW
**Address: http://daisy.uwaterloo.ca/
            ~alopez-o/polind.html**
Region: Mexico

Patriots against the New World Order

1995 has seen a great deal of media attention on "patriot" and "militia" groups in the U.S.. If you'd like to know what they think (without necessarily having to actually meet them), take a look at this interesting archive of documents. It includes both right- and left-wing perspectives on creeping totalitarianism, both in the U.S. and abroad.

Type: WWW
**Address: http://www.kaiwan.com/
            ~patriot/**
Region: World

Patriots Archive

Archived at this site are U.S. far-right political documents, including one-world-government conspiracy

stuff; a directory devoted only to documents about the arrest of Randy Weaver and the BATF/FBI assault on the Waco compound of the Branch Davidians; citizen militia documents; Bo Gritz documents; and other items of similar ideological bent.

Type: WWW
**Address: http://www.tezcat.com:80/
            patriot/**
Region: U.S.

PNEWS Conferences

PNEWS Conferences are for discussion, and serve as conduits for articles from left-wing publications and other sources. PNEWS Conferences provide radical alternative views with an emphasis on justice, humanitarian positions, protests, boycott alerts, activism information, and more. The Internet mailing list version is called PNEWS-L.

Type: Mailing list
Address: odin@shadow.net
Region: World

Political Science Resources

This is an excellent site for international research, as it includes sites, journals, and university political science departments from around the world, including official European Community sites, the latest from the frenetic and confusing Italian political scene, Israeli politics and other Middle East info, and more.

Type: WWW
**Address: http://www.uark.edu/depts/
            plscinfo/comp.html**
Region: World

Political Zine Archive

All sorts of interesting e-zines are archived here, including publications that cover Vietnam, Somalia, Peru, England, and elsewhere.

Type: Gopher
Address: gopher.etext.org:70/11/Politics
Region: World

Politics Today: The Inside Track

This weekly online newsletter provides an update on political developments around the world, such as dissension in the Russian government and impending armed conflict in Peru.

Type: WWW
**Address: http://140.190.128.190/SMC/
newsletters/pol.html**
Region: World

POLITIKA

POLITIKA is a discussion group that covers Turkish politics, in Turkish.

Type: Mailing list
Address: listserv@tritu.bitnet
Region: Turkey

The Radical Religious Right Page

Who would have thought that the Queer Resources Directory would be the place to find a shopping list of religious far-right Internet sites? But the truth is, this list contains many Net denizens who make Rush Limbaugh look like a bleeding-heart liberal—the sort of stuff that more traditional conservatives wouldn't touch with the proverbial ten-foot pole. Holocaust revisionism, anti-choice/pro-life organizations, and the Scriptures for America Identity Christian Archive are all here, as well as more "main-stream" movement sites from the likes of Focus on the Family (the Boulder, Colorado radio ministry that sponsored and campaigned for the now-defunct Colorado anti-gay ordinance) to the Wittgenstein Net page, for Christian critical thought.

Type: WWW
**Address: http://www.qrd.org/qrd/www/
rrr/rrrpage.html**
Type: Gopher
**Address: gopher.casti.com/11/gaystuff/
QRD/religion/anti**
Region: U.S.

The Right Side of the Web

If you're a conservative, liberal/left/libertarian/anarchist is not enough of a political spectrum to encompass your views. You'll welcome this site, which tries to provide the beginnings of an antidote.

Type: WWW
**Address: http://www.clark.net/pub/jeffd/
index.html**
Region: U.S.

The Seed: UK Alternative Information

Set up as part of a dissertation project on the alternative press, organizing, and the Internet, The Seed provides links to some of the most radical organizations in Europe, including England's Class War. Also available at the site is an often-updated news and announcements section for radical actions and activities, primarily in the U.K.

Type: WWW
**Address: http://web.cs.city.ac.uk/homes/
louise/seed2.html**
Region: England, Scotland, Wales, Northern Ireland, Europe

Situationist International Page

If you are old enough to remember what happened in Paris in 1968, when a surprise alliance of students, workers, and everyday Parisians took over the city for a moment of philosophical liberation, the word *situationist* may have meaning to you. If not, you should still take a look at this beautifully designed page, packed with critiques of consumer ("spectacular") society that go beyond tired left/center/right labels.

Type: WWW

**Address: http://www.access.digex.net/
~spud/SI/si.html**

Region: France, World

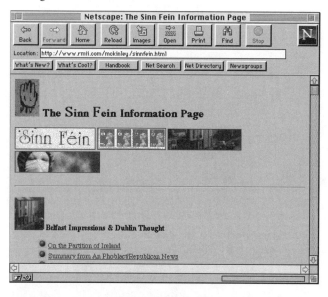

The Sinn Fein Information Page

Now that Sinn Fein, long described as "the political wing of the IRA," is taking an open leadership role in the politics of Northern Ireland, it's a good time to learn about this political party. This page discusses its history and archives related documents, including speeches and newspaper articles.

Type: WWW

**Address: http://www.rmii.com/mckinley/
sinnfein.html**

Region: Ireland

soc.politics

This is a moderated newsgroup for talking about political systems and problems. Many of the nation-specific newsgroups in the soc.culture. hierarchy also host the occasional political gabfest.

Type: Usenet newsgroup

Address: soc.politics

Region: World

Spunk Archive

This archive introduces the ideas and history of anarchist and anti-authoritarian thinkers, activists, and organizations. At this time there are almost a thousand files, primarily texts. Authors such as Peter Kropotkin, Mikhail Bakunin, Emma Goldman, Max Stirner, Hakim Bey, and Noam Chomsky—to name just a few—are represented, as are many publications, including *Practical Anarchy Online, Anarchy: A Journal of Desire Armed,* and *Red and Black Revolution.* As a practical joke on those searching for the infamous *Anarchist Cookbook,* a nonanarchist volume of vile bomb and poison recipes, there's an "anarchist cookbook" here with recipies for salsa, tofu scramble, and other goodies, contributed by actual anarchist cooks.

Type: WWW

**Address: http://www.cwi.nl/cwi/people/
Jack.Jansen/spunk/Spunk_Home
.html**

Type: Gopher

**Address: gopher.etext.org:70/11/Politics/
Spunk**

Type: FTP
Address: ftp.cwi.nl/pub/jack/spunk
Region: World

talk.politics

One of the reasons the talk.politics groups exist is that subscribers to other political newsgroups got tired of endless debates that prevented rational discussion on such matters as when to hold the next party convention or what Newt Gingrich *really* said about orphanages for the poor. So those who like to debate ad nauseum can now be exiled to this family. I've included just a few of the groups; see any complete listing of Usenet newsgroups to get the whole picture.

Type: Usenet newsgroup
Addresses: talk.politics.animals
            talk.politics.china
            talk.politics.cis (Commonwealth of Independent States—ex-USSR)
            talk.politics.crypto (political implications of computer cryptography)
            talk.politics.drugs
            talk.politics.guns
            talk.politics.libertarian
            talk.politics.medicine
            talk.politics.mideast
            talk.politics.misc
            talk.politics.soviet (more ex-USSR politics)
            talk.politics.theory
            talk.politics.tibet
Region: U.S., World

Terrorist Profile Weekly

This Web site contains information on just over a dozen "terrorist" organizations from around the globe, as defined by the U.S. State Department. The use of buzzwords is certainly a standard rhetorical tool in political debate, and labeling an organization with the "terrorist" moniker has long been used by state powers to delegitimize the opinions and actions of organizations with whom they are at conflict, so descriptions here should be taken with a grain of salt.

Type: WWW
**Address: http://www.site.gmu.edu/
            ~cdibona/index.html**
Region: World

Thomas Legislative Server: Library of Congress

Named after Thomas Jefferson, this site organized by the Library of Congress allows searches of both pending legislation and the "Congressional Record" of both the House and Senate of the U.S. government. You can also download bills to study at your leisure. The same database is available through the MARVEL Gopher, at the address below.

Type: WWW
Address: http://thomas.loc.gov/
Type: Gopher
Address: marvel.loc.gov:70/11/congress
Region: U.S.

U.S. Federal Government WWW Servers: InfoCern Listing

Broken down first by branch, then by individual agency, this page is linked with hundreds of U.S. government servers. It's an excellent starting point for researching legislation, regulations, or governmental policies of the United States.

Type: WWW
**Address: http://www.fie.com/www/
            us_gov.htm**
Region: U.S.

Yahoo's Guide to Political Parties and Groups

If you don't find any fellow travelers at the sites above, try this one. It includes links to European parties, U.S. parties, those pesky citizen militias, international Green groups, and just about everything else that's political and organized—even a who's who of groups that were working the booths at the most recent Lollapalooza alternative-rock festival.

Type: WWW

**Address: http://www.yahoo.com/Politics/
            Parties_and_Groups**

Region: World

RELIGION AND SPIRITUALITY

Because of its capacity to store and transmit huge volumes of information, the Internet has become an important resource for religious organizations and spiritual seekers. It makes scriptures instantly transportable, for example, and can help isolated practitioners find each other.

Some of the groups listed could be better classified as "cults" due to their total-control goals regarding followers and gurulike leaders. Use your judgement, and if you're not sure about a particular group, check in with FACTnet (an anticult group, also also listed below) or with another group that researches dangerous cults. I've also included "religious" groups that are "humorous," such as the Church of the SubGenius, here. Where else? But I hope no one with a serious interest in matters spiritual will be offended by the inclusion of these fringe elements with serious religious information. There should be something here for everyone.

Acem Hjemmeside

In Norwegian, this is about a worldwide movement having to do with meditation and yoga for inner and outer peace.

Type: WWW

**Address: http://www.oslonett.no/home/
            acem/**

Region: Norway

alt.meditation.transcendental

Here's a newsgroup for practitioners of Transcendental Meditation. For a more critical view of TM, see the FTP site.

Type: Usenet newsgroup

Address: alt.meditation.transcendental

Type: FTP

**Address: ftp.digex.net/pub/access/
            tm-dissent/**

Region: World

Avatar Mehere Baba Ki Jai!

Messages and articles by Meher Baba, as well as a biography and pictures of the spiritual leader, can be perused in Norwegian or English.

Type: WWW

**Address: http://www.oslonett.no/home/
            erics/index.html**

Region: Norway

Biblical Greek Studies List

B-GREEK is an electronic conference designed to foster communication concerning the scholarly (rather than personal) study of the Greek Bible. Anyone interested in New Testament Studies is invited to subscribe, but the list will assume at least a working knowledge of Biblical Greek.

Type: Mailing list
Address: **MAJORDOMO@VIRGINIA.EDU**
Send e-mail message with body:
     SUBSCRIBE B-GREEK.
Type: Mailing list
Address: **MAJORDOMO@VIRGINIA.EDU**
Send e-mail message with body:
     SUBSCRIBE B-GREEK-DIGEST
Contact: djm5g@virginia.edu (David John Marotta)
Region: Greece, World

Biblical Hebrew Studies List

B-HEBREW is an electronic conference designed to foster communication concerning the scholarly (rather than personal) study of the Hebrew Bible. Anyone interested in Biblical Hebrew Studies is invited to subscribe, but the list will assume at least a working knowledge of Biblical Hebrew and Aramaic.
Type: Mailing list
Address: **MAJORDOMO@VIRGINIA.EDU**
Send e-mail message with body:
     SUBSCRIBE B-HEBREW.
Type: Mailing list
Address: **MAJORDOMO@VIRGINIA.EDU**
Send e-mail message with body:
     SUBSCRIBE B-HEBREW-DIGEST
Contact: djm5g@virginia.edu (David John Marotta)
Region: Israel, World

Baha'i Faith

Baha'i is a modern religion that emerged in Iran (where its followers are now persecuted). It emphasizes the unity of world faiths and peoples. This mailing list echoes the newsgroup, which covers the tenets, history, and texts of the Baha'i Faith. Among the topics discussed are the relevance of Baha'i principles to current events and problems, and the relation of Baha'i to other religions, as well as more academic textual analysis.
Type: Mailing list
Address: **Send message <subscribe bahai-faith> to bahai-faith-request@oneworld.wa.com**
Type: Usenet newsgroup
Address: **soc.religion.bahai**
Region: World

Berita Dari Tanahair

This mailing list has a gateway to the Usenet group. It covers Malaysian, Singaporean, Southeast Asian, and general Islamic news. It is not a discussion list, but if you want to discuss the news, you can also subscribe to BERITA-D, created for this purpose.
Type: Mailing list
Address: **listserv@vmd.cso.uiuc.edu**
Send e-mail message with body: subscribe
     berita-l <Firstname Lastname>
Type: Usenet newsgroup
Address: **bit.listserv.berita**
Region: Malaysia, Singapore, Asia

Bhakti Yoga Home Page

This page has links to a fair amount of mostly Hindu literature, and a listing of contact addresses for Hare Krishna centers worldwide.
Type: WWW
Address: **http://webcom.com/~ara/**
Region: U.S., India, World

CATHOLIC

Discussion of the Catholic approach to Christianity is the subject of this discussion list. It has a gateway to the newsgroup.

Type: Mailing list
Address: catholic@auvm.american.edu
Type: Usenet newsgroup
Address: bit.listserv.catholic
Region: World

Christian Charity

For many religious people, manifesting their faith as good deeds for the needy is a central tenet. This Web page has leads to home pages for several charitable groups and missions in Italy, many doing international work, and most with a Christian ethic. In Italian.

Type: WWW
**Address: http://www.crs4.it/~gavino/
vs_info.html#aifo**
Region: Italy, World

Christian Discussion Groups

There are probably more newsgroups with a Christian flavor; these are just a few of the most popular ones. Several of these groups have Web pages or FAQs that can provide more information—see the Christian Resource List below for an address where you can find some of these.

Type: Usenet/BITNET newsgroup
**Addresses: alt.religion.christian
bit.listserv.catholic
bit.listserv.christia
rec.music.christian
soc.religion.christian
soc.religion.christian.bible-study
soc.religion.christian.youth-work**
Region: World

Christian Liturgy List

LITURGY provides an academic forum for discussion of all aspects of Christian liturgy. The list does not confine itself to any one historical period, geographical area or Christian tradition. Contributions are welcome from all historical and theological fields, as well as from those involved in other disciplines, such as literary analysis, comparative religion, and the sociology of religion.

Type: Mailing list
Address: mailbase@mailbase.ac.uk.
**Send e-mail message with body: subscribe
LITURGY <Firstname Lastname>**
Region: World

Christian Resource List

There are so many resources here that you'll just have to look for yourself. It includes Bibles and prayers in many languages, several introductions to Christianity, links to sites for specific denominations, and some commercial Christian sites. There are also documents on Christian history and literature, plus newsletters, online magazines, and pointers to mailing lists and newsgroups.

Type: WWW
**Address: http://saturn.colorado.edu:
8080/Christian/list.html**
Region: World

The Church of the SubGenius

To my knowledge, the Church of the SubGenius is the first "religion" to come out of the computer subculture. It started with some wacko programmers in Texas and has since become a worldwide phenomenon. Enter here, click on the Graven Image of Bob, and take a trip down the High Weirdness infohighway.

Type: WWW
**Address: http://sunsite.unc.edu/
subgenius/**
Region: World

College of Biblical and Family Studies Information Server

Placed online by the somewhat conservative Abilene Christian University in Texas, this site includes links to many Christian resources, from scriptures and Bible study groups to information about overseas Christian missions. It also has the online version of *Campus Crosswalk*, a newsletter for Christian college students.

Type: WWW
Address: http://bible.acu.edu/
Region: U.S., World

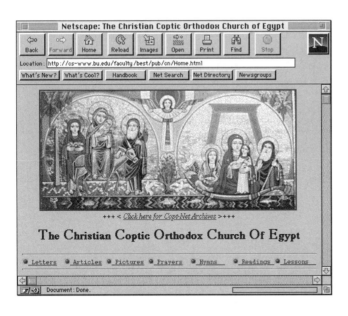

Copt-Net

These sites have been set up to serve the emigrant Coptic Christian community of Egypt. Newsletters, articles, readings, scriptures, and hymns are what you'll find.

Type: WWW
**Address: http://cs-www.bu.edu/faculty/
best/pub/cn/Home.html**
Type: FTP
Address: pharos.bu.edu/CN/
Region: Egypt, World

Dead Sea Scrolls On-line Exhibit

This contains several images of scroll fragments and other objects from the Qumran site. The accompanying text sets out to answer some of the questions raised in the heated debate about the authenticity, source, history, and so on of the scrolls and the scriptures they hold. This site is a fascinating example of a real exhibition (from the Library of Congress in Washington, D.C.) transferred successfully online.

Type: WWW
**Address: http://sunsite.unc.edu/expo/
deadsea.scrolls.exhibit/intro.html**
Region: U.S.

Dharma-Talk

This mailing list is an international forum for discussions and exchanging information regarding Buddhism, and for announcements of Buddhist-related events. List members may or may not be Buddhist adherents, and it is a multilingual list.

Type: Mailing list
Address: majordomo@saigon.com
**Send e-mail message with body: subscribe
dharma-talk**
Type: Mailing list
Address: majordomo@saigon.com
**Send e-mail message with body: subscribe
dharma-talk-digest**
Region: World

DIGNITY

Dignity is an organization for lesbian and gay Catholics. It works for change in the Church and offers an accepting place for gays and lesbians, including sometimes arranging for masses.

Type: Mailing list
Address: LISTSERV@AMERICAN.EDU
Region: World

Fight against Coercive Tactics Network

FACTnet is an anti-cult group. Their FTP site includes documents, texts of books, minutes from anticult conferences, and news about cults and cultlike groups around the world. Scientology comes in for special criticism.

Type: FTP
Address: ftp.rmii.com/pub2/factnet/
Contact: factnet@rmii.com
Region: U.S., World

Findhorn Foundation Home Page

Containing various information about the projects and progress of this longstanding alternative community in Scotland, this page focuses on spiritual matters.

Type: WWW
**Address: http://www.mcn.org/findhorn/
            home.html**
Region: Scotland

The Freethought Web

Ah yes, antireligious, antimyth myth-makers. For atheists, here's where to discuss the faith (and other people's faiths, too).

Type: WWW
**Address: http://freethought.tamu.edu/
            freethought/**
Region: World

Friends of Osho

Remember the Rajneeshis? They're ba-ack....

Type: WWW
Address: http://earth.path.net/osho/
Region: India, World

Fringes of Reason

This is a source for information on the wacko side of religion.

Type: WWW
**Address: http://phenom.physics.wisc.edu/
            ~shalizi/hyper-weird/fringe.html**
Region: World

Futhark

Pronunciation, meaning, and detailed interpretation of the Norse and Anglo-Saxon runes, including their religious significance and use in ritual, is the subject of this page.

Type: WWW
**Address: http://www.tu-chemnitz.de/
            ~mabo/runes.html**
Region: Germany

GASSHO

An electronic journal serving the global Buddhist community, GASSHO is intended to promote and support dialogue between monks, nuns, teachers, practitioners, scholars, and students. It is open to all schools and traditions of Buddhism.

Type: FTP
Address: **ftp.netcom.com/pub/dharma/ Gassho**
Type: Gopher
Address: **cis.anu.edu.au:70/ 1ftp%3Acoombs.anu.edu.au@/ coombspapers/otherarchives/ electronic-buddhist-archives/ buddhism-general/e-journals/ gassho-journal**
Contact: **dharma@netcom.com (Barry Kapke)**
Region: World

A Guide to Chabad Literature

This guide includes the huge "Chabad-Lubavitch in Cyberspace" archive of Chabad literature, with full books such as the basic text of the Chabad-Lubavitch philosophy known as the "Tanya," *Sefer HaYom Yom*, with a Chassidic thought for every day, and *Commentary on Pirke Avot* (*Ethics of our Fathers*), along with many articles about Moshiach, Chabad customs (*minhagim*), and locations of Chabad Houses.

Type: WWW
Address: **http://www.utexas.edu/students /cjso/Chabad/chabad.html**
Region: World

History of Islam Mailing List

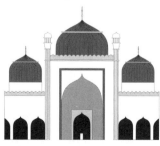

The list is for the systematic study of the history, ideology, beliefs, and values of Islam from its founding in A.D. 622 to the present. This includes the historical antecedents and historical analysis of modern phenomena. This is an academic list and includes information from study groups from around the world. It is moderated, but only to sift out irrelevant messages.

Type: Mailing list
Address: **listserv@ulkyvm.bitnet**
Send e-mail message with body: subscribe islam-l <Firstname Lastname>
Region: World

Indonesian Islam

This is a server on Indonesian Islam. It includes news, scriptures, history, and more. All documents are in Indonesian.

Type: WWW
Address: **http://budi.ee.umanitoba.ca/**
Type: Gopher
Address: **budi.ee.umanitoba.ca/**
Type: FTP
Address: **budi.ee.umanitoba.ca/pub/**
Region: Indonesia

IOUDAIOS Review

This is the serial electronic publication of *IOU-DAIOS*, the international electronic forum for scholarship on Early Judaism and Christian Origins. A review journal, it uses the electronic medium to provide thorough peer reviews quickly.

Type: Mailing list
Address: **listserv@yorkvm1**
Address: **listserv@vm1.yorku.ca**
Send e-mail message with body: SUBSCRIBE IOUDAIOS
Type: Mailing list index
Address: **listserv@yorkvm1**

Address: listserv@vm1.yorku.ca
Send e-mail message with body: INDEX
IOUDAIOS
Contact: dreimer4@mach1.wlu.ca (David
Reimer)
Region: World

Islamic Society of Stanford University

This student and faculty group maintains a Web page with lots of links to Islamic resources online, including scriptures, study groups, and discussion groups.
Type: WWW
Address: http://www-leland.stanford
.edu/group/ISSU
Region: World

The Jerusalem One Gopher Server

This is a very extensive collection of resources on Israel and the Middle East: some of the material is excellent, and some is of poor quality. Primarily geared to an Israeli or Jewish audience, it includes a collection of news archives from around the world; a large collection of mailing list archives that deal with such disparate issues as Touring Israel, the Arab Media, and a Rabbinical Question and Answer forum; a collection of Hebrew software; a very detailed archive on Holocaust history; and a list of Israeli and Jewish organizations worldwide.
Type: Gopher
Address: gopher.jer1.co.il/
Contact: lando@jerusalem1.datasrv.co.il
(Zvi Lando)
Region: Israel, World

Jewish Studies

The H-JUDAIC mailing list is the world's largest journal devoted to ongoing research and current events in Jewish Studies.
Type: Mailing list
Address: jewstudies@israel.nysernet.org
Address: h-judaic@uicvm.uic.edu
Contact: ajhyman@oise.on.ca (A. J. Hyman)
Region: Israel, World

Journal of Buddhist Ethics

The Journal of Buddhist Ethics is the first academic journal devoted entirely to Buddhist ethics. Research papers and discussion articles submitted to the journal will be subject to blind peer review.
Type: WWW
Address: http://www.cac.psu.edu/jbe/
jbe.html
Address: http://www.gold.ac.uk/jbe
.html
Type: FTP
Address: ftp.cac.psu.edu:/pub/jbe/
Address: ftp.gold.ac.uk:/pub/jbe/
Address: coombs.anu.edu.au:/coombs
papers/otherarchives/electronic-
buddhist-archives/buddhism-
general/e-journals/jbe
Type: Mailing list
Address: jbe-l@psuvm.psu.edu
Contact: jbe-ed@psu.edu
Region: World

Mage's Guide to the Net

This is a very difficult to read compendium of magical resources on the Net, from Egyptian to modern.

Type: WWW
**Address: http://www.iia.org/~widersb/
            mage_guide.txt**
Region: World

MSA-Net

Run by the Muslim Student Associations in North America, this list covers issues related to Islam and to the MSA. Only Muslims are admitted as a rule, but exceptions can be made in special cases.

Type: Mailing list
Address: msa-request@htm3.ee.queensu.ca
**Send e-mail message with body that
            includes the following informa-
            tion: your full name, your e-mail
            address, your postal address,
            your academic major or area of
            research, and your religion**
Region: Canada, U.S.

New Age Discussion

Here's a place for those with an interest in "new age" spirituality to discuss ideas and practices.

Type: Usenet newsgroup
Address: talk.religion.newage
Region: World

Objective Discussion of Religion

The OBJ-REL mailing list is intended to meet the needs of those who seek information and intelligent discussion on religion. Discussion on OBJ-REL is intended to be centered around such topics as the existence of God or gods, creationism versus evolution, reasons for the existence of religions, epistemology, religion and government, and more. Proselytizing is forbidden.

Type: Mailing list
Address: listserv@emuvm1.cc.emory.edu
Region: World

Orthodox Christian Page

Prayers, news, icons, and more from all world orthodox Christian communities (Greek, Russian, and so on) can be found here. It's a very restful stop for busy infobahn travellers.

Type: WWW
**Address: http://www.ocf.org:80/
            OrthodoxPage/**
Region: Russia, Eastern Europe, Greece, World

Orthodox Discussion Group

ORTHODOX is dedicated to the thoughtful exchange of ideas concerning Orthodox Christianity worldwide. Particular attention is paid to the rise of Christianity in Russia and her neighbors.

Type: Mailing list
Address: listserv@arizvm1.bitnet
Address: listserv@arizvm.ccit.arizona.edu
Region: Russia, Eastern Europe, Greece, World

The Oshun Festival in Western Nigeria

This is an interesting story about African religious traditions, as told by a European convert.

Type: Gopher
**Address: gopher.adp.wisc.edu:70/00/
            .browse/.METAASPCM/.ASPCM01
            /.00000016**
Region: Nigeria

Pagan Mailing List

This is a list for people who want to discuss the religions and philosophy of paganism, and to find out who's hosting the next 'bat. Activity tends to increase around the full moon.

Type: Mailing list
Address: mailserv@drycas.club.cc.cmu.edu
Send e-mail message with body: HELP
Region: World

Paganlink

This is a news and networking site for the U.K. and Ireland. Paganlink is a multidenominational organization, providing information of interest to people on all Pagan/Magical paths. The site has a very open, personal, and amateurish feel to it; a refreshing change from the glossy, formalized style generally found on the more conventional religious sites. Here they share their religion, their art, their magazines, and pointers to related topics.

Type: WWW
Address: http://www.tardis.ed.ac.uk/~
          feorag/paganlink/plhome.html
Region: England, Ireland

Pagan Resources on the Net

Here you'll find lots of links to various traditions.

Type: WWW
Address: http://www.netspace.org/~
          athomps/pagan/paganres.html
Region: World

The Principia Discordia

Written by a Marine buddy of Lee Harvey Oswald and first mimeographed in New Orleans in the office of DA Jim Garrison (of *JFK* fame), *The Principia*

Discordia is a strange psychoreligious document, presented here in hypertext form. It's proof of what government psy-ops can do to someone's mind.

Type: WWW
Address: http://www.willamette.edu/
          webdev/principia/body.html
Region: U.S.

The Purple Thunderbolt of Spode

"The Purple Thunderbolt of Spode" ("PURPS") is the Electronic House Organ of the Otisians, the followers of the God(dess) Otis and her huge pantheon of assorted deities and saints, some of whom exist on the Internet in mysterious places such as Hong Kong and Poland. Each issue of "PURPS" contains announcements of current events, various editorials and commentaries, letters, dream interpretations, texts of translated ancient writings, various stories and parables, news events pertaining to Otis, and an assortment of generally interesting stuff. "Even though we are considered as a serious religious order, people often find our material humorous," they say. Uh-huh.

Type: WWW
Address: http://www.tiac.net/users/ighf
Type: Gopher
Address: sit.sop.fau.edu:70/11/purps
Type: Mailing list
Address: listproc@sit.sop.fau.edu
Send e-mail message with body: subscribe
          hailotis <Firstname Lastname>
Contact: mal@sit.sop.fau.edu
Region: U.S., World

Religion in the Caribbean

This collection of home pages relates to religions practiced in the Caribbean countries and by Caribbeans overseas. Includes Voodoo in Haiti; Santeria in Cuba, Puerto Rico, and New York; and Spiritism.

Type: WWW
Address: http://www.nando.net/prof/ caribe/caribbean.religions.html
Region: Haiti, Cuba, Puerto Rico, U.S.

Religion Pointers

Here's a list of online religion resources, from Christianity to Taoism.

Type: WWW
Address: http://www.cs.vu.nl/~gerben/ religion.html
Region: World

The Religions of India

This Gopher offers a searchable index to the religions of India.

Type: Gopher
Address: info.anu.edu.au/11/elibrary/ country/India/religion
Region: India

Scientology

Several files on Scientology are available at the FTP site, including information on books and tapes, the catechism, and more. The Usenet newsgroup is primarily for "official" discussion: the Church of Scientology has gone after dissenters online through legal means, including an Interpol raid on a Finnish anonymous remailer that was transmitting anti-Scientology messages. Another source for critical information on Scientology is the Web site below, "Sloth's Suppressive Person Page."

Type: Usenet newsgroup
Address: alt.religion.scientology
Type: FTP
Address: ftp.doc.ic.ac.uk/usenet/usenet-by-group/alt.religion.scientology
Address: rtfm.mit.edu/pub/ usenet-by-hierarchy/news/ answers/scientology/users/
Type: WWW
Address: http://falcon.cc.ukans.edu/ ~sloth/sci/sci_index.html
Region: England, World

Shamanism Resources

For those looking to follow the path of prehistoric religion, various books and other pointers to shamanic resources are available here.

Type: WWW
Address: http://www.demon.co.uk/drci/ shamen/shamanism/shamanism .html
Region: England, World

soc.religion.shamanism

This is a moderated newsgroup for those interested in the many forms of shamanism. The FAQs are available in the FTP site below.

Type: Usenet newsgroup
Address: soc.religion.shamanism
Type: FTP
Address: src.doc.ic.ac.uk:/usenet/usenet-by-hierarchy/soc/religion/ shamanism/
Region: World

The Spirit of Raving

Rave is religion for many people, especially those nihilistic Gen X-ers, and this site has the testimonials to prove it. It also has files on techno's relevance to culture and history, "raving as a technoshamanistic activity," plus politics, humor, and general "good vibe" files. Of particular merit are files on connecting and networking, mostly within the U.S. and western Europe.

Type: WWW

**Address: http://hyperreal.com/raves/
              spirit/**

Region: World

SSREL-L

SSREL-L is a private list intended to facilitate discussion among persons interested in the scientific study of religion. Is is not for scientific justification or refutation of faith, nor is it for evangelization.

Type: Mailing list

Address: listserv@utkvm1.utk.edu

**Send e-mail message with body: sub ssrel-l
                <Firstname Lastname>**

Region: World

Tiamat-L

The list is specifically for those interested in exploring the use of the Internet as a magical tool and resource. Users on the list discuss magical techniques usable in cyberspace, and also organize and perform online, virtual group workings.

Type: Mailing list

Address: listserv@netcom.com

**Send e-mail message with body: Subscribe
                Tiamat-L**

**Contact: AShtoN@netcom.com *or*
owner-tiamat-l@netcom.com.**

Region: World

Tibetan Buddhism

This scholarly archive maintained by an Australian university includes scriptures, newsletters, a searchable database, and much more.

Type: WWW

**Address: http://coombs.anu.edu.au/
              WWWVL-TibetanStudies.html**

Region: Tibet

Transmissions

"Transmissions" is the electronic journal of Thee Temple ov Psychick Youth, North America. TOPY is an occult group with its roots in modern art and music, accompanied by a large helping of psychedelics and Crowley. The journal covers its public workings, and offers a stream-of-consciousness depiction of topics of interest to some in the Temple

Type: WWW

**Address: http://heimdall.riapub.com/
              topy.html**

Type: FTP

**Address: heimdall.riapub.com/pub/
              alamut/topy/transmissions**

**Contact: max@riapub.com (Max Delysid) *or*
              alamut@netcom.com**

Region: U.S., England

Tribe of Love Home Page

The Tribe of Love is a social movement originating in Rio de Janeiro that proposes a cultural revolution, based on the work of Wilhelm Reich. Considering this, it is not surprising that their particular brand of enlightenment relies on the free flow of energy throughout the body. Music and dance (especially Brazilian) also play an important part in their philosophy. Wacky new agers or enlightened humanists? You decide.

Type: WWW
Address: http://turnpike.net/metro/tribo
Region: Brazil, World

Universal Life Church

"An interdenominational congregation in cyber-space," the ULC have a bizarre Web page full of links to scriptures and ancient works from several religions, as well as files on Freemasonry and esoterica. They'll ordain anyone for a small fee.
Type: WWW
**Address: http://www.primenet.com/~
          ottinge/index.html**
Type: FTP
Address: ftp.primenet.com/users/o/ottinge
Region: U.S.

World Christian Resources on the Internet

This page is an admirable (and very successful) effort to bring together a wide variety of resources, including scriptures and information from other religions, country-by-country historical and cultural information, and theological Christian information. It's especially useful to missionaries or those working to support church missions.
Type: WWW
**Address: http://www.morningstar.org/
          world-christian.html**
Region: World

Ziontology

Here are several amusing satires on religious cults, including thinly veiled pastiches on the Moonies and Maharashi Mashesh Yogi—lots of fun.
Type: WWW
**Address: http://www.cis.ohio-state.edu/
          htbin/info/info/satire.info**
Region: World

ROMANCE

See also **Sex page 445**

The media thinks it's a hoot, but many people are finding long-distance love in cyberspace. I see it as a return to a period when people wrote long letters to each other and carried on torrid affairs that way. And that's pretty romantic, not pathetic. So if you're looking for a life partner (or just a cyber-fling), look into some of the resources below. Many of the "dating services" charge for some or all of their matchmaking tasks, so check prices before you leap.

I have mixed feelings about including the "mail order brides" listings, but it's true that some people do find real love this way. It's also true that some people (usually the "brides," but occasionally also the prospective husbands) end up with a great deal of heartbreak and exploitation. If a cross-cultural romance is your goal, there are many other ways to find Mr. or Ms. Right online—most of the alt.personals newsgroups and online "dating services" are quite international in scope.

I've also included a few sites that can't hook up mates, but may provide inspiration for the romantic in you.

alt.personals

There are a whole bunch of newsgroups in the "alt.personals" family. These are the right place on Usenet for personal ads. See the Web page below for a long list of them all, or subscribe to alt.personals itself for basic information on how it all works before going on to a specific newsgroup, such as alt.personals.jewish or alt.personals.big-folks. The alt.personals groups are more like the ads in the back of your local newspaper, although some are a bit more specific, steamy, and rude than what most papers will print.

Type: Usenet newsgroup
Address: alt.personals (and many, many more)
Type: WWW
Address: http://www.lib.ox.ac.uk/internet /news/alt.personals.html
Region: World

alt.romance

The alt.romance newsgroup is for talking about romance—what's romantic, what isn't, do nice guys ever finish first, dating do's and don'ts, that sort of thing. The multipart FAQ is at the Web site, along with some more romance links.

Type: Usenet newsgroup
Address: alt.romance
Type: WWW
Address: http://www.dina.kvl.dk/~ fischer/alt.romance/
Region: World

alt.romance.chat/The ARChive

The alt.romance.chat newsgroup is, as the name denotes, very chatty. Romance is often the topic, but as good-hearted souls the gang here likes to get silly. They even have net.food.fights. The Web page is a helper page for the Usenet group, with a link to the group, FAQs, and more.

Type: Usenet newsgroup
Address: alt.romance.chat
Type: WWW
Address: http://minerva.doe.mtu.edu/arc/
Region: World

AMOR!

This site contains advice in Spanish from a Latin lover, including romantic lines from poetry and prose that are sure to impress.

Type: WWW
Address: http://www.nando.net/prof/ caribe/AMOR.html
Region: Caribbean

The Art of Love: Works of Melinda Camber Porter

The Art of Love is a multimedia, one-woman, international traveling exhibition of Melinda Camber Porter's writings and paintings, initiated by Les Services Culturels of the French Embassy in New York. It has travelled to Boston, Chicago, Houston, San Francisco, and Washington, DC, and now it's on the Net. You can see all her romantic works from this tastefully designed Web stop.

Type: WWW
Address: http://adware.com/arts/ blakegallery/exhibit/welcome .html
Region: World

Babbs Personals/Les Annonces de Babbs

This site is just plain scary. The first image is of someone I'm not anxious to date anytime soon. She's got glowing green eyes, and her severed head is floating on gray paper with orange-yellow text. Parts of it are in French, and parts of it you'll never see because they get "edited" by some French person for "legal reasons." I assume these contained commercial solicitations because some of the uncensored ads are kinda tasteless. Many ads are in French, some are in English; international participation.

Type: WWW
**Address: http://www.labri.u-bordeaux
.fr/~goudal/Annonces/annonces
.html**
Region: France, World

Books about Love, Sex, and Marriage

This is an online bookstore's choice of reading selections in a romantic vein. You can purchase *In the Mood: How to Create Romance, Passion, and Sexual Excitement by Falling in Love All Over Again* by Doreen Virtue, *Enabling Romance: A Guide to Love, Sex, and Relationships for the Disabled* by Ken Kroll, and many more titles here.

Type: WWW
**Address: http://intertain.com/store/
new-browse/Love_Sex_and_
Marriage-Romance.html**
Region: World

The CD-ROMANCE Home Page

That's CD as in *compact disc*. This site is very commercial, very polished. It's plenty useful though, especially if you're looking for love on the wires. You can place ads, order the CD, meet someone "right here, right now!" in their Online meeting place, and so much more. You gotta love™ it!

Type: WWW
**Address: http://www.iquest.net/
cdromance/personals**
Region: World

The Cyrano Server

He's here and he wants to help. Say you're shy and love-struck, and sort of a dim bulb when it comes to using the English language—Cyrano can help. Just

fill out the form and Cyrano will use your information to write a love letter for you. My favorite categories are "steamy," "desperate," and "indecisive."

Type: WWW
**Address: http://www.nando.net/toys/
cyrano.html**
Region: World

E-mail-Order Brides

Your bride is in the mail! There's lots of information here—but who cares about that? Scroll down to the reason for visiting and click on links to Mail Order Brides. All us gals want to know is, where can we order up some *husbands* who are young, good-looking, and know how to cook, clean, and help with the kids?

Type: WWW
**Address: http://www.vix.com/pub/men/
romance/pen/intro.htm**
Region: World

Foreign Relations

It's an "International Picture Personals Magazine," and it's now on the Web. Hundreds of Russian women are waiting to correspond with and meet you. Too good to be true? Well, there's more. Coming soon will be links to meet women from the Philippines, Costa Rica, and Columbia. And not to be so one-sided, also coming soon will be links for foreign men wanting to meet American women. Can you spell "Green Card"? Can you spell "exploitation"?

Type: WWW
**Address: http://www.kiss.com/fr/index
.html**
Region: World

Hannu's Love

Photos of a happy Finnish couple who met via IRC chat, and a little of their love story, can be found here.

Type: WWW
Address: http://www.niksula.cs.hut.fi/~ haa/love.html
Region: Finland

IRC Romance

Maybe you can get a little romance of your own going on this Internet Relay Chat channel, devoted to the topic of pitching woo. There's more about it at the Web page.

Type: IRC
Address: #romance
Type: WWW
Address: http://minerva.doe.mtu.edu/arc/ ARC.faq
Region: World

Lucy Lipps

She's the siren of style. She's a cyberbabe (her own words). She lives in Houston, but works in Los Angeles, New York, Aspen, Miami, and London; and she has successfully developed her own time zone! So what does this have to do with romance, you ask? Everything—romance is what she does. She travels the globe giving advice to the lovelorn, she doles out online "Love Tips," and she has even published her "Little Black Book"—and you can see this all and more at the following URL.

Type: WWW
Address: http://204.145.251.200/ lucylips/
Region: World

match.com

This online personals service describes itself as "woman-oriented." It certainly has a pretty interface, if *that's* what they mean. You can browse user profiles, chat in one of the conference rooms, enjoy their online love-and-relationships magazine, and have the management make you a match. Straight, gay, lesbian, and bisexual ads are available.

Type: WWW
Address: http://www.match.com
Region: U.S.

MCS Online: Dr. Love's Office

He's got the cure for whatever is ailing you—broken hearts, lying hearts, cheating hearts—it doesn't matter. They've even made this service free to MCS Online customers, just to lower the price of rising health care costs. Just type your letter and send it in.

Type: WWW
Address: http://www.prairienet.org/~ connor/love.html
Region: World

Online Weddings

I've never seen anything like this. It looks like the text of a marriage posted online for all to enjoy (what is this world coming to?). Here's a sample:

<Rev.Strange> Okay, I think we're ready to begin. Ladies, Gentlemen, and less gentle folks of both genders: We are here to oversee the marriage of Mark and Nora. The Blushing Bride wishes to say a few words before we begin.

[Nora]: I know I sent e-mail to everyone that this would be logged, but I wanted to remind everyone again. If anyone gathered here wishes to have something they've said, or everything they said, struck from the log, send me e-mail, and I'll see to it. (Thanks Nora—that's awful nice of you.)

Type: WWW
**Address: http://sunsite.unc.edu/pub/
academic/communications/logs/
weddings/**
Region: World

The Pacific Century Club

Offering a "dignified and effective" way for men to meet the women of Japan and the Far East, this site leads you down some twists and turns before you can even get to see your potential future wife. But then again—they tell you right away that viewing the pictures of the women is not for amusement purposes—you need to be serious, and if you're not they tell you to go elsewhere. Well, excuuuuuse me!

Type: WWW
**Address: http://www.stw.com/pcc/pcc
.htm**
Region: World

Positive Planet

This is a Web site for *Positive Planet*, a magazine designed to help HIV-positive people find dating partners in a way that "feels normal." They list articles, provide links to personals, and generally offer help for HIV-positive people looking for love.

Type: WWW
**Address: http://www.qrd.org/QRD/aids/
hiv.dating.magazine**
Region: World

public.com Personals

Wow! What an ethereal and inviting home page. You've got your cherubs, your 3D marble icons, a neat little red logo—what more could you ask from a romance-related home page? And they haven't just been spending all their time in the design room, either—they list over 14,000 personal ads, as well as links to tons of romantic spots, like Sincere Singles, Mega 900 Personals, and the Carolina Singles page—many with photos. If you can't find love here, you're not really trying.

Type: WWW
**Address: http://www.public.com/
personals/**
Region: World

Rainbow Connection Mailing List

The Rainbow Connection Mailing List is devoted to the topic of Long Distance Relationships, so ubiquitous online that they now rate their own acronym: LDR. The Web page has information about subscribing to the list, a FAQ page, and links to home pages of some members. An international collection, they all seem to be smart, attractive people. Let this be clear, however: Rainbow Connection is not an Internet dating service.

Type: Mailing list
**Address: major@exxilon.xx.rmit.EDU.AU
Send e-mail message with body: subscribe
rainbow**
Type: WWW
**Address: http://www.wam.umd.edu/~
sek/rainbow.html**
Region: World

Rencontres

That's French for "encounters." European, Asian, North and South American, and occasionally African people of all persuasions post personals here with their e-mail addresses attached. Some are pretty steamy, some are quite romantic, and some are just looking for friends.

Type: WWW
**Address: http://www.easynet.co.uk/
          findlove/index.htm**
Region: World

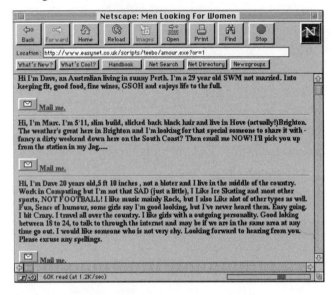

Phrantic's Trailerpark on the WWWeb

Fuscia flamingos are what greet you when you first log on, so you know it's going to be fun! It's been here since 1994, providing an online meeting place by "parking people's trailers" on their unlimited number of lots (all view sites, too—can you imagine?) and listing them in a neat column so the curious browser can easily stop by for a visit. It's a great concept, and well-executed—go get yourself a doublewide.

Type: WWW
**Address: http://www.cybernetics.net/
          users/phrantic/trailer.htm**
Region: World

Romance

Check out the definition according to *The Devil's Dictionary* by Ambrose Bierce, published in 1911. I won't spoil it for you—you have to log on and see for yourself.

Type: WWW
**Address: http://www.vestnett.no/search/
          devil/ROMANCE.html**
Region: World

Romantic Adventures

This is just a nice little list of helpful hints for keeping that spark alive, or just getting it glowing in the first place. No links, just some Valentine-y graphics and words to the wise.

Type: WWW
**Address: http://www.sos.net/romance/
          romantic.tips.html**
Region: World

Romantic Getaways

"Explore hidden beaches, dine in fine restaurants, and stay overnight in luxury accommodations with spectacular views. For a vacation whose memories will last a lifetime, visit the tropical paradise of Costa Rica." Does that sound like a travelogue, or someplace you want to take your sweetie right now? Check out their black-and-white sunsets—who needs color when you're in love?

Type: WWW
**Address: http://www.sig.net/~amt/roman
          .html**
Region: Costa Rica

Single Search National/International

It's a commercial match-making service that touts itself as being the largest match-making network in the United States or the world. You have to join, though—it's for serious singles only.

Type: WWW
Address: http://nsns.com/single-search/
Region: World

Singles Newsgroup

It's not necessarily romance—but where else can you list them? In soc.singles, you can read the rantings of lonely people as they deal with single life.

Type: Usenet newsgroup
Address: soc.singles
Region: World

soc.couples.intercultural

Cultural and racial differences can make relationships even harder to handle. This newsgroup is devoted to talking about how to handle them.

Type: Usenet newsgroup
Address: soc.couples.international
Region: World

The Virtual Meet Market

Okay, so they've had enough press already. Maybe it's the clever name that draws all the journalists, from *NetGuide* to *The Wall Street Journal*. It's just another one of the million places on the Net to meet that "someone special." The graphics aren't really all that unique or nifty, and the whole look of the page seems a little hurriedly thrown together—but there must be something here that everyone's shouting about.

Type: WWW
Address: http://wwa.com:1111/
Region: World

The World of Romance

Their own words: "The World of Romance is a gathering place for those interested in living a romantic lifestyle. Passion, creativity, excitement, and romantic relationships are the focus of the World of Romance." What a great focus, eh? And they do a decent job of covering some ground. They have links to lots of romantic cybergetaways. They have the word *Enjoy* flashing at the top, and cute little heart bullets for their links. If this frilly stuff isn't your thing it might make you say "eewww."

Type: WWW
**Address: http://www.sos.net/romance/
romance.html**
Region: World

WorldPort Personals

With so many of these Web personal services out there, you have to appear both friendly and professional, and combine ease of use with a look that also says you're established and here to stay. This site can be sort of a template for all that. They've got neat little professional-looking buttons, just a few easy links, and friendly graphics.

Type: WWW
**Address: http://www.worldport.com/
personals/**
Region: World

World-Wide Profile Registry

It's not necessarily romantic—but it could be. WWPR is a central database for personal profiles of Internet users from all over the globe. Just plug in the country, name, occupation, and so on, of someone you're looking for, and the search engines do their thing for you. And it's free! Maybe you'll find that lost love from years ago this way.

Type: WWW
Address: http://www.wizard.com/registry .html
Region: World

The World Wide Web Dating Game

It's very much like the TV game show that you might remember from years ago. One contestant asks questions of three other contestants, and picks a winner based on their answers. Then the happy couple can go out on a real date.

Type: WWW
Address: http://www.galcit.caltech.edu/~ aure/date/
Region: World

Yahoo Guide to the Personals

This is the personals list to end all personals lists. You've got your French links, Asian links, Russian links, CyberSex, magazines, personal ads, matchmaking services—why go anywhere else?

Type: WWW
Address: http://akebono.stanford.edu/ yahoo/Business/Products_and_ Services/Personals/
Region: World

See also Computers page 128; Engineering page 237; Environmental Data and Issues page 243; Health and Medicine page 310; Weather page 484

Since this directory is intended as a "general interest" book, this section is by necessity a brief survey of the scientific information available online. Since many of the Internet's founding organizations were and are in scientific fields, the scope of such data is indeed immense.

alt.misc.forteana

Fans of scientific weirdness will enjoy this newsgroup, where participants swap stories about rains of frogs, inexplicable physics, and other wacky phenomena.

Type: Usenet newsgroup
Address: alt.misc.forteana
Region: World

Asian Oil and Gas Internet Resources

People are getting so hyped about some hitherto untapped oil and gas resources in Asia that they're building artificial islands in the sea, with hopes of staking a claim that'll let them drill. Find out here about what's out there.

Type: WWW
Address: http://www.ntu.ac.sg/~asreid/ asianog.htm
Region: Malaysia, China, Hong Kong, Thailand, Vietnam

Astronomy

Hubble telescope pictures and other astronomical images and data are available on this Web page.

Type: WWW
Address: http://www.einet.net/galaxy/ Science/Astronomy.html
Region: World, Outer Space

AstroWeb

This is the place in cyberspace for astronomy and astrophysics information. This huge grouping of links includes publications, data sets, research results online, telescopes connected to the Net, images, educational resources, and more.

Type: WWW

Address: http://info.cern.ch/hypertext/ DataSources/bySubject/astro/ astro.html

Region: World

Atlantic Oceanographic and Meteorological Laboratory

Check here for graphically presented data on ocean acoustics, physical oceanography, and ocean chemistry.

Type: WWW

Address: http://bigmac.aoml.erl.gov/ aoml.html

Region: World

Atlas of the Drosophila Nervous System

Here you'll find everything you ever wanted to know about the common fruit fly's nervous system, with lots of pictures. Since it's the most popular research subject for geneticists, this should be useful.

Type: WWW

Address: http://brain.biologie.uni-freiburg. de/Atlas/text/atlasFi.html

Region: Germany

Australian National Botanic Gardens

The Australian National Botanic Gardens maintains a scientific collection of native plants from all parts of Australia. The plants are displayed for the enjoyment and education of visitors and are used for research into plant classification and biology. A herbarium of preserved plant specimens is closely associated with the living collection.

Type: WWW

Address: http://155.187.10.12/anbg/ anbg-introduction.html

Region: Australia

Biodiversity Resources

This WWW server is devoted to information of interest to systematists and other biologists of the organismic kind. You will find information about specimens in biological collections, taxonomic authority files, directories of biologists, reports by various standards bodies (IOPI, ASC, SA2000, and so forth), an archive of the Taxacom and MUSE-L listservs (now hypermailed!), access to online journals (including Flora On-line), and information about biodiversity and collections oriented projects (MUSE and NEODAT). Recently added are index images to the Biological Image Archive.

Type: WWW

Address: http://muse.bio.cornell.edu/

Region: World

Bioline Publications

This page is a conduit for several searchable electronic publications from Brazil on the subjects of microbiology, biotechnology, biodiversity, and bioinformatics.

Type: WWW

Address: http://www.ftpt.br/cgi-bin/ bioline/bioline

Region: Brazil

Bionet Newsgroups

This is a large set of newsgroups created especially for discussions related to biology. You can find out more about these newsgroups at the Web page, and get FAQs or see their archives at the Gopher site.

Type: WWW
Address: http://net.bio.net/
Type: Gopher
Address: net.bio.net/
Region: World

Brazilian Mycology

Fungi from Brazil are carefully catalogued and cross-referenced by Brazilian mycologists. Neat stuff!

Type: WWW
**Address: http://www.ftpt.br/cgi-bin/
bdtnet/fungilistbr**
Region: Brazil

Centro de Ciencias de Sinaloa

This is a regional multidisciplinary scientific research center in Mexico. Their site, in Spanish, includes information on its programs and plans in a variety of fields.

Type: WWW
Address: http://docs.ccs.conacyt.mx/
Region: Mexico

Chemistry in Israel

You can discuss Israeli chemistry through the mailing list here.

Type: Mailing list
Address: listserv@taunivm.bitnet
Contact: chemic-l@taunivm.bitnet
Region: Israel

Chemistry Pointers

This WWW Virtual Library listing provides dozens of leads to chemistry data, chemistry departments at universities around the world, and chemistry-related sites.

Type: WWW
**Address: http://www.chem.ucla.edu/
chempointers.html**
Region: World

Cognitive and Psychological Sciences on the Internet

It's a bit messy to read, but this list of university programs, Web sites, and archives related to psychology, psychiatry, and other cognitive research is quite complete, and very international in scope.

Type: WWW
**Address: http://matia.stanford.edu/
cogsci.html**
Region: World

COSMOS

This discussion list is on astronomy and related topics, with emphasis on current happenings, discoveries, and theory. In Spanish.

Type: Mailing list
Address: listasrcp@rcp.net.pe
**Send e-mail message with body: add
<Your E-mail Address> cosmos**
Type: Gopher
**Address: chasqui.rcp.net.pe:70/11/
servidores/cosmos**
Type: WWW
**Address: http://www.fcaglp.unlp.edu.ar/
~spaoli/cosmos.html**
**Contact: listasrcp@rcp.net.pe (Matthew
Waugh)**
Region: Argentina, Peru, World

Demography and Population Studies

Where is everybody, you ask? Look here and find out. This site encompasses census, population health, and other data, as well as links to archives of several demographics and population research mailing lists, and software for making predictions.

Type: WWW
**Address: http://coombs.anu.edu.au/
            ResFacilities/
            DemographyPage.html**
Region: World

European Commission Host Organization

Telnet in to search scientific databases here in eight languages, including French and German.

Type: Telnet
Address: echo.lu
Login: echo
Region: Europe

Geographische Informationssysteme

This Austrian geography discussion list is conducted in German.

Type: Mailing list
Address: listserv@awiimc12.bitnet
Contact: acdgis-1@awiimc12.bitnet
Region: Austria

History of Science and Technology

This journal puts scientific progress in perspective.

Type: FTP
Address: epas.utoronto.ca/pub/ihpst/
Region: Canada, World

International Atomic Energy Agency

No matter what you think of atomic power, this is a very interesting site to browse around in. Includes information on the ongoing program to reuse atomic waste in agriculture via irradiating crops, databases on nuclear energy, a library of online publications, and more.

Type: Gopher
Address: nesirs01.iaea.or.at:70/11/main
Region: World

International Centre for Theoretical Physics

This United Nations-sponsored organization brings together physicists from around the world to share major computing power and knowledge, with the hope of cracking some of the physics dilemmas that still exist. The linked Gopher site includes online versions of physics journals in several languages.

Type: WWW
Address: http://www.ictp.trieste.it/
Type: Gopher
**Address: gopher.ictp.trieste.it:70/11/
            others/pre-prints/Physics**
Region: World

Internet Resources Organized by Taxonomic Group

Say you want to know more about invertebrates. Where do you turn? If you're on the Internet you would naturally turn to this site. It can tell you where to go to get the latest breaking news on newts and fungus and even creatures with exoskeletons. If it's taxonomic, you'll find it here.

Type: WWW
**Address: http://muse.bio.cornell.edu/
            taxonomy/welcome.html**
Region: World

Islam and Science List

ISL-SCI is a new list dealing with issues concerning Islam and science, including history, sociology, anthropology, economics, politics, natural sciences, and exegisis.

Type: Mailing list
Address: listserv@vtvm1.cc.vt.edu
Region: Middle East, Africa, World

Japanese National Institute of Genetics

The Japanese are obsessed with genetics, to the point that pop fans trade information on their idols' blood types (which are supposed to indicate genetic inferiority or superiority). This site holds a large DNA database, which includes information about amino acid and nucleotide sequencing, among other resources.

Type: Gopher
Address: gopher.nig.ac.jp:70/1
Region: Japan

Jung-Psyc

If you'd like to chat about Jungian Analytical Psychology, try the Jung-Psyc list.

Type: Mailing list
Address: majordomo@creighton.edu
Send e-mail message with one-line body:
            subscribe jung-psyc <Your E-mail Address>
Region: World

Maghrebian Scientific Institute

The Institute's MIAST list is a forum for the discussion of science and technology in the Arab Middle East.

Type: Mailing list
Address: listserv@uiucvmd.bitnet
Region: Middle East

The Mini-Annals of Improbable Research

This newsgroup, echoed by the mailing list, publishes research news and satire from the *The Annals of Improbable Research*, which is probably the world's funniest spoof on science. It also provides news about the annual Ig Nobel Prize ceremony, which honors dubious "achievements that cannot or should not be reproduced," and other "science humor" activities.

Type: ClariNet newsgroup
Address: clari.feature.imprb_research
Type: Mailing list
Address: LISTSERV@MITVMA.MIT.EDU
Send e-mail message with body:
            SUBSCRIBE MINI-AIR <Firstname Lastname>
Contact: air@mit.edu
Region: U.S., World

Missouri Botanical Garden

This site brings together a variety of databases on plants around the world, as well as information about this U.S.-based botanical garden and related research.

Type: Gopher
Address: gopher.mobot.org
Region: U.S., Canada, Costa Rica, Peru, Guatemala, Argentina, China, West Central Africa

New Discoveries from China

Check out this huge list of the latest scientific breakthroughs being made in Chinese industrial and university labs.

Type: FTP
Address: ftp.fedworld.gov/pub/ntis/ chinese.txt
Region: China

Periodic Table

Even if you memorized it in high-school chemistry, you've probably forgotten it by now. Download a DOS program here that will display it graphically.

Type: FTP
**Address: ftp.edvz.univie.ac.at/pc/dos/
             chemistry/periodic.zip**
Region: World

Principia Cybernetica Web

Okay you eggheads—do you know what MetaSystem Transition Theory is? It's a world view that tries to predict the evolution of systems, including human systems like ethics, through high-falutin' mathematical and scientific calculations. This page is where hopeful futurists hang out. They're hopeful, because their projections say that humanity is about to experience a positive sea-change in smarts, perhaps easing some of the earth's serious problems. Let's hope they're right!

Type: WWW
Address: http://pespmcl.vub.ac.be/
Region: Belgium, World

Resource Guides for Science

There are so many guides to online and other resources to choose from here—in all branches of the sciences.

Type: Gopher
**Address: una.hh.lib.umich.edu:70/11/
             inetdirs/sciences**
Region: World

The Royal Botanic Gardens at Kew

Kew gardens are probably the most famous gardens in world, outside the long-gone Hanging Gardens of Babylon. You can "visit" the gardens, find out about their research projects, and access related scientific and botanical information.

Type: WWW
**Address: http://www.rbgkew.org.uk/
             index.html**
Region: England

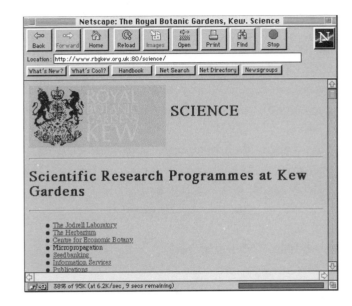

Science Television

All sorts of videos on mathematics are available from this site, as well as information on accessing them via satellite.

Type: WWW
Address: http://www.service.com/stv/
Region: World

sci Newsgroups

There are about 100 special science-related newsgroups available via Usenet that cover various scientific topics. Subscribe to sci.answers or see the Web page for a hotlinked list of the groups.

Type: Usenet newsgroup
Address: sci.answers (and many more)
Type: WWW
**Address: http://www.chem.ucla.edu/
sci_news.html**
Region: World

The Scientist

This online biweekly for scientists covers science funding, education, and jobs, current research projects, and prominent scientists.

Type: FTP
Address: ds.internic.net/pub/the-scientist/
Type: Gopher
**Addresses: hobbes.jax.org
gaia.sci-ed.fit.edu/**
Type: WAIS
Address: the-scientest
Region: World

Smithsonian Gopher

Stop here to harness the many scientific resources of the Smithsonian Institutes, including invertebrate zoology, paleobiology, entomology, and so much more.

Type: Gopher
Address: nmnhgoph.si.edu
Region: U.S.

Sneaky Science

Learn here about the cases of scientific fraud, including faked medical research. It happens more often than we'd all care to think! This site is run by two fraud researchers whose groundbreaking work at the National Institutes of Health (U.S.) got them fired rather than promoted. The mailing list is a separate but equally interesting resource for scientific fraud news.

Type: WWW
**Address: http://nyx10.cs.du.edu:8001/
~wstewart/**
Type: Mailing list
**Address: listserv@albnyvm.bitnet
Contact: scifraud@albnyvm1.bitnet**
Region: World

Structural Geology Resources on the Internet

Do you know which comes first, the mantle or the core? The people who run these sites do. They provide data, publications, maps, software, and other stuff that makes geology accessible.

Type: WWW
**Address: http://hercules.geology.uiuc.edu/
~schimmri/geology/structure.html**
Region: World

Third World Academy of Sciences

This organization provides support for scientists of the Southern Hemisphere and their research, providing educational assistance and grants.

Type: WWW
**Address: http://www.chem.ucla.edu/
chempointers.html**
Region: World

The Tree of Life

This is a series of biological and scientific resources organized in the form of a phylogenetic navigator.

Type: WWW
**Address: http://phylogeny.arizona.edu/
tree/phylogeny.html**
Region: World

Tunisian Scientific Society

TSSACT-L carries announcements about the activities of Tunisian scientists, while TSSNEWS has news about their discoveries.

Type: Mailing list
Address: listserv@utkvm1.bitnet
           (TSSACT-L)
Address: listserv@athena.mit.edu (TSSNEWS)
Region: Tunisia

Za Nauku

This is a newspaper of the Moscow Physics and Technology Institute, in Russian.

Type: FTP
Address: ftp.cs.umd.edu/pub/cyrillic/
              sov_news_digest/Fizteh_ZaNauku/
Region: Russia

SEX

See also Sexuality and Gender Issues page 450

It's said that when the first researcher on the early Internet got the idea of talking about sex online in a mailing list, Net traffic suddenly quadrupled. If the current volume of sex-related sites is any indication, this topic continues to have the same effect even today.

Many of the sex sites online are commercially oriented, or contain do-it-yourself porn. I'm not a prude, so I included a few here. This material is so easy to find that it's no challenge, and it's not much different from what you might find in a pornographic video or magazine. In a word (mine, perhaps not yours): boring.

More useful is information on sex, from how-tos to how to stay safe and healthy, to the professional side of sex. There's much more in that vein included here, along with a little racy humor.

I should mention that of all the places to visit online, sites having to do with sex appear and disappear faster than any other. When a new sex site is mentioned in one of the popular Usenet newsgroups, it can suddenly receive up to 20,000 calls per day—enough to make even the most tolerant network administrator reach for the "censor" button as this unexpected traffic blocks other customers from using the system.

This section is intended for mature adults only.

alt.sex

Entire books have been written about "talking dirty" online. The alt.sex. heirarchy of newsgroups has grown much too huge to list here, with choices that range from chat about various preferences and kinks to simply posting smutty pictures. Many service providers refuse to carry these groups, often simply to avoid overloading stressed servers. You can access many from links available via The Complete Internet Sex Guide (see below) and many other sex-related Web pages.

Type: Usenet newsgroup
Address: alt.sex (and many others)
Region: World

Atomic Books Catalog

This is a catalog of what you could call "intellectual smut": porn novels secretly written by major literary figures, artistic erotica, and books about sex and sexuality that might find their way into a college curriculum.

Type: WWW
**Address: http://www.clark.net/pub/
            atomicbk/catalog/sleazbk.html**
Region: U.S.

Bianca's Smut Shack

For a "Smut Shack," this place sure has a nice, good-timey, do-it-yourself (ahem) vibe to it—no slick, commercial stuff here. There are interactive sex-chat lines and places to post erotic stories. Some of it is extremely explicit, and there is no charge.

Type: WWW
Address: http://bianca.com/shack/
Region: World

The Blowfish Sexuality Information Center

This women-friendly site includes sex-related news, information about sex and health and sexual politics, and other resources. They also have a catalog of safe-sex supplies and toys linked in someplace.

Type: WWW
**Address: http://www.best.com/
            ~blowfish/blowsic.html**
Region: U.S., World

Brandy Alexandre Home Page

Alexandre is a semi-retired porn star (who has also written, directed, and produced adult films), but this isn't a pornography site. It includes her life history in the form of a series of FAQs, a little about her interests outside of work (reading, computing, and other non-erotic pursuits) and links to other information about the adult film industry.

Type: WWW
**Address: http://www.primenet.com/
            ~otrprod/**
Region: U.S.

The Complete Internet Sex Guide

If it has to do with sex, it's probably connected to this page somehow. Mailing lists, IRC chat groups, newsgroups (including German, Russian, Finnish, and Swedish ones), Web pages, and too much more to mention—just go take a peek for yourself.

Type: WWW
**Address: http://www.best.com/~craig/
            netsex.html**
Region: World

Cyber-Sex-Toys

This is a catalog of what they call "marital aids" under the laws of many states. Obviously computing is not the only technical field where intelligent minds have been at work lately, is all I can say after reading a few pages.

Type: WWW
**Address: http://www.webcom.com/~dml/
            sex/mainpg.html**
Region: U.S.

CyberSight Chat

These pages are sort of like BBS forums: You open up a "room," read the entries already there, and leave replies or messages of your own. Several of the "rooms" here are for discussions about sex or of an erotic nature.

Type: WWW
**Address: http://cybersight.com/cgi-bin/cs/
            newsic/news/**
Region: World

Cybersuck: Legal Whorehouses Home Page

This is a list of a few of the better-known licensed brothels in Nevada, with some brief information on negotiating the price and the work to be performed. Interestingly, when French prostitutes went on strike in 1975, they said that state-controlled legalized prostitution was far worse than illegal self-employment, though an improvement over some abusive pimps. Consider the meaning of an eight-hour day in this business!

Type: WWW
Address: http://www.panix.com/~zz/ ex2.html
Region: U.S.

Erotic City

The sex industry in Amsterdam is notoriously large, and is tolerated due to the Netherland's liberal laws. This page includes a sample of current exhibitions from the city's Erotic Museum, and ads from several sex-related businesses. I was particularly heartened to see an ad for a woman-owned co-operative brothel that formed to get better wages and improved working conditions for the employees.

Type: WWW
Address: http://www.euro.net/5thworld/ erotic/erotic.html
Region: Netherlands

A Girl's Guide to Condoms

This guide is written just for the ladies, to make up for the films that only the boys got to see in sixth-grade health class. Actually, I suspect that this goes into considerably more detail. Informative, and essential if you are sexually active.

Type: Gopher
Address: english.hss.cmu.edu/ 0F-2%3A2161%3AGirl%27s%20 Guide%20to%20Condoms
Region: World

Go Ask Alice!

This site is an archive of "Alice's" answers to questions about sexual health and relationships. These are *exactly* the kinds of questions you are probably embarrassed to ask your family doctor or mate about, and the answers are kind and well researched.

Type: WWW
Address: http://www.columbia.edu/cu/ healthwise/cat1.html
Region: World

Guide to Self-control

I hope this text is a parody, but the level of detail makes me suspect it's not. It's intended as a self-instruction course in how to avoid masturbation for young Mormons.

Type: Gopher
Address: english.hss.cmu.edu/ 0F-2%3A2161%3AA%20Guide% 20to%20Self-Control
Region: U.S.

The Idiot's Handbook of Love and Sex

This page takes a humorous view of the mixed signals we send each other when we're on the prowl or in relationships. There's some realistic information here among the cartoons and quips.

Type: WWW
Address: http://www.ida.his.se/ida/ ~a94johal/sex.chtml
Region: Sweden

InterSex City/The Point of No Return

Lots of commercial and noncommercial links are what you'll find on one of the Net's largest sex sites.

Type: WWW
Address: http://www.intersex.com/
Region: World

Just Say Yes

Calling an explicit, sex-positive sex-education pamphlet for teens controversial is an understatement—but here one is, excerpted online. Before you get angry, consider this: Are the scare tactics we use now really working to improve self-respect or lower the rate of teen pregnancy or STDs? Or would realistic, supportive information about sex be more helpful? This pamphlet has simply written information on birth control, pregnancy, safer sex, and more.

Type: WWW
**Address: http://cornelius.ucsf.edu/
           ~troyer/safesex/justsayyes.html**
Region: U.S., World

Links from the Underground: Sex

The guy who runs this site has an open mind and a sense of humor. You may find some of the material he includes somewhat offensive—or simply educational.

Type: WWW
Address: http://www.links.net/sex/
Region: World

Love, Sex, and Marriage Books

This is a shopping list from an online bookstore that carries all sorts of mostly mainstream books about sex, sexuality, and sexual health. Page back to other parts of the catalog (such as the Relationships section) for more titles that fit into this category as well.

There are books there for many interests, from *Foods For Fabulous Sex* to *Nice Couples Do: How To Turn Your Secret Dreams Into Sensational Sex*.

Type: WWW
**Address: http://intertain.com/store/
           new-browse/Love_Sex_and_
           Marriage-Sex.html**
Region: World

The Love Teachings of Kama Sutra

Taken from an ancient Indian poem intended to instruct husbands and wives on how to please each other in bed, this has become a classic of erotic literature. This version has been translated into English and has a few comments.

Type: WWW
**Address: http://www.ida.his.se/ida/
           ~a94johal/sex2.chtml**
Region: India

Male Infertility Overview

This is a guide to the causes and treatment of male infertility, written with some technical detail.

Type: WWW
**Address: http://www.mindspring.com/
           ~mperloe/shaban.html**
Region: World

Phone Sex Links

For those with an interest in phone sex, numbers to many such services can be found here. Most of them appear to be offshore companies.

Type: WWW
**Address: http://www.infotank.com/
           WildThing/Sex/**
Region: World

PONY

PONY is a support and advocacy group for people in the sex industry, including all current or former male, female, or TS/TV prostitutes, erotic dancers, nude models, X-rated actors, peep-show performers, and phone-sex operators.

Type: WWW
**Address: http://www.paranoia.com/faq/
             prostitution/pony.txt**
Contact: pony@virtualx.com
Region: U.S.

Radical Sex

This explicit page is a guide to the fringes of sex, including piercing, sex in public, S and M, and so on. Includes links to related businesses and book reviews.

Type: WWW
**Address: http://www.best.com/~haynes/
             radical_sex/radical_sex.html**
Region: U.S., World

The Safer Sex Page

Brochures, articles, and other information about HIV/AIDS and other sexually transmitted diseases can be found here, along with lots on condoms and other safer-sex strategies. The Safer Sex Forum section links you into an ongoing discussion on a single topic, which changes regularly. There's also data especially for counselors, and audio and video clips covering important issues like negotiating safe sex with your partner.

Type: WWW
**Address: http://www.cmpharm.ucsf.edu/
             ~troyer/safesex.html**
Region: World

Safe Sex: The Manual

This is an animated sex-ed film from the Netherlands. The Croatian film festival site here includes a clip in MPEG format.

Type: WWW
**Address: http://animafest.hr/filmovi/
             a5.html**
Region: Croatia, Netherlands

Sex and Love Addiction

If you have created an unhealthy obsession with sex (hopefully not by compulsively following up the links on this page) check in here for information on treatment, using the familiar 12-step boogie.

Type: WWW
**Address: http://www.wam.umd.edu/
             ~lihn/sexlove/**
Region: World

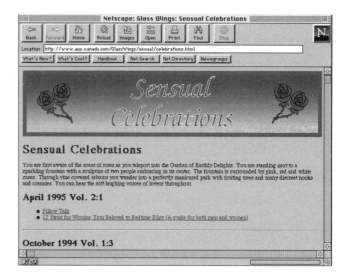

Sexuality: Health Information and Enjoyment

This set of sexology pages is an introduction to information on human sexuality, including all sexual persuasions and with a sex-positive slant. Health information, addressing sexual dysfunction, men's and women's sexual issues, sexual health, and more are covered. It has a warm, even sensual interface, too.

Type: WWW
Address: http://www.aus.xanadu.com/ GlassWings/sexual.html
Region: Australia, World

Sexuality Information

Planned Parenthood of Ottawa provides answers to your questions about STDs, contraception, parenting, and infertility here.

Type: WWW
Address: http://www.ncf.carleton.ca/ freeport/social.services/ppo/ info/menu
Region: Canada

The World Sex Guide

This series of FAQs compiled from the alt.sex.services newsgroup covers the topic of prostitution country by country, and sometimes by specific city as well.

Type: WWW
Address: http://www.paranoia.com/faq/ prostitution/
Region: World

SEXUALITY AND GENDER ISSUES

See also Health and Medicine page 310; Romance page 431; Sex page 445

No matter what floats your boat, there's probably a site on the Internet for networking and discussion about it. Gender-based issues, including men's and women's rights and community building, are also a growing segment of Net offerings.

Most of the sexuality information available in this list could be described as "alternative," meaning other than heterosexual monogamy. My guess is that with heterosexual monogamy being legal, accepted, and the dominant paradigm, there isn't much need for discussion about it.

ALTERNATES

This mailing list is for discussing alternative sexual relationships.

Type: Mailing list
Address: alternates-request@ns1. rutgers.edu
Region: World

Alternative Sexuality/Sexual Politics Resource List

This is a good resource page for various types of alternative sexuality, including gay, lesbian, transgendered, polyamory, and S/M. Includes links to interesting body art pages, "coming out" information, and a long list of mailing lists around the world as well.

Type: WWW
Address: http://www.phantom.com/ ~reive/altsex.html
Region: World

alt.feminism

This newsgroup seems to have a high propensity for flames, and they get in the way of sincere discussion. Many of the participants are men, some honestly trying to support women's equality, others obnoxiously "feminazi-baiting."

Type: Usenet newsgroup
Address: alt.feminism
Region: World

alt.feminism.individualism

This newsgroup is for independent-minded, anti-"victimology" feminist discussion.

Type: Usenet newsgroup
Address: **alt.feminism.individualism**
Region: World

alt.politics.sex

Conversation in this newsgroup ranges far and wide, from gender roles and the media to laws about sex.

Type: Usenet newsgroup
Address: **alt.politics.sex**
Region: World

alt.sex

As reviewed in the previous section, there are many newsgroups in the alt.sex category, including some for discussion of sexual issues and sexuality. Subscribe to alt.sex for information on other groups available and their focus, or just look here for the FAQs.

Type: Usenet newsgroup
Address: **alt.sex** (and many more)
Type: WWW
Address: **http://www.lib.ox.ac.uk/ internet/news/faq/by_category .alt-sex.html**
Region: World

alt.support.lesbigay

Lesbians and gays in search of an online support group can subscribe to this newsgroup.

Type: Usenet newsgroup
Address: **alt.support.lesbigay**
Region: World

alt.support.transgendered

Transgendered (transsexual) individuals can find support and understanding here.

Type: Usenet newsgroup
Address: **alt.support.transgendered**
Region: World

AUGLBC-L

The American University Gay, Lesbian, and Bisexual Community mailing list is a support group for lesbian, gay, bisexual, transgender, and supportive students. The group is open to all, and is also connected with the International Lesbian, Gay Youth organization (IGLYO).

Type: Mailing list
Address: **listserv@american.edu**
Send e-mail message with one-line body:
          SUB AUGLBC-L <Firstname Lastname>
Region: U.S.

aus.culture.lesbigay

Australian gays and lesbians discuss lifestyle, events, and other cultural issues here.

Type: Aus newsgroup
Address: **aus.culture.lesbigay**
Region: Australia

AUSGBLF

This mailing list is a general discussion forum for Australian gays, lesbians, and bisexuals.

Type: Mailing list
Address: **ausgblf-request@minyos.xx .rmit.oz.au**
Region: Australia

Australian Queer Resources Directory

The "AusQRD" is a library of things that may be of use to the Australian gay, lesbian, and bisexual communities. It contains news clippings, papers, articles; book, film, and play reviews; event announcements; and other resources. There's a link to New Zealand information here also.

Type: WWW
Address: **http://www.casti.com/qrd/world /pacific/australia/**
Region: Australia, New Zealand

The Australian Institute For Women's Research and Policy

Links to information about dealing with sexual harassment, rape, motherhood, and many other experiences, both positive and negative, that women face.

Type: WWW
Address: **http://www.gu.edu.au/gwis/ aiwrap/AIWRAP.home.html**
Region: Australia

BiCon'95

1995 will see the U.K.'s Thirteenth National Bisexual Conference. This page will keep you up to date on conference dates, workshops and plans, or you can contact the organizers directly via e-mail.

Type: WWW
Address: **http://sun1.bham.ac.uk/ J.W.Harley/bicon95.html**
Type: E-mail
Address: **bicon@bham.ac.uk**
Region: England

Bisexual Resource List

This is a compilation of resources useful to bisexual and bi-friendly people, including a calendar of events, mailing lists, Usenet newsgroups, and organizations around the world.

Type: WWW
Address: **http://www.qrd.org/QRD/www /BRC/brl-toc.html**
Region: World

The Blacklist

This list of lesbian, gay, bisexual, and transgendered people of African descent was first developed in response to requests for names to include in Black History Month 1994 celebrations. Includes some names that you may not expect.

Type: WWW
Address: **http://www.udel.edu/nero/lists/ blacklist.html**
Region: U.S., Africa, World

Canadian Gay, Lesbian, and Bisexual Resource Directory

There's lots here of interest, including upcoming events, publications, student groups, and Canadian companies that offer same-sex family benefits.

Type: WWW
Address: **http://www.ccia.st-thomas.on.ca/ ~cglbrd/**
Region: Canada

can.motss

This is a Canadian newsgroup for gays, lesbians, and bisexuals.

Type: Can newsgroup
Address: **can.motss**
Region: Canada

ClariNet Gay News

Subscribe here to a virtual clipping service of wire stories on gay issues and gay-related news.

Type: ClariNet newsgroup
Address: clari.news.group.gays
Region: World

Collected Queer Information

Information about the "Queer Nation" (the concept, not the political action group of the same name) and links to many related online resources are available here.

Type: WWW
Address: http://www.cs.cmu.edu/Web/ People/mjw/Queer/MainPage .html
Region: World

The Complete Internet Sex Resource Guide

This is a huge guide to all sorts of sex and sexuality resources online, including archives, Web pages, mailing lists, newsgroups, IRC channels, and BBSs.

Type: WWW
Address: http://www.best.com/~craig/ netsex.htm
Region: World

COUPLES-L

This discussion list covers sexuality issues for heterosexual couples.

Type: Mailing list
Address: LISTSERV@CORNELL.EDU
Region: World

The CyberQueer Internet Guide—The Queer Guide to Cyberspace

This is a big queer site, with lots of links. "Fight back with technology" is the rallying cry here—plenty of political activism links along with more general sex and sexuality resources.

Type: WWW
Address: http://www.cyberzine.org/html/ Queer/Publication/one/ cyberqueerpage.html
Region: World

CyberQueer Lounge

Choix d'Éditeur

No international Internet resource list would be complete without including the CyberQueer Lounge. Sorted by topic, this page takes you around the world in search of solutions in the areas of human rights, justice, and sexuality. Has many links to publications, resources for rural gays, gays in recovery, gay travel, and much more—including a scary section of far-right/anti-gay links. They're here, they're organized, and they even have a link to lawyer jokes—so get used to it.

Type: WWW
Address: http://www.cyberzine.org/html/ GLAIDS/glaidshomepage.html
Region: World

deviants Mailing List

Occasionally disgusting but not always, this is the home of ranting, experimental reports, news clippings, and other items related to sexual "deviance."

Type: Mailing list
Address: majordomo@csv.warwick.ac.uk
Send e-mail message with body: subscribe: deviants
Region: England, World

Dutch Queer Resources

Dutch gay and lesbian news, legal information, gay media from the Netherlands, sports, clubs, and other cultural assets are all online here.

Type: WWW

Address: http://www.xs4all.nl/~heinv/ dqrd/index.html

Region: Netherlands

EURO-QUEER

This venerable and very busy mailing list is for discussion on topics like legal issues, sexuality, films, "outing," and regional news. It includes subscribers from both Western and Eastern Europe, and there is some U.S. and Asian participation as well. Most messages are in English. FAQs are available at the first Web page below, and it's archived at the second. A digest version is also available.

Type: Mailing list

Addresses: majordomo@queernet.org

Send e-mail message with body: subscribe euro-queer

Send e-mail message with body: subscribe euro-queer-digest

Type: WWW

Address: http://www.qrd.org/QRD/ www/electronic/email/ euro-queer.html

Address: http://www.uni-konstanz.de/ %7Epascal/eq/

Region: World

EURO-QUEER-STUDIES

This mailing list is dedicated to networking among researchers in the field of European gay and lesbian history.

Type: Mailing list

Address: majordomo@queernet.org

Region: World

Euro-Sappho Information

Euro-Sappho is a lesbian discussion group for mostly European women. FAQs and related files are available at the Web site.

Type: Mailing list

Address: majordomo@seta.fi

Address: euro-sappho-request@seta.fi

Send e-mail message with body: subscribe euro-sappho <Your E-mail Address>

Type: WWW

Address: http://www.helsinki.fi/~kris_ntk/ esappho.html

Region: Europe

Father's Rights

Conversations in these newsgroups can get pretty heated. They are forums for discussing the rights of fathers—particularly in divorce and custody situations.

Type: Usenet newsgroup
Address: alt.dads-rights (Moderated)
Address: alt.dads-rights.unmoderated
Region: World

Feminist/Women's Studies Resources on the Internet

This is an easy-to-read guide to all sorts of sites, ranging from historical information to Web pages for feminists.

Type: WWW
Address: http://www.mit.edu:8001/ people/sorokin/women/ lhunt-wir/wir.homepage.html
Region: U.S., World

France Queer Resources Directory

Here you'll find laws; publications; gay resources for all of the major cities in France; and support, political, and religious groups for gays and people with AIDS. Available in French or English.

Type: WWW
Address: http://acacia.ens.fr:8080/ home/delmas/fqrd/fqrd.html
Region: France

Gay and Lesbian Liberation in South Africa

This Gopher site is small, but includes publications from an ANC-linked gay-rights advocacy group.

Type: Gopher
Address: wn.apc.org:70/11/gay
Region: South Africa

Gay, Lesbian, and Bisexual Mailing Lists

Many, many discussion lists can be accessed from this page, for all interests and many nationalities.

Type: WWW
Address: http://www.qrd.org/QRD/www/ electronic/email/lgbt.lol.html
Region: World

Gay London

Gay life in London is bustling. This page has much to offer, including a list of gay and gay-friendly bars, nightclubs and coffeehouses, support groups, and hotlines.

Type: WWW
Address: http://www.quipu.com/~elliot/ gay.london/gaystuff.html
Region: England

Gay, Lesbian, and Bi Usenet Newsgroups

The Web page's list of newsgroups, with hot links, is mostly U.S.-oriented. Archives of postings to these groups and many more are available at the Gopher site, including German, Norwegian, and other non-U.S. groups. The Web page is especially useful if your Internet service provider bans sex- and sexuality-related newsgroups.

Type: WWW
Address: http://server.berkeley.edu/ mblga/netnews-www.html
Type: Gopher
Address: gopher.infoqueer.org:1901/11/ netnews
Region: World

Gender Issues

This page is a resource for both men and women. It includes links to all sorts of information on issues that face each of the sexes, from men in prison to women in high-tech industries.

Type: WWW
**Address: http://www.einet.net/galaxy/
Community/Gender-Issues.html**
Region: World

Gender and Sexuality

This is a very interesting collection of links on sexuality, sexual practices, and gender identity, from the conservative Concerned Women for America to the radical art-world action group Guerrilla Girls.

Type: WWW
**Address: http://english-server.hss.cmu.edu/
Gender.html**
Region: World

German Gay Resources

This page has connections to German gay resources, including German-language newsgroups.

Type: WWW
**Address: http://bio5.chemie.uni-freiburg.
de/~dreyer/Gay_Conn.html**
Region: Germany

GRANITE

This list covers topics in the area of gender research.

Type: Mailing list
Address: granite@nic.surfnet.nl
Region: World

Hein's Ultimate Gay Links

A great source for gay/lesbian/bi information for Europe, the U.S., Canada, and Australia.

Type: WWW
**Address: http://news.xs4all.nl/~heinv/
heindoc/gayhttp1.html**
Region: World

ILGA Home Page

The International Lesbian and Gay Association sponsors a yearly international conference and advocates for homosexual rights. It is especially active in Europe. Find out more about ILGA activities, including the 1995 conference, at the sites below.

Type: WWW
Address: http://www.seta.fi/ (in Finnish)
Address: http://www.seta.fi/english.html
(in English)
Type: Gopher
Address: gopher.seta.fi/
Region: World

International Gay News

There are just a couple of links here, but they're full of news about legal and social developments around the world concerning gays and lesbians, including news from Sweden (where homosexual marriage is now legal), India, and elsewhere.

Type: WWW
**Address: http://www.geko.com.au/users/
QRD/world/world.html**
Region: World

InterSex City

A great many of the links here are to commercial services, but there are also some links to information about sexuality and alternative lifestyles, including swingers, naturism, various fetishes, and more.

Type: WWW
Address: http://www.intersex.com/
Region: World

Israel Queer Resources Directory

This page includes news updates, information on The Society for the Protection of Personal Rights For Gay Men, Lesbians & Bisexuals in Israel, AIDS treatment and prevention data for Israelis, and local events and community centers listings.

Type: WWW
Address: http://qrd.tau.ac.il/
Region: Israel

KHUSH Mailing List

KHUSH is a mailing list for gay, lesbian, and bisexual South Asians and their friends. It's for discussions of South Asian gay culture, experiences, and issues. A FAQ is available at the Web page.

Type: Mailing list
**Address: khush-request@lists.mindspring
            .com**
Send e-mail message with body: subscribe
Type: WWW
**Address: http://www.rahul.net/trikone/
            khush.html**
Region: Bangladesh, Bhutan, India, Maldives,
            Nepal, Pakistan, Sri Lanka

The Lesbian Avengers—London Chapter

The Lesbian Avengers is a nonviolent direct action group committed to raising lesbian visibility and fighting for gay rights. General information about its highly creative demonstrations and actions is available here, with a special emphasis on activities of the London chapter.

Type: WWW
**Address: http://www.cs.ucl.ac.uk/students/
            zcacsst/LA.html**
Region: England

Lesbisch? Schwul?—Lesbian? Gay?

Subtitled "Lesbian & Gay Homepage for Everyone," this site focuses on organizations, news, and events in Austria, with links to resources elsewhere. In German and English.

Type: WWW
**Address: http://www.oeh.uni-linz.ac.at:
            8001/homo/**
Region: Austria

Lovestyles

If you start running into terms that you haven't heard before while exploring the Net's sexuality resources (for example, what the heck is "polyamory"?), this is a glossary. You may find some of the definitions a bit mind-blowing, but there's certainly something to be learned here about options that you might not have been aware of.

Type: WWW
**Address: http://www.phantom.com/
            ~reive/lovestyle.html**
Region: World

Mail Men

This is a discussion group on men's issues: intimacy, fidelity, gender differences, and more are talked about here. Participants include men and women. The FAQ is available at the Web page below.

Type: Mailing list
**Address: mail-men-request@summit.
            novell.com**
Type: WWW
**Address: http://galaxy.einet.net:80/
            e-periodicals/mail-men.txt**
Region: World

MOMS

This is a mailing list for lesbian mothers and mothers-to-be.

Type: Mailing list
Address: majordomo@qiclab.scn.rain.com
Send e-mail message with body: subscribe moms
Region: World

Newsgroups from gay-net

This site has hyperlinks to some of the gay-net newsgroups, including gay-net.international and German-language groups.

Type: WWW
Address: http://rzstud1.rz.uni-karlsruhe.de /~uk2x/svsk/node9.html# SECTION00034000000000000000
Region: England, Germany, World

NOW Home Page

Everything you need to know about the biggest feminist organization in the U.S., if not the world, is available on this page. You'll find history; contact lists for regional and local chapters; current and back issues for the national newsletter, "NOW Times;" background materials on feminist issues; news and commentary on the issues NOW is presently focusing on in the U.S.; plus feminist struggles supported by NOW around the world.

Type: WWW
Address: http://now.org/now/home.html
Region: U.S.

Out Now!

This U.S. and international gay newspaper is now online. Nice illustrations, and news of both U.S. and international happenings is what you'll find here.

Type: WWW
Address: http://www.zoom.com/outnow/
Region: U.S., World

Outrageous Tokyo

This is an English-language gay magazine from Japan, which includes feature stories and listings of organizations, bars, clubs, and events for gays in Japan.

Type: WWW
Address: http://shrine.cyber.ad.jp/ ~darrell/outr/home/ outr-home.html
Region: Japan

The Plaid

This is a server for the transgender community, including transsexuals and transvestites. There's medical information about "the operation," mailing lists, newsgroups, IRC channels, and more. There's also European legal information regarding name/gender changes.

Type: WWW
Address: http://scratchy.csd.abdn.ac.uk/ ~mosaic/gender.html
Region: England, World

Polyamory

This is the page to have in your hotlist if you're loving more than one. It includes links to newsgroups, mailing lists, and other resources for those in long-term nonmonogamous relationships.

Type: WWW
Address: http://www.hal.com:80/ ~landman/Poly/
Region: World

Queer Asian-Pacific Resources

Check here for organizations, bibliographies, mailing lists, and more related to gays and lesbians in Asia, Australia, and New Zealand.

Type: WWW
Address: http://www.tufts.edu/~stai/ QAPA/resources.html
Region: Japan, China, Taiwan, Asia, Australia, New Zealand

Queer Nation Mailing List

This is a discussion group for members of the political action group Queer Nation.

Type: Mailing list
Address: majordomo@queernet.org
Region: U.S.

Queer Infoservers

Here's a list of gay, lesbian, and bisexual information resources online, organized by subject and by continent.

Type: WWW
Address: http://www.infoqueer.org/ queer/qis/
Region: World

Queer Resource Directory by Gopher

This Guide is linked into many gay and lesbian Web pages, but is also available via Gopher here for those without Web access.

Type: Gopher
Address: gopher.qrd.org/11/gaystuff/ QRD
Region: World

Queer Resources Directory

This is a good resource for the gay, lesbian, bisexual, and transgendered community. It has sections concerned with AIDS facts and treatments, resources and contact information for various support and activist groups, bibliographies of publications, movies, radio and other media, civil rights and domestic partnerships information, and more.

Type: WWW
Address: http://www.gnn.com/gnn/wic/ soc.06.html
Type: FTP
Address: nifty.andrew.cmu.edu/pub/QRD
Type: WAIS
Address: Queer-Resources
Region: World

Sappho Mailing List

This long-running mailing list for lesbian and bisexual women has been around for nearly a decade. FAQs and related links are available at the Web page. A digest version of the list is also available.

Type: Mailing list
Address: sappho-request@apocalypse.org
Address: majordomo@qiclab.scn.rain.com
Send e-mail message with body: subscribe sappho-digest <Firstname Lastname>
Type: WWW
Address: http://www.apocalypse.org/ sappho/
Region: World

SEX-L

This discussion list is for talking about general sexual issues and is open to people of all persuasions.

Type: Mailing list
Address: LISTSERV@TAMVM1.BITNET
Region: World

SEXTALK

If you enjoy intellectual talk about sex and sexuality, this list is for you.

Type: Mailing list
Address: LISTSERV@TAMVM1.BITNET
Region: World

Sexuality and Health

This Gopher server has information about birth control, sexually transmitted diseases, and pregnancy.

Type: Gopher
**Address: gopher.uiuc.edu/11/UI/CSF/
            health/heainfo/sex**
Region: World

Sex und das Internet

Prepared to enlighten reporters and researchers, this essay covers the issue of sex on the Internet and censorship, including information on feminism, sexuality, genetic-sciences, and other types of sites online that deal with sexual issues. In German.

Type: WWW
**Address: http://www.techfak.uni-bielefeld.
            de/fun/internet+sex.html**
Region: Germany, World

Slovene Queer Resources Directory

Information on gay, lesbian, and bisexual organizations based in Slovenia, local events (including the Slovene Gay and Lesbian Film Festival), the Slovene gay press, and local history have been put together here.

Type: WWW
**Address: http://www.kud-fp.si/~zoran/
            QRD/index.html**
Region: Slovenia

soc.bi

This newsgroup is for discussing issues related to bisexuality. The Web page for the newsgroup has links to FAQs and to other bi resources.

Type: Usenet newsgroup
Address: soc.bi
Type: WWW
**Address: http://sun1.bham.ac.uk/
            J.W.Harley/soc-bi.html**
Region: World

soc.feminism

This newsgroup is for discussions about feminism, including history, current events, books, and other publications, and ongoing efforts to achieve equal rights for women. FAQs are available at the Web site below, along with a large list of hotlinks to other women's and feminist Internet resources.

Type: Usenet newsgroup
Address: soc.feminism
Type: WWW
**Address: http://www.io.com/tittle/
            feminism/homepage.html**
Region: World

Society for Human Sexuality at University of Washington

This student group studies human sexuality, sponsors films and speakers on erotic or sex-ed topics, and maintains online archives at the Web and FTP sites below. The mailing list is for discussion of such topics and of the Society's activities.

Type: Mailing list
Address: majordomo@tower.techwood.org
Send e-mail message with body: subscribe sfpse
Type: WWW
Address: http://weber.u.washington.edu/ ~sfpse/
Type: FTP
Address: ftp.u.washingion.edu/pub/ user-supported/sfpse/
Type: E-mail
Address: sfpse@tower.techwood.org
Region: U.S., World

soc.men

Men's issues, problems, and rights are the topic of discussion in this newsgroup.

Type: Usenet newsgroup
Address: soc.men
Region: World

soc.support.transgendered

If you're thinking about having a little remodeling done, you probably want to ask around a bit first. Here you can meet people who've been there.

Type: Usenet newsgroup
Address: soc.support.transgendered
Region: World

soc.support.youth.gay-lesbian-bi

This a place for young gays, lesbians, and bisexuals to find social support and perhaps learn some new chants for the Parade this year. "Two, four, six, eight; how do you know your kids are straight?" has been suggested. It goes on from there.

Type: Usenet newsgroup
Address: soc.support.youth.gay-lesbian-bi
Region: World

soc.women

Women's issues and concerns are discussed in this newsgroup.

Type: Usenet newsgroup
Address: soc.women
Region: World

Think Pink Pages

Amsterdam is a legendary gay mecca, and this site has information about all it has to offer, including *Rainbow* magazine (the largest local gay publication), clubs, organizations, health resources, travel, shops, and more.

Type: WWW
Address: http://www.euro.net/5thworld/ pink/pink.html
Region: Netherlands

Transgender Forum

This is a tasteful and useful site for transvestites, transsexuals, and other "gender benders." It includes consumer information, links to a place to get large-size women's clothing, the latest news on legal and social issues, and a nice photo gallery from readers.

Type: WWW
Address: http://www.zoom.com/personal/ cindym/indextg.html
Region: World

Trikone Home Page

This is a page for South Asian gays, including a magazine, resource directory, and events listings.

Type: WWW

Address: http://www.rahul.net/trikone/ index.html

Region: Bangladesh, Bhutan, India, Maldives, Nepal, Pakistan, Sri Lanka

uk.gay-lesbian-bi

For gays, lesbians, and bisexuals in the U.K., this is an online discussion group.

Type: U.K. newsgroup

Address: uk.gay-lesbian-bi

Region: England, Scotland, Wales, Northern Ireland

Women Online

If you've been on the Net awhile, the question of why there are so many more men than women online may have already crossed your mind. This well-researched essay provides some of the reasons, along with some suggestions for increasing female participation.

Type: Gopher

Address: english.hss.cmu.edu/0F-2% 3A2161%3ATruong-Gender% 20Issues%20Online

Region: U.S.

Women's Info by Gopher

This is a compendium of items available by Gopher that relate to women or women's studies. It's a huge list that ranges from women's colleges in Korea to libraries with extensive collections of women's studies books.

Type: Gopher

Address: liberty.uc.wlu.edu:3002/ 7?women

Region: World

Women's Issues in Asia

This Gopher site has files on issues like the Thai sex trade and the Beijing Women's Conference of 1994.

Type: Gopher

Address: csf.Colorado.EDU/11/ipe/ Geographic_Archive/asia/women

Region: Asia

Women's Page

Lots of links to information of interest to women can be found here, such as women's professional organizations, women's health, domestic abuse, personal empowerment resources, databases, and more. A very complete collection.

Type: WWW

Address: http://www.mit.edu:8001/ people/sorokin/women/ index.html

Region: U.S., World

Women's Resources

This site includes information for and about women in the fields of health, business, feminism and ecofeminism, women's studies, human rights, high-tech industries, and education.

Type: WWW

Address: http://www.clark.net/pub/ lschank/web/women.html

Region: World

Women's Studies Links

An international collection of women's links can be found at this site, including Islamic education for women, Belgian feminists, and more.

Type: WWW

Address: http://www.yahoo.com/ Social_Science/Women_s_Studies/

Region: World

SPORTS

Whether you are strictly a fan or an avid amateur participant, there are many Internet sites that feature sports information and statistics. This section will be especially appreciated by readers who enjoy sports like soccer, hockey, and lacrosse, who may not get the daily updates via traditional media in the U.S. that football, baseball, and basketball rate.

You can also get information online about local leagues and "fantasy" sports where you play your imaginary all-star team against those assembled by others.

Aikido Dojos Worldwide

This site includes lists of Aikido schools (dojos) in Asia, Australia, New Zealand, Europe, and the Americas. There are also bibliographies about this martial art and other resources for students and teachers of Aikido.

Type: FTP
Address: cs.ucsd.edu/pub/aikido
Region: World

The Arte of Defense

This is a Web page about the art of Elizabethan fencing and rapier play.

Type: WWW
**Address: http://mac9.ucc.nau.edu/
             fencing.html**
Region: Europe

Australian Sporting News

Football, motorcycle racing, and cricket results can be found here, as can other sorts of Australian sports news.

Type: Gopher
**Address: megasun.bch.umontreal.ca:70/
             11/Australiana/OzSport**
Region: Australia

Caribbean Soccer and Cricket Pages

From The Caribbean Connection service, this is a collection of places where you can check in on your favorite West Indies teams.

Type: WWW
**Address: http://www.mrl.uiuc.edu/
             ~stuart/car6.html**
Region: Caribbean

Cricket Fan Mailing List

Stranded without your cricket fix? Try a subscription to this discussion list.

Type: Mailing list
Address: listserv.vm1.nodak.edu
Type: E-mail
Address: cricket@vm1.nodak.edu
Region: World

Cricket in India

Columns, features, and schedules on cricket in India can be found here. Nice interface—but it may be available by subscription only by the time you read this. Part of the IndiaWorld service.

Type: WWW
**Address: http://www.indiaworld.com/
             subscribe/rec/cricket/index.html**
Region: India

Croquet in Canada and Beyond

This surprisingly large and involved Web page covers the history of croquet, where to play in Canada, croquet competitions, and rules.

Type: WWW
Address: http://www.wimsey.com/~dims/
          Croquet.html
Region: Canada, World

ESPnet Sports Zone

This is the online version of ESPN, the cable and radio sports network, and much of the content here is tied to the broadcast services. Includes up-to-the-minute sports scores, and lots of sporting news.

Type: WWW
Address: http://ESPNET.SportsZone.com/
Region: U.S., World

eWire

This is a HyperCard e-zine that covers BMX freestyle biking, mostly in New England, and music (punk and ska), with color photos and audio samples. You can download it here; it requires a Macintosh and HyperCard software.

Type: FTP
Address: obi.std.com:/obi/Zines/eWire/
Type: E-mail
Address: wirezine@aol.com
Region: U.S.

Fantasy'Net Basketball

Pick your team with an online form, and see who comes out on top. With the baseball strike over, the site organizers are planning to start up Fantasy'Net Baseball.

Type: WWW
Address: http://www.ftn.net/~earnold/
          basket/
Region: U.S.

Fun.com

Links here are for mostly U.S. sports, including pro sports, fantasy baseball, youth leagues, and more.

Type: WWW
Address: http://fun.com/fun/sports.html
Region: U.S.

The Gaelic Games Home Page

Includes a history of the Gaelic Athletics Association, which is over 100 years old, and includes information about the sports of hurling and Gaelic football themselves.

Type: WWW
Address: http://info.cern.ch/hypertext/
          WWW/Daemon/User/Guide.html
Region: Ireland

GolfWeb

"Everything golf on the Web" is the motto, and this is a most comprehensive source for information about professional golf and just plain playing golf. There's even an online Pro Shop.

Type: WWW
Address: http://www.golfweb.com/
Region: U.S.

Great Outdoors Recreation Pages

Here you'll find information on hiking, biking, climbing, fishing, boating, skiing, bird watching, wildlife viewing, spelunking, windsurfing, hang gliding, and scuba diving: where to have lots of outdoor fun on every continent.

Type: WWW
Address: http://www.gorp.com/
Region: U.S.

The Greatest Finnish Sports Network in Internet!

And perhaps the only one? Find out here about the major ice hockey, soccer, and pesäpallo (similar, but not identical to, baseball) teams in Finland.
Type: WWW
Address: http://www.funet.fi/~don/
Region: Finland

Horse Racing in Holland

In Dutch, this is a page about horse racing. Most of the listings are for European races.
Type: WWW
Address: http://www.euronet.nl/users/ petport/rensport.html
Region: Netherlands

Ice Speed Skating Home Page

This is a very complete system for access to scores, history, world records, information about competitions and champions, and the latest news about competitive speed skating. It's mostly in English, with a little Dutch.
Type: WWW
Address: http://www.twi.tudelft.nl/Local/ sports/skating.html
Region: Netherlands, World

International Soccer

This is a personal page created to bring together international soccer scores and team home pages. It's still in the formative stages, but growing rapidly.

Type: WWW
Address: http://www.pitt.edu/~ktgst/ international.html
Region: World

Japanese Soccer

J-League scores and information, lots of links to information on Japan's chances for the next World Cup, and worldwide soccer information can be found here.
Type: WWW
Address: http://syrinx.gen.u-tokyo.ac.jp/ j-league/
Region: Japan

Korfball Home Page

This was a completely new sport to me, but it's played extensively in Africa, Europe, and Oceana. It's the only sport (other than mixed-doubles tennis, I suppose) with teams that include men and women on the same team. It looks to me like a combination of basketball and soccer.
Type: WWW
Address: http://www.earth.ox.ac.uk/ ~geoff/index.html
Region: World

Modern Arnis Århus

This is a form of Filipino martial arts, also known as Kali and Escrima. This site has a link to FAQs, newsgroups, and related sites.
Type: WWW
Address: http://www.daimi.aau.dk/ ~jpsdiry/arnis/
Region: Philippines

Motorsport Information

This site has statistics, race results, information about auto-racing events worldwide, and links to an extensive list of tracks on every continent.

Type: WWW

Address: http://www.bath.ac.uk/~py3dlg/ motorsport/motorsport.html

Region: World

Osmar's Sports Page

There's plenty here on "multisport" sports, like triathalons, plus long-distance swimming, running, and rock climbing. Many, many links.

Type: WWW

Address: http://www.earth.ox.ac.uk/ ~geoff/int.html

Region: England, World

La Pelote Basque

In French, this page talks about pelote, also called pelota or jai alai. It's played with a rubber ball and curved basket-like bat. It's popular wherever Basques live—including France, Spain, and Argentina.

Type: WWW

Address: http://ahuzki.univ-pau.fr/ Basque/PELOTE/pdg.html

Region: France, Spain

Recreation, Sports, and Hobbies

Lots of links and reviews on sports sites online are available at this graphics-heavy and opinionated site.

Type: WWW

Address: http://www.cs.fsu.edu/projects/ group12/title.html

Region: U.S.

rec.sport.olympics

This group discusses Olympic sports, Olympic athletes, and issues related to the Olympics, such as controversies over where they are to be located. The FAQs are available at the Web site below.

Type: Usenet newsgroup

Address: rec.sport.olympics

Type: WWW

Address: http://www.cs.cmu.edu/afs/ cs.cmu.edu/user/clamen/misc/ Sports/Olympics-FAQL.html

Region: World

rec.sports.soccer

This is one of the most popular sports groups online, and certainly the most international! See the Web page for its FAQs and for leads to more soccer information organized by country.

Type: Usenet newsgroup

Address: rec.sports.soccer

Type: WWW

Address: http://www.atm.ch.cam.ac.uk/ sports/

Region: World

SEA Games 1995

The South-East Asia games will be in Thailand this year. Find out about the men's and women's competitions in 28 sports, including Judo and Taekwondo, traditional Asian boat races, snooker, Asian sports like Sepak Trakraw and Silat Olahraga, and many "Western" sports as well.

Type: WWW

Address: http://www.chiangmai.ac.th/sg/ sg95.html

Region: Thailand, Myanmar (Burma), Laos, Cambodia, Vietnam, Brunei, Malaysia, Philippines, Indonesia

Shamrock Rovers Football Club Home Page

Interviews, photos, scores, and even club songs for this Dublin, Ireland soccer team can be found here. It's a good example of a home-grown sports-team page.

Type: WWW
Address: http://paul.maths.may.ie:8000/ Rovers.html
Region: Ireland

Skateboarding Discussion

Join in here for answers to all your skateboarding questions. It's especially useful for the beginner, or for the person thinking of trying to skate again after a long absence.

Type: Usenet newsgroup
Address: alt.skate-board
Type: WWW
Address: http://web.cps.msu.edu/ ~dunhamda/dw/faq.html
Region: U.S., World

Soccer in Mexico

This large and nicely illustrated page is a good English-language starting point for fans of the great Mexican teams. Includes statistics, details of their World Cup showing, and more.

Type: WWW
Address: http://www.cedar.buffalo.edu/ ~khoub-s/WC94.nations/ Mexico.html
Region: Mexico

Spelunking in Slovenia

On this page, take a journey through a cave in Kosiche, Slovenia, in English or Slovakian. Lots of cool photos.

Type: WWW
Address: http://www.tuke.sk/sh/sh-a.html
Region: Slovenia

Sport

That's the one-word name of this server, entirely in German, which covers sports in Europe and the world. Subjects include racing, football (soccer), tennis, and more. There are links to several German sports newsgroups too—including de.alt.sport for general sports chat in German.

Type: WWW
Address: http://sunwww.informatik. uni-tuebingen.de:8080/sport/ sport.html
Region: Germany, Europe, World

Le Sport

There's lots on French, European, and U.S. sports, in French, on this Web page.

Type: WWW
Address: http://gplc.u-bourgogne.fr: 8080/Sport/Welcome.html
Region: France, World

Sport Source

"S2" is a commercial online service for sports news and information. It includes sections for mountain biking, climbing, and other sports.

Type: WWW
Address: http://s2.com/
Region: World

Sports Gophers

If you want to access sports scores and more about hockey, football, baseball, and basketball, check out this Gopher site, which includes links to many more Gopher sites.

Type: Gopher

Address: gopher.panix.com/11/Misc/ Sports/

Region: U.S.

Sports in Singapore

From archery to tennis, there are lots of sports to play and watch in Singapore. Check here for facilities and other information.

Type: WWW

Address: http://www.ncb.gov.sg/sog/ sports/

Region: Singapore

Sports Links

Check here for a humongous list of Internet sports resources: the auto-racing section alone is over a page long.

Type: WWW

Address: http://www.yahoo.com/ Entertainment/Sports/subdir.html

Region: World

Sports Pointers

Many links to sites for many sports, from curling to Olympic events can be found here.

Type: WWW

Address: http://www.cs.cmu.edu/afs/ cs.cmu.edu/user/clamen/misc/ Sports/

Region: U.S., World

Sports Rules

This Gopher includes world rules from FIFA, the international soccer organization, and Aussie Rules football, along with lots of other sports information.

Type: Gopher

Address: wiretap.spies.com:70/11/Library/ Article/Sports

Region: U.S., Australia, World

Sports Scores

This is a rather difficult to use system for obtaining the latest sports scores. It has a search function, and covers U.S. and European sports and teams. It includes boxing, rugby, cricket, korfball, and many more sports. In Dutch.

Type: WWW

Address: http://teletext.iaehv.nl/cgi/tt2w ww/nos/gpage/600-1?181,310

Region: Netherlands, World

The Sports Server

Based in Canada, this Web page serves up news on baseball, NHL hockey, college and professional basketball and football. There's also an online chat area, NandO Sports Chat, and The Sports Page for daily updates on all kinds of sports from auto racing to tennis.

Type: WWW

Address: http://www.nando.net/ sptsserv.html

Region: Canada, U.S.

Il Subacqueo

This is Italy's leading scuba-diving magazine, available online (and in Italian).

Type: WWW

Address: http://www.nexus.it/subacqueo

Region: Italy

Swedish Football

Find out about the teams in the Allsvenskan ("all Sweden") soccer playoffs for 1995, their playing schedules, and scores.

Type: WWW
Address: http://www.nada.kth.se/ ~nv92-ego/eng.html
Region: Sweden

Swiss Soccer Match Reports

This site includes results and reports originally written for the Swiss Soccer Mailing List, which there's a link to as well. It includes both youth and adult amateur soccer.

Type: WWW
Address: http://err.ethz.ch/members/ neeri/soccer.html
Region: Switzerland

Usenet Sports Talk

The Web page will take you directly to some of the sports newsgroups, of which there are many in the alt.sport and rec.sport families.

Type: WWW
Address: http://www.cs.fsu.edu/projects/ group12/sports.news.html
Region: World

Windsurfing Resources on the WWW

This Web site includes lots on where to windsurf and where to talk about windsurfing. The rec.windsurfing newsgroup is the main forum for discussion online; it's archived at the FTP site below.

Type: WWW
Address: http://www.dsg.cs.tcd.ie/ dsg_people/afcondon/ windsurf/windsurf_home.html
Type: Usenet newsgroup
Address: rec.windsurfing
Type: FTP
Address: lemming.uvm.edu/ rec.windsurfing/
Region: Ireland, U.S., Canada, Sweden, Europe, Australia, New Zealand, Israel

Women's Sports Page

Here's a great page about women's sports, including baseball, basketball, bicycling, track and field, gymnastics, rugby, skating, handball, volleyball, canoeing, kayaking, and lots more. It also has links to pages about women's sports teams in the U.S., Canada, Hungary, Norway, Sweden, and the rest of the world. Includes international championships and Olympic sports.

Type: WWW
Address: http://fiat.gslis.utexas.edu/ ~lewisa/womsprt.html
Region: World

World Cup

History, statistics, a glossary of soccer terms, and yearly summaries of World Cup results are available here. There's also a link to a heavily illustrated page for the U.S. World Cup team.

Type: WWW
Address: http://www.cedar.buffalo.edu/ ~khoub-s/WC94.hist.html
Region: World

World Squash Federation

This site includes the rules of international squash, complete with all appendixes and guidelines for referees.

Type: WWW

Address: http://www.ncl.ac.uk/~npb/ WSF/rules.html

Region: England, Europe

The World Wide Web of Sports

Color pictures and tons of information for the serious sports fan grace this set of pages, which can be customized to fit your interests. There's lots on U.S. sports; also on world sports like soccer; international competitions like the Olympics, Commonwealth Games, Games of the Small European States, and European Youth Olympics; frisbee, cycling, and Aussie Rules football; and college sports, including lacrosse and curling.

Type: WWW

Address: http://www.tns.lcs.mit.edu/ cgi-bin/sports

Region: World

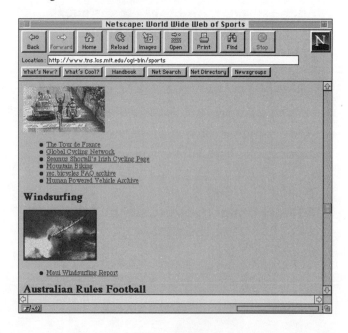

TELEVISION

Americans watch too much of it, it rots the brain, and the truth is that TV outside the United States is not a whole lot better. The same time-wasting soap operas, inane comedies, obfuscating news shows, and snore-o-rama military documentaries pervade the airwaves worldwide. On the other hand, non-Americans are smart enough to spend a lot less time with the box per day.

However, other people's awful shows can be high-camp humor to those who aren't subjected to them on a daily basis (this is the only way I can rationalize the otherwise unfathomable popularity of "Baywatch" in the world syndication market). Think of Australia's "Dame Edna," or the heinous-yet-hilarious British comedy "Are You Being Served?" So branch out and enjoy. With satellites and videos, you may actually be able to watch some of these shows. I've included many links to U.S. television information—not just for Americans, but also for the multitudes worldwide who are fed a steady diet of red-white-and-blue TV product.

There are also a number of Usenet newsgroups under the general alt.tv rubric, most of them for U.S.-based programming. See any comprehensive list of alt newsgroups for more information.

Adam

Information on the Swedish comedy show "Adam" is at this site. You can even e-mail star Adam Alsing, and go "backstage" for a weekly report. In Swedish.

Type: WWW
**Address: http://www.everyday.se:80/
hem/adam/**
Region: Sweden

Airwaves Television Page

This page gets brownie points for opening with a totally appropriate anti-TV rant from Frank Zappa. Includes a mostly-U.S. page of soap-opera links and lots of other links to TV-related pages around the U.S. and Europe.
Type: WWW
**Address: http://radio.aiss.uiuc.edu/~rrb/
tv.html**
Region: World

alt.aeffle.und.pferdle

This is the place to chat about those quirky German TV cartoon characters Aeffle and Pferdle.
Type: Usenet newsgroup
Address: alt.aeffle.und.pferdle
Region: Germany

British TV Discussion

You have a couple of options here. The newsgroup alt.comedy.british is for chat about all Brit comedies, while rec.arts.tv.uk covers all sorts of English shows, including dramas and soaps.
Type: Usenet newsgroup
**Addresses: alt.comedy.british
rec.arts.tv.uk**
Region: England

Banned in Britain

Look here for the list of videos banned in Britain, which includes some items you may be better off missing (*Bare in Prison*) and also some surprising

ones (*A Clockwork Orange*). If you live in England, this page also includes who to complain to about censorship. Also here is the "Melon Farmer's List," which presents a list of videos being shown on U.K. television that have been censored first.
Type: WWW
**Address: http://www.bath.ac.uk:80/
~su0bufs/melon.html**
Region: England

Britcomedy Digest

"Britcomedy Digest" covers all aspects of British comedies—radio, television, books, film, and plays. Past topics include "Blackadder," Monty Python, "Red Dwarf," "Terry Pratchett," "The Goodies," and "I'm Sorry I Haven't a Clue." These sites include archives of back issues.
Type: WWW
**Address: http://cathouse.org:8000/
BritishComedy/BD/**
Type: FTP
**Address: dixie.aiss.uiuc.edu:/pub/cat
house/humor/british.humour/**
Region: England

Deutsche Welle Radio and TV International

Available with a German, English, French, Spanish, or Portuguese interface, this page offers a day-by-day schedule of the satellite-TV and radio programs of this company. The listings themselves are all in German. Many of the shows are in the public-interest vein, including news shows, documentaries, and investigative reports, and the satellite broadcasts are available in Europe and the Americas.
Type: WWW
Address: http://www-dw.gmd.de:80/
Region: Germany, Europe, World

The Dominion

This is a promotional site for the Sci-Fi Channel, but it's pretty fun for SF fans also. Includes files you can download for free, show listings, and information on the Sci-Fi Channel's original programming for the U.S.

Type: WWW
Address: http://www.scifi.com:80/
Region: U.S.

Endemol Home Page

Endemol Entertainment is the largest independent TV producer in Europe. At their Web site you can find out about its facilities in the four countries where it operates, and get a little information on the shows it produces.

Type: WWW
Address: http://www.veronica.nl/endemol /information/television.html
Region: Holland, Germany, Portugal, Spain

European Satellite TV

This is a nicely written FAQ about the various satellite TV options available in Europe, and how the hardware works. Some data is specific to Scandinavia. It explains how to get European, Turkish, Arabic, and other shows.

Type: WWW
Address: http://xan.esrin.esa.it:2602/ Satellite-TV-Europe-FAQ.html
Region: World

Finnish TV

This is a searchable Web site about Finnish TV, in Finnish.

Type: WWW
Address: http://www.apu.fi/cgi-bin/tv
Region: Finland

Gays on TV

This is an eye-opening list of most of the gay, lesbian, and bisexual characters who have appeared on English-language television shows. It's interesting to see how often homosexuality is played "for laughs" and how frequently these characters are tragic victims of violence, and how rarely sexual orientation is simply incidental. They do try to "out" Ernie and Bert, too.

Type: WWW
Address: http://www.qrd.org/QRD/ browse/glbo.tv.characters.list
Region: World

Gerry Anderson Home Page

Ever seen "The Thunderbirds" or "U.F.O.," children's shows that combined animation and marionettes for a strange and unique effect? This page is dedicated to their creator, and has information on these and other shows he worked on.

Type: WWW
Address: http://www.brookes.ac.uk/ ~p0054463/fab.html
Region: England

i-TV

Stop in to see a "hyper-TV station" in action. Based in Edmonton, Alberta, i-TV has gone online with an Internet version of its daily broadcasts, including local and international news, sports, weather, and commercials. They bring together lots of Internet resources as well as the "report of the day." I stopped in not long after the terrorist bombing in Oklahoma City, and there were links to disaster relief organizations, a list of patients currently in the hospitals due to the bombing, links to local government and the

FBI, and even logs of IRC activity on #Oklahoma. Most impressive!

Type: WWW
Address: http://www.itv.ca/index.htm
Region: Canada

MuchMusic

It's like MTV, only Canadian. Their schedule, information on programs and VJs, and interesting links are here. Its French-speaking cousin, MusiquePlus, is apparently not yet online.

Type: WWW
Address: http://www.muchmusic.com/ muchmusic.html
Region: Canada

Nippon Hoso Kyokai

Link up here for information about Japan's premiere TV network. The site includes data on the network's sociological and market research programs.

Some text available in English, much more in Japanese.

Type: WWW
Address: http://www.nhk.or.jp/
Region: Japan

Pinoy TV!

Your guide to Filipino satellite TV and radio. Movies and old favorites from Filipino TV are most of the fare here.

Type: WWW
Address: http://www.bdt.com/home/ capjcruz/pinoytv.html
Region: Phillipines

Radio Television Hong Kong

This network is experimenting with Internet-based broadcasting, and also provides an online version of their news shows.

Type: WWW
Address: http://www.cuhk.hk/rthk/index .html
Region: Hong Kong

Red Dwarf

The absolute worst science-fiction TV series ever made, and all the funnier for it, "Red Dwarf" was an English space-opera comedy show that still commands a loyal following. Chat with other viewers via the newsgroup, or see the FTP site for episode guides, FAQs, scripts, audio files, recipes (?!), and more.

Type: Usenet newsgroup
Address: alt.tv.red-dwarf
Type: FTP
Address: toaster.ee.ubc.ca:/pub/red-dwarf
Region: England

Satellite TV Images

This could be described as an online video art project. It displays random images scanned from satellite broadcasts around the world. The images are also archived: The collection now features all sorts of exotica, from a snap of a news report on the Barbie Liberation Front to New Year's Eve in Moscow to a zouk ensemble in Martinique. Checking this out is much more fun than watching TV!

Type: WWW
Address: http://itre.uncecs.edu/misc/ images/images.html
Region: World

Screenwriters and Playwrights Home Page

The SCRNWRT mailing list is open to beginners, but it's surprising how many knowledgeable and serious TV writers use it for high-level exchange of information about projects-in-progress, studio problems, and the mechanics of the latest screenwriting software. However, 100 messages per day is not uncommon, so beware…. The excellent multipart FAQ on the intricate art of writing screenplays for TV is available at the Web site below—it's written by the pros, and has the kinds of tips you won't get in a college class (sample section: "Lies My Agent Told Me.") This page also has many links to other screenwriters resources. Invaluable.

Type: WWW
**Address: http://www.teleport.com/
           ~cdeemer/scrwriter.html**

Type: Usenet newsgroup
Address: listserv@tamvm1.tamu.edu
**Send e-mail message with one-line body:
           subscribe scrnwrit <Firstname
           Lastname>**
Region: U.S., World

Shortland Street Online

Described herein as "Drug of the Nation," "Shortland Street" is New Zealand's most popular soap opera. It's a tale of interpersonal intrigue, a little racy, and has that indefinable quality you might call "spunk." How popular is it? So much so that this site had to be moved from its previous home on an academic server to a commercial site in order to save some poor systems operator's job. See totally salacious and screamingly campy weekly summaries, an exercise in interactive scriptwriting, theme music, and lots of good humor.

Type: WWW
**Address: http://www.chch.planet.co.nz/
           shorters/shorters.html**
Region: New Zealand

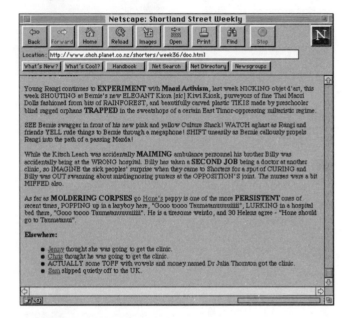

The Sofasphere II Project

This is a humor page about the couch potato lifestyles of the future.

Type: WWW
**Address: http://FTP.STD.COM/homepages/
           stevec/SSII/intro.html**
Region: World

South African Broadcasting Corp.

This public TV network in S.A. runs several stations in many languages. In fact, its Language Bureau home page, linked in here, is one of the best parts of its Web page. Its internal newsletter, *Interkom*, is also archived here.

Type: WWW
Address: http://www.sabc.co.za/
Region: South Africa

Take Two

Lots of TV links, including newsgroups for Australian, Chilean, UK, European, Canadian and U.S. TV, European satellite TV, and more.

Type: WWW

Address: http://www-bprc.mps.ohio-state .edu/cgi-bin/hpp/take two.html

Region: World

Tardis TV Archive

Links to information about shows and broadcasting in many nations. Several of the links include graphics or sound files.

Type: WWW

Address: http://src.doc.ic.ac.uk/public/ media/tv/collections/tardis/ index.html

Type: Gopher

Address: sunsite.doc.ic.ac.uk:70/1/media/ tv/collections/tardis

Region: U.K., Canada, U.S., Japan, Sweden

Television from Yahoo

A large collection of directories and subdirectories here divides the material to be searched by country of origin, type of show (comedy, cartoons, dramas, soaps, and so on), and genre.

Type: WWW

Address: http://www.yahoo.com/ Entertainment/Television/Shows

Region: World

Transient Images

This is a weekly e-zine about TV and movies. It includes the current TV ratings and lots of gossip, gossip, gossip.

Type: WWW

Address: http://www.cais.com/jpadgett/ www/home.html

Region: U.S.

Tusen och En Natt

Interview with Ylva-Maria Thompson, the hostess and star of one of Sweden's most poular erotic TV shows (yup, TV over there sure is different—this isn't even late-night cable). Smart discussion about sex information, in Swedish.

Type: WWW

Address: http://www.everyday.se:80/ hem/ylva-maria/

Region: Sweden

TV Galaxy

Lots of links to information about TV shows, networks, broadcasters, Gopher sites, and WAIS servers relating to the boob tube. Most of it's U.S.-based, but there's more.

Type: WWW

Address: http://www.einet.net/galaxy/ Leisure-and-Recreation/Television .html

Region: U.S., World

TVnet

Yes, you can even find out what's on TV tonight on the Net...and here's one place to do it. This very well-linked Web page provides access to FAQs about TV and particular TV shows, e-mail addresses and information on networks, linked listings of TV newsgroups, legal issues and news regarding television broadcasting, ratings, studios, information on world television station home pages, and yes, listings of programming in every time zone in the U.S. for any given day of the week. An excellent basic starting point for Internet television information searches.

Type: WWW
Address: http://tvnet.com/TVnet.html
Region: U.S.

TVnet—World TV List

Provided by the service above, this list has information about television stations around the world, arranged alphabetically by nation.

Type: WWW
**Address: http://tvnet.com/WORLDtv/
          worldtv.html**
Region: World

TV Tonite

If you live in the U.S., this is like having a free *TV Guide* in your computer. Includes broadcast and many cable listings.

Type: WWW
**Address: http://metaverse.com/vibe/
          tvtonite/tonite.html**
Region: U.S.

Xuxa's Home Page

"La Show de Xuxa" (and its many spin-offs) is the biggest hit on the air in the Spanish-speaking world. Hostess Xuxa is an unlikely but mighty cute combination of Madonna and Shari Lewis, a blonde bombshell with a flair for making money and fun times on her children's shows. This extensive page has information on all her shows and other projects.

Type: WWW
**Address: http://rt66.com/cj/xuxa/xuxa
          .html**
Region: Brazil

Right now, the best I can hope for in the way of international travel is a vicarious trip through some foreign Web pages. If they feature great photography, information about the wonderful food and warm, sandy beaches I'm missing, and tantalizing reports of bargains in the bazaar, it's almost heartbreaking—but better than nothing.

Maybe you're in the same boat as me, and "virtual travel" will pique your interest. Or maybe you're in that other boat. You know, the one leaving on a 'round-the-world cruise next Friday. You can get the latest on converting your currency, which credit cards will get cheers rather than jeers, where to go, where to stay, what to nosh on, and all the rest here.

If you're one of the lucky ones, are you *sure* you don't have room for a spare travel companion in your trunk? I don't take up much room, and I know some good jokes....

African Travel Links

It's a short list, but growing. Links include Africa-related material from the rec.travel archive, adventure travel company schedules, South African tourist information, and more.

Type: WWW
**Address: http://www.sas.upenn.edu/
          African_Studies/Home_Page/
          WWW_Links.html#Travel**
Region: Africa

alt.travel.road-trip

The Road Trip is a particularly American form of travel, as chronicled by Jack Kerouac and many others. It's *so* American that every summer I meet European and Asian tourists who are giving the crosscountry trek by car a try. This newsgroup is for exchanging anecdotes and information.

Type: Usenet newsgroup
Address: alt.travel.road-trip
Region: U.S.

Bad Trips

Isn't it funny how some of the best travel stories are about the worst experiences you've ever had? As long as you survive the bout with Montezuma's revenge, the bus ride from hell, or the border guard who claps you in irons, it'll prove you are an Intrepid Traveler (as opposed to an Ignorant Tourist) when you tell about it later on. Here are some true tales of travel horror.

Type: WWW
**Address: http://gnn.com:80/meta/travel/
           features/badtrip.html**
Region: World

Canadian Airlines Scheduling Information

The other airlines should see this Web page before they go online. It has an easy forms-based interface that gives you information on where they're flying and when (international flights only).

Type: WWW
**Address: http://www.cdnair.ca/documents
           /schedule.html**
Region: Canada, World

Caribbean Travel Roundup

This online newsletter is a first-person, seemingly honest insider sheet from people in the industry. Includes book reviews, coming events in the islands, advice from travel pros, and tips on getting good deals from those in the know.

Type: WWW
**Address: http://www.digimark.net/
           rec-travel/Caribbean/
           travel-roundup/9211**
Region: Caribbean

City Net

This information resource provides links to basic tourist, entertainment, and travel-related information for cities around the world. Updated daily, it's all available by text menus, by clickable maps (at the second Web address listed), or through a search feature that lets you look for a specific city, country, or region.

Type: WWW
Address: http://www.city.net/
**Address: http://wings.buffalo.edu/world
           /vt2/**
Region: World

Crash

This e-zine describes itself as a "guide to traveling through the underground." It includes low-budget/"alternative" travel tips, plus personal travel stories.

Type: Gopher
**Address: gopher.etext.org:70/11/Zines/
           Crash**
Contact: johnl@ora.com
Region: World

EINet Travel

This is a varied set of links to travel narratives, commercial travel sites, and nifty items like a list of airline 800 numbers.

Type: WWW
Address: http://galaxy.einet.net/galaxy/ Leisure-and-Recreation/Travel .html
Region: World

Electronic Tour Guide: Chicago

Part of the official home page for the city of Chicago, this online tourism office gives visitors information about upcoming summer activities in Chicago and other basic tourist information.

Type: WWW
Address: http://www.ci.chi.il.us/Chicago/ html/tourism/tourism-txt.html
Region: U.S.

Friends and Partners' Russia/CIS Travel

An excellent site with lots to offer about travel in the many regions that were once the U.S.S.R. Includes links to a Norwegian company that leads adventure tours in Siberia, many tourism-information pages from specific regions, a link that helps you get a tourist visa, and information on study tours and language-learning tours.

Type: WWW
Address: http://solar.rtd.utk.edu/friends/ travel/travel.html
Region: Russia, C.I.S.

GNN Travelers Center

So it's a little commercial around the edges—so are most travel magazines, and we don't let that ruin our fun, now do we? This set of pages is a good starting place for researching a potential excursion. Offerings include online guides to a number of off-beat destinations, including Jordan and Chechnya; travel information from Fodor's; and *Shoestring Travel,* an e-zine for budget travelers. There are also links to airlines elsewhere on the GNN system.

Type: WWW
Address: http://gnn.com:80/meta/travel/
Region: World

Holiday in Cambodia

This site includes fine photos and culturally sensitive text about this complex and fascinating Southeast Asian nation, now open for tourism by the adventurous.

Type: WWW
Address: http://none.coolware.com/entmt /cambodia/cambodia.html
Region: Cambodia

Hong Kong in Pictures

This selection from an exhibition shown at the Chinese University of Hong Kong explores the scenery and architecture of Hong Kong, along with the daily life of its inhabitants.

Type: WWW
Address: http://www.cuhk.hk/hk/scenery .htm
Region: Hong Kong

Images of Brazil

From soccer superstar Pele to gorgeous scenery to ladies in the famous Brazilian "tanga" (sub-bikini swimsuit), these photos in JPEG format will make you want to hop the next flight.

Type: FTP
Address: math.berkeley.edu/pub/
Preprints/P_N_de_Souza/Images
/Brazil/Fotos/
Region: Brazil

Indian Subcontinent Travel

Aside from the usual tourist information on the Indian subcontinent, Nepal, and Sri Lanka there is also a general tips document dealing with travel in South Asia.

Type: WWW
Address: http://IndiaOnline.com/travel
.html
Region: India, Nepal, Sri Lanka, Pakistan, Bangledesh

The Internet Guide to Hosteling

Why pay for a fancy hotel room when all you're going to do there is sleep? At hostels, you save dough and meet fascinating people. Here you can find a worldwide list of hostels, information on travel options for the have-backpack-will-travel crowd, and catch up on the latest news on the hosteling front.

Type: FTP
Address: ftp.crl.com/users/ro/overby/
hostel.welcome.html
Region: World

Journey to the East

There's much more at this site than travel information about the nations of South Asia. Online Indian spice merchants coexist here with tourist stuff, the Gyoto Tantric Choir, and home pages from Nepal.

Type: WWW
Address: http://www.eskimo.com/
~panther/east.html
Region: Nepal, India, Pakistan, Bhutan, Asia

Koblas Currency Converter

Planning a trip overseas and want to see how far your money will stretch? Designed by David Koblas, this site simply provides a weekly updated currency exchange versus the U.S. dollar.

Type: WWW
Address: http://gnn.com/cgi-bin/gnn/
currency
Region: U.S., World

Microstates

This is a fascinating site with all sorts of information about the world's tiniest countries and independent island nations, including lots of tourism pointers. There are even pages for specific Caribbean resorts, related newsgroups, and everything else you need to prepare for a truly "get away from it all" vacation or life.

Type: WWW
Address: http://www.microstate.com/
pub/micros/index.html
Region: World

The Money Abroad Page

This FAQ takes a continental approach to providing information valuable to the tourist about monetary issues (but not currency exchange), such as obtaining and using travelers checks in certain climes, acceptance of credit cards internationally, and so on.

Type: WWW
Address: http://www.inria.fr/robotvis/
personnel/laveau/money-faq/
money-abroad.html
Region: France, World

Northern California Wine Country

An online tour of wineries in Northern California Wine Country. The author of these pages assures readers that this is a noncommercial effort; hence, this is not a wine-industry advertisement.

Type: WWW
Address: http://www.paranoia.com/ ~steveo/sb_wine.html
Region: U.S.

Online Travel Center

This site provides links to about 15 or so excellent travel resources, like a searchable guide to online connections to governmental tourism offices world-wide, Viet-Web, and City Net.

Type: WWW
Address: http://www.newsouth.com/ L6.html
Region: U.S., World

Online Travel Journalism

Here you can find some personal travel narratives in text form. One of the most interesting is the true story of a hapless unemployed programmer who had the misfortune to be implicated in a series of bur-glaries, actually committed by his roommate of less than two weeks. He tells about his long journey through the Virginia prison system—talk about a "bad trip"!

Type: FTP
Address: ftp.spies.com/Library/Article/ Journey/
Type: Gopher
Address: wiretap.spies.com:70/11/ Library/Article/Journey
Region: World

PC Travel

This is an online travel reservations service. If you live in the U.S., they'll deliver tickets to your door via overnight mail.

Type: Telnet
Address: pctravel.com
Region: U.S., World

Peru: Que Bonito!

In Spanish, this site offers a virtual tour of Peru. Side trips include Macchu Picchu, the mysterious Nasca Lines, and the beaches of Lima.

Type: WWW
Address: http://www.rcp.net.pe/peru/ que _bonito.html
Region: Peru

Pierre Flener's Travel Archive

Here's an interesting collection of personal accounts of international travel. The pieces are all in the form of personal anecdote, most written by Turkish or European nationals, but in English.

Type: WWW
Address: http://www.cs.bilkent.edu.tr/ ~pf/travel/
Region: Belgium, Egypt, Guatemala, Jordan, Luxembourg, Morocco, Turkey, Turkmenistan, Uzbekistan, Venezuela

El Planeta Platica

"Eco-tourism" is traveling in ways that leave the "Ugly American" stereotype in the dust: avoiding swank, resource-grabbing hotels; using mass transit, bicycles, and your feet; treading lightly on natural resources. *El Planeta Platica* ("The Earth Speaks") is a well-written online newsletter about eco-tourism in South America. This site also has links to related resources.

Type: WWW
Address: **http://www.txinfinet.com/mader /planeta/planeta_current.html**
Region: Central America, South America

Prince Edward Island Travel Guide

One of the loveliest places in Canada, Prince Edward Island has beaches, lots of grassy meadows, and plenty to do for the visitor. Check in here for where to stay, local foods, places the kids will enjoy, the best golf courses, and many other items of interest.

Type: WWW
Address: **http://www.gov.pe.ca/info/vg/**
Region: Canada

rec.travel

This set of newsgroups is for talking about travel, planning for future trips, and exchanging stories of trekking triumphs and disasters. The rec.travel archives, available at the Web, Gopher, and FTP sites below, are an excellent source for both hard information and entertaining tales, often written to professional standards. Subscribe to rec.travel itself for worldwide information, or to one of the more specific newsgroups in the hierarchy. (By the way, rec.travel.marketplace is the place to look if you want to buy or sell airline tickets or other travel-related items.)

Type: Usenet newsgroup
Addresses: **rec.travel**
rec.travel.air
rec.travel.asia
rec.travel.cruises
rec.travel.europe
rec.travel.marketplace

rec.travel.misc
rec.travel.usa-canada
Type: WWW
Address: **http://www.digimark.net/ rec-travel/**
Type: Gopher
Address: **gopher.nus.sg/1ftp%3aftp server.nus.sg%40pub/misc/ travel/**
Type: FTP
Address: **ftp.remcan.ca/rec-travel/**
Region: World

Singapore Online Guide

This is an excellent example of what will certainly become the norm for government tourist bureau Web sites. Rich with graphic and cultural material, these pages cover a comprehensive field of topics, from deals and tours to seasonal festivals and local cuisine.

Type: WWW
Address: **http://www.ncb.gov.sg/sog/ sog.html**
Region: Singapore

Slovakia Tourist Home Page

Quite an impressively vast page for such a small region! Information pages for the major cities of Slovakia as well as the more historically interesting towns, and a variety of information relevant to the average traveler. This is a good spot to hit before visiting this tumultuous, though historically and architecturally beautiful region.

Type: WWW
Address: **http://www.tuzvo.sk/ homepage.html**
Region: Slovakia

Tour Guide to Bangladesh

This is quite a complete guide to Bangladesh for the prospective tourist, giving information on and photos of scenic natural areas, archaeological and historical sites, and tour information for the capital city Dhaka. There is also basic demographic and geographic data, as well as currency exchange information and visa requirements.

Type: WWW

Address: http://www.cif.rochester.edu/ users/outcast/tour/

Region: Bangladesh

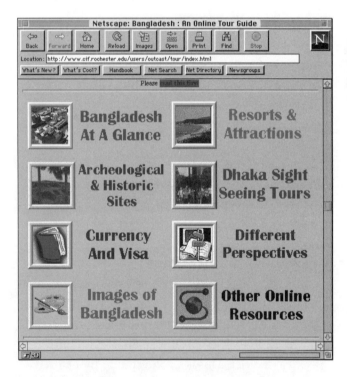

Tour in China

This site takes you on a mostly text-based virtual tour of China. You'll quickly understand what a vast undertaking an actual tour of the world's most populous nation would be. Except for listing Tibet as a province of China (I know that's official Chinese government policy, but it's inaccurate all the same), it's pretty honest, too. This is from the section on the Nei Mongu, the Mongul Autonomous Region in northern China: "…this region is only for strong and adventurous tourists who don't mind a mutton diet. The nights are cool. Winters are very cold and springs have sandstorms."

Type: WWW

Address: http://www.ihep.ac.cn/tour/ china_tour.html

Region: China, Tibet

Travel ASIA!

The travel guides created especially for Silk Route are the best part of this site, with all the essentials you'll need for a good trip. There are also links to other Asian travel sites, and to hotel and transportation information.

Type: WWW

Address: http://silkroute.com/silkroute/ travel/index.html

Region: Australia, Bangladesh, China, Hong Kong, India, Indonesia, Japan, Malaysia, Nepal, Pakistan, Philippines, Singapore, South Korea, Sri Lanka, Taiwan, Thailand, Vietnam

Travel Europe

This site provides links to dozens more that offer information on travelling in the many nations of Europe. It's very complete, and you can browse by city or country.

Type: WWW

Address: http://superior.carleton.ca/ ~jgreig/europe.html

Region: Europe

Traveler's Japanese

See the Language listings for more ways to get to get up to speed on any languages you may need for your trip. This one is an online phrasebook, with simple Japanese expressions you'll need for marketing, getting a taxi, ordering dinner…that sort of thing. It has audio files as well—very important with the Japanese language, since inflection can radically change the meaning of the same sound.

Type: WWW
Address: http://www.ntt.jp:80/japan/japanese/
Region: Japan

Travel Matters

This quarterly newsletter from acclaimed travel-book company Moon Publishing has travel narratives, health hints, and book reviews—including titles from other companies. The emphasis is on adventurous, relatively low-budget, eco-conscious/culture-conscious trips. It's free; just send them a note.

Type: E-mail
Address: travel@moon.com
Region: World

A Trip to Sub-Arctic Urals

This photo-essay takes you on a tour of the blue skies, cascading rivers, and ancient mountains of northern Russia, as traversed recently by the authors, their families, and a few friends in true wilderness-camper style. This rarely visited region sounds like someplace I would love to go.

Type: WWW
Address: http://solar.rtd.utk.edu/~asebrant/uralslog/story.html
Region: Russia

Macau Tourism Information

This Web page gives basic information about the province of Macau, technically a territory of Portugal but located in Asia. Tours, entertainment, shopping, transportation, and lots more are linked in, along with a colorful photo that telegraphs Macau's dual-culture personality.

Type: WWW
Address: http://sftw.umac.mo/Tourism_of_Macau/mac.html
Region: Portugal

U.S. State Department Travel Advisories

Before you buy a ticket for Kabul, check in here to see what the situation on the ground is. These assessments, which are updated regularly (and instantly in cases where there's a sudden change, such as a war), could save you a lot of grief.

Type: FTP
Address: ftp.std.com/obi/US.StateDept/Travel/
Type: Gopher
Address: gopher.stolaf.edu:70/11/Internet%20Resources/US-State-Department-Travel-Advisories
Region: World

Vanuatu: A Small Place in the South Pacific

Lots of gorgeous pictures, a little history, even a sound clip of a local radio broadcast. Not a travel brochure per se, which makes it all the more inviting.

Type: WWW

**Address: http://www.clark.net/pub/
kiaman/vanuatu.html**

Region: New Hebrides (Vanuatu)

Wandering through the Yucatan

This Web page is derived from entries in a travel journal written during a five-week backpacking trip through southern Mexico. There are some nice photos of Mayan ruins here also.

Type: WWW

**Address: http://www.netaxs.com/
~jduncan/Yucatan.html/**

Region: Mexico

Welcome Center for Virtual Vegas

Okay, here's the cheese…. Vegas, the ultimate tacky casino vacation paradise brought to you in living color. Sponsored by the Nevada Development Authority, this site will give you everything you need to plan your vacation to the "City of Sin," the city of speedy weddings and even speedier divorces, the real city that never sleeps.

Type: WWW

**Address: http://www.infi.net/vegas/vlv/
welcome.html**

Region: U.S.

WEATHER

You don't have to be a weatherman to care which way the wind blows: Whether you're wondering if it's time to sow the crops that your livelihood depends on or just planting pansies, knowing what to expect can be essential. If you're planning a trip, curious about when it'll be an auspicious time to set sail or go hiking, or collecting information for a high-school research paper on the climate in Peru,

here's a world's worth of sources to keep your personal weather report up to date.

There are probably 100 or more newsgroups concerned with weather as it affects specific cities, states, nations, or regions, such as ia.weather (Iowa) and pdx.weather (Portland, Oregon). Check with your service provider to get a list of any local newsgroups that they carry.

AHP_ARCHIVE-L

The Alberta Hail Project collected data about hail storms in Alberta, Canada from 1957 to 1986. Participants in this list discuss how the data should be preserved and used.

Type: Mailing list

Address: MAILSERVE@ARC.AB.CA

**Send e-mail message with body:
SUBSCRIBE AHP_ARCHIVE-L**

Region: Canada

Alfred Wegener Institute

Ocean and polar research goes on here. Read about the Institute's Antarctic research station and ocean measurements.

Type: WWW

**Address: http://www.awi-bremerhaven
.de/**

Region: Antarctica, World

Antarctica Images

Here you can find GIF-format weather-satellite images of Antarctica.

Type: Gopher

**Address: gopher.ssec.wisc.edu/11/amrc.d
/antarctica_images.d**

Region: Antarctica

Atlantic Oceanographic and Meteorological Laboratory: Hurricane Division

Information on the hurricane research and projects of the AOML, a U.S. research group, are made available here. Lots of images of hurricanes and data about them, including the current year's crop of pre-chosen hurricane names. By the way, accessing the FTP site via World Wide Web works well here, as the information is actually in HTML format.

Type: FTP
Address: aeolus.aoml.erl.gov/pub/www .d/HRDtest5.html
Region: U.S., World

Australia Bureau of Meteorology

Current forecasts and observations, climate data, and other weather-related information for Australia are available at this Gopher site.

Type: Gopher
Address: babel.ho.bom.gov.au/1
Region: Australia

Aviso Altimetrie

Oceanographers using satellites to study the oceans have created this Web page, which includes data on the satellites and their missions, and some of the results.

Type: WWW
Address: http://www-aviso.cls.cnes.fr/
Region: France, World

CALMET

This FTP archive is maintained by people who are working on software to help teach meteorology; it includes documents and programs.

Type: FTP
Address: ftp.met.ed.ac.uk/calmet/
Region: England

Canadian Satellite Images and More

This site offers lots of GIF images, organized by date and type—mostly of Canada and the polar region. There's also data on the polar ice caps, including historical information, and much more of interest here.

Type: FTP
Address: rainbow.physics.utoronto.ca/ pub/
Region: Canada

Centre for Atmospheric Science

These sites offer information on upcoming seminars, publications, and positions available at the center, which is part of Cambridge University. Includes information on their Atmospheric Chemistry Modelling Support Unit, a division that is writing software for creating computer simulations of the atmosphere. Some of the programs developed for this project are also available.

Type: WWW
Address: http://www.atm.ch.cam.ac.uk/
Type: FTP
Address: ftp.atm.ch.cam.ac.uk/pub/ugamp
Region: England, World

CLIMAT Mailing List

This list is for discussions of the CLIMAT system of data stations, which provide monthly means for a given country. Users of the data post various messages here for all users to read.

Type: Mailing list
Address: almanac@awis.auburn.edu
Send e-mail message with body: subscribe climat
Region: U.S., World

Climate Prediction Center—African Desk

Here you can find current data and recently archived data on African weather, plus predictions.

Type: WWW
Address: **http://nic.fb4.noaa.gov/products /african_desk/index.html**
Region: Africa

Cray Meteo-window

Want to run a meteorology imaging program on a Cray in Italy? Just Telnet to this site; the first time you drop in you'll get instructions on how to set things up so that the Cray can "see" your display (you have to send some e-mail to them first). Then you may be able to see images from the Meteosat weather satellite and of the Piedmont area of Italy.

Type: Telnet
Address: **cspnsv.csp.it 5000**
Region: Italy

Croatian Weather

This site provides a brief run-down on today's weather in Croatia and climatological mean monthly values. Text in Croatian or English.

Type: Gopher
Address: **madhz.dhz.hr/11/eng/ lokalni-info**
Region: Croatia

Current Weather Maps/Movies

Information at this site includes a number of high-resolution images in GIF format and digital movies of various areas: the U.S., Europe, Atlantic, Africa, Antarctica, and more.

Type: WWW
Address: **http://wxweb.msu.edu:80/ weather/**
Region: U.S., World

Current Weather Map: United Kingdom

Today's weather map for this region is available at the bottom of this Web page.

Type: WWW
Address: **http://www.doc.ic.ac.uk/**
Region: England, Scotland, Wales, Northern Ireland

The Daily Planet

 Of all the weather-related sites online, this one is probably the easiest to use for the amateur. It includes satellite pictures and forecasts, links to temperature and weather forecast for cities around the world, severe weather warnings and updates, a hypertext climatology textbook, and global links to more weather sites. Developed by the University of Illinois at Champaign-Urbana.

Type: WWW
Address: **http://wx3.atmos.uiuc.edu/**
Type: Gopher
Address: **wx.atmos.uiuc.edu/**
Region: World

Environment Canada

This is the Web site of the Canadian government's weather department. It includes forecasts, maps, and satellite images for Canada; long-range predictions; and information on the department's other programs.

Type: WWW
Address: **http://cmits02.dow.on.doe.ca/**
Region: Canada

German Climate Computing Center

This site, run by a supercomputer center that does climate research, is mostly in German. It includes information on their projects and staff, as well as some MPEG-format excerpts from climatology movies they've produced.

Type: WWW
Address: http://www.dkrz.de/index-eng.html
Region: Germany

GT-ATMDC

This mailing list is for discussing the dispersion of chemicals through the Earth's atmosphere.

Type: Mailing list
Address: Request@Interduct.TUDelft.NL
Send e-mail message with Subject: send gt-atmdc-info
Region: Netherlands

HAPEX SAHEL

This site is maintained by a group working in western Niger to understand the significance of the Sahel (Sahara desert) to global weather. You can examine the online data or spot images, and find out how to register to receive the official data.

Type: WWW
Address: http://www.orstom.fr/hapex/
Region: Niger, Africa

High-Resolution Africa Images

Current satellite images of Africa are available here, making weather data visual.

Type: WWW
Address: http://clunix.cl.msu.edu/weather/afr.html
Region: Africa

International Weather Observations

With lots of plots, maps, and data from around the world, this archive is maintained by Florida State University.

Type: Gopher
Address: metlab1.met.fsu.edu/
Region: U.S., World

Latest Weather in New Zealand

Here you can find JPEG-format images from New Zealand, courtesy of the VUW Institute of Geophysics. The FTP site archives the hourly images from the past two days; an MPEG version is in the works, they say.

Type: WWW
Address: http://www.gphs.vuw.ac.nz/../meteorology/maps.html
Type: FTP
Address: ftp.gphs.vuw.ac.nz
Region: New Zealand

Melbourne/Victoria Weather

Current forecasts and temperatures for the city of Melbourne and state of Victoria in Australia. Unfortunately, it has a terrible interface.

Type: Telnet
Address: 134.178.130.2 55555
Region: Australia

MET-AI

This discussion list is for those who want to talk about using artificial intelligence to solve meteorological problems.

Type: Mailing list
Address: met-ai-request@comp.vuw.ac.nz
Send e-mail message with body: subscribe
Region: New Zealand, World

Meteo Consult

Various weather data, including forecasts and weather images, is available here in Dutch, German, French, or English. There's also a link to an excellent commercial weather-information bureau in Germany: Meteofax Wetterdienste GmbH.

Type: WWW
Address: **http://www.meteocon.nl/**
Region: World

Meteosat

Here you can find GIF files of pictures from the Meteosat weather satellite.

Type: Gopher
Address: **gopher.rrz.uni-koeln.de/11/ themen/Wetter**
Region: Germany, World

Met-stud

A mailing list aimed at meteorology students around the world, met-stud is a forum for discussions about study programs and weather questions.

Type: Mailing list
Address: **listproc@bibo.met.fu-berlin.de**
Send e-mail message with body: SUB met-stud <Firstname Lastname>
Region: Germany

National Forecasting Contest

Discussions of all kinds of weather forecasting subjects, and particularly about the contest, are the topic of this list.

Type: Mailing list
Address: **listproc@bibo.met.fu-berlin.de**
Send e-mail message with body: sub nfc <Firstname_Lastname>
Region: Germany

The National Hurricane Center

Information on hurricanes, cyclones, and tropical storms can be found here, including images, movies, documents from the center, and more.

Type: WWW
Address: **http://nhc-hp3.nhc.noaa.gov/ index.html**
Region: U.S.

National Weather Service On Line

This Web site for the U.S. National Weather Service offers worldwide recent weather data and satellite images.

Type: WWW
Address: **http://hpcc1.hpcc.noaa.gov/nws /nwshome.html**
Region: U.S., World

The NOAA Weather Page

Lots of U.S. weather data, as well as pointers to weather servers all around the globe, are the subject here. It includes data about climactic changes that occurred in prehistory, too.

Type: WWW
Address: **http://www.esdim.noaa.gov/ weather_page.html**
Region: U.S., World

Oceanography Data

This archive holds maps and other oceanographic information, focusing on the North Atlantic. It includes some PC software as well.

Type: FTP
Address: **server.ices.inst.dk/dist/ocean**
Region: World

Russian Weather

You can check on recent and current weather in Moscow and St. Petersburg here.

Type: WWW
Address: http://solar.rtd.utk.edu/friends/ weather/weather.html
Region: Russia

sci.geo.meteorology

Discussions of all kinds of meteorological topics occur in this newsgroup.

Type: Usenet newsgroup
Address: sci.geo.meteorology
Region: World

The StormCast Project

At the Department of Computer Science at the University of Trømso, the staff of this project is working with distributed computing techniques, and have chosen weather as an application to test their theories. You can find out the current weather in Trømso, examine the data from the distributed StormCast program, and find out more about the project's staff from this page.

Type: WWW
Address: http://dslab3.cs.uit.no:1080/ StormCast/index.html
Region: Norway

Taiwan Weather

This is the official Taiwanese government site for weather reports. It includes links to weather information for other locales in Asia. All text is in Chinese.

Type: WWW
Address: http://www.cwb.gov.tw/
Region: Taiwan, Asia

University of Bayreuth

GIF format images from weather satellites archived here cover the entire world. They're organized by region.

Type: Gopher
Address: gopher.uni-bayreuth.de:70/11/ Service/Meteosat
Region: Germany, World

University of Edinburgh Satellite Images

In the images directory here you will find various weather-satellite images, mostly of Europe, in both GIF and JPEG formats.

Type: FTP
Address: cumulus.met.ed.ac.uk
Region: Scotland, Europe

University of Reading Meteorology Department

Various weather data and maps, including news about a project called the Airborne Southern Hemisphere Ozone Expedition, are available at this Web page. This department's staff is doing the data processing for the expedition. Some digital movies are also available on meteorological events.

Type: WWW
Address: http://typhoon.rdg.ac.uk/ typhoon.html
Region: England, World

Weather and Global Monitoring

Lots of images, organized by region or nation (Pacific, Antarctica, Japan, China, Korea, and so on) are available through this Web page, as well as forecasts and environmental information on Australia and other countries.

Type: WWW
Address: http://life.anu.edu.au/weather .html
Region: Australia, World

Weather Information

JPEG images of the U.K. and pointers to other sites are online here.
Type: WWW
Address: http://web.nexor.co.uk/users/ jpo/weather/weather.html
Region: England, Scotland, Wales, Northern Ireland

Weather Information, II

Pointers to many worldwide weather sites can be found at this Web page.
Type: WWW
Address: http://www.env.uea.ac.uk/ weather.html
Region: World

Weather Resources FAQ

Pointers to all kinds of weather resources, both on and off the Net: newsgroups, mailing lists, books, journals, and more.
Type: WWW
Address: http://www.cis.ohio-state.edu/ hypertext/faq/usenet/weather/ top.html
Region: U.S.

World Meteorological Organization

This is the meteorology group of the United Nations. You can find information on the organization, a directory of its staff, an FTP site with documents of the WMO, and pointers to the meteorological sites of member nations. Available in Spanish and English.

Type: WWW
Address: http://www.wmo.ch/
Type: FTP
Address: www.wmo.ch/
Region: World

The World Wide Web Virtual Library: Meteorology

A nearly complete index of worldwide meteorology sites is here.
Type: WWW
Address: http://www.met.fu-berlin.de/ DataSources/MetIndex.html
Region: Germany, World

Wxsat

This list isn't big on discussion, but it automatically sends you a blizzard of weather data every day: all NOAA/NESDIS bulletins on their satellites, plus some data on the Meteosat weather satellite. Best if you need to get lots of data without hunting for it. The FTP site is an archive of programs and graphics sent over the list.
Type: Mailing list
Address: wxsat-request@ssg.com
Type: FTP
Address: kestrel.umd.edu/pub/wxsat/
Region: U.S., World

WORKING ABROAD

Have you fantasized about living abroad while working at a dream job? If so, this section could give you the push you need to make those dreams a reality.

The Internet is still coming into its own as a job-search mechanism, unless the career you seek is in an academic or high-tech field. But other types of employers are starting to pay attention to the number of smart, skilled individuals who are online, and adjusting their recruitment efforts accordingly.

A few of the sites below are connected to professional recruitment agencies. Generally speaking, reputable agencies do not require payment up front to help you find work, as they are paid either by the employer or in some cases by deductions from your salary later on.

Another important source for job listings is the employers' own sites. If you've always wanted to work for Bank of America, Disney, CARE, Greenpeace, or the University of Jamaica, they are just five of the thousands of employers that maintain a presence on the Web. Often this presence includes current job openings and information about the company that might give you an edge over other applicants. In fact, Web-based businesses themselves (such as the flashier electronic magazines and information providers with a profit motive) seem to be in a hiring frenzy much of the time. Good luck with your search!

Academic Jobs in Holland and Beyond

This site consists of Nijenrode University's job openings for technical/academic personnel, plus worldwide academic openings.

Type: Gopher
Address: zeus.nijenrode.nl:70/11/Jobs
Region: Netherlands, Europe

Academic Position Network

APN lists open faculty positions around the world. The listings are divided geographically, so you can easily target a specific country.

Type: Gopher
Address: wcni.cis.umn.edu:11111
Region: World

Acadamie This Week's Chronicle of Higher Education

Along with a copious amount of U.S. listings, there's international employment information available here via a WAIS search engine, including some jobs outside of academia. The list is skewed towards Europe.

Type: Gopher
Address: chronicle.merit.edu:70/11/.ads/ .ads-by-search
Region: U.S., World

American Mathematical Society

You'll find here a small listing of international academic positions open in mathematics.

Type: Gopher
Address: e-math.ams.org:70/11/profInfo/ ProfOp/employ/ZZ
Type: WWW
Address: http://e-math.ams.org/web/ employ/employ.html
Region: World

Asia-Net

Looking for a job in Japan, China, or elsewhere in Asia? Look here first. Almost all of these positions require the ability to speak the language of the nation you'll be working in; the site also has information about proper application procedures and links to the Japan-Net and China-Net mailing lists for job-seekers. Note: Some jobs listed are for Japanese- or Chinese-fluent employees, but are actually located in the U.S. or Europe.

Type: WWW

Address: http://www.asia-net.com/

Region: Japan

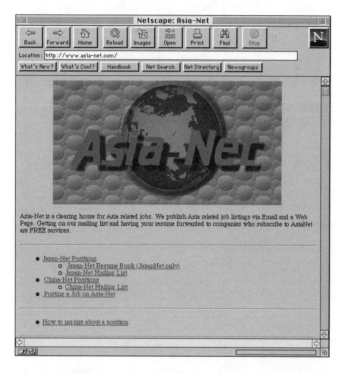

CareerMosaic

Sponsored by the world's largest employment search firm, this site has what computer dealers call "value-added" features. For instance, along with lots of mostly high-tech employers in search of new hires, there's information on résumé-writing (including multimedia résumés), and about co-op and internship opportunities for college students and others starting out on new careers. It's all U.S. companies, but some of them have operations overseas, so a

thorough search might turn up something in your country of choice.

Type: WWW

Address: http://www.careermosaic.com/

Region: U.S.

The Chicago Tribune Career Finder

This is a nice online classified ad listing of electronic, technical, and related industry jobs. Includes a limited search capability, although there's no way to search by region.

Type: WWW

Address: http://www.chicago.tribune.com: 80/home.html

Region: U.S., Canada

Commonwealth Education Jobs

The National Information on Software and Services (NISS) database contains University job listings in the U.K. and the Association of Commonwealth Universities. The Commonwealth includes many nations of the Caribbean, South Pacific, and Asian-Pacific, so there are well-paid academic jobs in some pretty exotic places here, like Fiji and Papua New Guinea.

Type: Gopher

Address: gopher.niss.ac.uk:71/11/G

Type: Telnet

Address: niss.ac.uk (select option AA or AB)

Region: England, Scotland, Wales, Northern Island, Australia, New Zealand, World

CyberDyne CS Ltd.

This very nice service is located in the U.K. In addition to their own job-search services, they include links to international job listings and some U.S. servers. Links are arranged geographically by region, including Asia, Australia, and Africa; jobs include high-tech, media, banking, medical, and other fields.

Type: WWW
Address: **http://www.demon.co.uk/ cyberdyne/cyber.html**
Region: England, U.S., Australia, World

CyberWeb: Jobs

Part of the Virtual Library system, this site brings together job-search links that can help you find a technical job in Utah, a medical job in the U.K., and anything in between.

Type: WWW
Address: **http://www.charm.net/~web/ Vlib/Misc/Jobs.html**
Region: U.S., World

Employment Opportunities and Resume Postings

Academic and scientific jobs for many U.S. institutions are listed here. You can also find all editions of the *Occupational Outlook Handbooks*, to find out which careers are hot and which are not, and other resources.

Type: Gopher
Address: **Gopher.Mountain.Net/11/ Employment%20Opportunities% 20%26%20Resume%20Postings**
Region: U.S.

FROGJOBS List

This mailing list can hook you up with a scientific job in France. It's intended for French grad students abroad and for foreign scientists hoping to find work in France.

Type: Mailing list
Address: **Listproc@list.cren.net**

Send e-mail message with body: **subscribe frogjobs <Firstname Lastname>**
Contact: **frogjobs@list.cren.net**
Region: France

Guides to Living and Working in Japan

The first Web page has an index to resources of interest to anyone planning to seek employment in Japan, including government, legal, travel, and sports information. Most important are its guides for foreign workers, including one especially for scientists. These are very thorough, covering everything from how to rent an apartment to what foreign parents need to know about the Japanese educational system.

The second Web page listed is a U.S.-based guide to Japan, which includes information on specific Japanese cities and work/study programs, doing business in Japan, and much more.

Type: WWW
Address: **http://www.ntt.jp/japan/index .html**
Address: **http://fuji.stanford.edu/japan_ information/japan_information_ guide.html**
Region: Japan

H.E.A.R.T—Career Connection's On-Line Information System

The Human Resources Electronic Advertising and Recruiting Tool is a large contract-placement service, with online listings from many fields. The service is free.

Type: WWW
Address: **http://www.career.com/**
Type: Telnet
Addresses: **career.com college.career.com**
Region: U.S., World

The Interactive Employment Network

A large employment Web site with multiple services, this page has links to openings at over 1,700 mostly U.S.-based employers. You can search according to global region, or post your resume/CV to their database. Few international listings.

Type: WWW
Address: http://www.espan.com/
Region: U.S., World

International Career Employment Network

Based at Indiana University, this site is an invaluable resource for foreign nationals seeking employment in the U.S. Information about visas, jobs, insurance, student life, and more can be found here. For U.S. readers, there are also job listings abroad, including academic and high-tech careers, through the *International Career Employment Network* newsletter and other sources.

Type: Gopher
**Address: gopher.indiana.edu/11/the
           university/life/intlcent**
Region: U.S., World

Job Bank

From the University of Texas at Austin, this site has mostly academic-related U.S. listings, but it also archives postings to the misc.jobs (international) and tx.jobs (Texas jobs) newsgroups.

Type: Gopher
**Address: gopher.utexas.edu:70/11/world
           /Jobs**
Region: U.S., World

Job Guide

This site is an impressive guide to job-search resources on the Net, with helpful tips on incorporating the Internet into your job search. Includes links to listings in all fields, including summer jobs, internships, and co-op opportunities for students.

Type: WWW
**Address: http://www.wpi.edu/~mfriley/
           jobguide.html**
Region: U.S., Canada, World

Job Listings Available via Dial-Up BBS

This list includes several computer bulletin boards accessible via modem that specialize in job listings. It provides the name of the BBS, the phone number, modem settings, type of positions listed, and whether or not fees are charged to access the BBS's services. Alternatively, you can send a message to the e-mail address below for a copy of the list. Includes U.S. and international opportunities in many career fields.

Type: WWW
**Address: http://rescomp.stanford.edu/
           jobs-bbs.html**
Type: E-mail
Address: hotlist@jobnet.com
Region: U.S., World

JobNet

This job-search helper can be searched by field and by geographical region. It includes a small but growing set of international job databases.

Type: WWW
Address: http://sun.cc.westga.edu/~coop/
Region: U.S., World

Job Placement in the Virtual Town

This nice collection of employment-related links is maintained by the University of California at Davis. Seems geared especially for the graduating student, so there's lots of information on getting started with your job hunt and finding entry-level positions.

Type: WWW

Address: http://www.cs.ucdavis.edu/virt-town/job.html

Region: U.S., World

Jobs by Gopher

Gopher Jewels is a compendium of the very best Gopher sites, so naturally its employment section is terrific. Includes the *Chronicle of Higher Education*'s international academic listings, and links to dozens of Gopher sites that specialize in law, science, medical, forestry, the arts, biology and biotechnology, and other positions.

Type: Gopher

Address: cwis.usc.edu:70/11/Other_Gophers_and_Information_Resources/Gopher-Jewels/1stuff/employment

Type: WWW

Address: http://galaxy.einet.net/GJ/employment.html

Region: U.S., Canada, World

Jobs by Net

Several mostly-U.S. employment sources are available through this site, including jobs in data processing and medical careers.

Type: WWW

Address: http://www.uwm.edu/Mirror/inet.services.html

Region: U.S., World

Jobs by Usenet

Try these newsgroups for some leads; they're the two biggest. Beware, some opportunities offered are less than legitimate: Don't pay up front for job information, for example. See the Web pages for a longer (but by no means complete) list of linked job-search newsgroups. The Gopher document is by far the best Usenet resource, as it has a huge list of regional U.S. job newsgroups and an even longer list of nation-specific newsgroups for all of Europe.

Type: Usenet newsgroups

Addresses: misc.jobs.offered
misc.jobs.contract

Type: Gopher

Address: gopher://una.hh.lib.umich.edu:70/00/inetdirsstacks/jobs%3Ariley

Type: WWW

Address: http://www.demon.co.uk/cyberdyne/cybenews.html

Region: World

Job Searching and Employment: Best Bets from the Net

This guide by Phil Ray and Brad Taylor is a selection of the best places to begin searching for jobs in various disciplines. They also include easy instructions on using the Internet in your quest. An excellent and well-maintained site with links to many employment information sources that list many U.S. and some foreign openings.

Type: WWW

Address: http://asa.ugl.lib.umich.edu/chdocs/employment/

Type: Gopher

Address: una.hh.lib.umich.edu/00/inetdirsstacks/employment%3araytay

Region: U.S., World

Jobs in Canada

This is a menu of links to Usenet newsgroups and Telnet sites that have information about employment opportunities in Canada. You can search by province.

Type: WWW
Address: http://www.wpi.edu/Depts/ Library/jobguide/canada.html
Region: Canada

Latino Employment Network

Positions are posted here for mostly academic positions in Latin American Studies and related fields.

Type: Gopher
Address: latino.sscnet.ucla.edu/11/ Employment%20Center
Region: U.S., Central America, South America

Medsearch America

Medsearch is a health-care and heath-care support job listing service, with some international contacts available as well as many U.S. jobs.

Type: WWW
Address: http://www.medsearch.com/
Region: U.S., World

NCS Career Magazine

This publication-cum-Web-site is a fine resource for finding work. It has postings from agencies and employers, plus the *Wall Street Journal*'s business listings, which can be searched using keywords for type, skill, and location (search on "overseas" for listings outside of the U.S.), as well as articles on improving your chances.

Type: WWW
Address: http://plaza.xor.com/careermag /index-text.html
Region: U.S., World

Nordic Linguistic Bulletin

A general linguistic information board with some international job offerings mixed in with other text bulletins. Postings are directly from employers, which are mostly academic.

Type: Gopher
Address: nora.hd.uib.no/11/Nordic%20 Linguistic%20Bulletin
Region: Norway, World

Nursing Jobs Online

Nursing is one of those portable skills that can take you around the world if you want it to. The Gopher sites here can hook you up with opportunities close to home or far away. The first is for the NURSE Gopher Service for Nurses in England, the second is the University of Tennessee at Knoxville's Nightingale service. The English service includes many listings from outside the U.K., incidentally, plus listings for spring- and summer-camp nurses in Europe (what a great idea for a working vacation!)

Type: Gopher
Address: nurse.csv.warwick.ac.uk/11/ jobs
Address: nightingale.con.utk.edu/11/ Communications/Positions
Region: U.S., England, Scotland, Wales, Northern Ireland, Canada, World

Ohio State University Business Job Finder

An outstanding Web site with links to general employment information; this includes many lesser-known sites, a significant number of them with international listings.

Type: WWW
Address: http://www.cob.ohio-state.edu/ dept/fin/osujobs.htm#Link3
Region: U.S., World

The Online Career Center

A good industry-sponsored free Web site with keyword searching available. Search on "overseas" for foreign job listings.

Type: WWW
Address: http://www.occ.com/occ/Home Page.html
Region: U.S., World

On-Line Job Services

This Internet meta-list is extraordinarily complete, with listings for recruitment companies, online résumé banks, specialty job-search services, career-development resources, job-search Usenet newsgroups, and more, including resources in Europe and Asia. For U.S. readers, it includes valuable links to Federal and state government job resources—and the listings maintained by local employment offices nationwide. Well worth checking into.

Type: WWW
Address: http://rescomp.stanford.edu/ jobs.html
Region: U.S., World

Papyrus Media's Careers On-Line

A U.K.-based international recruiter, their site specializes in listing jobs in the European Union nations and the Pacific Rim, including Hong Kong. The site also includes important links to information about visas, work permits, and immigration matters.

Type: WWW
Address: http://www.britain.eu.net/ vendor/jobs/main.html
Region: England, Europe, Asia, World

RPI Career Resources

Rensselaer Polytech has put together a very nice collection of links to U.S. and international resources for the job-hunter. One of the most useful is a link to professional organizations, which are always a good source of leads.

Type: WWW
Address: http://www.rpi.edu/dept/cdc/
Region: U.S., World

Russian and East European Institute Employment Opportunities

This listing includes academic and support positions, most of which require proficiency in one or more languages other than English.

Type: WWW
Address: http://www.indiana.edu/ ~reeiweb/indemp.html
Region: Russia, Eastern Europe

The San Francisco Chronicle and Examiner Job Placement Ads

The main problem here, as with all newspaper ads, is the inability to search by category. But it offers a wealth of employer data, including some foreign listings (particularly for Pacific Rim companies).

Type: WWW
Address: http://sfgate.com/classifieds/ files/770.html
Region: U.S., World

Singapore Teletext

I had a tough time accessing the file, but this site includes career opportunities in Singapore and with Singapore-based companies.

Type: WWW
Address: http://www.ntu.ac.sg/intv/ intv_ww2.html
Region: Singapore

TeleJob

This is the electronic job exchange board of the Associations of Assistants and Doctoral Students of the technological institutes of Zurich (AVETH) and Lausanne (ACIDE). There are plenty of interesting jobs here for young academics. The home page is in English with German and French versions available, but many job positions may not be listed in English.

Type: WWW
Address: http://ezinfo.ethz.ch/ETH/ TELEJOB/tjb_home_e.html
Region: Switzerland, Europe

Times Higher Education Supplement

This online version of the *London Times*'s supplement is invaluable to any teacher or professor seeking work overseas, or interested in the doings of their English counterparts. Includes worldwide job ads.

Type: WWW
Address: http://www.timeshigher.newsint .co.uk/
Region: England, World

TKO Personnel Inc.

This recruiter specializes in filling technical positions for companies in Asia, Japan, and the Pacific Rim region. They are interested in bicultural candidates only, which means you need proficiency in English and at least one Asian language, as well as the desired job skill. Some U.S. positions are listed here as well, with Asian firms or companies making products for the Asian market. Information is available in English or Japanese.

Type: WWW
Address: http://www.internet-is.com/tko/
Region: Japan, China, Korea, Asia, Pacific, U.S.

US to UK Moving FAQ

Are you an American who wants to live and work in one of the nations of the U.K.? This lengthy FAQ has all the information you need to get started, from the cheapest way to move your stuff and how to plug in your electric hair-dryer to important questions like "Will I be able to stand the food in the U.K.?" Of course, there's information on visas and work permits here too. Written by an experienced Yank expatriate.

Type: WWW
Address: http://www.biols.susx.ac.uk/ sandell/ukfaq/uk_faq.html
Address: http://www.charm.net/~web/ uk_faq.html
Address: http://www.biols.susx.ac.uk/ sandell/ukfaq/uk_faq.html
Type: FTP
Address: rtfm.mit.edu/pub/usenet-by- hierarchy/news/answers/ US-to-UK-moving-faq
Region: England, Scotland, Wales, Northern Ireland

WWW Home Servers Guide for the Companies in Japan

This is a page of links to the home pages of Japanese companies. Very useful and interesting.

Type: WWW
**Address: http://www.jicst.go.jp/
            dir-www/com.html**
Region: Japan

Yahoo's Listings of Employment Information

This is an absolutely fantastic service, with the usual huge assortment of frequently-updated links you can always expect from Yahoo.

Type: WWW
**Address: http://www.yahoo.com/Business
            /Employment**
Region: U.S., World

Appendix A: Internet Providers

It would be easy to write an entire book that contained nothing but the names and addresses of Internet service providers around the world. Instead, I've included contact information here for at least one in each nation that I could find providers for. If there was a choice between academic providers, such as universities, and private providers or companies that supply service to non-governmental organizations (NGOs), I chose the latter. Obviously, if you have academic connections you should use them first—you may even be able to obtain service for free. If there was a choice between a provider that offered only dial-up accounts and one that offered full Internet access, I listed the latter.

All of these providers were in business at press time, but because this is a very fast-paced field company names, status, and offerings may change. In some cases the companies listed are the only Internet providers in the nation, but in many cases they are not. Many of these firms maintain local-access nodes in cities or regions other than the one in which they are physically located. Please also note that you may need an additional country or city code or access number to reach some of these firms by telephone or fax, depending on your location—check with your long-distance carrier if you have trouble connecting.

If you are searching for a service provider, also see Chapter 6 for information about obtaining extremely complete lists via e-mail or FTP of companies that operate in various regions. These lists are regularly updated, and provide a wider picture of what's available than this admittedly small offering.

I have not included information on pricing or specific services offered because this information would almost surely be outmoded by the time you read this, and because fluctuating currencies make overseas prices difficult to describe accurately in terms of U.S. dollars. I can say that unless you are in a region where there is no choice at all, it pays to compare—even in the U.S. some providers charge as much as twice or three times the amount asked by their competitors for the same services.

Neither I nor Ziff-Davis Press are expressing support or endorsement for any company or service by including it in this list.

I owe a special debt of gratitude to the many individuals who maintain lists of Internet service providers online. I'd like to give particular thanks to Carl Benoit of Benoit LIPS (lips@best.be), who maintains a list of access providers around the world (http://www.earth.org/~lips—see Chapter 6 for how to order this list by other means), Peter Harrison, Randy Bush, and many others whose donated efforts should not go unrecognized.

Africa

Many areas in Africa are served only by FidoNet, if at all. If the providers below don't meet your needs, download "Connectivity with Africa by Randy Bush" via Gopher from rain.psg.com:70/00/networks/connect/africa.txt.

Algeria

Algeria Net
06 Rue Frederic MISTRAL Telemly
Algiers
Phone: (213) 2-612-715

Burkina Faso
ORSTOM
01 BP 182 - Ouagadougou
Phone: (226) 30 67 37 or (226) 30 67 39
Fax: (226) 31 03 85

Cameroon
ORSTOM
BP 1857
Yaoundé
Phone: (237) 20 15 08
Fax: (237) 20 18 54

Congo
ORSTOM
BP 181
Brazzaville
Phone: (242) 83 26 80
Fax: (242) 83 29 77

Egypt
EUnet Egypt
E-mail: ow@estinet.uucp
Phone: (20) 2 3557253
Fax: (20) 2 3547807

Ethiopia
Pan African Development Information System (PADIS)
Box 3001
Addis Ababa
E-mail: sysop@padis.gn.apc.org
Phone: (251) 1 511 167
Fax: (251) 1 514 416

Ivory Coast
ORSTOM
15 B.P. 917
Abidjan 15
Phone: (225) 24 37 79
Fax: (225) 24 65 04

Kenya
ELCI
E-mail: sysop@elci.gn.apc.org
Phone: (254) 2 562 015

Madagascar
ORSTOM
BP 434 - 101
Antananarivo
Phone: (261) 23 30 98
Fax: (261) 23 30 98

Mali
ORSTOM
BP 2528
Bamako
Phone: (223) 22 43 05 / 22 27 74
Fax: (223) 22 75 88

Niger
ORSTOM
BP 11 416
Niamey
Phone: (227) 73 20 54
Fax: (227) 72 28 04

Senegal
ORSTOM
BP 1386
Dakar
Phone: (221) 32 34 76 / 32 34 80
Fax: (221) 32 43 07

Seychelles
ORSTOM
Seychelles Fishing Authority Headquarters
Rue des Frangipaniers - BP 570
Victoria-Mahe
Phone: (248) 247 42
Fax: (248) 245 08

South Africa
Commercial Internet Services (CIS)
P.O. Box 395
Pretoria, 0001
E-mail: info@cis.co.za
Phone: (27) 12 841-2892
Fax: (27) 12 841-3604

Togo
ORSTOM
BP 375
Lomé
Phone: (228) 21 43 44 / 21 43 46
Fax: (228) 21 03 43

Tunisia
EUnet Tunisia
E-mail: mondher@Tunisia.EU.net
Phone: (216) 1 787757
Fax: (261) 1 787827

Uganda
MUKLA
Makerere University
Kampala, Uganda
E-mail: sysop@mukla.gn.apc.org
Phone: (256) 41-532-479

Zambia
ZAMNET Communication Systems Ltd.
Box 32379
Lusaka
E-mail: sales@zamnet.zm
Phone: (260) 1-293317

Zimbabwe
MANGO
Department of Computer Science
University of Zimbabwe
P.O. Box MP-167
Harare
E-mail: Rob_Borland@mango.apc.org
or
johnux@zimbix.uz.zw

Asia
China (People's Republic of)
China Research and Education Network (CERNET)
Wu Jian Ping
Head of the CERNET Technical Board
Professor of the Computer Engineering Department
Tsinghua University
Beijing 100084
E-mail: jianping@cernet.edu.cn
Phone: (86) 1-2595931
Fax: (86) 1-2595933

Hong Kong

Hong Kong Supernet
HKUST Campus
Clear Water Bay, Kowloon
E-mail: info@hk.super.net or postmaster@hk.super.net
WWW: http://www.hk.super.net/~rlowe/bizhk/
    bhhome.html
Phone: (852) 358-7924
Fax: (852) 358-7925

Internet Online Hong Kong Ltd
P.O. Box 47165
Morrison Hill, Post Office
Hong Kong
E-mail: info@iohk.com
Phone: (852) 768-8008

India

aXcess Online Services
Business India Information Technology Ltd.
3-10 Phoenix Mills Compound, Bombay - 400 013,
    India
E-mail: sharad@axcess.net.in
or
postmaster@axcess.net.in
Phone: (91) 22-493 7676
Fax: (91) 22-493 6578

UUNET India Limited
270N Road No. 10
Jubilee Hills
Hyderabad, A.P. 500 034
E-mail: info@uunet.in
Phone: (91) 842 238007
Fax: (91) 842 247787

Indonesia

University of Indonesia, Department of Computer Science,
Jl. Salemba Raya 4, P.O. Box 3442
Jakarta 10002
E-mail: postmaster@UI.AC.ID
Phone: (62-21) 727-0162

Japan

Japan has a rapidly growing demand for Internet access, and new firms are springing up to meet it seemingly overnight. For a fresh update, send the message "subscribe" (without the quote marks) to: efj-request@twics.com, or FTP to neoteny.eccosys.com/pub/efj/efj-faq.txt.

Cyber Technologies International K.K.
Otake Bldg. 304, 4-6 Daikyocho
Shinjuku-Ku, Tokyo 160
E-mail: sales@cyber.ad.jp
Phone: (81) 3-3226-0961
Fax: (81) 3-3226-0962

Global Online Japan
Oshima Building 302
1-56-1 Higashi Nakano
Nakano-ku, Tokyo 164
E-mail: info@gol.com (to receive information
    automatically)
or
sales@gol.com (to ask specific questions)
Phone: (03) 5330-9380
Fax: (03) 5330-9381

Malaysia
JARING/MIMOS
7th Floor, Exchange Square
Off Jalan Semantan, Bukit Damansara,
50490 Kuala Lumpur
E-mail: noc@jaring.my
or
mal@mimos.my
Phone: (60) 3-254-9601
or
(60) 3-255-2700, ext. 2101
Fax: (60) 3-253-1898

Nepal
Mercantile Office Systems
E-mail: kgautam@mosnepal.ernet.in
Phone: (977) 1 220773
Fax: (977) 1 225407

Pakistan
Brain Computer Services/Brain NET
730-Nizam Block
Iqbal Town, Lahore-54570
E-mail: info@brain.com.pk
Phone: (92) 42-541-4444
Fax: (92) 42-758-1126

Philippines
Email Centre
108. V. Luna Road, Sikatuna Village
Quezon City
E-mail: sysop@phil.gn.apc.org
Phone: (63) 2 921 9976

Phillippine Network Foundation Inc.
Phone: (63) 2 633-1956

Singapore
SingNet
Gopher: gopher.technet.sg
Phone: (65) 751-5034

South Korea
DACOM Corporation
140-716 DACOM B/D.
65-228, 3-Ga, Hangang-Ro
Yongsan-Ku, Seoul
E-mail: help@nis.dacom.co.kr
Phone: (82) 2-220-5232/3
Fax: (82) 2-220-0771

Sri Lanka
Lanka Internet Services, Ltd.
IBM Building, 5th Floor
48 Nawam Mawatha
Colombo 2
E-mail: info@lanka.net
WWW: http://www.lanka.net/
Phone: (94) 1-342974
Fax: (94) 1-343056

Taiwan (Republic of China)
Pristine Internet Gateway
3F, No. 2, Alley 2, Lane 244, Roosevelt Rd. Sec. 3
Taipei, Taiwan
E-mail: robert@pristine.com.tw
WWW: http://www.pristine.com.tw/
Phone: (886) 2 368-9023
Fax: (886) 2 367-0342

SeedNet

Taipei Service center

E-mail: service@tpts1.seed.net.tw

Phone: (02) 733-8779

Fax: (02) 737-0188

or

Hsinchu Service center

E-mail: service@shts.seed.net.tw

Phone: (035) 773311, ext. 512

Fax: (035) 788031

Thailand

Thaisarn Internet Service at NECTEC

E-mail: sysadmin@nwg.nectec.or.th

WWW: http://www.nectec.or.th/

Phone: (66) 2 248-8007

Fax: (66) 2 247-1335

Vietnam

NetNam

E-mail: admin@netnam.org.vn

Phone: (84-4) 346-907

Fax: (84-4) 345-217

Canada

See the Web site at http://www.well.com/user/peterh/phaphome.html for Peter Harrison's Access Provider (PHAP) list of North American Internet providers, or see Chapter 6 for more leads to other extensive lists. Many U.S. providers, notably Portal and IAT, also service many parts of Canada.

HookUp Communications

1075 North Service Road W., Suite 207

Oakville, Ontario L6M 2G2

E-mail: info@hookup.net

FTP: ftp.hookup.net/pub/info/Info-Brochure

Phone: (905) 847-8000

Fax: (905) 847-8420

UUNET Canada

1 Yong Street, Suite 1400, Toronto, ONT, M5E 1J9, Canada

E-mail: info@uunet.ca (to automatically receive information)

or

support@uunet.ca (to ask specific questions)

FTP: ftp.uunet.ca

WWW: www.uunet.ca

Phone: (800) INET-123

Fax: (416) 368-1350

Caribbean

Bahamas

CUNET

IBM Bahamas Ltd.

P.M.B. SS-6400

Nassau

E-mail: KBETHEL@UBAHAMAS.ORG.BS

Phone: (809) 322-2145

Fax: (809) 322-4649

Barbados

CUNET

Computer Center

University of the West Indies

Cave Hill Campus

P.O. Box 64

Bridgetown

E-mail: WILLIAMS@UWICHILL.EDU.BB

Phone: (809) 425-1310

Fax: (809) 425-1327

Bermuda

Internet Bermuda Limited

P.O. Box HM 2445

Hamilton HM JX

E-mail: info@ibl.bm

WWW: http://www.ibl.bm

Phone: (809) 296-1800

Fax: (809) 295-7269

Cuba

Instituto de Documentacion e Informacion Cientifica y Tecnica (CENIAI)

Jefe de Departmento Tecnico Red CENIAI

Industria y San Jose Capitolio Nacional

Apartado 2213

Habana

E-mail: jemar@ceniai.cu

Phone: (537) 62-6565 or (537) 62-0757

Fax: (537) 33-8237

Dominican Republic

REHRED (Academic and Research Network)

E-mail: sjb@acn.miami.com

or

pimienta!daniel@redid.org.do

Grenada

CUNET

Granada National College Tanteen

St. George's

E-mail: LINDY@GNC.EDU.GD

Phone: (809) 465-2090

Fax: (809) 465-5202

Jamaica

CUNET

University of the West Indies, Mona Campus

Kingston 7

E-mail: MANISON@UWIMONA.EDU.JM

Phone: (809) 927-2781

Fax: (809) 927-2156

Puerto Rico

Corporacion para la Red Cientifica Cientifica y de Investigacion Nacional de Puerto Rico (CRACIN)

Secretario de Relaciones Internacionales

P.O. Box 195355

San Juan 00919-5355

E-mail: ERivera@mxruc.clu.net

Phone: (809) 759-6891

Fax: (809) 759-8117

St. Kitts and Nevis

CUNET

College of Further Education

P.O. Box 295

Horsford Rd., Basseterre

E-mail: IDM@CFE.EDU.KN

Santa Lucia

CUNET

ISIS

P.O. Box GM 717

3 Castries

E-mail: ADANIEL@ISIS.ORG.LC

Phone: (809) 452-3702

Fax: (809) 453-7690

Trinidad and Tobago
CUNET
4 Serpentine Place
St. Clair
E-mail: SLAURENT@CARIRI.GOV.TT
or
LARS_J@NIHERST.GOV.TT
Phone: (809) 628-8523
Fax: (809) 622-7880

Central America
Belize
CUNET
University College of Belize
P.O. Box 990
Belize City
E-mail: OLDA@UCB.EDU.BZ
or
brian@ucb.edu.bz
Phone: (501) 232732
Fax: (501) 230255

Costa Rica
Red Nacional de Investiacion CRNet
Universidad de Costa Rica
San Jose
E-mail: gdeter@ns.cr
Phone: (506) 255911
Fax: (506) 2255911

Guatemala
MayaNet
Universidad del Valle de Guatemala
Apartado Postal #82
Guatemala City 01901
E-mail: furlan@uvg.gt

Phone: (502) 2-690791
Fax: (502) 2-380212

Nicaragua
Nicarao
CRIES
Iglesia El Carmen, 1 cuadra al lago
Apartade 3516
Managua
E-mail: ayuda@nicarao.apc.org
Phone: (505) 2 621312
Fax: (505) 2 621244

Panama
Universidad de Panama
Vicerectoria de Investigacion y Postgrado
Ciudad Universitaria Octavio Mendez P
Panama City
E-mail: barragan@huracan.cr
Phone: (506) 64 4242
Fax: (506) 64 4450

Eastern/Central Europe
Azerbaijan
InTrans
370000 Azerbaidjanskaya respublika
g. Baku, ul. Hagani, 18
E-mail: postmaster@insun.azerbaijan.su
Phone: 7 8922 930832

Belarus
EKSPO
210001 g.Vitebsk, ul. Kosmonavtov 4
E-mail: lav@ekspo.vitebsk.by
Phone: 7 0212 370898

Bulgaria

EUnet Bulgaria

E-Mail: postmaster@bulgaria.EU.net

Phone: 359 52 259135

Fax: 359 52 234540

Croatia

CARNet

E-mail: Predrag.Pale@carnet.hr

FTP/Gopher: carnet.hr

Phone: 385 41 629 963

Czech Republic

EUnet Czechia

E-mail: prf@Czechia.EU.net

Phone: 42 2 3323242

Fax: 42 2 24310646

Estonia

Ants Work

Deputy Director

Institute of Cybernetics

Estonian Academy of Sciences

Akadeemie tee 21

EE 0108 Tallinn

E-mail: ants@ioc.ee

Phone: 007 0142 525622

Fax: 007 0142 527901

(Note: also serves Latvia and Lithuania)

Georgia

Omega

380056 g.Tbilisi, pr. G. Robakidze, 3 kv., 5 korpus

Kazarova Narine Georgievna

E-mail: postmaster@aod.ge

Phone: 7 8832 985647

Hungary

EUnet Hungary

1518 Budapest PoB 63

E-mail: info@Hungary.EU.net

Phone: 36 1 2698281

Fax: 36 1 2698288

Latvia

(*See also* entry for Estonia)

Versia Ltd

Kleistu 5

Riga, LV-1067

E-mail: gene@vernet.lv, voll@vernet.lv

Phone: 371 2 417000, +371 2 428686

Fax: 371 2 428937

Lithuania

(*See also* entry for Estonia)

Amber Software Technologies, Inc., LT Branch

Litovskaya Respublika, G. Klaipeda 5800, a/ya 49

E-mail: root@mes.lt

Phone: 7 01261 99926

Romania

LOGIC

Calea Grivitei 136, 78122 Bucharest, Romania

E-mail: Tudor.Panaitescu@alliance-partners.sprint.com

Phone: (4-01) 617-6333

Fax: (4-01) 312-8443

Russia

GlasNet

Ulitsa Sadovaya-Chernogryazskaya, 4-16a

RU-107078 Moscow

Phone: 7 095 262 7079

Fax: 7 095 207 0889

JSV Relcom
123060, Moscow, ul.Raspletina, d.4, korp.1
E-mail: postmaster@kiae.su
or
support@kiae.su
Phone: 7 095 943 4735
Fax: 7 095 198 95 10

Slovakia (Slovak Republic)
EUnet Slovakia
MFF UK Computing Centre
Mlynska dolina
842 15 Bratislava
E-mail: info@Slovakia.EU.net
WWW: http://www.eunet.sk/,
Gopher: gopher.eunet.sk
Phone: (42) 7 725306
Fax: (42) 7 728462

Slovenia
Histria
Ziherlova 43 61
Ljubljana
E-mail: support@histria.apc.org
Phone: 386 (61) 211 553
Fax: 386 (61) 152 107

Ukraine
Apex Network Centre
17/315 pr. Gagarina
320095, Dniepropetrovsk
Phone: 7 0562 476995
Fax: 7 0562 410911
E-mail: vaget@apex.dnepropetrovsk.ua

Uzbekistan
Firma Kompyuternye Kommunikacii
700000 Tashkent, 1 Ulxyanovskii per., 3
E-mail: postmaster@ccc.tashkent.su
Phone: 7 3712 687956

Mexico
Internet de Mexico, SA de CV
Paseo de Echegaray 3 - 206
Nauclapan, Estado de Mexico
E-mail: info@mail.internet.com.mx
WWW: http://www.internet.com.mx
Phone: (525) 360-2931
Fax: (525) 373-1493

RepCom de Mexico, S.A. de C.V.
Av. Nuevo Leon 67 Despacho # 601
Col. Hipodromo Condesa, CP 06140
Mexico City, Mexico Distrito Federal
E-mail: staff@seinet.net.mx
Phone: (525) 211-2282
Fax: (525) 211-2391

Sistema Profesional de Informacion (SPIN)
Cuenca 87-4 Alamos 03400
Mexico City, Mexico Distrito Federal
E-mail: info@spin.com.mx
Phone: (525) 628-6220
Fax: (525) 628-6210

Middle East

Most Internet access in the Middle East is through private businesses, FidoNet or similar set-ups, or dial-out services. I was unable to find a FAQ with other pointers; you might contact GreenNet (support@gn.apc.org), a network maintained by the Institute for Global Communications, which has connections in some parts of the Middle East.

Egypt

EUnet Egypt
E-mail: ow@estinet.uucp
Phone: (20) 2 3557253
Fax: (20) 2 3547807

Israel

DataServe Ltd.
E-mail: info@datasrv.co.il
or
register@datasrv.co.il
Phone: (972) 3-647-4448
Fax: (972) 3-647-3833

Pacific

Australia

You can find a more extensive list of Australian service providers at http://www.cs.monash.edu.au/~zik/netfaq/org.html.

APANA
E-mail: info@apana.org.au
or
propaganda@apana.org.au
WWW: http://www.apana.org.au/apana/
Phone: (03) 571-0484

AUSNet
E-mail: tom@kakadu.com.au
WWW: http://www.ausnet.net.au/
Voice: (089) 483-555
Fax: (089) 480-232

Drasnian Technologies
12 Guinevere Way
Carine 6020, Western Australia
E-mail: admin@drasnia.it.com.au
WWW: http://drasnia.it.com.au/
Phone: (09) 447-6261 (a/h)

Spirit Networks
Canberra
E-mail: info@spirit.com.au
WWW: http://www.spirit.com.au/
Phone: (06) 281-3552
Fax: (06) 281-3552

New Zealand

You can get a FAQ on New Zealand connectivity that includes a larger list of public and private service providers from the Web page at http://www.cis.ohio-state.edu/hypertext/faq/usenet/internet-access/new-zealand/faq.html.

IBM Global Network
E-mail: bowden@vnet.ibm.com
Phone: 0800 105-765

PlaNet
E-mail: support@ak.planet.co.nz
Phone/Fax: (09) 3786006

South America

Argentina

Proyecto Wamani

Centro de Comunicacion de Informacion (CCI)

Talcahuano 325 - 3F

1013 Buenos Aires

E-mail: carlos@wamani.org.ar

or

eduardo@wamani.org.ar

Phone: 54 (1) 382-6842 / 793-1502

Bolivia

Academic and Research Network

Av. Mariscal Santa Cruz, No. 1175 (Obelisco)

Facultad de Ingenieria, Tercer Piso

La Paz

E-mail: clifford@unbol.bo

Phone: (591-1) 314990

Fax: (591-1) 314990

Brazil

Rua Vicente de Souza, 29 Botafogo

Rio de Janeiro, RJ

E-mail: saff@ibase.br

or

iyda@ibase.br

Phone: 55 021 286-4467/286-0348

Fax: 55 021 286-0541

Telex: 2136466 BASE BR

Chile

REUNA

Bernarda Morin 550-A

Providencia, Santiago

E-mail: postmaster@reuna.cl

Phone: (56) 2 274-0403

Fax: (56) 2 209-6729

Colombia

SAITEL - ITEC - TELECOM

Bogota

E-mail: hcaballe@itecs3.telecom-co.net

or

jserrano@itecs3.telecom-co.net

Phone: 571 334 8149

Fax: 571 613 1814

Ecuador

Corporacion Ecuatoriana de Informacion

ECUANET

P.O. Box 988

Guayaquil

E-mail: xbaquero@ecnet.ec

Phone: (593-2) 433-006 y 1410

Fax: (593-2) 437-601

Paraguay

LEDNET

P.O. Box 1718

Campus Universitario, Barrio Santa Librada.

Asuncion

E-mail: gbellas@ledip.py

or

postmaster@ledip.py

Phone: (595 21)334650

Fax: (595 21)310587

Peru

Red Cientifica Peruana

Alonso de Molina, 1698

Monterrico, Lima

E-mail: js@rcp.net.pe

Phone: (54) 14 35-1760

Fax: (54) 14 36-4067

Uruguay

Chasque

Miguel del Corro 1461
Montevideo 11200
E-mail: apoyo@chasque.apc.org
Phone: 598-2-496-192
Fax: 598-2-419-222

Venezuela

CONICIT

Sistema Automatizado de Informacion Cientifica y
Tecnologica (SAICYT)
Edificio Mapioca
v. Ppal. Lops Cortijos de Lourdes
Caracas 1071
Phone: (58) 2 239-0577
Fax: (58) 2 239-8677
Telex: 25205

United States

I concentrated on the larger national or regional firms
here; it's entirely possible that a smaller local company
might be able to provide you with better prices or services.

Many of the companies here are accessible from Canada
and/or Mexico as well, and most are accessible via the
Compuserve Packet Network (CPN) or Sprintnet, or
maintain local access numbers through other dial-up services (which have additional fees).

East Coast

Clark Internet Services

E-mail: info@clark.net
WWW: http://www.clark.net
Phone: (800) 735-2258
or
(410) 730-9764
Fax: (410) 730-9765

Phantom Access Technologies Inc. (MindVox)

E-mail: info@phantom.com
Phone: (800) 646-3869
or
(212) 989-2418
Fax: (212) 989-8648

Public Access Unix and Internet (PANIX)

E-mail: info@panix.com (to receive information
automatically)
or
staff@panix.com (to ask specific questions)
Phone: (212) 787-6160

Midwest

APK Net, Ltd.

1621 Euclid Avenue, Suite 1216
Cleveland, Ohio 44115
E-mail: info@apk.net (to receive information
automatically)
or
support@apk.net (to ask specific questions)
WWW: www.apk.net
Phone: (216) 481-9428
Fax: (216) 481-9425

Msen Inc.

628 Brooks Street
Ann Arbor, Michigan 48103
E-mail: info@mail.msen.com
WWW: www.msen.com
Phone: (313) 998-4562
Fax: (313) 998-4563

Ripco Communications Inc.
E-mail: info@ripco.com (to receive information
   automatically)
or
sysop@ripco.com (to ask specific questions)
WWW: http://www.ripco.com:70/1/ripco
Phone: (312) 477-6210

Northwest
Eskimo North
P.O. Box 75284
Seattle, Washington 98125-0284
E-mail: nanook@mail.eskimo.com
WWW: www.eskimo.com
Phone: (206) 361-1161

Teleport Inc.
319 SW Washington Street #803
Portland, Oregon 97204
Phone: (503) 223-4245
Fax: (503) 223-4372

South
Interpath
P.O. Box 12800
Raleigh, North Carolina 27605
E-mail: info@interpath.net
Gopher: gopher gopher.interpath.net
WWW: www.interpath.net
Phone: (800) 849-6305

Southwest
Crossroads Communications
E-mail: info@xroads.com
Phone: (602) 813-9040

Illuminati Online
P.O. Box 18957
Austin, Texas 78760
E-mail: info@io.com
WWW: http://www.io.com
Phone: (512) 447-7866
Fax: (512) 447-1144

West Coast
Information Access Technologies (IAT)
46 Shattuck Square, Suite 11
Berkeley, California 94704-1152
E-mail:info@iat.mailer.net (to receive information
   automatically)
or
support@holonet.net (to ask specific questions)
WWW: www.holonet.net
Phone: (510) 704-0160
Fax: (510) 704-8019

The Little Garden
3004 16th Street #201
San Francisco, California 94103
E-mail: info@tlg.org (to receive information
   automatically)
or
sales@tlg.org (to ask specific questions)
FTP: ftp.tlg.org
WWW: http://www.tlg.org/
Phone: (415) 487-1902
(Note: The Little Garden is building a network of affili-
   ates in other areas; contact them for information
   about one in your area.)

Portal Information Network
20863 Stevens Creek Boulevard, Suite 200
Cupertino, California 95014

E-mail: info@portal.com (to receive information automatically)

or

support@portal.com (to ask specific questions)
WWW: www.portal.com
Phone: (408) 973-9111
Fax: (408) 725-1580

The WELL

1750 Bridgeway, Suite A200
Sausalito, California 94965-1900
E-mail: support@well.com
WWW: www.well.com
Phone: (415) 332-9200
Fax: (415) 332-9355

National

CRL

P.O. Box 326
Larkspur, California 94977
E-mail: support@crl.com
FTP: ftp.crl.com/CRL- Info/Basic.Services.Info
Phone: (415) 837-5300
Fax: (415) 392-9000

Netcom Online Services

3031 Tisch Way
San Jose, California 95128
E-mail: info@netcom.com
WWW: www.netcom.com
Phone: (800) 501-8649
Fax: (408) 241-9145

Performance Systems International (PSI)

510 Huntmar Park Drive
Herndon, Virginia 22070
E-mail: info@psi.com

WWW: www.psi.com
Phone: (800) 827-7482
Fax: (800) FAX-PSI1

Western Europe
Europe

Along with commercial online services, such as CompuServe and Europe Online, there are companies that provide connectivity across national borders in Europe, including European telecommunications pioneer EUnet. I-COM does them all one better by sweetening the deal with low-cost dial access to the U.S. as part of their all-Europe service package.

I-COM

4, rue de Geneve B33
B-1140 Bruxelles / Belgium
Phone: (32) 2 215 71 30
Fax: (32) 2 215 8999

Austria
EUnet Austria

E-mail: info@Austria.EU.net
Phone: (43) 1 3174969
Fax: (43) 1 3106926

Belgium
Interpac Belgium

Av. Louise 350, Boîte 11
1050 Bruxelles
E-mail: info@interpac.be
Phone: (32) 2 6466000
Fax: (32) 2 6403638

Denmark

DKnet/EUnet Denmark

Fruebjergvej 3

2100 Copenhagen Oe

E-mail: info@DKnet.dk

Phone: (45) 39 17 99 00

Fax: (45) 39 17 98 97

Finland

EUnet Finland

Punavuorenkatu 1

FI-00120 Helsinki

Phone: (358) 0 400 2060

Fax: (358) 0 622 2626

France

FRANCENET

49 Rue du Faubourg Poissonnière

Paris

http://WWW.Francenet.fr

E-mail: infos@francenet.fr

Minitel: 36 15 Francenet

FTP: FTP.francenet.fr

Gopher: Gopher.francenet.fr

Phone: (33) 1 40 61 01 76

Fax: (33) 1 48 24 46 22

Germany

Interactive Network Informationssysteme GmbH i.Gr.

Spohrstrasse 24

D-60318 Frankfurt am Main

E-mail: johnny@interactive.nacamar.de

Phone: (49) 69 5974099

Fax: (49) 69 555442 / 555683

Interactive Networx GmbH

Hardenbergplatz 2

D-10623 Berlin

E-mail: info@unlisys.net

Phone: (49) 30 25431-0

Fax: (49) 30 25431-299

Greece

EUnet Greece

E-mail: postmaster@Greece.EU.net

Phone: (30) 81 221171

Fax: (30) 81 229342

Iceland

EUnet Iceland

E-mail: postmaster@Iceland.EU.net

Phone: (354) 1 694747

Fax: (354) 1 28801

Ireland

IEunet Ltd.

E-mail: info@ieunet.ie, info@Ireland.eu.net

Phone: (353) 1 6790832

Italy

ALPCOM

CSI Piemonte

c.so Unione Sovietica, 216 I-10136

Torino

E-mail: info@alpcom.it

or

secretary@alpcom.it

Phone: (39) 11 3187407

Fax: (39) 11 4618212

INET S.p.A.
v. A.Bono Cairoli, 34 I-20127
Milan
E-mail: info@inet.it
Phone: (39) 2 26821182
Fax: (39) 2 26821311

Luxembourg
EUnet Luxembourg
E-mail: postmaster@Luxembourg.EU.net
Phone: (352) 470261 361
Fax: (352) 470264

Netherlands
EuroNet Internet
Prins Hendrikkade 48
1012 AC Amsterdam
E-mail: info@euro.net
or
office@euronet.nl
Phone: (31) 20 625 6161
Fax: (31) 20 625 7435

Norway
DAXNET
Enebakkveien 304
Postboks 79 Abilds
N-1105 Oslo
E-mail: daxnet@datametrix.no
WWW: http://www.datametrix.no/
Phone: (47) 22 74 06 20
Fax: (47) 22 74 04 89

Portugal
Telepac Servicos de Telecomunicacoes SA
Rue Dr Antonio Loureiro Borges 1
1495 Lisboa
E-mail: henrique@telepac.pt
Phone: (351) 1 790 7000
Fax: (351) 1 790 7001

Spain
RedIRIS
Fundesco
Alcala 61
28014 Madrid
E-mail: secretaria@rediris.es
Phone: (34) 1 435 1214
Fax: (34) 1 578 1773

Sweden
Bahnhof
Phone: (46) 18-100899
Fax: (46) 18-103737
E-mail: info@bahnhof.se
WWW: http://www.bahnhof.se/

Switzerland
PING GmbH
Albisstrasse 48
CH-8932 Mettmenstetten
E-mail: aurelio@ping.ch
or
afink@ping.ch
WWW: http://www.ping.ch/
Phone: (41) 1 768 53 16
Fax: (41) 1 768 53 19

Turkey

TUVAKA

Ege Universitesi

Bilgisayar Arastirma ve Uygulama Merkezi

Bornova, Izmir 35100

E-mail: Esra@ege.edu.tr

or

Esra@trearn.bitnet

Phone: (90) 51 887228

U.K. (England, Scotland, Wales, Northern Ireland)

A U.K.-specific Internet access list is posted monthly to the newsgroups alt.internet.access.wanted, uk.net, uk.telecom, and uk.misc. It can also be obtained via FTP at ftp.demon .co.uk:/pub/archives/uk-internet-list/inetuk.lng.

Absolute Communications Ltd.

E-mail: sales@foobar.co.uk

Phone: (44) 0 116 2330033

Fax: (44) 0 116 2330035

Aladdin

5 Alexandra Road, Hedge End

Southampton, Hants, SO30 0ZZ

E-mail: info@aladdin.co.uk

WWW: http://www.aladdin.co.uk/

Phone: (44) 0 1489 782221

Fax: (44) 0 1489 782382

Demon Internet Ltd.

42 Hendon Lane

London N3 1TT

E-mail: internet@demon.net

FTP: ftp.demon.co.uk:/pub/doc/

Phone: (44) 0 181 349 0063

Fax: (44) 0 181 349 0309

Zetnet Services

Garthspool, Lerwick

Shetland GB ZE1 0NP

E-mail: info@zetnet.co.uk

WWW: http://www.zetnet.co.uk/

Phone: (44) 1 595 696667

Fax: (44) 1 595 696548

Appendix B: Print Resources

A long with the many FAQs and help files available online, you might like to read one or more of the books below to clear up any lingering questions on specific aspects of the Net. This is a mere fraction of the Internet books now available—as you probably know, if you have purchased this one recently!

If it's difficult to find these or other Internet books where you live, let me suggest contacting one of the best reasons to live in Portland, Oregon: Powell's Technical Books. Powell's either has every Net book under the sun, or will order it for you. Best of all, they're online and happy to mail books anywhere in the world. For more information, see their Web page at

http://www.technical.powells.portland.or.us/

Exploring the Internet: A Technical Travelogue by Carl Malamud (1992, Prentice Hall) If you want to know more about how the many networks around the world that became the Internet grew and got connected, try to find this book. Malamud is well-respected technical writer, and since he wrote this volume as a giveaway for people attending a computer-network trade show there is some technical detail. You can skip some of it, if need be. The welcome surprise here is that the book reads like a traditional travel narrative—sort of like what you'd get if you set famous British explorer/author Richard Burton off on a tour of the Net in 21 nations.

How the Internet Works by Joshua Eddings (1994, Ziff-Davis Press) If the whole concept of this worldwide network still seems a bit overwhelming, try this profusely illustrated book that explains its inner workings in detail, but does so relatively painlessly.

The IRC Survival Guide: Talk to the World with Internet by S. Harris (1995, Addison-Wesley) This was the first book spawned by Internet Relay Chat. It explains how IRC works, and includes information about specific IRC channels.

Net.sex by Nancy Tamosaitis (1995, Ziff-Davis Press) This slim volume covers sex and sex-related activity online. It's well written, and doesn't have the breathless tone of some competing books.

The Virtual Community: Homesteading on the Electronic Frontier by Howard Rheingold (1993, HarperPerennial) This dense, if somewhat disjointed, book about online communities brings together interesting stories and ideas from many of the best-known thinkers in cyberspace, including John Perry Barlow and Bruce Sterling. Rheingold explores the Net's beginnings and present, and speculates on its future as a medium for free expression.

What's on Internet by Eric Gagnon (1994/1995, Peachpit Press) Peachpit plans to make this book—devoted to spilling the beans on which Usenet newsgroups are hot (or not)—a regularly updated affair. That's a good idea, since the world of newsgroups is always expanding and changing.

The Whole Internet User's Guide and Catalog by Ed Krol (1994, O'Reilly & Associates) Of all the "beginner's guides to the Net," this is my favorite. Krol goes into serious technical detail in case you need to know, but also sets up his book so that you can skip the heavy stuff if all you want to do is get online fast with a minimum of fuss. Now that's a difficult trick!

Appendix C: Special Resources for Kids

With a Web browser, even grade-school kids can be Netsurfing in no time—in fact, once you get them started you may have a hard time getting your computer back.

How you want to handle access to the Net for your offspring or students will depend a great deal on their age and how you think they might handle stumbling onto one of its darker corners. It's true that pornography is as easy to find online as one of the kid-friendly sites listed below, and there's no easy way to put a lock on it.

Computing along with your kids is great for younger children, but teens are likely to resent your presence at the keyboard. Having a frank talk about what's out there and how you feel about it and reiterating these instructions regularly may be more effective at this age.

This will come as a surprise to many adults—mainly those who have conveniently forgotten the shenanigans they got into as teenagers—but there is an entire online underground for teens out there. Most of it is BBS-based, with teens running bulletin boards at night out of their bedrooms or basements. It's beginning to move to the Internet as access spreads. For the most part, it's a bunch of kids (still mostly boys, but there are an increasing number of young women online as well) hanging around and gabbing about "Star Trek," cars, the latest music, and who's got a crush on whom. The problems generally occur when adults enter this picture. Sometimes they try to lure teens into sexually explicit conversations, and sometimes they try to lure them to meet them offline. Often they pretend to be teenagers themselves, and since their faces are invisible there's no way to know until a face-to-face meeting occurs.

There have been documented cases of pedophiles using such ruses to lure children and teens into unsavory and potentially dangerous situations, so I urge you make a strict rule about offline meetings with new "net friends": there should be none unless they occur in a public place, such as a cafe or the mall, and with you present. You can hang discreetly in the background or insist on meeting your teen's new acquaintance as you prefer—the important thing being to ascertain that your son or daughter is dealing with someone close to their own age.

Kids and teens both should also follow the rule of not giving out real names, home addresses, or phone numbers until they have your permission to do so in each case.

I hope this information doesn't frighten anyone out of giving their teens access to the Internet. I recall well from my small-town, Bible Belt upbringing that creepy adults could occasionally be found hanging around the roller rink, the movie theater, the public parks, and even at church functions. If you've worked hard with your kids to make sure they know how to size up people and situations that could be detrimental to their well-being, the Net can actually be a safer way to practice their skills than some "real-life" scenarios—in the movie theater you may have to smack someone with your popcorn bucket, but online you can just hang up the modem.

There are not many places online created especially for teenagers, but they can enjoy most of the sites listed in this book, according to their interests. Incidentally, Internet search engines are especially useful for pulling in impressive items you can cite in high school research papers!

Younger kids seem to especially enjoy setting up their own folder of Web links. As with videos, they have favorites they want to see again and again. You may want to sneak in some of the educational experiences listed below.

Be sure to check out the section "Education," especially if you are homeschooling.

My daughter Carmen Waltz, a 13-year-old homeschooler and writer, checked each of these sites personally and wrote many of the reviews.

Adbusters

This Canadian magazine takes a strongly critical look at the role the advertising industry plays in our lives. There's information about it at this Gopher site, including some about *Big Noise*, their supplement for high-school kids. Not only is it fun to read, you can get paid for contributing the kind of stories they're looking for about kids and ads.

Type: Gopher
Address: gopher.well.sf.ca.us/00/ Publications/online%5Fzines/ Ad%5FBusters
Type: E-mail
Address: adbusters@mindlink.bc.ca (Jordan Reeves)
Region: Canada, U.S.

African Studies at the University of Pennsylvania

This very extensive and well-linked site from the African Studies faculty at UP provides graphics, information, and multimedia resources. It's the best launching point for any Internet research dealing with the African continent. It includes a section for primary and secondary school students and educators, supplying lists and links to online and other resources suitable for either research or classroom use, including classroom guides and hand-outs for teachers.

Type: WWW
Address: http://www.sas.upenn.edu/African _Studies/K-12/menu_K-12.html
Region: Africa

Buena Vista Movieplex

A virtual movie house from the Disney folks: You get to go inside the theater and watch clips from the films of your choice.

Type: WWW
Address: http://www.wdp.com/BUPM
Region: U.S.

Canada Schoolnet

This page has a list of really cool projects that kids are doing all over the world, including the Berlin Wall Falls Project, a UN project, and more.

Type: WWW
Address: http://schoolnet.carleton.ca/english /Web_Resources/intrnatl.html
Region: Canada

Canadian Kids Home Page

This page is a list of online activities for kids. I especially liked the Street Cents Online, a project by Canadian kids about getting good deals for your money.

Type: WWW
Address: http://WWW.OnRamp.ca/~lowens/ 107kids.htm
Region: Canada

Carrie's Education Links

This set of pages has a lot of cool stuff for kids of all ages to do and learn, ranging from finding out what's up at NASA to learning Spanish to tracking down information on Disney movies.

Type: WWW
**Address: http://www.mtjeff.com/~bodenst/
            page5.html**
Region: U.S., World

The Children's Page

In Italian and somewhat fractured English, this page from Padova Astronomical Observatory pulls together several fun resources for kids, from a "trip to Mars" using images sent back by NASA to pen pals, soccer, and skateboarding. There's also a section on basic astronomy for teenagers.

Type: WWW
**Address: http://www.pd.astro.it/bambini
            .html**
Region: Italy

EKIDS

This is an Australia-based mailing list for kids. Participants send e-mail about what's up at their school, movie reviews, and questions, which are bundled up and sent out as a monthly digest. It's archived at the Web site below.

Type: Mailing list
**Address: majordomo@citybeach.wa.edu.au
Send e-mail message with blank Subject link
            and body: subscribe ekids**
Type: WWW
**Address: http://www.citybeach.wa.edu.au/
            ekidsarc.html**
Region: Australia

Emma's Art Gallery

These are very cute drawings by "Emma." They remind me of Simon on "Saturday Night Live."

Type: WWW
**Address: http://www.primet.com/~sburr/
            gallery.html**
Region: U.S.

The Globe and Mail Newsfeed

This Toronto paper is delivered to Canadian classrooms via Internet. The Gopher site below includes an archive of the paper, plus classroom guides for teachers.

Type: Gopher
**Address: schoolnet.carleton.ca:419/11/
            Announ.dir/Newspapers/globe**
Region: Canada, World

HungerWeb

Run by the World Hunger Program, this page will soon offer interactive links between U.S. kids and street kids in the Dandora Shelter in Nairobi, including e-mail pen pals, photos, songs, and pictures to share. It also has papers and multimedia resources for K–12 teachers on hunger and relief efforts.

Type: WWW
**Address: http://www.hunger.brown.edu/
            hungerweb/**
Region: Kenya

Intercultural E-mail Classroom Connections

If you want to set up an e-mail pen-pal project between your class and one in another nation, this is a good starting point. There is also a form for posting requests for assistance with classroom projects from people in other parts of the world.

Type: WWW
**Address: http://www.stolaf.edu/network/
            iecc/**
Region: World

IT-Gener@tionen

This is a Swedish computer program for kids. The nine-person crew of IT-Gener@tionen takes their presentation to schools along with a mobile classroom full of computers that are hooked up to the Internet. Their site is in Swedish.

Type: WWW
**Address: http://www.everyday.se:80/hem/
itgenerationen/**
Region: Sweden

Japan Window

If you're curious about life in Japan, check in here. There's information about computers, science, money, government, travel, and everyday life. There's also a special "just for kids" area where you can learn some Japanese and find out how to do origami.

Type: WWW
Address: http://kiku.stanford.edu:80/
Region: Japan

The Jason Project

This is like a computer field trip. There are different virtual expeditions you can "go on," making it an ideal spot to visit with kids ages 7 to 12.

Type: WWW
**Address: http://seawifs.gsfc.nasa.gov/
JASON/HTML/JASON_HOME.html**
Region: World

The K–12 Online Library

These pages offer a list of good online educational resources, including teacher discussion groups, interactive projects, and much more. Teens and homeschooling families can find many useful items here.

Type: WWW
**Address: http://edweb.chidr.org:90/k12
.html**
Region: U.S., World

KidLink

KidLink is a project of Duquesne University (Pittsburgh, Pennsylvania), intended to bring kids between the ages of 10 and 15 from over 60 countries together in e-mail and other telecommunications exchanges. There are several ongoing projects at KidLink, including the Norway-based KIDCAFE one-to-one exchange, classroom-to-classroom exchange projects, and an online art gallery. Many languages are used here, so it's an especially good place to be if you're trying to learn another language.

Type: Gopher
Address: kids.ccit.duq.edu/
Region: World

KID Lot

Here, "KID" stands for Kids Internet Delight. It's another listing of places children will enjoy on the Net.

Type: WWW
**Address: http://www.clark.net/pub/
journalism/kid.html**
Region: U.S.

Kid Pub

This is a place for Net-savvy kids to publish their stories online, and for classes to publish their projects for all to see. There are also collaborative writing projects here.

Type: WWW
**Address: http://escrime-en-garde.com:80/
kidpub**
Type: E-mail
Address: KidPub@en-garde.com
Region: World

Kids on Campus WWW Tour

Every year Cornell University hosts Kids on Campus, a program that brings kids to the university. This year one of their offerings is an interactive tour of the Web, which you can try for yourself at this site. It includes links to pages on dinosaurs, space, volcanoes and earthquakes, the Smithsonian's Gem and Mineral Collection, sports, and animation, among other things.

Type: WWW
**Address: http://www.tc.cornell.edu/Kids.on
           .Campus/WWWDemo/**
Region: U.S., World

Kids' Page in Japanese
Entirely in Japanese, this page tells about the activities of a class that's experimenting with the Internet. They have their class newspaper here, among other things. If you're trying to learn Japanese you'll enjoy this.

Type: WWW
**Address: classhttp://kids.glocom.ac.jp/
           default.html**
Region: Japan

Kids Web
This is a collection of links to WWW pages of interest to kids, and a good starting point for an afternoon of exploration.

Type: WWW
**Address: http://www.primenet.com/~sburr/
           index.html**
Region: World

KiWePro—Texas Kids Web Project
This section is for kids in Texas, particularly junior high and high school youth, but kids from other parts of the world might enjoy seeing what they're up to. You can see the Web pages participants have made online here. Includes links to do-it-yourself information.

Type: WWW
**Address: http://198.213.61.243/ktask/
           kiwepro/kiwepro.html**
Region: U.S.

MathMagic!
This is a site dedicated to a new way of teaching mathematics, using computer technology while improving math skills. For kids K–12.

Type: WWW
**Address: http://forum.swarthmore.edu/
           mathmagic/**
Region: U.S.

The Ralph Bunche Computer School
This mini-school in inner-city New York has its own online newspaper, updates and requests for help on many ongoing projects, and links to other educational projects online. Especially interesting for middle-school students.

Type: WWW
Address: http://mac94.ralphbunche.rbs.edu/
Type: Gopher
Address: ralphbunche.rbs.edu/1
Region: U.S.

Scholastic Central
U.S. students know Scholastic as the *Weekly Reader* company. This is their Internet site, with *Press Return*, a student-written online newsletter; The International Arctic Project; and links to pages about children's horror writer R.L. Stine. *Press Return* is also available at the FTP site below.

Type: WWW
Address: http://scholastic.com:2005/
Type: FTP
Address: ftp.wais.com/pub/scholastic/
Region: U.S., World

SchoolsNET Home Page
SchoolsNET is the Australian K–12 Internet initiative. If you're looking for information about Australia, or to make contact with Australian classrooms or kids, this site is for you. There's a pen-pal archive here, many interesting links

(including Web pages at schools in Tasmania and other parts of Australia), and some classroom resources for teachers, too.

Type: WWW
Address: http://www.schnet.edu.au/#z3
Region: Australia

Theodore the Tugboat Online Activity Centre

This is an entire section dedicated to a happy little tugboat named Theodore, who Canadian kids may know from an educational TV show. There are lots of online activities here for young children.

Type: WWW
Address: http://www.cochran.com/tt.html
Region: Canada

Uncle Bob's Kids Page

There's tons of information here about various things kids enjoy, like Michael Jordan, dinosaurs, the Animaniacs cartoon series, the Muppets, and "Newton's Apple," a PBS science show. It's very easy to use.

Type: WWW
Address: http://gagme.wwa.com/~boba/ kids.html
Region: U.S.

The Virtual School

Hundreds of learning resources are clustered here in "classrooms" that you can use. Includes items related to everything from learning French to studying astronomy.

Type: Gopher
Address: schoolnet.carleton.ca:419/11/ Virtual.School
Region: Canada, World

Voices of Youth

This page documents a United Nations-sponsored interactive online project. It includes 3,000 messages from youth in 81 countries.

Type: WWW
Address: http://www.iisd.ca/linkages/un/ youth.html
Region: World

The Web as a Learning Tool

This page has links to information about art, music, wildlife, science, and other topics of interest. There's also a selection of online newspapers from around the world.

Type: WWW
Address: http://www.cs.uidaho.edu/~connie /interests.html
Region: World

What to Do When It's 40 Below

This is a cute little section about what kids do when it's cold outside, from drinking hot chocolate and cuddling up with a good book, to playing in the snow. It's written by youngsters from Alaska with lots of first-hand experience.

Type: WWW
Address: http://www.upk.northstar.k12.ak .us/below.html
Region: U.S.

Cut Here

Cut Here

Ziff-Davis Press Survey of Readers

Please help us in our effort to produce the best books on personal computing.
For your assistance, we would be pleased to send you a FREE catalog
featuring the complete line of Ziff-Davis Press books.

1. How did you first learn about this book?

Recommended by a friend . . . . M   -1 (5)

Recommended by store personnel . . . .   M   -2

Saw in Ziff-Davis Press catalog . . . .   M   -3

Received advertisement in the mail . . . .   M   -4

Saw the book on bookshelf at store . . . .   M   -5

Read book review in: _____ M   -6

Saw an advertisement in: _____ M   -7

Other (Please specify): _____ M   -8

2. Which THREE of the following factors most influenced your decision to purchase this book? (Please check up to THREE.)

Front or back cover information on book . . .   M   -1 (6)

Logo of magazine affiliated with book . . . . . .   M   -2

Special approach to the content . . . .   M   -3

Completeness of content . . . .   M   -4

Author's reputation.   M   -5

Publisher's reputation . . . .   M   -6

Book cover design or layout . . . .   M   -7

Index or table of contents of book . . . . M   -8

Price of book . . . .   M   -9

Special effects, graphics, illustrations . . . .   M   -0

Other (Please specify): _____ M   -x

3. How many computer books have you purchased in the last six months? _____

(7-10)

4. On a scale of 1 to 5, where 5 is excellent, 4 is above average, 3 is average, 2 is below average, and 1 is poor, please rate each of the following aspects of this book below. (Please circle your answer.)

Depth/completeness of coverage   5 4 3 2 1   (11)

Organization of material   5 4 3 2 1

(12)

Ease of finding topic   5 4 3 2 1   (13)

Special features/time saving tips   5 4 3 2 1   (14)

Appropriate level of writing   5 4 3 2 1   (15)

Usefulness of table of contents   5 4 3 2 1   (16)

Usefulness of index   5 4 3 2 1   (17)

Usefulness of accompanying disk   5 4 3 2 1   (18)

Usefulness of illustrations/graphics   5 4 3 2 1   (19)

Cover design and attractiveness   5 4 3 2 1   (20)

Overall design and layout of book   5 4 3 2 1   (21)

Overall satisfaction with book   5 4 3 2 1

(22)

5. Which of the following computer publications do you read regularly; that is, 3 out of 4 issues?

Byte . . . .   M   -1 (23)

Computer Shopper . . . .   M   -2

Corporate Computing . . . .   M   -3

Dr. Dobb's Journal . . . .   M   -4

LAN Magazine . . . .   M   -5

MacWEEK . . . .   M   -6

MacUser . . . .   M   -7

PC Computing . . . .   M   -8

Please turn page.

PLEASE TAPE HERE ONLY—DO NOT STAPLE

6. What is your level of experience with personal computers? With the subject of this book?

	With PCs	With subject of book
Beginner	M -1 (24)	M -1 (25)
Intermediate	M -2	M -2
Advanced	M -3	M -3

7. Which of the following best describes your job title?

Officer (CEO/President/VP/owner) . . . . M -1 (26)
Director/head . . . . M -2
Manager/supervisor . . . . M -3
Administration/staff . . . . M -4
Teacher/educator/trainer . . . . M -5
Lawyer/doctor/medical professional . . . . M -6
Engineer/technician . . . . M -7
Consultant . . . . M -8
Not employed/student/retired . . . . M -9
Other (Please specify): _____ M -0

8. What is your age?

Under 20 . . . . M -1 (27)
21-29 . . . . M -2
30-39 . . . . M -3
40-49 . . . . M -4
50-59 . . . . M -5
60 or over . . . . M -6

9. Are you:

Male . . . . M -1 (28)
Female . . . . M -2

Thank you for your assistance with this important information! Please write your address below to receive our free catalog.

Name: _____
Address: _____
City/State/Zip: _____

Fold here to mail.

3296-18-22

_____
_____
_____

BUSINESS REPLY MAIL
FIRST CLASS MAIL   PERMIT NO. 1612   OAKLAND, CA

POSTAGE WILL BE PAID BY ADDRESSEE

Ziff-Davis Press

5903 Christie Avenue
Emeryville, CA 94608-1925
Attn: Marketing

NO POSTAGE
NECESSARY
IF MAILED IN
THE UNITED
STATES